EMPRESS

WITHDRAWN
UTSA Libraries

EMPRESS
QUEEN VICTORIA AND INDIA

MILES TAYLOR

YALE UNIVERSITY PRESS
NEW HAVEN AND LONDON

Copyright © 2018 Miles Taylor

All rights reserved. This book may not be reproduced in whole or in part, in any form (beyond that copying permitted by Sections 107 and 108 of the U.S. Copyright Law and except by reviewers for the public press) without written permission from the publishers.

For information about this and other Yale University Press publications, please contact:
U.S. Office: sales.press@yale.edu   yalebooks.com
Europe Office: sales@yaleup.co.uk   yalebooks.co.uk

Set in Adobe Garamond Pro by IDSUK (DataConnection) Ltd
Printed in Great Britain by TJ International Ltd, Padstow, Cornwall

Library of Congress Control Number: 2018944754

ISBN 978-0-300-11809-4 (hbk)

A catalogue record for this book is available from the British Library.

10 9 8 7 6 5 4 3 2 1

**Library
University of Texas
at San Antonio**

For Shalini

CONTENTS

CONTENTS

ILLUSTRATIONS

1. Dwarkanath Tagore, sketch by Queen Victoria (1842). Royal Archives / © Her Majesty Queen Elizabeth II 2017.
2. Sutlej Campaign Medal by William Wyon (1846). © The Fitzwilliam Museum, Cambridge (CM.1445-2009).
3. Franz Xaver Winterhalter, *Queen Victoria* (1856). Royal Collection Trust / © Her Majesty Queen Elizabeth II 2017 (RCIN 406698).
4. Joseph Nash, *The Indian Court* (1854). © Victoria and Albert Museum, London.
5. The Maharaja Duleep Singh on the Lower Terrace, Osborne (1854). Royal Collection Trust / © Her Majesty Queen Elizabeth II 2017 (RCIN 2906553).
6. Prince Arthur and Prince Alfred in the costume of Sikh princes, Osborne (1854). Royal Collection Trust / © Her Majesty Queen Elizabeth II 2017 (RCIN 2906169).
7. Maharaja Duleep Singh, sketch by Queen Victoria (1854). Royal Archives / © Her Majesty Queen Elizabeth II 2017.
8. Lady Canning, *Delhi from the Lahore Gate of the Palace* (1858). Photograph by Jonathan Turner. Reproduced by courtesy of the Harewood House Trust.

9. Thomas J. Barker, *The Relief of Lucknow* (1858). Royal Collection Trust / © Her Majesty Queen Elizabeth II 2017 (RCIN 813930).

10. Bust of Queen Victoria on a postage stamp, Nabha state (*c.* 1876). Author's collection.

11. Crown of the Emperor Bahadur Shah II. Royal Collection Trust / © Her Majesty Queen Elizabeth II 2017 (RCIN 67236).

12. Statue of Queen Victoria, Bombay (1872). © British Library Board (Photo 937 (28)).

13. Vasily Vereshchagin, *The Prince of Wales at Jaipur, 4th February 1876* (1876). By kind permission of the Victoria Memorial Hall, Kolkata.

14. Lala Deen Dayal, 'The Duke of Connaught having breakfast at Bala Hissar, Golconda Fort, Hyderabad', from the H. J. Barrett Album (1889). The Alkazi Collection of Photography (ACP: 99.23.0003(00039)).

15. Prince Albert Victor, the Maharana Fateh Singh of Udaipur and the Maharaja Kumar Bhupal Singh of Udaipur, Udaipur (1890). © Maharana of Mewar Charitable Foundation, Udaipur (2008.06.0395i_R).

16. Imperial Assemblage Medal (1877). Royal Collection Trust / © Her Majesty Queen Elizabeth II 2017 (RCIN 443439).

17. Imperial Assemblage, Coronation Pavilion and Amphitheatre by Bourne and Shepherd, from the Dhar Album (1877). The Alkazi Collection of Photography (ACP: 95.0079(00021)).

18. Empress Mills, Nagpur. Courtesy of Tata Central Archives, Pune.

19. Queen Victoria as Empress of India, by W & D Downey & Co. (1877). Royal Collection Trust / © Her Majesty Queen Elizabeth II 2017 (RCIN 2105735).

20. Queen Victoria at her accession, from Ambika Chandra Ghosh, *Rajarajeswari Victoria* (Calcutta: Arundoday Roy, 1895). By permission of the National Library, Kolkata.

21. Queen Victoria at the deathbed of Prince Albert, from Ghosh, *Rajarajeswari Victoria* (1895). By permission of the National Library, Kolkata.

ACKNOWLEDGEMENTS

This book has evolved over some time and I have received much support and incurred many debts of gratitude along the way. To begin, I must thank my colleagues at the University of York and in the School of Advanced Study at the University of London, who allowed me the time and space to be a historian alongside my day jobs. In this respect I am particularly grateful to my head of department at York, Mark Ormrod and to John Local, the academic co-ordinator for Arts and Humanities, for their kindness and guidance. In London, the vice chancellor, Sir Graeme Davies, and Roger Kain, the dean of the School of Advanced Study, ensured that I had the means to carry on my research for this book. Without Elaine Walters, the unflappable and tireless administrator of the Institute of Historical Research, I could never have combined my own studies with the demands of running the IHR. I will long retain warm memories of the six years spent in her professional company.

I was trained in the early 1980s as a historian of Victorian Britain, albeit one who was encouraged to peer out at the rest of the world in order to bring the metropole into focus. Plotting the interconnections between Empire and the domestic polity in this manner led me ultimately to the monarchy, and then, inevitably, to India. There I was not a complete novice. Peter Marshall introduced me to the history of British India as an undergraduate. At Cambridge in the 1990s I learned much, in different ways, from Susan Bayly and from the late Sir Christopher Bayly. However, in unravelling the full story of Queen Victoria and India, I have entered uncharted territory, encountering only a few stray historians along the way, reliant instead on the expertise of archivists, curators and librarians. I benefited hugely from being given access to the Royal Archives at Windsor. There Pamela Clark, Allison Derrett and Sophie Gordon guided me through the royal correspondence and photographs, accompanied by some splendid baking. Bridget Wright introduced me to the Royal Library. At the Royal Collections in St James's Palace, Jonathan Marsden and later Agata Rutkowska expedited my enquiries. Across India good will, luck, persistence and wonderful food sustained my fieldwork. In Delhi, Mushirul Hasan eased my journey into the National Archives of India and helped open doors in Bhopal, Bikaner and Chennai. Also at the National Archives Jaya Ravindran was so welcoming and generous with her time. Elsewhere in India I gained much from many small acts of kindness. I would like to single out the following librarians and curators: Joyoti Roy at the Alkazi Foundation in Delhi, Chittaranjan Panda and Jayanta Sengupta at the Victoria Memorial Hall in Kolkata, Sanam Ali Khan at the Rampur Raza Library (a visit made memorable by taking tea in her ancestral home), Dr J. V. Gayathri at the Mysore District Archives, Sonika Soni and Bhupendra Singh Auwa at the Mewar Palace Archives in Udaipur, Pankaj Sharma and Giles Tillotson at the City Palace Museum in Jaipur, Nagender Reddy at the Salar Jung Museum in Hyderabad, and Ashim Mukhopadhyay at the National Library in Kolkata. Two researchers – Saptadeepa Bannerjee in Kolkata and Raghav Kishore in London – assisted me in collecting material. Other friends and colleagues shared findings and references or copied correspondence from archives in India, Germany and the USA that I was unable to consult in person: thanks in this regard to Zirwat Chowdury, Dane Kennedy, Prashant Kidambi, Cindy McCreery, Samira Sheikh and A. R. Venkatachalapathy. Horst Gehringer and Oliver Walton guided me in and out of the archives in Coburg and Gotha. Richard Virr at McGill University in Montreal made available vital copies of correspondence, and Russell Lord let me view photographs in the Metropolitan Museum in New York, whilst Roy Ritchie introduced me to the riches of the Huntington Library at Pasadena, and to kumquats. Sandy and Michaela Reid kindly allowed me into their Jedburgh home to consult the archives of their distinguished ancestor. Many hours have been spent in the Asia and Africa Reading Room of the British Library in London, where the staff have been unfailingly diligent and friendly.

For permission to consult and quote from records in their possession, I acknowledge the permission of Her Majesty Queen Elizabeth II; the Royal Commission for the Exhibition of 1851; the British Library; Lambeth Palace Library; The National Archives, Kew; News International; the Royal Society of Arts; the Dean and Chapter of Westminster Abbey; the Deputy Keeper of the Records, Public Record Office of Northern Ireland, and the Marchioness of Dufferin and Ava; the University of Birmingham; the Churchill Archives Centre, Churchill College, Cambridge; Cambridge University Library; the Trustees of the Devonshire Collection, Chatsworth House; Durham University Library; the National Archives of Scotland; the University of Sussex; the Marquess of Salisbury, Hatfield House; Suffolk Record Office; the Library and Museum of Freemasonry; the Bodleian Library, University of Oxford; the West Yorkshire Archives Service; Liverpool Record Office; the Hartley Library, University of Southampton; Hampshire Record Office; the Borthwick Institute for Archives, University of York; McGill University; the Huntington Library, San Marino; Nehru Museum and Memorial Library; Mumbai University Library; Bikaner Palace; the National Archives of India, and the State Archives of Andhra Pradesh, Baroda, Bikaner, Karnataka, Madhya Pradesh, Tamil Nadu, West Bengal and the District Archives of Delhi and Mysore. The publication has been made possible by a grant from the Scouloudi Foundation in association with the Institute of Historical Research.

Early versions of the ideas and arguments that follow were tried out at various seminars, conferences and lectures. For their hospitality, commentary and suggestions on those occasions, the following scholars are due warm thanks: Shigeru Akita, Peter Bang, Asma Ben Hassine, Fabrice Bensimon, Franz Bosbach, Judith Brown, Joya Chatterji, Ariane

Chernock, John Cookson, Ian Copland, David Craig, Santanu Das, Rajat Datta, Christiane Eisenberg, Lawrence Goldman, Anindita Ghosh, Peter Gray, Holger Hoock, Duncan Kelly, Harshan Kumarasingham, Colin Kidd, Jörn Leonhard, Claude Markowitz, Philip Murphy, Andrzej Olechnowicz, Jurgen Osterhammel, David Washbrook, Yvonne Ward, Lucy Worsley and Jon Wilson.

I am blessed with a superb publisher. Robert Baldock and Heather McCallum deserve a special mention for their advice and encouragement, and above all for their patience. I am grateful to Marika Lysandrou for her calm efficiency in the final stages and to Christopher Shaw, who did the proofreading. Thanks too to Andy Lawrence at Keele University Digital Images Services who drew the map of British India, Tony Stewart for his linguistic skills and Brendan Bell for applying his magic touch to some of the illustrations.

Scholarship of this kind relies on friendship. I have been lucky to enjoy the empathy and succour of many friends in the last decade, of whom the following have been most supportive: Justin Biel, the late Asa Briggs and his wife Susan, David Cannadine, Sam Cohn, the late David Eisenberg, David Feldman, Orlando Figes, Jo Godfrey, Joseph Hardwick, Michael Hulme, the late Jane Moody, Tony Morris, John Morrow, David Moss, Mark Roseman, Claire Scobie, Gavin Schaffer, John Shakeshaft and Karina Urbach. I am especially grateful to Michael Bentley, Jonathan Fulcher, Prashant Kidambi, Doug Peers, Minnie Sinha and Susie Steinbach for reading drafts of the book and pointing up where I needed to go back and think some more. Any errors or flaws of course remain my own.

Finally, as ever, my family have sustained me over the years of completing this project. For reminding me of the true meaning of life, I am grateful to my children: Helena, Patrick, Sarah and Vivaan, as well as my grandson, Leo. And to my wife, Shalini, words cannot really express my deep appreciation of her wisdom, faith and devotion. Hopefully, the dedication of the book says it all.

NOTE ON THE TEXT

For ease of reference and consistency, this book uses romanised script for Indian words; that is to say, proper nouns in Hindi, Urdu and other Indian vernaculars are written in their western form. Place names in India are mainly given in their Anglicised, nineteenth-century format, accompanied by the modern-day version where appropriate, for example Calcutta (Kolkata). Names of Indian persons have generally not been modernised, so Duleep Singh and not Dalip Singh, Jamsetjee Jejeebhoy not Jamshedji Jijibhai, etc., except when the modern form is in more common usage.

The Indian currency in this period was the rupee, subdivided into smaller denominations of annas and pice. One rupee was worth about 1s 4d, so there were fifteen rupees to the British pound, and the pound in 1877 (the year that Queen Victoria became Empress of India) was equivalent to £40 in today's value.

ABBREVIATIONS

BL	British Library
CWMG	*Collected Works of Mahatma Gandhi, Gandhi Heritage Portal* (www.gandhiheritageportal.org)
DIB	C. E. Buckland, *Dictionary of Indian Biography* (1906, repr. New Delhi, 1999)
HC Debs	*Hansard*, House of Commons debates
HL Debs	*Hansard*, House of Lords debates
ILN	*Illustrated London News*
INC	Indian National Congress
IOR	India Office Records, British Library
Letters of Queen Victoria	*The Letters of Queen Victoria: A Selection from Her Majesty's Correspondence Between the Years 1837 and 1861*, ed. A. C. Benson and Vct. Esher, 3 vols (London: John Murray, 1907)
	The Letters of Queen Victoria: Second Series. A Selection from Her Majesty's Correspondence and Journal Between the Years 1862 and 1885, ed. G. E. Buckle, 3 vols (London: John Murray, 1926–8)

	The Letters of Queen Victoria: Third Series. A Selection from Her Majesty's Correspondence and Journal Between the Years 1886 and 1901, ed. G. E. Buckle, 3 vols (London: John Murray, 1930–2)
MSA	Maharashtra State Archives, Mumbai, India
NAI	National Archives of India, New Delhi, India
NMML	Nehru Museum and Memorial Library, New Delhi, India
NNR	Native Newspaper Reports, 1868–1901, IOR L/R/5
NPG	National Portrait Gallery, London
ODNB	*Oxford Dictionary of National Biography*
PRONI	Public Record Office of Northern Ireland, Belfast
QLB	'Quarterly Lists of Books published in the provinces of India, 1867–1947', BL SV412 (now digitised at https://data.bl.uk/twocenturies-quarterlylists/tcq.html)
QVJl.	Queen Victoria's Journals, RA VIC/MAIN/ QVJ (W), Princess Beatrice's copies (www. queenvictoriasjournals.org/)
RA	Royal Archives, Windsor Castle
RCIN	Royal Collections Trust
TNA	The National Archives, Kew, London
ToI	*Times of India*
Transfer of Power	Nicholas Mansergh (ed.), *The Transfer of Power, 1942–7,* 12 vols (London: HMSO, 1970–83)
V&A	V&A Collections, Victoria and Albert Museum, London

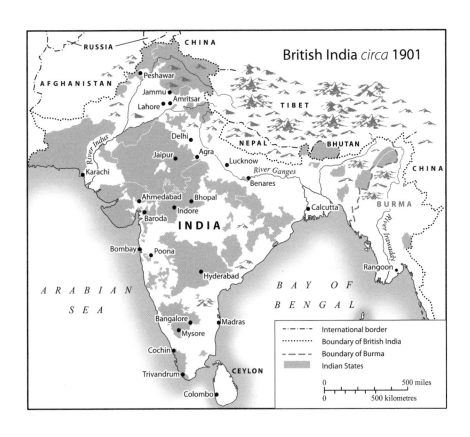

British India *circa* **1901**

RUSSIA
CHINA
AFGHANISTAN
Peshawar
Jammu
Amritsar
Lahore
TIBET
River Indus
Delhi
Jaipur
Agra
NEPAL
BHUTAN
Lucknow
River Ganges
CHINA
Karachi
Benares
Ahmedabad
Bhopal
Indore
Calcutta
BURMA
Baroda
INDIA
River Irrawaddy
Bombay
Poona
Hyderabad
Rangoon
ARABIAN
SEA
BAY OF
BENGAL
Bangalore
Madras
Mysore
Cochin
Trivandrum
CEYLON
Colombo

— · — · — International border
·········· Boundary of British India
— — — — Boundary of Burma
▨ Indian States

0   500 miles
0   500 kilometres

INTRODUCTION

Shortly before she became Empress of India in 1876, Queen
Victoria asked her courtiers to find out whether she was already
known by that title. She thought so. She herself had used it
on occasion, for example in June 1872. On being told that three envoys
from Burma would not prostrate themselves before her on being
received at court, the queen declared, '[A]s Empress of India, I must
insist on this.' The following year, she inquired of the Liberal government 'how it was that the title of Empress of India, which is frequently
used in reference to her Majesty has never been officially adopted'.
At the time the Duke of Argyll, then secretary of state for India,
suggested that the title had been used in the text of the 1858 proclamation that had transferred the Government of India from the East India
Company to the Crown. Experts scrutinised the proclamation in all
its different vernaculars, from Persian, Urdu and Hindi through to
Gujarati, Malayalam and Tamil, but to no avail: there was no trace
of the word 'empress' in any version.[1] So in 1876 the search resumed.
Lord Carnarvon, secretary of state for the Colonies was sure that the
title was in use in Australia. The queen's resident churchman, the dean
of Windsor, chipped in with some historical corroboration, showing
that Athelstan had worn an imperial crown. A schoolgirl wrote in to

1

point out that, according to her geography schoolbook, the queen was indeed 'Empress of India'. Semi-official proof was found too. The India Office unearthed a telegram to the Emir of Kabul in which the queen was referred to as 'Empress of India'.[2] It was too little and too late to change anything. Benjamin Disraeli's government went ahead with the Royal Titles legislation. For the first and only time in British history, a reigning queen became an empress as well.

Queen Victoria's ministers may have suffered from mild amnesia over her imperial title. By the time the history of her reign came to be written total memory loss had set in. There has never been a full study of the British monarchy and India. Queen Victoria personified British rule in India for almost half a century, formally from 1858, when the Crown took over from the East India Company, and by statute from 1876, when she assumed the title of Empress of India. After her death in 1901, her son (Edward VII), grandson (George V) and two great-grandsons (Edward VIII and George VI) all went on to be Emperors of India. Another great-grandson, Louis Mountbatten, was there in 1947 as the last British viceroy when the curtain came down on the Raj. This long relationship between the British royal family and the Indian subcontinent has eluded full analysis. As her reign came to an end there were some attempts both in India and in Britain to put Queen Victoria's rule in India into historical perspective, but the queen herself barely merited a mention in the chronological sweep.[3] Later, the prospect of devolution of power to India produced some potted constitutional histories of the status of the Crown in India. Written as British authority in India was waning, these dry tomes were prescriptive as much as descriptive, and hardly bothered to distinguish one monarch from the next.[4] The Crown and not its wearer was the point at issue.

Since Britain withdrew from Empire, the political temperament has been set against telling a story of modern India with the monarchy as part of the plot. Postcolonial anger, embarrassment and indifference keep the topic off the agenda. Proud of their republican present, contemporary India and Pakistan remain sensitive about reminders of the colonial past. Disputed treasures, such as the Koh-i-Noor diamond, now part of the crown jewels in the Tower of London, or colonial atrocities such as the Amritsar massacre of 1919, still pop up in diplomatic crossfire. Symbols of empire have been renamed; for example, in Mumbai the main railway station, the Victoria Terminus (1887), changed its name to the Chhatrapati Shivaji Terminus in 1996. Or they have been replaced. In Udaipur a statue of Mohandas Gandhi now sits on the plinth once occupied by one of the queen-empress. Many imperial relics have simply been removed altogether from prominent public display.[5] In modern India the past *is* a foreign country, and its name is imperial Britain. Its emblems are no longer welcome; they speak of conquest, not of consent.

Yet on her death in 1901 Queen Victoria's imprint on India was everywhere, indelible and undeniable. There were statues large and small, starting with the first that went up in Bombay in 1872 and the last in Ayodhya in 1908. There was, and still is, the Victoria Memorial Hall in Calcutta, Lord Curzon's ostentatious tribute to the queen-empress.[6] After her death gazetteers and other topographical surveys listed hundreds of public buildings – hospitals, schools, colleges, clock towers, parks, bathing tanks, gardens, libraries and factories – that had been erected by public subscription in honour of the queen.[7] All this might be read as an exercise in official patriotism. Foreign regimes tend to encourage cults through such monuments. Except that only the Victoria Memorial Hall was a project conceived by officialdom, and even that relied on voluntary contributions as well. Elsewhere, the public iconography of the queen was the product of civic organisations. Some of this was princely patronage, but there were plenty of examples of less grandiose projects, supported by a wide range of Indians.

Set in stone, and set in type too, Queen Victoria was a literary phenomenon of nineteenth-century India. By 1901, around 200 biographies, verse collections and eulogies had been published since 1858 about Queen Victoria and the rest of her family.[8] In addition, her own diary – *Leaves from the Journal of Our Life in the Highlands* – was translated into several Indian languages. Queen Victoria's reign coincided with the flourishing of vernacular print culture across India, as printing press technology, improved communications and greater literacy expanded the reading public.[9] An empire of information gave way to an empire of education and entertainment, over which the Government of India kept a watchful eye through its surveillance of the publishing industry as well as its monitoring of the native newspaper press, in the process leaving behind a rich record of demotic text.[10] Biography and history were popular subjects, and within that genre Queen Victoria received plenty of attention, the texts sometimes accompanied by portraits of the queen. She was eulogised in poetry and song as well, particularly in Bengali: Sourindro Mohun Tagore was a one-man industry of celebratory verses devoted to the queen and her family. Queen Victoria also featured in the *ghazals* of Urdu poets, notably those who were exiled from the King of Delhi's court after 1857, and who found refuge in Jammu, Lahore and Rampur, sometimes writing under commission from their princely patrons, on other occasions independently.[11] Many of these writers and poets, who cut their teeth on Queen Victoria, are today revered as part of a literary renaissance in colonial India that paved the way for political nationalism in the late nineteenth and twentieth centuries.[12] During her reign there was less of a contradiction between nationalist poetics and loyalism than might be supposed.

The queen was also the object of much attention from India. Tokens of loyalty and esteem poured into the British court from the princes of India. Their generosity fuelled the success of the famous 1851 exhibition at the Crystal Palace in London's Hyde Park, and they bankrolled two major late Victorian institutions, the Imperial and Colonial Institute in Kensington and the Indian Institute in Oxford. Indian professions of loyalty also came in the shape of addresses, presents and memorials, usually sent on formal occasions such as her accession to the throne, the transfer of power in 1858 and during her two jubilees in 1887 and 1897, but also at times of celebration and bereavement in the royal family.[13] The Indian princes led the way in this form of direct contact with the monarch, but with the mushrooming of literary societies, schools and colleges, trade and municipal associations, and *sabha* and *anjuman* organisations from the 1860s onwards, memorials came from a larger cross section of Indian society. Indeed, so persistent were Indian memorialists that the Government of India frequently changed

4

the rules on direct communication with the queen so as to limit the traffic. At times it seemed as though effusions of Indian loyalty did not require encouragement so much as containment.

Such a culture of loyalism is easier to measure than to interpret. Undoubtedly, the colonial state played its part in the fabrication of Queen Victoria, managing the monarchy in India in ways that are similar to the cults of the emperor that emerged at the same time in Tsarist Russia, the France of Louis Napoleon, Meiji Japan after 1868, and the Austria-Hungary of Franz-Josef.[14] However, British rule was always spread thinly on the ground in India. With fewer than 1,000 officials and around 160,000 European settlers at most, it is hard to conceive how some 250 million Indians could be dragooned into silent adoration of the queen. More nuanced explanations of loyalism are required. Indian reverence for the queen might be seen as 'clientelism' or collaboration; that is to say, loyalism was a device by which concessions might be extracted from the colonial power.[15] There is mileage in this, particularly when it comes to examining parts of Indian society such as the Indian princes, the mercantile communities of Bombay, Calcutta and Madras, and the *zamindars* of Bengal, all amongst the most vocal cheerleaders for the Crown throughout the queen's reign. But the popularity of the queen spread well beyond Indians who made their living out of the Raj.

There are other explanations on offer. Indian loyalism, especially of the type that permeated the rhetoric of the early years of the Indian National Congress, formed in 1885, has been written off as typifying the timid outlook of the pre-Gandhian generations of intellectuals and activists. Traditional and conservative in their social views, they were cautious in their demands for political change, their faith in European liberalism a symptom of their colonial captivity. Patriarchy in private and imperial patriotism in public went hand-in-hand.[16] It is perhaps inevitable that Indian nationalism of Queen Victoria's reign should be so judged as supine and conformist. Looking backwards to India before Gandhi in this way emphasises the immense distance travelled by later generations of Indian patriots and freedom fighters, whose opposition to the Raj was so uncompromising. Except that Gandhi was also a loyalist, prominent in the support he gave to the Crown whilst a lawyer and newspaper editor in the British colony of Natal in southern Africa.[17] Loyalty to Queen Victoria was not just incidental to nineteenth-century Indian nationalism, a polite addition for the sake of form – it was central to its ideology. This points to other possible interpretations of Indian loyalism. One argument, advanced by the late Christopher Bayly, is that the institution of the British Crown in India after 1858 sanctioned older forms of Indian indigenous patriotism, as traditional ideas about 'good counsel', virtuous rule and *dharma* were turned against officials. In this way, opposition to British rule developed within what Bayly termed the 'cocoon of loyalism'.[18] Similarly, another recent historiographical intervention suggests that Crown rule helped to create the space for 'imperial citizenship', the means by which Indians could forge a hybrid identity as the queen's subjects, aspiring through empire to gain the status and rights that were denied them because of their race. Entry into imperial institutions both in India and in Britain – the civil service, the universities, associational life, ultimately the Westminster Parliament itself – was successfully contested by Indians, behaving as both subjects and citizens of the Crown.[19] Such reformulations of loyalty in the age of Empire as these might be applied more generally to India under Queen Victoria. The monarchy authorised ways of belonging to a wider imperial identity that transcended class, religion, nation and ethnicity.

Empress is a study of the impact of India upon Queen Victoria, and at the same time the influence of the queen over Indian political and cultural life. Victoria never visited India. Although she received a variety of Indians at court, for much of her reign India was lived in her imagination, stimulated by sources at home and on the subcontinent. She started out with the martial and evangelical prejudices of her age, wanting to conquer and convert India. That did not last. The Indian rebellion of 1857–8 changed her views completely, as it did for many Victorians – only that Queen Victoria moved in the opposite direction, becoming more sympathetic to India and its people, not less, and growing more tolerant and less instinctively racist than her fellow-Britons. By the 1880s, many of her courtiers at home and senior officials in India thought she had gone too far that way, instinctively taking the side of Indians in various disputes with the viceroys' rule. In India, the queen was made known through different means. Now and then, the lead was taken by the Government of India, for example in the official visits to the Indian subcontinent by members of the queen's own family. Missionaries did their best to inculcate the image of a Christian monarch. Mostly, however, the queen existed in the Indian imaginary in all its literary, religious, political and cultural forms. Indian people took hold of Queen Victoria and made her their own. By the end of her life she was as much an Indian maharani as a British monarch.

Three themes are interwoven throughout the chronological narrative of the book. Firstly, I emphasise the agency of the queen. I argue that when it comes to India Queen Victoria needs to be seen less as a constitutional monarch hedged in by protocol of the sort with which we are familiar nowadays, and more as a dynastic imperial ruler of the long eighteenth century. Historians have overemphasised the quiescence of Queen Victoria, unduly preoccupied with the symbolic role she played in the 'propaganda of Empire' that emerged in Britain from the 1870s. The actual voice of the queen is seldom heard in these studies of the 'democratic royalism' of the era.[20] Queen Victoria has been silenced for too long. After all this was the Europe of her age and not ours. By the time the Government of India transferred from the East India Company to the Crown in 1858, most of Europe was ruled over by dynastic monarchs in ever-enlarging empires: the Romanovs in Russia, Louis Napoleon in France, Franz-Josef in Austria-Hungary, followed not long after by the Wilhelmine imperial monarchy of Germany. To these Continental empires were added overseas annexes: the Portuguese in Brazil, the French in Mexico (albeit briefly) and the Dutch in Indonesia. Only the Spanish colonial empire was in retreat. This was the heyday of viceregal rule; that is to say, a system of government in which the apparatus of European monarchy was applied to remote colonies and dependencies.[21] Queen Victoria was an important part of this new more global monarchy of the nineteenth century. With her marriage to Prince Albert, alongside the existing Hanoverian connections of her own family, she became connected to many of the smaller Protestant courts of Europe, a sphere that widened down to her death as her own children and grandchildren were married into Continental royalty. Some of this dynastic influence is touched upon in older studies of the queen and foreign policy. In two cases – Ireland and Canada – the place of the Crown in colonial governance has been examined at length.[22] In India her prerogative powers were even more extensive, the norms of parliamentary government applied less. As head of the Anglican church overseas, as titular head of the armed forces in India, and eventually as sovereign, in theory the queen had greater powers of patronage and control over India than anywhere else. India became an extension of her court. Men who began their careers as part of the royal entourage at home – for example, the 1st Marquess of Dalhousie, Charles Canning and Lord Dufferin – went on to assume command in India, taking their habits of intimate correspondence with the queen with them. A constant stream of traffic from the Raj also passed through the queen's court: military officers, churchmen, civil servants, travellers, philanthropists and Indian royalty, bringing to the queen information and stories from India. It is not fashionable to suggest that there was a 'court' interest in nineteenth-century British politics.[23] At times, however, in Indian affairs the queen behaved like a monarch of old, exploiting her own back-channels of communication, pushing for the promotion of her favourites, and leaning on politicians sympathetic to her views. Denied a political role at home, she found it instead in her Indian dominion.

Secondly, the book considers the uses to which the Government of India put the name and fame of the queen. In the aftermath of the Indian rebellion of 1857–8, the full apparatus of the Crown was rolled out as a means of pacification and reassurance. At the heart of this exercise lay a text: the queen's proclamation of 1858. With its promises of clemency, toleration and equality, the proclamation was immediately dubbed the 'Magna Carta' of India, and went on to achieve a status almost as potent as that of the queen.[24] That was not all. The name of the queen underpinned the law, finance and currency, the new Indian Civil Service and the newly amalgamated army. Here lay the roots of the 'ideology of the Raj', normally dissected by historians without any reference to the Crown. A notable exception is Bernard Cohn's brilliant examination of the Imperial Assemblage of 1877.[25] Cohn's work apart, British royalty in India is seen as incidental, or ornamental to imperial authority, the gloss and not the substance of the Raj. This is only half the story. For instance, much has been written about how colonial rule in India after mid-century was Janus-faced: liberal and inclusive in theory, but authoritarian and racist in practice.[26] Queen Victoria stood for this duality. Formally, she constituted colonial authority in India, giving sovereignty and legitimacy to the state, sanctioning the policies carried out in her name. At the same time, as a female monarch, she represented justice and charity. She was a beacon of beneficence in ways in which British bureaucracy in India could never be, either before 1858 or after. Abstract and remote, the fictive power of the queen both buttressed and softened the rule of colonial difference. There was no masterplan. Sometimes Indian officials and commentators spoke as though there was: how they had discovered the mystery of the lure of kingship in the east, an orientalised understanding of status and symbolism. For the most part, however, the usage of the queen by her officials was banal. Once the East India Company yielded power, sovereignty passed automatically to the Crown. The Government of India accordingly attached the queen to the nomenclature and motifs of the new regime. Little did they know what a runaway success she would be. In time it turned out that they had created a Frankenstein of the proclamation and the benevolent image of the queen that went with it. By the end of her reign officials dared not invoke the queen's words of 1858, for fear of the expanded notions of liberty and citizenship that it set out. After her death, the Government of India went on putting out fires using the monarchy, but with diminishing returns, and with less reliance on the proclamation.

Thirdly, the book charts the diffusion of representations of Queen Victoria in Indian political culture. Not least because of the 1858 proclamation, the queen developed iconic status in India. Direct criticism of her was extremely rare. She largely escaped the satirical cartoonists' pen, appearing only on occasion as a benign Britannia.[27] There was no one version of the queen that dominated. Hindus might associate her with deliverance from Mughal rule, Muslims might see her as the champion of minority rights. She was seen to be on the side of economic modernity and liberal reform. After 1858 she represented the idea of the beneficent state, alert to the cries of the peasants and victims of famine. She was looked up to by the principal movements of religious reform in nineteenth-century India, amongst them the Brahmo Sumaj. But she also was a guiding light to Muslim educational reform for men such as Syed Ahmed Khan. Over time she came to be seen as the ally of Indian nationalism. Indeed, for the Indian National Congress, the monarch was their greatest weapon, not their fiercest foe. Above all, Queen Victoria's identity as a woman, and particularly after 1861 as a widow, stimulated the idea of her as an exemplary female. Some of the ways in which the queen was drawn into the sexual politics of Empire are hinted at in classic scholarship on gender and the nation in colonial India, but they remain undeveloped.[28] She was invoked in discussions about female education, widow status and marriage reform, about the *zenana* (the Indian convention of female seclusion), and in the campaigns for the caring professions. In all these ways, by the 1880s, the epithet of 'mother of India' began to be applied to Queen Victoria, around the same time that 'mother India' entered common parlance.[29] She occupied an imaginary space, helping to define a national community, at no time more so than during her two jubilee years of 1887 and 1897, events that spanned the first decade or so of the Indian National Congress. After her death in 1901, it was as though India awoke from a 'strange hypnotism', as the nationalist Bipin Chandra Pal described colonial rule.[30] Her successors never had the same reputation in India as model monarchs. The Crown came to be seen as inseparable from the Government of India, and the wider system of British imperialism. By 1930 a rhetoric of republicanism had taken over: secular and socialist, with an Islamic counterpart. By the time of the last royal proclamation of June 1948, announcing the abolition of the imperial title, there was nothing left in India of the royal appeal or appeals to royalty. So nervous and tense were the British that India and Pakistan were almost the very last new members of the Commonwealth to host a royal visit. The mood had swung the other way.

The passage of time is a distorting mirror. India may now be the largest democratic republic in the world, but for ninety years it was the most extensive monarchical empire ever known, less populous than the India of today, but greater in its girth (including modern-day Pakistan, Bangladesh and from 1886 Burma). At the apex of the Raj for much of this time presided a diminutive white woman, ensconced in a retro-Gothic castle some 4,000 miles away. How Indian people, princes and queen first encountered each other, how they drew together and how they were forced apart, is recounted in the book that follows. It is a history of modern monarchy with the monarch restored to life. It is a case study of the imperial dimension to British politics and culture during the nineteenth century. Most of all it is a missing chapter in the story of the making of modern India.

CHAPTER 1

CROWN AND COMPANY

'Her Majesty seems to take a deep interest in Indian Affairs and . . . is not ill-informed on the subject.' So wrote John Hobhouse, president of the Board of Control to Lord Elphinstone, governor of Madras, shortly after Victoria came to the throne in 1837. The news was double edged. It was rumoured that Elphinstone, a courtier to William IV, had been exiled to India as the young princess had grown too fond of him.[1] It was about as close a connection that Victoria had to India in the early years of her reign. For Victoria was a 'Whig' queen, tutored in the realities of constitutional monarchy by Lord Melbourne, the prime minister, and his Whig colleagues. They managed the choice of her husband, they supplied the staff of the royal household, and Lord Melbourne himself guided the eighteen-year-old queen through her first meetings of the Privy Council, initiating her in her new responsibilities in domestic and foreign policy.[2] Not that there were too many of these. For Queen Victoria was also a 'Whig' queen in that she was the first new monarch of the era ushered in by the Whigs' 1832 reform act, her crown prerogative substantially limited by the powers of Parliament and an expanded electorate keen to root out the excesses of royal rule which had dominated the later years of her Hanoverian predecessors.

Nowhere in the new queen's realm were the reins on her power held tighter than in India. Since the late eighteenth century Britain had governed the presidencies of Bengal, Bombay and Madras through the East India Company.[3] The Company also administered British relations across the rest of the Indian subcontinent. The Company did not hold power without responsibility. The governors were accountable to the British Parliament via the president of the Board of Control who sat in the Cabinet. Successive renewals of the East India Company's charter in 1813 and 1833 loosened the grip of the Company, opening up India to missionaries, ending the Company's monopoly over trade in and out of India, and removing the influence of Company stockholders from any say in Company policy. Most important of all, the 1833 charter renewal invested the Board of Control with full authority over the Company and centred that authority in Bengal, with the governor there becoming governor-general of all of British India. For the first time, British policy in India was made as much in London as in Calcutta. The modernising instincts of the era began to take over. Free trade, state education and legal codification were all experimented with in India in the late 1820s and 1830s, despite not yet being established practice back home.[4] In this so-called 'dual government' by Company and Parliament there was no room for anyone else. Certainly not for an ageing monarchy whose track record at managing overseas conquests was poor. Much ambiguity and potential confusion remained, however. In theory the British Crown retained patronage over one part of the armed forces in India – the royal troops – and also had the final say over the selection of the three governors, as well as senior judicial and ecclesiastical appointments. The monarch was the head of the Church of England in India, and, since 1813, the Crown had been the nominal sovereign over all Indian territories. Who exactly was in charge?

This chapter explores how the role of the Crown in the Government of India was understood at the outset of Queen Victoria's reign. For many, it was Whig business as usual in India. But not everyone saw it this way. For some, Victoria symbolised national regeneration and a fresh start. Indian rulers responded to her accession by welcoming her imperial authority. Victoria's accession also coincided with the expansion of the evangelical mission to India – new bishoprics were established at Madras in 1835 and Bombay in 1837 – and the new queen became a focal point for various Christian campaigns. With her marriage to Prince Albert in 1840 and the change of government in Britain from Whig to Tory under Sir Robert Peel the following year, Victoria severed her dependence on the Whigs, and began to see India through different eyes.

Empire by Treaty

By 1837, there were over forty separate treaties formalising relations between Britain and India. Not one of them mentioned the British monarch. From the Treaty of Allahabad in 1765 through to the contentious agreement with the King of Awadh concluded by the governor-general, Lord Auckland, shortly after Victoria came to the throne, the details of British government in India were set out in an assortment of official documents, negotiated between agents of the East India Company and the ruling houses of the various Indian kingdoms and territories.[5] These treaties confirmed financial and military arrangements, and specified the extent to which the British government could interfere in the internal administration of each state. Many had been concluded amidst the dying embers of battle, as Britain consolidated its hold over India during the later eighteenth and early nineteenth centuries with Mughal authority waning in the north and centre of India, and Maratha chiefs and their French allies being swept aside in the south. These treaties also covered trading concessions, and by the 1830s were being used by the British government in India to regulate sati (widow-burning) and female infanticide. Their remit was not confined to the Indian subcontinent. Nepal (1816), Burma (1826) and (as a temporary protectorate) Java (1811) were all brought under British control through the mechanism of the Company treaty. The same formula was extended across the Indian Ocean to Arab states and to eastern Africa, mainly to enforce compliance with the abolition of the slave trade.[6] Taken together, the treaties provide a compendium of British supremacy in India. Oddly, no one saw fit to list them until the early 1830s, and a full assessment was not provided until the mid-1860s.[7]

Without exception, the East India Company and not the Crown signed off these treaties. Since the revolution of 1688–9, the Company had distanced itself from royal patronage, and operated with considerable autonomy, virtually a sovereign state in its own right.[8] Company men on the spot were the treaty signatories along with the Indian ruler. In this way the Treaty of Allahabad of 1765, which at the stroke of a pen placed millions of Indian peasant cultivators under Company rule, was a gentleman's agreement between Shah Alam II, the Mughal emperor, Robert Clive, the commander of the East India Company forces, and John Carnac, commander of the Bengal forces. In theory, Company officials could make treaties like this in India on a whim. Only from 1784 was it required that all treaties had to be ratified by the governor-general in Council, who in turn reported to London. By then the British Parliament was still reeling from the scandals surrounding the Nawabs of Arcot, the rulers of the Carnatic region of eastern India. Allied by Company treaty to the British forces in their fight against French and Maratha armies, the Nawabs ran up huge debts to finance their troops, and many of their creditors were English and Scottish MPs. The 'Arcot interest' in the House of Commons proved at the time an irresistible lobby, and the Nawabs in turn appealed for support by writing to George III (and to Queen Charlotte), amplifying their complaint with diamond jewels.[9] Sorting out the debts of the Nawabs took decades. The incident served as an enduring reminder of the need to keep the English constitution out of Indian politics. Some of the most important treaty settlements of the period – such as the Treaty of Seringapatam – were stamped with the military imprimatur of the 'Commander-in-Chief of the Force of His Britannic Majesty', but even these documents made it clear that the legal authority on the British side was the Company. All of this made perfect sense within the context of trade and rule overseas by a chartered company. Introducing the person of the sovereign to the treaty might present problems. It elevated the Indian signatory to a status that the Company was reluctant to recognise, and it created the possibility of Indian rulers considering themselves lieges or allies of the British Crown, with the right to approach the monarch directly, as had the Nawab of Arcot. Controlling the Crown at home meant distancing it from sources of venality in India.

Inevitably, in the absence of the monarch in person, the Company itself came to play the role of de facto sovereign. This was partly by design. Victorious over Tipu Sultan in Mysore, and over the Mughal stronghold of Delhi, Richard Wellesley, the governor-general, set about turning the Company seat of Calcutta into the capital of British India. The new headquarters was a palace. Government House was completed by 1803, and included a throne room, where the governor-general's throne dwarfed a jewelled stool captured from Tipu. Government House became the focal point of Calcutta society, and also the venue for delegations of Indian rulers.[10] It was as much Irish as English. There were obvious parallels between Dublin Castle, the seat of the Lord Lieutenant of Ireland, and Government House. Dublin Castle had got its own throne room or 'presence chamber' in the 1780s, where Irish lords swore allegiance to the British Crown, and the Lord Lieutenants of Ireland enjoyed viceregal powers not unlike those developing in India. Both Wellesley and his successor Cornwallis swapped the top post in India for its equivalent in Ireland.[11] In other respects, Wellesley and his successors fashioned a more improvised style of kingly rule without the king. They began the convention of approving dynastic succession in Indian states. In 1803 Wellesley's brother Arthur attended in person the installation of Krishnaraja Wadiyar III, the new Maharaja of Mysore, and in 1819 the Marquess of Hastings went to Lucknow to authorise the enthronement of the King of Awadh, Ghazi-ud-Din Haider Shah.[12] Governors-general at Calcutta also started the practice of firing royal salutes to mark the accession of new rulers in the Indian princely states. In use from 1803, the gun salute was a significant step in applying royal protocol by proxy to India.[13]

As was the durbar tour. Dating from the years of Mughal rule, durbars were ritual meetings of rulers with their dependents from whom they were owed homage. Durbars involved the exchange of visits and gifts – *nuzzer* – the form of the visit, and the value of the gift depending precisely on the status of the two parties involved. Beginning in 1814 with Lord Moira (governor-general 1813–23 and known as the Marquess of Hastings from 1816), the Company incorporated the ritual of the durbar into a new routine of regular tours of Indian treaty territories allied to or indirectly controlled by the British. Travelling by river in a golden barge with a regiment of soldiers, and making encampments along the route, Moira held durbars at Benares (Varanasi), Lucknow and Bareilly, and met the sons of the Emperor of Delhi at Allahabad. He evidently disliked the fawning ceremonial involved, believing it only served to keep up the appearance and not the reality of Indian princely power. Company officials were not supposed to take gifts from Indians, so anything of value presented at the durbar was immediately sent back to the *toshakhana* (treasury) in Calcutta and sold off.[14] Hastings's successors Amherst and Bentinck followed suit with durbar tours of their own. By the 1830s, governors-general were spending as much time 'up-country' on the road, river and in the saddle as at their desk in Calcutta.[15] For the Company, the durbar tour was the means of keeping tabs on the extent of lands and loyalty under British control. Some Company officials favoured cosying up to the courts. From Rajputana James Tod envisaged a new romanticised feudalism, calling for William IV to lead local rulers under the 'banner of that chivalry of which your Majesty is head'.[16]

Ultimately, the Company legitimated royalty in India by leaving intact the Mughal emperor. Although defeated at the battle of Delhi in 1803, the Emperor Akbar II was allowed to maintain his court inside the Red Fort in Delhi.[17] One explanation for this state of affairs was that the Company was authorised by an imperial *farman* to administer former liege states of the empire. For its part the Company was content to leave Akbar II inside his gated enclave with his poets and painters. But it was an awkward stalemate. Hastings refused to show deference to the imperial title, whilst Akbar II did not recognize the Company as the paramount power. Over the years that followed the formal powers of the Delhi emperor were reduced by the British. The Nizam of Hyderabad and the Nawab of Awadh were encouraged to become royal rulers in their own right, and so end their obeisance to the emperor at Delhi.

The nizam refused, but a king of Awadh was proclaimed, as we have seen, at Lucknow in 1819. This only served to cause confusion. Frustrated by the Company, Akbar II turned to the British monarchy for redress, sending his portrait to the dying George IV, a gift that was accepted by his successor, William IV. In 1832, Akbar II followed up by sending a delegation to Britain, headed by the Bengali reformer (and former Company servant) Ram Mohan Roy, who quickly became the toast of Unitarian and liberal activists in London and around the country. Although lionised for his efforts to end sati, Ram Mohan Roy's mission was not an official success. He only got as far as meeting the king's brother, the Duke of Sussex, and tragically died before making the return trip to Calcutta. Furthermore, the squeeze on Akbar II was tightened. In 1835 the residual title of 'emperor' was downsized to 'king', and the emperor's image was removed from coinage in India.[18] When his son Bahadur Shah Zafar succeeded him in 1837, a few months after Victoria became queen, there was thus little left of the imperial reach of the Mughal throne. The new kings of Awadh were in no better state. In an era when new monarchies were being invented across Europe and Latin America, the court at Lucknow was neither puppet nor master. The Awadhi court also looked to the British court for recognition. In 1835, the new King of Awadh sent over gifts to William IV, and his 'ambassador' was received at St James's Palace by William IV and Queen Adelaide.[19] The pattern was becoming clear. The retention by the Company of the forms of royal rule in India left the lines between Company and Crown blurred, and when the Company paid no heed to Indian royalty, the British Crown was expected to respond. So much for undivided sovereignty.

A Whig Queen

The death of William IV and accession of Victoria was announced on 20 June 1837 in London and at the beginning of September in Calcutta. In London there was no reference to India or indeed any other part of the Empire in the proclamation of the new monarch, nor at her coronation a year later. Her official title was 'Queen of Great Britain and Ireland, and Defender of the Faith' and although the shorthand 'Queen of these realms' was also used, there was nothing to indicate that Queen Victoria's dominion stretched beyond the British Isles. In India a more expansive view was taken. The circular of the governor-general informed the princely houses of India of the accession of Victoria to the 'imperial throne'. In a sermon marking the event in Calcutta, an exuberant chaplain described how the new queen 'can look east and west and north and south, and view in every quarter, dominions that own her sway'.[20]

Sway, however, was not the same as rule. In Britain and in India it was taken for granted that Victoria would abide by the constitutional norms of the day limiting her power. For example, the East India Company Court of Directors were quick to send her an address of congratulations. At their July meeting, leading lights of the Company were all effusive in their admiration for the new queen, but could not avoid lacing their laudations with a hint that she might let them get on with matters their own way: they prayed 'that the welfare of the millions of subjects in your Majesty's Indian territories intrusted to Parliament by our charge, may be preserved and advanced under your Majesty's mild and beneficent sway'.[21] The same line was taken in India. When the Raja of Alwar attempted to a send a *nuzzur* of gold directly to Victoria on the occasion of her succession, he was told that this was not possible, as 'the Governor-General is the representative of the British nation and power', and 'he is willing to receive in Her Majesty's name the expression of the good will of her Indian allies and the homage of her Indian subjects and dependents'.[22] Lord Auckland, the governor-general, saw no special reason to mark Victoria's accession officially. The townspeople of Calcutta sent an address of congratulations to the queen, but the absence of any government representation at the public meeting convened to agree the address was noted.[23] In India there was also some incredulity at the news of the accession of a female ruler. From Rajahmundry (Rajamamaherdravaram) in Madras it was reported that one local raja found it beyond his comprehension 'how she was to contrive to reign, and how *men* were to agree to obey her'. Back in Calcutta, Emily Eden, sister of the governor-general, Lord Auckland, recorded the remark of James Prinsep, the man at the mint charged with stamping rupees with Victoria's head: 'I wish we had never changed the stamp; I should not wonder if the natives were to mistrust a coin with nothing but a woman's head on it.'[24]

Only the princely states of India responded to the accession of the new British monarch with a sense of decorum. The governor-general's September circular was despatched to forty-one royal houses. Over the next four months, more than half of them sent back their formal replies to Calcutta, enclosing *kharitas* (formal letters) of congratulation to the queen, via the governor-general. Some were ornate ornamental addresses, some came with separate accounts of the ceremonial firing of cannon, drumrolls and elephant fights organised to accompany the pronouncement. The Maharana of Udaipur went into silent seclusion for the day.[25] From Lahore in the Punjab came perhaps the most eloquent of all the addresses, from Maharaja Ranjit Singh, the 'lion of the Punjab'. The 'letter of felicitation' undoubtedly lost something in its translation from Persian into English, but the sentiment was clear, invoking a sacred garden paradise. Tidings of the new queen, the letter declared, meant that 'the gardens of dominion received fresh attraction and the bowers of imperial sway assumed throughout a verdant aspect. It has caused the Salsabil[26] of joy to permeate from all sides and opened the channels of felicity in every direction'.[27] Without waiting for approval from Calcutta, Ranjit Singh entrusted the letter to the safe keeping of his military aide, General Jean-Baptiste Ventura, to take to London and deliver in person to the queen.

Ranjit Singh's personal epistle was timely diplomacy. The letter came just at the moment when the armed forces of Ranjit Singh's Sikh kingdom were joining with the British in overthrowing the Afghan king, Dost Mohammad Khan, and replacing him with Shah Shuja Durrani.[28] Queen Victoria was drawn further into this pact when Lord Auckland finally met Ranjit Singh one year later on the banks of the Sutlej river at the end of November 1838, ahead of the invasion of Afghanistan. In front of their large entourages, Auckland and Ranjit Singh exchanged gifts, and, as Auckland later described, 'one of them, I was sure, he would receive with more than ordinary satisfaction': a portrait of the queen, drawn by his sister, Emily Eden, and 'framed at Delhi in Gold & Jewels'.[29] This presentation was not only most probably the earliest unveiling of the likeness of Queen Victoria in India, it was also the first instance of the British authorities using the image and name of the queen to ease their way through the complexities of imperial rule. Lord Auckland may have been reluctant to proclaim the new sovereign with pomp and circumstance in Calcutta, but he had no hesitation at all in presenting her portrait to Britain's most valuable ally of the era. It suggests a neat irony, to which this book will return frequently. Constitutional propriety both in Britain and in India relegated Queen Victoria to a minor role in Indian statecraft; power relations on the ground demanded she show her face whenever possible.

Defender of the Faith

If politicians were keen to dampen down expectations about the new queen in India, there was one section of British society for whom Victoria was the rising star: the evangelical church. As Charles Blomfield, the Bishop of London, described her at her coronation, she was 'called to the seat of imperial power in all the freshness and fulness of youthful hope and promise'. For Sydney Smith, canon at St Paul's, she was a 'patriot queen', albeit a Whig one – for religious toleration at home and peace abroad.[30] Some of the first acts of Victoria's reign signalled her status as Defender of the Faith in the Empire. On the eve of their departure, she met with India's two new bishops: George Spencer (Madras) and Thomas Carr (Bombay), and issued a 'Letters Patent' authorising the expansion of the activities of the Society for the Propagation of the Gospel in Foreign Parts, one of the Church of England's leading missionary organisations.[31] There was more than dry formality to this. Victoria was at her most evangelical in these years. The Bishop of London, responsible for the overseas dioceses of the Anglican church and a keen supporter of Christian conversion of subject peoples, was Victoria's bishop, especially when she was resident at Buckingham Palace. He preached her coronation sermon. Her journals record him frequently in attendance at court, and also her enjoyment of his sermons. There were other early signals of her evangelicalism. Never a great reader, she spent a good part of the autumn of 1838 working her way through the biography of William Wilberforce, the hero of the campaign against the slave trade, but also the leading light of the Clapham Sect, which did so much to expand the Anglican mission overseas, including to India.[32]

In India the missionary churches of Britain had made great strides in the quarter century since they were allowed into the Company's territories. The see of Calcutta (1813), was subdivided in the mid-1830s to create Anglican bishops for Madras and Bombay. By then Protestant missions had been particularly successful in establishing stations and churches in southern India, the joint Church Missionary Society/ Society for the Propagation of the Gospel community at Tinnevelly (Tirunelveli) at the southernmost tip of India being the flagship. The Wesleyans had a foothold in Madras. Further north, the churches were moving steadily beyond their original settlements in Bengal. The pioneering Baptist mission, led by William Carey, was in Serampore (Svirampore), where they had established a college, and then in Calcutta, Delhi and Allahabad.[33] From the see of Calcutta, new zeal was added to the Anglican enterprise by the fifth bishop, Daniel Wilson, appointed in 1832, and made the metropolitan bishop for all of India in 1835. He claimed to have established nineteen new churches in his first four years, as far afield as Agra and Lucknow.[34] The Church of Scotland was not far behind its English brethren. Led by Alexander Duff, an overseas mission and later a college were founded in Calcutta.[35] Catholic missionaries were also supported, with the Company subsidising in fits and starts Portuguese and French missionaries in Madras and in western India, and providing for Catholic chaplains in the army.[36] Historical opinion differs on the extent to which Christian missions in India in these years were united in their drive towards conversion,[37] but they were certainly effective at rousing public opinion both in Britain and in India, and the accession of a new monarch provided an opportunity to intensify their campaigns.

Evangelicals were alarmed by British policy in India at the time of Victoria's accession. First, there was the British government in India's support for non-Christian religions – the observances of Muslims and Hindus in India. Public pressure, especially from women at home in Britain, had pushed the Indian government of Lord Bentinck into banning sati in 1829, but the ban only applied to the presidencies, and opponents of sati continued their campaigns, invoking Victoria along the way. One writer hoped that 'the beneficent rule of the young Island Queen of the West' be remembered for ending these 'wretched sacrifices'.[38] Moreover, in the name of toleration, religious festivals, temples and other forms of worship were supported by the state, most controversially in the shape of the pilgrim tax (levied on everyone so as to provide public funds for Hindu and Muslim pilgrimages). Both the tax and the Jagannath temple at Puri, the principal destination for Hindu pilgrims, were condemned by evangelical churchmen, who mobilised their congregations into a frenzied campaign. Over 400 public petitions calling for the suppression of 'idolatry' in India poured into Parliament in Victoria's first year.[39] Their supporters were quick to point out the contradiction between the advent of a new Christian queen and the persistence of state support for what was deemed an idolatrous religion. 'Shall the British government continue its patronage of this system, when by it the enthronement of our Queen is disgraced,' thundered John Eley, a Leeds reverend, just days before Victoria's coronation, whilst a few days later a Unitarian minister in Newcastle hoped that 'under her sway' the 'debasing power of idolatry' would be destroyed.[40]

However, it was another issue – the expansion of the Church of England in the Indian subcontinent – on which evangelical expectations of the new queen focused over the longer term. Spurred by the success of the new bishops in Madras and Bombay, the Church of England pushed for additional sees elsewhere in the Indian subcontinent. In 1841 the Bishop of London co-ordinated the new Colonial Bishoprics Fund, an initiative of the Society for the Propagation of the Gospel, supported at its inaugural public meeting by William Gladstone, then an opposition Tory MP.[41] Much of the work of the Fund was focused elsewhere in the Empire. But its efforts were felt in India and its surrounding territory too. Encouraged by his superior in London, the Bishop of Calcutta, Daniel Wilson, was instrumental in establishing a new diocese at Colombo in Ceylon (Sri Lanka) in 1845, and a decade later laid the foundations for the first English church in Rangoon (Yangon) after the East India Company forces invaded Burma (Myanmar). In India Wilson pressed ahead with plans to increase his establishment in Calcutta, so as to be able to send out more missionary clergy to the north-west and south to Madras, and to create a new subdivision of the diocese at Agra, in the heart of the old Mughal empire.[42] In 1845 he returned to Britain to muster support. He found none from the Court of Directors of the East India Company, and at the Board of Control Lord Ripon proved reluctant to intervene. However, Wilson secured an audience with the queen in March 1846, and returned to Calcutta with her personal gift of ten pieces of gold communion plate for the new cathedral in the city, duly consecrated two years later. A small token, perhaps, but much was made by Wilson of this royal contribution, and churchgoers in Calcutta seldom missed a chance thereafter to show their affection for their queen.[43]

Queen Victoria was an unwitting accomplice of the evangelical mission in India in the late 1830s and 1840s. Missionary publications detailing the onward march of the Christian church in India were sent to her and to Prince Albert.[44] Her regular dealings with the Bishop of London at a moment when the Anglican episcopate was going global undoubtedly reminded her of her duties as a Protestant monarch in a burgeoning empire. But in matters ecclesiastical, as in affairs of the state, she remained a Whig queen, and the Whigs in government were as indifferent to missionary creep in India as the East India Company was firmly opposed. Not for the first time in her life, Victoria became the focus of religious reform movements in India without getting involved herself. For her views about India to take shape, there needed to be a change of scene and of male company. That came with her marriage in 1840 to Albert, and the exit of the Whigs from government a year later.

East India Men

Until the change of government from Whig to Conservative in the late summer of 1841, Victoria was kept away from Indian affairs. The Whig prime minister, Lord Melbourne fed her snippets of information, especially as Lord Auckland's ill-advised invasion of Afghanistan unfolded, alarming her with news of Ranjit Singh's death in September 1839 and the self-immolation of some of the women at his court which accompanied his demise.[45] Otherwise, her lines of communication were poor. Hobhouse, the president of the Board of Control, was frequently at the Palace in his ministerial capacity and as a dinner guest, but he revealed little of official business to the queen, even when prompted by Melbourne.[46] All began to change however with Victoria's marriage to her cousin Prince Albert of Saxe-Coburg and Gotha in February 1840, an important turning point in her life as monarch, not least in relation to India. A married queen, and the prospect of a dynasty to follow, augured well for the survival and security of her reign. Breaking with the protocol followed at her accession, Government House in Calcutta led the way in announcing the marriage with fireworks and illuminations.[47] Effusive addresses of congratulation were sent from the citizens of Madras and Bombay, first for the marriage, and then over the next two years to welcome the first babies of the next generation of royals: Princess Victoria (born November 1840) and Albert Edward, the Prince of Wales (born just under a year later). Inevitably, the Prince of Wales, as future king, attracted more excitement than his elder sister.[48] These were not exclusively European celebrations. In Bombay, one of the principal Parsi businessmen of the city, Jamsetjee Jejeebhoy, played a conspicuous role in helping to organise the addresses.[49] Princely states – in the Carnatic, Gwalior, Sindh and Indore – sent addresses or celebrated with durbars and fireworks.[50]

That Victoria's marriage and her motherhood generated more headlines in India than her accession and coronation is not surprising. Crowning a monarch was one thing, finding a mate and producing a male heir was another, as anyone familiar with the House of Hanover in Britain, or with the princely houses of India, could attest. Her union with Albert, and the progeny it produced at a rapid rate (nine children in seventeen years), firmly established Victoria's as a monarchy built to last. Escaping the first two assassination attempts of her reign in 1840 and 1842 – both widely reported in India – helped too.[51] The story of

Albert's role here, as family patriarch, has been told many times. But just as important was the way in which he bolstered Victoria's political presence. Lord Melbourne and his ministers now had her consort to engage with as well as Victoria, and, although Albert was as youthful as the queen, he was not naïve on constitutional matters. Until his death in 1861, Albert contributed to a double-headed monarchy, undertaking public roles that Victoria could not, and developing expertise and interests that lay beyond her reach.[52]

One of these was the Anti-Slavery Society, a large meeting of which Prince Albert presided over in June 1840. It was the first occasion on which he spoke publicly, most probably pushed into participating by the queen, deeply impressed as she was by the example of William Wilberforce.[53] By the 1840s, the work of the Society had moved away from slavery in the British West Indies (abolished in 1833), and was focused instead on curbing slavery in America, on ending the slave traffic in coastal Africa and persuading the remaining slave powers such as Brazil to end the transatlantic trade. Additionally, at the moment when Albert guested at its convention, the Society was campaigning to outlaw the remaining pockets of slavery in India, and also pressing Parliament to monitor more closely an invidious new form of slavery: forced migration of poor Indian labourers to plantation economies in the West Indies and elsewhere – the so-called 'coolie' system.[54] Albert did not reappear at another Anti-Slavery Society meeting, but two years later the new prime minister, Sir Robert Peel, did pass on to him a lengthy memorandum dealing with slavery in India.[55]

From the Anti-Slavery Society, it was a natural step for Albert to become involved in another evangelical cause: the Society for the Propagation of the Gospel overseas, the oldest and most influential of all the Christian missionary organisations in Britain. He became its president in 1851, and delivered an address at its 150th anniversary celebration of that year. It was an unmemorable oration, being a short review of the Society's achievements, save for the prince's observation that the Society had helped to 'carry Christianity to the vast territories of India and Australia, which are at last again to be peopled by the Anglo-Saxon race'.[56] This was a curious statement. Given the occasion and his audience, it is likely that he was echoing some of the rhetoric of the Society and the evangelical churchmen they supported overseas. In endorsing the missionary enterprise in such unequivocal language, Albert was firmly attaching the monarchy to the export of Christianity to India. Where Victoria had been no more than a silent talisman for evangelical aspirations, Albert was turning out to be a more vocal champion.

Albert's greater role in public affairs coincided with the return of the Conservatives to government in 1841. As the administration of the country changed, so too did the personnel of the Court. For the first time India became more embedded in Queen Victoria's immediate world. Two changes in the royal household were to prove of long-term significance. In 1842 Lady Charlotte Canning and Lady Susan Ramsay were made ladies of the bedchamber. Their husbands joined Peel's government (Charles Canning as under-secretary of state at the Foreign Office in 1841, James Ramsay as vice-president at the Board of Trade in 1843).[57] Both men went on to fill the top post in India: Ramsay (better known as the Marquess of Dalhousie) was governor-general from 1848 until 1856, when he was succeeded by Canning, who became the first viceroy after the transfer of the Government of India from the East India Company to the Crown. Both men took their wives with them to India. By the time he went to India in 1848 the Marquess of Dalhousie was already a trusted servant of the court. In 1842 he organised the queen's first major visit outside London and the Home Counties – to Edinburgh – ensuring the greater visibility of the young monarch.[58] Slowly but surely, the links in a chain which would connect Victoria to India across her long reign were emerging. Peel's ministry also kept the queen up to date with news from India. Lord Fitzgerald, president of the Board of Control from 1841 to 1843, was especially assiduous. It was Fitzgerald who brought to court her first Indian visitor – Dwarkanath Tagore, the Bengali businessman and philanthropist – whom she sketched.[59]

Peel's government also introduced two Indian political heavyweights into Victoria and Albert's world: the Duke of Wellington and Lord Ellenborough. Both had a decisive impact on the royal view of India during the 1840s. Arthur Wellesley, Duke of Wellington, returned to his old post of commander in chief of the Army in 1842. In that role he struck up a friendship with Albert, and, indeed, took the young royal family under his wing more generally. Soon after his appointment, the duke hosted the royal visit to the naval docks at Portsmouth, and, later in the year, Victoria and Albert visited Walmer Castle, one of the duke's residences, perched on the edge of the Kent coast.[60] He carried the sword of state at the christening of the Prince of Wales in 1842 and later became godparent to their third child, Arthur, born in 1850 and destined for a military career, the latter event captured in Franz Winterhalter's 1851 group portrait of the royal couple with their infant son, receiving a gold casket from the duke, who might easily be taken for one of the adoring Magi. The Duke of Wellington was a key influence on Victoria and Albert's understanding of Indian affairs in the 1840s. Unlike his predecessor as titular head of the armed forces, Lord Hill, Wellington was a veteran of warfare in India. His reputation had been forged in the wars against Tipu in the south of India forty years previously, and he remained attached to the strategy of keeping India lightly governed but heavily fortified. Now in his seventies, Wellington was something of a handicap to civil government at home – his jitters over the Chartists in 1842 and 1848 brought much ridicule. However, he retained his renown as a military strategist. Successive volumes of his despatches from the era of the French and Napoleonic wars – including those from his Indian campaigns – were published to critical acclaim in the late 1830s. As Britain's invasion of Afghanistan went from bad to worse in the early 1840s his public pronouncements on Indian affairs carried weight.[61] The duke also encouraged Prince Albert in his military career, and in his side interest in army reform. Albert had received military training as part of his schooling, and shortly after his marriage to Victoria he was given command of a cavalry regiment of the British army, the 11th Hussars, their cherry-coloured trousers matching the livery of the Saxe-Coburg and Gotha house. From this point on Albert took a keen interest in the British way of warfare, and by the end of the decade was regularly writing memoranda on recruitment and the size of the military establishment, on training and practice in peacetime, and

British campaigns in India. So impressed was the duke by Albert's military acumen that he suggested in 1849 that Albert might succeed him as commander-in-chief.[62]

Peel's administration contained one other senior politician who now came to influence royal views about India. The new president of the Board of Control was Edward Law, Lord Ellenborough, and within a year he had moved closer to the action in India, going out to succeed Auckland as governor-general, thereby beginning an almost uninterrupted Conservative party monopoly on the head of the Indian government throughout the rest of Victoria's reign. Seldom can a change of office have produced such a turnaround in policy. A veteran of the Duke of Wellington's Cabinet of 1828–30, Ellenborough had been a cocksure and strident critic of the Whigs at home and in India during the ensuing decade. He disliked the close relationship that the Whigs enjoyed with the bankers and stockholders of the East India Company. He opposed the Anglicising policies of Bentinck and Auckland, and on arrival in India dramatically set about bringing the Afghan war to an end, before embarking on even more decisive intervention in Sindh and across the seas in China.[63] Victoria and Albert, as the next chapter narrates, looked on in wonder.

Once in Calcutta Ellenborough lost no time in taking the unusual step of writing to Victoria separately on all matters connected to Indian affairs. This was unprecedented. Previously, governors-general had sent their official despatches and confidential correspondence to the East India Company Court of Directors and to the president of the Board of Control, who then used his discretion in passing on information to the monarch. Ellenborough broke with that protocol, sending a monthly résumé of the latest news in India directly to the queen.[64] In so doing, he started up a convention that was followed by nearly all of his successors. For Ellenborough, this was more than a simple courtesy. He envisioned a special position for the British monarch in India. As he explained to Victoria, during his first durbar tour in 1843: 'were your Majesty to become the nominal Head of the Empire . . . [t]he princes and chiefs would be proud of their position as the Feudatories of an Empress'. He went on, explaining that if the princes were given reason to feel 'confidence in the intentions of their Sovereign', they would co-operate in the improvement of their dominions and the lives of their subjects. Finishing with a flourish, he told Victoria that he could 'see no limit to the future Prosperity of India' if it were governed with careful regard for the 'interests of the People . . . and not the pecuniary advantages of the Nation of Strangers to which Providence has committed the rule of this distant Empire'.[65] This was a truly remarkable letter. Ellenborough put the idea of 'empress' into the young queen's mind, over thirty years before it became her official title. Such audacity. For the direct assumption of power over India by the Crown ran counter in every respect to the past eighty years of British intervention in India. How far could Ellenborough take the queen and her ministers with him on this new course?

CHAPTER 2

WARRIOR QUEEN

The first vessel anywhere in the world to bear the new queen's name was the wooden sloop steamship *Victoria*, which slipped out of the Bombay dockyard in 1839. For the next fourteen years it plied an unspectacular passage back and forth to Aden and Suez, shuttling passengers, as well as the mail.[1] The main action lay not in the Indian Ocean but to the north and east. Between 1842 and 1853 the British Empire in Asia grew like never before – into Sindh and the Punjab (part of what is modern-day Pakistan), into coastal China and down into Lower Burma (nowadays the Irrawaddy delta region of Myanmar). It was probably the bloodiest decade of small colonial wars of Queen Victoria's reign, and the armed forces of the East India Company, both navy and troops, led the way.[2]

HMS *Victoria* escaped the fray, but the queen did not. From being a mere cipher in Indian affairs under the Whigs, Victoria became more directly associated with the burgeoning Empire from the early 1840s onwards. As Walter Arnstein has argued, her role as a 'warrior queen' was at least as important as her public identity as a young mother and wife. Now treaties were signed off in her name – most famously, the Treaty of Waitangi, establishing the new Crown colony of New Zealand, but also others in Asia and the Arabian Gulf. Her signature replaced that of the East India Company in treaties such as those with Muscat (1839) and Aden (1843), and the Treaty of Nanking (1842) which opened up Chinese ports to British traders and annexed the territory of Hong Kong island.[3]

Such changes did not simply reflect a difference of legal nomenclature, they also demonstrated increasing interest in the affairs of Empire, on the part of Victoria and Albert. With her domestic ministers reluctant to endorse a more martial monarchy – Sir Robert Peel quashed the proposal for a new military order to celebrate the birth of the Prince of Wales[4] – the queen turned to India. Here the influence of Lord Ellenborough was decisive. In his short governor-generalship of 1842–4, Ellenborough did more to upset the East India Company than anyone in his position before or after. Victoria took Ellenborough's side, and her views on the paramountcy of the Crown over the Company began to harden. Limited by convention as to what she could say publicly, her resolve took shape over the issue of campaign medals for all the victories in India and China during this period, as she insisted they be struck and awarded in her name. It was the beginning of a new royal style in India. As the Punjab kingdom fell, the symbols of rule transferred to her, as the story of the famous Koh-i-Noor diamond describes. By the time the charter of the Company was renewed for what turned out to be the final time in 1853, pressures in India and in Britain had moved control further in the direction of the Crown.

The Runaway Elephant

Vain and headstrong were just two of the more polite comments made about Lord Ellenborough, who left London at the end of October 1841 for Calcutta to replace Lord Auckland as governor-general. He departed bragging to the queen that 'we shall be in possession of the Emperor of China's Palace' by her birthday, and within a few months he was able to boast of reversing the unremitting bad news of the campaign in Afghanistan.[5] Victory at Jellalabad in April 1842 meant that British forces could retreat from Afghanistan with hostages saved and some dignity preserved, after both sides of the conflict suffered great losses.

The British forces exacted heavy retribution as they looted and burnt their way back over the border.[6] Further east it was clear by the spring that the combined forces of the Royal Navy and the East India Company navy were winning out in China. Captured Chinese flags were sent by the War Office to Buckingham Palace, to the evident pleasure of the queen.[7]

In his first year in India Ellenborough thus brought to an end two campaigns: the wars in Afghanistan and China. The pressure to open up the Chinese trade was an Indian as much as a Chinese question, insofar as the ending of the Company's monopoly in 1833 led to the growth of an overseas trading community in China. The opium trade, a legal enterprise, was spearheaded by merchant houses operating out of the ports of Gujarat and Bombay. Some of the most vocal agitators for free trade with China were the merchants of Bombay, who had also been effusive in their congratulations at the accession and marriage of the new queen.[8] For their part, Victoria and Albert identified with their new Chinese acquisition. Albert suggested their eldest child be known as Princess Victoria of Hong Kong. At the end of November, delighted at the news of the Treaty of Nanking, Victoria cut out from the newspaper its formal announcement, including the clause that Hong Kong was to be 'perpetually ceded to her Britannic Majesty', and placed it in her private journal.[9]

Ellenborough was not simply tying up loose ends. He was determined to leave his stamp on India.[10] He took personal command of the final stages of the exit from Afghanistan, and then proceeded to rule by proclamation. In the first of these official pronouncements, confirming the end of hostilities in Afghanistan, Ellenborough made public his criticism of Lord Auckland, upholding the principle of non-interference in neighbouring sovereign states. This was supplemented by a circular sent to the rulers of Nepal, Hyderabad, Nagpur, Awadh and elsewhere, describing the recapture of Ghazni and Kabul in Afghanistan, and the treaty with China 'dictated by the queen', and warning them to preserve tranquillity in their own states.[11] At the end of 1842 he held a durbar at Ferezepore, on the banks of the Sutlej, so that Dost Mohammad Khan, the Afghan Emir held prisoner by the British since 1839, could pay homage to him before returning to Kabul.[12] Ellenborough also sent in the Bombay army to mop up lingering rebel activity amongst the Emirs of Sindh, who remained defiant of the truce in Afghanistan. In Sindh, ignoring expert advice, Ellenborough gave Charles Napier carte blanche to turn a mission of control into one of conquest. By the following March, the Emirs had been defeated in decisive battles at Miani (Meeanee) and at Hyderabad, and the province was subjugated. The region bounded by the Indus river was added to British control, a territorial gain to which Ellenborough added a showy flourish of free trade by proclaiming the abolition of all the riverine custom duties and tolls. Napier made sure that the queen's birthday in this newest acquisition of the colonial Empire was marked with full military salutes.[13]

To cap it all, in an extraordinary act of theatre, Ellenborough authorised the removal of the sacred sandalwood gates of the mausoleum of Sultan Mahmud at Ghazni and their restoration to the temple at Somanath in Gujarat. In his proclamation of 16 November he set out the route that the escort of the gates would take across the Punjab. Justified as restitution due to the Hindus of India, whose shrine had been looted eight centuries previously, Ellenborough made what turned out to be his biggest mistake. The gates were known to be replicas. Muslims in India protested, whilst the English-language press in Calcutta and Bombay launched into the governor-general for interfering in religion, and appearing to support idolatry.[14] Back in Britain Ellenborough opened himself up for criticism and ridicule all round. The pre-eminent cartoonist of the day, 'H.B.' (John Doyle) cast him as an elephant running mad.[15] Old India hands castigated him for his ungentlemanly attack on Lord Auckland, and for not leaving military leadership to the generals. *The Times* accused him of an 'apish affectation of Orientalism'.[16] Early in 1843, Parliament reassembled, as news of the Somanath and Sindh proclamations was being reported. Ellenborough was quickly exposed as the government's Achilles heel, his governing style roundly condemned. Zealous Anglican MPs, led by Robert Harry Inglis, laid into his decision to use the forces and resources of the British government in India to support Hindu 'idol-worship'. Peel defended his errant governor-general as best he could, whilst expressing in private his own misgivings.[17] Over the annexation of Sindh the opposition proved more resilient, and it took a careful doctoring of the blue books to turn Napier's aggressive invasion into an act of necessity caused by the warring Emirs.[18] Sindh turned out to be the trap into which the elephantine Ellenborough finally fell. Within a year, the East India Company had successfully sought his recall, and his successor – his brother-in-law Sir Henry Hardinge, secretary at war in Peel's Cabinet – was sent out to undo the damage.

One person stood by Ellenborough throughout these turbulent two years: Queen Victoria. She had become close to Lord Auckland's successor in India. Apart from a six-month gap in 1843, Ellenborough wrote directly to the queen every month, enclosing copies of each of his infamous proclamations. During the same period she heard first-hand from Peel as soon as news came in from India. From the Board of Control Lord Fitzgerald furnished further private information, for example sending extracts from Lady Sale's journal of captivity in Kabul long before the book became available publicly. And Lord Stanley corresponded regularly from the War Office about the China campaign.[19] Where the Whigs had let Indian news only drip through to the palace, with the Conservatives it was in full flow. Some of it was dirty water. Plenty of politicians, including Peel and his foreign secretary, Lord Aberdeen, pointed out to her Ellenborough's faults. However, she warmed to his policies in several ways. When he issued medals in her name for the victorious troops of the Afghan and Chinese campaigns, she recorded her support, only wishing that she had herself sent the order. In the summer of 1843 she asked Peel to include in the upcoming queen's speech, which would open the new session of Parliament, 'something relative to the new Possession of Sindh'. Peel deflected her, reminding her that the Court of Directors of the East India Company believed the annexation of Sindh to be 'untenable'. Victoria persisted nonetheless, stating her intention to send public letters of support to both Ellenborough and Napier. Out came the rule book. Peel reiterated that 'the regular and constitutional channel for conveying the opinion of your Majesty . . . would be through your Majesty's servants'. Still the queen did not desist. When it became clear that Ellenborough was to be recalled, she expressed her view that this was 'very unwise' and also a 'very ungrateful return for the eminent services Lord Ellenborough has rendered to the

Company in India'. She concluded ominously, '[t]he Queen would not be sorry if these gentlemen knew that this is her opinion.'[20]

Queen Victoria's admiration for Ellenborough had limits. On the one hand, as she confided to her journal as Parliament tore his policies apart, 'I must say that with the exception of the Samnauth Proclamation, & an occasional want of judgement [he] has done a great deal.' Equally, when she and Albert finally spent time with Ellenborough on his return from India, he 'did not impress either of us very favourably', coming over for all his intelligence as conceited and contemptuous of others.[21] It was the principle that Ellenborough stood for in India that attracted Victoria. The manner of his fall from power led her to talk with Peel 'of the very bad system, on which the whole of the Indian possessions are managed. The East India C. have a negative Power, which is quite absurd, & prevents everything going on well.' Peel agreed, suggesting that the present arrangements could not survive, and that it would all end 'in the Crown having the management of the whole'. Just over two weeks later, Peel proposed a solution which would mean that the Company 'should not appear to triumph over the Crown by naming their own Governor'. Henry Hardinge would go out as both governor-general and commander-in-chief of the Army, an act which, Peel explained, would be 'recognised as <u>my</u> appointment by sending out one of my own Ministers', and moreover one who had sanctioned Ellenborough's policies.[22] The triumph of Peel over the Company did not spell the end of the dual government. The fundamental difference between wielding the power of the Crown and yielding power to the Crown remained. However, an important line had been crossed. Peel was the first minister to put into Victoria's head the idea of direct rule by the Crown over the Indian subcontinent. Hardinge, Ellenborough's successor, now became the first governor-general to put the queen's head on the medals and awards symbolising the new British presence in the north-west of India.

The Queen's Army

Issuing victory medals to East India Company forces in the queen's name was one of Lord Ellenborough's more impulsive pronouncements.

Ellenborough's order broke with protocol in several ways, as members of Peel's Cabinet observed on hearing the news.[23] Such an award, it was argued, should have been issued by the queen, campaign medals in India were not generally given to both Company and royal troops, and there was a reluctance to single out some regiments for distinction from the swathe of forces who fought without special honour. However, Ellenborough wanted to cover the Crown in the laurels of victory. He had already suggested that the cavalry regiment which led the line earlier in the year at Jellalabad – the 15th Hussars – be renamed Prince Albert's Own.[24] Now he wanted to draw in the queen as well. She was supportive, naturally enough, and the Duke of Wellington stepped in to reassure his colleagues in early December.[25] So William Wyon at the Royal Mint was instructed to come up with an appropriate medal.

Wyon faced a challenge. Not in depicting Victoria, whom he had been drawing since she was fifteen, and whose bust he had already engraved for the first coinage in domestic circulation of her reign; the dilemma was that monarchs did not normally feature on British war medals. There was one famous exception proving the rule, and that was the prince regent (admittedly a monarch-in-waiting) wearing a laurel on the 'Waterloo medal', given to all soldiers – officers and men – who served on the victorious battlefield in June 1815.[26] Otherwise, monarchs were invoked at times of conciliation or peace, as George III had been on the 'peace medal' distributed amongst Native American tribes during the war of 1812.[27] In India, until 1842, monarchs never appeared at all. Between 1778 and 1839, eleven different campaign medals were struck for the native and European regiments in India, as tokens of their success in battles on the Indian subcontinent from Gujarat to Mysore, but also further afield in Egypt (1801), Java (1811), Mauritius (1811), Nepal (1814) and Burma (1824). Initially, Britannia and the British flag were depicted, before a more settled image emerged of the sepoy soldier, his foot holding down an enemy troop. Inscriptions detailing the battle were in English and Persian. Sometimes, a little more imagination was applied. The Burma medal of 1824–6, for instance, depicted an elephant crouching before the British lion. But there was not much in the pattern book for Wyon to go on. Ellenborough clearly could not wait and a simple medal was approved from Simla for the soldiers who served under General Nott in the retreat, showing the mural of a crown, with the date of the battle of Jellalabad added.[28]

Wyon's Afghan medal was sent out in 1843. It used the standard bust of the queen already in circulation on domestic coin, added the motto 'Victoria Vindex' and left room on the obverse for the name and date of the battle, to which Kandahar, Kabul and Ghazni were added.[29] In September 1843, a similar medal was struck for those who served in the Sindh campaign. This marked a true turning point – 'the first opportunity', cooed the *Bombay Times*, 'on which special permission has been given to the Company's troops to wear, in any portion of Her Majesty's dominions, decorations won in India'.[30] Wyon's China medal took another year to complete. His original design pulled no punches, depicting the British lion pinning down the Chinese dragon, an image that particularly pleased Prince Albert, who preferred it to the alternative of 'a composition representing the signature of the treaty'. Albert noted drily, 'modern acts of Diplomacy are rarely happy subjects for artistical representation'. In the end diplomatic etiquette won the day – lions and dragons were rejected as too provocative, and the royal coat of arms with a faux palm tree in the background was chosen for the medal instead. Something of the martial was retained: the motto read 'Armis Exoposcere Pacem' ('they demanded peace by force of arms').[31]

At the same time as Victoria was becoming modelled at home as the epitome of genteel femininity, in India and China a completely different image – that of a warrior queen – was being stamped out with each military conquest. No British monarch before or since has been so indelibly linked to the representation of war in the colonial theatre. Ellenborough started something that proved impossible to stop. The two Sikh campaigns produced more medals. Now Wyon was in his stride, depicting not only Victoria (as 'Regina', rather than 'Vindex'), but also the angel of victory in the first Sutlej medal, and, when that opportunity for peace with dignity had been missed, in the second Punjab medal, three years later, a mounted British officer was shown receiving the weaponry of the surrendering Sikh leaders.[32] All of these medals were seen and approved by the queen. She also took the unusual step in 1848 of insisting that the official notice of the award of the Companion of the Bath to Major Herbert Edwardes, Company agent and hero of the siege of Multan in the second Sikh war, was announced before the Company gave their own medal to Edwardes.[33] Nor were these new medals just a passing fancy. In 1851, a retrospective 'Army of India' medal was issued, its recipients the veterans of East India Company military and navy campaigns from 1799 to 1826.[34] The past was being rewritten. Battles fought in India before Victoria was even born were now being commemorated in her name. How times had changed. On their return to government in 1846, the Whigs resented the chalice that had been passed on by Peel and Wellington. The 3rd Earl Grey, at the Colonial Office, complained to Hobhouse about awarding medals in the queen's name, when the number of royal troops involved was relatively small.[35] It was to no avail. In 1854 the 'India General Service Medal', with Victoria on one side and 'Victory' on the other, was established to cover all manner of minor campaigns in India.

Loot from Lahore

Medals were one thing, prizes of war another. Under Ellenborough's successors as governor-general – Sir Henry Hardinge (1844–7) and Lord Dalhousie (1848–56) – Queen Victoria became more involved in Indian conquest. It started with the exchange of gifts and ended with the taking of war booty. In all this Hardinge and Dalhousie acted as her cheerleaders. Although not a man of the court, Hardinge grew close to the queen shortly after his appointment in 1844. She encouraged him to write to her often – which he did – and he sent on to her sketches drawn by his son Charles of events and personalities from the time, most of them recording the fall of the Sikh dynasty.[36] Dalhousie was similarly attentive, enclosing private letters marked for the queen with his formal despatches, in particular sharing her confidence over the failures of his commander-in-chief, Hugh Gough.[37] Queen Victoria pushed for honours for both governor-generals as swiftly as possible: Hardinge was made a knight commander of the Order of the Bath on going out to India, and elevated to the peerage within a few weeks of the conclusion of the war in the spring of 1846. Dalhousie arrived in India as a knight companion of the Order of the Thistle, and became a marquess within weeks of his military triumph in the early summer of 1849. In both cases, the queen was prominent in supporting her favourites.[38]

In turn Hardinge and Dalhousie brought the queen around to their way of thinking about India's northern frontiers. Across the nineteenth century there were few military minds more devoted than these two men to the doctrine of making India impregnable from the mouth of the Indus (modern-day Karachi) to the Malay peninsula. Hardinge used the two treaties which concluded the first Sikh war to leave the Sikh royal family intact (the boy-heir Duleep Singh on the throne, with his mother, the Maharani Jind Kaur acting as regent), but took over key forts and defences along the river borders with Afghanistan, and also turned Kashmir into a buffer state in the north-west ruled over by the Maharaja of Jammu. In July 1847 Hardinge boasted to the queen that 'Your majesty's Eastern Empire has this remarkable feature of unity & strength which renders it almost impenetrable against any external aggression,' a cordon stretching, effectively, he stated, from Karachi to Singapore.[39] Hardinge's peace did not hold. The resistance of the Hindu ruler of Multan, the Dewan Mulraj Chopra, turned into a drawn-out second Sikh war, with the Afghanistan forces of Dost Mohammad Khan pitching in, and the British suffering heavy losses at the battle of Chillianwala in January 1849. A month later, the British won out at the battle of Gujrat. Without awaiting instruction from London, Dalhousie accepted Duleep Singh's surrender, packed the boy maharaja and his mother off to exile and promptly annexed the whole of the Punjab. It was now, he told the queen, 'a portion of your Majesty's Empire in India'.[40]

On the map next to Kashmir and the Punjab nestled the kingdom of Nepal. There were no fights to pick with the Nepalese. War between the Company and the Gurkha forces back in 1816 had left the two sides in accord. Besides, the Nepalese were busy bickering amongst themselves. In 1846 most of the court and government were slain in a coup, from which Jung Bahadur emerged as chief minister. He exiled the incumbent royals and placed the king's son, Surendra Bikram Shah, on the throne. In 1850, Jung Bahadur decided to visit Europe. Despite widespread reports of blood on his hands, Dalhousie encouraged Queen Victoria to meet with him, arguing that it would be good for the fractious Nepalese to be shown the military might of Britain. Dalhousie provided an escort for the trip from Calcutta – Captain Orfeur Cavenagh.[41] Jung Bahadur arrived in London via Paris, and, once doubts were allayed over whether he was who he said he was, he was given an audience with the queen, effectively her first official meeting with anyone from the Indian subcontinent. Jung Bahadur brought with him fifteen boxes of furs and armour, and, once the visit was concluded, elaborate arrangements were made for an exchange of portraits of the Nepalese royal family (or what was left of them), with those of Victoria and Albert.[42]

Treasures and booty flowed most freely from the Punjab. Dalhousie sent back captured armoury, and the contents of the Lahore treasury, including its most lustrous jewel of all, the Koh-i-Noor diamond. The toing and froing of gifts with the Punjab had already begun under Ellenborough's guidance in 1843, when silver plate was sent out from the queen to Sher Singh, who had thrust aside his nephew to become Maharaja of Lahore in 1841, only to be assassinated two years later. Inconveniently, the plate was already en route when Sher Singh died. In a spirit of economy, Lord Ripon suggested that the gift might be diverted to Mehmet Ali, the self-proclaimed Khedive of Egypt, and the queen approved.[43] Soon, the traffic became one way. As part of the Treaty of Amritsar that settled the first Sikh war, the Maharaja of Jammu was required to send a quantity of Kashmir shawls over to the queen each year as a tribute. The East India Company intervened in this practice, stopped the transmission of shawls and changed the tribute to a simple cash remission. When Dalhousie found out, he reinstated the original practice, and so for the rest of the reign a parcel of shawls from Kashmir arrived every year at Windsor Castle.[44] Booty from battle first arrived in 1847. Hardinge sent on to Windsor a battle-axe taken from the Emirs of Sindh, which was reputed to be the weapon of Nader Shah, the conqueror of Delhi in 1739. Doubts were cast over its authenticity. Its inscription was deemed by the orientalist scholar Horace Hayman

Wilson to be Hindi not Persian. Nonetheless it still found its way into the royal residence – albeit in the toilet at Windsor.[45]

More than anyone else, Dalhousie nurtured the queen's appetite for trophies of war from the Sikh campaigns. In June 1848, the queen requested that Sikh cannon taken in 1846 at Aliwal and the Sutlej be sent to England, so that she might place them on the terrace at Windsor. To this consignment were added fourteen six-pounder guns. A year later she requested more. Additional cannon and guns – this time howitzers – were relatively straightforward, but the chain mail asked for from the battlefield proved harder to obtain. Eventually, suits of armour previously worn by Sher Singh and Dhian Singh (younger brother of the Maharaja of Jammu, assassinated in 1843 at the same time as Sher Singh) were sent, and in 1850 Duleep Singh gave a suit of armour to the queen as well.[46] Then, on his own initiative, Dalhousie decided to make a present to the queen of Sikh regalia from the Lahore palace. There were two particularly choice items: the golden throne of Ranjit Singh, and the Koh-i-Noor diamond. The Koh-i-Noor had been wrung from the hands of one Indian dynasty after another since the fourteenth century, passing from Hindu rulers to Turkics to the Mughals, who fitted it into their peacock throne, and then on to Persian and Afghan raiders, finally coming into Sikh possession in 1830. Ranjit Singh's throne was deemed too bulky to send immediately (it eventually arrived in London via Calcutta in 1853).[47] The Koh-i-Noor was more portable, and Dalhousie took personal charge of it, transporting it all the way from Lahore to Bombay. Sewn into a small leather bag by his wife, and strapped around his midriff in a cashmere belt, the precious stone never left his body, even when he took his bath, as he dangled it over the rim to keep it dry. Duly delivered to the docks, the diamond then lay awaiting shipment for two months, finally reaching the queen at the beginning of July 1850. Her delight was evident. In 1849 she copied out into her journal Dalhousie's letter announcing that the jewel, 'a historical emblem of conquest', was now hers, and on 3 July 1850 she took delivery of the gem in person at Buckingham Palace.[48]

Having survived the passage from east to west, the Koh-i-Noor and the rest of the Lahore treasury faced a greater struggle through the choppy waters of protocol. The East India Company were aghast that the sovereign could receive such a large haul of war booty. This defied every rule developed over the years in dealings with Indian states and rulers. If the Koh-i-Noor was a gift exchanged on the termination of hostilities, then it had to be treated as though it was the accompaniment to a treaty. The diamond was therefore the property of the Company not the Crown, and it was the Company's right to present it to the queen, which was precisely what Sir Archibald Galloway, chair of the East India Company, proposed. Hobhouse recognised the logic, for it was a classic Whig formulation, but on this occasion he out-manoeuvred Galloway and took the side of his governor-general and the queen. Hobhouse pointed out that the queen had never been a signatory in any treaty, and so the Koh-i-Noor could only be considered as war booty. Under international law, as war booty, its rightful destination was the sovereign head of state.[49] And so the matter remained stalled as the spoils of war made their long journey west.

Meanwhile a solution to this impasse came with the arrangements being made for the Exhibition of all Nations two years hence. A deal was struck between the Company and the Board of Control, with the consent of the queen, that the items from the Lahore treasury would be lent to the Exhibition by the Company – in whose possession they currently lay – before a selection of them was sold to the queen at the end of the Exhibition. They would be submitted as examples of the manufactured wares of India. The Company also promised to under-write the costs of the Exhibition to the tune of £10,000, not an inconsequential sum.[50] As we shall see, the Koh-i-Noor became the centrepiece of the 1851 exhibition; its appearance there was entirely fortuitous. It provided a short-term solution to the problem of who owned the booty from the Sikh wars. Later in 1851, a delegation from the Company visited the queen to hand over in person more than 100 items from the exhibition, including the heist from Lahore. Items of less value were purchased by the Crown and set on one side for the School of Design that was intended as a permanent legacy of the exhibition.[51] In the end everyone was happy. The exhibition secured its main attraction, the Company kept face and gifted back to the Crown most of the disputed items of war booty, and the queen kept the Koh-i-Noor. Prince Albert sent it off to Amsterdam to be cut and polished, and in 1856 Franz Winterhalter depicted the queen wearing the gem in a brooch.[52] The queen of diamonds had found its way onto the state robes of the Queen of India. To this day there is perhaps no more visible sign of the centrality of India to the British imperial imagination than the Koh-i-Noor, yet it did not end up on the royal breast by accident. From first to last, the queen herself sought out and made sure she hung onto the most symbolic trappings of conquest from her eastern dominion, from cannons to armour to jewels. The tables had been turned. The sovereignty over Indian civil and military affairs that for so long had been informally vested in the East India Company was now moving to the monarch. Ellenborough, Hardinge and Dalhousie – all were loyal Tories and one a devoted courtier. Yet throughout the Indian campaigns of the 1840s, in the background, it was the queen herself who proved the most covetous trophy hunter of all.

Double Trouble

By the time the loot from Lahore was handed over to the queen, pressure was growing for the Government of India to follow as well. Not to her in person, but to the Crown, that is to say the ministers acting on her behalf. In 1852, as the clock ticked down on the East India Company's charter (it was subject to renewal every twenty years), a series of parliamentary select committees opened up British government in India to an unprecedented degree of inquiry and speculation.[53] And, as Parliament gathered evidence about the operations of the Company in India over the previous two decades, some thoughtless gunboat diplomacy in Burma led to full-scale war there, and placed Lord Dalhousie's policies under even more scrutiny. Lord Derby's short-lived ministry set up the review of the Company's work in India in April 1852. The double Government of India, which had survived almost seventy years, was now found wanting in so many ways. The parliamentary inquiry was both a review of what the Company had been charged to do since 1834, and an investigation of the viability of dual power. As an investigation of the dual authority, witness testimony showed again and again the confusion caused by the co-existence of crown and company. Questions were raised about the efficiency of having two distinct navies: the Royal Navy and the Company marine, about the very different cultures of command, discipline, promotion and reward in the royal European regiments and in the army of the Company.[54] Concerns were expressed about to whom soldiers owed loyalty – the Company or the Crown?[55] Finally, the existence of two jurisdictions of civil and criminal law in India – the queen's courts and the *sudder*, or Company courts – baffled many in Parliament and angered petitioners from Calcutta and Bombay in particular.[56]

War in Burma added to the troubles of those trying to defend the Company. By 1852 Dalhousie had earned a reputation that was increasingly for adding territory to British India and asking questions afterwards. The incident that triggered the war was a reprisal action by Commodore Lambert of the Royal Navy, who blockaded Rangoon in defence of 'Her Britannic Majesty's subjects' when their property was seized. Company ships and troops were sent in to assist in the stand-off, which stepped up to full-scale war when the King of Ava refused to yield to British demands.[57] Once victorious, Dalhousie took the decision to annex a portion of Burma – Pegu (Bago) – into British Indian territories. Back in Parliament the sequence of events in Burma raised a fundamental question: who had the power of recall? Namely, that if the Company had not wanted to support the governor-general in his annexation of Pegu, whose authority would have prevailed?[58] It turned out to be a hypothetical question, for, as the Aberdeen coalition took up office, the annexation of Pegu was announced from Calcutta as a fait accompli, without any treaty negotiation, and in the name of the governor-general.

Throughout the debates on the future Government of India, the queen was frequently invoked. Defenders of the Company admitted that a simple way to resolve the jurisdictional problems in the Indian courts would be to pool the judges from both systems and call them all the queen's courts. The authority of the Company might be strengthened, argued George Campbell, by moving the seat of government to

Agra, and by making all Indian people the subjects of the queen. The Company had become the focus of so much odium, argued another loyal servant, Marshman, that it would be as well to transfer the name of government to the Crown and improve reverence for authority that way. In terms of military morale, the discrediting of Company authority was having the same effect – let fidelity be declared to the queen instead, argued Henry Maddock.[59] Other commentators went further and argued that authority should be exercised in the person of the monarch. For the first time in her reign, there were calls in public for Victoria to become the sovereign of India. John Sullivan, former Company official, suggested to Parliament that she be made in name what she was in reality, 'the Queen of Hindostan or India', and one of her sons be made viceroy.[60] A fuller case was put a year later by James Silk Buckingham, sometime Indian newspaper editor and MP. No friend of the Company, which had thrown him out of India, he now returned the favour. In his *Plan for the Government of India*, he called for the queen to be proclaimed as sovereign of India, for the Crown to take over the debts of the Company, and for her rule in India to be characterised by acts of peace and improvements to public works.[61] The germ of an idea that had been suggested in private by Lord Ellenborough back in 1843 now began to grow.

In the end, Lord Aberdeen's ministry avoided dealing with many of the issues brought up by the select committees. When Sir Charles Wood, the president of the Board of Control announced the new bill for the Government of India at the beginning of June 1853, there was no question of delay, as the Company's charter only had eight months to run, and the session of Parliament only three. The queen made her own anxiety lest the bill be postponed known to Aberdeen.[62] The bill left to one side reform of the courts, of administrative recruitment in India, and of the armed forces. Amongst other changes, the queen gained new powers over the choice of directors of the East India Company. Not only were they no longer allowed to canvass for election, but three of the eighteen directors were to be appointed directly by the queen. The queen also retained oversight over appointments in India, with new members of the Council there subject to her 'approbation'. Whilst only a small shift of power, the 1853 legislation moved the Government of India further down the road towards the Crown. Some of the most doughty defenders of the Company realised its days were numbered.[63]

In the diplomatic relations with the kingdoms that surrounded India, and across the seas to imperial China, Queen Victoria thus became the fixed image of Britain as a colonial power around mid-century, displacing the Company Raj. In the Punjab, as the tussle over loot and medals shows, the emergence of the new royal symbolism was dramatic and publicly contested by Whig politicians back in Britain. Elsewhere, change was more subtle. When a British envoy was sent from Calcutta to Rangoon in 1855 to ratify the terms of the annexation of Pegu, the reclusive King of Ava, wanting to know who had sent him, asked him about the welfare of the 'English ruler'. The king's mouth was full of *paan*,[64] so it was difficult for the envoy to follow exactly the words used, but he noted that the king chose an expression that could refer to either the queen or to the governor-general.[65] Within a few years there would no longer be any ambiguity over who was really in charge.

CHAPTER 3

EXHIBITING INDIA

Maharaja Duleep Singh, the deposed heir to the Sikh kingdom, spent the summer of 1854 with the royal family, first at Buckingham Palace and then at Osborne House. A series of portraits survive as a record of these visits. In London Duleep Singh sat for Franz Winterhalter, with Queen Victoria looking on appreciatively, as a majestic full-length study in oils took shape. At Osborne, where Victoria and Albert enjoyed drawing and experimenting with the new medium of photography, he was sketched by the queen and he also posed for the camera for Ernst Becker, one of the children's tutors. The royal family liked to dress up, and, during the maharaja's stay, photographs were taken of Alfred and Arthur, the two younger princes, attired in Indian costume made specially for the occasion: a turban each, embroidered velvet *kurta*, *pajama*, slippers and pearls.[1] Duleep Singh was an exhibit as much as he was a guest. These portraits carry all the hallmarks of orientalism – the distorting lens through which the western imagination has viewed Asian civilisation, romanticising its antiquity whilst at the same time asserting its backwardness in the face of European progress. It is tempting to explain away the royal family's infatuation with Duleep Singh, and their interest in India more generally, as a facet of nineteenth-century orientalism, but there was both more and less to it than that. Victoria and Albert enjoyed a uniquely privileged vantage point from which to view Indian culture. They were surrounded at court by scholars, travellers and soldiers whose tales and researches helped form their knowledge of Britain's eastern empire. The royal couple lent their patronage to museums and exhibitions that featured the arts and industry of India. Moreover, the court of Albert and Victoria increasingly became the destination for Indian princes and maharajas, and their agents, seeking redress from the Government of India. From such materials as these, Victoria and Albert developed their understanding of India and its history.

In the early 1850s, for the first time in Queen Victoria's reign, the Indian subcontinent came home to Britain. One manifestation of this was the princely exiles. Duleep Singh was not the only Indian royal adopted at court. From the tiny southern Indian state of Coorg (Kodagu) came Princess Gouramma, and Queen Victoria also took up the cause of the last of Tipu Sultan's sons, Prince Ghulam Mohammed. By far the biggest exposition of India, however, came in the 1851 Exhibition of All Nations at the Crystal Palace in Hyde Park. The 'Indian court' was one of the most memorable features of the show, so successful that it was repeated at a Dublin exhibition two years later, again at the 1862 International Exhibition of All Nations in Kensington and also inspired a wave of new museums in India. The presiding genius behind the 1851 exhibition was Prince Albert. This chapter begins by looking at India through Prince Albert's gaze, before turning to the 1851 exhibition, and then finally the story of the royal family's encounter with Duleep Singh and Princess Gouramma.

Prince Albert and India

Prince Albert's knowledge of India was rooted in a German, as much as an English, tradition. With the encouragement of Baron Bunsen, the Prussian ambassador to London, German scholars steered Albert's interest in art and architecture.[2] This was no less true of his Indian studies. At university in Bonn he encountered leading Indologists, particularly August Wilhelm Schlegel, whose work on the common origin of western and eastern languages inspired a generation. Albert went on to give support to German Sanskrit scholars who came to England, notably Bunsen's protégé, Max Müller, and later in the 1850s Georg Bühler and Theodor Goldstrücker, both of whom who advised him on his book collecting and on the organisation of his library.[3] Albert's personal library reveals much about the German flavour of his understanding of Indian culture. Some eighty titles relating to India, published between the 1830s and late 1850s, are collected there. German scholarship and travel literature are conspicuous. German, especially Prussian, military acumen was in demand amongst Indian states for help with training native armies, and the dynastic connections of the smaller German duchies via the house of Coburg with the queen meant that restrictions on their travel in India were usually lifted. A series of military officers and curious aristocratic and royal travellers created a genre of German language expertise on India in the 1830s and 1840s. Leading the way was Charles von Hügel, a Bavarian who served in the Austrian army and wrote a bestseller about his travels to the Punjab and Kashmir in the early 1830s. He passed through London in 1845, dining with the royal couple on several occasions.[4] Another chronicler of the Sikhs was Leopold von Orlich, whose memoir was also published in 1845, as was Henry Steinbach's (an English officer of Prussian origin) account of the Punjab. Orlich settled in London after 1848, where he worked on a large history of British India, unfinished on his death in 1860.[5] Finally, and closest to the royal family, there was Prince Waldemar, the second son of the Crown Prince of Prussia, who witnessed the first Sikh war, and whose sketches and narratives of his travels were published in German in the mid-1850s. Waldemar visited the court in July 1847, and joined the royal entourage (including Baron Bunsen) that visited Cambridge that month for the installation of Albert as Chancellor of the university.[6]

German scholarship on India, such as this, differed from its English equivalent in a number of ways. It was less interested in the history of the East India Company, and it was not as preoccupied as the English evangelicals with conversion to Christianity. There was a fascination with and respect for the martial traditions of the Sikhs. There was sympathy for their religion, dating as it did from around the same time as the European reformation. German scholars saw Sikhism as fusing together the Hindu and Islamic traditions. Like Protestant Christianity, Sikhism was based on a single book – the *Granth* – and on worship of one god. German commentators saw Guru Nanak, the founder of Sikhism, as a man who had renounced worldly goods, and committed himself to a life of contemplation and pilgrimage. Nanak's descendants were respected for taking up arms to defend their religion. It was a narrative history that was shaped not least by the eye of the beholder: small German Protestant princely houses, hedged in by more powerful states and rubbing against the southern Catholic underbelly of Germany.

Albert also took an interest in another branch of German scholarship on India, one that was not confined to German scholars, but in which they led the way. This was Aryanism, not the twentieth-century variety made infamous by Nazi ideology, but a set of philological studies emergent around the 1830s that identified a common point of origin for the languages of both east and west, and in particular looked to the Sanskrit texts of ancient Hindu culture for evidence. The principal Sanskrit practitioner in England was Horace Wilson, holder of the Boden chair of Sanskrit at Oxford University. His patronage and that of Baron Bunsen and Albert helped introduce a range of German Sanskrit scholars into Britain. Foremost amongst them was Max Müller, who came for a brief visit in 1846, sponsored by the East India Company, and ended up staying for a lifetime, securing an academic post in Oxford.[7] Most of his early years in Britain were spent translating into German the *Rig Veda*, one of the four books of the Hindu *Vedas*. In the 1850s Müller became more of a public figure, advocating the introduction of Sanskrit and other oriental languages to the curricula of the East India Company colleges, so that Company men could better understand the peoples of northern India. In 1857 Müller became a candidate for the Boden chair at Oxford as Wilson's successor, an appointment that required the holder of the post to be an Anglican. The election to the chair was dominated by the evangelical desire to link Sanskrit study to the work of missionaries in India. Müller's rival Monier Monier-Williams saw Sanskrit as the means to undermine the oral culture of popular Hinduism. His strident arguments, likening the influence of Indian Brahmins to the Catholic priesthood, and his campaigning methods ended up defeating Müller's bid for the professorship.[8] Whilst there is no evidence that Albert took any interest in the election – it was not his university after all – two of his pronouncements in the decade suggest he subscribed to Müller's gentler brand of Aryanism. His comments at the jubilee meeting of the Society for the Propagation of the Gospel in 1850, discussed in chapter one, and later in the decade his design for the insignia for the new 'Star of India' order of chivalry (described in the next chapter), indicate that he believed in a common origin for Indo-European civilisation. For her part Victoria did not catch up with Müller until the 1860s. In 1864 he gave a lecture on the languages of India at Windsor Castle, and she noted down his argument about the linguistic links between east and west. More poignantly, she observed how his voice reminded her of Albert's. Whilst Monier-Williams enjoyed the patronage of the Prince of Wales in the 1880s, Müller kept in regular correspondence with the queen, sending each successive volume of the translation of the *Vedas*, unperturbed by the royal reply that she was unlikely to read them. In 1887, as part of the queen's jubilee celebrations, he did provide the Sanskrit inscription for the memorial to Albert erected in Windsor Park in 1887.[9]

Albert viewed India as a prince as well as an armchair scholar. He took pride in his small royal house, the Coburgs, that could date its existence back to the Holy Roman Empire, and enjoyed a remarkable network of connections through marriage to the principal monarchies of Europe.[10] At Bonn, his history and law teachers were disciples of Friedrich Karl von Savigny, the historical jurist who had shown the links between the customary laws of the smaller states of the later Holy Roman Empire and the original Roman law, a marked difference of emphasis from those who rooted the origin of modern sovereignty in the changing map of Europe after 1648: that is to say the growth of the centralised Bourbon monarchy and its modern descendant, revolutionary and Napoleonic France.[11] During the German revolution of 1848–9 Albert fell in behind his brother Ernst in supporting the Prussian king's plan for a confederation of princely states operating under the leadership of the Prussian monarchy, as a middle way alternative to the status quo of the Austrian-led Bund, and a republic of nationalities advocated by the Frankfurt parliament.[12] In Germany, the chamber of princes ideal came to nothing, but the seed of an idea was sown. By the end of the decade, Albert was turning closer to home, to the British Empire, as a theatre for princely influence. In 1860 he spoke proudly of two colonial tours being taken simultaneously by his two eldest sons, of the:

> curious coincidence, that nearly at the same time . . . though almost at the opposite poles, the Prince of Wales will inaugurate, in the Queen's name, that stupendous work the great bridge over the St Lawrence in Canada, while Prince Alfred will lay the foundation stone of the breakwater for the harbour of Cape Town.[13]

The colonies, and later India, might provide a vocation for his sons. In other words, Albert's understanding of India was not an adjunct to Victoria's. He shared some of her instinctive evangelicalism and was as covetous of military success in the 1840s as she was. He also encouraged her to think of the Indian empire – and the colonies more generally – as a family enterprise. But Albert's views were also rooted in German scholarship of the period and in the revival of orientalist studies in Britain, a body of work that drew affinities between European and Indian culture.

India on Display

As president of the Royal Society of Arts, Prince Albert was the genius behind the most extensive display of Indian culture ever seen in Britain: the Indian court at the 1851 'Exhibition of All Nations' at the Crystal Palace in Hyde Park. The Indian exhibits ranged from priceless ornaments such as the Koh-i-Noor diamond of Lahore and the ivory state chair from Travancore to machinery, metal, ceramic and textile handicrafts, weaponry and raw produce. Prince Albert played his part. He encouraged the Royal Society of Arts in 1849 to include works from the colonies in its annual exhibitions. He also tried to secure expert Indian knowledge to assist, inviting the veteran Indian administrator and historian, Mountstuart Elphinstone onto the Exhibition Commission, but they had to make do instead with the chairman of the East India Company.[14]

The Indian court was one of the stars of the show in 1851. Three weeks after its opening *The Times* observed that 'the tide of spectators sets eastward [towards the Indian and foreign sections] with a far stronger current than towards the rest', and as the exhibition entered its final month, the paper concluded that 'the Indian collection is not only the most attractive, but the most instructive display' of all.[15] India took up more space at the Crystal Palace than all the other British colonies combined. Only the United Kingdom, Austria, Belgium, France, the states of the German Zollverein and the USA had a larger exhibition footprint than India, and only the UK and France displayed wares that were more valuable. There were so many consignments of exhibits from India that the East India Company had to clear two floors in its ware-house to store them all.[16] The centre of attention was the Koh-i-Noor diamond, its lustre only outshone by the glass of the Palace itself. Case after case featured other jewellery (some misleadingly classified under mining and minerals), carpets, shawls and furniture, machinery and tools, musical instruments, and weaponry, both ornamental and prac-tical (the latter included in the 'naval architecture and military engi-neering' section).[17] The Indian court was a triumph over expectation. Early previews of the Indian exhibits had drawn a distinction between India's glorious past as represented in its gems and guns, and a lethargic present comprising a land fecund with raw materials and resources but without the industrial know-how to develop them. By the close of the exhibition, the ingenuity and vibrancy of Indian crafts and design had won over many commentators.[18]

Indian princes and chiefs played a significant part in gathering goods for despatch to the Exhibition. Without their participation many of the exhibits that grabbed the headlines would not have featured at all. The ivory state chair from Travancore, the howdah from the Nawab Nizam of Bengal, shawls, scarves and carpets from Kashmir, a model of one of the largest diamonds in the world from Hyderabad, bedsteads from

Benares, silks from Nagpur, leather from Cutch, cloths from Lucknow, ivory from Jodhpur and Nepal, and swords, daggers, axes and pistols from almost everywhere – all of these were ordered specially for the exhibition by the princes, not the Company resident.[19] Commissioned from local handicraft workers deploying traditional skills and styles, and using local materials, these manufactures all satisfied the exhibition's requirement for examples of industrial arts peculiar to the region. However, they were luxury goods, fashioned for the princely courts. Indeed, they were fit for a queen. Several of the princes made it clear that these were gifts for Queen Victoria. The Raja of Travancore sent the ivory state chair overland to Madras and thence to London, stipulating that it was a contribution to the exhibition, but also a 'slight token of my profound respect for your Majesty's exalted person', a 'friendly but humble tribute' from a faithful ally and dependent.[20] Similarly, the Nawab Nizam of Bengal insisted that the howdah was a present for the queen. Somewhat reluctantly, the President of the Board of Control and the East India Company relaxed the rules on this occasion and allowed the Nawab's present through, and agreed that letters of acknowledgment should be signed by the queen and sent directly to the two Indian princes.[21] The examples might be multiplied. Despite the superior quality of much of this finery, the Indian princes' submissions were not considered for exhibition awards by the prize juries. However, twenty-five Indian princes were singled out and given Exhibition medals (nine of them received a presentation catalogue from the Company as well), in recognition of their contributions.[22]

Victoria, Albert and their children made many visits to the exhibition after its official opening on 1 May. On 16 July, they were guided around the Indian court by Dr J. Forbes Royle, one of the men responsible for assembling the wares on show there. Victoria wrote it up in her journal afterwards: '[the Indian section] is of immense interest, & quite something new for the generality of people, these . . . articles having hitherto, only come over as presents to the Sovereign'.[23] This observation suggests that Queen Victoria was sharing her India with the nation. The exhibition exposed to the public a version of Indian civilisation and culture confined until then to the private view of the monarch.

Moreover, her comments imply that she was lifting the lid on royalty, inviting the public in to gaze upon the instruments and tokens of high diplomacy, of which they normally knew nothing. Displayed to show the variety of Indian products, arts and manufactures, there was no disguising their original provenance as gifts: symbols of homage intended for the queen.

So successful was the Indian court in 1851 that the Royal Society of Arts combined forces with the East India Company to plan a much larger 'Exhibition of the Arts and Manufactures of India' to be held in London in the spring of 1853. The follow-up event was intended in particular to furnish information about the prices of Indian wares, and their costs of production, details that had been missing from the Crystal Palace show. The East India Company promised to supply illustrations of suitable items for the new exhibition and instructions were again sent out to India for the collection of exhibits. However, the project floundered. No one could be found to back the exhibition, nor could a large enough venue be secured. Little support was forthcoming from India either. Alexander Hunter, from the Madras School of Art, spoke for many when he pointed out that too few inducements were being offered to exhibitors from India, with none of their transport costs covered. Finally, in the autumn of 1852, plans for the London exhibition were dropped, and, with the approval of Prince Albert, who helped select a few items from Windsor, it was diverted to Dublin, where a meagre 100 square feet was found within the 'Great Industrial Exhibition' of May 1853. The Society halted the call for produce from India, hastily brought in Japanese exhibits from the royal collections in The Hague – Queen Sophie of the Netherlands was Victoria's cousin – and relied on the East India Company, Buckingham Palace and the Royal Asiatic Society for the rest. Consequently, Indian produce again ran second best to gems and guns, with ornamental weaponry dominating the show, including the 'Gough compartment', a miscellany of loot taken by the former commander in China and India. A hint of India's economic future was displayed: a relief map showing the subcontinent's principal rivers and railways.[24] Albert and Victoria dutifully made their way to Dublin to view the exhibition, but made no comment on the Indian artefacts on display, which their intervention had helped to salvage.

Not until the 1860s did India begin to get exhibition coverage that fully focused on its produce as opposed to its arms and ornaments, and by then the Indian sections enjoyed less space and received less attention than those devoted to other countries. At the successor exhibition to Crystal Palace, opened by the Duke of Cambridge, the queen's cousin, in London in Brompton in 1862, India was only given the same amount of area for its displays as Egypt. But organised by Royle's successor at the India Museum of the East India Company, J. Forbes Watson, the smaller space was given over mainly to raw produce and handicrafts, with scarcely a gun in view.[25] Likewise, three years later, in the Dublin exhibition, there was once again weaponry and gems from the royal collection, but this time there were also raw materials direct from India, supplied by the Lahore museum, under the superintendence of Baden-Powell.[26] Then in May 1886 India returned to South Kensington, in the shape of the 'Imperial and Colonial Exhibition', a pet project of the Prince of Wales, opened by the queen in a glitzy ceremony, which included a rendition of the national anthem in Sanskrit, and anticipated the jubilee festivities of the following year. By then some things had changed when it came to putting India on show. Not just products, but prisoners from the jail in Agra and other artisans were sent over as examples of traditional craftsmen. Intrigued, the queen commissioned their portraits. Moreover, the Indian sections of the exhibition were laid out according to the different presidencies, in such a way as to emphasise the diverse commodities, both natural and man-made, of the modern 'Indian empire'. Even so, the old prejudices remained. A few months later, the Indian exhibits were sold off by auction, the catalogue advertising the array of 'ancient and modern war implements' and 'quaint musical instruments'.[27]

One further legacy of the 1851 exhibition and its royal patronage was the increase in demand for particular Indian fabrics and textiles. Shawls from Kashmir displayed at the Crystal Palace had excited interest in 1851, and the queen's annual receipt of examples of the finest specimens was widely known. Soon after the exhibition she lent one of her shawls to a textile factory in Scotland and unknowingly triggered a new consumer industry, the distinctive Paisley design, based on the Kashmiri teardrop motif. For two decades the Paisley version of the Kashmir shawl dominated the market.[28] The queen also lent her name to the entrepreneurial project conceived by Forbes Watson in the mid-1860s to market Indian fabrics by circulating through provincial England pattern books of motifs, designs and colour schemes, which might be put to a variety of uses in clothing and the domestic interior.[29] In these ways, the roots of the influence of Indian arts on English design reached all the way back to royal patronage of the 1851 exhibition. When the Indian empire came home to Britain, so often its first port of call was the court. Royalty was the filter through which the eastern exotic became ordinary.

Indian Exiles

Away from the Crystal Palace, Victoria and Albert collected Indian exhibits of their own in the early 1850s, in the form of adopted royal children. There were two: Princess Gouramma, daughter of Chikka Virarajendra, the Raja of Coorg (Kodagu), and the Maharaja Duleep Singh, who been taken into custody by the British in 1849. Queen Victoria was godmother to many infants, including the African American Sara Bonetta in 1851, and, from New Zealand, the son of a Maori chief, who was baptised Albert Victor Pomare at Buckingham Palace in 1863.[30] Her Indian adopted children received special treatment. Both were welcomed almost as new siblings, their acceptance into the royal home marked by rituals of conversion and depiction.

Princess Gouramma arrived at the court via the Basel mission in Mysore. Persuaded by the mission, the Raja of Coorg negotiated with the East India Company to have his daughter, then aged eleven, brought up in England, under the guardianship of the queen. In exchange he hoped for the return of his wealth, seized by the British in 1834. He had already used his children as bargaining chips. Another daughter had married Jung Bahadur, the chief minister of Nepal in 1850. Gouramma was brought over from India by Mrs Drummond, the wife of a retired major in the Bengal cavalry, and came to Buckingham Palace at the beginning of

June.[31] As the terms were agreed about her adoption, the queen showed off Gouramma to her own children, and commissioned Franz Winterhalter to paint her portrait. The queen watched the sitting and made her own sketches of the Indian princess. Gouramma also played with the royal children. At the end of the month she was christened in the chapel of Buckingham Palace. The Archbishop of Canterbury performed the service, Lord Hardinge and James Hogg (of the East India Company) were Gouramma's sponsors and, with all the royal family in attendance, the queen led Gouramma to the font, naming her Victoria.[32] Controversy flared after the baptism, when her father objected that Gouramma's guardian, Mrs Drummond, was not of sufficiently high social standing and claimed that he had been misled into the wardship of his daughter. As a compromise Gouramma remained looked after by Mrs Drummond but at the homes of various families with connections to the Government of India, such as the Hoggs, the Hardinges and the Woods.[33] Her father's grudge against his treatment by the Company continued until his death in 1859, whilst Gouramma eventually married a lieutenant colonel, John Campbell, and with him she had a daughter of her own, Edith.[34] Queen Victoria celebrated the little princess Gouramma as a Christian convert from the east. Winterhalter's portrait shows Gouramma in her Indian clothes: a fitted blouse, pleated sari with a wide embroidered *pallu*, gathered by a gold belt. She is heavily jewelled with an elaborate headpiece. In her hand she holds a small Bible. The queen also commissioned the sculptor Carlo Marochetti to capture the moment of Gouramma receiving her crucifix, executed in pale marble. The queen then had the bust painted to enhance Gouramma's facial features.[35]

An almost identical pattern was repeated with Duleep Singh. He arrived at Buckingham Palace two years after Gouramma, in the summer of 1854. As an eight-year-old boy, Duleep Singh had been taken into the care of the British forces under Henry Hardinge, who pitied the plight of the 'beautiful boy'. Dalhousie was far less sympathetic to Duleep Singh, 'a brat begotten of a *bhistu*[36] – and no more the son of old Ranjeet than Queen Victoria'. Nonetheless after the surrender of the Punjab in 1849 Dalhousie authorised the boy to be placed into the guardianship of Sir John Login, former surgeon at the British residency in Lucknow, and his wife, Lena. As temporary governor of the citadel at Lahore, Login was in charge of the dispersal of the Lahore treasury. Duleep Singh proved one piece of booty over which he was especially careful. Whilst his mother was exiled to Kathmandu, the young maharaja was taken to Fatehgarh for his safety, and there began his western education with the Logins, converting to Christianity in 1853. The switch of faith surprised many, including Dalhousie. In the meantime, arrangements were made for what portion of the Lahore treasury would be kept for the prince, for the costs of his maintenance in England, with some set aside for the construction of a tomb for Ranjit Singh at Amritsar.[37]

By the time Duleep Singh arrived in London, he was a well-groomed fifteen-year-old, with good English and refined manners, as the queen noted. Just as she had with Gouramma, she sat and watched Winterhalter paint Duleep on successive days, as well as sketching him when he joined the family at Osborne. Winterhalter's portrait is a grandiose full-length study, depicting Duleep as a proud Sikh ruler, richly dressed, adorned with pearls, a sheathed sword in his right hand, and a temple in the background. One small detail hints at his conversion. Around his neck is a miniature portrait of Queen Victoria, the very same one that had been given to Ranjit Singh by Lord Auckland in 1839. Two years later, as she had done with Gouramma, Queen Victoria commissioned a bust from Marochetti of Duleep, and had it coloured, although was disappointed with the result.[38] As well as sketching Duleep Singh, the queen kept a record of their conversations that summer. She went over the details of the narrative of his life, getting him to confirm some of the awful events – in particular, the murder of his uncle, Sher Singh, astride an elephant while Duleep was his passenger – and she questioned him about his conversion to Christianity and the ostracisation he had suffered from his family as a result. In an ironic twist she revealed to Duleep Singh some of her own souvenirs of the Punjab. She showed him Charles Hardinge's sketches of him as a small boy, and let him see the Koh-i-Noor, which he was allowed to stroke. But she ensured that he did not view the captured Sikh arms on the terrace. Her fondness for Duleep was clear, but there was also a certain wallowing in his submissiveness. Passing on her congratulations for his sixteenth birthday she noted he 'would have come of age, had we not been obliged to take the Punjab'.[39]

Duleep Singh returned to stay with the royal family at Windsor and Osborne again over the next two years, and on each occasion the queen was able to observe the progress of his education under the guidance of the Logins. Some of this took a conventional form. There was a lot of hunting and shooting in the Scottish Highlands, and a tour to Europe at the end of 1858. Other episodes in the grooming of the maharaja reflected Prince Albert's enthusiasms. He was taken on a tour of the sites of Staffordshire in March 1856, including a descent down a pit-shaft, and later that year attended the Birmingham cattle show and helped set up a refuge home for Indian lascars. He joined a volunteers regiment in 1859, and once he left London in 1859 to live at Mulgrave House, near Whitby, he represented the queen at various local functions.[40] By the time he was a young adult, Duleep Singh was pining for the Punjab. To the consternation of Queen Victoria, he remained close to his mother. Duleep yearned to return to India, and finally travelled there in 1861, bringing his mother back with him to England, only for her to die two years later. He made another trip to India to scatter her ashes, and passing through Cairo on his return he met and married Bamba Müller, a young woman of German and Abyssinian descent who lived in the American mission there. They settled down to country life on a Norfolk estate, raising a family of six children, the first of whom, Victor Albert Duleep Singh, born in 1866, became the queen's latest godson.[41] Duleep Singh's frustrations in forced exile in England radicalised him, and by the 1880s he was planning to renounce his Christianity, return to India and claim his succession as Sikh leader. He sought allies for his restitution as far as Cairo and Moscow, and finally died in Paris in 1893, separated from his homeland and from his family. For much of his life Duleep Singh proved a headache for the British government at home and in India, and on occasion he was a major strategic risk. Despite his reputation as a pampered prince, he remained a credible focal point for Sikh nationalism throughout his lifetime.[42]

For all his justifiable resentment against the British, Duleep Singh was considered an intimate member of the queen's extended royal family until his death. From the marriage of Princess Vicky in 1858 through to the funeral of Prince Leopold in 1884, he attended every major royal ceremony, including the funeral of Prince Albert in 1861 and the thanksgiving for the recovery of the health of the Prince of Wales in 1871. On each occasion he sat on one side of the queen (her own children were on the other) along with the other foreign princes, mostly those from the smaller German states who were related to Victoria and Albert.[43] Queen Victoria's own dedication to Duleep rarely wavered. She defended him from suspicion that his loyalties lay elsewhere during the Indian rebellion of 1857–8.[44] In 1868 she pressed Disraeli's government to make further provision for Duleep Singh's growing family, although that had not been part of the original terms under which he was included in the civil list (the public funds used to finance the royal family).[45] Even in 1886, once his machinations with Russia were known, and she conceded that he was 'off his head', she still insisted that the government look after his family properly, in the event of his not returning to Britain. There was a final meeting between the queen and the maharaja in Grasse in the south-east of France in March 1891, two years before he died.[46]

Queen Victoria's obsession with these two young exiles in the mid-1850s defies simple explanation. She undoubtedly had a genuine sympathy for the Indian royals whom her own government had done so much to displace. It extended to the old as well as the young. The same year that Duleep Singh came to the court, she had an audience with Prince Ghulam Mohammed, the last living son of Tipu Sultan, who had come to London to argue the case for ongoing support for his own sons and any descendants they might have.[47] To support his claims Prince Ghulam republished the history of Tipu, already reasonably well known. The queen noted in her journal her respect for Prince Ghulam's quiet dignity as he went about his appeals, whilst observing that had Tipu survived then all might have turned out very differently. Her magnanimity always came from belonging to the winning side. There was also a strong element of mothering. Tipu was widely depicted as a neglectful father.[48]

Queen Victoria's wrath against Duleep's mother and also her contempt for the Raja of Coorg betrayed the same indignation over poor parenting, the very reversal of the patriarchal household that she and Albert had developed around their own children. Her own maternal instinct was more than matched by Prince Albert's vision of a princely confederation that might include his own sons, as well as the minor German princes and Duleep Singh. They were of royal blood after all. After his death, Victoria remained loyal to Albert's dynastic aspirations, with her inclusion of all the princes in all the family ceremonies thereafter. Particularly in the case of Duleep, there was also a heavily romanticised appreciation of Sikhs and Sikhism, fuelled by the first-hand accounts from the battlefield and also by travel literature popularised by various German and English writers in the 1840s. As a war-like but conquered people, there was not a little vanity and conceit contained in the way in which the royal family not only captured Duleep in his Sikh finery, but also appropriated it for themselves.

Most telling of all, the addition of these young India royals to the court represented the high-water mark of Queen Victoria's evangelical aspirations for India. This can be seen in the rituals around conversion, that is to say, Gouramma's baptism at the Palace, and Duleep being made to recount the trials he suffered surrounding his own conversion. It is also evidenced in the portraits and busts that the queen commissioned of the two, depictions emphasising their racial difference, whilst at the same time detailing the tokens of their new allegiance to a western monarch and to a Christian god. Here was Christianity in India making rapid strides at her very feet. Three days after she introduced Gouramma and Duleep Singh to each other for the first time, she wrote to Lord Dalhousie, saying how she approved of their future marriage (it never happened), and also how she hoped that the growing network of railways in India would 'facilitate the spread of Christianity which has hitherto made very slow progress'.[49] The Bible and the steam engine – religion and industry: for all their curiosity about the east, Victoria and Albert understood India from a largely western perspective. The year of rebellion, 1857–8, changed all that.

CHAPTER 4

'THIS BLOODY CIVIL WAR'

N ews of the revolt in India reached London in July 1857 just as Queen Victoria met with members of the royal family of Awadh, whose court at Lucknow was at the centre of the uprising against British rule in 1857–8. Few noted the coincidence at the time, or since. Malika Kishwar, the mother of the deposed King of Awadh, along with the king's brother Mirza Sikandar Hashmat, her grandson and heir-apparent, Mirza Hamid Ali, and a retinue of more than 100 had arrived at Southampton the previous summer. Leaving the deposed king in Calcutta, the royal party was accompanied in its mission by an English agent, Major Robert Wilberforce Bird, and, it was claimed, immense sums of money to help make the case for reversing Lord Dalhousie's annexation. Despite losing £50,000 worth of jewels overboard en route through the Red Sea, the Awadhi delegation remained in Britain for almost a year.[1] To the amusement of the news-papers, the 'Queen Mother', as Malika Kishwar was dubbed, was in purdah throughout.[2] Queen Victoria also wanted 'to get a sight of her Royal Sister'. The Board of Control found itself caught between the wishes of 'our own Majesty who sometimes patronises these deposed despots' and a determination to avoid political intrigue back in India.[3] A promise having been extracted that the Awadhis had booked their passage home, an audience at Buckingham Palace was arranged for the beginning of July 1857. The occasion – the only time when Victoria met face to face with a Muslim woman from India – was carefully staged. The malika was secluded from the vision of Prince Albert and the visiting princes in the closet in the White Drawing Room of the Palace. Malika Kishwar presented an address from her son, in which he described the friendly relations between his court and George IV and William IV, refuted the allegations made against him and appealed to Queen Victoria's 'responsibility of distributing justice to all the inhabitants of the British territories'.[4] To no avail. By the time the Awadhis got to the queen in London, army mutinies were sweeping across northern India, from Bengal through the North-West Provinces, into the Punjab, and down into the region around Gwalior and Bhopal. An emperor had been reinstated at Delhi, the ex-King of Awadh was locked up in Fort William, the British Residency at Lucknow lay under siege and the king's estranged wife, Hasrat Mahal, had taken control of the court.

This encounter with the Awadhi court at the outset of the Indian rebellion of 1857 tells us a great deal about the wider role of Queen Victoria in the Indian revolt, and, conversely, about the changing place of India in Victoria's own statecraft. As the unsuccessful Awadhi mission demonstrates, the queen was perceived as a court of final appeal – the last resort for Indian rulers at odds with the East India Company. The Awadhis were only the latest in a succession of rulers of states annexed by Dalhousie who brought their grievances to London with the hope of redress from the monarch. The episode also emphasises how Victoria was a Christian queen within a European culture infused with a heightened sense of religious difference and superiority. By the mid-1850s she had come to stand for much of the evangelical Protestant ideology of British India. Her support for the expanding Anglican church in India and her adoption of princely converts to Christianity, such as Duleep Singh and Gouramma of Coorg, had cemented the idea that she was not neutral when it came to the Christian religion. In the 1840s, this had aroused little comment at home or in India. By 1857, the situation was very different. Britain's intervention with France in the Crimea in defence of Christian minorities, together with the war against the Shi'a

Shah of Persia in 1856, demonstrated Britain's willingness to fight in the name of religion. Inevitably, as the revolt in India came to turn on a clash of religious cultures, so Queen Victoria became invoked not for her tolerance but for her Protestant zeal. In this way, Victoria, far removed from the scene of battle, symbolised many of the tensions over which the rebels were battling.

The rebellion also proved a turning point for Victoria herself. Throughout 1857 and 1858 India consumed the energies of the queen. With Albert and her cousin George, the Duke of Cambridge and recently appointed commander-in-chief of the Forces, she pressed the Cabinet of Lord Palmerston for a faster and more resolute military response from Britain. She sought her own channels of information about the unfolding events. Once the rebellion was suppressed, Victoria and Albert turned their attention to the post-war settlement – the transfer of the Government of India from the East India Company to the Crown. The royal couple intervened to ensure that royal prerogative was upheld. Then, when Lord Derby and his ministers drafted the proclamation announcing the transfer of power to the peoples of India, it was the queen and her consort who changed fundamentally the tone of the document in ways that ensured it would become known as the 'Magna Carta' of Indian liberties.

The Infidel Victoria

The Indian rebellion of 1857–8 had many causes and a variety of effects. Social change, modernised communications, religion, new taxes and old grievances, all combined to turn a fairly regular occurrence in British India – a mutiny amongst the Indian regiments of the army – into widespread, organised revolt.[5] The mutiny spread like wildfire. One by one across the army garrison towns of northern India during May and June 1857, ordinary Indian soldiers – 'sepoys' – took up arms against their commanding officers. The outbreak was triggered by the mutinies of the 3rd Light Cavalry at Meerut and various infantry regiments at Delhi on the 10 and 11 May. In both cases the troops had been incensed by the practice of greasing rifle cartridges using animal fat. Across the Bengal presidency, sixty-four regiments mutinied (over half the total army). The old Mughal capital of Delhi became the epicentre of the revolt. The former King of Delhi, Bahadur Shah Zafar, was returned to the city and proclaimed emperor at the end of May. Rebel governments were also established at Jhansi, Kanpur, Lucknow, Malwa and Moradabad, all of which swore allegiance to the restored court of Delhi.

The rebels singled out Queen Victoria as the enemy. On 6 June 1857 Nana Sahib was proclaimed peshwa at Kanpur. In announcing his assumption of power, he accused Queen Victoria of being behind a plan to Christianise forcibly the sepoys in the Indian army. A similar rumour, claiming that the queen had personally approved of a decision by the governor-general in Council to convert all sepoys was expressed at Lucknow. Then, in early July 1857, a pamphlet invoking a holy war against Britain – entitled *Fateh-i-Islam* – argued that servitude under a Muslim king would be better for Indian rajas than 'under the infidel Victoria and the English'.[6] Unprecedented levels of violence on both sides now followed, although losses were disproportionate. British fatalities numbered around 11,000, three-quarters of these from disease, whilst rebel deaths exceeded 100,000. Sepoy killings of European officers and civilian residents were countered by British forces slowly but steadily annihilating the rebel armies and the communities from which they were drawn, as well as undertaking bloody reprisals for months after the revolt had subsided, including ritual executions by cannon and public hangings. Initially caught unawares, Britain poured European and colonial troops into India from west and east – from the recent war in Persia, together with several regiments from the Cape and from Ceylon, and diverted troops en route to China[7] – all to contain the revolt, and drew on every ounce of loyalty to be found in India itself. A force of British and European volunteers was offered from Calcutta but rejected by Viscount Canning, the governor-general, but otherwise military support from the states ringed around the North-West Provinces proved crucial. Gurkha troops were provided from Nepal by Jung Bahadur, whilst to the south-west the armies of the Maharaja of Gwalior and Tukoj Rao Holkar of Indore rallied and cordoned off routes to the

Rajput states and to the coast. To the north-west of the rebel areas, the Punjab held back from taking up arms against the British, despite serious early outbreaks of mutiny in regiments at Ambala, Lahore, Peshawar and elsewhere.[8] Undoubtedly a risky strategy at the time, the steps taken by Sir John Lawrence to pacify and then mobilise Sikh forces from the Punjab allowed the British to protect the vulnerable north-west frontier from the threat of Afghan and Russian incursion, and to retake Delhi by September 1857. Bahadur Shah was captured, his two sons and a grandson were executed in his presence and he went on trial the following January. Still the revolt continued as the Rani of Jhansi, the most potent female icon of the rebellion, held out and joined other leaders such as Nana Sahib converging on Gwalior, where they were eventually defeated in June 1858. By the end of 1858 Awadh returned to British control, and lingering pockets of resistance in Bengal and Bihar had been suppressed as well.

Although confined to northern India, the revolt was so much more than a series of isolated military uprisings. Mutiny in the Indian army revealed Britain's garrison state at breaking point. As the boundaries of British India expanded in a north-westerly direction, the army had become ever more reliant on Indian troops serving on declining rates of pay far from their home villages. European regiments had been siphoned off to serve in the wars in the Crimea and in Persia, and then towards the end of 1856 several units were despatched to China.[9] With the advent of the telegraph, news of disaffection in the army travelled more speedily than in previous decades, and where accurate information could not be conveyed rumour did its own work.[10] Since the Registration of the Press Act of 1835, newspapers in India had been relatively lightly regulated, and by 1857 there were many vernacular weeklies and news-letters. Curbs on printing presses were introduced through emergency legislation in June 1857, and censorship rolled out to include the English language press, but with limited effects.[11] Economic modernisation was also at work in rural northern India, as local markets opened up to the free trade competition of British goods, and, unprotected by the law, landowners sold off struggling estates and farms.[12] Western-style liberalisation of the economy thus created an unstable mix of winners and losers, some ripe for revolt, others primed to show loyalty in return for concession and benefit.

Above all, at the heart of the revolt lay religion and political power. The spark which ignited the flames of mutiny – the greasing with animal fat of soldiers' cartridges – signified colonial arrogance towards Islam and Hinduism, stoking the fear that sepoys would be subjected to Christian conversion. The restoration of the Mughal emperor at Delhi gave legitimacy to traditional forms of dynastic rule in India, which decades of Company administration had done much to undermine. Although modern scholarship has proved kinder, much of the blame at the time for the religious and political disaffection that lay behind the revolt was laid at the door of the Marquess of Dalhousie, the governor-general of India.[13] In the Dalhousie era evangelical Protestantism had certainly been spurred on. Restrictions on the remarriage of Hindu widows had been lifted, greater protection provided for the property rights of native Christian converts, and encouragement given to missionary work in schools and in villages in Bengal and the North-West Provinces. In April 1857, the Society for the Propagation of the Gospel revised its plans for the expansion of the Anglican church in India, calling for three new sees: two in the north – Agra and Lahore – and one in the south, at Palamcotta (Palayankottai) in Madras. There was also evidence of growing evangelicalism in the army in 1857, through the work of so-called 'missionary colonels', such as Lieutenant-Colonel William Mitchell and Colonel Stephen Wheeler of the 34th Cumberland foot regiment, stationed at Kanpur.[14] British opinion at the time was adamant that the rebel movement was 'primarily of Mahomedan origin' to such an extent than Bahadur Shah Zafar was tried in January 1858 for leading an international Muslim conspiracy.[15] More recently, historians have identified the jihadi and Wahabi elements in the rebel movement, but also emphasised how the revolt united Hindus and Muslims against a common Christian enemy.[16] Religious differences focused enmities like nothing else. The first mutiny at Meerut, it was rumoured, was planned around an attack on Christian civilians and soldiers worshipping on a Sunday.[17]

During his time in India Dalhousie had also pushed through the most extensive annexation of territory to Britain in the Indian subcontinent since the end of the Maratha wars.[18] The subjugation of the Punjab in 1849 was accompanied by the imposition of direct rule across India: from Satara and Sindh in the west, to Rajputana and the North-West Provinces, to Tanjore and Arcot in Madras, Nagpur and Jhansi in central India, as far south as the Berars in the kingdom of Hyderabad, to the north-east in Sikkim, and all the way round to Pegu in Burma. Dalhousie did not invent the infamous doctrine of lapse, whereby Britain took control of states in which a ruler had died and where there was no natural replacement heir, but he certainly applied it with vigour. Moreover, Dalhousie aspired to expel Muslim rule in northern India. In 1851 he undertook an extensive tour of the conquered north-west frontier, conducting durbars at which a series of Sikh rajas swore personal fealty to him in the same way that they had previously honoured the Mughal emperor. At Peshawar Dalhousie noted how Britain had stopped 'the tide of Mahometan conquest' after over eight centuries and subjugated the 'fanatical & furious barbarians, whose faith is a cloak for every crime'. At Pinjore Dalhousie sat on the golden throne of Ranjit Singh to receive the Maharajas of Patiala and other Sutlej chiefs. These tours continued into the North-West Provinces. At Rampur singers assembled by the Nawab sang 'Rule Britannia'.[19] Dalhousie's critics accused him of assuming the powers of a 'deity', whilst he defended the expense and the long absences from Calcutta that his durbars entailed, pointing out that they were not 'mere gaudy show', but critical to the stability of British power.[20] Under Dalhousie the Government of India also ensured that northern India was made aware of British prowess beyond the north-west frontier, for example translating into Urdu news of allied success at the battle of Alma in the Crimea.[21] Finally, in 1856, Dalhousie moved ahead with the annexation of the Muslim kingdom of Awadh. He shrugged off his own colleagues' concerns about the legitimacy of the move and delayed his departure from India until it was completed. With pathos he described for Queen Victoria the moment of submission when the King of Awadh handed over his turban to the British resident: 'the deepest mark of humiliation and helplessness which a native of the East can exhibit . . . when the head thus bared in supplication was one that had worn a royal Crown'.[22]

For Dalhousie annexation was much more than another chapter in the piecemeal expansion of British India. In absorbing territory Dalhousie was displacing ancient Muslim and Hindu kingdoms and princely states, and their religious and ceremonial infrastructure. Through his durbar tours he appropriated older forms of Mughal royal style in order to enforce allegiance to Christian Britain and its queen. His administration encouraged depictions of native rule as decadent, corrupt and immoral, for example William Knighton's salacious account of the court at Awadh,[23] and choked off official and unofficial communications amongst Indian royal houses and between their rulers and London. It took its toll. Exhausted and bereaved (his wife, the queen's former lady-in-waiting, died in India in 1853), Dalhousie returned home in 1856. He was so ill on reaching England that his chair had to be hoisted on deck so he could wave to Queen Victoria and Prince Albert as they sailed past on the royal yacht down the Solent. But he had left a tinderbox behind, with the queen perched on its lid.

News from India

Queen Victoria was oblivious to how the leaders of the Indian revolt denounced her personally, but she quickly discerned the root cause of the mutinies. Writing to Charlotte Canning, the governor-general's wife, the day after she had received the Awadhi delegation, she asserted that 'a fear of their religion being tampered with is at the bottom of it'.[24] Her immediate concern, however, lay with the inadequacy of Britain's military reactions to the uprising. Throughout the summer months of 1857 she kept in close contact with the news reported from India, communicated directly from the War Office and Horse Guards to Buckingham Palace whilst she was in London, and then by telegraph straight into Osborne House during the summer months. Queen Victoria blamed the spread of the mutiny on reductions in the European army in India, and on the dual fighting force (crown and Company troops) that created a divided command.[25] En route to Osborne House on 16 July she met with Palmerston and his Cabinet colleagues and 'spoke to them *most strongly* about the necessity of recruiting the whole army, of taking energetic measures at once, & not miserable half measures'. But the 'dilatoriness and senselessness' of Palmerston's government in the face of the revolt continued to alarm Victoria. On arrival at Osborne she and Albert wrote a long memorandum on the army in India, calling for the integration of the European and native soldiers. The following weekend they took the steamer over to Portsmouth to watch the departure of Albert's brigade, the 3rd Rifles, as part of the troop reinforcements going east.[26] Over the next two months Queen Victoria repeatedly called on Palmerston to increase the supply of extra troops, not just from other parts of Asia but from Canada and the Mediterranean as well. Gradually, helped by the intercession of Lord Clarendon, the foreign secretary, Palmerston's Cabinet heeded her advice and the urgency of the situation, agreeing to call up the militia and send out extra battalions from home as well as from Malta and Canada.[27] As in the 1840s, Queen Victoria's instinctive reactions to events in India were those of a warrior queen. True, she sanctioned Lord Palmerston's proposal to hold a day of state prayer.[28] Mostly, however, it was her voice of military command that prevailed. She saw Sir Colin Campbell, appointed by Palmerston to lead the British forces in India, before he left for India in July 1857, and once back in London and Windsor during the first half of 1858 she met and spoke with many returning officers and army wives, getting first-hand information about the battle scenes and their experiences.[29]

In this way the queen stood apart from much of the response to the Indian rebellion that so captured the British literary imagination. Contemporary magazines, newspapers and so-called eyewitness accounts rendered the violence and bloodshed of the mutiny as the 'rape' of British India, dwelling particularly on the ferocity with which the sepoy rebels attacked European women and children.[30] Queen Victoria was certainly aware of the atrocities, sharing in the wave of emotional indignation that broke over Britain from late August. 'If only they had been shot down,' she wrote in her journal of the European women and children murdered and dumped in a well at Kanpur, 'it would not be so ghastly but everything that can outrage feelings, – every torture that can be conceived, has been perpetrated'.[31] However, the sensational reportage did not hold her attention. Plenty of contemporary officer accounts of the British campaign against the rebels in India survive in the Royal Library at Windsor, but only Adelaide Case's *Day by Day at Lucknow* (1858) is there to represent the more popular genre of female non-combatant memoirs.[32] By November 1857 Queen Victoria was telling Canning that she thought the 'unChristian spirit shown by the public' would not last and she was asking for evidence of the ill treatment of women.

For this Queen Victoria turned to Charlotte Canning. Of all the nineteenth-century vicereines, Charlotte was the closest to the queen, having served at court for thirteen years as a Lady of the Bedchamber. She kept a diary and was a prolific watercolourist and photographer.[33] From Charlotte Canning Queen Victoria received the most detailed accounts of the rebellion and the British counter-offensive, from the early scares over the greased cartridges through the major incidents of the rebellion as it spread north-west, and on to her husband's post-revolt tour of northern India in 1859–60, which she carefully documented with brush, pen and camera. Charlotte Canning's letters supplied Queen Victoria with a corrective to the lurid narratives of the events, particularly at Kanpur and Lucknow. She pointed out to Queen Victoria that most of the stories of the sepoy horrors arose from the mutilations that were carried out upon the bodies of the dead, but there was no credible evidence that violent sexual assault had occurred whilst they were alive. Concerned that she seemed to 'talk of "poor dear sepoys"' and to have 'softness or tenderness towards them', Charlotte Canning assured the queen that she only wanted to test some of the stories. It seemed to work. Other visitors to Buckingham Palace confirmed that there had been 'dreadful exaggeration of the cruelties'. In fact by May 1858 Charlotte Canning herself feared that there had been 'too great a reaction' the other way, and that in accepting the evidence against mutilation, all the 'treachery and cruelty' should not be forgotten.[34]

Charlotte Canning also encouraged Victoria to seek visual representations of India. She passed on news of the work in India of two photographers, Dr John Murray and Felice Beato, who were amongst the first to record the aftermath of the fighting. Editions of both photographers' work were later purchased for the queen, but it was Charlotte who initially brought them to her attention, describing in particular detail Beato's views of Lucknow.[35] Victoria took her own initiative as well. At the beginning of February 1858 she commissioned the Swedish court painter Egron Lundgren to go to India to depict the battle scenes. Lundgren reached India in time to witness the final stages of the British campaign. Amongst other works, he recreated the relief of Lucknow, providing rough sketches which were then turned into book illustrations and an oil painting by Thomas Jones Barker.[36] In 1859, Charlotte Canning added to Victoria's Indian portfolio by sending on her own watercolours and ink drawings. Many of these were of picturesque scenes – ancient buildings and landscape views – but battlefields were included as well, notably depictions of Farrukhabad, Kanpur and Lucknow.[37] Such sources as these suggest that Victoria was more familiar than most with the topography of the Indian rebellion. Taken together, the work of Murray, Beato and Charlotte Canning presented to Queen Victoria an eastern sublime ravaged by war – beautifully ornate mosques and palaces stockpiled with armoury, disempowered colonial buildings pockmarked with cannon-fire and bullet holes, loyal over-dressed sepoy regiments resting battle-weary in arid settings. These were dissonant images, neither glorifying nor sentimentalising the aftermath of the revolt, but displaying the chaos and disorder wrought by war.

The Transfer of Power

By October 1857 it was becoming clear that the future Government of India would not lie in the dual authority of the East India Company and the queen's ministers. Or, as Lord Palmerston informed Queen Victoria in his own colourful way, there would be an end to:

> the inconvenience of administering the Gov^t of a vast country on the other side of the Globe by means of two Cabinets, the one responsible to your Majesty & to Parliament, the other only responsible to a mob of Holders of Indian stock, assembled for 3 or 4 hours, 3 or 4 times a year.[38]

Palmerston's government began the work of drafting a bill which would transfer power to the Crown, or rather to the ministers of the Crown, who would be subject to the usual constitutional checks and balances provided by Parliament. Opinion in the press and amongst Indian experts was divided.[39] A growing crescendo of voices called for the Crown to displace the Company and become the sole authority in India. 'The veil which has hitherto concealed the Crown from the eyes of the people of India', declared John Henry Treemenheere, 'must now be rent asunder.' A 'virtual sovereign', the Crown would drive forward the moral reform of India, some writers argued, as they called for European colonisation and conversion of the subcontinent under the queen as empress.[40] Here lay a simple logic. What better way to Anglicise India in the aftermath of the rebellion than to invest power in the queen?

Curiously, the Crown and its powers remained imprecisely defined as Indian constitutional reform was considered during the winter of 1857–8. Both government and opposition understood the 'Crown' to imply greater ministerial control over the Government of India, or simply over the Company itself. Palmerston's Cabinet got as far as drafting a bill that would have substituted the Company and the Board of Control with a small council in Britain chosen by nomination. Palmerston was also advised to move the seat of British government from Calcutta to Agra, and to take steps to put an end 'to the prevailing indifference of our rulers to Christian truth'. All of this, Palmerston explained to the queen, would mean more power exercised in her name.[41] She was uncertain. Reading over the clauses set out in Palmerston's initial bill at the end of January, 1858, Queen Victoria enquired, 'Is this absolute power?' Her own take was unequivocal. She expected to be given more direct responsibility for India, including sight of all despatches to and from India, just as she was entitled to see all Foreign Office despatches. She sought a unified command under the Crown of the Indian army. She also wished to retain complete control of the patronage and appointments within the Indian civil service as well as the Indian military.[42] Absolutely.

Palmerston and his colleagues resigned in February 1858. To Lord Derby's Cabinet now fell the task of reforming the Government of

India. Charged with transferring power in India from Company to Crown, Derby and his ministers also wanted to hang on to power at Westminster. Derby's was an unstable majority. Having defeated one ministry, a headstrong House of Commons was capable of despatching its successor, and it was anticipated that the new government's India bill would provide the earliest opportunity for a showdown. Hence the Conservative bill conceded an elective element to the new Council, doubling its size and giving some of Britain's largest urban constituencies the right to choose Council members, much to the queen's consternation. An early version of this bill also pandered to other popular demands, including evangelical pressure. The executive remit of the governor-general was extended, and a new bishopric at Agra was promised. A clause contributed by Prince Albert committed the new Government of India to other 'public works' in addition to railways. The new elective element pacified the Commons (just as it enraged Victoria).[43] Nonetheless, the Conservatives managed to embroil themselves in a crisis six weeks later. A despatch from Lord Ellenborough, Conservative president of the Board of Control, had carried garbled versions of Governor-General Canning's Awadh proclamation of March 1858, itself designed to penalise landholders who were still holding out against the British. The despatch was leaked to politicians outside the Cabinet and then exploited by both sides of the debate, namely those MPs who felt that Canning was not harsh enough on the rebels, and those who felt the Awadhis had some cause to complain.[44]

Almost no reputation emerged untarnished from the furore over this infamous 'Oude proclamation'. Ellenborough resigned, Canning – 'too "civil" by half' as *Punch* caricatured him – felt misunderstood and Derby limped through the next few weeks fearing that his government would fall. No reputation, that is, save that of Queen Victoria. For it was the queen who refused to allow Derby to dissolve Parliament and so bring on the fourth change of government in three years. She chided her prime minister for not having shown her the offending despatch before it was sent to India. When Derby, having reshuffled his son, Lord Stanley, to be president of the Board of Control for the last two months of that office, chose the novelist Edward Bulwer-Lytton as Stanley's replacement, Queen Victoria objected.[45] Whilst Parliament continued to work out what elements of the royal prerogative might be entered into the new India bill, here was the queen acting out some of its principal features: the right in future to see all despatches to India, and the right to be consulted on Cabinet appointments. Moreover, with the confusion over Canning's policy in India and the political disarray at home, Queen Victoria began to emerge as a solution to the problem of authority in the aftermath of the Indian revolt. As the Conservatives' India bill neared the end of its long journey through the Commons with its seventy-one clauses more or less agreed – the Company's powers to be transferred to a secretary of state, advised by a Council comprising fifteen members, with a viceroy appointed by the Crown – MPs began to talk up a new role for Queen Victoria in giving moral force to the change of government. Leading the cheers as ever was Disraeli, who suggested to the queen that the bill was 'only the ante-chamber of an imperial palace' and that her name should now be impressed upon Indian native life. But radicals joined in as well. John Bright called for a proclamation to be made in the name of Victoria and to include an amnesty, the upholding of native property titles and adopted heirs, and a statement on religious toleration.[46]

Still Queen Victoria was not satisfied. In the bill that left the Commons at the beginning of July she was 'shocked to find that in several important respects the Gov[t] have surrendered the Prerogatives of the Crown'. Without her agreement alterations had been made to key clauses. Competitive examination was now proposed for the Indian civil service, and Parliament was to be given the final say in the raising of the Indian army. The queen conveyed her horror to Derby, for it was 'to him as the Head of the Gov[t] that she looks for the protection of those Prerogatives which form an integral part of the Constitution'. Somewhat conciliated by Derby's promise to uphold Crown influence in the Indian army, the queen relented, and the bill passed through the Lords.[47] There it survived a late rally by the Archbishop of Canterbury, who, whilst respecting that there could be no more proselytism or interference with Indian religion, insisted that the Government of India should not be indifferent to the question of conversion to Christianity.

It should declare against caste, make the Bible compulsory in schools, end state support for Hindu and Muslim festivals and stop discrimination against native converts. Derby offered some reassurance but not much. A cleric proved easier to brush aside than a queen. One final royal touch was required to the second clause of the act: all previous powers of the East India Company would now be exercised not 'on behalf' as in the draft but instead 'by and in the Name of Her Majesty' and it was duly promulgated on 2 August.[48]

Queen Victoria pulled off a remarkable achievement with the Government of India Act. Since her accession, politicians had clipped her constitutional wings on virtually all domestic matters. By the 1850s the idea that the royal prerogative was no more than a useful fiction had become a commonplace to the extent that when Walter Bagehot described the monarchy a few years later as the 'theatrical' element in the English constitution, few disagreed.[49] Victoria's influence over the bills transferring power from the Company to the Crown belies her reputation as a constitutional monarch with limited powers. Throughout the discussions in Cabinet and the debates in Parliament she sought clarification on every point that touched on her role. She also kept the politicians to the task in hand, not letting either the change of government in February or the crisis over the 'Oude' proclamation in May slow the momentum behind Indian reform. Victoria's stance on several key components of the clauses proved of crucial significance. Her insistence that any elective element in the new Council be balanced with a nominated equivalent, her requirement that she see all Indian despatches, and her refusal to relinquish all military patronage indicate a fuller interpretation of royal prerogative than is usually understood; but these key clauses also reveal her distrust of parliamentary management of India, especially over troop numbers – a factor she believed lay behind the vulnerability of the army in 1857. They pointed to a future in which the monarch played more and not less of a role in Indian affairs. The Government of India Act passed, despatches began to arrive at Windsor by the cartload, and Victoria and Albert immediately returned to their obsession with reforming the Indian army. Her work done, the royal couple left for Potsdam in Prussia, to join Princess

Victoria, newly pregnant with their first grandchild, the baby who would become the ill-fated heir to the Prussian empire (Wilhelm, the future Kaiser). From Potsdam Victoria applied the finishing touches to the transfer of power in her own dominion. As time would tell, the last strokes were by far the most important.

The Indian Magna Carta

The new Government of India was made in England, but needed to be proclaimed in India. Lord Derby and his Cabinet colleagues now turned to draft a proclamation. Derby recognised that it was important that it should be said in the words of the queen. Insofar as the proclamation reiterated what had been agreed in Parliament, it was reasonably straightforward. The Crown was to assume direct authority from the East India Company, the governor-general was to become a viceroy, all existing treaties with native rulers were to be accepted, employment in the public service was to be open to Europeans and natives alike, equal and impartial protection was to be given to all subjects in the exercise of religion and in the maintenance of property rights, and there would be an amnesty. The principle of religious neutrality continued to present problems. The queen's official title included the phrase 'Defender of the Faith' and Derby's Cabinet colleagues wanted to retain this wording. At the same time, explicit recognition of the monarch's Christian religion sat awkwardly in a document which promised not to 'undermine any native credo or customs, or to propagate any form of religious beliefs'. As one minister observed, this phrasing 'if it speaks the Queen's mind, it represents her to India as indifferent to Religious truth, whereas all that is required is that she should be impartial'. He went on:

> [s]he subscribes to the S.P.G. the very object of which is here condemned, and is, and cannot but be a Christian Queen . . . We had agreed to found a bishopric at Agra, and we must either do that, or permit others to do it, & from time to time found other Bishoprics; but the language . . . would seem to preclude the Queen from that exercise of her Prerogative.[50]

A way around this obstacle was to emphasise how the queen's devotion to Christianity made her tolerant of other religions.

Thus far had Lord Derby reached when he met with the queen on 9 August to update her on the eve of her departure for Germany.[51] At the same time a new crisis began to brew over the references to religion in the proclamation. Whilst Derby was carefully consulting on how to encompass both Christianity and the religions of India in the same text, Lord Stanley received a deputation of British missionary societies, stated to them that religious neutrality would guide future policy in India, and that no steps would be taken in India to give to 'the opinions of Europe in apparent preference to those which were found existing in the country'. Disraeli reported to Stanley that these words – relayed as Stanley referring to Christianity as 'the religion of Europe' – had caused considerable dissatisfaction, and one that was not confined to 'the ultra-religious circles'. Disraeli went on: '[No] Government can stand that is supposed to slight the religious feelings of the country. It is as important to touch the feelings and sympathies of the religious classes in England as to conciliate the Natives of India.'[52] Lord Derby and his Cabinet faced an obvious dilemma: how to appease evangelical opinion at home and at the same time offer meaningful words of pacification in India. They were also obliged to give voice to the queen throughout the proclamation. As Spencer Walpole reminded Stanley just before the draft was sent on to Prussia, 'the Indian proclamation is likely to be one of the most important State Papers ever issued by the Ministers of the Crown', its tone needed to be high, and throughout references to the British government should be replaced with the queen, 'partly for the purpose of acting, as it were, upon an oriental imagination, – and partly for the purpose of convincing the people that the transfer was something real and complete'. Not so important as all that: Derby carelessly left his copy of the draft behind in London when he left town.[53] Fortunately, Lord Malmesbury, the foreign secretary, was more careful, and, as part of the royal party in Potsdam, he was deputed to show the draft proclamation to the queen. She did not like what she read.

Anticipating Queen Victoria's reactions was never easy, as many nineteenth-century prime ministers found to their cost. She told

Malmesbury immediately that the proclamation 'must be almost entirely remodelled'. It was a question of substance and one of tone. She wished all references to the British government to be substituted by the royal 'we'. She suggested (as Derby had assumed she would) that the way around the religious neutrality issue was to say that the deep attachment she felt for her own religion meant she would not interfere with the religion of the Indian people. She wanted a greater commitment stated to 'future prosperity and general welfare' than the vague reference in the draft to the 'relief of poverty', and she wanted something said about the privileges of subjects of the British Crown whilst at the same time making a guarantee to preserve ancient laws and usages. Above all Queen Victoria wanted the proclamation to rise to the occasion of what she called 'the commencement of her new reign'.[54] Or, as Malmesbury told Derby, '[T]here is not half bellows enough in it for the personal address of a Great Queen to an Oriental Hemisphere' – in its present form it was 'too much like a respectable magistrate's notice after a parochial [meeting]'. Malmesbury, who found Victoria 'the most fidgety person I ever saw within the reach of a Minister', then conveyed her instructions for the proclamation to Lord Derby:

> The Queen would be very glad if Lord Derby would write it himself in his excellent language, bearing in mind that it is a female Sovereign who speaks to more than 100 millions of Eastern People on assuming the direct Government over them after a bloody civil war giving them pledges which her future reign is to redeem & explaining the principles of her Gov^t. Such a document should breathe feelings of Generosity, Benevolence, and Religious feeling, pointing out the privileges which the Indians will receive in being placed on an equality with the subjects of the British Crown & the prosperity following in the train of civilisation.[55]

Two things then happened, or rather did not happen. First, Lord Derby replied to acknowledge receipt of the queen's revisions, but revealed that the draft had already gone to the printers so he could not check it against the suggested changes from Potsdam, although he assured Malmesbury that he had avoided all the points to which Victoria had taken exception. He and Stanley, as well as George Clerk (now the new permanent under-secretary), had moved on to another thorny topic: how the proclamation, and in particular the phrase 'Defender of the Faith', would translate into the Indian vernacular. Derby hoped, somewhat unrealistically, that it might come out benignly as 'Protectress of Religion'.[56] Secondly, learning no doubt from Stanley's candour on meeting the missionary delegation earlier in the month, the Cabinet went quiet on the final text contained in the proclamation. Until news reached London at the beginning of December that the transfer of power had been proclaimed throughout India on 1 November, no one was any the wiser outside of the Cabinet and the court as to what it actually said. Those in the know gave little away. In a speech at the Mansion House in early November, Derby stated that a 'message of peace and mercy' had been sent out from the queen to her Indian empire, whilst the Duke of Argyll told a meeting of the India Christian Association in London later that month that the proclamation was limited in its scope, and simply removed the 'screen' between the Company and the Crown.[57] Evangelical natures clearly abhorred the vacuum. As late as October the missionary lobby assumed that the assumption of power by the queen would accelerate not diminish the spread of Christianity. For example, Lord Shaftesbury claimed in a speech at Leeds in October that even without government aid 'clouds upon clouds' of Bibles could descend on India.[58] Seldom can a document of such magnitude have been kept under wraps for so long and caused such speculation.

When it eventually appeared the final version of the proclamation clarified the new British position of religious neutrality in India and set off a series of evangelical criticisms.[59] The proclamation did incorporate most of the concerns expressed by Victoria and Albert. The omissions were significant, however. Two stand out. Despite what passed down into folk memory in India, there was no reference in the proclamation to Indians enjoying the same equality as other subjects of the British Crown. The nearest the proclamation comes to this is in the seventh paragraph, where the queen declares to 'hold Ourselves bound to the Natives of Our Indian Territories by the same obligations of Duty which bind Us to all our other Subjects'. This did not go as far as Victoria wished, when she called for Indian subjects to be 'placed on an equality with the subjects of the British Crown'. Nor did the proclamation refer, as she had wanted, to 'the commencement of her new reign', a point of less importance perhaps, but the sentiment denoted the fresh start she hoped for her Indian realm.

One final instalment of the transfer of power remained. Back in December 1857, Lord Palmerston had suggested to the queen that an Indian order of knighthood be established as a means of rewarding and strengthening the personal bonds of loyalty between Queen Victoria and the loyal Indian princes. Eighteen months later, the queen returned to the idea, recommending it to Lord Canning. Canning assumed that the queen wanted to keep the new order exclusively for Indians. He made enquiries around British India about how it might work, only to be told that it would not get very far unless both Europeans and Indians were eligible to join. Indian elites, Canning was informed, would not look favourably at an honour set aside just for them.[60] So, instead, a new order of chivalry, the 'Star of India' was established for senior Indians and Europeans. Prince Albert took up the project with great energy, designing its ribands and mottoes, in consultation with the new Liberal secretary of state for India, Sir Charles Wood. Albert's stance on India – somewhere between evangelism and toleration, antiquity and modernity – is captured by his ideas for the new Indian order. His preferred title was the 'Eastern' or 'Morning Star'. As he explained to Wood, '[t]he Eastern Star preceded the three Kings, or wise men when they did homage to the infant Christ & maybe taken as the emblem of dawning Christianity, as such it would have a memorable meaning which may remain concealed from the Indians, & yet be one day recognised in history.' At the same time, Albert pointed out, '[a]s the light of the world came from the east (like the Sun) & the human races are supposed to have spread from the East, the emblem might be eligible on that account & not uncomplimentary to the Indians'. Albert also enthusiastically drafted a list of Latin mottoes that might accompany the order, eventually settling on 'lux caeli dux noster' (heaven's light our command).[61] Albert's blueprints did not impress either Wood or Canning. Between them the two statesmen pointed out that Latin mottoes were fine for British orders such as the Garter, but not for 'Princes whose ancestors were sitting on their Thrones four or five centuries before the Garter . . . [was] dreamt of'. It was explained to Albert too that as far as Indians were concerned their country was not in the east, but in the west, for example Muslims in India faced west to pray to Mecca. 'Indians do not think of . . . themselves as Orientals', Canning helpfully reminded the court. For good measure Canning also pointed out that 'star' in Hindi was 'satara', the family name of the Maratha dynasty that the British had defeated in 1804. And so these discussions rambled on for the best part of nine months. Further names for the order were canvassed: the 'Imperial Star' (rejected as the British Crown was a royal one), the 'Celestial Star' (a tautology), the Star of Peace (no good, as the Hindi equivalent of peace was 'agreement after war' or 'sleep'). At one stage an exasperated Albert suggested it should be known as the 'golden impossibility' since no one could agree, and eventually the Star of India was settled on.[62]

From a distance the Star of India looks like an attempt to impose western ideas of status and hierarchy on princely India, cloaked in the kind of medieval mystique beloved by the Victorians. In some respects, the new honour did just that. It was modelled on the Order of St Patrick, the Irish equivalent of the Order of the Bath, and over time its membership came to read like a who's who of British Indian society. In the aftermath of the Indian rebellion, however, the Star of India was more a roll call of loyalty, with particular emphasis given to those chiefs who had supported the British in 1857–8. Canning was insistent that the awards be made for service more than in recognition of blood ties or 'ancient dignity'. From a long list the initial Indian recipients were whittled down to eight: five Hindu princes (the Maharajas of Gwalior, Kashmir, Indore and Patiala and the Gaekwar of Baroda) and three Muslim rulers (the Nizam of Hyderabad, the Begum of Bhopal and the Nawab of Rampur). This was a very different cadre from before 1857, when the Company's table of gun salutes had begun with the kings of Delhi and Awadh, and included many of the smaller rulers of northern India.[63] The Order was also established to mark the queen's 'new reign'. The first investitures in 1861 were organised to fall on the anniversary of the proclamation.

The new Order of the Star of India was launched on 1 November 1861, simultaneously in Allahabad and London. Four Indian rulers made the trip to Allahabad: the Maharajas of Gwalior (extra blue ribbon was ordered to suit his extravagant tastes), Patiala and Kashmir, and the Begum of Bhopal (who declined the special title of 'Lady Knight'), whilst the other Indian recipients were admitted at investiture ceremonies in their own courts. To Canning's amazement and anger, the Nizam of Hyderabad initially refused, explaining that such awards ran counter to his religious beliefs.[64] In London, the first knights were Albert, the Prince of Wales and Duleep Singh. Sadly, the Buckingham Palace ceremony was one of the last such public occasions for Albert. He fell ill later that month with a typhoid attack and died on 15 December. The Star claimed a victim in India too, for Charlotte Canning succumbed to a fatal bout of malaria on her return to Calcutta. Charles Canning's spirits sank immediately. He followed his wife to the grave seven months later, with barely time to organise her memorial stone at Barrackpore. Time stood still for Queen Victoria too. Already in mourning for her mother, the Duchess of Kent, who had passed away earlier in the year, she now became the most famous widow in the world, disappearing from public view for the best part of a decade.[65] In India, by contrast, she was everywhere, as the Government of India, anxious to secure the new Raj, circulated her name, and her image, far and wide.

CHAPTER 5

VICTORIA BEATRIX

'A new era has dawned upon India; the reign of Victoria Beatrix has commenced', declared veteran Indian expert John Kaye, as reports of the publication of the queen's proclamation in India on 1 November 1858 reached London a few weeks later.[1] No expense was spared in spreading the news throughout the Indian subcontinent. Overseen by Charles Canning's private secretary and linguist extraordinaire Lewin Bowring, the proclamation was translated into the principal vernacular languages of India, and read out in full at formal ceremonies in the major towns and cantonments of the three Presidencies (Bengal, Bombay, Madras), in the princely states and across the seas to Singapore, Malacca and the Straits Settlements. Everywhere, the trappings of the East India Company were removed, and the royal standard substituted in their place, most poignantly in Bombay harbour, where with one hoist of the ensign the ships of the East India Company navy became the fleets of the Royal Indian Navy. Lithograph presses went into overdrive as thousands of copies of the proclamation were printed. In the Punjab, for example, every village was given one. Public celebrations – fireworks, illuminations, feeding of the poor and nautch-dancing – marked the event, from Peshawar to Mysore, from Calcutta to Bombay, from Gujarat to Travancore.[2] Addresses – some ornate, some handwritten, in some cases containing signatures than ran into the thousands – were sent onto the queen, many of the memorialists pledging their loyalty as the queen's subjects at the start of her 'direct sovereignty' and her 'royal supremacy' in India.[3]

All happened in haste. Canning only received the final text of the proclamation from London in the middle of October, and many local officials reported getting their copy and translation as late as 27 October. Not everywhere made the day of destiny on time, and even those that did slipped up. The Bombay Custom House flew the Union Jack upside down, a bad omen some thought. In Madras, only the troops were present at the ceremony, as there had been no time to advertise the event: 'all was solemn, gloomy and dull'. Victoria's new title also proved difficult to translate, there being no obvious female equivalent in Hindustani: was she a begum, or a maharani, or padishah? Fortunately, a simpler title suggested itself. One illumination at the Auckland Hotel in Calcutta proclaimed Victoria as 'Empress of India'.[4] Despite the rush, the diffusion of the queen's proclamation throughout India was of huge significance. Never before had there been so conspicuous an iden-tification of the British monarchy with the Indian empire. Rarely had so much resource been put into translating and disseminating an offi-cial announcement across the whole of the Indian subcontinent and beyond. The proclamation was the manifesto of a monarch. It made a series of pledges to the people of India: to respect their religions and laws, to treat them in the same manner as the queen's subjects else-where, to open up the administration of the country to Indians, to modernise public utilities, to end the policy of annexation, and to offer clemency to those who had taken up arms against British rule. In short, as the Christian socialist J. M. Ludlow put it, the proclamation was 'British India's Magna Charta'. In future India's governors would be judged against the words of the queen. 'They may violate every one of its promises,' Ludlow declared prophetically, 'but every promise will survive its own violation – and avenge it.' An irreversible step had been taken in India. Sidelined from power by the English constitution at home, the queen now constituted English authority in India. As the 8th Duke of Argyll observed, 'the personal authority of the Sovereign' was now in India brought 'within the circle of political contention'.[5]

This chapter explores the immediate consequences of the transfer of power from Company to Crown: how it was implemented, and how it was interpreted. The queen's proclamation was paternalist and Tory in tone. Carrying out its pledges became the task of liberals. Empowered by the Indian Councils Act of 1861, Charles Canning, the new viceroy, gathered a reforming executive around him, its legal and financial members drawn from the bright lights of liberalism back in Britain. James Wilson, editor of the London free-trade tribune *The Economist*, arrived to take up the finance post, and Henry Maine, a precocious professor of law at Cambridge, accepted, at the second asking, the law portfolio. Indian expertise was not considered important. Neither Maine nor any of the legal members of the Executive Council down to 1877 had experience of India. Instead, they all signed up to the principles of liberal governance: freedom of trade, freedom of contract under the law and freedom of opinion. These ideas worked well enough at home, even if they sometimes required the strong arm of the state to enforce and regulate them. Early Victorian Britain had gone through a revolution in government; now it was India's turn for a dose of what James Fitzjames Stephen, Maine's successor in 1869, called 'benevolent despotism'.[6] After 1858 the Government of India set about turning the Company state into a liberal state. The currency and the post were overhauled, the legal system codified, the civil service and the army reorganised. When all that was done, the Government turned its attention to reform in the princely states. This Indian revolution in government was far more extensive than its British equivalent, and historians have given it due attention.[7] What they have overlooked completely is the extent to which the queen's proclamation loomed large in both the projection of British power in India after 1858, and the ways in which it was debated and contested. To re-establish control after the rebellion, the queen's status, and the queen's image, were played out by the Government of India in an unprecedented fashion. At the same time, the guarantees of equality given in the queen's proclamation created a discursive space within which Indian claims for inclusion within the imperial polity could be made. One way or another, the queen proved central, and not merely ornamental, to this new phase of the Raj.

Sovereigns

The Government of India did not stop at the proclamation in directly associating the name of Queen Victoria with British dominion over India after 1858. Words were one thing. Amongst a population with low levels of literacy, images were another. The reorganisation of the Indian coinage and the paper currency, as well as the expansion and centralisation of the postal system, offered the opportunity of establishing a more fixed image of the queen's sovereignty amongst her new subjects. In 1862 the famous 'Company rupee' was withdrawn. In its place came the queen, her head and shoulders engraved into the new coinage issued from 1862 onwards. She featured on all denominations, from the gold *mohur* 'sovereign' to the tiny copper *anna*. She also adorned the new banknotes, made legal tender by the Paper Currency Act of 1861.[8] Outside of British India, creating a uniform coinage posed difficulties. Many of the princely states maintained their own mints, and, although they obediently removed the image of the Emperor of Delhi, they were mostly reluctant to add the queen. They either preferred an image of their own chief, or no image at all (particularly so in Muslim states such as Bhopal and Hyderabad). Closing down the mints of the native states became a government priority. Separate currencies placed obstacles in the way of trade and encouraged forgery. But, economic utility aside, it was the symbolism of the indivisible sovereignty of the queen's rule that lay behind the drive to a uniform coinage across the whole of India. In 1871, Mayo, the viceroy, spelled out what was at stake. 'I cannot help thinking', he wrote to the Duke of Argyll, the secretary of state for India:

> that it would be extremely desirable, that on coins which will pass from hand to hand among the people of India that recognition of suzerainty, which was thought necessary and insisted upon by the Mahomedan Emperors, would be suggested by a Power which exercises an influence in Hindoostan which was unknown to the rulers of Delhi.

In other words, Queen Victoria. Mayo's successor, Northbrook, agreed, and in 1876 the Native Coinage At was passed, requiring princely states to give up their mints and hand over the manufacture of coinage to Calcutta.[9] Few complied, but the passage of time and the free flow of the new Indian rupee did its work in marginalising the smaller currencies.

The new rupee fabricated Queen Victoria across India, and beyond, into the currencies of Ceylon and British territory in east Africa.[10] Admittedly, some of her own officials doubted its potency at first. How could the effigy of a woman displace the Company coin, especially amongst Hindus and Muslims, who were not used to depictions of female power?[11] Yet considerable effort went into designing the new coin so that it had Indian appeal. Queen Victoria had featured on the old Company rupee in the last two decades of its issue, her bust taken from the same designs used on British coinage at home. Now, in 1862, an Indian version of the queen was substituted. Her nose was straightened and made more prominent, her hair was plaited, a crown was added to her head, and a string of pearls draped around her neck and over an elaborately embroidered blouse. An additional enhancement featured in the banknotes of the 1862 issue: her eyes were darkened. To both the coins and the notes the queen gave her approval, on the recommendation of her secretary of state Sir Charles Wood. They would, he assured her, bear 'the unmistakeable sign of being issued by the Sovereign, namely the representation of the Sovereign, with same ornaments and accessories on both'.[12] Thus she remained in the currency of British India for the rest of her reign, cast permanently as a young woman, orientalised in her appearance.

Queen Victoria's image, tailored for Indian use, also featured on postage stamps throughout the subcontinent after 1860. The first stamps, designed by Henry Thuillier, the Surveyor-General of India, used the standard depiction of the queen from the British 'penny black'. However, in the early 1860s the Indian Mint commissioned a fresh portrait from Thomas De La Rue, the London printer. He depicted the queen's bust in an oval vignette; she wore a simple laureate crown with her hair tied back. This was a less regal image than the 1862 currency issue, but, like the coinage and banknotes, the postage stamps caught Queen Victoria as a youthful woman. This remained the standard Indian postal stamp for almost all of the reign. Not until the 1890s did age catch up with the queen on the stamps, when a completely new portrait of the queen as empress, wearing a small crown, partially covered by a shawl, was produced, her eyebrows darkened, with exposed ear and ear jewellery.[13] As with the currency in India, postage was not standardised across India, except insofar as mail needed official stamps to be sent outside native states. Six states did opt to become 'convention' states, permitting them to counter-stamp the Government of India stamp with the name of their own state. Some of them applied the airbrush to the image of Queen Victoria. Compare for example, the standard Government of India 1866 stamp with the counter-stamped version of the same portrait for the states of Nabha, Chamba or Faridkot, just ten years later. The queen's eyes are larger and darker, her nose and mouth much fuller than in the original.[14] As likenesses these images on coin, banknote and postage stamp rendered the queen almost unrecognisable; as representations of female monarchy in an eastern setting they served an important purpose.

Subjects

Equality before the law was *the* great promise of the queen's proclamation of 1858. As we have seen in the previous chapter, Queen Victoria's personal insistence that Indians be treated on an equal footing to all her other subjects was actually watered down in the text of the proclamation. Instead of 'equality', it was stated that the queen was bound to do her duty to Indians in the same way as she was obliged to all her other subjects. In principle, the new Government of India accepted this definition of a common imperial subjectivity. Within weeks of the proclamation, Canning confirmed that, as far as the amnesty clause was concerned, no distinction was to be made between Europeans and Indians, when cases of clemency for murderous acts during the rebellion were judged. 'To give a more restricted sense to the term' – that is, to limit the amnesty to Europeans – 'would be to make the spirit of the proclamation more exclusive, and to exhibit the Crown as less considerate of the lives of Indian subjects than the literal and legal meaning of the words used'.[15] However, this noble sentiment was quickly spirited away in the legal reforms that took place in India in the early 1860s, as well as in some of the key decisions of the courts.

Three major pieces of legislation defined the new liberal India: the Code of Civil Procedure (1859), the Penal Code (1860) and the Code of Criminal Procedure (1861). Although already on the statute book when they arrived, these laws were shaped by Henry Maine and James Fitzjames Stephen, the first two legal members of the Viceroy's Council. Both men came to India wearing their liberalism on their sleeves, untainted by the world-weariness so endemic to Indian administration.[16] As it turned out, their advanced views did not survive the long journey east. The rebellion of 1857–8 had altered many men's minds, the Indian legal fraternity more so than most, and a hardening of attitudes was apparent immediately.[17] Immunity from prosecution for Europeans in the district courts was effectively upheld by the new Code, and by the Indian High Courts Act of 1861. There would be no return to the 'Black Acts' of the 1830s, whereby native judges had been allowed jurisdiction over all cases, irrespective of race. In the new legislation, only a Justice of the Peace (JP), and not an ordinary magistrate, could refer accused Europeans to the higher courts, and JPs tended to be white men. This flew in the face of the queen's proclamation, or so it seemed to the British Indian Association, the mouthpiece of Bengali landowners, which protested to Canning, reminding him of the 'spirit' of the queen's words.[18] In theory, anyone who had risen through the Indian Civil Service could be a JP. In 1872 Stephen closed that particular loophole, amending the Criminal Procedure Act so that only JPs who were British subjects could judge in such cases. For the purposes of the Act, 'British subjects' meant those who were 'born, naturalised or domiciled' in any of Britain's European, American, Australasian or African possessions, but not in India. A Maltese merchant, or a khoikhoi tribesman from southern Africa, or a New South Wales sheep farmer could be a JP in India, but not an Indian. The queen's proclamation proved of little use in this regard. As Henry Maine advised in January 1866, the term 'subject' in all statutes relating to India 'expressly contrasted' the British subject and the native Indians.[19]

There was no such ambiguity about the status of the queen's proclamation when it came to matters penal, however. Loyalty to the Crown was written directly into India's new Penal Code, in operation from

1862. Originally drafted by Thomas Babington Macaulay and others back in the 1830s, the Penal Code was finally published in 1860. On the face of it, as with other aspects of the law, the new version of the Penal Code was simply an update registering the new nomenclature of the Crown instead of the Company.[20] However, a new section was inserted in the chapter of the Code covering offences against the state. Here it was proposed that the full weight of the English law of treason be applied to India. Canning and his Council extended to India the British statute, introduced at the height of the last Chartist risings in 1848, which made collecting arms to levy war against the queen an offence punishable by transportation. In India the law would be stretched further to include the government alongside the queen.[21] The Code cited the proclamation as defining the relationship of 'allegiance' between the queen and her subjects. In return for her protection, her subjects should give a 'true and faithful obedience'. If they did not, if they chose to 'wage war against the Queen', and, by extension, the Government of India, then they would be prosecuted.[22] In later versions of the Penal Code, the reference to the 1858 proclamation was dropped, but the sections relating to the penalties for 'waging war' against the queen remained, and in 1870 a new crime of conspiracy to overthrow the queen was added.[23] Between 1858 and 1901, four men were tried for 'waging war against the Queen', that is attempting to overthrow the Government of India. They were Vasude Balwant Phadke in Poona in 1879; Shivaji IV, the Maharaja of Kolhapur, in 1881; the King of Ava in Burma in 1886; and the Senapati of Manipur in 1891. The law actually proved blunt and ineffective. Only in Phadke's case was there an implicit reference to the queen's rule, insofar as he was reported to desire a republic, and he was duly tried, convicted and transported, dying in captivity in Aden in 1883.[24] Only in Manipur was there a successful capital conviction, as we shall see in a later chapter. Nonetheless, the insertion of treason into the new Indian Penal Code showed the determination of the Government of India to wield the might of the monarch when crime against the state reared its head. Strikingly, it was the only mention of the proclamation in any of the new legal codification for India introduced after 1858. Not so much Victoria Beatrix as Victoria the Punitive.

Any Magna Carta worth its name would surely respect the principle of *habeas corpus*, or no detention without trial, a fundamental right of the English since their own Magna Carta in 1215. Yet, when tested, that extension of liberty to India also proved elusive. In 1870, two Bengali Muslims – Amir Khan and Hashmadad Khan – were arrested on suspicion of belonging to the jihadist wing of the Wahabi sect.[25] They were imprisoned and, when no date was set for their trial or even arraignment, an appeal was made to the Calcutta High Court. It was by no means straightforward. Under Company rule *habeas corpus* had been routinely set on one side. So the barrister who brought the appeal, Thomas Chisholm Anstey, threw in the queen's proclamation and its guarantee of equality, to help his plea. All fell flat. Not only did the court reiterate that *habeas corpus* did not apply in the *mofussil* (that is, outside Calcutta, where the Khans had been arrested), but in any event the viceroy had the right to take suspects into custody without trial.[26] The case caused controversy, as Indian Muslims were accused of not recognising English law, as Wahabis believed India lay within the domain of Islam. That put the matter back to front. For it was actually English law – in this case *habeas corpus* – that refused to recognise Indians. This 1870 ruling was occasionally tested but never overturned, and *habeas corpus* remained precarious in India thereafter. Once more, the queen's proclamation seemed undone by the work of British officialdom.

The fiction of the queen as the fount of justice for India was perpetuated insofar as she was the court of final appeal in both civil and criminal cases. In civil matters, the Judicial Committee of the Privy Council in London had since 1833 embodied the sovereign's role as supreme arbiter, albeit without requiring her physical attendance at its hearings. Appeals for redress from both Europeans and Indians in India took up an increasing amount of Privy Council time during Victoria's reign. Before 1858 there was an annual average of seven appeals from India. From the 1860s, the rate climbed exponentially. By the early 1870s some two-thirds of appeals to the Privy Council in civil matters were of Indian origin.[27] Not that taking a case from India to London was straightforward. There was the cost of arranging transcripts and organising witness depositions. In 1863 further hurdles were erected. Only appeals involving disputes over 10,000 rupees were permitted, and financial securities had to be provided upfront in the event of all the costs being awarded against the appellant. Still the tide was not stemmed, despite two successive legal members of the Viceroy's Executive Council – Stephen and Arthur Hobhouse – arguing in 1872 that final appeals should rest with the Indian higher courts. Then, in 1874, another condition was added: the appeal must also involve a 'substantial question' of law.[28] The number of cases levelled off in the 1880s, but India kept the Privy Council busy well into the twentieth century, and so kept alive the queen's reputation as judge in the last resort, 'a star chamber' whose proceedings were transparent and trusted compared to the viceregal machinery in India.[29] Not so in criminal cases. Although the queen also retained the prerogative of appeal for these, by 1876 it was noted that this was exercised very rarely. Similarly the governor-general and then the viceroy acted as gatekeeper in matters of pardon and commutation. After 1858, there was no change to the 1855 enactment that commutation of sentences such as death and transportation remained the final decision of the governor-general, although the royal prerogative to pardon was retained. As late as 1890 this ruling still presented some confusion, the practical solution being that the hangman's noose usually intervened before any appeal for royal clemency could reach London.[30]

So, as quickly as new legal channels between the queen and her subjects appeared to open in 1858, judicial reform and practical administration in the years that followed sealed them shut, or at best put in place powerful disincentives. Maine and Stephen had embedded racial difference in the law. They left behind them a legal code that bore little relation to the paternal rhetoric of the queen's proclamation of 1858. The imperial jurisdiction of the Privy Council over civil matters aside, most legal routes to the Crown proved dead ends. In 1882, in the case of *Empress v. Tegha Singh*, the Calcutta High Court even went so far as to rule that the acts of the Indian legislature took precedence over the queen's proclamation.[31] Effectively, the queen's words had no binding legal status. And, by the mid-1870s, the principle that the local courts and the supreme court of India (that is, the Viceroy in Council) had the final say on whether anything should be appealed to London was well established. But it was not well known. The spirit of the proclamation lived on. In 1872, in an unusual breach of convention, twenty-two memorials addressed to the queen slipped through the net at Bombay and made it all the way to Buckingham Palace, where they were diverted and returned to India by Colonel Thomas Biddulph, the watchful keeper of the Privy Purse.[32] Written in Marathi and Persian as well as in English, they were the stuff of the lower courts of the Bombay presidency – mostly inheritance and property disputes – hardly fit business for a queen, however encompassing her rule was supposed to be. But they point to an abiding belief after 1858 amongst Indian litigants in the remote justice offered by the Crown, no matter how much the Government of India confuscated the procedures, nor how extensively men like Henry Maine attempted to modernise Indian law.

Servants

In 1858 Queen Victoria took over formal control of thousands of civil servants and soldiers from the East India Company. The switch of employer – from Company to Crown – came a long way down the list of clauses within the Government of India Act. In fact, the alteration was almost forgotten until a hastily drawn-up supplement was bolted on to the proclamation of 1 November 1858. New legislation was required to transfer the Company army into the regular Queen's army, and that only came two years later. The Indian Civil Service (ICS), by contrast, had already been reformed in 1853. Indeed, India was the guinea pig for the new principle of competitive entry to administrative positions, gradually applied in Britain following the Northcote–Trevelyan report of 1854. Yet both for the army and for the civil service, the transfer of power in India had more immediate and direct effect than many of the other changes made in 1858, and not all of it met with approval. Designed to quell and control the mutinous Indian rebels of 1857, the new terms of service for soldiers and civilians as employees of the Crown in turn provoked backlash amongst Company hands in India.

A new broom had swept through the Indian Civil Service following the renewal of the Company's charter in 1853. A new competitive exam was introduced.[33] Anxious that they would miss out on promotion and pensions, and wary of 'competition wallahs' overtaking worthy plodders, existing Company servants protested against the new system, demanding compensation.[34] But the new service, formalised by the Indian Civil Service Act of 1861, quickly established itself. There were now calls to make the Indian Civil Service explicitly a royal cadre, with its own uniform, and a new Royal India College to be specially created in either Oxford or Cambridge for the preparation of candidates for the examinations.[35] No pressure came from the Palace to follow this through. Queen Victoria remained ambivalent about the Indian Civil Service. As late as 1890 she lamented the inferior quality of its recruits, regretting that 'gentlemen' no longer entered the administration, implying that she preferred patronage to merit.[36]

In India there was no such hesitation about the benefits of the new Indian Civil Service. The promise to throw open administrative positions to qualified Indians, already made in the 1833 East India Company Charter, and now amplified in the queen's proclamation, became a beacon of hope to the educated elite of India. It was a chance to assert loyalty, an incentive for public service, and a means of influencing the colonial power. But there were stumbling blocks. Entry examinations had to be taken in England. Hindus broke caste if they travelled overseas. Not surprisingly, Indian admission to its own civil service remained limited. By 1878 there had only been ten successful Indian candidates; by 1884 there was only one more. Through the years Indian candidates had presented themselves, for example eight in 1867 and seven in 1872, but were rarely successful. Demands for equal treatment in the ICS came from both Britain and India with increasing regularity from the late 1860s. In Bombay, led by a Parsi merchant, Dadabhai Naoroji, the local branch of the East India Association took up ICS reform. In 1868 Naoroji and the Bombay Association submitted a petition to Stafford Northcote, the secretary of state for India. Henry Fawcett, the radical MP for Brighton, took up the Bombay petition, debuting in his role as unofficial 'member of Parliament for India'. Fawcett referred to the queen's proclamation of 1858, explaining to the House of Commons that Indians believed it to be 'the charter of their liberties', and hence the basis for demanding easier access to the ICS. Fawcett supported the plan for ICS examinations to be held simultaneously in Bombay, Calcutta and Madras. Fawcett's intervention went nowhere. Changes to the system of ICS entry were made slowly, but hardly in the spirit of the queen's proclamation. An Indian statute of 1870 allowed the various branches of the Government of India to nominate Indians to join the minor branches of the ICS. In 1878, Lord Lytton as viceroy proposed that a section of this 'statutory' service, based on the hybrid maxim of 'selection by merit', should be closed and reserved for Indian appointments made this way without examination. Critics called it 'the re-establishment of jobbery'. The new system added forty-eight new Indian civil servants by 1886, hardly boosting the meagre proportion of native civil servants (5½ per cent of 950 officials overall).[37] Thirty years after the proclamation, the ICS had indeed been transformed, but not quite as planned. By design, Indians were being kept in their place in the ICS.

For Indian nationalists of Naoroji's era, and indeed for the generation that followed, the sclerotic pace at which the ICS was opened up proved the largest breach of faith in the principle of equality affirmed in the queen's proclamation of 1858. Naoroji aired his disappointment – in his speeches to the first few meetings of the Indian National Congress (est. 1885) and once he was an MP in the British Parliament (1892–5). In 1893 he denounced the 'Anglo-Indian system' for using 'every subterfuge' to defeat the spirit of the 'proclamations of the Sovereign', comparing the British in India unfavourably with their Mughal predecessors, who had populated their administrations with the very same Indians that they had vanquished.[38] Native admission to the ICS was seen as an instant panacea for many of the ills that beset the Raj in the second half of the nineteenth century: famine and unpopular taxation especially. Within an Indian polity in which there was little realistic chance of representative government any time soon, improved entry to the corridors of power was the next best thing. An ICS run by Indians as well as for Indians was never ruled out by the British, but it was never made easy. Jawaharlal Nehru's later verdict on the ICS in 1934 – 'neither Indian, nor civil, nor service' – points to a missed opportunity. From a truly Indian ICS a loyal creole bureaucracy might have been forged, as happened elsewhere in the British Empire, for example French Canada. Instead, Indians were relegated to positions of petty power, trained to pen-push, but never trusted to take control.

In the other main portion of the queen's Indian service, loyalty carried a higher premium. The army constituted the largest element of Her Majesty's servants in India after 1858. Victoria and Albert, together with her cousin, the Duke of Cambridge, had long coveted a more direct control of the army in India. The experience of divided command in the suppression of the rebellion of 1857–8 had only strengthened their resolve. Clauses 56 and 57 of the Government of India Act of 1858 transferred the armed forces of the East India Company to the Crown, and the Crown lost no time in taking up the command.[39] Within weeks of the Act being passed the Duke of Cambridge was instructing Jonathan Peel, the secretary of state for war, with his future intentions. Albert was soon ready with his own plans. He envisaged an army of India, still split across the three presidencies as far as native regiments were concerned, but led by one all-India corps of officers, which would rotate around the different divisions. In his scheme, all the European regiments – both the soldiers of the Company and the royal troops – would be incorporated into the regular army of the line, that is, under the command of the Crown. That was essentially what the queen desired too, her domain to be secured by her own army. With the queen anxious for complete control, and the Duke of Cambridge, as commander-in-chief of the Armed Forces, keen to take precedence immediately over the India Office, Albert counselled patience. Amalgamate the two armies of India into the regular army, and the rest would follow.[40]

However, that was not the view of Parliament, in the first instance at any rate. In March 1859, a commission, chaired by Peel, reported on the way forward. On merging the two armies, its views were split: the majority favoured retaining the local army, raised exclusively for service in India and under the command of the viceregal authorities and the secretary of state for India. A minority report gave the case for the Crown, calling for the maintenance of the separate armies of each presidency, and the combining of native and European regiments under a single command.[41] Learning of the outcome of the Commission in February, ahead of publication, the queen was furious. She spelled out to Lord Derby her preferred course of action: the abolition of the local army, the transfer of command and recruiting to the head of the regular royal army, a reduction in the number of native regiments, and the introduction of Crown patronage over the appointment of senior European officers and military cadetships. Prince Albert joined in, writing directly to Peel, and, to complete the royal battery, the Duke of Cambridge (a member of the Commission) pitched in as well to lobby Lord Derby. Wincing at the 'great pain' the queen's remonstrations caused him, but mindful of likely parliamentary opposition to any attempt to enhance the authority of the Crown over the army, Derby did his best to dodge the bombardment from the Palace and the Horse Guards (the Duke of Cambridge's HQ) that continued unabated through March and April.[42] Relief only came for the embattled prime minister when the Liberals under Palmerston returned to power. An old Whig now filled the new office of secretary of state for India: Sir Charles Wood. The prospects for amalgamating the army in India looked even dimmer. The Whigs believed in government by Parliament, and Parliament liked to think it controlled the army, wherever its operations. Fearing the worst, the queen made an early move on her new minister, pressing Wood to implement the changes required by the Palace. Wood deflected her ultimatum, saying that he needed to get his feet under the table of his new ministry, and also await the return of Parliament. Frustrated and fuming, the queen threatened Wood that she would not approve any new commissions in the existing Indian army until he made a decision about its reform.[43] Royal brinkmanship once more.

Then something happened to prevent a stand-off between Crown, Cabinet and Parliament – another 'mutiny' in India, but this time of British troops. Throughout the debates around Indian army reform in the immediate aftermath of the rebellion of 1857–8, no one had thought to consult the European soldiers themselves. In May 1859, almost two years to the day after the start of the sepoy mutiny, a regiment of European troops at Meerut began a protest – or a 'strike', as they called it – objecting to serving the Crown.[44] Graffiti suggested it was personal. 'John Company is dead, we will not soldier for the Queen' was scrawled on the washhouse walls at Meerut. The protests spread: to Allahabad, Baharampur in Bengal, and to the hill cantonment of Dagshai. At issue was the question of whether the soldiers were obliged to switch service, or whether they might be discharged and re-enlist, or be paid a bounty to move from one regiment to a new one, as was the convention. Company troops were limited to service in India; soldiering for the queen might take them anywhere in the world. Many believed they had been offered the right to a discharge from comments made by Lord Palmerston during the debates on the Government of India bill in 1858. Fearful of having to turn European soldiers on fellow Europeans, the Government of India moved swiftly to quell the outbreak. Three ringleaders at Meerut were identified. Special hearings were conducted at several of the principal army towns to find out how widespread was the mood of resistance. In their statements, many soldiers claimed they were loyal subjects of the queen, but not her servants. Having sworn an oath of attestation when they joined the Company army, and with the Company now disbanded, they felt no obligation to the Crown, unless incentivised by the bounty payment. Of the 837 soldiers interviewed at Lahore, 73 per cent stated they were dissatisfied with the way their transfer had been handled. Extra troop ships were quickly laid on for those who wished to be discharged, and by the summer of 1860 some 10,000 troops had been shipped out.[45] As a statement of disloyalty amongst the rank and file, the 1859 mutiny was a powerful one. The authorities in India and in Britain subsequently recognised that European soldiers' 'rights had been overlooked' in the transfer of government from Company to Crown. One commentator went so far as to suggest that, instead of the change of employer being made by the 'stroke of a pen', a general order should have been issued, in which the queen offered all Company troops a bounty to re-enlist in the regular army, referring in 'stirring language' to their recent brilliant exploits.[46]

Preoccupied with securing Indian loyalty after the rebellion, the British government had taken for granted the patriotism of its own forces.

The 'white mutiny' of troops in 1859 quickly undid the work of Peel's Commission. From India it was reported that Lord Clyde (commander-in-chief of the Indian army) and General William Mansfield (commander of the Bombay army) were not only sympathetic to the discontented troops, but also felt that the incident proved the days of the local army were numbered. Clyde also had the ear of the queen and the Duke of Cambridge. Wood, the new secretary of state, who on taking office had been minded to deliver the Commission's recommendations, changed tack completely.[47] The following summer he brought forward legislation which did away with the local army altogether. European company troops were absorbed into the regular army, and three native armies were maintained in the Presidencies, together with the Hyderabad contingent and the Punjab frontier force. The East India Company's military college at Addiscombe was closed. A new officer corps was brought in, over the course of time picked from the regular army and directly from the army staff college at Sandhurst. The sepoy regiments were disbanded, and 'irregular' Indian infantry and artillery established, with their own native officers.

The court had got its way. India now felt the force of only one army, and it was the queen's. As Wood's Indian army bill left the House of Commons en route for its final reading, Lord Clyde stayed over at Osborne House, his table talk 'very strong about amalgamation of the Army'.[48] This was a royal army in India in every sense. Its overall command lay with the queen's cousin, the Duke of Cambridge. The queen herself ensured that going forward her views on senior military appointments in India were made known. Army institutions over which she enjoyed patronage – Sandhurst, the Royal Artillery and the Royal Engineers – now staffed the officer corps in the Indian army. The new Indian irregulars fought in the name of the queen, the buttons on their tunics embossed with the crown of England.[49] By the mid-1860s the reorganisation was complete. The new Indian army comprised 62,000 British officers and rank-and-file, and 125,000 Indians. The native regiments were unlike the old sepoy units. They were drawn deliberately from the 'martial' peoples of India: Punjabi Sikhs and Muslims, Gurkhas, Jats, Santhals, Balochis and Pathuns. They were recruited into clannish regiments, serving alongside their neighbours, kith and kin.[50] They were expected to fight anywhere, not just in their immediate vicinity as in the old days. The last campaign fought by the dual army was in Sikkim in 1860, the first of the new era was in Bhutan in 1864–5. Then, in 1867, 13,000 British and Indian troops sailed from Bombay to fight in Abyssinia, setting a pattern for overseas deployment during the rest of Queen Victoria's reign[51] – 40,000 troops went to Egypt in 1882, 8,500 to the Sudan in 1885, and 9,000 to Burma between 1885 and 1887. This reformed and streamlined, multipurpose and amphibious Indian army soon became the model for a projected inter-colonial army, first mooted in 1867. Less than a decade after worried military men thought African troops might be required to suppress the rebellion in India, Indian regiments were being proposed as a new cheap fighting force for Africa.[52] For years the native regiments had been the Achilles heel of the Indian empire. Now pockets of loyalism that were to last through to 1947 emerged in the principal recruiting areas of the Indian army such as the Punjab. Waging war *for* the queen and later for the emperor, and by 1914–18 suffering great casualties in doing so, became the hallmark of Indian imperial patriotism, however much it was taken for granted by the British, who never allowed recruitment to extend beyond the home-lands of the 'martial' races, and who dismissed out of hand Indian enthusiasm for establishing their own volunteer forces.

Sannads

The queen's proclamation applied not only to British India, but to all the native or princely states as well. Numbering some 560 altogether, the princely states comprised just under 40 per cent of the Indian subcontinent, and around 20 per cent of its population.[53] There were so many, because they were mostly very small, concentrated in a strip that swept westwards from Bengal and Orissa (Odisha) through Bhopal and Gwalior, fanning north up into Rajputana and the northern and eastern parts of the Punjab, to Kashmir, and up against the frontier with

Afghanistan, and south-west into Gujarat. There were also many small independent states dotted about the Deccan plateau within the British presidency of Bombay. To the south lay the three largest princely states of all: Hyderabad, Mysore and Travancore. Victoria became queen of them all, assuming the paramount power that had previously been held by the King of Delhi. His crown and throne came to Windsor in the new year of 1861. They were not in good shape. Charles Wood told Prince Albert that the 'head-dress' could not really be called a crown; it was more of a skullcap. And the throne was in fact two 'old and worn' chairs, remarkable only because the king had used them.[54] As symbols of sovereignty the personal effects of Bahadur Shah II were not at all impressive. Fortunately, the words of the queen set out in the 1858 proclamation were, and had as much influence over the princely states as they did over British India. Letters of congratulation from several prominent Indian maharajas – Benares, Bikaner, Jind, Mysore, Nabha, Patiala and Udaipur – joined the many similar civilian addresses received by the queen upon the transfer of power in 1858. In Hyderabad, the nizam held a special durbar to mark the occasion.[55] Princely India was thus cemented into the fabric of British India, and so it remained for the next ninety years. The British Raj could not exist without the strategic security and revenue provided by the Indian states; the royal families of the princely states required the Raj to shore up dynastic rule. There was something for all in the queen's proclamation.

As far as the princely states of India were concerned, the key phrases of the proclamation were the queen's assertion that Britain had no desire to extend 'Our present territorial Possessions' and that the 'Rights, Dignity and Honour' of native princes would be respected 'as Our own'. No one needed to read too much between the lines to know that this meant an end to Dalhousie's doctrine of lapse, whereby Indian states without a legitimate direct family heir were annexed to Britain. It also implied acceptance of the right of adoption, that is to say, the succession passing to someone chosen specially for the role even if not related to the incumbent ruler. During the remainder of the queen's reign the promise of the proclamation to respect the integrity of these states was kept, more or less. Only one new territory was added to British India – Upper Burma in 1886 – and technically it was outside British Indian territory. Native rulers were replaced by temporary British administrations in a handful of cases: Karauli (1882), Rajpipla (1884–7), Cambay (1890–92) and Makrai (1890–93). Ruling dynasties were ousted and new chiefs chosen by the Government of India in several other instances: Tonk (1871), Suket (1878), Bharatpur (1900), Jhalawar (1896) and, most dramatically of all, following conspiracies against the British representatives, in Baroda (1875) and Manipur (1891).[56] These, however, were exceptions. Somehow, the queen's words worked wonders. As Lewin Bowring later put it, the minds of the Indian princes were 'tranquilised' by the proclamation.[57] Calmed, certainly, but were they sedated as well?

Queen Victoria's first crop of viceroys did not take the deference of the Indian princes for granted. Canning, Lord Elgin and Mayo all undertook extensive durbar tours in order to bind the princely states into union with the British. The long journeys in the saddle endured by both Canning and Elgin destroyed their health, whilst Mayo was assassinated as one of his expeditions neared it conclusion. Lord Lawrence travelled less and lived longer, but his durbars were by far the largest. It is tempting to see these durbar tours as early versions of the famous Delhi durbars of 1877, 1903 and 1911, when the Indian princes swore fealty in acts of collective submission to their British rulers who had superseded the Mughals. That would be misleading. These earlier durbars were more like diplomatic summits, in which the terms of Indian princely allegiance to the British Raj were negotiated and settled. As formal occasions, they were inevitably accompanied by ritual pomp and ceremony, but the business they transacted suggested that the viceroys of the 1860s, as they laid down the foundations of the new Raj, did not rely on the habits of deference and obeisance routinely attributed to eastern potentates. Canning set the tone early on. At the time of the transfer of power in 1858 he told Lord Stanley that 'ostentatious' ceremonies of homage to mark the occasion were inappropriate. Better that he set out to meet the native chiefs on their own territory. During his second durbar tour in 1860, Canning declared to Charles Wood that Indian princes did not need cajoling into showing 'loyalty and reverence for the Queen's name'.[58] Just over two years later, Canning's successor Elgin made the same point, albeit in a slightly different way. He told Charles Wood that:

> I know that it is customary with certain people whose opinions are entitled to respect to act on the assumption that all Orientals are children, amused and gratified by external trappings and ceremonies and titles, and ready to put up with the loss of real dignity and power if they are only permitted to enjoy the semblance of it.

On the contrary, Elgin argued, 'the Eastern imagination is singularly prone to invest outward things with a symbolic character, and that relations on points of form are valued by them because they are held necessarily to imply connections of substantial matters'.[59] In other words, subjection to the Raj involved both heart and head. The authority of the queen, articulated by the proclamation, underpinned the terms of the union between the native states and the Raj. The proclamation was a covenant between the queen and the princes, mediated by the viceroys.

Someone who understood these maxims well was Scotsman Charles Umpherston Aitchison, an Indian civil servant across whose desk most of the significant diplomatic dealings with the Indian princes passed. First as under-secretary from 1859 and then as secretary from 1868 he worked in the foreign department of the Government of India for almost twenty years (except for three years when he was posted to Lahore). Aitchison compiled what proved to be the definitive listing of all the treaties and agreements that bound the states of India, surrounding territories and dependencies in the Persian Gulf. What started life in 1862 as a snapshot of princely northern India became by the time of its fifth edition in 1929 a fourteen-volume guide to the architecture of British rule in India.[60] For his insights into the principles of Crown paramountcy after 1858 Aitchison is an invaluable guide, both as draughtsman and as commentator, yet rarely have historians consulted him.

Aitchison had little time for the argument that British authority over the princely states was derived from the power originally enjoyed by the

Mughals. Rather, he argued that de facto supremacy had been built up over many years, and was underwritten by successive treaties and charters. In this respect the importance of the queen's proclamation was that it promised to uphold all the original agreements made by the East India Company, and not to transgress any single treaty with a native state. Aitchison described a mutual relationship between the British government and the Indian states. The latter did not enjoy the principle of nationality, but they did have sovereignty. They could expect Britain not to advance its own interests at their expense, but equally they needed to show 'active co-operation' in furthering imperial interests. Their nationality was vested in the British government, with whom they had a unity of interest, which the queen personally expected them to fulfil.[61] In support of his argument, Aitchison turned to Henry Maine for confirmation of the type of sovereignty applicable to the princely states. Maine had argued in a series of minutes while legal member of the Viceroy's Council that the princely states enjoyed what he described as 'demi-sovereignty', similar to the situation that had prevailed in the eighteenth-century Prussian empire, or more recently in the Confederation of the Rhine, or German Bund. The Indian states were under the protection of the British sovereign in their internal affairs, but obliged to conform to external obligations laid down by the paramount power. Maine, who like Aitchison disregarded any precedents set by the Mughals, stated that this kind of 'demi-sovereignty' was in fact a standard model in modern international law. It was not so much a throwback to the era of Akbar as an eastern variation of the European state system recalibrated by the great powers after 1815. Aitchison's doctrine thus bore a striking resemblance to the late Prince Albert's vision of princely independence within an imperial framework. Aitchison later singled out Lord Lawrence for applying this modern version of the 'feudatory principle' during his term as viceroy, but its genesis can be found in the durbar tours of Canning a few years earlier.[62]

In the late autumn of 1859 Canning set out on a series of circuits of northern India. Taking an 18,000-strong retinue of Indian soldiers with him, he met face to face with the Indian princes in order to explain the transfer of power. Canning kept Queen Victoria in the picture throughout. Over the next fifteen months there were twenty-five durbars, starting with a meeting with the royal family of Awadh in Lucknow in October, and ending with the first Indian investiture of the Star of India at Allahabad in November 1861. All told, the ceremonies involved some 1,300 native chiefs. The durbars mixed private visits and public meetings, thereby avoiding any hierarchy, either of Europeans over Indians or amongst rival Indian chiefs. Charlotte Canning accompanied her husband, photographing and sketching as they travelled, and William Simpson, the famed artist of the Crimean war, went along too. Both sent back these durbar snaps to the queen, some of the first likenesses she had seen of princes in India.[63] Canning used these durbars to deliver individually tailored messages from the queen, telling of her gratitude for the loyal support of the chiefs, reiterating the pledges of the proclamation and summoning civic spirit. For example, at Lahore in February 1859, he told the Punjab chiefs that they were needed – not only to fight. The 'Government of the Queen also claims your service', Canning declared, in times of peace, and they should expect to be appointed as magistrates and revenue officials, not for their own private gain, but for the public good. At Lucknow in November 1859, he spoke to the Taluqdars of Awadh, 'in the name of the Queen your sovereign', saying that now that their estates had been restored, they might be improved. By May 1860, Canning felt able to report back to the queen of what he had found across northern India: 'a deeply founded disposition to loyalty in these Princes and Chiefs which needs only to be evoked by a steady, generous and considerate, but at the same time firm treatment, in order to become a main bulwark of Your Majesty's authority throughout India'.[64]

More than 150 *sannads* – treaty agreements – were issued following Canning's durbar tours of 1859–61, formalising the promises contained in the queen's proclamation, namely that native titles, properties and succession would henceforth be honoured by the Government of India. Virtually all of the *sannads* stated that Her Majesty was 'desirous that the governments of the several Princes of Chiefs of India who now govern their own territories should be perpetuated' and promising that on failure of natural heirs the British government would confirm the adoption of a successor 'in accordance with religion and race'.[65] The *sannads* re-established the Raj as an empire held together by treaty, only this time in the name of the Crown, not the East India Company.

Reforming princes now joined the Viceroy's Legislative Council, established by the Indian Councils Act of 1861. A consultative body, lacking the teeth of the Viceroy's Executive Council, the Legislative Council was nonetheless a sign of changing times. Starting with the appointment of Ishwari Prasad Narayan Singh, the Maharaja of Benares, at the beginning of 1862, seven maharajas joined the Legislative Council as 'non-official' members in the 1860s. Distinguished not only for their support during the rebellion of 1857–8, they were also princes whose territories were considered models of enlightened administration. Some, for example Metab Chand, the Maharaja of Burdwan (Bardhaman), and Ram Singh II, the Maharaja of Jaipur, had turned over their state revenues to famine relief. Yusef Ali Khan, the Nawab of Rampur, whom Canning met at Fatehgarh in November 1859, modernised banking in his state. Vijayarama Gajapati Raju III, the Maharaja of Vizianagaram, and the Maharaja of Benares were both patrons of education. Membership of the Legislative Council brought them regularly to Calcutta, creating the opportunity to forge new friendships, for example between the Maharajas of Jaipur and Vizianagaram.[66] These princes were conspicuous in their public displays of affection to the queen and loyalty to Britain. The Maharaja of Benares translated her Highland journals into Hindi, the Maharaja of Burdwan paid for a statue of the queen in Calcutta. From a land where drought killed millions, they sent their support for the parched people of England. The Maharaja of Benares funded a well in a Cotswold village in 1864, and in 1867 the Maharaja of Vizianagaram commissioned a drinking fountain in Hyde Park, London.[67] Perhaps they were only a decorative element to the viceroy's government – apart from the Maharaja of Vizianagaram, they rarely intervened in legislative council debates in the 1860s – but the queen welcomed 'the attempt to introduce a native element to the government'.[68]

One prince who was not sent a *sannad* nor invited onto the Viceroy's Council was the Maharaja of Mysore. Since 1831 the kingdom of Mysore had lain under the direct rule of the British. Krishnaraja

Wadiyar III was effectively a puppet king, subject to the watchful eye of the Commissioner Lieutenant-General, later Sir Mark Cubbon. There being no treaty to uphold, the threat of annexation in the event of a lapse of rule still hung over the Wadiyar dynasty.[69] The ageing Wadiyar saw the queen's proclamation of 1858 as his chance to resolve the situation. Celebrations in Mysore to mark the transfer of power were more effusive than those that took place in other courts. The maharaja wrote directly to the queen, expressing his gratitude for how his country had been restored to him when a child. Passing over the years of direct British control, he told the queen of how much he valued her respect for ancient rights, usages and customs, as well as for the freedom of religion, and for the promise of clemency: 'so merciful and humane an act could only emanate from the heart of a British Queen'. With Cubbon departed – the octogenarian Commissioner left Mysore in 1860, dying at Suez en route home – Wadiyar III also let it be known that he had no intention of letting the state lapse. He wanted to see his own monarchy fully restored, and he turned to the queen, or the 'Empress of Hindostan' as he called her, for assistance. Presents were sent – horses, cattle, jewellery – and later, come the first opportunity, the wedding of the Prince of Wales, followed by the birth of a grandson, Prince Albert Victor – more congratulatory addresses came from the Wadiyar to Windsor.[70] Canning and Wood quickly twigged what was going on, bemoaning the behaviour of 'these pensioner princes', but also aware that Queen Victoria and Prince Albert 'think that we have been very shabby indeed' towards the maharaja.[71] A *kharita* from the queen, acknowledging the presents, was delivered to Wadiyar. It only encouraged him more. Agents came to London to make his case. They appealed to the queen's proclamation of 1858 – 'a document worth more than the 70,000 British bayonets now in India' – and the liberal press of London chimed its approval.[72] For a couple of years the fate of Mysore hung in the balance, annexation always a possibility. Then in 1867 the Government of India decided to recognise the adopted heir to the throne. Wadiyar III would not be restored, but his grandson, Chamarajendra, born in 1863, would be groomed under British tutelage and become maharaja on turning eighteen. Moreover, he would be allowed to name his successor, so the Wadiyar dynasty effectively was reinstated in Mysore. Explaining the decision to the House of Commons, Stafford Northcote, the secretary of state for India, likened the new policy to 'the great Emperor Akbar and his successors availing themselves of Hindoo talent and assistance'. For Indian ears, Northcote gave the announcement a royal tweak: 'Her Majesty desires to maintain that family on the throne in the person of His Highness' adopted son.'[73] In fact, the queen made no pronouncements on Mysore, either privately or publicly, yet both the maharaja and the Government of India played her as a bargaining tool.

The Mysore case proved instructive. Other Indian princes were now encouraged to reach out to Queen Victoria and press their own claims, for example Tukoji Rao II, the Maharaja Holkar of Indore. Aggrieved over being forced to cede territory to the British after the rebellion of 1857–8, following a question mark over his loyalty, Holkar took on John Dickinson, veteran Indian lobbyist, to make representations on his behalf in London. Dickinson encouraged Holkar to ingratiate himself with the royal family in England, to make himself 'personally known to the Queen'. As he explained, 'if your Highness would show yourself in our imperial Court and take your place there as one of the first of the Indian princes, and the recognised head of the Maratha Power, you would gratify our royal family, and make valuable acquaintances among our aristocracy.'[74] Another example was the Nawab of Tonk, removed from his Rajputana state for allegedly ordering the murder of a political rival and his family. He too petitioned the queen directly, he too found an agent, a retired army officer, Iltudus Thomas Prichard, to make his case in London. There were plenty more where these wronged princes came from. In 1872, Frederick Chesson, long-time secretary to the 'Aborigines Protection Society', bundled together Tonk, the Nawab of Surat, the Ranis of Tanjore and others into a collective appeal for public attention, invoking the queen's proclamation.[75] It was an odd development, this alliance of radicals, legal guns-for-hire, ex-army officers and Indian royalty, seeking protection from the queen, but it speaks volumes about the momentum gathered by the 1858 proclamation within a few years of its pronouncement.

Lobbying also began to be carried out in person. In 1876 Sir Salar Jung, the wily prime minister of Hyderabad, came all the way to Windsor. Assured by his agent, the banker Thomas Palmer, that the 1858 proclamation meant that Hyderabad's debts to the East India Company might be renegotiated, Salar Jung sought out a private audience with Queen Victoria. Salar Jung's visit to Europe had several purposes, not least to seek finance for the railway being projected for the state. From the queen, however, he wanted restitution of the Berars, the lucrative cotton districts of the state that had been annexed to British India in 1853.[76] Lytton, the viceroy, had hoped to hold back Salar Jung at Calcutta. Salar Jung could not be restrained, however, despite suffering a fall in Paris. Wheelchair-bound, he met with the queen at the end of June 1876.[77] The encounter left both parties unsatisfied. It was reported to Queen Victoria that the Hyderabadi minister had not been allowed to discuss anything 'but the heat of the weather', and she wondered whether he might be offered another visit. This was ruled out. For good measure Lytton warned the queen that Salar Jung had brought with him enough cash and jewellery to bribe Parliament several times over. Her door remained open nonetheless. At the end of August she complained to Disraeli that it was 'unfortunate' that Salar Jung had not been permitted to state his own case, which every one of her subjects had the privilege of doing.[78]

The most controversial test of princely power in India in the first two decades of Crown rule came in Baroda, a princely state dispersed across several small tracts of territory to the north of Bombay presidency. Its ruler, the Gaekwar, Khanderao, was a moderniser and conspicuous supporter of the queen. In 1866 he funded a statue of her that was erected in Bombay. However, in 1870 he died suddenly and was succeeded by Malhar Rao, his less favoured brother. Soon the new Gaekwar and the British resident Colonel Robert Phayre were at loggerheads, the Gaekwar accused of corruption in his administration, to which he responded with charges of overzealous interference by Phayre. In 1874, as a sign of good intentions, the Gaekwar brought in Dadabhai Naoroji from Bombay as his dewan, and the Government of India, for its part, made plans to replace Phayre.[79] Then chaos ensued. An attempt was made to poison Phayre, and the Gaekwar was implicated in the plot. A commission of inquiry was appointed, its membership equally divided between three Europeans and three Indians (Jayajirao, the Maharaja of Gwalior, Ram Singh, the Maharaja of Jaipur, and Dinkar Rao, the former Dewan of Gwalior). Despite trial by media, in which the new Gaekwar was depicted as an uncivilised savage, the Indian commissioners concluded that his alleged role in the assassination attempt was unproven. Still, the viceroy was advised to remove the Gaekwar from power, on the grounds that he had not administered his state properly. It was a weak charge, a clumsy compromise, and the English press quickly pounced on the manoeuvre.[80]

A royal solution was found. Queen Victoria had been kept informed of the trial, and she knew there were misgivings amongst British officials over the extent of the Gaekwar's guilt. She expressed her concern over this first ever removal of an Indian prince under her rule, observing that the act should not happen without her public sanction. Whilst she could not be mentioned in the sentence passed on the Gaekwar, she requested that she be referred to in some other way, not least to register her gratitude to the three Indians on the commission.[81] So she was. Back in Calcutta, Charles Aitchison drew up a 'proclamation' announcing the removal of the Gaekwar, and introducing Queen Victoria as the peacemaker. Wanting to mark the services of the previous Gaekwar, the proclamation explained, the queen was re-establishing a native administration in Baroda, and in so doing was pleased to accede to the request of the previous Gaekwar's widow, Jamnabai, that she adopt a suitable person from the family line as the new ruler.[82] To help tidy up matters, Holkar of Indore's dewan, Madhava Rao, was sent to Baroda to assume ministerial duties there. Furthermore, the education of the adopted heir, Gopalrao, now renamed Sayajirao, was entrusted to an English tutor. Not one maharani, but two – the former Gaekwar's widow and the queen – were credited with mopping up the mess of their menfolk. The whole episode closed out with a visit from the Prince of Wales to Baroda at the end of 1875, diverted from Bombay by the Government of India, to give the new occupant of the throne the royal seal of approval. It was a telling moment; a precedent had been set. When Indian affairs became critical, the monarchy was mobilised into action.

With varying degrees of success, the native chiefs of India were thus drawn into the Raj of the queen after 1858. Through *sannads*, durbars and courtly diplomacy, the Government of India used the name and the authority of the queen to ease its passage through princely India. The queen was deployed as an instrument of colonial rule in a manner that was hardly appreciated or even known about back in Britain. Yet it was a policy that created its own dilemma. The more that royalty was dangled before the princes, the closer contact many of them desired with their queen. Whilst only a handful ever travelled to the English court, many others chanced their arm through agents, or through sending presents and memorials. Such traffic proved hard to control, but the Government of India did its best. In 1861, following the flurry of presents sent to the queen in the wake of the transfer of power from Company to Crown, an initial attempt was made to control gift diplomacy in particular, and direct contact with the queen more generally. Henceforth, presents and memorials had to be approved first by either the local government (the presidency and the provinces) or by the Government of India at Calcutta. Charles Wood drew up a template letter that might be sent to any Indian prince considering an unsolicited offering to the queen. Having sorted out the new order of the 'Star of India', Wood was now accomplished at such tasks, knowing his sovereign and her sensitivities all too well. 'Beautiful as are the gifts which your Highness has presented to the queen and interesting as they are in her eyes,' the pro-forma reply to princes stated, 'Her Majesty commands me to say that the most acceptable part of the offering is your Highness' very friendly letter.' He signed off with an intimate touch worthy of a manual on etiquette: 'Kind words from a distant friend are the most precious of all gifts.'[83]

But the gifts – and the words – continued to come. Exceptions to the new rules were easily found: a silver couch from Munger in Bihar, jewellery from the Maharaja of Patalia. So in 1867, it was ruled that all correspondence addressed to the queen must be transmitted via the Government of India. Still there was no ebbing of the flow. The following year, the viceroy, Lord Lawrence, complained that more needed to be done to prevent Indian princes and 'noblemen' using presents to the queen as the means of making a 'request for indulgence or favour'. Part of the problem was that the queen proved willing to accept such presents. 'It is a rather troublesome business altogether,' observed Northcote, the secretary of state for India, 'as there is no saying where this sort of thing is to stop.' The Government of India tried to stop direct contact from the queen's side. In 1873, as the Palace was deluged with memorials from India congratulating the Prince of Wales on his recovery from serious illness, the 1867 rules were reiterated, this time with the stipulation that the queen would reply to Indian addresses only on special occasions.[84] Five years later the screw tightened further, with a new protocol that the Government of India would use its discretion to decide which memorials would go to the queen, and whether a reply from the viceroy would suffice. In 1881 a further obstacle was introduced. All vernacular addresses must be accompanied by an English translation and be checked for legibility and spelling. Finally, in 1906, it was ruled that the Government of India would consider correspondence to be sent on to the king-emperor only in cases in which the Indian memorialist had already addressed the local government or the authorities in Calcutta.[85] In the half-century since the queen's proclamation the Government of India had been transformed from postman to the sovereign to censor of the royal mail.

For the princes, as for the people of India, there was real meaning to the transfer of government from the East India Company to the queen after 1858. Sovereignty had been an elusive element in Company rule. By the 1840s there was much confusion in Britain and India about the dual power of the Company and Crown within the territories under direct British administration, and diminishing clarity about the status of independent and ceded states. After the rebellion of 1857–8, Britain needed a quick fix in India to reassert control and to dismantle rival claims to power. Legitimacy was found in the shape of the queen, a distant monarch who symbolised clemency, justice and fairness. She was written into everything that the Government of India did after 1858; her name and status lay at the centre of the new architecture of imperial rule. Lest she appear only to be a symbol, or cypher, successive viceroys encouraged a style of governance in which the queen appeared to be present, as interested in the workings of the Indian empire as were her officials. The queen was a genie let out of the lamp, to magic away the terror and strife of the rebellion. As with all genies, it was hard to predict what her effect might be. The Government of India underestimated the influence that the queen's proclamation of 1858 would have over the political culture of the Raj, certainly in her lifetime. The queen's words, which the Government of India had itself done so much to publicise, were turned to over and again as the means not to resist British rule, but to make it more accountable. British officialdom underestimated something else too. No one anticipated that the queen would herself abide to the letter by the new powers of prerogative granted to her by the legislation of Lord Derby's government in 1858. She and Prince Albert plunged into Indian affairs with a passion that surprised and alarmed her political advisers. Queen Victoria took seriously her responsibility to fellow rulers in India, with whom she expected to be in direct communication, whatever conventions were invented to prevent that happening. She proved proprietorial over her formal powers of command, especially in the army, less so in the Indian Civil Service, an institution to which she never really warmed. For the next forty years the queen hardly ever missed an Indian despatch. The Raj radiated royal rule and she was its centre. She personified power in India much as the tsar did in imperial Russia, or the kaiser in Germany. She was an empress in practice as well as in name.

CHAPTER 6

QUEEN OF PUBLIC WORKS

'It is Our earnest Desire', declared the queen's proclamation of 1858, 'to stimulate the peaceful Industry of India' and 'to promote Works of Public Utility and Improvement'. Just as the transfer of power from Company to Crown signalled the advent of a new style of government in India under a just monarch, so too were expectations raised about the material progress of the Indian people under a beneficent queen. Enlightened rule would produce economic advancement, or, as the tireless colonial statistician Robert Montgomery Martin put it in 1862, capturing the heady optimism in London of the immediate aftermath of the proclamation, '[e]very year of tranquillity and good government in India . . . [gives] . . . scope to unfettered enterprise and capital'.[1] In the 1860s and 1870s, Queen Victoria came to symbolise British intervention in the Indian economy. She was seen as the agent of modernity as India's railway network expanded, its major waterways became canalised and its communications revolutionised by telegraph and by rapid steamship travel. She adorned the entrance to one of the country's first cotton mills in Nagpur – Jamsetji Tata's 'Empress Mills' – and she was written into the stonework of the new Gothic-style buildings of India's boom city of the period, Bombay.

Inevitably, by the time of her diamond jubilee almost forty years later, the state of the Indian economy under Crown rule gave little cause for self-congratulation. The resources of India had been exploited by the British much as they were previously in the days of the East India Company, only now on a grander scale. Government-backed investment in the railways drove Indian capital out of the country and into the London stock exchange. Native Indian industry was strangled at birth by the lack of protective tariffs. The oft-repeated promise that the financial burdens of India would never be visited on the English taxpayer left Indians paying for British 'foreign policy' in India (wars against Afghanistan (1878–80), Burma (1885–6) and other territories on the Indian frontier, the invasion of Abyssinia (1868) and the occupation of Egypt (1882)), as well as the costs of viceregal government in India itself. After 1858 there were new taxes imposed on the urban middling classes – principally the income and stamp taxes – and old taxes hiked up for the poor peasant cultivator – most onerously, the salt tax. Above all, British administration of the Indian economy proved helpless at best and directly culpable at worst during successive famines in the Punjab, in Bihar and Orissa, and Rajputana in the 1860s through to the central and southern Indian catastrophe of 1876–7 and on to the nationwide famine of 1897. Between them these famines resulted in around 15 million deaths. This British 'drain' on the Indian economy – of lives and incomes – became a standard weapon in the armoury of Indian nationalists from the 1880s onwards, and remains a compelling indictment of the policies of the Raj down to this day.[2]

Curiously, Queen Victoria escaped censure in this damning critique. She remained associated with all the trappings of 'civilisation' brought by the British to India after 1858, and none of the curses. Economic nationalists such as the Bombay Parsi, Dadabhai Naoroji, who coined the 'drain' theory and who was one of the first Indian MPs in the British Parliament, and Romesh Chandra Dutt, the Bengali civil servant, translator and historian, both excluded her from their catalogue of complaints. Likewise, one of the principal British opponents of the policies of the Raj, William Wedderburn MP, could write in 1897 of the 'skeleton at the jubilee feast' – juxtaposing famine and the royal celebrations – without even mentioning the queen.[3] How was this possible? This chapter opens by describing the ways in which Queen

Victoria became synonymous with the application of British and indigenous capital and enterprise to India after 1858, before turning to examine how her reputation for sympathy for the plight of the Indian people developed during the famines down to the end of her reign. Finally, the analysis turns to look at how the queen emerged as a symbol of paternalism amidst economic protest in India, a rhetoric driven not least by evangelical reformers and missionaries.

The Age of Improvement

God and the queen were essential elements in the British rhetoric of economic progress in India after 1858. The older providential language of military subjugation and religious conversion was recast as a new mission to modernise the country's infrastructure. Iron, steel and brick would go where the Bible could not and without recourse to the sword. Railways were rolled out – just under 5,000 miles of track by 1871 – and the great rivers of northern India adapted for transport and irrigation.[4] Viceroys enthused over the transformation. Looking out at the worshippers on the river Ganges at Haridwar in 1863, Lord Elgin (Viceroy of India, 1862–3) noted that it was 'curious to see the old Faith, washing itself in the sacred waters of the Ganges, and the new faith, symbolised in the magnificent works of the Ganges canal'. Seven years later, Lord Mayo (viceroy, 1869–72) described to the Rajputana chiefs assembled at Ajmer how:

> [h]ourly is this great empire brought nearer and nearer to the throne of our Queen. The steam-vessel and the railroad enable England, year by year, to enfold India in a closer embrace. But the coils she seeks to entwine around her are no iron fetters [for] [t]he days of conquest are past; the age of improvement has begun.[5]

Officials invoked Queen Victoria in this technological transformation of the Indian empire, especially in the expanding web of railways. From its commencement in the 1840s, railway development in India had been promoted as the arm of Christian evangelism, a 'true religion' combining the arts and sciences, with improved locomotion the key to spreading the 'truth of God's word'. The official opening of the first major line between Burdwan (Bardhaman) and Calcutta in 1855 was preceded by a long religious service conducted by the Bishop of Calcutta, with illustrative readings taken from the Old Testament and blessings offered to the East India Company and to the governor-general.[6] After 1858, this same Anglican ceremony recurred as more lines were unveiled, only this time with the queen rather than the Company being blessed. At Lahore in 1858, before a gathering of 200 Punjabi chiefs at the opening of the Punjab railway, the Government of India held a Christian service to mark the event, where the queen was toasted as the 'Empress of Hindustan'.[7] During the years of rebellion and its aftermath, the railways were turned over to military require-ments and later in the 1870s and 1880s to famine-relief projects. Only later in the century did they become predominantly passenger rail-ways.[8] But, whatever their purpose, the opening of each new line and junction was the occasion for either or both church and monarch to grace the proceedings, albeit in name only, and give it their seal of approval. Elgin held a durbar for local maharajahs, alluding to the queen, at the commencement of the Benares–Jabalpur line in February 1863. Sir John Lawrence (viceroy 1864–9) organised a similar gath-ering as the Calcutta line connected to Lahore via Amritsar in October 1864. He also sent on photographs of the new railway station at Lahore to the queen as well.[9] As late as 1878, when the novelty of the railways had begun to wear off, the same sacred service with the same invoca-tions of the queen was performed by the Bishop of Lahore at the opening of the 'Empress Bridge' across the Sutlej at Bahawalpur.[10]

Railways were not the only new technology associated with the queen's name. For a time during the 1840s and 1850s rivers and canals vied with the railway as the best choice for India's economic future. Projects such as the Ganges canal, opened at Roorkee in 1854, received the same Anglican baptism as their railway counterparts. As the canal was extended in the later 1850s and 1860s, its new features received the royal appellation: the 'Queen's channel' at the Solani aqueduct, the structure guarded by four stone lions, and the 'Victoria feeder', a channel cut to link the Ganges canal to the Yamuna river at Allahabad.[11] Similarly, the queen was an unwitting champion of advances in steamship links to the west and east of the Indian subcontinent. The East India Company had been reluctant to develop steamship navigation. So promoters and commercial companies looked instead to the monarch for endorsement, as they pursued lucrative mail contracts and passenger lines. A royal charter was given to the Peninsular and Oriental Company in 1840 and to the India and Australian Mail Steam Packet Company in 1847.[12] The greatest fillip of all was given to steamship connections between Britain and India when the Suez Canal opened in 1869, and it too came with royal approval. The Prince and Princess of Wales visited the completed project in March 1870, shortly after it was officially inaugurated, opening the sluices of one of the feeder canals.[13] The first steamship India-bound to use the new route followed in 1872. Once Benjamin Disraeli had flamboyantly bought the Egyptian Khedive's shares in the canal in the queen's name in 1875, the canal was incorporated into the imperial Indian mindscape. Queen Victoria was delighted: it 'gives us complete security for India', she confided to her journal.[14] Steamship business to and from India – passengers, mail, troops and goods – multiplied, and the shipping companies branded their vessels accordingly. The P&O, for example, launched the *Kaisar-i-Hind* in 1878, and the *Victoria* in 1887, both Bombay-bound through the Suez Canal on their maiden voyages.[15] Although she never travelled so far east, the queen was there in spirit in the passage to India.

New technologies also brought Queen Victoria's own words closer to her Indian dominion. The expansion of the telegraph system within India was initially slow, confined as it was to the main railway routes. But as the means of instant communication across seas and land between Calcutta or Simla (increasingly, from the 1860s, the summer retreat for the viceroy and his government) and London, it was irreplaceable.[16] The first formal address made by the queen to the people of India via telegram followed the recovery of the Prince of Wales from illness in January 1872, and it was followed almost immediately by another address lamenting the assassination of Lord Mayo. Further telegraphic messages from the queen to the viceroy were promptly published in the newspapers during the second Afghan war.[17] Whilst the telegram format did not allow much to be said, it did mean it could be said quickly. During the queen's jubilees of 1887 and 1897, as hundreds of loyal telegrams came in from India, the Palace responded speedily with almost instant messages of gratitude sent back telegraphically by way of the viceroy.

Railways, steamships, the telegraph and above all the Suez Canal shifted the axis of British India from east to west, from Calcutta to Bombay. Bombay grew exponentially after 1850, perhaps the first example of an 'Asian tiger' metropolis, the largest city of Britain's overseas territories.[18] Bombay's commercial development coincided with the transfer of power from Company to Crown. The city famously became the site for an ambitious rebuilding of its civic centre in Victorian Gothic style, then in vogue back in Britain, especially in church design. No other city in India proved such an attractive playground for English architects and civil engineers of the Gothic revival. The story of the distinctive architecture of nineteenth-century Bombay is well documented, especially from the British side: the *dirigisme* of Henry Bartle Frere, the governor, the elastic budgeting of Arthur Crawford, the municipal commissioner, and the pattern books of English designers such as Henry Conybeare and George Gilbert Scott.[19] Invariably, however, accounts of Bombay's Victorian Gothic leave out the eponymous queen. Closer inspection reveals how Queen Victoria herself shaped from afar the style that bore her name.

The physical redevelopment of Bombay owed much to the loyalty to the British Crown of the predominantly Parsi, Jewish and Brahmin mercantile community of the city. They owned or bought up land in Colaba, in Back Bay and around the old harbour and fort and donated it to the city for public purposes. Two generations of the Parsi merchant house of the Jejeebhoys – Jamsetjee (1783–1859) and Cursetjee (1811–77) – along with other Parsi businessmen such as the Framji Cowasji (1761–1851), Cowasji Jehangir Readymoney (1812–78) and Dinshaw Petit (1823–1901), poured money into the city. They funded schools, hospitals, housing for the poor, drinking fountains, waterworks, veterinary care and the new University of Bombay.[20] This was classic philanthropy, turning private gain into public virtue, opium into opulence. It was also conspicuous patriotism. Jamsetjee Jejeebhoy was an attentive admirer of the British royal family. With the Brahmin magnate, Jaganath Shunkerseth, he put up the capital for the Victoria Museum and Gardens, which opened in 1862, a monument to the new Crown government. One of the museum's supporters was Bhau Daji Lad, a local doctor and educationist, who stated that there was 'no fitter monument, no better *nuzzar*' than the museum; it was a 'permanent monument of the devotion of the people' to the queen. Jejeebhoy's patriotism was rewarded. He was made a baronet a year before he died, having been the first Indian to be knighted in 1841.[21] His son, Cursetjee, along with Shunkerseth, led the city's celebrations of the transfer of power in 1858.[22] Framji Cowasji's loyalty was more entrepreneurial. A keen horticulturist, in 1838 he sent the first mangoes to Britain via steamship, as a gift to the queen.[23] In Bombay, Cowasji Jehangir Readymoney, living up to his name, invested in the Back Bay reclamation, Elphinstone College and the Crawford Market, whilst back in Britain he funded a drinking fountain in Regent's Park and contributed to the 'Albert Orphan Asylum' in Bagshot, near Windsor.[24] And Dinshaw Petit endowed the Victoria Jubilee Technical Institute in 1887.[25]

Another loyal Victorian and Bombay philanthropist was David Sassoon, a Jewish merchant from Baghdad, who came to Bombay in the early 1830s, fleeing persecution. Like his Parsi neighbours he gave over land to the city's development, especially around the docks that to this day bear his name. He also founded various institutions, most notably the Mechanics Institute and the Industrial and Reformatory Institution. He paid for the clock tower in the Victoria Gardens. When Prince Albert died, and the new museum became the Victoria and Albert Museum, it was David Sassoon who in 1864 dedicated the pedestal for a statue of the Prince Consort in the museum. His son Albert Sassoon then commissioned the full statue of Prince Albert for the Museum (unveiled in 1869) and gave two further lump sums to the Reformatory Institution. One donation commemorated the visit by the Duke of Edinburgh to the city; the other marked the recovery of the Prince of Wales from illness. Albert Sassoon also commissioned an equestrian statue of the Prince of Wales, after his visit to the city, eventually erected in 1879.[26]

With the statue of Queen Victoria (unveiled in 1872) at one end of the Esplanade Road and the Prince of Wales at the other, the royal family framed the new city centre. Perhaps this imperial loyalty of the Parsis and Jews of Bombay was *sui generis*. It might be wrong to extrapolate from it a more widespread enthusiasm for the British monarchy. As religious minorities and ethnic outsiders under the nominal protection of the Crown, families like the Jejeebhoys and Sassoons had more reason than most to be faithful. At the same time, there were plenty of other philanthropists in Bombay, such as the Brahmins Shunkherseth and Bhau Daji Lad, whose patriotism was just as enthusiastic. However their allegiance is interpreted, the magnitude of their gratitude in the built environment of Bombay is striking, and was made known to the queen, not least through a volume presented to her in 1886.[27]

Gothic may not have looked very modern, but it was emphatically monarchical. In an age of industry and republican democracy the Gothic style was a romantic return to the late middle ages when kings and clerics ran the show. For the first industrial city of the empire, Gothic was an entirely appropriate form for Bombay. Ornate steeples and *campanili* softened the effect of factory chimneys, churchlike public buildings imposed solemnity on municipal gatherings. So, once the loyal businessmen of Bombay had sown the seeds for the redevelopment of the city, incurring risk where other capitalists were reluctant to go, the government took over. Steered by Bartle Frere and benefiting from one of the largest public share issues ever known outside Britain, the rest of the new city centre took shape in the 1860s and 1870s. The old ramparts around the Fort were cleared and, in the space created across from the Esplanade, a series of government buildings went up: the High Court, the Mint, the Secretariat, the Telegraph Office and the University. The Port Trust took over further reclamation schemes, and new docks were added in the 1870s and 1880s: the 'Prince's Dock' and 'Victoria Dock'. The queen featured prominently in the new buildings. The letters 'V. R.' were inlaid in the entrance to the High Court and the University's clock tower chimed out 'God save the Queen' on weekdays.[28] Then in 1878 work began on perhaps the most grandiose building to be named after Queen Victoria during her lifetime – the Victoria Central Terminus, the new home of the Great Indian Peninsular Railway. Designed by Frederick William Stevens and opened ten years later, the 'VCT' symbolised both the predominance of Bombay as a railway hub and the modernity of the monarch. With its stained glass, glazed tiles, multiple spires, arched window openings and doorways, and central dome, the 'VCT' might have been mistaken for an overgrown basilica. Yet it was state of the art in its own way. The vaulted dome was a marvel of modern engineering, the train platforms and sheds amongst the longest in the world at that time. Electric light ran throughout the building. There was a restaurant too, although the owner stuck to his temperance principles for the first two years of business. The 'VCT' was, according to the newspapers, one of the 'best modern buildings in India'. The queen was there too. The dome was topped with a female colossus symbolising 'progress'. Beneath the dome was a smaller statue of the queen.[29] Starting with the tour of Prince Albert Victor in 1889 and through until the opening of the Gateway to India in 1924, the 'VCT' now became the ceremonial starting point for all royal and viceregal arrivals. Thus, Bombay modern, in its late nineteenth-century version, 'belonged unmistakeably to Queen Victoria's world', as Asa Briggs observed in his classic *Victorian Cities*.[30] Likewise Queen Victoria belonged to Bombay, not simply as a required feature of the city's colonial iconography, but as a celebration of its social and economic progress.

Except that she had a rival: her own son. To boast of its rapid success and transformation, the city Corporation planned a major international exhibition for 1885. Jules Joubert, a French Australian who had masterminded the Calcutta Exhibition of 1883, offered to manage the spectacle, and the governor of Bombay, Sir James Fergusson, gave his approval. Then fate, or rather, the Prince of Wales, stepped in, announcing his own plans to emulate his father and act as patron of an 'Imperial and Colonial Exhibition' to be held in London in 1886. Bombay might seek to trump Calcutta, but there was no way the city could rival a royal project in London, especially when it was rumoured that the prince was 'put out' by the prospect of a similar event in

Bombay. Plans for the city's own extravaganza were shelved, and many of the exhibits intended for showcasing Bombay in India were appropriated instead for an English audience at home.[31] It was a snub, and a right royal one too.

Famine Queen

Poverty sat alongside 'progress'. The first two decades of the queen's direct rule saw some of the worst recorded outbreaks ever of famine in India. In the 1860s there were three major famines: in the Doab region of the Punjab, spilling over into Awadh and Rajputana in 1860, in Orissa and Bihar in 1865–6, and in the Rajputana states in 1868–70. Drought and crop failure were compounded by British refusal to interfere in the market, allowing exports out of the affected areas to continue, and providing little in the way of relief until it was too late. Despite the recent 'great famine' in Ireland and, moreover, the Irish experience of some Indian administrators, lessons had not been learned.[32] For some Indian experts, this hands-off policy amounted to a missed opportunity to effect some good for the people of India. There were precedents, after all. Responding to the Orissa famine, retired Madras army colonel George Thomas Haly noted how the Mughal government had dealt with such catastrophes in its day by improving systems of irrigation and communication to head off further calamity. Arthur Cotton, champion of the canalisation of India, told the Social Science Congress meeting in Manchester that the Orissa famine was the moment for a 'wise, sympathising, capable Government' to show itself to the Indian people: 'If, when this harvest failed, Her Majesty had issued a proclamation, assuring the people that the Government were caring for them . . . it would never have been forgotten.'[33] The queen had been deployed on famine duty before. The Whig government of the late 1840s had sent her to Ireland to smooth over the discontent rife there following the famine. When famine conditions temporarily hit Lancashire in the early 1860s, Queen Victoria made a very public contribution of £2,000 as Duchess of Lancaster to the relief fund set up in London to ameliorate the condition of the cotton-factory workers.[34] Might the same gestures work for India? The Raja of Travancore had reached into his own pocket to support the starving in Lancashire in 1863.[35] A reciprocal act was overdue. In March 1868, at her private secretary's suggestion, Queen Victoria asked Stafford Northcote, the secretary of state for India, whether it might be made known to 'these poor People, how her heart bleeds for them, & how deeply she sympathises with them under such unparalleled sufferings'. Northcote welcomed the idea, but considered it too late in the day, some two years after the famine had hit.[36] However, when famine conditions returned six years later, this time in Bengal, the queen's intervention was better timed.

In 1874 the second major famine within a decade to strike Bihar, in the north-western corner of Bengal, was dealt with very differently from almost all of the other famines in British India in this period. When the first reports of crop failure were circulated, pre-emptive plans were made by Lord Northbrook, the viceroy, and Sir Richard Temple, lieutenant-governor of Bengal, both to buy in sufficient grain from Burma and also to employ thousands of relief workers to help with distribution.[37] Back in Britain, Disraeli, the new prime minister, singled out in the queen's speech on the opening of Parliament dealing with the Indian famine as a priority of his government. A relief fund was launched by the Lord Mayor of London, with the queen as patron, around the same time as one was organised in Calcutta. It was to this latter fund that the queen contributed 10,000 rupees (around £1,000) in January 1874, a donation that was publicised in the newspapers the following month. In all the relief subscriptions totalled £131,000 in India, and £146,000 in London, with the Government of India matching the combined sum. They were applauded as model schemes of intervention in food crises. The combination of foresight, extraordinary expenditure and voluntary aid from near and far helped to avert a second Bengal disaster in 1874. Later in the year, as the British Parliament was prorogued, Lord George Hamilton, the under-secretary of state for India, lauded the work of Northbrook and Temple, who had defied 'Political Economy' and saved 'Her Majesty's subjects' from death by starvation.[38]

Small though it was, the queen's donation to the Calcutta relief fund at the beginning of 1874 enhanced her reputation for generosity, amongst Bengalis in particular. Later in the year a deputation from the British India Association of Calcutta – the principal lobby for the presidency's landowners – thanked Northbrook and Temple for their actions: 'the first time in the history of British rule in the East that the State recognised its duty to maintain its suffering subjects at a time of general scarcity' they declared, going on to say that it is 'observable that this policy of Your Excellency's Government has been in conformity not only with Indian notions of a Sovereign's duty to his subjects, transmitted from historic times both Hindu and Mahomedan, but with the highest teaching of modern political economy'. The largest landowner of all in the state, Metab Chand, the Maharaja of Burdwan, turned his appreciation into raising funds for a statue of the queen, the first in Bengal, eventually unveiled in Calcutta in 1878. And, from Mithila in the north of Bihar, Northbrook sent on a translation of a song for the 'Great Queen of London', praising her resolution that 'no ryot should be allowed to die for want of grain'.[39] The actual amount of royal support mattered less than the spirit in which it was given.

Catastrophic hunger and death returned to India within a few years, and this time in the fuller glare of the European media. The famine of 1876–8 began on the Deccan plateau of south-central India and spread to most of the south of the subcontinent, with outbreaks in pockets of the north as well. Disraeli's government again promised to do all in its power to help, pledging in the queen's speech that 'every resource will be employed not merely in arrest of this present famine, but in obtaining fresh experience for the prevention or mitigation of such visitations for the future'. Not quite every resource. In the new year of 1877, Lord Lytton, presiding over the Imperial Assemblage at Delhi, held an emergency council that decided to send Sir Richard Temple south to Madras to oversee the relief operation. On this occasion Temple's watchword was parsimony. Rigorous tests were brought in to determine and limit who was to be given relief, daily supplements were reduced from previous levels, and there were no attempts to bring in emergency supplies of grain. Strikes amongst relief workers ensued in Bombay and Temple's own colleagues protested against the severity of the measures being taken.[40] From London Queen Victoria watched on, no longer simply reliant on despatches from India for news of conditions there. This latest famine was better covered in the press than any previous. Temple's critics disseminated their dissent in lectures, pamphlets and magazines. Florence Nightingale joined the fray. The illustrated *Graphic* newspaper, which specialised in realist depiction of poverty in Britain, now found a subject of equal challenge in India. The *Pall Mall Gazette*, a pioneer of investigative journalism, despatched Henry Hyndman to cover the crisis. For Hyndman the famine brought into sharp focus the flurry of new British interest in India brought on by the Bengal famine, the tour of the Prince of Wales and the imperial title taken by Queen Victoria.[41] *Punch* made the same point, albeit more dramatically, in a cartoon titled 'Disputed empire!', which depicted the queen seated on her throne, wearing her imperial crown with her mace in one hand, trying to ward off the grim reaper (also crowned) with her free hand.[42] Noticeably different, too, was the queen's own interest in this new famine, which she described as 'fearful', 'terrible', 'frightful' and 'distressing', as she became more aware of its spread and scale across the year. Although she expressed confidence in Temple's handling of the crisis, she urged Lytton to travel south to take over personally the management of the famine in the summer of 1877, and welcomed the slight change of policy that the viceroy's appearance brought about. Lytton tried to work some royal balm into the misery, using the occasion of the queen's birthday to issue a special 'famine' *Gazette*, listing honours for those involved in the famine operations.[43]

The next instance of widespread famine came in 1896, lasting through to the summer of 1897, the year of the queen's diamond jubilee. It commenced in Bundelkhand, and spread eastwards to Bengal and south to Madras and Bombay, combining in Bombay with an outbreak of bubonic plague. Relief measures followed the guidelines laid down in the new famine code of 1880, but no one bothered with the cautionary advice on charitable aid. The globe shrank in response to the crisis. Volunteers went out from Britain to assist in the relief operations, and contributions came in from Canada and Australia.[44] Over £500,000 was raised in Britain by the Lord Mayor's 'Mansion House Fund', and just under £1 million given in India. The royal family chipped in. The queen led off the donations from the court with £500 and the Duke of Connaught spoke at the launch of the Lord Mayor's fund.[45] In India, the queen was once again directly associated with the charitable efforts under way. This was partly a case of the government taking advantage of the queen's good reputation. In the North-West Provinces, for example, in June 1897, almost a million people on relief work were given three days' wages in advance of the diamond jubilee holiday to honour 'the great Maharani under whose gracious auspices the abundant relief and charity of the preceding months had been dispensed to them'. Elsewhere, villagers spoke of the protective instincts of the queen: 'the talk around the humble firesides and in the homes of the people is that it is the Great Queen who could have so successfully dealt with such a vast and unbounded calamity' reported a famine official from Bengal. Another official in Bombay reported that the 'motto' of the relief workers was 'the kind and humane message of the Mother Queen Empress to do everything possible and spend anything to save every life of her subjects from starvation'.[46]

Never mind that British famine policy in India remained committed to non-interference in the market, and became increasingly bureaucratised. Famine recurred once more during Queen Victoria's reign, in 1899–1900, affecting many of the regions hit hardest three years earlier, especially in Bombay, but there was no change in the government's parsimonious response. Never mind, as some noted, that once in India charitable aid was quickly diverted into public works rather than food distribution. Then as now the act of giving was more significant than the fact of receiving. One thing remained constant across the famine years in India, however: in the midst of suffering and death, Queen Victoria was believed to be on the side of paternalism and state intervention, for saving lives, not simply alleviating misery.

Immoral Economies

Queen of charity, queen of industry – but there was one Victorian value with which Queen Victoria was seldom associated in India after 1858: free trade. Liberalisation of the economy was the leitmotif of the new regime. Retrenchment in public expenditure, commercialisation of the rural economy and the abolition of taxes on trade and consumption were all principles that had been fought for and won in Britain in the 1840s and 1850s. Now they might be exported to India. The appointment of James Wilson, the proprietor and editor of the London *Economist*, to the finance portfolio in Charles Canning's first viceregal council heralded the change. *The Economist* had led the charge towards free trade in Britain from its first issue in 1843.[47] Wilson brought with him to Calcutta two policies close to his heart: the income tax and, as we have seen in the last chapter, a paper currency, adorned with the image of the queen and intended to modernise and monetise Indian commerce. Liberals liked the income tax, if only as a necessary evil. Direct taxation did its work of raising revenue with more reliability and less opposition than taxes on consumer products such as food and tobacco. Moreover, liberals thought India was lightly taxed, even arguing that the Indian middle class was not paying its way.[48] Wilson's *Economist* made a slightly different case. India's tax base was too narrow. It was dependent on land revenues collected by tax-farming *zamindars*, on behalf of the government. A shift to taxing personal property and income was required. Those who benefited from British rule in India would in future make a direct contribution to the costs of government. So Wilson unleashed his income tax on India in February 1860.[49]

India, however, was not Britain. The new income tax was widely denounced. From Madras it was condemned as a 'direct contravention' of the 1858 proclamation, and it was confidently predicted that the queen would use her power to veto the measure.[50] Opposition was not confined to better-off Indians now within reach of the tax-gatherer. Wilson's senior colleagues were appalled as well, their tongues loosened by his premature death in August 1860. Men who had preached free trade at home sang from a different hymn sheet in India. London recalled Charles Trevelyan, the governor of Madras, only fourteen months into his post because of his outspoken criticism of the new income tax. The viceroy was even rumoured to be opposed, preferring, it was later claimed, 'to govern India with a European army of 40,000 men without the income tax than with 80,000 men with it'.[51] Critics deemed the income tax unsuitable for India. Witnesses giving evidence to Parliament a decade later, including Trevelyan, were agreed. Its harsh methods were seized on by journalists as evidence of the shameful officialdom carried out on behalf of 'England, ruled over by a Queen whose name in India is held in reverence almost as that of the deity'.[52] Lord Northbrook abandoned the policy in 1873. It returned, barely disguised as a 'licence tax', in 1878, sparking riots in Surat, before becoming an income tax once again in 1886, confined to non-agricultural incomes.

Without an effective income tax, the land continued to bear the brunt of revenue collection after 1858. Not that its yield increased very much. In India as in Ireland, British free trade maxims struggled to break through. Whether collected by the middleman (the *zamindar*), or directly from the peasant cultivator (the *ryot*), rents were fixed, discouraging agricultural improvement. The 1858 proclamation, mused one Bengali reformer, might have been the moment for a proper land settlement in Bengal, emancipating the *ryots* from the servitude imposed by *zamindars*, ensuring that the queen reigned 'in their hearts forever'.[53] As India entered more and more into the global economy after 1860, the familiar signs of a lopsided cash-crop sector alongside subsistence communities began to appear, encouraged by a new planter class. Cotton production and its ancillaries, such as indigo, brought a greater commercialisation to some parts of the economy. Squeezed out by planters and moneylenders, Indian peasants turned to protest in two widely publicised instances: in the indigo plantations of Bengal and in the cotton fields of the Deccan in 1875. In both cases Queen Victoria was seen as standing on the side of the *ryot*. In Dhaka, Dinabandhu Mitra published a play, *Nil darpan*, to draw attention to the condition of the indigo cultivators, having witnessed their plight in his travels as a postmaster. In the preface to the play, Mitra signalled the new paternalism of the queen: 'most kind-hearted Queen Victoria, the mother of the people, thinking it unadvisable to suckle her children through maid-servants, has now taken them on her lap to nourish them'.[54] The play was widely circulated, not least because of its translation by the missionary James Long. Long was prosecuted for libel by the Government of India, and used his trial to raise awareness of the plight of the indigo workers, desiring only, he claimed, to avoid another mutiny.[55]

Similarly, in the Deccan riots, the protests were triggered by a story that the queen 'had sent out orders that the Marwaris [the moneylenders] were to give up their bonds', so freeing the peasant farmers from their debts.[56] Popular protest thrives on whispers and rumour, on the appeal to a higher moral authority. After 1858 Queen Victoria's omnipotence, rightly or wrongly, was thought to extend into the heart of rural India.

Missionaries, evangelicals and disgruntled Indian officials all encouraged the fiction that the queen could dispense economic justice. They did so by homing in on the tax burden borne by ordinary Indians. For, unable to rein in expenditure, reluctant to impose a comprehensive income tax, and facing falling revenues from the land, the Government of India resorted to tried and tested means of rescuing the finances: taxes on consumption. By the early 1870s, liberals such as Charles Trevelyan and Henry Fawcett were complaining that the Indian government had abandoned treating revenue as fixed, and gone over to a new economy of 'annual borrowing'. Each projected deficit was made good by increasing indirect taxes.[57] By 1880 the three principal forms of customs revenue – duties on salt, opium and alcohol – accounted for almost as much revenue as the land. In particular, the yield from salt duties soared, increasing fourfold between 1860 and 1890.[58] India had lurched from low taxation to high. Free trade, which for Victorians meant the removal of duties, was in retreat in India. Critics blamed the Government of India, as it controlled the manufacture and sale of these commodities. One woman was credited with having the power to do something about it: Queen Victoria.

Of all the Indian revenues, the duty on salt was the most elastic. Like the Mughals and the East India Company before them, the Government of India managed all salt manufacture in the territories under its direct control. Salt of the earth, lake, sea and mountains was produced under the watchful eye of officials, who collected the tax at the point of production, leaving tradesmen and sellers to pass on the additional cost to the consumer. Elaborate measures were taken to prevent the illegal private manufacture of salt (especially from coastal waters), and to restrict smuggling across the borders from the princely states into British India, the most ingenious of all being the 'great hedge' customs line separating

Bengal and Rajputana. The salt duty was effectively a poll tax, salt being the one commodity that everyone needed and everyone consumed.[59] Unseen and uncontested, the salt duty was the first tax to be raised in times of budget deficit. Yet the salt tax made liberals uneasy. One governor, Vere Hobart in Madras (1872–5), protested forcibly when the viceroy, Lord Northbrook, adjusted it upwards. Allusions to the unpopularity of the *gabelle* on the eve of the French revolution were common.[60] In the House of Commons, George Balfour, former colleague of Charles Canning when viceroy, led a campaign for its abolition. In 1875 he came up with a simple solution: the queen should break with Asiatic tradition and use the occasion of the Prince of Wales's visit to India to issue a proclamation doing away with the salt duty. In such a manner, 'Asiatics' would come to believe that 'by eating this free salt they really owed fidelity to the Empress of India'.[61] Another liberal, another admirer of the queen as benevolent despot. India did strange things to British sensibilities.

Opium was also a state monopoly in India. By the 1870s, the opium trade was not just confined to export from India to China, but increasingly it was supplying Indian users as well. Queen Victoria knew all about Indian opium. Back in 1851 at the Great Exhibition she had listened and watched with interest as Dr Royle opened up a poppy to explain the structure of the plant and to show how its seeds were extracted.[62] Anti-opium campaigners knew about Queen Victoria too. From the mid-1870s they used her name and authority to criticise the 'poppy plague'. As its name suggested, the Anglo-Oriental Society for the Suppression of the Opium Trade, formed by Quakers in 1874, primarily targeted the Chinese end of operations. Still, it held Queen Victoria responsible. Now that she was empress, argued the Society's magazine, the *Friend of China*, in April 1876, 'it is a strictly logical, though not a very pleasant deduction, that the queen is made responsible for the growth, manufacture and sale of a destructive poison'.[63] Practically, as the magazine admitted, it was the Government of India and Parliament who were culpable. Queen Victoria, however, was too good a moral exemplar to miss. Why could she not intervene 'to remove . . . the dark stain from the lustre of her glittering crown' asked a delegate to the Shanghai Missionary conference in 1877. Why had the occasion of the new title of empress not been used to do away with a policy inherited from the East India Company, demanded the industrialist and philanthropist Samuel Mander in the same year.[64] In the early 1890s, the anti-opium campaign stepped up a gear, and was instrumental in pressurising William Gladstone's government into setting up a Royal Commission to investigate the traffic in India, China and Burma too. The Society intensified its propaganda, claiming that in the name of the queen-empress, the Government of India was now extracting opium revenue from Burma, 'the subjects of the Queen-Empress' in India suffered from the same 'havoc which they wrought with a light heart among the Chinese'.[65] Additional pressure came from India. Invoking the motto of the royal order of the 'Star of India' – 'heaven's light our guide' – Sunderbai Powar, who ran a zenana mission school in Poona, publicised the anti-opium speaking tour she had made in northern India during 1891–2.[66] Ultimately, the Royal Commission of 1894–5 settled very little, and it was not until the early twentieth century that public pressure and market forces combined to end the trade. Some of the evidence presented to the Commission did however suggest that Queen Victoria was invested with special powers over the opium trade, if only she would use them. One user in Ajmer allegedly told a missionary that she wanted the queen to send out a medicine to cure her addiction. Another witness told of rumours in Bombay that the queen planned to close down all the opium dens of the city.[67] The name of the queen was as powerful as the drug itself.

The drink trade in India also came under the evangelical spotlight. The sale of alcohol was controlled by the Government of India, which extracted a tax – *abkari*[68] – from all liquor stores. Whereas alcohol consumption in the British army in India was tightly regulated, the state monopoly on drink was left alone in the interest of maximising revenue. The tide of temperance reform ebbed and flowed after 1858. Driving drink out of the queen's army remained a pressing concern. Some wanted total abstinence, others temperance (drinking in moderation), whilst some simply settled for pale ale, a low-alcohol brew especially developed for soldiers in India.[69] Hindu reformers also made the liquor traffic an issue. One of the leaders of the Brahmo Sumaj movement, Keshub Chandra Sen, came to Britain in 1870 and spoke at a meeting of the principal domestic temperance organisation, the UK Alliance. As 'one of the most loyal subjects of Her Majesty Queen Victoria', it grieved him to witness the state-owned drink trade, one of the 'blots on the administration of India'.[70] In the 1880s, the anti-alcohol lobby in India grew in strength. The Salvation Army arrived in India in 1882, upsetting many with its militant methods, including its campaign for abstinence from intoxicants. In 1888, William Caine, the president of the British Temperance League, visited India, attended the meeting of the Indian National Congress at Allahabad, and two years later helped found the Anglo-Indian Temperance Association. Within a few years this was a nationwide movement, largely run by Indians, topped up by itinerant lecturers from Britain.[71]

One of these was Thomas Evans, who made a habit of bringing the queen into the battle against the bottle. He argued that the legalised sale of liquor broke with the 'solemn promises' of the queen's proclamation of 1858, which had pledged not to interfere with Indian religion, abstinence from alcohol being the norm for both Hindus and Muslims.[72] Evans's naming and shaming of the queen had little impact, however. Despite the touchstone status of the 1858 proclamation there is no evidence that Indian temperance reformers took up this kind of argument, either in the lectures and meetings of the Anglo-Indian Temperance Association or in the influential Kayastha temperance movement run by Brahmins in Gwalior. The queen remained off-limits in the rhetoric of the temperance movement in India. Off-message as well. Whilst she supported the campaign to drive drunkenness out of the Indian army,[73] she was no fan of the opposition to the drink trade, finding temperance reformers an overzealous lot. To one of them – Basil Wilberforce, grandson of William, and rector of St Mary's in Southampton – she took particular objection. Wilberforce visited India in 1890, partly for his health and partly to persuade more Indians to take the pledge and give up alcohol.[74] The queen had no desire to lead a moral majority either in India or at home.

Despite the best efforts of evangelicals and other opponents of the burgeoning Indian fiscal state, Queen Victoria eluded criticism. Royal handouts during the famine years were magnified by her officials into momentous acts of grace. If anything, by focusing so centrally on the queen, the clamour over salt, opium and *abkari* enlarged her omnipotence. She personified paternalism, not the coercion of the market, a moral force that lingered on, later reworked by Gandhi and his followers during the 1920s and 1930s, as they mobilised against the Raj and its control over the basic commodities of life such as salt. In 1880 a Bengali lament referred to Queen Victoria as *dina janani* (the 'mother of the poor').[75] Even from a distance the woes of her Indian people were believed to be close to her heart. So, when her sons and heirs began to travel to India, it was hoped they came as messengers.

CHAPTER 7

ROYAL TOURISTS

In the summer of 1861 it was prophesied in the Punjab that a king would 'come from west to east' and 'rule the Country without dipping the end of his little finger in blood'. Missionaries worked this up as a sign that Christianity was nigh. Charles Canning, the viceroy, remarked tartly that 'if the Emperor of Russia or Louis Napoleon would drop down in India they would find they were not unexpected'. The rumour focused on the deposed Sikh dynasty and the hope that Duleep Singh might return, but Sir Charles Wood mentioned it to Prince Albert as a pretext for sending out to India the Prince of Wales.[1] Albert died, the project was shelved, and, when a prince did finally come, he came from the east, not the west. The arrival from Australia via Singapore and Penang of Prince Alfred (the Duke of Edinburgh), Victoria's second son, at Calcutta on 22 December 1869 marked the first occasion when British royalty alighted on Indian soil. His visit was followed by the tours in 1875–6 of his elder brother, Albert Edward the Prince of Wales, and by the Prince of Wales's eldest son, Prince Albert Victor, the Duke of Clarence, in 1889. Additionally, Arthur, the Duke of Connaught (Victoria's third son), served in India for six years during the 1880s. Queen Victoria never visited India. The furthest east she journeyed was Tuscany. So these visits by her sons were important. The tours made the British monarchy visible across most of the Indian subcontinent, bridging the divide between the virtual sovereignty of the queen and the proxy powers of the viceroy. Royal visits made real the extent and purpose of the British Empire in India, emphasising its military might and geographical girth, its durability in the shape of two generations of heirs to the throne, and its modernity, as the itineraries featured ceremonial openings of new railway lines, docks and other public works. Whilst historians have noted the impact these visits had as media events back in Britain, less has been made of the way they reshaped the meaning of monarchy in the Raj.[2]

For the tours were the first major test of Indian attitudes towards British rule since the transfer of power in 1858. The times were not propitious. Prince Alfred's visit came amidst widespread famine and popular resentment over the austerity measures the Government of India had taken to deal with dearth in Orissa in 1866. In 1872, the viceroy, Lord Mayo, was assassinated and fears abounded of Wahabi conspiracy. In these circumstances, unsure as to how royalty might be received in India, the Government of India did its best to manage the tours, leaving as little as possible to chance. Much remained outside their control: not least the royal tourists themselves.

'A walking proclamation': Prince Alfred in India, 1869–70

Prince Alfred spent four months crisscrossing India.[3] He was a reluctant tourist, wanting his mother to cut him some slack and shorten the length of his naval commission.[4] There were good reasons for his lack of enthusiasm. By the time he reached India, Alfred had been on a sea voyage around the world for more than two and a half years. In Sydney there had been an attempt on his life and in New Zealand he had been plunged into the lingering embers of the Maori wars.[5] His global tour interrupted by the unsuccessful assassin in Australia, Alfred's original Indian schedule had to be postponed, and when he did arrive the Calcutta police were told that a suspected Fenian sympathiser, embedded in a circus troupe, had followed his ship, the *Galatea*, from Melbourne.[6]

For the choreography of Prince Alfred's visit to India, there were no real precedents for the government to follow. Previous calls on the colonies by the British royals had been to dependencies without viceroys, that is to say, parts of the British Empire which were not under direct rule: settlement colonies with their own assemblies and a governor-general as the representative of the Crown. The Viceroy of India, in contrast, was invested with the full powers of the monarch. This immediately raised the question of whether a royal prince outranked the holder of the viceregal office. It was decided that he did not, and so Alfred was the viceroy's guest for the parts of the tour when Lord Mayo was present, otherwise he took precedence as the queen's representative. Other matters of protocol were more intractable. One was the issue of scale. Great durbars were envisaged at first, then the tour was cut back in size, owing to the scarcity produced by extensive famines in Rajputana and in the Punjab. Mayo proposed one durbar only, at Agra, but eventually cancelled this too, and instead summoned the Indian chiefs to Calcutta.[7]

Nonetheless, a royal visit was unprecedented. There were expectations of largesse on both sides. Alfred himself told Lord Mayo that he had anticipated 'oriental magnificence', whilst the Benares Gazette predicted that the prince's 'circle of wealth will come'. The prices of glass and lights rocketed in Calcutta and Bombay, as the Anglo-Indian communities of both cities prepared illuminations of public buildings, with gossipy talk in Calcutta that poor homes were also required to be lit up for the occasion. The military manoeuvres underpinning Alfred's tour were substantial. For example, for his visit to Agra, nineteen cavalry and infantry regiments were transferred just from Bengal alone. Partly for love of sports, partly for the sake of tradition, British officials decided that hunting should form an integral part of the princely tour, only made possible by extensive preparations of kraals and access roads occupying several months beforehand, undertaken by thousands of labourers.[8]

Scarcity was not the only factor in the Government of India bearing down on the costs of the trip. Since the transfer of power from Company to Crown in 1858, Indian officials had shown increasing concern at the volume of gifts passing directly from native chiefs to Queen Victoria, and anticipated the prince's tour being used by Indian maharajas to offer presents with the expectation of receiving the same in return. The India Office in London sanctioned £10,000 to cover the costs of a full-scale durbar, including exchange of gifts, at Agra, only for Mayo to cancel the durbar. Hoping to avoid criticism, the viceroy's officials suggested setting aside £8,000 of this sum to cover the gifts to be given by Prince Alfred on tour with the proviso that he would not keep any; everything would be passed on to the *toshakhana* (the government treasury) and sold off. Sensing this would cause offence, the Duke of Argyll, secretary of state for India, overruled Mayo, stipulating that Prince Alfred could give and receive gifts, but the gifts from native chiefs required approval and should be modest: 'curiosities, ancient arms, or specimens of local manufacture, and gifts of such like nature, which would in fact be more objects of interest than value'.[9] In fact, this protocol proved an open invitation to the Indian chiefs to line up not simply souvenirs, but the most ornamental weaponry, carpets and precious stones that could be found in their home states.

For the first and only time before the onset of air travel, Calcutta was the start of a royal visit to India. The *Galatea* sailed all the way up the River Hoogly to Fort William, and a line of people two and a half miles long thronged the Maidan as the royal party landed and made its way to Government House. On horseback heading the greeting party for the prince were the viceroy, the governors of Bombay and Madras and the Maharajas of Gwalior, Jaipur, Rewa, Bharatpur, Alwar, Dholpur and Kapurthala, with the Begum of Bhopal (and her daughter) following behind in a carriage. The two weeks spent by the prince in Calcutta were, as befitted the historic capital of British India, as Anglo-Indian as they could be. There were fireworks and illuminations, which took over most of the city, a grand levée, Hebrew prayers, a visit to the Mahomedan Literary Society, a Hindu reception at the Seven Tanks Hall, including Vedic blessings given by professors from the Sanskrit College and nautch dancing, addresses from the University and from the Chamber of Commerce, sports and Sikh games, a fancy dress ball and a visit to the opera (Donizetti's *Lucrezia Borgia*). Good use was made of the *Galatea*, as the individual visits of the native chiefs took place there, and on the eve of the prince's departure a ball was held on board. The welcoming procession and the fireworks generated the largest audiences and the most conspicuous displays of loyalty: the letters of 'God Save the Queen' lit up in gas along the East Esplanade of the Maidan, together with a revolving portrait of the queen, and huge transparencies hanging over the main buildings, including the motto, 'God bless the Empress of Hindostan'.[10]

At most of the formal occasions during the prince's time in Calcutta, Europeans outnumbered Indians: for example, by about eight to one at the Government House levée on the second day of the visit. However, the centrepiece of the Calcutta programme was the chapter meeting of the Star of India. Then the Indian presence dwarfed the British: seven maharajas to one prince. Suggested by Queen Victoria as a substitute for the cancelled durbar, Mayo encountered a problem straight away. Unlike his elder brother, the Prince of Wales, Prince Alfred was not a member of the order. So the principal object of the meeting was his own investiture, to be overseen by the most senior members of the order, the Knight Grand Commanders, who on this occasion were drawn from the Punjabi and Rajputana maharajas. Mayo's officials struggled to work out the correct protocol. Charles Girdlestone looked to the example of the Prince of Wales's installation as a Knight of the Order of St Patrick the previous year in Dublin, but found it inconsistent. He turned for advice to a colleague in the Bengal Civil Service, 'whose tastes and reading have lain towards heraldry and medieval ceremonies'. From this discussion came a plan to hold the investiture in the Throne Room and Marble Hall of Government House, with the viceroy in the throne as the Grand Master of the Order and the rest of the members of the order seated before him as an audience in rows. The royal warrant approving the chapter would be read in English and Hindustani with the queen's title referred to 'Empress of Hindustan'.[11] However, once it became obvious that Government House would not be able to accommodate all those called to Calcutta, then the venue moved to the viceroy's durbar tent in the grounds, specially constructed for the occasion.

What followed was a piece of impromptu theatre in which the Indian princes took the lead. The throne remained, but the chairs

seating the princes and other members of the order fanned out in an arc
from the other side of the throne. The prince was brought into the tent
by the British officials, followed by the Begum of Bhopal and Lady
Mayo, and then a procession of 'banners, esquires and pages'. As the
prince knelt before the grand master, the Maharaja of Gwalior formally
invested him, and the Maharaja of Jaipur pinned the Star onto his robe.
Outside the tent sixty-five elephants, several with canopied howdahs,
awaited the prince's inspection, including his own on which had been
placed Dalhousie's silver howdah.[12] This extemporised ceremonial
contained very little that could be considered as a display of deference
by the Indian princes. They met with Prince Alfred as senior members
of the Order into which they admitted him. The act of an Indian maharaja pinning the Star of India onto an English prince is a significant
reversal of the usual colonial roles. Only the silver howdah denoted how
the British were first amongst equals; only the seating plans in the nave
indicated an order of hierarchy – and it was one amongst the Indian
princes and not one that separated Indians and Europeans.

As Prince Alfred left Calcutta, other parts of the Government of
India's protocol slipped away. The ban on extravagant presents was
circumvented. The pundits at the Seven Tanks had given a silver hookah
and a gold attar server. The Maharaja of Rewa had topped that with a
diamond valued at £2,500 (hardly the 'very small offering' Mayo
described to Argyll).[13] The prince now headed off to hunt on the estates
of the Maharaja of Benares, with a visit to the holy city of Benares to
follow – to give him, as Mayo told the queen, a better idea of a 'native
city' than anywhere else in India. Accolades started to flow. Passing
through Burdwan en route to camp at Murshidabad, he was guest at a
breakfast provided by the local maharaja, a visit which was later celebrated in a Sanskrit address provided by the Bengali poet Taranatha
Tarkavcaspati. Then, in Benares, the poet Bharatendu Harischandra
tried to present an offering of flowers to the prince. Prevented by
William Muir, the lieutenant-governor of the North-West Provinces
from doing so in person, Harischandra invited fellow poets to his house
and he read to them a biography of the prince. This gathering then
published verses 'expressing their heartfelt joy on the advent of the

Royal Prince to this city'.[14] The prince did not notice this 'native' welcome. He was similarly unimpressed by the Ganges at work, where an eclipse of the moon led 50,000 pilgrims to flock into the water, confiding to his mother that he did not know how many drowned, but suggested that those who did 'will be consoled by going to heaven quicker than their neighbours'.[15] Travel was not broadening his mind.

Mutiny memories then hoved into view, as the prince moved towards Delhi. At Agra there was a gun salute as the prince entered the town and the Taj Mahal was turned over for a fete attended by the Nawab of Rampur, his family and almost fifty local chiefs. A visit to the Church Missionary Society orphanage at Sikandra, where a choir sang the national anthem in Hindustani, was followed by a viewing of Akbar's tomb. Alfred also attended a ball given by the local regiment and another by Lady Muir, the lieutenant-governor's wife.[16] Four days were spent in Delhi, encamped in the grounds of Ludlow Castle. Loyal addresses presented to the prince alluded to a complete break with the Mughal past. They spoke of 'living among the monuments of a mighty empire passed away'. Then the prince rode the Delhi ridge along the route taken by the mutinous regiments in 1857, looking back to the conquered city.[17]

From Delhi Prince Alfred travelled into the Punjab. The chiefs turned out en masse at Lahore, a reminder of the loyalty that had helped save the Raj in 1857–8. The most powerful of them (Kashmir, Patiala, Bahawalpur, Jind, Nabha, Kapurthala and Malerkotla) greeted the prince on his arrival, and a fuller contingent awaited him in an elephant procession through the Akbari gate of the walled city the following day. A state banquet and a ball in the recently opened Palladian-style Montgomery Hall were laid on, as was a visit to the city museum and its exhibits of antiquities, guided by its curator Baden Henry Baden-Powell.[18] Time was set aside for an exchange of presents with chiefs, and here the rules on gifts were stretched to the limit. The Maharaja of Kashmir came with two shawls worth £1,250, which had taken three years and over 300 men to weave and decorate. In public the prince was told he could not accept these, although he might present them instead as a gift to the queen. The northern portion of his tour drawing to a close, Alfred retraced his steps back to Amritsar, viewed the temple and tank, and then made the long journey to Awadh, glimpsing the Himalayas on the way. At Lucknow and Kanpur he paid respects at the memorials from 1857–8, sending his mother flowers picked from the Residency at Lucknow, and from the infamous well at Kanpur. He also met up in the Kaiserbagh Palace in Lucknow with those Taluqdars of Awadh who had remained loyal in 1857–8. Addressing him as the son of 'our Mighty Sovereign and Empress', they presented Alfred with an ornamental sword and shield. Another interlude of hunting, this time in the Terai, offered two weeks of respite before the prince proceeded south.[19]

As they bade farewell to Prince Alfred at Jabalpur, where he attended the ceremony marking the completion of the junction linking the northern and western parts of the Great Indian Peninsula Railway, Mayo and his colleagues reckoned the trip had been a success.[20] By arrangement the prince had made no speeches, except at Lucknow and Jabalpur, and he had disappointed some commentators by dressing plainly and seldom appearing in uniform. He had, however, obediently made his way through the different versions of India that the government had put on display. The legacy of the Indian revolt was everywhere. Then, having spent two and half months in the northern half of India, the prince sped through the rest of his tour in four weeks. Visits to Bombay and Madras were not planned when the trip was first plotted in 1868. Bombay was added as the prince approached the Indian subcontinent towards the end of 1869, hard to avoid once it was clear that the railway connections would be completed. It then made sense to include Madras as well, as the *Galatea* could sail south from Calcutta and collect its captain. There were even plans, which did not come to fruition, to take the prince overland to Madras via Hyderabad, but, not for the first time, the nizam's kingdom eluded British ceremonial.[21]

Bombay welcomed Alfred off the train with a deputation comprising the governor, William Vesey-FitzGerald, and Indian princes drawn from the length and breadth of the presidency: notably, the Gaekwar of Baroda, the Raja of Kolhapur, the Rao of Cutch and the Nawab of Junagarh. Costs began to spiral out of control. The municipal illuminations budget was overspent, the presents exchanged between the prince and the Indian chiefs quickly 'ran up the score' and the Gaekwar had to be persuaded to limit his extravagance to funding a new sailors' home. The prince met with the influential Parsi community and received an address in Pahlavi (ancient Persian) from its priests. The highlight, as such, of the six-day stay in the city was a banquet given to the prince in the Elephanta caves, then a dilapidated remnant of the ancient site of Hindu worship. Journalists from Calcutta sniped at the insensitivity of a military band playing for the guests a rendition of the 'The Roast Beef of Old England'.[22] On reaching Madras, the tour became even more crass. The prince arrived by train and joined a formal procession from the railway station to Government House. Passing by the crowds and through the triumphal arches the pecking order of the carriages revealed that Indian princes were deemed less important in this part of the country. The first four vehicles were occupied solely by the governor and his official colleagues, with the first native chief, the Raja of Travancore, one of Victoria's most assiduous admirers, to be found only in the fifth carriage. In the days that followed there were the usual formalities including a banquet and municipal address to the prince, and also an address from native Protestant Christians, the only such memorial of a royal visit otherwise low on missionary gestures.[23] Having completed his obligations in Madras, the prince rejoined his ship, bound for more hunting in Ceylon.

Most of Prince Alfred's visit to India had gone to plan. Indian princes in the north had been gratified, and civic vanity in Bombay and Madras had been satisfied. The rules on gifts had not really worked. Mayo's secretary, Owen Tudor Burne, was able to tot up the account so that presents in did not completely overwhelm presents out, but only by excluding from his calculations the Rewa diamonds and the Kashmiri shawls. The diamonds went into the *toshakhana*, and the prince took everything else home with him, putting some of the hoard on public display two years later. The prince's gifts to the Indian princes – British-made watches, swords with a personalised inscription, stereoscopes and guns – were described by vernacular papers as mundane in comparison to the finery given to the prince. Also noted was the absence of any philanthropic gestures, with amends only being made as the prince left, by way of a donation sent for local schools in Bombay. There had been no budget for the trip, but whatever expenditure had been estimated was undoubtedly exceeded. Mayo contributed heavily from his own pocket towards the costs.[24] The press had not been encouraged to attend. Mayo had invited along William Howard Russell, by then a veteran of reporting the Crimean war, the suppression of the Indian rebellion and the American Civil War, but he made his excuses. Outside of the main cities the prince's route had been hard to follow, with the newspapers reliant on officials in the royal party for details of his whereabouts. Publicity stills were produced – 4,000 photos of Prince Alfred, but only as mementoes on his departure.[25] However, Prince Alfred had made his mark and, more importantly, that of the queen. The *Madras Times* called him a 'walking proclamation'. There were calls in India and in England for Alfred to be made viceroy.[26] He was just happy to finally reach home. Four years later he married into the Russian imperial family. Less arduous, perhaps, than a trek around India, but equally effective as an act of royal diplomacy.

Shahzardah: The Prince of Wales in India, 1875–6

The visit of Albert Edward, Prince of Wales, to India five years after his younger brother was a different kind of royal tour of India, in scale and in purpose.[27] The Prince of Wales travelled for longer and went further. The tour lasted five months (eight including the voyages out and back), and took the heir to the throne – or Shahzardah as he became known – on a traverse of the Indian subcontinent. Placating the princes of northern India took less priority, and the western and the southern states and cities received equal treatment. It was a marathon and also a spectacle. Parliament provided £60,000 (around £2 million at today's prices) to cover the prince's expenses outside India, including the fitting out of his ship, the *Serapis*, and for presents for the native princes. The Government of India contributed another £30,000, much of it earmarked for the special train carriages commissioned for the journeys and the costs of security. In all the major towns visited by the prince, subscriptions averaging between £40,000 and £60,000 were raised to pay for civic entertainments, and vast amounts were also spent on the whitewashing of public buildings, and on improvements to princely palaces, temples and mosques. Together with the sumptuous hospitality and bejewelled court retinues of the Indian princes and chiefs, such an outlay made the prince's India tour one of the most extravagant royal occasions of the Victorian era. As several historians have shown, it was certainly one of the best publicised.[28] Facilitated by the spreading Indian railway network and the subterranean telegraph (which had reached India in 1869), the prince's tour was extensively reported back in Britain and beyond. Veteran special correspondents William Howard Russell of *The Times* (*The Times* spent £10,000 alone on the trip) and William Simpson of the *Illustrated London News*, as well as up-and-coming newsmen such as G. A. Henty of the *Standard*, ensured almost daily coverage back home of the ceremonies, military display and sport.[29] Russell's reports were syndicated to the *Chicago Daily Tribune*, Henty's to the *New York Times*. Curious and well-heeled types joined the tour at various points, and some who just missed it, for example Julia Stone, wife of the US Consul, wrote it up in apparently authentic travelogues as though they had been there.[30] In India, the Prince of Wales was both hunter and hunted.

This level of media interest in the tour is unsurprising. The Prince of Wales was far more of a news story than his brother. The waywardness of his youth behind him, he was the centrepiece of London's *beau monde*, and, during the queen's long mourning, he had become the familiar face of the royal family, opening new buildings, supporting charities and travelling overseas through North America and the eastern Mediterranean. Moreover, since his marriage in 1863, the Prince of Wales had become a focus of attention in India. Flouting official restrictions, Indian rulers had sent gifts at the time of his wedding to Princess Alexandra of Denmark. Then, when the prince recovered from serious illness in 1872, the wave of thanksgiving services in India generated so many addresses from Indian states and municipalities that Queen Victoria was obliged to telegraph her gratitude.[31] So from the moment information about the prince's trip to India emerged in March 1875, editors, journalists and enterprising publishers fed anticipation of the event. The press was brought into the planning of the tour at an early stage, with *The Times* and the *Illustrated London News* given official accreditation, and Russell of *The Times* appointed as the prince's 'honorary private secretary'. The principal London newspapers and Reuters' news agency vied for berths on the *Serapis* and inveigled their way into the hunting parties that were being organised for the prince.[32] Ousted from the official tour, the *Graphic* published a special advanced issue about the Indian visit, just days after the prince had left London, describing sights and destinations that the prince was likely to see. Similarly, before he arrived in India, maps plotting the prince's route were published in London – not always with complete accuracy.[33] In India too, the tour drew attention soon after it was first announced. A Tamil biography of the prince was published in Madras. A new illustrated journal devoted to the trip – the *Royal Tourist* – was projected in Calcutta. From across India entries were sent into a princely poetry competition run from London by William Sparks Thomson, proprietor of the Crown Perfumery Company.[34] Once started the frenzy did not stop. The entre-preneurial Calcutta Anglophile, Sourindro Mohan Tagore, prepared poetry and song, and portraits of the royal couple were circulated in Calcutta.[35] All this before the prince had barely arrived.

The tour was much more than a media show, as compelling as that aspect of it may seem to the modern eye. In the first place, it was the prince's show. Neither Disraeli nor Lord Northbrook, the viceroy, came up with the idea of a second princely voyage to India so soon after the first. Queen Victoria took a lot of persuading. An aspiring prince regent, Albert Edward had been champing at the bit for some time, wanting a larger share of the family business. The India branch attracted him. He shared his wish with Disraeli to go to India, and somehow *The Times* leaked the story of the planned visit in its 20 March edition.[36] The queen was indignant that she had not been consulted. Faced with a fait accompli, she gave her 'very unwilling consent' to the trip, and over the next few months the Prince of Wales's people talked with her people about arrangements.[37] The queen had several objections. Firstly, she feared for the health of the prince, still delicate after his recovery from typhoid fever a few years earlier. Exposure to epidemic illness en route and in India, together with the hot climate even in the cool season, as well as the sheer intensity of the proposed itinerary, worried her. Dr Joseph Fayrer, formerly resident surgeon at Lucknow and Lord Mayo's doctor, who had accompanied Prince Alfred on his tour, was selected as the Prince of Wales's medical adviser, his first duty being to prepare a memorandum on the risks attached to the voyage out, around and into India.[38] Secondly, the queen feared for the prince's morals, not so much because of where he was headed, but because of whom he intended to take with him. The prince enjoyed louche company, and wanted some of the most louche to accompany him to India. The queen singled out three of his party as especially risqué: the Duke of Sutherland ('devoid of all idea of etiquette'), Lord Carrington ('his character is not respectable') and Lord Charles Beresford. But she deferred to Disraeli and all three were allowed to go. They were counter-balanced by the Bible and the sword. Robinson Duckworth went as chaplain (Queen Victoria thought him unnecessary as 'there will be chaplains everywhere'), and General Dighton Probyn, veteran of the war of 1857–8, went too ('distinguished & safe'). Fortunately, the queen did approve of the chief co-ordinator of the whole operation, Sir Henry Bartle Frere, the former governor of Bombay.[39]

Then the queen had one further concern, overriding all others. People in India might think that the Prince of Wales was the monarch and not she. She refused to sanction any situation where the prince might take precedence over the viceroy, her representative in India. The prince was to travel not as her proxy, but as the 'first subject of the realm' and as the guest of the viceroy.[40] This meant no durbars, nor any distribution of royal honours by or to the prince. She even refused to countenance the prince conveying a message from her to the people of India during his visit, and she did not like the idea of a commemorative medal being struck to mark the occasion.[41] The prince was irritated by his mother's interference, resenting the 'sort of guardianship' being assumed over him. The trip was his idea, and at the age of thirty-three he knew what he was doing, having consulted experts such as Fayrer and Frere.[42] Nonetheless, although giving way on some of the detail – a silver medal, not a gold one, was issued – the queen held steadfast to her prerogative. The two durbars originally scheduled for Agra and

Lucknow were cancelled. Careful arrangements were put in place to ensure that, at the Star of India investiture being organised for the Calcutta portion of the prince's trip, he would be afforded only a secondary role. Most significantly of all, the viceroy had to tear up his own itinerary and start again. Lord Northbrook had planned to meet the prince at Calcutta, two months into the trip, and travel with him on the north-western section of the tour, before returning him to Bombay for his departure. This would have meant the prince arriving initially at Bombay and going straight into formal ceremonial visits with the Indian rulers, effectively as the queen's representative. Instead, Lord Northbrook altered his diary, travelled to Bombay ahead of the prince's landing there and spent an exhausting week making durbar with the Indian chiefs.[43] In this way, the queen retained her top billing, and the Prince of Wales was kept in his place.[44] Except that he was going to be in India, and the queen was not. Here lay another reason why the prince's visit was such a watershed in the history of the Raj. He was a monarch in the making, the first heir to the throne to visit India, the 'future Emperor', and he had to be seen to be believed.[45]

The prince's tour was masterminded by Frere, whose modernising instincts had already made a huge difference to the city of Bombay. Now he looked backwards to find the future. Frere subscribed to the conventional Victorian stereotype of the Orient as feudal, somewhere where power was expressed through rituals of homage and deference. 'Royalty should be seen in the flesh by the People of India', his biographer explained. 'The Eastern mind . . . seeks for a visible chief to bestow its allegiance, and cannot rest on the idea of power latent in a code or constitution.'[46] Never mind that Bartle Frere's Britain lacked a code let alone a written constitution, or that by 1875 many educated Indians were word-perfect in their knowledge of the queen's 1858 proclamation, Frere stuck to his script and designed a tour programme that would reveal the body of the monarch-to-be across the length and breadth of India. He was not expected to say very much: he was advised that, unless he was fond of languages, there was no need to learn any Hindustani.[47] But he could expect a packed engagement calendar. As news of the trip broke in India, invitations from the princely states began to flood in. In the larger towns and cities en route, Frere looked for opportunities for the prince to be associated with the burgeoning infrastructure of the Raj: opening docks and railways. The Government of India ordered a special railway saloon carriage to take the prince onwards from Calcutta, a vehicle notable for its extended balconies at each end, on which the prince could be seen as he steamed into and out of the stations. Making the prince so visible did carry the risk of leaving him an easy target. Frere ensured that his security was as detailed as possible, for example guards lined the whole route from Delhi to Lahore at regular intervals.[48] Careful choreography was crucial to the trip's success. Frere wanted as many people as possible to see the prince, and in as modern an environment as India could provide.

By the time he left Britain for the voyage east, the Prince of Wales was carrying many expectations alongside his large entourage. What had started out as a 'lark' – the prince and his pals enjoying some hunting in between social calls on Indian maharajas – had assumed by the late summer the character of a 'royal progress', according to Disraeli. The queen remained sceptical to the last. She imagined scenarios in which the prince would have to abandon his tour: war with Russia, war with Prussia, even war with Burma. She expected the costs of the trip to sink the project once Parliament scrutinised the bill.[49] In fact, the House of Commons, in a rare moment of generosity towards India, insisted that the Indian taxpayer be spared from paying all the prince's expenses. Queen and Parliament assuaged, the final stages of preparations for the prince's embarkation in October were made. The personnel of his tour party now ran in to double figures. An Indian troop ship, the *Serapis*, was requisitioned and fitted out for the journey, its crew numbering 499. Fifteen other vessels (including state barges and a state galley ship) travelled with the *Serapis*, thousands of visitors viewing the flotilla before it set sail.[50] The prince was seen off by Lord Salisbury and with the blessing of the Dean of Westminster. Still no formal approval came from the queen. Her parting shot criticised the prince for not only leaving the Princess of Wales behind, alone, but also for not insisting that the princess come and live with the queen at Windsor during her husband's absence. Last-minute arrangements were made for regular telegraphic communication between the royal couple – the princess was permitted to send fifty words per week – and on parting Edward gave Alexandra a gift of a carriage and four small ponies, possibly to hasten her escape if she was held captive by the queen.[51] Alexandra went with him as far as Calais. Finally, at the end of September the prince set sail for the Mediterranean, calling in at Athens, Cairo and Aden, before crossing the Indian Ocean to Bombay.

The self-styled second city of the Empire mounted an extravagant reception to welcome the prince on his arrival on 8 November. He certainly had a captive audience. The viceroy (Lord Northbrook), the governor of Bombay (Sir Philip Wodehouse) and the maharajas of Kolhapur, Udaipur and Cutch had been waiting the best part of two weeks. So too had two of the boy princes, the Maharaja of Mysore and the Gaekwar of Baroda, travelling outside their states for the first time.[52] Northbrook had failed to coax another boy-prince, the Nizam of Hyderabad, out of his palace to come to Bombay, and caused offence when he sought medical proof that he was unfit to travel. Salar Jung, the prime minister, keen for a one-to-one with the Prince of Wales, came instead, probably what the Hyderabad court wanted all along.[53] As for the Indian princes who did attend, strict instructions were laid down regarding the gifts they might bring and the number of armed retainers that could accompany them. They had been required to send on photographic portraits, and details of their family lineage and histories of their territories had been compiled for the purposes of the prince's visit. Municipal bodies and civic associations in Bombay were warned that the prince should not be asked for subscriptions to any cause, nor petitioned about any matter. Street decorations for the welcome reception were provided by local prisoners.[54] Despite all the protocol, the landing of the ship and procession brought out the crowds, one reporter estimating that there were over 200,000 people present. As the boat docked, the Indian princes gathered on the gangway. The prince alighted in military uniform, wearing a pith helmet. Transparencies lined his route into town, screaming Bombay's recent progress, although it was another banner that caught the reporters' eyes: a 'Tell Mama we're happy' slogan draped over houses and shops in a Muslim neighbourhood of the city.[55]

The Prince of Wales spent two weeks in Bombay. On his birthday –
9 November – he hosted a reception for the Indian princes at
Government House, and on the following day he attended a levée at
the governor of Bombay's residence. Gifts were exchanged. A tea service
from Baroda stole the show, although the Maharaja of Kolhapur's presentation of a Maratha ceremonial sword from the seventeenth century
was perhaps more symbolic.[56] Significantly, however, all this took place
with the viceroy of India at the prince's side. The exchanges that really
mattered had taken place when the viceroy met with the Indian rulers
in the days before the Prince of Wales arrived. The queen's supremacy
remained unaffected. His work done, the viceroy headed back north.
The only event that the Prince of Wales presided over in an individual
capacity was the laying of a foundation stone for the docks in Bombay
harbour. He undertook this function on behalf of the Freemasons, of
which he had become grand master the previous year. As the local lodge
boasted, snubbing their fellow masons in Madras and Calcutta, it was
'the only Masonic ceremony' that the prince attended during his tour.[57]
But it was with a trowel and mortar in hand, not an orb and sceptre.

After a short excursion to Poona, the prince's itinerary now took an
abrupt turn to avoid outbreaks of cholera across Mysore. The tour
would continue by sea, direct to Ceylon via Goa, and then onwards by
sea and rail to Madras. The revised route meant 'extreme disappointment' for many in the south, but it did provide the opportunity for
some additional diplomacy.[58] On 18 November, the prince's party left
Bombay for Baroda, 250 miles to the north, a trip laid on at short
notice, partly at the behest of the acting regent, Madhara Rao, and the
Maharani, the Gaekwar's mother, anxious for a show of British paramountcy to help cement her infant son's authority. Thousands of Indian
workers were dragooned into preparing the town's railway station and
its thoroughfares, and also getting ready the area selected for the prince's
quail-hunting and pig-sticking on the return journey.[59] The Baroda trip
was the first application of the royal touch to the prince's Indian tour.
On arrival at the railway station he stepped up a silver ladder to get into
the howdah mounted on an elephant, an ornamental umbrella held
aloft over his head, as he rode alongside the Gaekwar's elephant to the

British Residency. As the Gaekwar's guest he watched men wrestling and beasts brawling (buffaloes, elephants and rhinoceroses). Indeed the Prince of Wales spent more time in Baroda in the company of the animal kingdom than the human. Apart from a formal dinner at the Makarpura palace, at which the prince and Madhara Rao gave speeches, most of the mini-itinerary was given over to animal sports. That was partly the point. The rituals of hunting and animal fighting were a time-honoured way of affirming the regal status of both the newly enthroned Gaekwar and the visiting heir to the British throne.[60]

Mission accomplished in Baroda and back in Bombay, the spruced-up *Serapis* was ready to sail again. A series of visitors came on board in the days before departure: more Indian princes, the Aga Khan, several members of the Jejeebhoy family, and Professor Monier-Williams, the latter seeking support for his planned Indian Institute in Oxford.[61] The sea voyage took the tour party first to Goa, territory held by the Portuguese. Then, hugging the Malabar coast (although not too tightly as there was cholera onshore), the *Serapis* travelled south, arriving at Colombo, capital of Ceylon, on 1 December.[62] Unlike India, Ceylon was a Crown colony, theoretically enjoying more self-government than its Indian neighbour. However, like the Indian mainland, Ceylon had experienced revolt. In 1848 martial law was proclaimed on the island after rebels restored the native Buddhist Kandyan monarchy. Almost thirty years on, colonial authority remained brittle.[63] The Prince of Wales was enlisted to ramp up support for British rule. On disembarking he drove into town under triumphal arches. One was laden with fruit, another formed from two elephants on either side of the road, their raised trunks touching. Dinner with the governor, Sir William Gregory, was followed by a torch-lit elephant procession, as royal a reception as could be laid on.[64]

The prince had come to Ceylon mainly to look for elephant, but first he was required to gaze over the relics of Ceylon's departed monarchy. The governor journeyed with him to Kandy, the old royal capital in the centre of the island. There they viewed one of the Kandyan kings' most sacred remains, the Buddha's tooth. The prince and his companions took it all in with a mixture of disdain and levity. Dr Fayrer thought that the tooth was probably that of a seal, and the prince wound up Reverend Duckworth by asking him to converse with a Buddhist priest on the subject of nirvana.[65] However, for Gregory, the visit helped dampen nostalgia for the old days of native monarchy. As he told Lord Carnarvon, the Kandyans 'yearned for the visible presence of a king'. The visit of the prince had done just that: '[t]hey have no longer to deal with abstractions. They have seen the heir to the Crown.'[66] By way of return, the prince got his elephants. More than 1,000 men had spent weeks preparing the site for the hunt at a camp outside Ruwanwella. After three days' wait in heavy rain the prince finally cornered and shot his first elephant. Or rather a team of Ceylonese enticed the elephant from the trees, trapped and wounded the animal, leaving the prince to fire the fatal bullet – a metaphor for British rule in India, perhaps.[67] The visit to the island ended back in Colombo with a levée and a ball at Government House. Then the *Serapis* made its way back across the sea to Tuitcorin (Thoothukudi). The prince opened a new railway branch and proceeded up the line to Tinnevelly for a flying call on the Christian missionaries there. Meeting the delegation on the railway platform, the prince was presented with a Tamil Bible.[68]

The tour now turned north, making the long overland trip by train to Madras via Madurai. After the bustle of Bombay, and the humidity of Ceylon, Madras was cooler in every sense. The municipal authority had been parsimonious in their preparations. The prince was met at the railway station, the building covered in calico for the occasion, as though in a bed gown observed one of the party, and the rest of the town still seemed asleep. Indeed there was 'hardly anyone to be seen'. Local journalists put their finger on the problem. No one knew which of the pith-helmeted pink Europeans was in fact the prince.[69] Into this Madras malaise stepped the governor, the 3rd Duke of Buckingham and Chandos. The duke and his three daughters (he had recently been widowed) now applied royal gilding. The duke suggested that the prince appear in public with a golden umbrella held over his head, to signal his state of majesty and to single him out from the white faces around him. The prince now made up for the earlier cancelled tour dates. Audiences were held for the Maharaja of Mysore and the Raja of

Travancore, the Nawab of Arcot, and, from behind a screen, the Princess of Tanjore. Time was also squeezed in for the laying of a foundation stone for the new docks (local freemasons were invited to watch), and for a day at the races (with a spot of hunting) at Guindy.[70]

The prince, with his golden umbrella, now headed to Calcutta, where he was due for Christmas and for the investiture of the Star of India on New Year's Day. The Calcutta programme closely resembled what had taken place at Bombay. Rulers from northern India came to meet the prince, viewing from a platform as the ship drew up on the Maidan. The Burmese court sent a delegation too. Day one of the Calcutta stay was given over to visits from and exchanges of gifts with the Indian princes, and with a state banquet at Government House in the evening. It was the first time that any of the British press had come face to face with the more legendary ruling houses of India, and they made full use of the opportunity to exoticise them. Bourne and Shepherd, the leading firm of Calcutta photographers, were also on hand to capture the occasion.[71] The prince was expected to match the princes with a stylish flourish of his own. A portable teak throne finished in silver was provided for him at Calcutta. But he declined, preferring to sit on a sofa when receiving the Indian rulers. After a brief interlude for Christmas Day, the packed calendar resumed. There was a visit upriver to Barrackpore, to pay respects at the Canning memorial. On 28 December there were return visits made to the Indian princes, and then the whole world seemed to turn up at the governor's levée; over 200 presentations were made to the prince, including some of the grandsons of Tipu Sultan, the British Indian Association of Calcutta (the *zamindars*' lobby), and the Calcutta lodge of the freemasons, the latter affronted that they had to stand in line to meet him. Other stops on his Calcutta visit, although scripted, were harder for the British authorities to control. The prince attended a 'native entertainment' at Debendranath Tagore's house at Belgatchia and also visited Calcutta University, where he collected an honorary degree. There were two visits to the racecourse, one to watch a polo match.[72]

On 1 January, starting at 8 a.m., the main event of the Calcutta visit took place: the Star of India investiture. It was the only occasion during the tour when the prince acted in the name of the queen, and it was a grand affair. Each of the new knights were given their own tent, from which they emerged one after another to be admitted into the order, the Prince of Wales pinning the star and riband onto their robes.[73] That ceremony over, the prince rushed off to unveil an equestrian statue of Lord Mayo, return to the racecourse, dine at Government House and close out the first day of 1876 with a trip to the theatre. During the dash across the city, an Indian approached the prince's carriage and managed to throw something into the royal lap. It turned out to be a missive and not a missile, an Indian petitioner managing to skirt the security.[74]

Boarding the prince's special train for the first time, the tour party left Calcutta and turned north-west, across Bengal to Bankipur. At Bankipur indigo workers tried to petition the prince but were turned back. Then on to Benares, where the Maharaja of Benares hosted his visit at Ramnagar, presenting the prince with a copy of his translation of the queen's Highland journals, and another royal accessory: a gold walking stick.[75] More regalia came his way at Lucknow, the next stop, as the Taluqdars of Awadh gave him their crown. Now he was looking like a royal. There were mutiny memories too: an inspection of army veterans from the siege of Lucknow, a visit to the memorial at the Residency and, a few days later, a service at the memorial church at Kanpur.[76] History and memory combined with even more force at Delhi, reached on 11 January. A crowded procession led the prince from the railway station to his tented camp on the ridge above the old city. There was a ball in the peacock chamber of the Red Fort and a dinner in the zenana court. Just to rub in British superiority six grandsons of the ex-King of Delhi were presented to the prince.[77] Delhi had been chosen for the first major military show of the tour. On 12 January the prince led a review of 20,000 troops, organised by Major Frederick Roberts, followed two days later by a reconstruction of the offensive against the rebel soldiers back in 1858.[78] It was an important statement of British military might, reliving the heat of the battle that had decisively seen off the last serious challenge to British power.

After six days in Delhi, the tour pushed further north, entering the Punjab capital of Lahore on 17 January. The by now familiar routine kicked in: a levée and a ball, principally for Europeans, a visit to the 'Soldiers' Industrial Exhibition', and a fete in the Shalimar Gardens.[79] Unlike in 1870, the Punjabi and Kashmir chiefs did not come to Lahore to meet British royalty. Instead, the prince went out to them. Travelling via Wazirabad, where he opened the 'Alexandra' railway bridge over the Chenab river, the prince went north to Jammu, entering the capital of Kashmir in an elephant cavalcade. The enemy felt very close. Russian-made goods were noticed in the bazaar. Alongside polo, acrobatics and a sacred dance performed by *lamas*, another mock battle was organised.[80] The prince's party now turned back east, via Lahore to Agra, calling at Amritsar and Patiala on the way. At Amritsar they visited the jail, and, at the prince's suggestion, several prisoners were released as an act of royal clemency. At last he was behaving like a king-in-waiting. The prince also saw the Sikhs' Golden Temple – temple and tank illuminated for the occasion – but declined to remove his footwear on entering the site. Just to prove he was a prince, if not an observer, of all faiths he also met with another missionary delegation.[81]

As the tour came towards the end of its third month, enthusiasm and energy was beginning to flag. One eyewitness to the prince's Amritsar stopover found his manner peremptory. Physical fatigue and sports injuries were setting in too. The prince proved hardier than most of his companions, but even he succumbed to illness at the beginning of February. His physician was not surprised: 'how can anyone keep well long in so much racket and fatigue,' moaned Fayrer.[82] Agra afforded some respite. A plush camp was pitched outside the town: tents equipped with furniture and fireplaces became the prince's base for the next two weeks. From there he visited the town of Agra, entering astride an elephant as in Jammu. Two visits were made to the Taj Mahal, one by moonlight. From Agra he made a series of excursions: a day's shooting in Bharatpur; a visit to Fatehpur Sikri to see the ruins of Akbar's city, and, more significantly, to Gwalior and Jaipur, where the local rulers competed to impress their royal visitor. At Gwalior, Sayaji Rao, the maharaja, did not stint in his preparations. He constructed a completely new palace – the Jai Vilas Mahal – and the prince was his first guest. Arriving by carriage, the prince was met outside the city by his host and 14,000 troops, a reminder of the potency of his loyalty. The new palace was not quite finished – 'Buckingham Palace repainted,' gibed the *Telegraph* correspondent – but still the guests marvelled at the fittings.[83] Anything Sayaji Rao could do, the Rajputana princes could do better. The tour returned to Agra, stopping in at Dholpur on the way, where another palace – in Italianate red sandstone – had been built just in time. From Agra the prince went back into Rajputana, heading for Jaipur, where there were no new palaces awaiting him. Instead the Maharaja of Jaipur had painted the city pink in readiness for the visit. There was no stopping the one-upmanship. Reaching Jaipur, past welcome signs in giant letters placed on the surrounding hills, and passing under a series of triumphal arches to the background noise of 'God save the Queen' played on whistles, the prince and his companions transferred from their carriages to howdahed elephants to enter the city, the stately procession caught for posterity in the enormous oil painting made by the Russian artist Vasily Vereshchagin. Vereshchagin depicts the procession in daylight, but it was even more striking than that, for it was a torch-lit spectacle, taking place in the evening. The following day the prince laid the foundation stone of the Prince Albert Museum, the ceremony conducted from a podium over which a royal crest was suspended.[84] Jaipur had also been selected for another hunting expedition, the press corps in contention to get the scoop of the prince's first kill. As the prince enjoyed another assisted success – shooting down an already wounded animal – Reuters was the first to telegraph the news back to London, where it was taken as final proof that Edward was fit to be king. As one songster expressed it, 'The hunting is over, the victory won! / The crown has been earned and everything done,' and it went on: 'He has won it by valour, no man about Town / Ever brought like the prince, a wild Elephant down / And now he must wear an Imperial Crown.'[85]

The tour now began to wind down. The prince and a smaller group went off to hunt for three weeks, firstly in the Terai, then they crossed the border into Nepal as the guests of Jung Bahadur, the prime minister, for more stalking and shooting. On 5 March the prince and his colleagues left Nepal, travelling back across Awadh by horse-drawn carriage to Lucknow. They paused to meet with the Nawab of Rampur at Pilibheet (Pilibhit). At Lucknow they rejoined the train, arriving in Allahabad on 7 February for the penultimate ceremony of the trip, a second investiture of the Star of India.[86] There remained one more maharaja to see: Tukoji Rao II, the Maharaja Holkar of Indore. The prince travelled along the shiny new railways of his state to meet him. Then the party sped south to Bombay, where the smallpox was closing in, halting only for a farewell dinner with the governor, Philip Wodehouse. Afloat once more, the prince dashed off a thank-you letter to the people and princes of India, and, in a final act of modest munificence, donated money to local Bombay causes.[87]

On 11 March the *Serapis*, laden with wild animals, flora and fauna, left Bombay harbour and made its way home. As if he had not seen enough royalty already, the Prince of Wales called in on more en route, Isma-il Pasha of Egypt and the kings of Spain and Portugal. The *Serapis* finally docked at Portsmouth two months after leaving Bombay. The royal ladies were pleased to have the prince home, the Dean of Westminster gave thanks for his safe return, and the commodity culture spawned by the tour picked up where it had left off. The *Serapis* was opened up to the public, then the exotic menagerie was transferred to London Zoo. The hoard of gifts from the princes of India went on display at the South Kensington Museum, before an 'Indian' room was made for them at Marlborough House, the prince's London home. Some of the journalists turned their copy into instant bestsellers.[88]

In terms of political capital at home, the Prince of Wales's tour of India was a triumph. The heir to the throne had shed his reputation for lazy indifference, and proved more daring, diplomatic and dedicated than anyone had expected. In India, the effects of the prince's visit were more mixed. Frere, designer-in-chief of the tour, told Queen Victoria that India had now fully submitted to imperial authority.[89] Certainly, India had seen the heir to the throne, the present and future of the Raj had been viewed in person by thousands of Indians. As the Mahomedan Literary Society of Calcutta concluded nothing had been quite so important as making visible the person of the monarch.[90] The prince had fulfilled some Indian expectations too. His criticism of British officials and their rough handling of Indian chiefs in Bombay and at other stops later in the tour was widely reported. Newspapers picked up on his every small act of charity and compassion and highlighted them as examples of his princely virtue. Alongside this went the complaint that he was not being shown the real India, that he would be unable to inform the queen of the real plight of her Indian people. Writers from Bengal and Poona urged the prince to give a 'correct account' to his mother of what he had witnessed. The *Hindoo Patriot* urged him to 'tell her that all that you have seen so glittering is not gold'.[91] There was not much point being a royal messenger if he failed to deliver the message.

Heirs and Graces: The Later Tours

Although nothing quite so grand as the Prince of Wales's tour ever happened again, a pattern was set for other royal tourists to follow. Later visits by members of Queen Victoria's extended family went further and lasted longer, but they always had princely India at the centre of their itinerary, and they all included a spot of diplomacy alongside the hunting and bunting. The Duke of Connaught and Strathearn, Queen Victoria's third son, was not merely a tourist, but a resident royal. In October 1883 he took command of the army at Meerut, moved on briefly to command at Rawalpindi in October 1885, before promotion to commander of the army in the Bombay presidency, a post he held for four years.[92] In effect, he was the only member of the royal family to serve in India during the queen's lifetime, and in combining a civilian and military appointment in Bombay, the only royal to get a seat at the table of the Government of India.

The duke's duties were predominantly military. However, in February 1884 he embarked on a tour of inspection to Agra and Mathura and coupled it with a hunting foray with the Maharaja of Bharatpur. Later that year he visited Kashmir. Although a 'private visit', he was received by various chiefs along the way through the Punjab.[93] Then in 1885, the duke made the first of two decisive interventions in

Indian foreign policy. In March he travelled to Rawalpindi in the Punjab to join the viceroy, Lord Dufferin, in his sensitive negotiations with the Emir of Kabul. Cajoled by gifts and cash, arms and men, the emir finally agreed to an alliance with the British. Adding the duke to the discussions helped to assure the emir that he was not being treated by the British as a mere feudatory prince, concluded the *Times* correspondent.[94] Four years later the duke was despatched on a special trip to Hyderabad, specifically tasked with coaxing the nizam out of his cosy circle of courtiers and making him more accustomed to European visitors.[95] The visit was an important step forward in relations between the British and the nizam. Before the trip, viceroys had remained wary of venturing to Hyderabad. After the duke had smoothed the path, they visited more regularly.

The Duke of Connaught also acted as chaperone for the last royal visit of India during the queen's lifetime. In the winter of 1889–90, her grandson, Prince Albert Victor, made what proved to be the most extensive of all the princely tours of the period, his travels taking him from Travancore in the south to Burma in the east and as far north as Darjeeling at one end of the Himalayas and Rawalpindi at the other. Supposed to be the guest of the viceroy, sojourning in India on a private visit undertaken for the sake of his health and to take him away from the scandal sheets at home, Albert Victor's tour eventually took on all the characteristic features of the earlier royal visits. At first all was unremarkable. Only eight Indian states had expressed any interest in meeting the prince.[96] His ship was kept waiting in Bombay harbour for two hours before anyone realised it was there, and he disembarked to be met by a 'beggarly array of empty benches and glaring yellow chairs'. Prince Albert Victor was whisked off to Poona, where his uncle, the Duke of Connaught took over hosting his visit to the presidency. There followed a meeting with the Indian rulers, and later with the Aga Khan, and sirdars from the Deccan and then, accompanied by the duke, the prince went to Hyderabad.[97] Before 1889 no British royal had met the nizam; now two had come along to his kingdom in the same year. No expense was spared by the Hyderabad court to welcome their first ever heir to the throne, with £200,000 lavished on the occasion, highlights including a dainty dish ('fluffy cakes') set before the prince from which birds flew out.[98]

From Hyderabad the royal party travelled into Mysore, a state that had been left off his father's tour. The prince caught up with the new Maharaja of Mysore in his ornate wooden palace, lit by electric light for the occasion.[99] Then the party moved on to Courtallum (Kuttalum) in Travancore, travelling in a carriage specially made for the occasion, provided by the Raja of Travancore, a throne on hand in case the prince wanted to hold a durbar.[100] There was a quick stop in Madras, then the prince became the first royal to visit Burma. The security situation was too tense to accommodate a ceremonial occasion, with the route from Rangoon to Pegu heavily policed. So the party moved on to Calcutta. Not that anyone was ready for them there. Preparations in Calcutta had been tardy too, with one government department passing responsibility for the visit to the city to another. The European community could not agree on how to fete the prince. In the end two maharajas – Darbhanga and Vizianagaram – came to the rescue, underwriting the costs of the occasion.[101] Such occasions were few and far between. Prince Albert's Calcutta itinerary involved almost exclusively European 'official society' with only a select band of Indians – the Maharajas of Cooch Behar and Darbhanga, Sourindro Mohan Tagore and the Nawab of Murshidabad – amongst the landing party. Although the viceroy, Lord Lansdowne, was adamant that many native gentlemen were anxious to see Prince Albert Victor, only one event, the quaintly named 'Calcutta Community Fete' on the Maidan, was set aside for the prince to meet Indians.[102] In vain did one local address memorial 'hope that His Royal Highness will kindly enquire into the condition of the dumb millions of the . . . Indian subjects'. Moreover, dissent was in the air. Students disrupted the proceedings of the welcome committee.[103]

Out of Calcutta, the tour resumed its routine aspect, and the prince fell back into the tracks left by his father and his uncle. There was more hunting around Benares, Nepal and Baroda. He made all the mutiny visits: to Lucknow and Kanpur, with veterans and survivors as his guides, and a tour of the site of the siege along the Delhi ridge. In the Punjab the ceremonies were more lavish: howdahed elephants at Lahore, military parade at Rawalpindi, a Sikh ceremony (a 'christening') at Amritsar, a durbar at Patiala.[104] On the return trip family duties resumed. At Agra Queen Victoria requested that the prince call in on the father of Abdul Karim, her *munshi* (secretary); he entered Jaipur on an elephant just as his father had; and he unveiled a statue of the queen at Udaipur. By now Albert Victor was going through the motions, observing to his grandmother that 'everyone was being nice to him' only because he was a prince.[105] As he returned to Bombay, the city was better prepared for his visit. The Indian National Congress and their republican guest, Charles Bradlaugh, had gone home. There was a week of festivities and civic ceremonies, including the laying of the foundation stone of a leper asylum funded by Dinshaw Petit.[106] Then the prince resumed his tour, to Hong Kong and Japan, before returning home in the summer of 1890.

The tour of Prince Albert Victor fitted into the patterns established by Prince Arthur in 1869–70, and the Prince of Wales in 1875. However, there were some important differences. The large cities were kept at arm's length. Bombay was bypassed at first as the meeting of the Indian National Congress was imminent, Madras only given a cursory nod, Calcutta carefully negotiated to keep the prince away from as many Indians as possible. Little was left to chance, lest the prince become embroiled in Indian politics. The Government of India had learned to be cautious.

Princely tours brought the British monarchy to India, putting Queen Victoria in touch, albeit indirectly, with the Indian people. There would be two more tours, one in 1905–6 and one in 1921. However, these visits never matched that of 1875–6. In 1905 Prince George, Duke of York, was tied up by protocol, and, in 1921, Prince Edward was parachuted into the aftermath of the Amritsar massacre, the trip dogged by boycott. The more that India became accessible to royal tourists, the less they saw of India. The Government of India wanted to show off the heir to the throne to princely India. But officials disliked mixing in monarchy with everyone else in India. The visit of Edward in 1875–6 was really the only occasion when a Prince of Wales was unleashed on British India, exposed to the towns and cities, and allowed to meet

Indians. Even then Indian newspapers complained that he had not been shown the real India. In the end, only one person came to see royal tours as a key part of the Raj, and that was Queen Victoria. Her sons were fulfilling their father's aspirations, turning India into a family affair, making the passage to India, whilst she remained at home. Was this not the way an empress was supposed to behave?

CHAPTER 8

QUEEN-EMPRESS

Not long after his death in 1881, Benjamin Disraeli featured on a Parisian cigarette card, depicted bowing before Queen Victoria as he conferred on her the title of Empress of India. The French always had a high estimation of Disraeli, but he could no more make Victoria an empress than he could communicate with Prince Albert in the afterlife.[1] The queen's new title required an act of Parliament. However, the idea stuck, and Disraeli has been credited ever since as the architect of the new imperialism at home, and overseas, decisively so in India. The imperial title, together with the purchase of shares in the Suez Canal in 1875 and the annexation of Cyprus in 1878, comprised a stroke of brilliant *realpolitik* by the ageing prime minister, protecting routes to the east and confirming the importance of India to British geo-politics. At the beginning of 1877, Lord Lytton, India's new viceroy, hand-picked by Disraeli, proclaimed the new title of empress at an Imperial Assemblage in Delhi. For many the story of the British Raj starts here. All the ingredients are in place: a compliant monarch, a high-handed politician or two, exotic eastern spectacle and the people of India caught somewhere between abject homage and complete indifference.[2] On closer inspection, the story is more complex. Queen Victoria wanted to be known as empress as much as Disraeli; in fact, she assumed the title was already a commonplace. Far from applying a masterly touch, Disraeli so mishandled the Royal Titles legislation in 1876 that politicians across the spectrum, from peers to republicans, opposed the measure. In India, in spite of Lytton's flashy theatre, a more positive response emerged, as many Indians believed the switch from queen to empress would bring reform. In the end, Queen Victoria herself appreciated the change of nomenclature most. She marked the occasion with a new honours order for women in India, tested the reach of her new powers in Afghanistan and Egypt, and sent out her third son, the Duke of Connaught, to take on senior command in India.

The Blot on the Queen's Head

No one was keener on the title of Empress of India than the queen. By 1876, her eldest daughter was a crown princess imperial, her second son had married into the Russian imperial family, and her eldest son and heir had just returned from a hugely successful royal tour of India, which had all the trappings of an imperial procession. Across Europe she could survey a world in which since Albert's death kingdoms had given way to empires: in Germany, Italy, Portugal (Brazil) and until recently France. Imperial rivalry struck hardest nearest to home, as Queen Victoria's correspondence with her daughter, the Crown Princess of Prussia, attests. In 1873 mother and daughter bickered over whether the Prussians in Germany or Englishmen in the east were the worst offenders.[3] So when Disraeli came up with a plan to give her a new title in India, he met with support. Of the proposed forms of title suggested by Disraeli she preferred 'Queen-Empress' or at least a separation of the two, for while India was a dependency Britain was an ancient kingdom. She also returned to her long-held wish that dukedoms be created for the colonies, positions to be held by her sons.[4] Disraeli consulted with his lord chancellor, Hugh Cairns, about how the announcement might be made. A senior Indian official looked into the implications of the proposed title in India.[5] Referring to the precedent of the Act of Union in Ireland (when the monarch's title had last been altered) Disraeli warned that it 'must be an affair of legislation & not of prerogative'. He told the queen that it would be mentioned in the royal speech at the beginning of the new session with a 'short act' to follow.[6]

The act may have been intended to be short, but the debate over the next three months was drawn out and acrimonious. Unveiling the government's intentions on 17 February, Disraeli caught the House of Commons by surprise. He avoided spelling out what the new title would be, claimed some change had been considered by Lord Derby's Cabinet back in 1858, and made loose references to the royal prerogative, clearly irking some of the Liberal opposition.[7] In the days that followed confusion grew over the wording of the title, concern lest the colonies misunderstood its implications, and disapproval that the form was un-English, conjuring up connotations of the French empire of Bonapartism, or, even more ominous, Russian despotism. Robert Lowe, the liberal maverick who had scuppered his own party's reform bill ten years earlier, led the line.[8] Disraeli expressed his surprise to the queen over the opposition. Backdoor channels were opened with the Liberal leadership, via Lord Granville and the Duke of Argyll. That only made matters worse, for when the Liberal leadership did meet, they were united in their disapproval of the bill. Disraeli was authorised by the queen to consult further with the opposition over the wording of the title, but still their criticism was not assuaged. The queen grew more irate by the day. Told of the Liberals' inflexibility, she sent a note in blue pencil to Henry Ponsonby, her private secretary: 'The Queen must insist on <u>Empress</u> of India as she has constantly been styled so + it <u>suits</u> Oriental <u>ideas</u>.'[9] She turned to Theodore Martin, Albert's biographer, asking him to find someone to write to the newspapers making it clear that she wanted the new title. However, newspaper opinion moved speedily in the opposite direction. By the time the bill re-emerged for its full second reading in the Commons three weeks later, a full-scale crisis was under way.[10]

A further bombshell dropped on the eve of the debate. It was rumoured that the queen herself did not want the title, that it was being imposed on her by Disraeli. To contain the damage as much as possible, Queen Victoria agreed that Disraeli could tell Parliament that a change to her domestic title of Queen had never been intended, and that her sons need not take colonial titles 'habitually'.[11] Still the opposition continued. Disraeli was accused of not consulting the other colonies, nor making any enquiries in India. As to the title, critics argued that there were no precedents for a dual appellation: 'queen' must ordinarily give way to 'empress'. Disraeli and his colleagues brazened it out, rejecting claims that they wished to 'sultanise' British government in India and denying that there would need to be a huge recall of currency. They cast around for existing usages of the title.[12] Going into the second week of the debate in committee, Disraeli produced a trump card. A schoolchild had found that her geography book referred to the title, as did *Whitaker's Almanack*.[13] Nothing annoyed the opposition quite as much as these cheeky revelations and they pushed for a division which the government narrowly won. So the bill limped through to its committee stages in the Lords where further obstacles awaited. Lord Shaftesbury pressed for a different title – 'Lady Paramount' and our 'Sovereign Lady' were proffered but ignored – and the bill was squeezed through.[14]

The fuss continued. As the queen left for the Continent, and Parliament went into recess for the Easter break, public meetings were held up and down the country. The republican movement, dormant since the beginning of the decade, revived. Joseph Cowen, the Newcastle MP, was its figurehead, and James Thomson, the poet, added his own indictment.[15] Within a few weeks, a humorous pamphlet, *The Blot on the Queen's Head*, dashed off pseudonymously by Edward Jenkins, the MP for Dundee, was a runaway bestseller, its circulation passing the 100,000 mark by the end of the year, its catchy title giving *Punch* and other satirists copy for weeks on end.[16] Debate outside Parliament ranged from practical suggestions about titles to lurid prophecies of Britain becoming a despotism. Disraeli was the focal point of the attacks. Anti-Semitic caricatures of Disraeli reached a crescendo, but any form of eastern derogation fitted the bill. He was portrayed as a sultan, a Russian who would turn the Brighton pavilion into the Kremlin and a Jewish pedlar encouraging Victoria to trade in her English crown for the new imperial one.[17]

Disraeli had badly misjudged the mood of the country, and the temper of the queen. Between one viceroy and the next he had not sought out opinion in India, and only seems to have confided in his colonial secretary, Lord Carnarvon, once his course was decided. The clamour did not die down. Both sides toyed with extraordinary means to achieve their ends. The radical MP Henry Fawcett announced his intention to push for a compromise title, the 'Queen of India', on the resumption of Parliament. According to Disraeli, the Liberal leadership contemplated holding a Privy Council meeting in the queen's absence and coming out in support of Fawcett. The queen suggested a counter move: she could summon a quick Council immediately on her return to formalise the title. Neither ruse materialised. However, the Royal Titles Act had to be accompanied by a proclamation, specifying the wording of the new royal style in all future foreign and colonial diplomacy.[18] Again, Disraeli slipped up, confirming that the imperial title would not be used in the United Kingdom. However, he made no mention of its possible application to other colonies and dependencies. This gave the opposition a further opportunity to derail the bill.[19] No one, it seemed, was really happy with the imperial turn. Far from triumphing with the Royal Titles bill, at each stage Disraeli brought further unpopularity to his government. In the years that followed, the title was not only not used in Britain but disowned altogether. The slightest intrusion of 'empress' into domestic usage prompted hostility in the House of Commons.[20] Empire was not for the absent-minded British. Disraeli had also managed to offend the queen. She passed from curiosity as to why the change was necessary to outrage that it should provoke so much opposition. Having endured such a rough ride at home, the new title would be puffed up as much as possible in India. For that the government turned to the new viceroy, Lord Lytton.

The Imperial Assemblage

Robert Bulwer-Lytton was not an automatic choice as the next viceroy of India. It was a shock to Lytton as well. He explained to Disraeli that he lacked the requisite knowledge, possessing an 'absolute ignorance of all facts and questions concerning India'.[21] Plucked from the diplomatic pool, he was the famous son of an even more famous father, Edward

Bulwer-Lytton, the novelist. Lytton had served abroad at Paris, Copenhagen, Vienna and Athens, postings as notable for the amount of poetry he produced under the *nom-de-plûme* of Owen Meredith as for any great policy successes.[22] Nonetheless, a career spent in the capitals of Continental Europe, witnessing the demise of the French and Austrian empires, and the advent of the German, was a not inappropriate preparation for India. Lytton had been present at the height of Louis Napoleon's imperial pageantry in France. He witnessed the crushing of the German princes during the Schleswig-Holstein crisis of 1864, and the breakaway of the Hungarian nobility from the Austrian empire. In a pair of articles published in the early 1870s he indicated the moral to be learned from the recent history of the Continent. Britain's European neighbours, he observed, had failed to cultivate and maintain the dynastic and monarchical principle, and so keep the loyalty of princes and nobility. France's 'middle-class monarchy' had been a sham, lacking national sentiment. Germany had become a militarised bureaucracy.[23] Lytton also made some interesting contacts in his diplomatic travels. In Athens in 1863 he met Ernest Renan, the controversial author of *The Life of Jesus* (1863) and champion of the French national revival. Lytton was disappointed by Renan. Another French man of letters in Athens impressed him more: Arthur de Gobineau, the race theorist. Lytton reviewed his *Traité des écritures cunéiformes* in 1867, dwelling particularly on Gobineau's revelations about the role of talismans and symbols in the 'eastern mind'.[24] Some of these ideas stayed with Lytton, resurfacing on his arrival in India.

Lytton's appointment was made public in March 1876, as he travelled east, meeting by arrangement the returning Prince of Wales on board the *Serapis*. Reaching Calcutta in the middle of April, he declared to Disraeli that he intended to announce the proclamation of the queen's new title with 'much theatrical effect & political significance'. To the queen he was even more grandiose. He promised 'to give every possible éclat to the queen's assumption of a title, which conspicuously places Her authority upon that ancient throne of the Moguls, with which the imagination and traditions of your Majesty's Indian subjects associate the splendour of supreme power'.[25] By the beginning of May

1. Dwarkanath Tagore (1794–1846), Bengali landowner and merchant, grandfather of the artist and poet Rabindranath Tagore. Dwarkanath Tagore was the first Indian whom the queen met. She sketched him on 24 June 1842, commenting in her journal: 'He was in his Native Dress, all of beautiful shawls with trousers in gold & red tissue, & a tartan as in this little sketch.' Tagore died in London in 1846 during a later trip and is buried in Kensal Green cemetery.

2. One of the first ever Indian army medals to feature the monarch, Victoria is depicted here as a warrior queen by William Wyon to mark the defeat of the Sikh armies during the Sutlej campaign of 1846. Queen Victoria saw and approved the designs.

3. A 'historical emblem of conquest', the Koh-i-Noor was taken by the British from Lahore after the overthrow of the Sikh dynasty in 1849 and sent to the queen by Dalhousie, the governor-general of India. She treasured the acquisition and refused to hand it over to the East India Company, allowing it out of her grasp for the Crystal Palace exhibition of 1851 but coveting it as her own. Prince Albert had the diamond cut, polished and made into a brooch, here featured in Winterhalter's portrait, for which Victoria sat in May 1856. Unusually, Winterhalter presented the queen in a formal pose, crowned and without any background or additions, the brooch signalling her Indian empire.

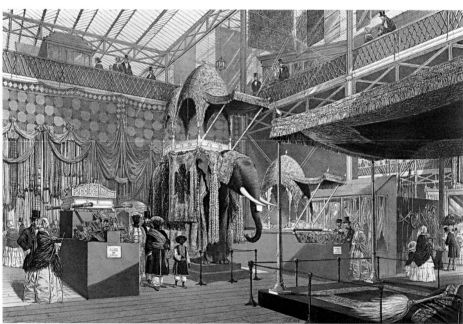

4. Queen Victoria visited the Indian court of the Crystal Palace exhibition on 16 July 1851, and was shown around by Dr J. Forbes Royle. The centrepiece of the court was the ornamental canopied seat, the howdah, given as a gift to the queen by the Nawab Nizam of Bengal for the exhibition. In fact, when Victoria saw the display, the howdah was not complete: there was no elephant. Throughout May and June the exhibition organisers hunted for one. They deemed borrowing a live animal from the Zoological Gardens in Regent's Park too risky, and rejected an offer from a basket-maker to fashion one out of wicker for £4 as too 'make-do'. Finally, a stuffed elephant, late of a menagerie in Essex, was tracked down, joining the exhibition at the end of July.

5. Duleep Singh (1838–93) photographed at Osborne House, Isle of Wight, the queen's summer residence, shortly after he arrived at court in the summer of 1854. The queen met him for the first time on 1 July, noting in her journal that 'He has been carefully brought up, chiefly in the hills, & was baptised last year, so that he is a Christian. He is 16 & extremely handsome, speaks English perfectly, & has a pretty, graceful & dignified manner. He was beautifully dressed & covered with diamonds.' Kitted out in ill-fitting English court clothes over a short *kurta*, Duleep Singh here looks less than dignified compared to the magnificent full-length oil portrait completed later that month by Franz Winterhalter.

6. Prince Arthur (1850–1942, and from 1874 known as the Duke of Connaught and Strathearn) and Prince Alfred (1844–1900, and from 1866 known as the Duke of Edinburgh) in specially tailored Indian costume, photographed at Osborne House in 1854. A Kashmir shawl – an annual tribute to the queen from the Maharaja of Jammu, with its distinctive 'teardrop' motif – is draped over the bench for effect. Both princes went on to see India for themselves, Alfred as part of his world tour of 1867–70, and Arthur in military command in the 1880s, and later on various official visits.

7. Queen Victoria sketched Duleep Singh at Buckingham Palace in the middle of July 1854, as he sat for a portrait being painted by Franz Winterhalter. As she sketched, Prince Albert and the queen chatted with John Login, Duleep's guardian. Login told them that 'the Sikhs are a far superior race to the other Indians, & that the founder of their religion had evidently been a man anxiously seeking for the truth; – that the women kept up superstition, as we both observed they did in many countries. They were very ill educated & schools for girls were much needed. If they could be started, it would make an immense change.' (QVJl., 13 July 1854).

8. Charlotte Canning (1817–61), former Lady of the Bedchamber to Queen Victoria, accompanied her husband Charles to India in 1856 when he took up his post as governor-general. She became the queen's eyes and ears on India around the time of the rebellion, sending commentary on the unfolding revolt. Then in 1858 she joined her husband, now viceroy, on his journeys around the country, painting, sketching and photographing as she went, and sharing some of her works with the queen. This watercolour, made at the end of 1858 looking out over the rooftops of the old city of Delhi from the tower of the Lahore gate of the Red Fort towards Jama Masjid (Friday mosque), shows the precise spot of the *hauz* (bathing tank) in front of the Fort where European prisoners were executed on 16 May 1857.

9. Barker's painting, *The Relief of Lucknow*, which Queen Victoria and Prince Albert viewed on 9 May 1860, used drawings supplied by Egron Lundgren, a court painter, who had been commissioned by the queen to travel to India and record what he saw. The picture shows British army generals James Outram, Henry Havelock and Colin Campbell meeting after having broken down the rebel hold on Lucknow, the battlefield smoke still drifting over the city's landmarks.

10. Nabha, a princely state in the Punjab, issued its own postage stamps, choosing a common image of Queen Victoria with added features to make her more familiar in an Indian setting: an embroidered headband, an elongated nose and enlarged eyes. Coinage and paper currency of the period included similar images, all of which were seen and approved by Queen Victoria.

11. More of a head-dress, this crown was used by the King of Delhi on formal occasions during the 1840s and 1850s, then assumed new significance during his short-lived reinstatement as emperor in 1857. An old man, and in poor health, Bahadur Shah Zafar paid dearly for his disloyalty. Two of his sons and a grandson were executed by the British following the recapture of Delhi, their severed heads presented to the king. Found guilty following a long trial, Bahadur Shah Zafar was exiled to Rangoon where he died in 1862. His crown, looted by the British, was purchased at auction by Prince Albert for the queen.

12. Paid for by an Indian prince, the Gaekwar of Baroda, this statue of Queen Victoria, the first in India, signified Bombay's special relationship with the Crown. The city's philanthropists were conspicuous in their loyalty, naming many new public buildings after members of the royal family. The statue joined another in the city of Prince Albert (1869) – the work of the same sculptor, Matthew Noble – and in 1876 there arrived from Britain an equestrian statue of the Prince of Wales, completed by Joseph Boehm. Times changed. The queen's statue was tarred in protest during the 1897 jubilee. And in 1965 it was removed (without the canopy) to the Bhau Daji Lad Museum, where it now stands, wearing away, in the garden.

13. During the Prince of Wales's tour of India in 1875–6, the Indian princes competed fiercely to stage the best show. Ram Singh II, the Maharaja of Jaipur, had the city painted pink to welcome the prince. Vasily Vereshchagin, a Russian artist, captured on canvas the prince's entry into the city, exercising some artistic license in doing so for the procession actually took place at night, whereas he shows it during the daytime. Later, Lord Curzon purchased the vast canvas for the Victoria Memorial Hall where it hangs to this day.

14. Not until 1889 did British royal diplomacy reach the Nizam of Hyderabad, the most powerful of India's Muslim princes. Earlier attempts in 1870 and 1875 had failed, then in 1889 Prince Arthur, the Duke of Connaught, visited twice, on the second occasion accompanying Prince Albert Victor. Here, on the first visit in January 1889, Prince Arthur takes breakfast after reviewing the nizam's troops. The photographer only managed to catch the prince's pith-helmet (centre-right of the table) as he sat alongside the Duke of Oldenburg (also pith-helmeted and obscured).

15. Prince Albert Victor (1864–92, the Duke of Clarence and Avondale, and the eldest son of the Prince of Wales, seated front and centre with the maharana in white to his left) visited India during the winter of 1889, his trip arranged partly to get him out of London, where rumours were rife that he was caught up in the Cleveland Street male brothel scandal. Here he meets with the Maharaja of Udaipur, having unveiled a statue of his grandmother the queen in the city. The photograph is a rare example of the maharaja and his own son and heir (the little boy seated facing the prince) together in public, a display of the dynasty's durability, in much the same manner as the prince, as son of the heir to the imperial throne, signified continuity in the British royal family – except that he died two years later.

16. Struck to mark the pronouncement in India of her new title of queen-empress, gold and silver medals were presented to the invited dignitaries at the Imperial Assemblage in Delhi on 1 January 1877, as well as to other Indian and European officials across the country. The medal, approved by the queen, depicted her wearing an imperial crown, and featured her title as 'Kaiser-i-Hind' on the reverse. Lord Lytton, the viceroy who masterminded the event, managed to lose his medal in the mud. Extravagant in every detail of the occasion, Lytton ordered too many medals. Years later, the Calcutta Mint melted down the unused stock.

17. The Imperial Assemblage of 1 January 1877 took place on the outskirts of the city of Delhi, the old Mughal capital. The same site was used later for the durbar of 1903 to mark the accession of King Edward VII, and for the coronation durbar of King George V in 1911. This photograph, taken by the Calcutta firm of Bourne and Shepherd, shows the main amphitheatre for the Indian princes, with their banners designed by Lockwood Kipling, as well as the dais from which the proclamation of the new title of queen-empress was made.

18. Queen Victoria's new title of empress was celebrated by events and memorials across India. In Nagpur in the Bombay presidency, Jamsetji Tata named his new cotton factory 'Empress Mills'. It was a bad omen, for later that year the mill was badly damaged by fire. In 1886, Tata built new premises in Bombay, this time opting for 'Swadeshi Mills', a name that reflected resentment at the stranglehold exerted by Britain on Indian domestic industry, ringed in as it was by tariffs and British monopoly of trade.

19. William Downey photographed the queen on the occasion of the pronouncement of her new title of queen-empress. The portrait was produced for the English market, so no imperial crown was on show. Instead, Queen Victoria sits on the ivory throne presented to her by the Raja of Travancore in 1850 and wears the sash of the Order of Neshan Aftab, presented to her by the Shah of Persia in 1873.

20. A popular subject for Indian biographers and writers of didactic literature, Queen Victoria was depicted in a variety of ways. Illustrators often took an English image and adapted it for an Indian audience. Here in a Bengali work of 1895, Thomas Sully's portrait of the queen on her accession in 1837 is reworked to show a young Indian royal.

21. In the same work, Prince Albert's deathbed scene, the subject of a composite photograph by Leopold Manley (1863), shows Queen Victoria as devoted companion, anticipating the status she went on to enjoy in India as a widow.

22. Shah Jahan (1838–1901), the Begum of Bhopal, one of three women from the same dynasty who ruled the Muslim state during the nineteenth and early twentieth centuries. Shah Jahan corresponded directly with Queen Victoria, and was sent copies of her Highland journals and the authorised biography of Prince Albert.

23. Suniti Devi (1864–1932), Maharani of Cooch Behar, visited Queen Victoria's court with her husband during the jubilee year of 1887, later modelling herself on the queen as a matriarchal princess.

24. Chimnabai II (1872–1958), wife of the Gaekwar of Baroda (also pictured), attended Queen Victoria's court with her husband on two occasions. She looked on the queen as a role model for modern women in Indian public life.

25. Lady Hariot Dufferin (1843–1936), wife of the viceroy, led a campaign to establish women's hospitals and nursing education across India, using the queen's 1887 jubilee to raise funds. She was aided by this collection card designed by Lockwood Kipling.

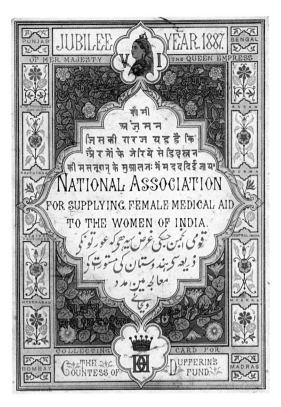

26. The queen-empress together with some of the principal princes of India in a photographic montage produced for the golden jubilee of 1887.

27. A typically regal portrait of the queen-empress, imperial crown aloft, at the time of the 1887 jubilee. This was the frontispiece illustration to a Hindi account of the jubilee celebrations in London, published in Lahore.

28. Twenty-two Indian cavalry formed an escort for the queen's carriage during the procession through the City of London on the occasion of her diamond jubilee in 1897, and also attended her during other events in the jubilee calendar. Here they are shown entering Buckingham Palace at the end of the route, leading in the royal carriage.

29. Abdul Karim (1863–1909), the queen's *munshi*. The son of a Muslim clerk, he joined the royal household shortly after the 1887 jubilee, one of a number of Indian servants taken on by the queen and other members of her family. Soon the *munshi* was teaching her Hindustani. 'I am so very fond of him,' declared the queen, to the dismay of the rest of her household.

30. Rafiuddin Ahmad (1865–1954), a Muslim lawyer from Poona, scooped two interviews with the queen in 1891–2, breaking the news that she was learning Hindustani. She described him as a 'staunch but liberal-minded Mahomedan' and passed on his opinions on a range of topics to her Indian officials.

31. Jagatjit Singh (1872–1949), the Maharaja of Kapurthala, a princely state in the Punjab. He met with the queen at Balmoral in October 1900, the last Indian visitor of her reign. Ironically, his grandfather Randhir Singh had died in 1870 en route to London, attempting to become the first Indian prince to have an audience with Queen Victoria.

32. The Victoria Memorial Hall, Calcutta, Lord Curzon's tribute to the queen, nearing completion at the end of 1920, in a race to be ready for the visit of the Prince of Wales (the future Edward VIII).

his plans for a great assembly of Indian princes had taken shape, and his officials set to work on the details of what would be prove to be the most spectacular ceremonial occasion of the British Raj to date.

For someone who was by his own admission an Indian novice, Lytton had moved quickly. The ink had barely dried on the Royal Titles Act at home, yet Lytton set to his task with guile and ingenuity. Whilst he was ably assisted by his colleagues, the inspiration was all his own. Lytton had two main aims. First, he wanted to make up for the damage done at home to the queen's new title from the opposition speeches, by evoking what he called the 'enthusiasm of the Asiatic mind'. Left to itself, he told Lord Salisbury, Indian political sentiment was dumb and insensate. Basing his notions on what he called 'a careful study of the native character', Lytton's plan was to reach out to the princes and chiefs of India, who had been unduly neglected by the British. Here was a great 'feudal aristocracy' which might be flattered into loyalty to British rule by appropriate titles, gifts and displays. Salisbury, whose family had been flattering English royalty for over 300 years, thought it all a good idea. In this way, Lytton assured the queen, British India might avoid the fate of crumbling empires such as the Austrian.[26] Secondly, Lytton wanted to make a display of the overwhelming military power of British India, to send out a message to Russia in particular, but also to the other European powers, who might be counting on the instability of the Ottoman Empire to further their eastern spheres of influence. Invitations to the January meeting would be sent out to the French and Portuguese envoys in India.[27]

Plans for the proclamation meeting, or durbar as it was known initially, took shape over the next three months. It was all done in secret, lest the newspapers of both countries pour further scorn on the imperial project. The details were finalised on 10 August at the second of two special viceregal council meetings. The date for the occasion, 1 January 1877, was settled early on, although plans for a three-day holiday extravaganza were soon scaled back because of famine conditions in the south and west of India. The venue was only agreed at an advanced stage of the discussions. Bombay was still being considered as a possibility in late July, but logic suggested somewhere more northern and central: Agra, Jabalpur or Delhi, and the latter was deemed by far the best because of 'accessibility by railway, command of space for encampments, and historical associations'.[28] Once Delhi was chosen, more detailed consideration was given as to how the city, still battle-scarred from the rebellion almost twenty years previously, might be made over for the occasion. Lytton took two key decisions. The first located the meeting on a plain to the north-west of the city, effectively the same position from which the British forces had mounted the siege of Delhi in the summer of 1857. The choice was dictated mainly by geography, but also by history. The kidney shape of the site enveloped and looked down on the city. Secondly, keen to secure the attendance of Muslim princes at the durbar – especially the Nizam of Hyderabad, whose failure to meet with the Prince of Wales at Bombay in 1875 still prickled – Lytton proposed returning the Fatehpuri Masjid and Zeenat-ul Masjid mosques in Delhi to their rightful owners. In an even more calculated move, he contributed to the repairs of the Jama Masjid, the largest mosque in Delhi, and part of the planned route of the procession to the durbar meeting. These gestures were not just for local consumption. Lytton also had one eye on the unfolding tensions in Constantinople. It was reported to Lytton that the Muslim community in Bombay was especially supportive of the anti-Russian stance taken by Disraeli in the crisis.[29]

Time and place settled, Lytton then spent much time designing the symbolic and decorative aspects of the durbar, above all the measures intended to rope the princes and chiefs into the new imperial order. In some ways, it was business as usual. Lytton continued the traditions of his predecessors. An increase and enhancement of gun salutes was proposed. Existing Indian orders of nobility such as the Star of India were extended. Queen Victoria was particularly keen that the highest tier of the order, the Grand Cross, might be now given to non-Christian princes. Lytton even resurrected another order which no one in London knew anything about – the Order of British India.[30] Lytton wanted more. He planned to reconstitute the Indian princes as a new order of aristocracy, for which they would need new titles and heraldry. A 'herald's college' was planned for Calcutta, and, borrowing from the example of fourteenth-century Venice, a *Libro d'oro* of the native nobility was begun. Banners displaying the shields, arms and colours of each ruling house were ordered for the durbar, initially from Calcutta, but later in the year the Mayo School of Art at Lahore took over the task, with its principal, John Lockwood Kipling, seconded to the viceroy's staff for the duration of the preparations. Lytton also wanted an Indian privy council composed of senior British officials as well as princes.[31] Finally, Lytton commissioned an artist, Val Prinsep, to come out from England to depict for posterity his grand event, paid for by subscriptions from the wealthier princes with copies of his finished work to be then distributed to the VIP guests who attended.[32] Traditions were being invented, their provenance as much medieval as Mughal.

By the middle of September certain features had been amended. The occasion would be an 'Imperial Assemblage' and not a durbar. Durbars were held under cover, and no tent could possibly accommodate all those expected to turn up. Lytton also wanted to avoid the exchange of lavish presents that a durbar usually entailed, as well as the petty squabbling over precedence and hierarchy.[33] Inducements were offered to minor princes that the Government of India would pay the costs of their travel, and special arrangements were made in Delhi to house the entourages of those coming from afar. The nizam was given Metcalfe House, the former home of the British agent in Delhi, roofless since being stormed by the rebels in 1857, now hastily refurbished for the occasion.[34] To encourage more favourable treatment from the newspapers, Indian and European editors were accommodated at government expense as well.[35] In addition, to sweeten the proceedings further, acts of grace were planned: the release of prisoners and issuing of pardons, the feeding of the poor in the main towns of the presidencies, and government funding for fireworks and illuminations throughout India.[36]

The viceroy also inserted the queen more prominently into the event. On Lytton's initiative, a commemorative coin was designed for distribution. Minted in gold and silver formats, the coin bore the queen's image together with her new designation 'Kaiser-i-Hind' in Persian and Hindi characters, and 'Empress of India' in English. Special currency was issued too, comprising annas of the smallest denominations.[37] Salisbury explained to Lytton that the Indian translation of the title had taken some time to agree. The Assyrian expert and Indian Council member Sir Henry Rawlinson had advised on the translation, as had another member of the Council, Sir William Muir, an Islamic scholar. 'Kaiser-i-Hind' was not without controversy. It was a male title, not a female one. Salisbury, ever the dour pragmatist, said this was because the government did not wish to change the sex on the coinage from one reign to another. The vernacular title also came as a surprise, for Disraeli had been adamant that only the English version, 'empress', would be used.[38] The queen was unruffled by the name, but more concerned with her image. She vetoed the first two versions of the coin. She thought her nose was too long and forehead too flat, then found her face and cheek 'too full and heavy'.[39] Other items for Lytton's programme followed. The queen asked that the royal standard be flown at Delhi and on all subsequent such ceremonial occasions. Disraeli requested that a portrait of the queen wearing her imperial crown should be placed in the viceroy's pavilion. A copy of Heinrich von Angeli's painting of the queen, completed the previous May, was sent out once a crown and a veil had been added.[40] Lytton took up these ideas, and conjured up more of his own. He relaxed his own rules regarding gifts, and ordered British-made watches inlaid with a picture of the queen to be sent out for presentation to the Indian chiefs at the private visits scheduled ahead of the January assemblage. The party planning went on and on. Lytton dreamed up a scheme for a new imperial crown, its jewels to be provided by the leading princely houses of India. He also wanted a philanthropic fund announced in London for hospitals and leper asylums in India: £100,000 was his target.[41] Salisbury dissuaded him from the latter, and the new imperial crown was also parked as a luxury and not a necessity. In the thinner air of Simla, the viceroy was letting his imagination run wild. As Disraeli commented, Lytton's 'proclamation schemes' now read like the Arabian nights.[42] It was time to come down to the plains and focus on the main show.

By the middle of December the site for the assemblage was ready. Tens of thousands of people and animals made their way to Delhi. The Gaekwar of Baroda, for example, sent on ahead an entourage of 520 men, 114 horses, 24 bullocks, 21 camels and 10 elephants. The Maharaja of Jaipur, who had less of a journey, brought 1,000 men, 300 horses, 300 bullocks, 130 camels and 15 elephants. And the Maharaja of Jodhpur topped them both, attended by almost 1,700 men, although only 15 elephants.[43] Soon these stage armies were joined by the main cast. Official welcomes with royal gun salutes and conveyance in the viceroy's carriage were given to the crème of the Indian courts, starting with the Begum of Bhopal. On 23 December Lytton arrived at Delhi railway station. Accompanied by Lady Lytton, his children and all his senior colleagues, he made a three-hour processional tour by elephant through the city and out to the encampment. Indian princes and their retinues lined the whole route, interspersed with a 'thin red line' of royal troops. A viewing area was set aside in front of the Jama Masjid for visiting foreign dignitaries and envoys.[44]

For the next ten days the camp of the Imperial Assemblage hummed and fizzed: a pop-up suburb blinking brightly over the old city of Delhi. Estimates of the number of visitors ran as high as 100,000 (the population of Delhi itself was only 160,000). The camp had its own streets, latrines, sewage control and extensive signage. Lytton's domain at the camp was gas-lit (courtesy of the prince-engineer, Ram Singh II, the Maharaja of Jaipur). There was a special police force, a telegraph office and several hospital tents.[45] In the days leading up to the proclamation Lytton honoured the old durbar rituals by making return visits to all the chiefs. Commemorative medals, banners and gifts were exchanged. The princes brought so many presents that an iron cage was required to house them all. *Amour propre* was respected: the Maharaja of Gwalior and the Maharaja of Kashmir were made honorary generals in the Indian army. Knuckles were rapped. Lytton admonished Salar Jung, the prime minister of Hyderabad, for using the occasion to agitate for the return of the Berars territory taken by Dalhousie in 1856. Lytton also upbraided Salar Jung for wrongly translating the viceroy's words to the nizam at their meeting, substituting 'friendship' and 'alliance' for what Lytton actually said, 'loyalty' and 'allegiance' (Lytton then made the government translator state to the nizam that what he really meant was 'obedience' and 'fidelity').[46] The tête-à-têtes were important. Lytton ensured that acts of obeisance to the viceroy, and hence to the queen, took place in private.

The preliminaries over, the ceremony of the proclamation took place on 1 January.[47] Prinsep's group portrait makes it look an intimate indoor occasion, but contemporary photography reveals the sheer physical scale of the event. Two crescent-shaped tented galleries housed the Indian princes, each entourage assembled behind its heraldic banner. These two spectator tents formed arcs around and equidistant to the main circular pavilion – an open-sided bandstand of a marquee, on which the viceroy's throne was placed, the queen's portrait hanging above. Once everyone was in place, the announcement of the queen's new title was signalled by trumpets, and by the playing of the national anthem. Major Osmond Barnes, veteran of the rebellion of 1857–8 and the Abyssinian campaign, acted as herald, wearing a tabard emblazoned with the royal coat of arms, reading out the proclamation, with a translation following in Urdu. Lytton then spoke, explaining the purpose of the queen's new title. It is doubtful that anyone could hear what he said, such was the distance – at least 100 metres (328 feet) – between the pavilion and the viewing area. In a short, peremptory address, Lytton began with the proclamation of 1858 and welcomed the 'union of the empire with the princes and peoples of India'. He praised the soldiers and official and non-official Europeans, as well as the princes for their loyalty. He did not hold out much of an olive branch to anyone else. Native Indians, hopeful of a share in the government of their country, were told that 'present conditions' demanded 'supreme supervision and direction of their administration by English officers'. The enemy without was also warned. Foreign powers were told that no one could 'now attack the Indian Empire without assailing . . . the unlimited resources of the queen's dominions and the courageous fidelity of her allies and feuda-tories'. So far, so good. Surprisingly, there was no protocol for how the ceremony was to end. Several Indian princes – Gwalior, Udaipur, Jaipur and Salar Jung (on behalf of the nizam) – made short impromptu speeches of their own, as did the Begum of Bhopal, the only female ruler there. But the crowds had already begun to peel away. A banquet followed in the evening. The day had gone more or less as planned, with a few slips. Ironically, Lytton managed to lose his own commemorative gold medal in all the excitement.[48]

Lytton regarded his spectacle as a success: 'no mere pageant . . . a great historical event'.[49] As a display of military might, and imperial loyalty, the assemblage achieved its ends. Lytton's officials reported to London that sixty-three chiefs had attended, and that 'their united territories exceed the combined areas of England, Italy and France'.[50] Not only had princely India been officially incorporated into the Raj, but also hundreds of Indian men (and in a few cases women) had been rewarded with titles and other new forms of status. Indeed, it was the Indian state bureaucracy rather than the princes who were the principal beneficiaries of Lytton's largesse in 1877. Magistrates, engineers, councillors, clerks, police inspectors, famine-workers, surgeons and builders figured prominently in the honours list. A line was drawn with the past too. The mutiny slate was wiped clean, with almost 16,000 prisoners released, including those who had not been given amnesty in 1858.[51] Had it all been worth it? Lytton claimed that the Imperial Assemblage had not blown a hole in his budget, although his accounting methods seem dubious. The military outlay was 'only' £23,000, he explained to George Hamilton, the under-secretary of state for India, equal to more or less the sum set aside for such expenditure for the whole calendar year. As to the rest, Lytton guestimated that the increased railway traffic stimulated by all the toing and froing would more than balance the books.[52]

What did the rest of India make of the viceroy's parade? Embedding the Indian press meant that the event was fully if not favourably reported. The *Civil and Military Gazette* welcomed Lytton's comments about the white community in India, wishing there had been more of the same sentiment, and the *Bangalore Spectator* thought it right that the strength of the paramount power had been impressed upon the princes.[53] However, most newspapers saw Lytton's address as a missed opportunity. No real concessions had been made. There was nothing in his address about introducing representative government, let alone opening up the administration to native Indians. Some of the vernacular press went further in its criticism, not only lamenting the failure to uphold the principles and hopes of the transfer of power in 1858, but also finding the new imperial title both unnecessary and unworkable, since it referred to a male ruler. The expense of the proceedings at a time of famine was deplored, and the subservience of some of the princes regretted. A young Rabindranath Tagore composed a song condemning the princes for hugging the 'golden chair' at a time of want.[54] The *Indian Charivari* seemed to get it right, depicting Lytton as a fairground attendant, the provider of an imperial peep show.[55]

With the passage of time, the Imperial Assemblage has become less of an object lesson in imperial vanity and more of a case study of colonial power. Bernard Cohn called it a 'ritual . . . of subordination' on the part of the Indian princes, as the British appropriated the old feudatory ceremonial of the Mughals, and invented a few more traditions of their own. More recently, Julie Codell has described the 1877 assemblage as part of the performance of 'feudal subjugation', the first in a sequence that 'anticipated modern fascist rallies'. Some of the evidence certainly points this way: for instance the choice of Delhi, the old Mughal capital, as the venue, still smarting from the battering the British gave it in 1858. Then there were the rhetorical allusions to the age of Akbar.[56] However, this verdict is too harsh. In the first place, Lytton wanted to empower Indian princes, not to devalue or degrade them. Lytton's pageantry was influenced as much by a medieval European imaginary as the precedents set by the Mughals. The Imperial Assemblage brought to life scenes from Lytton's own lyric fables and poems: knights convened around the round table of a king, tournaments and processions to show off valour and might, and the inauguration of a new chivalric brotherhood of nobles. In this way, the British wanted to fold the Indian aristocracy into their own monarchical order, not separate them, avoiding the alienation of local elites that Lytton had witnessed in Europe. Secondly, there was less submissiveness on the part of the princes than is often claimed. Individual pledges of loyalty, symbolised in the exchange of gifts and the taking of *attah* and *paan* all took place in private, through the return visits exchanged between the viceroy and the princes. Apart from being spectators, there was little about the choreography of the ceremony on 1 January to indicate that the princes were paying deference. Depictions of the event, such as Prinsep's, showing Lytton addressing a captive audience, mislead. The crescent-shaped accommodation was designed to avoid any hierarchy amongst the princes. Moreover, some of them came to the dais and issued their own addresses at the end of the ceremony. None of them made any public show of obeisance to the viceroy. Thirdly, it was the princes themselves who profited most from the Imperial Assemblage. They returned to their territories with their authority and status validated. For the Nizam of Hyderabad, the long trip to Delhi was the first time he had left his state. An elaborate chronicle of his journey was published.[57] For others, such as the Begum of Bhopal and the Gaekwar of Baroda, the trip to Delhi was part of a new strategy of making excursions across India and overseas, as they fashioned themselves as improving rulers.[58] Court poets were commissioned to describe the event, whilst other commentators emphasised how the grandeur of the occasion was derived from the attendance of so many Indian princes.[59] Lytton's Delhi show was as much a catalyst for catapulting Indian princes into modernity as it was a throwback to an imagined feudal past.

Beyond Delhi the proclamation of the new imperial title had impact too. It was overlooked at the time, and since, that the proclamation was an India-wide event. The governments of each of the three presidencies made small sums available – between 1,000 and 2,000 rupees – for all the principal towns and communities to mark the occasion. Full reports exist for each event, suggesting that the proclamation was as stage-managed an event in the rest of India as it was in Delhi.[60] Yet the British involvement was confined to ensuring that the event took place, providing an official to read the proclamation, and leaning on local elites to give their patronage. Some places observed the formality of a durbar, and many chose to spend their funding on illuminations and fireworks. There was spectacle too: triumphal arches, bearing the queen's new title in English, Urdu or in the local vernacular. Most dramatic of all was the proclamation at Ajmer, where fireworks were set off from rafts on the Ana Sagar lake, climaxing with 'the fiery design of a giant coming out of a well with a board in his hand, bearing the inscription in the vernacular [Marawi] of "God bless the Empress"'.[61]

Elsewhere, the proclamation presented an entrepreneurial opportunity. In Nagpur, Jamsetji Tata, a Parsi industrialist from Baroda, opened his new factory on 1 January, naming it 'Empress Mills'.[62]

Outside Delhi, the prevailing tone of the proclamation proceedings was one of charity and mercy, not ceremony.[63] From Tanjore in Madras, where the famine was striking hard by the new year, Henry Sullivan Thomas, the local revenue collector, explained that the government funding was being used to give 'distressed' widows a piece of simple white cloth, in the name of the 'widowed' queen. Distribution of alms and food to the poor was widespread. Benares witnessed the most extensive operation, with 15,000 indigent people fed. Prisoners were released; local chiefs came forward to pay for public buildings and utilities – clock towers, *dharamsalas* and bathing tanks; a new *serai* (palace) to commemorate the proclamation was promised at Cachar in Assam.[64] In these ways, Victoria's new title was associated with public philanthropy, minimal in its practical effects amidst the famine, but significant as acts of royal kindness and in accordance with older traditions of kingship and rule in India. Addresses from public bodies marking the occasion of the proclamation underlined this sentiment. From Dharwad in Mysore Victoria was likened to the 'virtuous and beneficent' kings and queens 'whose names are taught to every Hindu child'. Conversely other memorialists, including those from Farrukhabad and from Syed Ahmed Khan's 'Mahomedan Congratulation Committee' in Aligarh, compared Victoria to the great Muslim rulers.[65] Elsewhere, the new imperial title elicited hopes of reform. In Alibag in Bombay presidency, a memorial was published calling for various privileges in the spirit of 1858 to be granted, including reductions of land rent and salt duties, and the widening of native Indian representation in legislative matters. Reform was also the dominant theme of congratulatory addresses from several places in the heart of British India: from the 'inhabitants of Calcutta' (calling for popular election of the supreme and popular legislatures'), from Secunderabad, the British canton town across the river from Hyderabad (recalling the 'Magna Carta' spirit of 1858), and most fulsomely from Poona, demanding a new imperial council of the Indian princes, and an opening up of the higher ranks of the army and civil service to Indians.[66]

In 1877 the queen was not so much Mughalised as domesticated, appropriated by Indians for Indians.

Outside of these meetings, there were also many other smaller acts of homage to the new empress. Poems, acrostics, addresses, books, songs and musical arrangements: a variety and profusion of compositions appeared to mark her new title. Some were published, but many were just collected and collated by local officials, and sent on to Delhi. There they languished. Lytton, the poet-diplomat par exemplar, wrote disparagingly to the queen of every Indian who could 'write a few words' turning their hand to 'enthusiastic effusions'.[67] Taken together, however, they do provide revealing testimony to the range of meanings now associated with Victoria's name and rule, and the kinds of causes with which she was becoming identified. Prose and lyrics came from familiar names. Sourindro Mohun Tagore followed up the verses he had published for the Prince of Wales the previous year with two more works – *Victoria-Giti-Mala, or a Brief History of England in Bengali Verses* and *Victoria Sámrájyañ, or Sanskrit Stanzas* – and sent on another twenty-seven works as well. Bowmanjee Cursetjee Cowasjee, from Bombay, added to the poems he had produced for the Prince of Wales, this time producing a lyric entitled 'India's National Anthem'. Tagore went one better a few years later. Commissioned by Frederick Harford, a canon of Westminster Abbey, he composed a national anthem in Sanskrit and Bengali, and sent it on to the queen.[68] Others appeared in 1877. The son of Vedam Venkataraya Sastry, the Tanjore poet, republished for the latest event his father's verses written in 1858 and 1875.

However, there were new sources of loyal sentiment too, coming from Indians who had carved out their own niche in the Raj: schoolteachers such as D. V. Panandhikar, who translated the loyal Marathi songs sung by the pupils of his Bombay school; minor government officials – a translator from Sindh, a deputy collector from Kanpur, a superintendent from Dhaka, a small courts judge from Rangoon – all composed verses for the queen-empress. Different writers fashioned alternative versions of loyalty. Some of these were sectarian. A series of Telugu verses, published in Madras, compared the British deliverance of India from Mughal rule to Hannibal saving Carthage from the Romans.[69]

Tagore included a lyric in *Victoria Samrajyan* praising Victoria for taking the place of the 'powerful Mohamedans' who had deprived India of her own native religion. Invocations as a Hindu deity were common. Mahant Narayan Das, head of the *math* near the Jaganath temple in Puri, and veteran of the Orissa famine relief operation, saw Victoria as the incarnation of Lakshmi (the goddess of wealth, fortune and prosperity), whilst Mooradan, a court poet of Jodhpur, claimed her as a Chakravarti (a universal benevolent ruler). A Bengali poem likened her to Durga, the warrior goddess.[70] Queen Victoria was also likened to Muslim women rulers – Bilqis and Qaidafa – and to Persian kings such as Nausherwan, renowned for their justice. Chroniclers now included her in the genealogy of the sovereigns of Delhi and previous Indian dynasties.[71] Other writers bolted on to their verses calls for reform. Moung Un's poem from Rangoon was accompanied by a plea for hospitals for the poor with free food, and for public schools. From Bombay, Bowmanjee Cursetjee supplemented his anthem with a book published the following year, complaining about the 'drain' of wealth from India and calling for the recruitment of Indians to judicial and local government appointments.[72] As ever in Queen Victoria's India, the language of reform was cloaked in the guise of loyalty.

Lytton remained oblivious to this tidal wave of loyalism. On his return to Calcutta he reiterated his views that Indians might join the government administration only gradually. He poured scorn on the pretensions of the educated elites of Calcutta, deriding the city's university for turning out 'more free-thinkers than wise thinkers'. He also began a dispute with the British India Association of the city over the cotton duties and other aspects of his policy.[73] Later that year Lytton brought in the controversial Vernacular Press Act, subjecting native newspapers to severe scrutiny ahead of publication. The urbane tone of government in the months leading up to the Imperial Assemblage vanished as swiftly as it had arrived. In the end, despite Lytton's best efforts, the 'British Indian Empire', as it was formally known after 1877, looked just like its Continental European counterparts: barracks, bureaucracy and broken promises. Back in London, casting her eye over Lytton's India of famine, plunder and treachery, Annie Besant, rising star of socialism, summed up the mood with a sarcastic sneer. Although 'blessed with an Empress, an English Moguless, Lady Paramount of all mere native rulers', the Indian people 'do not love us, and they are not content with our sway'.[74] A damning verdict on Lytton's *annus mirablis* of 1877, it was a partial one for all that. Across India, away from the main event at Delhi, the cult of Queen Victoria was alive and well.

Crown Orders

While Lytton was proclaiming her new title to thousands in Delhi, the queen sat down to a small celebration dinner party of her own at Windsor Castle. Around the table were some of her immediate family and courtiers, including Disraeli. Lytton had telegraphed earlier with news of the proceedings at Delhi, and she had already used her new signature for the first time: 'V. R. & I.' That evening she wore only Indian jewels: the Star of India and the pearls, diamonds and rubies that had been gifted to her via the Prince of Wales from the Maharajas of Indore and Gwalior, and from Sir Jung Bahadur, the prime minister of Nepal. Arthur, her son, led the toast, 'to the Queen and Empress of India'.[75] It was a quiet affair but there was no dampening of the queen's enthusiasm for India.

India, and the role of the Crown in India, was plunged into further controversy in 1878, as Disraeli's ministry manoeuvred for position around the 'eastern question', attempting to check Russian influence on either side of the enfeebled Ottoman Empire. Matters came to a head at the Berlin congress of the European powers held in the midsummer. From the east, in India, Lytton switched from diplomacy to armed intervention in an attempt to counter Russian influence over the Emir of Afghanistan. And, from the west, ostensibly to protect Constantinople, Britain augmented its forces in the Mediterranean. A large contingent of some 5,000 Indian cavalry and troops arrived in Malta in May 1878, and, when the diplomats at Berlin agreed that the island of Cyprus should come under British protection, the India regiments were sent there. In his usual blithe way, Disraeli assured the queen that the acquisition of Cyprus was vital, as it meant the 'welding together' of the

Indian empire with Britain.[76] It became a family affair. The Duke of Cambridge, the queen's cousin and commander-in-chief of the Forces, went out to inspect the troops, including the Indian contingent. Prince Alfred sailed by in his yacht, and, most significantly of all, the Duke of Connaught led his own regiment during the occupation of the island.[77] At home the Indian empire was swept up into the anti-Russian warmongering mood of the moment, as jingoistic songs rang out in the music halls, and cartoonists punned and penned away, depicting the carving-up of Turkey, lest Russia's predatory instincts were repelled.[78] Without much effort (or indeed resistance) on her part, Queen Victoria was once again being identified as a 'warrior queen'.

One man was not amused. William Gladstone, leader of the opposition, stepped up the Liberal attack on Disraeli's foreign policy towards the end of 1878 as war unfolded in Afghanistan. As in 1839 the British responded to the appearance of a Russian envoy in Kabul by despatching a force to fight the emir, Sher Ali Khan, once he made it clear he would not accept a similar delegation from British India.[79] This aggressive move was very much Lytton's own. He skirted around both political and military advice in India. Lytton justified the forward policy to the queen and kept her informed at every stage.[80] Although the emir died, and his son, Mohammad Yaqub Khan, signed a treaty agreement with the British in May 1879, war broke out again later in the year, when the new emir's younger brother, Ayub Khan, led a rebellion, forcing the emir's abdication and taking over rule for himself. Ayub Khan was a different proposition from his brother. His forces defeated the British and Indian troops at Maiwand in July 1880, and he laid siege to Kandahar later that year. In dealing with the new emir, who was eventually seen off by troops under the command of Major-General Frederick Roberts, Lytton was once more instrumental in making decisions about strategy and tactics, which he reported directly to Victoria.[81] Gladstone was appalled, accusing Disraeli of 'abridging the rights of Parliament' by making use of the treaty- and war-making powers of the Crown to invade Afghanistan.[82] If this was the new imperial style, then it was time to put the genie back in the lamp.

In this way, the Afghan war became central to the general election, held in the spring of 1880. There was much debate too about the queen's new title and the different tone it had given to foreign and imperial policy under Disraeli. Once the outcome of the election was known – a sizeable majority for Gladstone's Liberal party – Disraeli and Lytton both resigned on the same day, their Indian foreign policy amongst other things repudiated by the electorate. The queen recorded her state of shock at this news. Not only would she have Gladstone to contend with, but, for the first time since the beginning of her reign, a new Liberal prime minister had appointed a Liberal viceroy. Writing to Lord Hartington, the new secretary of state for India, she voiced fears lest India be mixed up in party politics, as had happened too much of late.[83] Too much party politics, or was the queen simply backing the wrong party?

The Afghan war did not go away with the advent of a new administration under Gladstone. However, the queen cut a lonelier figure in ministerial discussions over the summer of 1880 and beyond. She persistently badgered Hartington over not giving up Kandahar, suggesting at one point that the proclamation of 1858 did not rule out further annexation if necessary.[84] This was an extraordinary interpretation of a document that she and Prince Albert had infused with the language of harmony. When the Cabinet proved resolute and set on withdrawing forces from Kandahar, she insisted that the timing of the announcement be delayed until a stable ruler was in place in Kabul. In particular, she tried to keep any mention of Afghanistan out of the queen's speech at the opening of the 1881 session of Parliament.[85] Ultimately, Gladstone's Cabinet prevailed, and in March 1881, the withdrawal of British forces was confirmed. Later that year, a renewed assault on Kandahar by Ayub Khan was repelled, and relative calm returned to the region.

The queen's stance on Afghanistan was untypically forward, and supplies the only occasion when she personally recommended an extension of her Indian realm. She was emboldened by what she heard from officers returning from the campaign.[86] She undoubtedly felt hubris at Gladstone, his Midlothian campaign, and the way in which he had made her monarchy an election issue. She was rueful over the demise of her prized prime minister, Disraeli, whose last contribution in Parliament was a question in the House of Lords about Kandahar on 18 March (he died on 19 April). Above all, the reawakening of her martial tendencies suggests that she had been taken in to a certain extent by the rhetoric and pretensions of Disraeli and Lytton. They convinced her that the proclamation of her new title had smoothed over criticism of the Crown both in India and Britain, and they impressed upon her just how vulnerable India was in the great power struggles of the late 1870s. Different voices in the queen's ear might have made her less hawkish.

A further legacy of Lytton and Disraeli's foreign policy remained: the bombardment of Alexandria and the subsequent occupation of Egypt late in 1882. Together with France, Britain invaded Egypt in order to depose Ahmed 'Urabi (known by the British as 'Arabi Pasha'), an army colonel who had seized power in 1878.[87] Once more, a large Indian expeditionary force, including 5,700 native officers and troops, was sent via the Suez Canal, with 1,360 kept in reserve at Aden, again under the command of General Sir Herbert Macpherson. The queen's son, the Duke of Connaught, also had a command – as an honorary colonel of the 13th Bengal Lancers – and was active in the battle of Tell-el-Kebir, a role that caused the queen great anxiety, and then relief, when she was able to read aloud his letters written just after the battle had been won. She later commissioned a painting of his heroic role.[88] Queen Victoria proved as proud of her Indian troops as she was of her son. On a 'never-to-be-forgotten day', 18 November 1882, she watched the parade at Horse Guards of the victorious regiments from Egypt, the Bengal Lancers led by the Duke of Connaught.[89] A few days later she met a selection of the officers and men of the Indian contingent – thirty-nine officers, including twelve Indians – and presented them with an Egyptian campaign medal that incorporated, for some of them, a special Tell-el-Kebir clasp.[90] Her old idea of getting 'an Indian guard' to be permanently based at the court was rekindled, and a new scheme took shape: a military command in India for Arthur, her soldier son.

His eyes on a bigger prize, the Duke of Connaught himself first devised the idea of serving in India. Back in September 1881 he told Lord Hartington that, as he wanted eventually to succeed the Duke of Cambridge as commander-in-chief in Britain, some further Indian experience was desirable. An appointment was duly found, as a regimental commander in the North-West Provinces, and Arthur and Louischen, his consort, travelled out in 1882. Queen Victoria pressed for a political officer to accompany the Duke of Connaught so that he might gain a grasp of civil affairs as well as those of the army. Naturally, the Whigs sidestepped that request.[91] The queen bided her time, and waited for the Tories to return to office. In the summer of 1885 she pressed for Arthur to be given a larger challenge, the command of the Bombay army. She solicited support in India, and at home found Lord Salisbury not opposed to the move. All seemed set for the elevation of Prince Arthur to the upper echelons of the armed forces of India.[92] There was a problem. Cometh the hour, cometh Lord Randolph Churchill, Lord Salisbury's secretary of state for India. When he threw a tantrum over the plan to give a command to the Duke of Connaught – only calmed apparently by a dose of calomel – Salisbury was forced to listen. Not only did Churchill oppose the duke's appointment, he was also surprised to find out that the queen communicated directly with her viceroys. A full Cabinet meeting was held, with fourteen out of sixteen supporting Churchill's insistence that the duke could not go to Bombay, as his role would spill over into civil matters and become politicised. 'A good deal annoyed', Queen Victoria accepted an alternative post for Arthur at Rawalpindi. A year later, when Bombay finally fell vacant, Randolph Churchill had moved on and the duke was appointed without any fuss.[93] There, he proved a diligent commander, with some diplomacy thrown in. He joined Governor Reay's Legislative Council, attending only during the sessions of March 1888, never speaking, but casting his vote when required.[94] The Duke of Connaught arrived too late to see action in the queen's latest Indian conquest: Burma, that is to say, the kingdom of Ava. Queen Victoria treated the Burmese annexation as a royal acquisition nonetheless. Apologising for being 'greedy', she asked Lord Dufferin, the viceroy, to find her some jewels to mark the defeat of the Konbaung dynasty. King Thibaw's crown was duly sent on, as well as captured guns, to her evident pleasure.[95] The old warrior instincts were alive and well. Now there was more than just booty to signify the queen's Indian empire. She had at last got her way, her persistence had paid off, and Prince Albert's wishes had been fulfilled. India had a resident royal prince.

In the end, the queen's new title meant more in India than in Britain. Certainly, the British liked empire, but they did not like to be thought of as an imperial people, and they abhorred mixing up their ancient island constitution with the trappings of Continental absolutism. So the queen's title was for export only. In India, the idea of an 'empress' was also a novelty. Lytton did his creative best to mark the inauguration of the new Indian empire. He need not have tried quite so hard. Without too much orchestration from above, the pronouncement of the imperial title in India produced a wave of popular endorsement, presaging new opportunities for co-operation and collaboration with colonial rule, and reform and development under the eye of a watchful matriarch.

CHAPTER 9

MOTHER OF INDIA

'The regeneration of civilisation in India must come from the women,' declared the Duke of Connaught, Queen Victoria's third son, soon after he arrived in India.[1] It was an odd statement for a soldier-prince to make. By the 1880s, the 'woman' question was beginning to dominate Indian social reform movements in India. A variety of issues preoccupied campaigners: the age of consent and the institution of child marriage, the treatment of widows, female education and health, and the control of prostitution in army cantonments (the notorious 'Contagious Diseases' legislation). Some of these were causes particular to India; others were extensions of pressure-group activity back in Britain.[2] The Duke of Connaught's view also embodied western stereotypes about the 'effeminate' Bengali man, and the enervated state of Indian men in general, physically inferior and morally backwards compared to their imperial rulers. From this colonising perspective, it was a small step to envisage a future for India in which women, suitably enlightened by British influence, might lead the way.[3]

Even so, the Duke of Connaught's intervention was unusual. At home, the royal family was not known for intervening in public debates about the place of women in contemporary society. Queen Victoria herself was a confirmed anti-suffragist: she opposed votes for women. She also disliked widowed women who remarried. In India, however, it was a different story. Royals were less restrained. The Duke of Connaught and his consort, Princess Louise of Prussia (known in the family as 'Louischen'), became prominent supporters of opening up the public sphere to Indian women – through schools and hospitals. Queen Victoria herself took an active interest in female education in India, one legacy of which was the large number of schools named after her. She also endorsed the provision and training of European and Indian nurses, an activity channelled through the Countess of Dufferin, whose husband was viceroy between 1884 and 1888. Most significantly of all, Queen Victoria became an unlikely role model for a diverse range of women and women's organisations in late nineteenth-century India, from queens and princesses, to Hindu social reformers, and on to missionary and other European societies active in south Asia in these years. As this chapter describes, in the last quarter of Queen Victoria's reign, the royal touch in India was increasingly a woman's touch.

Widow

With her new status as Queen of India in 1858 quickly followed by the death of Prince Albert at the end of 1861, Queen Victoria's settled image became that of a widow. Widowhood in Britain was a common enough state, although the queen set new standards for grief in the way she observed mourning for the rest of her life. In India, widowhood was even more salient, especially in Hindu culture.[4] This softer image was based on the narrative the queen and her courtiers constructed of her life with and without Albert. The projection of the queen as a devoted widow, continuing the work of her late consort, Prince Albert, did not come from the Government of India, although it observed official mourning on the death of the queen's consort at the end of 1861. Flags were lowered to half-mast, officials and British subjects were expected to dress in black, with the period of mourning effectively extended into the following May, as the queen's birthday ball due towards the end of that month was cancelled. In Bombay a memorial to Albert quickly took shape as the planned 'Victoria Museum' was given an injection of £10,000 by the government and the name of the new institution adjusted accordingly to the 'Victoria and Albert Museum'. Albert was remembered as devoted to the 'nobler branches of the Arts' and the 'humbler classes of a great industrial community'.[5] Indian responses followed. They focused far more on Albert the family man. For example, an 1863 memorial poem, 'largely read by the Gujarati-speaking community' of Bombay presidency, devoted one-third of the whole text to Albert's marriage, children and the education he gave to the Prince of Wales, his son and heir.[6]

However, it was the queen herself who, indirectly, gave the greatest stimulus to the Albert industry in India. India, she told Sir John Lawrence in 1864, was her late husband's sacred legacy. She wished his name to be looked upon with love by her Indian subjects.[7] Telling her version of their life together was a means to this end. In the two decades after his death, three studies of Albert's life and influence were published in England: Charles Grey's *Early Years of the Prince Consort* (1867), the queen's own *Leaves from the Journal of Our Life in the Highlands* (1868) – followed by a further instalment in 1884 – and Theodore Martin's *Life of the Prince Consort*, published in five volumes between 1875 and 1880. Queen Victoria had a hand in all of these. Charles Grey was the prince's former secretary and now the queen's, and his memoir was written under her 'direction'. She used Arthur Helps, clerk to the Privy Council, to prepare her own Highland journals for publication, and in 1866 she commissioned Martin to be the prince's biographer.[8] All three of these works made their way to India. Grey's volume, together with the edition of her Scottish Highland journals, became the queen's gift of choice in the exchange of presents with Indian royalty for the next thirty years. The Highland journals themselves were translated into three Indian editions: into Marathi by Ganapatarava Jadhava in 1871, then into Hindi by the Maharaja of Benares in 1875, and finally into Gujarati by Mancherjee Bhownagree in 1877. *More Leaves from the Journal of Our Life in the Highlands, 1862–1882* was also translated into Gujarati in 1886, and presented by Bhownagree to the queen that year. Martin's biography appeared in an abridged Hindi version in 1892 (replete with a different subtitle in which Prince Albert was described as 'father of the future emperors of India').[9] What image of the royal couple did these narratives convey?

Grey's memoir gave Albert's backstory. *The Early Years of the Prince Consort* was an account of just how well fitted for British royal service the Coburg prince had been on the eve of first meeting Victoria. The book described his schooling and university years, the mentoring given by King Leopold of Belgium, and his tours of central Europe and Italy. It was also an intimate account of their love match, how their courtship was as much a meeting of two hearts as two dynasties. Initially intended for private circulation only, Grey's book went into four editions in its first year, and over time became the queen's preferred memoir of Prince Albert, part romance, part exemplary tale of lives groomed for public service. There was no Indian edition of the memoir, although one was contemplated by William Nassau Lees, principal of the Mohammedan College in Calcutta and part proprietor of the *Times of India*, who assured Grey that a Hindustani translation would give 'Her Majesty's Indian subjects some idea of how a virtuous and good Prince can make his life conducive to the welfare and happiness of the subjects of his sovereign'.[10] Clearly a book with a message.

Leaves from the Journal of Our Life in the Highlands continued the dedicatory tone, but with Queen Victoria now installed alongside her consort, making it a work of pious devotion from a grieving widow, as well as an account of how the royal couple had managed their realm. As its title suggested, *Leaves from . . . the Highlands* was a memoir of family life from the 1840s to the early 1860s, taking in trips to and eventual residence in Scotland, as well as visits to Wales, Ireland, the Channel Islands and Devon and Cornwall, all aboard their paddle-steamer yacht. Readers were given an unusual insight into the private world of the royal family. Victoria and Albert were revealed as caring but controlling parents. The queen noted how she intended to make the Prince of Wales 'Earl of Dublin', and she described the wedding of her eldest daughter Vicky into the Prussian royal family. Prince Albert featured throughout as a renaissance Prince, sharing his knowledge of the topography of Europe as they traversed the glens and lochs of Scotland and the coastline of Ireland. He was also described as a keen mountain-walker and stag-hunter. In addition to being a family portrait, *Leaves from . . . the Highlands* was a travelogue of the closest parts of the queen's dominion. Her commentary highlighted the national differences between the English, the Scots and the Welsh, the variety of topography across the British Isles, and also the loyalty on display in the three nations. Particularly, in the 1840s, when she and Albert made their first visits across the border to Scotland, she described an itinerary that was a scenic tour of the history of Anglo-Scottish warfare down to the union of 1707. The journal was instructive, showing the queen as a devoted wife and mother, and as royal ruler, travelling to all the compass points of her kingdom, realms now united after centuries of strife and rebellion. Published in 1884, *More Leaves from . . . the Highlands* continued the story of 'our life', with Albert's ghostly presence supplying a constant point of reference for Queen Victoria, as she retraced journeys originally undertaken at his side, and recalled examples of his wisdom.

In India, the translations of the queen's works were themselves acts of devotion, presented to Queen Victoria via her sons when they visited India, or in person when the translators were in England.[11] Ornate, illustrated with woodcuts and hand-finished, the Indian editions of the Highland journals were expensive, published by subscription, and so well out of the reach of most Indians. Despite their limited circulation, they broke some new ground. The Marathi edition of the Highland journals included, it claimed, 'for the first time' in such ventures, Hindu ladies amongst its subscribers. The books were intended to furnish lessons. The Gujarati edition was welcomed as showing the duties of princes to the people, 'a fitting pendant to the splendours of the Delhi durbar'.[12] Published in Indian editions either side of the tours of her two sons, the Prince of Wales and Prince Alfred, *Leaves from the Journal of Our Life in the Highlands*, depicted a pious and devoted but active widow. She no longer seemed the 'warrior queen', a genre now re-emerging in stories about the rebel Rhani of Jhansi. Rather, she now belonged to a new trend of public-spirited noble Indian women and queens.[13]

Mother

The princely tours developed another aspect of Queen Victoria's persona in India: that of mother. Mothering her people was partly a religious and educational trope. Missionaries in India used stories of the Christian queen as a handmaiden to their evangelical work – for example, the accounts of the queen's life produced by the Reverend Babu in Tamil and Telugu in the mid-1870s. The apocryphal story of the queen presenting a Bible to an African chief, and attributing 'England's greatness' to Christianity, was retold in a Bengali pamphlet, *Maharanir Sakshya / The Testimony of the Queen*, published by the Christian Tract Society in 1895. And, after Queen Victoria died, 15,000 copies – a huge print run for this kind of ephemera – of *The Queen and her Bible*, another Bengali work, was rushed into print in Calcutta.[14] Queen Victoria's two jubilee years and her death also saw the advent of a spate of Tamil popular biographies destined for a school-age readership, the publicity suggesting they were suitable as prizes, or presents.[15]

However, much of the vernacular print culture also focused on the idea of Queen Victoria as a mother figure. Significantly, as 'mother of India', Queen Victoria emerged around the same time as her native counterpart, 'Bharat Mata' or 'mother India'. Indeed, in the original story of *Bharat Mata*, written by Kiran Chandra Banerjee and published in Bengali in 1873, the feminine character of 'India' is described as petitioning Queen Victoria. Other Bengali publications for the 1870s also placed 'Bharat Mata' alongside the queen, in her role as the source of justice and wisdom.[16] There was no contradiction between idealising India as a nation in the form of a woman under the care of the remote queen as an empress. Indeed, down to her death, prominent Indian reformers, including nationalists, authored popular celebrations of Queen Victoria, revering her domestic virtues. A few examples will suffice. The Hindi writer, Bharatendu Harischandra, who had eulogised Prince Alfred during his passage through Benares in 1870, hailed the queen at the time of Britain's invasion of Egypt in 1882, not least because Indian troops were involved. Another example was Ichharam Surayam Desai, a Gujarati journalist and author of *Hind ane Britannia* (1886), a sharp indictment of British rule. Desai was prosecuted by the British, but that did not stop him penning a jubilee life of the queen in 1887, which dwelled on the moral character of her life as a widow.

Then there was Bipin Chandra Pal, member of the Indian National Congress, who famously broke with the old guard of nationalist leaders in 1905, pushing the movement towards *swadeshi* (home-made goods) and *swaraj* (self-rule). Yet back in 1891 he also produced a life of the queen, praising her private virtues, her kindness towards her subjects and her vow of perpetual widowhood.[17] In each case, latter-day scholars have breezed past these tributes to the queen, sitting awkwardly as they do in the oeuvre of men so associated with the burgeoning of Indian nationalism in the final years of the nineteenth century. As a metaphor for the parental empire, 'mother of India' could rest comfortably, for the moment, alongside the emergent nation.

Sisters

There were not many women wielding power in nineteenth-century India, but those who did found in Queen Victoria their champion.[18] Some had lost power. The annexation policy of Dalhousie and his pre-decessors before 1857 resulted in a long trail of displaced maharani and their families, many of whom were supported in exile with Government of India pensions.[19] At the opposite end of the spectrum, there were states where women ruled outright, most famously Bhopal. Other states experienced the rule of queen regents – notably Rajkot (1862–7), Balrampur (1882–94), Nandgaon (1883–91), Cooch Behar (1857–60, 1863–83) and Mysore (1894–1902) – a stand-in role accepted by the Government of India when the male heir was still in his minority. Across this spectrum of female power in India there was one constant: Queen Victoria as role model.

Sisterly exchange did not begin well. The assumption of power in India in 1858 by a British queen brought a strident riposte from another first lady. Hazrat Mahal, the Begum of Awadh, the first wife of the King of Awadh, issued a 'counter-proclamation' from the 'parents of the people of Oudh'.[20] The begum picked through Queen Victoria's proclamation, pouring scorn on the idea that the queen would honour treaties, tolerate non-Christian religions, observe clemency and forgiveness, and improve the condition of the people. The document challenged the new royal authority, as well as Queen Victoria's status as the motherly queen of the Indian people. There is no evidence that the queen saw the begum's proclamation, and anyway Hazrat Mahal was soon whisked away by the British to silent exile in Nepal. Another female royal took up the chalice, contesting the claims of the 1858 proclamation in a more public fashion. The Rani of Tanjore was the heir apparent to Shivaji II, who died in 1855. In 1860 her supporters accused the queen of disregarding her own promises in her refusal to undo the annexation of Tanjore and allow the succession to take place. Such betrayal was 'so flagrant a falsification of their just and loyal expectations'. Appeals were made on her behalf to the spirit of the 1858 proclamation, the 'Magna Carta' of the Indian chiefs.[21] At the same time, the princess herself adopted a different kind of private diplomacy towards Queen Victoria. Writing to the governor of Madras, she claimed that she revered the queen as her 'mother' and the 'mother of her subjects'.[22] She tried unsuccessfully to get on the itinerary of the Prince of Wales's tour in 1875. Unperturbed she sent on a gift of a gold girdle for Princess Alexandra, and in 1880 she opened a medical school as a memorial to the visit – or, in her case, the visit that never was – of the Prince of Wales.[23] On her death in 1885, the Government of India refused to recognise the claim to the throne of her son.[24] Yet, the Tanjore maharanis continued to observe loyalty to the Crown. This was most conspicuous at the jubilees of 1887 and 1897 and suggests that the queen represented a unique channel of communication, separate from the government. Moreover, there was always the chance of redress, as the treatment of Mysore had shown. Another deposed dynasty, the Bhonsles of Satara in the ghats, south of Poona, made a similar appeal to Queen Victoria in 1874 through the last maharaja's widow, asking the queen, on whom the 'Ruler of the Universe' had conferred the 'sovereignty of the world', to undo the injustice of the East India Company.[25]

The queen was also kept informed about the progress of women in other states. From Travancore in the south of India, Lady Anne Napier, wife of the governor of Madras, described in copious detail to the queen the workings of what was regarded as a reforming princely state. In letters home to the queen, Lady Napier sent on photographs and her own watercolour depictions of Travancore, accompanied by commentary praising the modern dress worn by women in public, and the accomplishments of the daughters of the state's dewan (prime minister). On her return to Britain, Lady Napier travelled directly to stay with the queen at Balmoral, telling her more stories from the south.[26] Travancore women were at the forefront of loyal demonstrations, producing their own separate addresses for the queen for the 1887 jubilee, whilst the Travancore court sent a specially commissioned portrait, by Ravi Varma, of the maharani. Ironically, what Lady Napier did not reveal to Queen Victoria was the fact that the wives of the maharajas of Travancore had no real royal status: they were drawn from a lower caste, and kept apart from the court. So, the portrait sent was of the raja's sister.[27]

The most sustained contact enjoyed by Queen Victoria with female Indian royalty was with the Begums of Bhopal. For over a century, almost continuously, one dynasty of Muslim women ruled the large central Indian state.[28] The first two begums did not observe the purdah. They were well travelled within India, and beyond. Two of them made the pilgrimage to Mecca: Sikander Begum in 1870 and Kaikhusrau Jahan in 1903.[29] Two incidents brought them to wider attention. Firstly, Sikander Begum wrote an account of her trip to the Hajj, originally in Urdu, but translated into English by the wife of the Bhopal agent in 1870, and published in Calcutta and London, stimulating wide interest.[30] Secondly, Shah Jahan travelled to Calcutta to receive the Star of India, an occasion when she was photographed. This striking portrait of the tiny, bejewelled ruler went global.[31] Both Sikander and Shah Jahan sought direct correspondence with Queen Victoria. Shah Jahan authorised the presentation of sculptures in 1854 and Sikander exchanged gifts with the queen and endowed a school named after her in 1867. However, it was during the second reign of Shah Jahan that the relationship really developed. In 1870 Shah Jahan asked Lord Mayo if she might write to the queen, on a monthly basis, in order to practice her English.[32] In 1874 she sent to the queen a series of books: an Urdu history of Bhopal, in which Shah Jahan placed the alliance between Bhopal and the British Crown at the centre of her story, and the account of the Hajj journey of her mother. In return the queen sent her the two works that she had commissioned to remember Albert: Grey's *Early life of the Prince Consort*, and the Highland journal.[33] How might we interpret these exchanges? Even though they never met, the begum was high on the queen's loyalty list. Over twenty years later she recalled her in exact detail to Mary Curzon, who was about to travel to the state.[34] Queen Victoria proved less sympathetic when the begum ran into trouble, sparked by her husband, Siddiq Hasan Khan. He was a noted Islamic scholar, but he was also suspected by the British of being part of the Wahabi movement. In Bhopal he excited jealousy, accused at court of wanting to overthrow his wife's rule. Told of the situation by Lord Dufferin, Queen Victoria criticised her 'foolish marriage'.[35] Clearly, her advice on making the right match had been to no avail.

Queen Victoria wanted to do more than just correspond with the royal women of India. In 1876 she suggested that a new order of honours be established in India exclusively for women. This was the Order of the Crown of India, agreed to by Salisbury and Lytton in the summer of 1877, and intended for notable women of India: female members of the royal family, Indian princely spouses, vicereines and other wives of senior Government of India officials.[36] It was the only order in British history ever to be restricted to women. Although across its existence – no awards were made after 1947 – it became dominated by Europeans (86 out of 109 Companions in total), half of the sixteen awards to Indian women came in the first instalment in 1878. Of these some followed the normal hierarchy of the Indian states: Bamba Singh (the wife of Duleep Singh), the Begums of Bhopal, the Maharani of Mysore, the Gaekwad of Baroda, the Begum Sahiba of Hyderabad. Room was also made for the Princess of Tanjore. And, in a signal that royal marriage was not the only criteria for inclusion in the order, the Maharani of Kasim Bazar, a small estate in northern Bengal, was made a Companion for her contributions to the famine relief campaigns earlier in the decade. Outside of this order, two other Indian women were elevated to maharani for their efforts in the famine relief: Sham Moini of Dinajpur (in Bengal) and Haro Dundari Debia of Siarsol (also in Bengal).[37] As far as the queen was concerned, the native aristocracy of India, so important to the stability of the Raj, included women, even if their role was a minor one. The investiture ceremonies that followed certainly confirmed the secondary status of these women at court.[38] At Hyderabad, the nizam was simply sent a packet containing the regalia and left to pass it on to his consort. At her investiture the Gaekwad of Baroda was screened off, with the wife of the British resident pinning on the new order. In Tanjore there was a more formal event, but the princess's acceptance speech was read out on her behalf. Only in Mysore did the maharani appear in public and read out an address. However, despite their seclusion, there could be no doubting the personal connection that the new order established with the queen. At Kasim Bazar, the maharani read out her acceptance speech in Bengali from behind a screen, praising the queen as the 'monarch of the world' and the 'sovereign Mother of India'.

So, by the time she became empress, Queen Victoria had made links to a small but devoted sisterhood of Indian female rulers. Her Indian royal admirers were reformers, moderately independent in their personal lives, and in the administration of their state. In the next generation, a different type of royal progressive emerged, reformist not so much in power, which they did not exercise, but in their attitudes towards the place of women in Indian society. Two maharani stand out: Suniti Devi, the wife of the Maharaja of Cooch Behar, and Chimnabai, the consort of the Gaekwar of Baroda. Cooch Behar was a small state in the northeast of Bengal. The maharaja married the daughter of Chandra Sen, the leader of the Brahmo Sumaj, an unusual pairing of a Calcutta progressive and a small royal dynasty.[39] Suniti joined her husband in attending the queen's jubilee celebrations in London in the summer of 1887, staying on until the following year. Recalling the visit over three decades later she painted a picture of unconventional intimacy at the English court: face to face kissing on being presented to the queen, and dancing. What was excluded from her later account was also significant – the story of her dress. Already en route to England, she and the maharaja received word that Queen Victoria wished the Indian royal visits to her jubilee to appear in their 'native dress'. For the Cooch Behar couple this presented a slight problem, as they had already been tailored and kitted out in European finery as they passed through Calcutta at the beginning of their trip. Hasty rearrangements were made with tailors en route. When they appeared at court all was in place; that is to say, Suniti wore a sari, but unlike at home her head was uncovered. Never one to miss a trick, the queen noted the substitute clothing – 'a sort of Eastern dress of European materials' – and observed that the maharaja had arrived without his diamonds.[40] The couple's son, inevitably named Victor, was born on their return to Bengal, with Queen Victoria as godmother. Over time Suniti went on to fashion herself as a western-style matriarch at her own court, wearing European dress. She also developed an expertise on the role of women in Indian history. She authored a biography of Buddha's wife, Yasodhara, a study of Rajputana princesses, and an account of women in the *Mahabharata* and the *Ramayana*.[41] Suniti's later verdict on Queen Victoria was fairly formulaic – 'a good wife, a good mother, and a good woman all round' – yet her autobiography places her time spent with the queen as a formative moment in her life, presaging her emergence as a public presence alongside her husband.

An even more globetrotting royal couple were the Gaekwar of Baroda and his second wife, Shrimant Lakshmibai Mohite (1871–1958), who became Chimnabai II on their marriage in 1885. Sayajirao had been placed on the *gaddi* (throne) of Baroda following the infamous attempt to murder the British resident Colonel Phayre. Chimnabai was in purdah. As a couple, they too met with the queen, on two occasions, in 1892 and 1900.[42] As the Gaekwar described in an article published after their second visit, Chimnabai 'enjoys [in Britain] to the full the liberty she lacks in Baroda', where women remained in seclusion, and 'not even myself can at the present time lift up the veil'.[43] Chimnabai herself developed this narrative of European modernity and Indian conservatism into a political programme. Her encyclopaedic primer for social reform led by women, *The Position of Women in Indian Life*, published in 1911 to coincide with the coronation of George V and Queen Mary, had royal exemplars leading the way: Razia Begum (the Sultana of Delhi in the thirteenth century), Nur Jahan (the wife of Jahangir), Ahalya Bai (the Queen of Malwa in the eighteenth century), the present Begum of Bhopal, and Queen Victoria, under whose 'sway' the greatest empire the world had ever known had expanded.[44] Chimnabai went on to become an influential voice in the women's movement in India, supporting the Gaekwar's efforts to open up education to girls in Baroda. In these ways, courtly encounters with Queen Victoria served as important rites of passage for a younger generation of royal women in India, signifying their membership of a small club of consorts.

Daughters

Revered as a mother of India, Queen Victoria was careful not to be drawn into the politics of gender. The woman question in India took centre stage as philanthropists in Britain developed India as a field of mission, and predominantly Hindu reform movements in India challenged the traditions of caste and family life. The queen's own interest in the condition of women in India dated back to the late 1860s. In 1867 she met Manockjee Cursetjee, on a visit to London, drumming up support for schools in Bombay.[45] The following year she was introduced to Mary Carpenter, pioneer of the 'ragged' school movement in England, who also travelled to India.[46] And in 1870 Keshub Chandra Sen, of the Brahmo Sumaj, visited the Palace.[47] These meetings bore fruit. In 1870 Carpenter established the National Indian Association in London, with Sen leading the partner organisation in India. Amongst its aims was the raising of support and awareness of schools for girls in India, a project that was secular in character, explained Carpenter, upholding the queen's pledge of 1858 not to interfere in Indian religion.[48] In 1874, Queen Victoria deputed her second daughter, Alice, to be president of the NIA, an honorary role fulfilled from afar in Darmstadt in Hesse, where she was consort to Louis IV, the Grand Duke of Hesse, until her death four years later. In India, Mary Carpenter continually used the name of the queen to support her activities. In 1876 she presented the queen's Highland journals as gifts on her travels and brought home addresses and small tokens of gratitude for the queen from her trip.[49]

A decade later, the queen's daughter-in-law, Louise, the Duchess of Connaught, took up the cause. The only female royal ever to have lived in India, until Edwina Mountbatten arrived for a brief stay in 1947,

Louischen played an active auxiliary role alongside her husband when he was based in Poona and Bombay as commander-in chief of the Bombay army. They both learned Hindi and tried it out in public. Louischen joined the Bombay governor's forceful wife, Lady Reay, in fundraising in the city for schools and hospitals, coming to know the Sorabji family, who were the mainstay of the Poona Female Training College, and of the Victoria High School, which opened in September 1888. Some of this she described in detail to the queen in regular letters home.[50] Most significant, however, was her support for female education. In addition to aiding the Sorabjis, she made a series of visits around the presidency to see female training colleges. On these occasions it was usually her husband who spoke on her behalf, the duke explaining that she in turn was speaking on behalf of the queen. On one occasion – at Rajkot in 1889 – this ventriloquism was dispensed with, and Louischen spoke in public, probably the only female member of the queen's wider family to do so in her lifetime.[51] In this way, through the patronage first of Mary Carpenter and then of her own family, Queen Victoria's name was associated with the development of Indian schools for girls and young women.

Another Indian female cause to which the queen gave her blessing was nursing and the provision of hospitals for women in India, especially pregnant women. In 1882, Lord Ripon, the viceroy of India, had passed on to the queen the evidence of Pandita Ramabai, given to a government enquiry, about the problems in providing expert maternity care.[52] This testimony was followed up in 1883 by the dramatic case of the Maharani of Panna, who petitioned the queen via an English missionary, Elizabeth Bielby. The queen was sympathetic, but wary of becoming caught up with missionary endeavour. The episode turned complicated and toxic when it became clear that maharaja and maharani were at odds, and that Miss Bielby was a loose cannon.[53] However, the idea was planted. Two years later, Queen Victoria met with another pioneer, Mary Scharlieb, and, with no missionary in sight, gave full endorsement to her work in Madras, becoming patron of Scharlieb's Caste Hospital for Women in the city. The queen's 'moral influence' was deemed indispensable to this venture.[54] Around the same time,

Queen Victoria gained a new ally in the reform of Indian nursing at the seat of the Indian government in the person of Lady Dufferin, who accompanied her husband, the new viceroy, out to India at the end of 1884. Before she left, there was the customary audience with the queen.[55] Once Lady Dufferin had arrived in Calcutta, and then Simla, her ideas took shape.

The 'National Association for Supplying Female Medical Aid to the Women of India', or the 'Countess of Dufferin Fund' as it became known, was the single largest project of philanthropy outside Britain to which the queen's name was attached in her lifetime. Henry Ponsonby, her private secretary, hinted at its magnitude, probably unintentionally, referring to it as the 'Women of India Fund'.[56] The Fund raised money both for medical schools and hospitals, specifically to train up Indian nurses who would then work in dedicated women's hospitals. Launched in July 1885, the project was emphatic in its neutrality on questions of race and religion. Missionaries would not be employed, and, although English women and men would be hired as medical teachers and senior staff in the hospitals, the bulk of the investment would go into the future education of Indian nursing expertise.[57] Initially, Lady Dufferin did not risk associating the queen's name with a start-up scheme. However, within a few days, the queen had insisted that she do so. Once royal assent was granted, the queen became part of the brand image. Her own contribution was modest – £100 – but a 'Queen-Empress Gold Medal' was struck using that sum, and given as a prize to the best students.[58] In 1887, with the queen's backing, Lady Dufferin led a widely publicised drive for donations, using the golden jubilee celebrations as the draw. Income from donations leapt from around £650 to £3,500 within the space of twelve months.[59]

Over the next decade or so, the 'Countess of Dufferin Fund' grew in size and reach, with successive vicereines – Lady Lansdowne, Countess Elgin and Lady Curzon – all presiding over the scheme. By 1896, seventy hospitals had been established and around 3 million women had been treated. On Lady Dufferin's return to Britain in 1888 she set up a UK branch, with another royal, the Princess of Wales, as president.[60] The medical establishment in Britain sniped at its work, deeming it amateurish. The queen's physician Joseph Fayrer chipped in with objections too.[61] Over time the Fund has been criticised as an example of Victorian bourgeois do-gooding, shipped out, all its prejudices intact, to India. However, it was a success, not least because of the queen's patronage. As the hike in donations at the time of the golden jubilee in 1887 demonstrated, substantial support came in precisely because the queen gave her backing.[62] The Fund was careful to uphold the queen's 1858 pledge – the principle of non-sectarian support – taking action against local branches that employed missionaries as teachers or doctors, and coming down hard on any reports of proselytising.[63] Despite the exhortation to draw back the purdah, included in Rudyard Kipling's poem, 'For the Women' (1887), penned for the opening of Lady Aitchison's hospital in Lahore, lifting the veil was never part of the organisation's modus operandi.[64] More than anything else, the Fund ensured that the queen was revered as a caring monarch. In the longer term the Fund left a legacy of memorial hospitals and nursing scholarship funds patronised by the monarch. The Fund also created a problem: the royal touch could be decisive, and there were many other causes deserving of the queen's patronage.

For, as the 'mother of India', a flood of claims now arrived at the queen's door. Religion could hardly be set on one side with many of them. Campaigners for change in the law applying to child-widows appealed to the queen, with a concerted attempt in 1887 to gatecrash the golden jubilee. Reformers took up the case of Rukhmabai, a child bride (now grown-up), making a direct call on the queen to intervene and change the law by decree. Behramji Malabari, one of the Indian supporters of Rukhmabai, claimed in the *Indian Spectator* that the queen stood for 'free' and not enforced widowhood: she 'has been a living Sati all these years'. He also pointed out that the queen herself was the daughter of a widow who had remarried.[65] The 'Rukhmabai Defence Committee', led by Mancherjee Bhownagree and others, including Adelaide Manning of the National India Association, tried to raise sufficient funding to take the case to the Privy Council, where the queen was advised on cases brought for appeal, and by such pressure shame Lord Dufferin, the viceroy, into taking action.[66] Three years later, the campaign revived when Malabari visited England and a women's petition bearing hundreds of signatures was presented to the queen. Despite the mediation of Manning at the India Office, Ponsonby refused to let the queen's name be used as an endorsement on the grounds that it would offend Hindu opinion in India.[67] Even without getting involved, the queen was assumed to have a direct interest in the issue.

Purdah was another Indian convention in which Queen Victoria declined to interfere. Emancipating Hindu and Muslim women from domestic seclusion became one of the western missionary societies' principal campaigns of the late nineteenth century.[68] The queen was held out as an example of a widow who lived out her virtuous life in public, invoked in vernacular biographies circulated by evangelicals, in homely anecdotes retold in stories of missionary labours and in instructive literature aimed at women. For example, reworking an episode from the queen's *More Leaves*, one missionary used a picture of her reading the Bible to a sick old man as a lecture aid.[69] The *Telugu Zenana Magazine*, a reforming periodical published in Madras, began its first issue with a feature on the queen.[70] As with the agitation around Rukhmabai, missionaries tried to cash in on the queen's two jubilees. In 1887 in Delhi, the Baptist Missionary Society held a 'ladies durbar', attended by over 700 women in purdah, together with girls and boys from zenana schools, each of the children given medals stamped with the insignia of the queen.[71] Significantly, the queen *did* give tacit support to breaking the custom of purdah in China. In 1897 Queen Victoria accepted two tracts documenting the conditions of Chinese women from the Church of England Zenana Mission Society, but there is no record that she was ever presented with equivalent literature about India.[72] Queen Victoria was of course no stranger to the zenana. She had met the Begum of Awadh back in 1856; during 1885 Lady Dufferin described in her letters home her own visits to Indian women in purdah; whilst the Duchess of Connaught passed on to the queen her account of Brahmo Sumaj ladies who opposed purdah.[73] Safely returned from India, the Duke of Connaught turned out for the Bible Society, endorsing its stance on reforming the zenana.[74] However, as the missionaries knew full well, in

India, the queen's own hand was invisible. For example, in 1890, Charles Townsend, a visiting Baptist and Liberal party activist, complained of a pamphlet he had been given on his arrival. Drawn up by a *panchayat* of *pandits* and translated into many vernaculars, it reminded 'All Faithful Hindoos' that the queen's proclamation of 1858 guaranteed religious neutrality, and therefore she could be counted on to stop the activities of lady missionaries in the zenanas.[75]

In these ways female missionaries tried to work the queen's famed omnipotence to their advantage, just as their male counterparts were attempting the same over alcohol and opium. There were other instances of this tactic. Opponents of the Contagious Diseases regulations, introduced in India in cantonment towns in the 1860s, circulated the rumour that the queen was opposed to the measure, her concern heightened as she had daughters of her own.[76] However, Queen Victoria kept out of the missionary mania generally, no more so than when it touched upon religious sensitivities around the domestic sphere, keen as she was to avoid the evangelical fervour that had beset India before 1857. Her courtiers understood these limits, being careful to lend her name to schemes of education and nursing that were modernising, but not invasive of Indian culture. The queen's reputation as a benign matriarch remained intact. Her reputation for philanthropy grew without undermining her status as a totem of toleration.[77] Social reformers were not the only ones mobilising the queen. As 'mother of India', she became central to the Indian political imaginary as well.

CHAPTER 10

PATRIOT QUEEN

The murder of Lord Mayo, her fourth viceroy, in February 1872 shocked Queen Victoria. The news was telegraphed direct to Windsor Castle four days after the fatal attack at Port Blair on the Andaman Islands in the Bay of Bengal, a British penal settlement. She pasted the telegram into her journal.[1] Mayo's assailant, Sher Ali Afridi, was assumed to be a Wahabi, an Islamic sect, some of whose followers were committed to jihad. Three months earlier, one of Mayo's senior colleagues, John Paxton Norman, the chief justice of the Calcutta High Court, had also been killed, on the steps of the Town Hall by a suspected Wahabi, a Punjabi named Abdullah. In the event neither assassin was proved to be a jihadist. But the panic over Muslim 'fanaticism' was unabated and undiscriminating. In 1871, in an inquiry commissioned by Lord Mayo, it was claimed that several fatwas had even been issued against the queen herself.[2] Her alarm lingered over several months, from receiving the telegram accounts of Mayo's death in February, through to May, when Mayo's widow came to Windsor and recounted the viceroy's dying moments, and on into August, when she met with Major Owen Tudor Burne, Mayo's private secretary, who had been at his side when he was slain. Burne told the queen that 'powerful Wahabees at Calcutta' were behind the deadly deed.[3] Safe haven at court was found for both: Lady Mayo became a lady-in-waiting, and Burne was taken on as Argyll's political aide-de-camp.

Political assassinations were in fact rare in India. There were only three more such killings during Queen Victoria's reign, all in 1897, described in the next chapter. Queen Victoria stood more chance of being assassinated at home in Britain than her representatives did in India. She survived eight attempts on her life.[4] In contrast India simmered with loyalism throughout her years of direct rule, conditional at times, but instant when required. When the queen survived her eighth assassination attempt in 1882, over 100 memorials and addresses poured in from India to congratulate her on her escape. Nationalism in India never assumed the violent or separatist form that it did in other parts of the British Empire such as Ireland. Indeed, the nascent years of Indian nationalism saw the apotheosis of Queen Victoria's popularity. Why was this so? This chapter explores the place of Queen Victoria within early Indian nationalism, in both its Hindu and Muslim variants. It also considers a different kind of nationalism – the views of the Anglo-Indian community – which were never more virulent than in 1883, when the reforming viceroy, Lord Ripon, tried to increase Indian representation in the judicial system. For the queen had many Indian subjects, only some proved to be less subject than others.

Voices of India

By holding out a broader definition of imperial subjectivity, the queen's proclamation of 1858 gave new life to Indian reformers. The language of loyalty and adherence to the royal pledge became a conspicuous element in the rhetoric of Indian patriotism in the 1860s and 1870s, both amongst Hindus and Muslims. Before the rebellion of 1857 the queen had hardly figured in the petitions and memorials sent to Britain from civic and political associations in India. After 1858 she was rarely absent. The British Indian Association of Calcutta, founded in 1851 by Bengali *zamindars* and the city's merchants, registered this transformation. The BIA was most fulsome in its praise for the queen, hailing 'with delight the proclamation of our gracious sovereign whereby she assumed the direct administration of her Asiatic empire'. The editor of the BIA's mouthpiece, the *Hindu Patriot* (est. 1853), Kristo Das Pal, penned anonymously a pamphlet declaring Hindu fidelity to the queen, and it was he who wrote the 'native' address presented to the Prince of Wales during his stay in Calcutta in 1875–6.[5] Such sentiments were not limited to Bengal, coming from further afield too. For example, faith in the words of the queen came from the Indian members of the East India Association, an organisation set up in 1868. For example, Dadabhai Naoroji, later one of the first Indian MPs in Parliament, invoked the proclamation of 1858 in his plea for Indian reform.[6] There was something exclusively Indian about the idea of the queen as a benign force, looking out for the interests of her subjects overseas.

Of late, historians have not been sympathetic to these early genera-tions of Indian nationalists. Their place in the pantheon of patriots and martyrs of the modern Indian republic is uncertain. Not only was theirs the voice of an elite, but they modelled their political aspirations on a western European version of nationalism.[7] Conditions for nationalism in India were there – through the expansion of education, urbanisation and the opening up of the public sphere – yet it was a slow-burning process, not least because its leaders were so wrapped up in playing the game the British way.[8] Such a way of writing the early history of Indian nationalism throws out the baby with the bath water. There was nothing automatic about devotion to the Crown. It was there for a reason. The proclamation of 1858 was the only statement of its kind in the world, in which a monarch made a pledge to a subject population. Loyalism was deployed as a political device, a language of politics, enabling Indian reformers to push back the envelope of colonial power as much as possible.

After 1858 the queen became more important than the British Parliament for many Indian reformers. The language of the queen's proclamation of 1858 had asserted a direct relationship between monarch and Indian subject: were not Indians and Britons in India therefore entitled to expect a royal remedy to their problems? Such a claim was tested in 1871 when a petition of grievances was sent from India. Co-ordinated from Kanpur, the petition had been signed by hundreds of townspeople, Indian and European, from across the North-West Provinces.[9] Although the petition was discussed in Parliament, it was addressed to the queen. She was requested to set up a commission to investigate a long list of concerns: the Indian financial deficit, the public works programme, the income tax, the powers of the viceroy and the composition of his Legislative Council, and the state of the Indian army. Despite a powerful speech by Henry Fawcett, the radical MP for Brighton, the House of Commons refused the request for a Royal Commission on India. Liberals – Fawcett's own party – argued that as a parliamentary select committee on Indian finances had just been established, there was no need for a Royal Commission. It was a significant rebuke. Despite the transfer of power, Parliament jealously guarded its privileges, and, in Britain, that meant restraining the prerogative powers of the Crown. There would be no royal initiative.

Here lay a curious paradox, one that would dominate Anglo-Indian radical politics until independence in 1947. The most doughty proponents of Indian reform in Britain were themselves no lovers of royalty. As the honorific title of 'MP for India' transferred from one radical to the next – John Bright to Henry Fawcett to Charles Bradlaugh – it passed from the mildly republican end of the spectrum to the most extreme. A dialogue of the deaf ensued. Much of the explicit loyalism to the Crown that was a marked feature of the reform movement in India became diluted in the metropole. The cause of India was pressed into the mould of domestic radicalism, or it was hitched to the cause of the Irish Home rule, which was much further than most Indians wished to go. The queen's proclamation of 1858 was never mentioned by British friends of India. So when the first Indians came forward as candidates for Parliament in Britain, they did so under the auspices of advanced radicalism, their loyalism to the queen held in check. The first campaign came in 1885 – that of Lalmohan Ghose at Deptford. Then, in 1886, Ghose stood once more, and was again unsuccessful, as was Naoroji. Naoroji made his credentials clear – 'I am an Indian subject of the Queen' – and stated his aspiration to be the representation of 250 million people. But in his campaign he stuck to English issues, home rule and the like, and made no reference to India.[10] To be taken seriously as radicals in Britain, Indians left their loyalism at home.

Back in India, however, loyalism and radicalism remained in tandem, even when a more critical tone developed during the years of Lord Lytton's viceroyalty. Take, for example, the Poona Sarvajanki Sabha, founded in 1878, and often seen as the birthplace of Indian nationalism. The Poona Sabha's starting point was the 'broken pledges' of the 1833 Charter and of the 1858 proclamation regarding Indian entry into the Civil Service. It also condemned the way in which Lytton's famine policy had deviated from the paternalistic promises made in the queen's speech at the opening of Parliament in 1877. In 1880 the Poona Sabha issued an 'Address to the free electors of the United Kingdom', decrying the Government of India's 'contravention of Parliamentary Statutes and Royal proclamations', and, when a Liberal parliamentary majority was secured, the Sabha issued another address, including amongst its many demands a 'royal' commission of inquiry into Indian affairs.[11] *The Bengalee* took imperial loyalism to a different level, stating in 1877 that, if only Queen Victoria would visit India, she would awaken a semi-dormant 'loyalty to her person as distinguished from loyalty to the throne – such as has rarely been witnessed since the day when Germans, Magyars, Croats and Slavs exclaimed with one voice that they would stand by their King [*sic*] Maria-Theresa, an Empress Queen like ours?'[12] Loyalism did not come more effusive than this.

Muslim leaders in India also pledged allegiance to the queen after 1858. At the time of the 1857 rebellion, there was a widely held British view that the uprising was an Islamic jihad, not least because the mutineers placed the last Mughal king, Bahadur Shah, back on his throne at Delhi. In that context, loyal Muslims had a steeper hill to climb than Hindus, for, not unlike English Catholics in the same era, they needed to demonstrate that their loyalty to the head of their faith could coincide with their allegiance to the Crown. The most eloquent and persistent proponent of Muslim loyalism during Queen Victoria's reign was Syed Ahmed Khan, a lawyer and educationist, who had worked for the East India Company before 1857, and whose father and grandfather had both served in the Mughal court at Delhi in its twilight years.

In the aftermath of the 1857 uprising Syed Khan took on the leading English historian of the mutiny, John Kaye, and challenged his claims that Muslim disloyalty lay at the heart of the revolt. Syed Khan's privately printed pamphlet pointed up the causes of rebellion: ignorance, neglect, interference by the British, misunderstanding by Indians, but not disloyalty founded on Islamic ideology. Syed Khan welcomed the queen's proclamation of 1858. It was 'merciful and considerate', possibly even of divine origin, he wrote.[13] A decade or so later, at the height of the Wahabi panic in the early 1870s, Syed Khan restated the grounds of Muslim loyalty to the Crown. William Hunter, stalwart of the viceregal administration, had written a provocative pamphlet questioning whether Muslims could ever be loyal subjects of the queen. Hunter argued that Sunni Muslims owed their loyalty to an extra-territorial power, the Sultan of Turkey, head of the Islamic caliphate. Syed Khan carefully unpicked Hunter's argument, demonstrating that there was no contradiction in Indian Muslims being faithful to their own religion as well as to Queen Victoria.[14] The same case was put even more strongly by the Mahomedan Literary Society of Calcutta two years earlier. Speakers at one of its monthly meetings concluded that India was a true state of *Darul Islam* despite the Christian Queen Victoria being the sovereign. Under the queen's protection Muslims were free to worship according to their faith. Moreover, Queen Victoria was the staunchest ally of the Sultan of Turkey. She had received him at her court, and on more than one occasion her government had taken his side against Tsarist Russia. To undertake jihad against the British in India would therefore be to break faith with the caliphate.[15] In this way Muslim loyalty was far less conditional than that of Hindu nationalists: it sought fuller inclusion in the Raj, rather than further constitutional reform.

Indian Muslim associations looked to the queen as their guardian. Education and not political activity became their route to imperial citizenship. Syed Khan led a campaign to set up college at Aligarh for young Muslim men, an enterprise that he declared would be under the 'protection of the Empress'. Funding came in from the Government of India, and from the leaders of several princely states, Muslim and Hindu alike: the Nizam of Hyderabad, the Nawab of Rampur, the Maharajas of Benares and Vizanagram, amongst others. On 8 January 1877, the new Mohammedan Anglo-Oriental College opened its doors, the ceremony performed by Lord Lytton, en route back to Calcutta from the Imperial Assemblage, giving the queen's new title of empress its first official outing after the proclamation a week earlier. Twenty years later the college was going strong: twenty-four staff, across the college and its school annexe, with over four hundred pupils.[16] Here was loyalty to the Crown based on working with, and not against, the Raj. At the opening ceremony of the College, Syed Khan described Indian Muslims as 'useful subjects of the Crown', their loyalty stemming not from 'servile submission', but because of a 'genuine appreciation of the blessings of good government'. His son went further – for him there was no distinction between the government and the queen: 'British rule in India and the person of the Empress were one and the same thing.'[17]

So there was a gulf of difference between Hindu and Muslim loyalism in the quarter-century after 1858. In each case, however, the queen was central and not incidental to their schemes. For Hindu nationalists the queen, in the shape of the 1858 proclamation, provided the very justification for political activity. For Muslims, the queen offered protection as they ventured into the public sphere through educational reform. Performing loyalty to the Crown became a tried and trusted means of asserting an Indian presence in the civic spaces allowed by the Raj. At no time was this better exemplified than in the outpouring of sentiment at the time of Queen Victoria's escape from assassination in March 1882. Aside from the two jubilees of 1887 and 1897 this was the single largest volley of memorials sent to Queen Victoria from India.[18] They came from all over India, without official intervention, mainly from princes, chambers of commerce and municipal associations. Conspicuous amongst the memorialists were two associations from the vanguard of Muslim and Hindu associational life: the Mahomedan Literary Society of Calcutta, and the residents of Poona, seedbed of Hindu nationalism.[19] To understand the wave of loyalism to the queen-empress at this particular moment, we need to turn to the viceroyalty of Lord Ripon.

Ripon engel appan[20]

There were not many radical viceroys in the British Raj. Arguably, there was only ever one: George Robinson, the 1st Earl of Ripon. Sandwiched between two Tories, Lords Lytton and Dufferin, and selected by William Gladstone, whose own tiptoeing towards radicalism had by the 1880s become a sprint, Ripon's appointment 'astounded' Queen Victoria. Never before had she had to contend with such a clean slate: a new Liberal government at home and a new Liberal government in India. Elevated to the House of Lords in 1871, Ripon's politics and his faith seemed to take one unconventional turn after another, as he converted to Catholicism, embraced the co-operative movement, and supported the moderate strain of Irish nationalism.[21] Arriving in India in June 1880 he made it clear that he had come with his liberal baggage intact. The new viceroy told the Poona Sabha that he would honour Lord Canning's treaty *sannads* granted to the Indian chiefs in the 1860s. He promised the Corporation of Calcutta that he would treat the queen's subjects in India 'with the same equal justice, the same consideration, and the same regard for their interests' as 'the Englishmen who dwell most near to her throne'. And he assured the Mahomedan Literary Society of Calcutta that he would act 'strictly upon the Queen's Proclamation' in regard to religious impartiality.[22] Ripon quickly got down to work, undoing some of Lytton's legislation, and introducing much of his own. Out went the unpopular (and largely ineffective) Vernacular Press Act of 1878. In came India's first factory legislation. Commissions were tasked with reforming agricultural conditions in Bengal, and improving education. Ripon tampered with the Arms Act, another Lytton measure of 1878, and the bane of Indian nationalists. Fighting off the views of his own council, he reduced the salt tax.[23]

Two measures in particular cemented Ripon's reputation as a reformer. Firstly, in May 1882, Ripon's council introduced an elective element to local government in the provinces of India, devolved responsibility for public works, education and financial administration, and gave further tax-raising powers to municipal, district and local boards.[24] It was the first major concession of representative institutions by the British in

India, although over time the process of adoption was drawn out and choked by official resistance. 'Ripon' town halls and other municipal edifices were erected, most strikingly at Madras, but also at Multan in the Punjab. Secondly, and more controversially, Ripon attempted to resolve the issue as to whether native Indian judges could preside over the trials of Europeans in the district courts. The Criminal Procedure Amendment Bill, or the 'Ilbert bill' as it quickly became known, denoting the name of the legal member of the Viceroy's Council, Courtenay Ilbert, who was charged with drafting the legislation, broke with tradition. Since Thomas Babington's Macaulay's ruling of 1836 – the so-called 'Black Acts' – native magistracy had operated in civil cases in the provincial or *mofussil* courts, although not in the presidency towns of Bombay, Calcutta and Madras. But native judges were effectively excluded from criminal courts with jurisdiction over Europeans. By 1883, it was clear that action needed to be taken. The first qualified Indians had now completed the twenty years of Indian Civil Service required before they were eligible for appointment to the higher grade of magistrate, and there was now no legal bar to them judging all cases. It all seemed quite straightforward. Ilbert, a doyen amongst parliamentary draughtsmen, the viceroy's legal adviser, was asked to prepare an amendment that simply adjusted the judiciary to the passage of time.[25] The most civil of civil servants, Ilbert cannot have expected to go down in history as the instigator of legislation that triggered the loudest European backlash of the Raj.

Opposition to the Ilbert bill was fiercest in Calcutta and across Bengal more generally. In March 1883, the European and Anglo-Indian Defence Association was formed in Calcutta to co-ordinate petitions and other pressure-group opposition. The queen's proclamation of 1858, and native Indian faith in its promises, came under fire. The language of the proclamation, declared the anti-Ilbert bill memorialists, had only been 'guarded', leaving everything to political expedient, and to the 'unfettered discretion of the Government'. It was a 'specious sophism' to change the law just because Indians held the queen's words in such high regard. Besides, Englishmen in India had a Magna Carta of their own, that of 1215, and it spelled out the inalienable rights of the Englishman before the law.[26] As during previous moral panics, European women were deemed to be at peril, with much attention drawn to a recent case of a white women being raped. Most highly prized within the agitation of Calcutta Europeans was the petition to the viceroy from the English ladies of Bihar, who pointed out they that too 'had been confided to the care of the Queen'. The appeal from women to their queen, suggested *Som Prakash*, a Bengali newspaper published in Changripotta (Shubhashgram), might influence her unduly.[27] Indians pleaded that their patriotism was more powerful, claiming that the Ilbert bill fulfilled the pledges of the queen's 1858 proclamation, a far more important 'Magna Carta' than the document of 1215, which only applied to England.[28] A neat irony: the 1858 proclamation was, after all, exclusively designed for India.

Simultaneously, criticism came from Britain as well. One of Ilbert's predecessors as legal member of the Viceroy's Council and now a High Court judge in London, James Fitzjames Stephen penned a series of letters to *The Times*. He queried Ilbert's credentials for the job, and stated that the queen's proclamation had 'no legal force whatever'.[29] The leader of the opposition, Lord Salisbury, stepped in too, warning a Birmingham audience at the end of March of the danger of a man of colour judging a white person. Salisbury's Conservative party went on to compile a dossier against all of Ripon's policies to date, bundling in local government reform and the Bengal land commission.[30] Ample publicity was given in Britain to the Calcutta campaign, with most of the missives being republished in London. In turn, the radical wing of the Liberal party leaped to Ripon's deference.[31] So, by the time the Viceroy's Council returned to its business in May, there was a full-blown reaction against the Ilbert bill in India and a partisan free-for-all raging in Britain. For Ripon and Ilbert it was the opposition in India that weighed most heavily. Ilbert knew that changes were necessary but he wished to keep the principle of the bill.[32] Eventually, a compromise was reached, with white defendants retaining the right to have a jury with at least half its membership comprising fellow Europeans. Ilbert and Ripon, as well as some of the Indian members of the Legislative Council, held out for the principles of the queen's proclamation, but they were in the minority.[33] The colour bar was restored.

Queen Victoria watched on with increasing 'alarm' as the Ilbert bill unravelled: 'so contrary', she informed Ripon, 'to the expectations which were entertained beforehand of it'. In her first response in late April, Ponsonby told Ripon on the queen's behalf that she did not think he had brought forward the bill 'rashly'. However, she havered over whom to blame. Lord Kimberley, the secretary of state for India, had suggested to her in May that it was an 'injudicious' measure, and she herself told Ripon that the feelings of the European community might have been ascertained before Ilbert made his proposal. She hoped Ripon might modify the bill 'so as to prevent the bitter antagonism of races', feelings that had recently shown a 'decided improvement'.[34] As the bill was being revised during the autumn Queen Victoria wrote again to Ripon, sharing her hopes that the Duke of Connaught's impending visit to Calcutta might 'smooth feelings of antagonism and bitterness'. At the same time, Ponsonby made discreet enquiries about whether her executive power in India might definitively settle the question. 'Kindly explain to me the Indian constitution,' he asked an official at the India Office; if the Viceroy's Council passed the bill, did it still need to go to the secretary of state or to Parliament, so that '[t]he Queen does not approve or do anything?'[35] Ponsonby rarely pushed without a nudge from the queen. It was as clear an indication as any of her desire to assert her prerogative and see through Ripon's reform.

In January 1884 the Ilbert bill, substantially revised to appease European objections, was finally passed. The bill and the outcry it provoked defined Ripon's viceroyalty. The whites of Calcutta prickled with indignation. They stayed away from his levée at the end of 1883. Employees of the East India Railway, as well as some of the European volunteer regiments in Calcutta, publicly demonstrated their opposition.[36] Conversely, Ripon was celebrated as a hero of Indian nationalism. The closer he appeared to be to the queen's pledges to India, the more he was praised. The Poona Sabha memorialised the queen, requesting that Ripon's stint as viceroy be extended. A Marathi verse addressed to the queen lamented Ripon's return to England: the viceroy had 'raised true and everlasting trophies of thy greatness'. His final months in India were marked by eulogies in the press and his departure from Bombay in December 1884 saw the kind of festivities that were usually reserved for arriving royalty.[37] Some of his British colleagues, such as Fergusson in Bombay, could not wait to see him go, but there was no taking away from the popularity of Ripon, and, by proxy, Indian admiration of the queen. When Ripon returned to London, he met with Queen Victoria and told her of the 'extraordinary loyalty to me [the queen] personally' that existed in India. Wilfrid Scawen Blunt, who had raced over to India to document the white mutineers of Calcutta, summed up the Ripon effect on India simply if not very elegantly. The Indian population, he noted, 'grow yearly more and more estranged from their Anglo-Indian masters, they yearly look with more and more hope to England and to her who sits upon the English throne'.[38]

National Union

The Ilbert bill had sunk a wedge between European and Indian loyalties to the Crown. The Indian National Congress, formed in 1885, drove it deeper.[39] From the beginning, the INC laid claim to loyalty to the monarch as one of their weapons of choice. The INC wore their patriotism like a uniform. Every congress meeting closed out with three cheers for the queen. An 'airquake' of hurrahs was given in her golden jubilee year, or her 'first half century' as the INC memorial ambitiously referred to the anniversary. A triumphal arch with the words 'Long live the Empress' greeted delegates on their arrival at the INC camp at Allahabad in 1888, and a further three portraits of the queen and one of the Prince of Wales hung inside the meeting hall.[40] At each gathering speakers took their stand on the promises of the queen's proclamation of 1858, 'cherished as a great charter', its pledges embodying 'the germs of all we aim at now'. In 1894, all the delegates stood up to applaud the famous document. On three occasions the queen's letter to Lord Derby, in which she instructed him to use language in the proclamation that showed sensitivity to the people of India, was read aloud: by Madan Mohan Malaviya in 1888, Rungiah Naidu in 1894 and Rahimatulla Sayani in 1896.[41] Other delegates referred to the queen as 'our beloved mother Empress'. So emphatic was INC loyalty that staid English observers found it 'obtrusive'.[42] Nothing quite rallied Indian nationalists as much as the queen's wise words of 1858.

The loyalist stance of the INC was more than polite rhetoric or show. The INC called for a relaxation in the laws that prevented Indians from contributing to the civic life of British India. First and foremost, the INC wanted the repeal of the Arms Act of 1878, which banned the carrying of hand weapons. The INC's main criticism was that the Arms Act stifled Indian military volunteers. What better indication of Indian loyalty to the Crown than choosing to serve in its fighting forces, especially with a covetous neighbour, Russia, bearing down from the north? As Bipin Chandra Pal, a delegate from Sylhet, asked at the 1887 Congress:

> What . . . are all our professions of loyalty worth in the face of the Arms Act? The Nizam may offer sixty crores instead of sixty lacs for the defence of the Empire, ten thousand jubilee celebrations may be organised, the Government may publicly acknowledge the sincerity of these loyal demonstrations, British newspapers may trumpet them forth to the whole world; but the question is will foreigners believe, will Russia believe, in the truth and sincerity of these demonstrations in the face of the Arms Act?

It was a good point. Corps of volunteers existed for Europeans. There were around thirty by the late 1880s.[43] The INC wanted a taste of the action too. Furthermore, the INC sought to open up Indian access to the regular army, breaking with the policy of recruiting exclusively from the 'martial races'. In 1887 three of the Congress's eleven resolutions were related to military service: removing the Arms Act, establishing Indian volunteer units, and setting up an Indian military college for the Indian princes wanting an army commission.

A second measure of radical loyalism taken up by the INC was the older demand of improving Indian entrance to the Civil Service. The hostility shown towards Indian magistrates during the Ilbert bill demonstrated that suspicion of Indians in government administration was ingrained, even when they had surmounted all the obstacles placed in their way. The rules had been reviewed and even revised. But the fundamental problem remained: the tyranny of distance. The INC made the holding of ICS admission examinations in India a key demand. It also placed faith in the Indian Public Service Commission that began its enquiries in 1886, reporting at the end of the following year, members of the INC giving evidence, only to find its faith misplaced when the Commission rejected simultaneous examinations.[44] Thirdly, the INC emphasised the essential Englishness of its political demands. At its first meeting in 1885 the INC repeated the old demand for a Royal Commission in London to examine the state of the country and recommend reforms. Delegates defended institutions such as trial by jury whenever they appeared to be undermined in India.[45] The INC also pressed for the widening of the representation in the legislative councils of India, in the presidencies, as well as in the Viceroy's Executive Council, by allowing existing civic bodies (chambers of commerce, universities, district boards and so on) to elect candidates. In 1887 Surendranath Bannerjee described this entitlement to better representation as one due to Indians as 'British subjects'.[46] Two years later, a wide-ranging reform bill was introduced at the Bombay congress. It set out the INC's largest demands to date. For advice on details, the INC turned to one of the most notorious Englishmen of the day: Charles Bradlaugh.

The choice of Bradlaugh as advocate for the INC made sense in many ways. He had supported the original Ilbert bill back in 1883, and, once admitted to the House of Commons in 1886, he lost no time making good his claim to be 'member for India', putting twenty-seven questions and five motions relating to India before Parliament, and proving partic-ularly vocal in his criticism of famine policy in Madras, the plight of the Maharaja of Kashmir and the bias against Indians trying to enter the ICS.[47] In other respects, his politics went against the grain of the moderate loyalism of the INC. The most infamous atheist of the Victorian era, his views on religion did not recommend him to Indian audiences. At best he earned quizzical sympathy.[48] His support for female contraception was not mentioned by his Indian hosts. Above all, Bradlaugh was a republican. In 1874 he had called for the impeachment of Britain's royal family, noting in passing the support given by George III for the rapacity and greed of Warren Hastings as governor of Bengal in the 1770s. His anti-monarchism continued as he fought his way into Parliament after 1880. In 1889 he proceeded to attack the payments given from the civil list to the younger members of the royal family, including the queen's eldest grandson, Prince Albert Victor, just then preparing to visit India.[49]

Shaking off ill health, Bradlaugh came to India specifically to attend the INC's fifth meeting. Whilst he could not take the INC down a republican road, he did steer it in a much more radical direction. The second resolution of the Bombay congress reiterated the call for reform of the Indian councils, first made three years earlier. This time, however, with Bradlaugh's input, a two-stage election process was introduced, not unlike the French and American systems, whereby voters would elect a primary college that would then both elect and nominate candidates for the various councils. Stopping short of direct democracy, Bradlaugh's plan nonetheless introduced a popular element, by extending the franchise for the elections to the primary college to all males over the age of 21, subject to certain qualification later settled as all those who paid at least 50 rupees rent, or who paid direct taxes, or whose income was over 150 rupees per year.[50] Bradlaugh set to one side nomination and partial election by corporate institutions, the hallowed formula for widening the representation. No one had ever advocated enfranchising so many Indians before. The details of the bill were rushed into print. Eardley Norton lauded Bradlaugh's document as a new 'Magna Carta' for India, but in truth there was little in it that went back to the thirteenth century find the future.[51] Bradlaugh's bill would have catapulted India into the democratic unknown. In the new year of 1890 he returned to Britain with his bill, primed to press it on Parliament as Lord Salisbury's government prepared its own legislation on the Indian Councils. But Bradlaugh never had his day in the sun. The India Office delayed its plan and, by the time the Indian Council Bill came before the House of Commons in 1891, Bradlaugh was dead and buried. Amongst the 3,000 mourners at his funeral was a young Mohandas Gandhi.

Bradlaugh had been an instant hit in India, although perhaps not in the way he intended. There was no real change in the careful loyalism of the INC. Bradlaugh must surely have bristled when he heard the INC welcome his bill as one 'founded on the solemn promises of the Queen'. He cannot have missed how many of the addresses presented to him at the Bombay meeting – printed on silk and contained in caskets – combined reverence for the queen-empress with gratitude for his duties.[52] The Indian Councils were reformed in 1892, but without any further concession to the elective principle. Indeed, the INC returned to its moderate programme, limited to calling for a broader base for nominations to council membership.[53] Bombay and Bradlaugh's visit was a high watermark in the early years of Indian nationalism. Delegate numbers levelled off thereafter, only rocketing up again at the INC meetings held during the First World War. Some successes were scored in Britain. Naoroji was finally elected to Parliament in 1892 as MP for Finsbury Central. In 1895 there was a Royal Commission under the chairmanship of Lord Reginald Welby, a former Treasury official, to investigate the finances and expenditure of the Indian government. The INC gave evidence; unsurprisingly the Commission gave the Indian government a pretty clean bill of health.

In India the INC faced a barrage of criticism, its loyalty to the Crown contested at every turn. No matter how much the INC asserted its patriotism, it received short shrift from the governing classes. Lord Dufferin signed off his viceroyalty at a St Andrew's Day dinner at the end of November 1888 by denouncing the INC as a 'microscopic minority' bent on exciting 'hatred against the public servants of the Crown' and fomenting military insurrection and popular revolt, instead of encouraging reform of Hindu social practices.[54] The slightest hint that the INC was stoking dissent towards the queen was seized on by officials as a conspiracy. For example, a tract published by the INC in Tamil and circulated in Madras appeared to liken the Indian empire to a despotism, in which the queen-empress professed to take an interest in Indians whereas in fact she ignored all their appeals. From this and other charges Allan Hume and Eardley Norton defended the INC.[55] But the organisation remained under the severest scrutiny. Its activities during 1888 were subject to surveillance, as Dufferin turned over the 'Thugee and Dacoity' department of Special Branch to monitoring the

INC (as well as other organisations). The INC membership was also affected by an India Office ruling in 1892 that Indians who held official appointments could not be members of the INC nor the temperance movement.[56] For the Government of India, patriotism and politics were an unholy mixture.

For Muslim reformers in particular, the INC's was a spurious loyalism. Alarmed at the formation of the INC in 1885, Syed Ahmed Khan, assisted by the principal of the Anglo-Oriental College, Theodore Beck, set up the United Indian Patriotic Association (UIPA) three years later, its mission to dent the appeal of the INC to Muslim Indians. It was an unusual step, first as a Muslim campaign with an avowedly political purpose, and secondly, one that ventured beyond the borders of the North-West Provinces. Drawing in funding from the Nizam of Hyderabad, amongst others, by 1890 the UIPA had received support from 53 *anjumans* promising not to send delegates to the INC, sent a petition to Parliament with just under 30,000 signatures opposing Bradlaugh's bill and conducted a publicity campaign in Britain.[57] An effervescent force – it survived no longer than a year – the UIPA nonetheless niggled away at the INC, exposing its more vulnerable points, that is to say its representativeness, and its declared moderation. The UIPA tore into Bengali Brahmin dominance of the INC, arguing that introducing a more elective element into Indian's councils would mean Hindus outnumbering Muslims four to one, or as Khan put it more offensively, 'the whole [Viceroy's] Council will consist of Babu So-and-so Mitter, Babu So-and-so Ghose, and Babu So-and-so Chukerbutty'.[58] Here was an early outing of the demonology of 'Congress-raj', an Indian future for 30 million Muslims in which the benign despotism of British rule gave way to Hindu majority rule. In the late 1880s, this line of attack was flanked by another argument, namely that the INC's loyalism was only skin-deep. The INC were, according to Syed Ali Bilgrami, one of the Nizam of Hyderabad's ministers, and prominent member of the UIPA, '*soi-disant* patriots' playing a 'subtle trick' of showing loyalty to the throne whilst throwing 'seditious abuse at the administration'.[59] What the INC really desired was a republic, claimed Syed Khan; what it would create, warned Beck, were the conditions for another mutiny.[60]

There were thus a variety of nationalisms in late nineteenth-century India. Each had their own version of the queen-empress as the embodiment of the Raj. For moderate Muslims, such as Syed Khan, the language of loyalism was a way of fending off the spectre of Wahabism, as well as the majoritarianism of the INC. In turn, the INC used the rhetoric of imperial patriotism to contest the policies of the Raj, and press for the pledges of the proclamation of 1858 to be upheld and fulfilled. At the same time, as the conflict over the Ilbert bill revealed, the small but vocal British community in India were always poised ready to seize the Crown as their property, the embodiment of rights that were peculiar to the English race. From afar, Queen Victoria looked on and lamented at what was going on, anxious at the antagonism between the races. Significantly, one nation – India – was largely absent from these languages of loyalism in the late nineteenth-century Raj. Muslims contested the idea of the political nation based on Hindu predominance, yet also kept the caliphate at a distance. The INC looked to a wider imperial citizenship of shared rights across the British Empire. The whites of the presidency towns clung to a residual sense of Englishness, defined where it mattered most, in the privileged status they enjoyed under the law. Historians may look in vain for an authentic or mature Indian nationalism before 1900. That does not mean that India was politically quiescent or blindly deferential. The figure of the queen-empress offered a way of articulating citizenship without talking about the nation.

CHAPTER 11

JUJUBILEE

'Only in India,' claimed a Bengali newspaper, observing the queen's jubilee celebrations in 1887, was it 'possible for a man to set fire to his own dwelling-house in order to enjoy the lurid spectacle of a great and devastating fire.' *Bangabasi's* ridicule had two targets. Krishna Chandra Banerjee, the editor, criticised the British rulers for 'intoxicating' the country with anniversary festivities, and lamented how easily the Indian people set aside their misery in a show of loyalty. Banerjee suggested that the ceremonies should be called the 'jujubilee'.[1] In Bengali, a 'juju' was an imaginary monster used to frighten children; in Hindi, as in English, it meant a magical charm. Banerjee's censure was understandable. In 1887 and again in 1897, the popularity of Queen Victoria seemed to reach new heights in India. Jubilee addresses, gifts and memorials of all shapes and sizes were sent from India on both occasions. In 1887 there were almost 1,100 loyal addresses from India, double the combined total of the rest of the colonial empire, and almost 50 per cent more than were generated back in Britain. In 1897, there were fewer, but they still ran into the hundreds. In between the two jubilees, India supplied most of the funding for the Imperial and Colonial Institute, opened in London in 1893 as a permanent memorial of the first jubilee.[2]

227

How much of an exercise in orchestrated loyalty were the two Indian jubilees of 1887 and 1897? The Government of India had good reason to take matters into its own hands on both occasions. The viceroyalty of Lord Ripon unleashed new forms of popular politics in India, particularly through the expansion of municipal government. At the end of 1885, the Indian National Congress held its first meeting, wrapping its demands for reform in the rhetoric of loyalism, but calling for change nonetheless. It was potentially a heady brew. A decade later, in 1897, Indian opinion remained unpredictable, as famine ravaged most of the country, cholera broke out in Bombay, its impact deepened by the heavy-handed and insensitive measures of control implemented by the colonial authorities, and a massive earthquake hit Bengal. Three British officials were assassinated during the jubilee celebrations of that year.

At the same time, there was much that was spontaneous, and a great deal that was distinctly regional about the Indian jubilees. Patriotism by fiat only went so far; local communities did the rest of the work, and from the abundance of surviving evidence it is possible to chart the extent and the limits of Indian loyalism at the height of the Victorian era. The chapter that follows compares and contrasts these two royal jubilees in India, and in the decade that intervened tells the story of how Indian efforts kept alive the flagging fortunes of the Imperial and Colonial Institute in London.

Managing Loyalty: The Golden Jubilee of 1887

If it had not been for Indian enthusiasm Queen Victoria's first jubilee might never have happened. In the late summer of 1886, the India Office opened discussions with Lord Dufferin, the viceroy, about if, when and how Queen Victoria's jubilee might be marked in India. At home the queen made it known that she expected a thanksgiving ceremony in Westminster Abbey around 21 June (the day of her accession): 'a short plain service without a sermon'. Later she added a naval or army review and requested the attendance in London of a guard drawn from colonial and Indian cavalry regiments, as well as some of the Indian princes.[3] She also held out for a new Albert memorial, this time an equestrian one. Brushing aside advice, she insisted that the monies raised for a philanthropic project by the 'Women's Jubilee Offering' be spent on the statue, a bronze work by Joseph Boehm, unveiled in 1890 in Windsor Great Park, complete with an inscription around its pedestal in English, Gaelic, Latin and Sanskrit, the latter provided by Professor Max Müller, detailing the dedication, 'a token of love and loyalty from the daughters of her Empire'.[4] Whilst the Albert Memorial in Kensington Gardens had hailed a Renaissance prince, closer to home Queen Victoria wanted a reminder of her consort's imperial vision.

No such follies were proposed in India – not on this occasion anyway. Dufferin suggested a distribution of honours, and a release of debtors from prison. Richard Cross, the secretary of state for India, went along with this, concerned only that expenditure on celebrations in India should be as limited as possible.[5] There this desultory conversation closed for a few months. Meanwhile, in India, plans for the jubilee unfolded with more speed. Assuming that 1 January – the anniversary of the Imperial Assemblage – would be the jubilee day, preparations commenced in Madras and Bombay during the autumn of 1886.[6] In November, Dufferin and Cross resumed their dialogue, deciding that India's jubilee would be held before the main event in Britain, but in the middle of February, before the onset of the heat and the rains. The queen disliked this proposed 'celebration by anticipation'.[7] Confirmation of the date for India's jubilee came just in time to put a brake on preparations already under way. However, the viceroy's office only gave guidance in mid-January as to how the jubilee holiday should be observed. A telegram of 17 January encouraged the 'usual' celebrations: fireworks, illuminations and a feeding of the poor. Three weeks later the viceroy sent a *kharita* to all native rulers and to all senior officials in British India, confirming arrangements. The viceroy's office also circulated a sample text to be used in formal speeches and addresses. It described the highlights of the queen's reign, emphasised her personal virtues and listed the benefits of her rule over the 'teeming millions' of India: peace, the spread of railways and other public works, and improvements in education. Then, in a heavy-handed move, the government stipulated that all addresses of congratulation had to be approved by British officials. Public money would only be available for illuminations, and localities were encouraged to save some of the funds raised for permanent memorials, in the shape of public buildings and municipal facilities.[8]

For an event of such significance, it was all very hurried, with barely one month's notice of official plans for the jubilee. But last minute did not mean light touch. The viceroy's officials explained that 'we do not want to take the initiative but we wish to know as early as possible what is intended'.[9] As coded statements go, this one covered all bases. Government outlay would be minimal, but its oversight extensive. In the days leading up to 16 February, localities sent on to the Government of India detailed plans of proposed events, together with the text of the local address to be sent to the queen. Inevitably, some Indian princes and chiefs wanted to do things as grandly as possible. The Maharaja of Mysore sent an ivory flower-stand depicting Lakshmi, whilst the Raja of Travancore gifted an ornamental figure of Siva framed by elephant tusks. Many wanted to telegram the queen directly. Protocols on sending gifts to the queen were relaxed for the occasion, subject to their formal approval by the Government of India.[10] Between gifts, memorials and other visible displays of affection a remarkable degree of uniformity emerged. Was it coincidence or control?

Or routine? Many of the men who made Lytton's extravaganza work in 1877 were still on the scene ten years later. One of them, Owen Tudor Burne, wrote a timely piece in January 1887 on the ideas that had gone into the many local durbars at the time of the Imperial Assemblage.[11] So when it came to Indian royal ceremonial there was a tried and tested formula already in place. More – and less – was expected of the Government of India this time. Newspapers were quick to spot any undue interference by officialdom. From Allahabad, Bombay and Lahore came complaints that the poor were being forced to give a few annas to support the festivities. Fundraising momentum faltered when the viceroy issued another circular calling for subscriptions to be raised simultaneously for the Prince of Wales's pet project, the Imperial and Colonial Institute back in London. Then Lady Dufferin chipped in, piggy-backing onto the jubilee fundraising with an appeal for donations to her female hospitals.[12] By the beginning of February some critics had had enough. Involving the royal family, and allowing officials to take over the arrangements, was detracting from the spontaneity of the jubilee. Besides, it was argued, there was one obvious way in which government interference would be welcome: a symbolic act of grace to reward the queen's subjects at this historic time. Some newspapers called for 'largesse', recalling how Akbar had tuned gold into coin on such occasions. Others looked for more tangible reforms, such as repealing the Arms Act, introducing more representative institutions, opening up the Indian Civil Service to more Indians, and the redress of past wrongs, such as the restoration of Indian kings and princes to their thrones.[13] The Government of India went some way to address this clamour, although not very far. Complicated plans were drawn up to release 25,000 prisoners, and also to distribute a whole series of honours to higher and lesser orders of Indian nobility. There were no gold coins, but a jubilee medal designed by Sir Frederic Leighton was struck, Randolph Churchill being forced to apologise to the queen for leaving off the 'I' for Imperatrix in 'VRI' on the first version of the medal. None of this really satisfied anyone. In India the local elites who came forward to claim their honours were criticised for their fawning deference.[14] At home, the release of so many convicts alarmed politicians: questions were asked about the prisoner amnesty in both Houses of Parliament. Assurances were given that this was simply an 'ancient Oriental custom' and would not be part of the jubilee in Britain.[15]

However, a western custom worried the viceroy. Mindful of the Indian National Congress, Dufferin's government wanted politics kept out of the jubilee. Hence the decision to vet every single address intended for submission to the queen. Those emanating from municipal associations and *sabhas* were policed closely. The slightest demand for reform, for example a proposed address from Barisal in Bengal, calling for educational reform and summoning up the spirit of the 1858 proclamation, was only let through after careful scrutiny.[16] Mostly, however, the government came down hard on addresses that offended taste or grammar rather than patriotism. In Bombay presidency, the Jubilee Committee of Jambusar were told that their illustrated address showing a kneeling daughter representing their town showing her love to her mother by placing a garland of 'Peace, Prosperity and Progress' around Queen Victoria seated on a throne 'cannot be regarded as fit for presentation to Her Majesty'. In another intervention, the Literary and Social Club of the Native Christian Community of Bandora in Goa were told to change a reference to the queen managing to 'reduce' the once turbulent peoples of India to loyal subjects to having managed to 'convert' them instead.[17] Evangelical bias was more welcome than political radicalism.

All this censorship made for a mundane uniformity. Many of the addresses and speeches were formulaic. They were dull recitals that started with a potted biography of the queen, and then moved on to describe the achievements of her rule in India and the benefits bestowed on the 'teeming millions' – a phrase that stuck like glue – of her Indian subjects, before closing with a homily on her domestic virtues and the deep sympathy she had often shown for the plight of the Indian people caught up in famine and pestilence. There was an uncanny sameness about the addresses, as though they had been copied from a single source. They had. Many were carbon copies of the text circulated by the viceroy at the beginning of February. The same eulogies also rang like a chorus through many of the vernacular biographies that poured from the presses in 1887.[18] Moreover, the jubilee of the queen – her personal milestone – became conflated with the progress of British rule in India. Government officials tried to turn the jubilee into an upbeat endorsement of the achievements of British administration, especially since 1858. This fell flat. Many Indian localities skirted around that piece of protocol by making the queen, and not the Government of India, the focal point of their celebrations.

Depicted in a transparency, or in a photograph, or by a reproduction of a portrait, Queen Victoria was carried aloft on elephants, or inside carriages and palanquins, in the processions leading to the durbar, and then placed on a dais, or inside an improvised *pandal* marquee or on a throne during the ceremony itself. Local Indian officials addressed her image, sometimes paid homage with a bow or salute, or prostrated themselves before her. The city of Madras celebrated the jubilee in June as well as February and on the second occasion thousands of copies of a *carte de visite* photograph of the queen were distributed freely during the procession. Indianised depictions of the queen were common, the elongated nose and darkened eyes of the coinage and the postage stamps now transposed into print. For example, a Hindi account of the jubilee in London – *Landan-jubili* – published in Lahore in 1888, included a coloured portrait of the queen, fair-skinned but dark-eyed, whilst the *Bombay Gazette* illustrated its coverage of the June celebration with a head shot of the queen with dark eyes and unadorned except for a flowing head scarf. Triumphal arches were another recurring feature in the celebrations, illuminated by electric lights, candles and torches, or simply made to glisten with *ghee* and oil, with variations on the queen's title inscribed on the sides and centrepiece of the arch: 'Kaiser-i-Hind', 'Queen-Empress', 'Queen-Mother'. Hindus drew the queen into their own forms of worship: for example she appeared in the guise of Lakshmi, the goddess of prosperity, in a temple at Ranaghat in Bengal.[19]

The jubilee in India unleashed local philanthropy rather than im-perial grandeur: the repair of temples and mosques, the building of bathing tanks, the endowment of scholarships for schools, both English and vernacular.[20] In this way the memorials of 1887 and ten years later tell us more about civic patriotism than they do an unqualified loyalty to Britain. Official causes could hardly compete. Only a trickle of jubilee subscriptions found their way into the funds being raised for the Imperial and Colonial Institute. Many local committees agreed from the outset that they would not donate to the Prince of Wales's Institute project. Even in Bombay, where the prince's brother, the Duke of Connaught, was a member of the jubilee committee, it was decided that 'no portion' of the funds would go to London, but instead would be used for the Victoria Technical Institute in the city.[21] By the end of 1887 only a small amount had been raised in India for the Imperial and Colonial Institute.

Despite these snubs, Lord Dufferin declared the jubilee a success. '[O]fficialism has for once stood to one side', he stated in his official speech from Calcutta, 'and has left the Nation face to face with its Empress.' From London, Cross, the secretary of state, chimed in cheerily, saying he didn't know 'if natives can cheer', but if so Dufferin must be suffering from 'deafness' now.[22] On the ground, British officials patted themselves on the back for getting the tone of the occasion right. The Commissioner of the Northern District Bombay described the local celebrations as 'an enthusiastic expression of unmistakeable loyalty, without a single symptom of coldness, or even unsympathetic warmness', whilst the Collector at Kaira (Kheda) in Gujarat stated that the 'proceedings are the spontaneous results of native feelings, and have been inspired as little as possible by official leading'.[23] Such sentiments breathe a sigh of relief as much as triumph. The Government of India had left little to chance in 1887. Every single detail of the jubilee celebrations across India had been agreed in advance, and the flow of loyal addresses and gifts was rigorously controlled all the way from village, town hall and princely palace back to Windsor. Yet there was no disguising the magnitude of the event. Queen Victoria heard first-hand about the proceedings in Poona and Bombay. The Duke and Duchess of Connaught both described to her how a million people had turned out in Bombay, her statue brilliantly lit up for the occasion: 'never has there been such a universal display of loyalty to one person in India'.[24] A selection of literary tributes were sent on to the queen. By the time the main jubilee came round in Britain, around 200 addresses from India, all contained in elaborately crafted caskets and cases, had been sent to Buckingham Palace. On behalf of the queen the viceroy announced her gratitude, and separate acknowledgements were sent to all the princes.[25] India had led the way; now it was the turn of the rest of the Empire.

Four months later, in June 1887, Indian nobility visited London to take part in the jubilee celebrations there. In all, eleven Indian chiefs and nobles attended the June celebrations, each of them accompanied by a British official. Additionally, thirteen cavalry officers were sent over, at the queen's request, to join the guard of honour that accompanied the queen during the various processions and military reviews featured in the jubilee schedule. Taken together, it was the largest and most impressive deputation of Indians ever to visit England during the queen's lifetime. Key states were represented: Hyderabad (by Nawab Bashir-ud-Daula, a brother-in-law of the nizam), and Jodhpur (by

Pratap Singh, the maharaja's brother). The Gaekwar of Baroda came, seeking remedies for his ailments. Holkar of Indore also came in person, to the evident dismay of Dufferin, but to the delight of the London press who seized upon him as the most newsworthy of the visitors. There were also chiefs from smaller states prized by the British for their record in administrative reform, for example Cooch Behar (both maharaja and maharani, who arrived at the beginning of the summer), Bharatpur (the maharaja's brother-in-law, Ganga Bakhsh, was sent), the Rao of Cutch and the Thakur of Morvi (Morbi).[26] As Indian princes went, the Government of India felt assured that the modern and liberal side of the Raj was being despatched to represent India.

Except that was not really what the queen wanted. Towards the end of April, she indicated her desire that all her Indian visitors when in her presence wear Indian costume. This caused consternation. Most of the visitors had already departed from India, explained Dufferin, and anyway they were mostly westernised: the Maharaja of Cooch Behar never wore native dress, whilst Gurnain Singh (representing the Maharaja of Kapurthala) 'is thoroughly European in all his habits'. Indeed, west was not always best. Dufferin warned that Holkar's 'only notion of a smart get-up is to make himself look as like an English jockey as possible'. Nonetheless, Dufferin ensured that new wardrobes of 'oriental costume' were organised in time.[27] There was more to all this than the queen's usual insistence that Indians look Indian. The Indian guests were effectively acting as a semi-official party representing the queen's Indian dominion. They enjoyed pride of place at the jubilee service in Westminster Abbey on 21 June, riding on horseback in a group immediately in front of the queen's carriage, the cavalry escort at the rear. In the Abbey, they sat in the choir stalls, with other dignitaries from the colonies.[28] Then on 27 June they attended a reception at Windsor Castle, where they presented their own gifts and addresses to the queen in person, taking precedence over deputations from Bombay, Calcutta and Madras, all led by Englishmen. In return Holkar was knighted, and five of the other chiefs became Knight Commanders of the Star of India. The Thakur of Morvi stole the show, riding into the quadrangle of the castle on a fully caparisoned Kattiawar charger, which he duly handed over to the queen. A few weeks later the eleven Indians joined the queen at Hatfield House as the guests of Lord Salisbury, the prime minister, whilst the cavalry escort took part in a fete at Hyde Park, and in the military review at Aldershot on 2 July.[29] India thus took part in two jubilees in 1887, one at home and one in London. The delay between the two celebrations meant that the large volume of addresses generated in India in February could be sent on and included within the wider roll call of imperial loyalty on show in June, with Indian deputations on hand to present the tributes from India. From first to last, India was woven into the queen's golden jubilee.

Loyal Legacy: The Imperial Institute

As soon as the jubilee was over, the government announced that there would be a permanent memorial of the fiftieth year of the queen's reign. This was the Imperial Institute that eventually opened in 1893. First mooted in 1886 following the Imperial and Colonial Exhibition, as a building and organisation that would carry on the mission and aims of that exhibition, the initiative took on a grander ambition after the jubilee. The Prince of Wales presided over the project, Lord Rothschild and the Earl of Carnarvon were amongst its backers, and Lord Herschell, Gladstone's former lord chancellor, chaired the organising committee. An architectural competition for the building was announced and won by Thomas Collcutt. Contributions were invited from the British public and from India and the colonies. Lord Herschell went off to India to solicit interest and money there.[30] A site for the new institute was selected in South Kensington, in the heart of Albertopolis, and the foundation stone laid at the beginning of July 1887. Arthur Sullivan supplied an ode for the occasion, and the queen's Indian visitors joined the ceremony.[31]

The new Institute did not struggle for business. In 1890 a school for modern Oriental studies, the forerunner of today's School of Oriental and African Studies, was founded, and Max Müller gave the inaugural address. From 1892, the Institute ran an agency for colonial trade information.[32] Financial support was harder to come by. By 1891 one-third of the funding for the Institute had come from India. But interest was flagging, and the view was growing that the best way to extend the philanthropic initiatives of 1887 was to invest in local projects in India.[33] With the completion of the building and the opening of the new Institute scheduled for 1893, there was a danger that the project would not be completed on time to everyone's embarrassment. At the eleventh hour two Indian princes – the Maharajas of Jaipur and Bhavnagar – and a wealthy merchant from Bombay – Sir Cowasji Jehangir – stepped in and made up the difference: £40,000 each from Jaipur and Jehangir, and £3,000 from Bhavnagar.[34] Ready money from India once more.

The extra funding from India made all the difference, and the opening of the Institute took place at the beginning of May 1893. It was a moment of royal pomp to which Gladstone's government turned a blind eye. The satirical weekly *Moonshine* depicted the prime minister hiding under a table as the queen-empress and the Prince of Wales squabbled over arrangements. It was no less grand for all that. Arthur Sullivan performed a reprise, this time composing a march, another ode was dashed off as well, and the Irish historian and Unionist W. E. H. Lecky penned the inaugural address.[35] At the queen's insistence, India was foregrounded for the occasion. A cavalry guard was sent over specially from India, and stood out amongst the other colonial troops, to the evident pleasure of the queen. One of the guard left a rich account of his sojourn in England.[36] An ornate ceremonial key fashioned in an Indian style was used to unlock the doors of the new building. Once inside, the queen gazed over the proceedings from the throne of Ranjit Singh. The overseas visitors included three Indian princes – the Thakur of Gondal, who came with his wife, the Maharaja of Kapurthala and the Maharaja of Bhavnagar.[37] Not for the first time India had supplied more money, momentum and material for a London extravaganza than had been found anywhere else in the empire. Or, on this occasion, even from home. Lecky's inaugural address described how British civilisation had freed India from barbarism, but the successful launch of the Imperial Institute suggests it was India that had rescued the Prince of Wales's pet project from the philistines. Even so, Indian philanthropists had to accept a modest footprint in the new building. Jaipur got a special room, Bhavnagar a corridor. There was also a memorial for Lady Reay, mother of the former governor of Bombay, unveiled by Lord Reay. By the time of Queen Victoria's diamond jubilee in 1897 the Imperial Institute was regarded as a flop. Its programme of activities in no way fulfilled its original mission statement. Ironically, the Imperial Institute never rivalled Monier-Williams's Indian Institute at Oxford, bankrolled by railway magnate Thomas Brassey and Bhagvat Singh, the young Thakur of Gondal, and also patronised by the Prince of Wales.[38]

Critics lined up to attack what had become an embarrassing white elephant. Henry Labouchere, a rich, radical MP and proprietor of one of the pioneers of investigative journalism, *Truth*, led the onslaught.[39] Labouchere called the Imperial Institute 'a monument of reckless extravagance, purposeless effort, and incompetent administration'. His newspaper exposed its real debts, amounting to £40,000. Without directly blaming the Prince of Wales for the origins of the crisis, Labouchere called for him to take some responsibility for the Institute going forward, perhaps by transferring the assets of the 'wreck' to the Prince of Wales Hospital Fund.[40] In the end it was a university and not a hospital that came to the rescue. In 1899 the University of London stepped in to agree to write off its mortgage and its remaining debts. Officially handed over as a 'gift to the nation' in 1901, the multi-functional site became the property of the amorphous federal university, with some residual activity left to the Imperial Institute, now confined to the west wing. The space allotted to India in the transferred building was substantially reduced, effectively limited by the eve of the First World War to a shared conference room, and some storage space.[41] Its Indian patrons had good reason to be aggrieved over the rise and fall of the Imperial Institute. The Institute had been originally conceived at the 1886 Imperial and Colonial Exhibition, an event also presided over by the Prince of Wales, and one that had led to a similar exhibition planned for Bombay being abandoned. The Government of India had tried to divert funds to the Institute from the voluntary subscriptions raised for the queen's first jubilee in 1887. That the project had only been saved with a large infusion of capital from India left a sour aftertaste that lingered over the

1897 jubilee, and later over schemes to memorialise the queen after her death.

Feast and Famine: The Diamond Jubilee of 1897

Larger in scale than the golden jubilee of 1887, the diamond jubilee of 1897 was less of a spectacle. Overseen in London by the Prince of Wales, aided by the latest technology, which allowed the queen to press a button and electronically telegraph the empire simultaneously with a special jubilee message, and attended in London by the principal colonial leaders, the celebrations of the sixtieth year of the queen's reign were tempered by the fact that she herself was in her late seventies.[42] Queen Victoria's own preference was for minimal fuss. She wanted neither an exclusively state nor a church ceremonial; however, she did endorse involving the Empire, including India. By the end of February plans were in place for the queen to make a procession through central London, culminating in a drive-by of the steps of St Paul's Cathedral. An Indian guard of honour was to be at her side throughout. As far as the queen was concerned, the complement of Indian officers, mounted on horseback, was more important than the attendance of Indian princes in London.[43] This suited the Government of India. From the start, the viceroy, Lord Elgin, discouraged Indian chiefs from travelling to London. Indian princes were asked to stay at home, in some cases to tend to their famine-stricken people.[44] In the end only eight Indian chiefs came, alongside other Indian dignitaries such as Sir Jamsetjee Jejeebhoy. Of the Indian rulers, five came from states ranked in the hierarchy of salutes: Hari Singh, the Maharaja of Jodhpur; Sir Pratap Singh, regent of Jodhpur; Jagatjit Singh, the Maharaja of Kapurthala; Bhagvat Singh, the Thakur of Gondal (who came with his consort); and Sir Waghji II Rawaji, the Thakur of Morvi. Of these not all were welcome. Elgin pointedly observed that the rank of the Maharaja of Kapurthala could not excuse his reputation as 'dissipated & a spendthrift'. Both he and the Thakur of Gondal were suspected of turning up simply in the hunt for honours, Gondal's case being pressed by a persistent Monier-Williams, grateful for his donation to the Indian

Institute in Oxford. Four princely heirs who were attending Eton College were also invited to attend the torchlit procession at Windsor the day after jubilee day.[45] Less fuss was made of the princely visitors who did make it to London in 1897 than had surrounded those who came ten years earlier. They were not part of the jubilee procession through London, and only three of them (the Maharaja of Kapurthala, the Thakur of Morvi and the Thakur of Gondal) were presented to the queen. The Maharaja of Kapurthala went home happy, however, collecting his gong – he was made a Knight Commander of the Star of India – at a dinner with the queen on 10 July. The Thakur of Gondal was also a dinner guest, staying overnight at Windsor a few days later, but he only left with a promotion up the rank of the Order of the Indian Empire.[46]

The Indian guard of honour received much better treatment than the princes. Two Indian military contingents came to London in 1897. Firstly, there were 10,000 soldiers who formed part of the Imperial Service Troops, led by 17 native officers, specially selected from across the Indian princely states, the cost of their attendance charged to their own state treasuries.[47] Pride of place, however, went to the second Indian detachment, an Indian escort of twenty-two officers. Accompanied by three English officers and Field Marshal Sir Garnet Wolseley, the commander-in-chief of the Armed Forces, they rode right alongside the queen's carriage in the procession that made its way through the streets of London on 22 June, captured for posterity in one of the first newsreel films ever made, and also in John Charlton's sumptuous painting of the scene outside St Paul's Cathedral.[48] They were singled out in commentary on the occasion, and praised by the India Office: Hamilton thought Pratap Singh's horsemanship was especially impressive. The Indian escort was also invited to Windsor ahead of jubilee day for an audience with the queen, when they were shown the state apartments, as well being included in other events of the jubilee, such as the military review at Aldershot on 1 July. At Windsor the queen gave her own distinctive mark of approval, commissioning Rudolf Swodoba to paint portraits of some of them. They were also on hand as her personal guard at special ceremonies arranged for the presentation of jubilee addresses, not just from India but also from across the country and overseas. On 5 July the Indian escort returned to Windsor to bid farewell, and the officers were given jubilee medals by the queen, who touched the hilts of their swords before they left, and received their loyal address from Pratap Singh.[49] It was all an emphatic show of the queen's need for an Indian presence right at the heart of her jubilee. Just as Abdul Karim, her *munshi*, had become a part of her own secretariat close at hand, so too these guards now acted as her military attendants throughout the celebrations. The more she aged, the more the queen retreated behind an Indian cordon.

In India the government's instincts were for a quiet jubilee; 'nothing . . . on a large scale,' advised Elgin, the viceroy.[50] Nature, hunger and pestilence intervened to prevent a grand event. An earthquake hit Calcutta on the eve of the jubilee, toppling local landmarks, including the steeple of St John's Cathedral. There was widespread famine as well as outbreaks of cholera and the plague. Adding a mobile population to the mix would not help. Furthermore, the Government of India was reluctant to orchestrate celebrations on the scale of 1887. Some form was duly observed: 20,000 prisoners were released, to the consternation of some princely states, and there was a full distribution of Indian honours.[51] But ten years on Indian loyalty to the Crown was hard to predict. A noisy celebration of the queen's reign was as likely to raise hopes as much as cheers, so precise rules were set. There would be no addresses, memorials or gifts sent directly to the queen: they would all need to go through the viceroy's office. Any deputation that wished to present an address would need to travel north to Simla, where the viceroy was based in the summer months, to deliver the memorial at the Town Hall, the deputation restricted to a maximum of six people.[52] The vernacular and European press were perturbed by the draconian turn in arrangements, and Elgin only made matters worse when he made light of the Simla arrangements.[53] This time round, officials also were more inscrutable in their censoring of loyal memorials. An address from the Poona Sabha was rejected, and a disproportionate number of planned addresses from the Punjab were turned away, mostly on the grounds that they were too political.[54] So the official jubilee day, presided over by the viceroy at Simla, was a muted occasion, with only forty deputations making the long journey north. The viceroy and the queen exchanged telegraph messages, Queen Victoria saying '[f]rom my heart I thank my beloved people. May God bless them.'[55]

The sober goings-on in the hills at Simla in no way set the tone for the diamond jubilee elsewhere around India. Throughout the length and breadth of India, officials had been instructed to 'yield the initiative' in taking steps to commemorate the queen's diamond jubilee to the 'spontaneous action of the community at large'.[56] For the most part that is what happened. Across the Punjab a chain of fires extended along the hilltops from the Himalayas down to the Jumma and Indus rivers and southwards to the hills of the border with Balochistan. In Assam the highest peaks were lit up by bonfires. At Puri in Orissa the Jagannath temple was illuminated in a fantastic show. At the Nainital hill station in the North-West Provinces the local lake was transformed by a Venetian-style fete.[57] As in 1887, celebrations followed a typical pattern. There were local processions, many with an image of the queen held aloft or carried in a palanquin. Prisoners were released, there was distribution of food and clothing to the poor, and festive elements followed: sports and wrestling matches and schoolchildren singing, against a backdrop of illuminated streets and public buildings. Permanent memorials to the queen's jubilee were funded out of public subscriptions: bathing tanks, markets, buildings and equipment for female hospitals and dispensaries, veterinary hospitals, libraries and reading rooms, parks, and endowments for educational scholarships and prizes. Local rulers chipped in with munificence both traditional and modern. In the Gujarat state of Junagarh, the Nawab established a new bacteriological laboratory. In Travancore, the raja gave money for an orphanage and a library.[58] Controversially, in Rajputana funding was put up for the 'Indian Princes Victorian Health Institute', led by the Maharaja of Dholpur, in actual fact a vivisection unit, that in turn provoked the opposition of the Indian Anti-Vivisection Society, which claimed that the queen's 'never failing womanly sympathy for the weak and helpless' was at odds with this new initiative so 'against the sanctity of life'.[59] As always, the queen was all things to all people.

The jubilee of 1897 was less regimented than ten years earlier. Colonial authority stayed at home, leaving the field free for local communities to engage with the anniversary in their own way. The effect of this was that more attention was focused on the queen, and less on the fact of British rule. Evidence of this can be seen in Mysore in southern India, for which a particularly good record of the diamond jubilee celebrations exists.[60] The jubilee events in Mysore were co-ordinated from the cantonment town of Bangalore. There was inevitable military precision. Close attention was paid to the timing of events, and to the geography of the festivities and sports that were laid on. The Government of India was also on hand. At Bangalore the deputy commissioner addressed the jubilee procession, praising the gathering for their 'spontaneous enthusiasm'. A local judge took pains to explain to the prisoners released as a jubilee gesture why they were being given their freedom.[61] However, these cumbersome interventions aside, the jubilee in Mysore was left to honour the queen according to its own preferred style. At the centre of the proceedings was the Maharani of Mysore, acting as queen regent whilst her son was a minor. She led the procession from her palace to the site of the new hospital, where she laid the foundation stone.[62] Elsewhere in Mysore state, the processions placed Queen Victoria at the centre. At Shimoga (Shivamogga) a picture of the queen was unveiled and then placed in an open palanquin at the head of a procession of 1,000 people. At Anekal her photograph was carried in a coach at the head of the procession. In Kolar district soldiers and police saluted her portrait, before joining a procession of the temple gods. At Soraba, town leaders prostrated themselves before her image.[63] Partly a civic festival, partly a religious ceremonial, the jubilee in Mysore eluded the best-laid plans of local officials.

Subject to less official monitoring in the 1897 celebrations, the queen's role as the mother of India and widow-in-chief now came to the fore. In Bombay, the municipal corporation praised her 'womanly and motherly heart'. For the young Raja of Pudukkottai in southern India the queen was, according to the speech he made, the 'right example of Spotless Womanhood, perfect Wife, perfect Mother, perfect Friend'.[64] Some cheap biographies dwelled on the queen's long years of widowhood, a biography published in Calcutta noting that '[a] widow is debarred from all joys and pleasures; she must live in the strictest seclusion; she must force down the gushing spring of womanly love'. More Tamil histories of the queen appeared. In one her heavily Indianised portrait adorned the cover.[65]

Compared to the jubilee of 1887 there was there was much more dissent over the celebrations. There was resentment at viceregal influence, particularly over the summons to Simla. As in 1887 there were hopes that there might be fewer royal acts of favour – honours and the like – and more acts of grace, especially charity. And reform. India had demonstrated so much loyalty, despite widespread famine and poverty and, once again, as in 1858, 1877 and 1887, Indians had received so little reward in terms of political concessions. Two Bengali tributes sneaked in pleas for the queen's aid for her famine-stricken people.[66] Mostly, it was the Government of India that bore the brunt of criticism, not least when it was rumoured that it had planned to profit from the party by selling copies of the queen's diamond jubilee speech.[67] In Lahore there was public opposition to the erection of a statue of the queen to mark the diamond jubilee. Also in Lahore, the launch of the 'Victoria Diamond Jubilee Hindu Technical Institute' was accompanied with grumbling about the destructive influence of foreign competition on indigenous manufactures.[68] But now, for the first time in her reign, the queen was not immune from criticism. Her independence from British officialdom, for so long her strength, was deemed a disadvantage. As the *Dacca Prakash*, a Bengali-language newspaper published in Calcutta declared, she had little power to do good, only power to do evil which she chose not to use, whilst for the *Jami-ul-Ulum*, an Urdu paper from Moradabad, she was a 'mere signing machine'.[69]

Elgin had low expectations of the jubilee in 1897, and he almost achieved them. Hamilton, the secretary of state back in London, congratulated Elgin on his jubilee speech in which he had 'glided over the temporary difficulties'.[70] Then terror struck. On the day of the jubilee a government official (John Ross, the secretary to the deputy commissioner) was murdered at Peshawar, capital of the North-West Provinces.[71] Simultaneously, in Poona, 1,000 miles to the south, Charles

Walter Rand, chair of the Special Plague Committee in the town, together with his military escort, Lieutenant Ayerst, were shot dead by three brothers, Damodar, Balkrishna and Vasudeo Chapekar. The assailants were quickly rounded up, tried and later executed. In Poona, the British authorities identified a conspiracy, some even attributing it to the influence of the Indian National Congress. Damodar Chapekar later confessed his hatred for the queen – 'a female fiend who devours her own progeny' – describing how he had helped to tar the face of her statue in Bombay, and, on the day of the jubilee, created an effigy of her using old shoes and other materials from a rubbish tip, with her photograph perched on top.[72] But the Bombay police threw their net wider, and entrapped an influential Marathi nationalist. Bal Gangadhar Tilak, editor of the *Kesari* newspaper, was arrested and put on trial for citing disaffection. Tilak had proven radical credentials. He had been a member of the Poona Sabha and the INC. He also led the local campaign to memorialise Shivaji, the seventeenth-century Maratha warrior king who took on the Mughals and the Adil Shahis.

Tilak's trial that summer, and his eventual conviction and imprisonment, was a defining moment in Indian nationalism, as he appealed to an indigenous Indian tradition of heroic patriotism.[73] However, the trial also demonstrated the contested manner in which the queen's name had come to be used by 1897. The three main charges brought against Tilak all related in one way or another to the diamond jubilee.[74] The articles that he penned in *Kesari* for which he was indicted were part of a series devoted to the queen's jubilee. In the first he claimed that Shivaji provided a precedent for resisting rule through violence. In the second he was critical of the showy aspects of the jubilee, singling out for ridicule the fawning behaviour of the Indian princes who travelled to London, and referring to the Prince of Wales as a 'circus-wallah'. At the same time, Tilak made clear that he was loyal to the queen-empress, and only wished that she might be associated with acts of charity towards the Indian people in her jubilee year. Finally, and most significantly, Tilak was charged with bringing the name of Queen Victoria into disrepute by comparing her to Dharmaraja, or, in the epic *Mahabharata*, Yudhishthira, the 'monarch of the world', king of the

Pandavas, who spent 109 years on earth before entering heaven, symbolising piety and compassion for his fellow creatures. It was a bold move. The INC had spent over a decade cutting their cloth to fit the rhetoric of constitutional liberalism, invoking the queen's proclamation and asserting their rights as imperial subjects – all without much impact. Now here was one of them incorporating the queen into a quite different Indian moral universe, giving legitimacy to a Marathi nationalism by comparing the queen to past Indian rulers both mythical and real. Tilak's was not the first attempt to do this. However, by choosing the jubilee to make his intervention, and against the background of heavy-handed policing of the famine and the plague, his appropriation of the queen was timely, clearly angering the Bombay government.

A low-key jubilee in 1897 thus ended in high-resolution Indian discontent. The Government of India had not tried to manage the second jubilee in the way they had controlled the first, and what few rules they had laid down had been widely resented. Without too much intervention from above, India threw its own show in 1897, paying tribute to the mother of India, celebrating her womanly virtues, and naturalising her into Indian traditions, filtered by religion and region. The Government of India was right to hold back. Militant views lurked beneath surface loyalism, revealing themselves at those points where it was impossible to separate out the queen from the acts of government carried out in her name. Any attempt to project the queen further invited a backlash. Back in May 1897, Arthur Godley, the senior civil servant at the India Office, had counselled against a republication of the queen's proclamation of 1858 to coincide with the jubilee. 'This is hardly the moment,' he told Hamilton, 'to remind the world that the queen promised to make no distinction of race. The less said about it the better.'[75] With the volume turned low on official patriotism, the way was cleared for nationalists such as Tilak to turn the jubilee into an opportunity to craft a more indigenous version of India's story, and her destiny. Queen Victoria was included in that narrative, but she was there as an Indian monarch as much as an English one.

CHAPTER 12

THE LAST YEARS OF THE QAISARA

In July 1891 'Louischen', the Duchess of Connaught, celebrated her thirty-first birthday in the new wing of Osborne House. Everyone sat down to dinner for the first time in the 'Indian room'. It was unfinished. Nonetheless, the queen spent the summer showing off the new addition to her home, also known as the 'durbar room'. The room took up all of the ground floor of the new extension to Osborne House. Originally conceived as a state dining room, it soon became more of a family space. John Lockwood Kipling, principal of the Mayo School of Arts in Lahore, designed it, and Bhai Ram Singh, a Sikh craftsman, carried out the work. From India Kipling and Bhai Ram Singh had already made a billiard room for Bagshot House, the Connaughts' home. Now Bhai Ram Singh travelled west for a larger commission. Hired at £5 per week, he arrived at Osborne in January 1891. Scheduled to complete the commission in six months, he stayed until April 1892, lodging in nearby Cowes, superintending the London contractors and in turn being supervised by the Duchess of Connaught. Despite the delays, the queen was 'delighted' with his work, believing the room to be 'unique in Europe'. The wooden and plaster décor mixed Hindu and Mughal features, there were carpets woven by women prisoners at Agra, and hangings chosen by the queen. Indian portraits and jubilee gifts from India lined the corridor leading to the new wing. Airy and spacious, the durbar room served as an alternative family dining room in the summer, and most Christmases were spent there as well, including the queen's last in 1900. Amateur dramatics – the royal family's favourite *tableaux vivants* – were played out there too.[1] Alongside Indian rooms, there were Indian servants. The Connaughts brought one back with them when they returned from Bombay in 1890, and in 1887 Queen Victoria's long-standing desire to have her own Indian attendants was gratified with the arrival at court from Agra of two Muslims: Hafiz Abdul Karim and Muhammad Bakhsh. Abdul Karim, elevated from manservant to *munshi* in 1888, remained at court until the queen's death in 1901, teaching the queen Hindustani and, to the consternation of courtiers and politicians, seeming to become as close to the queen as John Brown had been in the 1860s and 1870s.

The queen's last years were in some ways her most Indian. With the Connaughts, who had seven years in India behind them, as her constant companions, with her durbar room to dine in, and above all, with her Indian servants at her side, Queen Victoria recreated her eastern dominion at home. For her officials, this sounded alarm bells. For her Indian public, it made her more popular than ever, so much so that on her death she was celebrated as an Indian monarch as much as a monarch of India. As the *fin de siècle* Raj became more British, the domestic life of the queen-empress grew more Indian. This final chapter discusses the causes and consequences of this last twist in the Indian history of the Victorian monarchy. It commences in the princely state of Manipur in 1891, when the queen, to her regret, was unable to intervene and prevent the only execution of a reigning prince during her reign. Then the chapter turns to describe the presence at court of not just the *munshi* but also another Indian Muslim, Rafiuddin Ahmad. Finally, the chapter surveys reactions in India to the queen's death in 1901.

Manipur

In 1891 Queen Victoria's annual holiday on the French Riviera was interrupted by news of a murderous seizure of power in Manipur, a small

British protectorate on the northern frontier of Burma.[2] In 1886 the independent ruler, Maharaja Chandrakirti, had died and a power struggle ensued between his successor, his son Surachandra Singh, and two of his other sons, Tikendrajit (known as the Senapati, or the 'military commander') and Kulachandra. The Senapati led a palace coup. Surachandra abdicated and was replaced by Kulachandra, whom the Government of India, reluctant to annex the state, now recognised as legitimate ruler. At the same time, a military force was despatched to punish the Senapati. It proved a disaster. The leader of the expedition, James Quinton, the chief commissioner of Assam, was captured and killed along with several others including the local resident, Frank Grimwood, whilst loyal troops, led by the redoubtable Ethel Grimwood, wife of the resident, managed to escape, later releasing her dramatic captivity story to the newspapers. Mutiny memories were revived, and more recent colonial disasters such as Isandlwana in southern Africa were recalled. Tales of treachery and mutilation of corpses quickly circulated.[3] Reinforcements were sent from Burma, joined by Gurkhas, and the coup was ended, with the princes and other ringleaders put on trial.

The whole episode left the queen 'full of anxiety'. She sympathised with the plight of the prisoners: what Mrs Grimwood went through 'must have been dreadful'. Of more lingering concern for the queen, however, was the treatment of the Manipuri princes. In Grasse, she swotted up on the history of British dealings with Manipur. On her return to Windsor at the beginning of May, she sought out Richard Cross, the secretary of state for India. She complained that the attempted seizure of the two brother princes at the durbar arranged by Quinton under the pretext of recognising the new regime created the 'appearance of treachery'; it was 'incredible and unpardonable conduct' for which Quinton had paid with his life. As reports of the trial and verdict reached London during June, she urged that Tikendrajit and Kulachandra be treated with clemency, preferring banishment or life imprisonment instead of execution (the 'Queen is naturally averse to hanging a Prince', observed Cross).[4]

Then Queen Victoria received the heroine of the hour, Ethel Grimwood, at Windsor. She wanted to award Grimwood the Victoria

Cross or the Crown of India, but settled, on her secretary of state's advice, on the Red Cross. In her conversation with the plucky survivor, the queen noted how even Mrs Grimwood blamed another coup conspirator, Lungthoubu Thangal (known as 'Thangal General') and not the Senapati for the killings.[5] Back in Imphal, the princes' lawyer, Manomohan Ghose, appealed to the queen for clemency. Lord Lansdowne, the viceroy, and Cross held their breath lest she interfered, a course of action that would be 'catastrophic', warned the viceroy. Kulachandra was spared death, but nothing more could be done for the other two. On 13 August, the Senapati and Thangal General were executed, on order of the viceroy, and on the same spot where Quinton and his colleagues had been slain. 'I regret it,' the queen wrote in her journal, 'as I think our whole conduct in that affair is not clear.' Cross sighed with relief, telling Lansdowne that the 'Queen was convinced that the peoples of India believed that she could of her own will have spared any execution'.[6] Still Queen Victoria did not let go. After the execution she contacted Ethel Grimwood via Harriet Phipps, one of her court staff, seeking further information. Grimwood expressed her sorrow for the prince, and absolved him of responsibility for her husband's death, but still felt he 'deserved to suffer' for what he had done to others.[7]

The Manipur crisis revealed many of the queen's usual Indian traits. There was the distrust of local British officials in India and an instinctive tendency to take the side of a native prince. She was forthright in her criticism of Lansdowne and wanted John Gorst, the under-secretary of state for India, reprimanded.[8] Even after the Senapati had been identified as the villain of the piece she continued to argue that he was more wronged than wrongful. His seizure by British officials at the durbar was underhand, she insisted, and anyway his punishment did not fit the crime. He had not been found guilty of murder. Nor was he responsible for the bloody reprisals: she pointed out to Cross (as Charlotte Canning had to her in 1857) that the beheadings had taken place after the victims had been killed. She also demanded that proper provision be made for the widows and children of the executed prince.[9] Then there was her thirst for first-hand testimony. As in 1857, when she relied heavily on Charlotte Canning's eyewitness accounts, in 1891 she based her view of events almost entirely on Ethel Grimwood's narrative. As in 1880 over the retreat from Kandahar, she thought she could pummel her ministers as well as the viceroy around to her way of thinking. In this respect, Queen Victoria proved ignorant of the uses to which the Government of India had been putting her authority since 1858. The Senapati, Thangal General and Kulachandra were all found guilty of 'waging war against the Queen'. The queen was clearly unaware of the long reach of this law applied in her name. 'Why shd. the Indian penal code be so different to ours?' she demanded of Cross.[10] Manipur was the only occasion during her reign when the charge of 'waging war against the Queen' in India could be made to stick. The queen was left in an invidious position. Unable to intervene to commute the sentences of death, she turned out to be the prince's executioner and not his saviour. Her warrant sealed his fate. Cross was made to feel the full force of her anger. After the executions had taken place, she told him of her 'strong feeling that the principle of governing India by fear, & by crushing them, instead of only by firmness & conciliation is one wh. never will answer in the end, and the Queen Empress shd. wish to see more & more altered'. For his part, Cross suspected that voices in the queen's ear were turning her against her own officials in India. He pointed to one source in particular, the Indian servants in the royal household.[11]

The *Munshi* and the *Maulvi*

By the time of the Manipur crisis in 1891 it was no secret that the queen had taken on an Indian retinue. In October 1887 she sent a public letter to the Government of Bombay Presidency, thanking her subjects there for their jubilee gifts and greetings. In the letter she mentioned that she now had two Indian servants, and that she was learning Hindustani.[12] The two Indians referred to were Abdul Karim and Mahomet Bahksh, sent over by John Tyler, the superintendent of the Agra jail, to assist the queen during the jubilee. They were the first of the series of Muslim manservants, all from Agra, who joined the royal household in the late 1880s and 1890s. The longest-serving of them was Abdul Karim, or the *munshi* as he became known when the queen upgraded him from servant to secretary in 1888.[13] Abdul Karim and Mahomet Bahksh quickly became fixtures at court. The queen commissioned two of her favourite artists, the painter Rudolf Swoboda and the sculptor Joseph Boehm, to complete their likenesses, and she herself sketched Abdul Karim's portrait. They joined the royal family in their *tableaux vivants*, in which they were usually cast as Arab characters. Queen Victoria laid down elaborate guidelines for the court livery that her new Indian servants were to wear, a hybrid of a red European tunic bearing the royal crest, Indian turban and a silk sash around the waist.[14] There was to be no hiding their racial difference, the fact that they were Indians at court, rather than just courtiers who happened to be Indian.

In acquiring her own Indian servants, the queen was, to some extent, following the example of her children. The Prince of Wales had returned from India in 1876 with his own Indian cavalry guard. The Duke and Duchess of Connaught came back from India for the 1887 jubilee bringing with them their own Indian servant, Stephen Damuda, a Christian orphan. The Connaughts could also speak and read Hindustani. Queen Victoria was particularly keen to acquire spoken Hindustani and to practise writing the script as well. She gave instructions to her new Indian servants that they were to converse with her only in Hindustani, albeit slowly. For the next decade or so, interrupted only by his trips home to India, she took daily language lessons from Abdul Karim.[15] Abdul Karim also began to act as an interpreter for the queen, when there were Indian visitors to court, starting with the Gaekwar of Baroda in December 1887.

More than anything else that she did as queen-empress, Queen Victoria's adoption of the *munshi* as her right-hand man caused widespread concern amongst Palace staff and at the India Office. Abdul Karim was everywhere. Not only was he in daily attendance upon the queen at Windsor and Buckingham Palace, but he also went with her on her travels. From July 1891 he was listed in the court circular whenever the queen's public engagements were reported.[16] He was soon given his own home: Frogmore Cottage at Windsor, a specially built house at

Balmoral and Arthur's Cottage at Osborne. The queen lobbied hard to extend favour to Abdul Karim's father back in Agra: official honours and land. She insisted that Abdul Karim be given special status when he visited India, allowed to carry arms, excused from customs on arrival and invited to a viceregal durbar. Throughout his time in her service she pressed for various awards and titles of dignity to be granted to him.[17]

No one likes a court favourite, least of all a foreign one. Resentment towards Abdul Karim grew. He was accused of being involved in the theft of a brooch, of bullying the other Indian servants, and of briefing the press with his photograph and with puffed-up stories about his life and role at court. The palace rumour mill began to doubt that the *munshi* was all he seemed. In 1894 enquiries were made in India about his family and their status there. It was revealed that his father was simply the apothecary and not the surgeon-general at the Agra jail.[18] From doubts about his true identity, it was a short step to questioning his loyalty. Rightly or wrongly, by the mid-1890s the *munshi* was believed to be influencing the queen with a pro-Muslim outlook on Indian affairs. In turn the queen was suspected of sharing confidential information and documents with the *munshi*, which the India Office feared were being leaked to intermediaries associated with the Emir of Afghanistan. Hamilton, the secretary of state for India, threatened to stop showing the queen despatches lest she pass on state secrets. When the *munshi* returned to India in the spring of 1896 his movements and contacts were closely monitored by a force led by Sir John Lambert, former deputy commissioner of the Calcutta police.[19] In 1897 matters came to a head during the queen's sojourn at Cimiez on the French Riviera, when the *munshi* met up in the Excelsior Hotel with one Rafiuddin Ahmad, of the 'Moslem Patriotic League', to share, it was supposed, sensitive diplomatic information. Ahmad was expelled from the hotel and from the holiday. With the Prince of Wales, and Prince Louis of Battenberg (husband of Princess Victoria of Hesse, Queen Victoria's granddaughter) briefing against the hapless *munshi*, the queen was confronted by her physician, James Reid, and persuaded that the situation was not only dangerous but potentially a huge embarrassment.[20]

Thereafter, Abdul Karim was not around as much. He spent almost the whole of the queen's final year, 1900, in India, and, apart from the occasional complaint, his behaviour at court roused little comment. Yet, on her death, all traces of the *munshi* were hastily removed. The new king, Edward VII, packed him off back to India with a generous grant of land. His correspondence with the queen was destroyed and, when her journals and letters from the last fifteen years of her life were published between 1930 and 1932, the *munshi* was mostly edited out of the story.[21] Lord Cromer, the consul-general of Egypt, summed up the mood of many when he claimed that all Queen Victoria's ideas about India came from the *munshi*, and, by implication, that they were all wrong.[22] This harsh judgement can be disregarded. The queen had been steering her own course as far as Indian politics were concerned long before the advent of the *munshi*. There is no firm evidence that she either passed on the secrets of state to him or that he plied her with advice about India that was unavailable elsewhere. To conclude otherwise would be to credit Abdul Karim with more guile and intelligence than he possessed, and to afford none to the queen. The queen had her own ideas about Muslim India at the close of her reign, and if there was a voice in her ear it was not that of the *munshi*, but of his friend the *maulvi* (lawyer), Rafiuddin Ahmad, to whom we now need to turn.

Rafiuddin Ahmad was a young Muslim from Poona, who came to London in 1889 to study for the bar at Middle Temple. Soon, he became one of the principal spokesmen for moderate Indian Muslim loyalism in England.[23] He joined the National Indian Association in 1890, and shortly afterwards helped establish the 'Moslem Patriotic League'. By then Rafiuddin Ahmad had already come to public attention as a defender of Islam, chiding the English theatre for allowing the Prophet to be portrayed onstage, and also explaining to an English audience the importance of purdah for Indian Muslim women. He chummied up to the poet laureate, Lord Tennyson, visiting him at his home on the Isle of Wight. He visited Constantinople in 1891, for which he had no diplomatic accreditation, but managed to see Sultan Abdul Hamid II, the head of the caliphate, on more than one occasion during the visit.[24]

At the end of 1892 Rafiuddin Ahmad pulled off a sensation, publishing in *The Strand* magazine facsimiles of pages from the queen's Hindustani journal, copied by Her Majesty 'expressly for this article'. There were two extracts: one described the visit of the Shah of Persia to London in 1889, the other the queen's grief at the death of Prince Albert Victor earlier in 1892. Ahmad noted how he had been shown the diaries during a visit to Balmoral, an occasion when he also heard the Duke of Connaught 'break the conversation in Hindustani'. The article lavishly praised the queen for her oriental studies, remarking on how they set an example to the princes of India, how they confirmed her bond with the Indian people and how they exerted a positive influence over the caliphate. Ahmad duly acknowledged the role of the *munshi* in the 'rapid progress' made by the queen in learning Hindustani, and his portrait along with that of the queen, and of course the *maulvi*, accompanied the piece.[25] Instant notoriety came with the scoop. Profiles of Ahmad, the 'orientalist scholar', followed in newspapers. Doors began to open. He became a regular visitor at court. The Prince of Wales granted him an audience, and he was on the guest list for the wedding of George the Duke of York to Princess Mary of Teck in July 1893, an occasion which he wrote up for *The Strand*. The queen gave her customary seal of approval by inviting Ahmad to sit for a portrait by Rudolf Swoboda.[26] No other Indian during her reign sped so fast from obscurity to acceptance at court. Yet the *maulvi* has eluded detection entirely.

Quite how Rafiuddin Ahmad worked his way into the confidences of the royal family is unclear. He had at least two audiences with the queen.[27] The queen sang his praises to Cross, the secretary of state, in May 1891, revealing that Lady Harris, wife of the governor of Bombay, had been his patron since his arrival in London. 'He is remarkably clever & most loyal & anxious to bring about the best of feeling between England and India,' the queen informed Cross, and went on to describe him as 'a staunch but liberal-minded Mahomedan' whom Cross would do well to meet.[28] Abdul Karim may have shared the extracts from the queen's diaries with Ahmad during his second visit, with or without the queen's consent, or the queen may have herself facilitated the publication. She certainly did nothing to prevent their publication. Moreover, she imbibed some of his ideas. In 1892, not long after her audience with Rafiuddin Ahmad, Queen Victoria expressed her anxiety over the status of Indian Muslims as a political minority to Lord Lansdowne, the viceroy, in relation to the new Indian Councils Act, echoing Ahmad's stance.[29] In 1894, Ahmad took up the cause of Indian Muslims caught up in the plague scares surrounding the pilgrim traffic to the Hajj at Mecca. He was introduced at the Foreign Office as Abdul Karim's brother, met with Sir Henry Fowler, the new secretary of state for India in Lord Rosebery's Cabinet, and was instrumental in improving the inspection of ships, something he later claimed had brought 'unfeigned satisfaction' to Indian Muslims.[30] Finally, towards the end of 1894, Ahmad stepped up his criticism of the Indian National Congress, arguing that the sectarian riots that had broken out in Bombay were the result of political provocation. Again, the queen was prompted into action, sending a telegram to her viceroy, the Earl of Elgin, asking him to provide further information.[31]

Rafiuddin Ahmad was clearly a persuasive charmer. It is unlikely that he knew Abdul Karim before he came to London, but once he met him in 1891, the *munshi* most probably became his channel of communication to the queen. The lack of surviving correspondence hinders a definitive conclusion, but it seems plausible to argue that the *munshi* amplified the views of Ahmad, and encouraged the queen to consult his journalism for herself. For example, in 1898 she recommended that the new viceroy, Lord Curzon, consult Ahmad's article in the *Nineteenth Century* calling for a new university in India to be dedicated to the higher education of Muslims.[32] As ever, on Indian affairs, the queen followed where her instincts dictated, not where she was pushed. In other words, she adopted a position more tolerant of Muslim views in the 1890s as she wished to avoid strife between the races, in much the same manner as she had despaired over the European backlash in Calcutta against Ripon's legal reforms in 1883. She reached out to Ahmad, not because he was the *munshi*'s friend, but rather because his views tallied with her own concerns.

As far as the court and the India Office were concerned, however, Ahmad's friendship with the *munshi* was a breach of security. He was ejected as we have seen from the queen's hotel in 1897, and monitored again by the police in 1898.[33] No smoking gun was found to connect him to the emir. To the twitchy British he was a 'ruffian' agitator, a 'Mahomedan intriguer' and possibly a spy.[34] To the queen he was an informant, but of the benign variety. He helped her develop a new perspective on the condition of Muslims in India, on the growing danger of sectarianism. She remained several steps ahead of her blinkered officials. Learning Hindustani, confiding in the *munshi* and taking guidance from Ahmad were all ways of steering a course independent of the Government of India and the India Office. The queen recommended it to others. In March 1899 she suggested to Lord Curzon that he employ an interpreter, so that Anglo-Indian views did not dominate.[35] Curzon had no need of a *munshi*, and, as we shall see, the youngest and most headstrong of all her viceroys had his own views about the role of royalty in the Raj.

Beyond the royal household Queen Victoria wanted Indians to serve in other parts of her realm. In 1896 she backed a proposal that Indian princes sit in the House of Lords.[36] Three years later, during the South African war, the queen urged that Indian forces be deployed, and was subsequently pleased to see 11,000 sent out as auxiliary, non-combatant support. But she wanted more. Might the troops be joined by senior Indian officers who could be given roles of command, she pressed George Hamilton, the secretary of state for India, on several occasions in 1900. Again, she had in mind Indian princes. Her suggestions were politely but firmly brushed aside by Hamilton, despite support from the viceroy, not a little amused to find the octogenarian queen still as alert, involved and Indophile as ever.[37]

In Memoriam

By the summer of 1900 Queen Victoria was ageing fast. She made an overseas trip to Ireland in April and hosted a large garden party at Buckingham Palace in July, where the royal couple from Baroda and the Maharaja of Cooch Behar were amongst the guests.[38] Her aides now closed in around her, limiting her travel to only her royal residences, and stemming the flow of visitors to the court. Despite this seclusion, her door remained open to Indian princes. Avoiding every obstacle set up by the India Office, the canny Maharaja of Kapurthala made his way to Balmoral at the end of October, where the queen was expecting him. Hamilton, the secretary of state, was aghast, not only as the audience with the queen took place without official sanction, but also because the maharaja was *persona non grata*, owing to the 'debauchery' of his rule.[39] Kapurthala was not the last Indian in the queen's schedule. Prior to the onset of her final illness, the Thakur of Morvi arrived in England, and sent on to the queen some vases, about which she wrote enthusiastically to Curzon just eleven days before her death.[40] There was an Indian presence too at the queen's last official engagement, on 2 January 1901, when Queen Victoria, with Abdul Karim at her side, received Lord Roberts, commander of the British forces in South Africa. Roberts came to Osborne House accompanied by six Indian cavalrymen orderlies. Veteran of the Indian rebellion of 1857–8 and the second Afghan war, ringmaster of the military review at the Delhi Assemblage in 1877, and commander-in-chief of the Madras Army in the 1880s, Roberts personified the royal army in India since the transfer of power in 1858.[41] It was a fitting end to a public life lived in Britain, but magnified in India.

During the next fortnight the queen's condition worsened. From 15 January, daily reports of her health were telegraphed to the viceroy, and printed in the government *Gazette*. By the 18 January the updates were coming in more frequently: several a day, and then by the hour. Public prayers for the queen's recovery were ordered in various parts of India. On 22 January Queen Victoria died, her immediate family, physician, nurses and the Bishop of Winchester at her bedside. Her body was removed to the dining room, and the royal household, including Abdul Karim, were allowed in to make their farewells. Then she was taken to the chapel at Osborne to lie in state until the funeral. There, the queen's coffin was laid upon a dais covered with the Royal Standard, with the Scottish lion and the Irish harp showing at each end. Beneath the Royal Standard lay an Indian shawl, and an Indian carpet was laid on the floor of the chapel. In death as in life, India was never far away from the queen.

On hearing the news, India ground to a halt. The Government of India declared three days of mourning, and stipulated that all government employees wear black crepe. Many of the princely states went further. Four days of mourning were declared in Mysore. In Hyderabad, the nizam interrupted an execution just as the noose was being tightened on the condemned man, and gave him a pardon.[42] Memorial meetings were organised to coincide with the funeral in London on 2 February. Curzon led the way, joining his officials for a service in Calcutta Cathedral. A similar service took place in Bombay, although the lines from the 'Dead March' imploring that the queen's soul be delivered from the 'gates of hell' were removed as inappropriate after objections.[43] As ever, official staging of the monarchy gave way to local, more spontaneous reactions from Indians. The black crepe protocol issued by the government offended many, both for its officious tone and for its choice of colour, white being the convention for mourning in India.[44] Perhaps the most striking moment of all came on the Calcutta Maidan, held at the same time as the Anglican service in the cathedral. In a ceremony organised by local Hindus the queen's portrait was placed on a stand and draped in white. Across the Maidan effigies of the goddess Lakshmi were carried aloft in one of the largest gatherings of Hindus ever seen in the city. In other cities the queen's death was marked in local style. In Bombay, for example, wreaths of white flowers appeared from nowhere to be laid around her statue.[45]

Remembering the queen the Indian way continued in the weeks following her final internment in the mausoleum at Frogmore in the grounds of the Windsor Castle estate. Hundreds of memorial meetings were convened across India during February, and through the months that followed there was a steady outpouring of biographies, tributes and offerings.[46] Two versions of the queen-empress emerged. On the one side was an Anglo-Indian queen, who had extended Christian civilisation to the east. For example, in the praise offered by *The Empress*, an illustrated magazine published in Calcutta, the queen was lauded for the protection she had given to Indian Muslims and to the women of India. At the same time, stories began to be told of the Indian dimensions to the queen's life. The 1858 proclamation took pride of place, not least because the viceroy referred to it as 'the golden guide to our conduct and aspirations' in his eulogy delivered to his Council on 1 February, his comments interpreted as a very public rehabilitation after the contempt shown towards India's 'Magna Carta' by the British governing class in the 1880s and 1890s.[47] Indian commentary in 1901 focused on how the queen in her last years had taken on Indian Muslim servants and learned Hindustani. The *munshi* was given pride of place in the narrative. The queen, apparently, had given him his own palace for his family's use. An illustrated memorial volume depicted the *munshi* at the queen's side during the last visit of Lord Roberts. The *Friend of India* even claimed that the *munshi* and another Indian servant had kept vigil over the queen's body as it lay in the chapel at Osborne, an erroneous story that originated in the London press and gathered pace in India.[48] The queen was also celebrated as a widow. As *The Bengalee* put it, the queen was revered more as a woman that as a sovereign, her life of posthumous devotion to her husband summed up the ideal of Indian widowhood. India had lost not so much a great queen as a mother. Dinshaw Wacha, the president of the Indian National Congress, declared her to be 'an affectionate mother and the type of the highest and most exalted womanhood'. As K. C. Duraisamy, a newspaper editor from Bangalore, observed, 'the women population are the greatest mourners' for the 'mother of mothers'. So the tributes to her as mother and widow went on, with her opposition to widow remarriage added in as well. She was revered by Lajjaram Sharma Mehta, the Hindu nationalist, as an ideal of Indian womanhood, and by the Tamil writer Vidhvan Periya Subbar Reddiar as a 'maiden wife and sovereign'.[49] There was no allusion to her colour – the epithet 'great white Queen' would only come later. In India, much more so than back in Britain, the queen was remembered as a female sovereign, the mother of India.

To this roll call of her Indian empathies was added an Indianisation of the queen. She was incorporated into Hindu deity: Queen Victoria was the Adya-Sakti[50] of our mythology, explained Sourindro Mohun Tagore. She was included in the telling of the 'Lays of India', delivering India from the 'anarchy' of its former rulers. She epitomised a divine presence, 'as a Sovereign in a limited monarchy, but as the visible agent of the invisible Providence', as Subramania Iyer, founding editor of the *Hindu* newspaper, described her at a meeting in Madras.[51] A 'Hindu pundit', writing in the *Madras Mail*, credited Queen Victoria with reviving respect for kingship, as she summoned from the Sastras the natural obedience shown by Hindus towards monarchs. For *Nava Yug*, a Bengali newspaper in Calcutta, the queen was a *jagadhatri* (protector of the world). She had returned India to prosperity, of the sort not known since the time of Rama, according to *Kalpataru*, a Marathi paper from Bombay. So deified and reified, Queen Victoria left life as a reincarnation of India's golden age. It was an Indian version of the queen that faced strong competition.

For one man had his own idea of how Queen Victoria should be commemorated: Lord Curzon, the viceroy. With indecent haste – the queen was only just buried – he outlined his ideas for a 'Victoria Memorial Hall', a 'Valhalla' for India. Curzon likened his project to Nelson's Column, and to the Albert Memorial. But he wanted something even more spectacular: a building that would be 'stately, spacious, monumental, and grand', to which people would flock from across India. Curzon's acolytes promised a new Taj Mahal, a tribute to the empress of the nineteenth century as fine and fitting as that completed for the empress of the seventeenth. The building, Curzon explained, would serve two purposes, first as a monument to the queen, and secondly as a museum or 'national gallery' of modern India, that is to say, India under British rule, 'worthy both of the queen and of the Victorian age'.[52] This latter stipulation proved controversial. Curzon viewed India's indigenous history through a distorting lens, one that celebrated the impact of the west and sidelined the achievements of the east. So the Victoria Memorial Hall would foreground India's history since the eighteenth century and leave the deeper past to others.

Curzon's plans developed quickly. Within days, dependable maharajas such as those of Jaipur, Kashmir and Mysore had stumped up large contributions, and over the following weeks a formidable nationwide organisation was established, a pot of funds began to fill and exhibits were donated or pledged. By the end of February Curzon was able to announce his scheme in more detail. The memorial would comprise a central hall, containing a statue of the queen, and around its walls her words in English and in the vernacular – from the proclamation and from her other messages to India – would be inscribed in gold. This centrepiece would lead on to a series of galleries, featuring the history of India since the Mughals, and represented by sculpture, painting, treaties and *sannads*, maps, newspapers, native arms and musical instruments.[53] There would also be a Princes' Court. But of India's own pre-history, into which so many Indian eulogies had managed to incorporate the queen, there would be no reference.

Critics lined up over the Calcutta memorial. Firstly, it was objected that a national monument should be in Calcutta. Secondly, that it should celebrate a particular version of Indian history, both in chronology and in content. And, thirdly, that a hall of the dead was to be preferred to more practical and useful schemes for the living.[54] Rival schemes of memorialisation emerged. Some had a national remit. The Indian Women's Victoria Memorial, although based in Bengal, had the Maharani of Mysore as its figurehead. Elsewhere, other places asserted their claim to be the rightful location for a memorial monument to the queen, for example Bombay and Karachi.[55] In the main, philanthropy was preferred to pomposity. Schemes came forward for education, most notably technical institutes, such as the one established in Madras. There was a revival of fundraising for medical causes, principally nursing, but also for hospitals. The Dufferin fund for the training of nurses and doctors revived, with a new 'Victoria Memorial Scholarships' scheme for training midwives, and several specialist facilities were set up, such as the Institute for the Blind in Bombay.[56] Indian initiatives looked forwards as well as backwards.

Curzon marked the demise of the queen and the advent of the new era with one other grand gesture: the imperial durbar of 1903. Soon after the accession of Edward VII, Curzon suggested that the new king should come to India for a parallel coronation event there. Little enthusiasm for the idea could be found in Britain. The king's private secretary explained that the king could not be spared for such a long period as a royal visit to India would entail. There would have to be a full tour, and not just a single event in Delhi.[57] Daunted but not defeated, Curzon proceeded anyway with plans for a Delhi durbar to coincide with the world tour of Prince Arthur and his wife, Louise. With the Connaughts and Ernest Louis, the Duke of Hesse (a grandchild of Queen Victoria), as royal guests, Curzon himself ghosting the role of the king-emperor, and Mary Curzon, the vicereine, matching her husband all the way for glamour, much to the amusement of the satirical press, India was promised an occasion both awesome and traditional. 'To the East,' the viceroy told his Council at Simla in October 1902, swiping away complaints about the costs of the impending durbar, 'there is nothing strange, but something familiar, and even sacred, about the practice that brings Sovereigns into communion with the people in a ceremony of public solemnity and rejoicing after they have succeeded to their high estate.'[58] Except that the sovereign stayed away.

Of all the Delhi durbars, Curzon's 1903 pageant was the most spectacular. Held on the same spot as Lord Lytton's Imperial Assemblage of 1877, it was less elaborate than its predecessor. Nor was it as momentous as the appearance of Edward VII's successor George V and Queen Mary at Delhi in December 1911. The 1903 durbar did, however, outshine the others in the sheer scale of its organisation, much of it caught on moving film.[59] Bhai Ram Singh and Ganga Ram, a civil engineer from the Punjab, were commissioned to build and decorate the Indo-Saracenic durbar pavilions designed by Swinton Jacob, veteran of the Public Works department of Jaipur. The 1903 durbar was an international extravaganza, a show put on for an audience back in Britain as much as for the princes and people of India. Compared to 1877, when there was only a handful of unofficial invitees, there was a huge influx of overseas guests, some 1,222 in all, from as far afield as Japan, South Africa and Australia. Only 159 Indians came, most of whom were princes and chiefs. Admittedly, the Indian maharajas came with thousands of followers, and the set pieces of the event – the elephant procession, the military parade – featured them in all their finery. However, there was no missing the wider message of some of the occasion. The time-honoured rituals of the durbar were ignored; there were no return visits of viceroys and chiefs. Curzon dominated the proceedings of the formal proclamation, speaking for thirty minutes, hand on thigh, foot disrespectfully placed on the bottom of the throne. Then, in the most marked break with tradition, all the princes showed their deference in full public view, one by one approaching the dais, from where the viceroy leant down to hear them swear their loyalty. Curzon later claimed that his durbar simply revived an old policy. 'We touched their hearts with the idea of a common sentiment and a common aim,' he told an audience at the Guildhall in London the following year. 'Depend upon it, you will never rule the East except through the heart, and the moment imagination has gone out of your Asiatic policy your Empire will dwindle and decay.'[60] But Curzon's durbar contained a range of innovations that came more from his imagination than anywhere else. Those with longer memories, such as Charles O'Donnell, who had attended Lytton's assemblage in 1877, were shocked by Curzon's 'peacocking Imperialism' and especially by the affront given to the Indian princes.[61] No words of royal sympathy or pledges of justice marked the occasion, just the viceregal boot of authority.

Royal India was never the same again after the death of the queen. Some things carried on as before. In 1905 the Prince of Wales – the future George V – toured India, not long after Curzon's controversial decision to partition Bengal into separate Muslim and Hindu provinces. The visit was a carbon copy of earlier royal tours, officials poring over the records from 1875–6 to ensure that they had the correct protocol.[62] The old magic was still there. Friendships were resumed, most notably with Ganga Singh, the Maharaja of Bikaner, who had been made the prince's aide-de-camp in 1902, and who would go on to serve in Lloyd George's Imperial War Cabinet a decade later.[63] But, as the Prince of Wales journeyed across the subcontinent, the terrain of Indian politics was being transformed. Muslims gathered at Aligarh used the occasion of the prince's visit in March 1906 to begin discussions about forming a new political organisation that later in the year became the All-India Muslim League, a rival to the Indian National Congress.[64] Prince George was kept on a tight leash, the Government of India insisting that no memorials or requests be presented to him at any stage of the trip.[65] In January 1906, whilst in Calcutta, the prince did lay the foundation stone of the Victoria Memorial Hall, on land halfway between the cathedral and the old prison.[66] However, the atmosphere had changed, with not much left of the spontaneous enthusiasm that had once accompanied the appearance of royalty in India. Lord Minto, who succeeded Curzon as viceroy, dragged his heels over getting on with the Victoria Memorial Hall.

As the fiftieth anniversary of the transfer of power approached in 1908, Minto vetoed plans for a general amnesty of prisoners. A new proclamation in the name of Edward VII was issued, steered by the secretary of state, John Morley, not least to boost army morale and ease tensions on the north-west frontier. It reflected on a half-century, surveying 'our labours . . . with clear gaze and good conscience' and cautiously promised more reform.[67] Cracks began to show. In 1909 statues of Queen Victoria at Benares and Nagpur were defaced.[68] When Edward VII passed away at the beginning of May 1910 there was little of the unorchestrated outpouring of grief witnessed at the death of the queen. Edward was remembered as 'the world's peacemaker', but, aside from a public letter sent during the 1907 famine, memorialists struggled to recall whether he had brought peace to India. Subscriptions were raised to commemorate the late king-emperor with an equestrian statue in Delhi, the Indian army coming up with a large part of the funding. Hardly any Indians attended the unveiling of the foundation stone, laid on a site between the Fort and the Jama Masjid by George V in December 1911.[69] At the 1911 durbar, the only time a serving monarch and his consort showed up in India, the Gaekwar of Baroda refused to dress in ceremonial costume for the occasion, and deliberately turned his back on the royal couple as he retreated from the throne.[70] Nonetheless, India fought for king, empire and country in the First World War, and some of the Indian princes – from Bikaner, Patiala, Cooch Behar, Jodhpur, Ratlam and Kishangarh – were selected for service in Europe. India remained loyal. Its loyalism was taken for granted.

Nowhere registered the waning of royal India quite so poignantly as the Victoria Memorial Hall. By 1907, although 4 million rupees had been raised and architects appointed, limited progress had been made on the construction of the memorial. There were problems in the supply of the marble. Subsidence was found to be affecting the site selected for the building. Between the heaven of the cathedral and the hell of the prison lay a lot of swamp.[71] None of Curzon's successors showed much enthusiasm for the project. Curzon lamented that had he stayed in India, the job would have been completed. Minto, he complained, was at best 'perfunctory'. Finally, in 1913, Lord Carmichael, the governor of Bengal and a trustee of the National Gallery in London, took some interest, securing the plot on the Maidan for the Memorial Hall.[72] Wartime restrictions on tools and materials slowed works further, and by 1918, although an end to the construction was in sight, so too was the depletion of the trustees' working capital. Curzon canvassed amongst Indian princes, testing the water for a further call on their generosity, but even the Maharaja of Bikaner, so loyal and lavish in the past, counselled against such a move. The Victoria Memorial Hall was eventually completed in 1920. However, that still left the grounds around and approaches to the building to be done. As the date of the opening ceremony approached, with the visiting Prince of Wales due to cut the ribbon, money was again running short, and loans were taken out in India and in London to make up the shortfall.[73] George Frampton's statue of the queen, which had been sitting at the other end of the Maidan waiting for its new home since 1901, was shunted into place. At last, on 28 December 1921, Victoria's 'Taj' was opened to the public, 'an enduring token of the affection which all, Indians and Europeans, princes and peasants, felt for Queen Victoria'.[74]

It had taken four viceroys, two king-emperors and one world war to see through the Victoria memorial project from start to finish. In that time, the Raj had changed so much. The capital was on the move, from Calcutta to New Delhi. The oldest part of British India – Bengal – had been split and then put back together again. Guns had been turned on the festival crowds at Amritsar. A terrible beauty had been born: Mohandas Gandhi's movement for *swaraj*, or self-rule. Curzon's version of India, frozen into the marbled splendour of the Victoria Memorial Hall, already belonged to a different age. So too did Queen Victoria. To this day her gargantuan bronze statue sits outside the Hall. She is slumped on her throne, looking north across the Maidan to the old Fort William where it all began. In her hands she clutches an orb and a sceptre. One piece of regalia is missing. No crown, either hollow or imperial, adorns her head.

EPILOGUE

The queen was dead, but the Empire lived on for almost a half century more. The new republic of India was finally proclaimed on 26 January 1950, following the granting of independence and simultaneous partition of India and Pakistan in August 1947. Pakistan became an Islamic republic on 23 March 1956. There was no straight road taken from imperial monarchy to republic. Narratives of national identity in the Indian subcontinent can tell an uncomplicated story of the coming of the modern states of India and Pakistan – of the journey from 'rebellion to republic' – as though the final form of polity chosen was always a pre-ordained outcome. As Jawaharlal Nehru, one of the architects of the new India, observed, when introducing the draft constitution for the new state in 1946, it was impossible to 'produce monarchy out of nothing . . . [India] must inevitably be a republic'.[1] Yet the exit from empire, and the rejection of the British monarchy, was considerably more drawn out and complex than this. The idea of the modern republic was novel and untried; the concept of monarchy was almost as old as time itself. The monarchies of Europe had endured and survived the revolutionary era after 1789, and adapted across the age of empire to become multinational, composite systems of rule, of which the Raj in India was a shining example, for better or worse. Republics, especially large ones, by contrast, had a bad nineteenth century, descending into civil war (America, France, Mexico, Spain, Uruguay). In this context, the genesis of India as a republic was as much an act of invention as one of faith.

On the British side, there were no precedents for monarchy giving way peacefully to a republican alternative. The American revolution of 1776 was so seared into the British psyche that colonial rule thereafter steered away from outright confrontation with settlers and indigenous elites. Only two territories managed to break away from the British imperial fold in the nineteenth century: the Orange Free State and the Transvaal. The fact that Britain refused to recognise the Transvaal's adopted name, the 'South African Republic', shows how alien the idea of the republic remained.[2] For Indians too, nationalists included, it proved difficult to conceive India without the monarchy. Until the end of the First World War the Indian National Congress and the All-India Muslim League sought 'home rule' for India under the Crown. After the Amritsar massacre of 1919, anti-British feeling intensified in India and during the 1920s the first calls for an independent republic were made. But there was no unanimity about what form a republic might take.

By way of conclusion, this chapter charts how the lure of monarchy in India waxed, waned and finally crashed to the ground in the first half of the twentieth century, and how the idea of a republican future took hold. One led to the other – in other words, the ways in which the Government of India persisted in the symbolism of the British monarchy, long after Queen Victoria's death, directly contributed to the emergence of the republic as the solution to India's woes. The Raj overplayed its hand. From being its strongest asset, the monarchy became its weakest link. Without Queen Victoria, royal India was exposed as an imperial sham.

Raj and *Swaraj*

After 1901 new times brought a new, less deferential tone to Indian nationalism. Criticism of the founding fathers of the INC became common, and dissenting versions of India's past began to be told. For some it was a complete volte-face. Bipin Chandra Pal, who less than two decades earlier had written a fulsome biographical tribute to Queen Victoria, now championed a 'new spirit' of patriotism, one that celebrated India as the motherland. Influenced by Rabindranath Tagore, Chandra Pal derided Lord Curzon's 'outlandish Walhalla' – the Victoria Memorial Hall – and called instead for a 'Walhalla of our own', made up of festivals and celebrations of Shivaji, the Hindu king. Chandra Pal railed against the INC's ritual devotions to the visiting Prince of Wales and to the king-emperor at the 1905 meeting of Congress at Benares. 'Devoted attachment to the person of the sovereign', he declared, was no basis for national sentiment.[3] Other histories of India that had been dormant now emerged, for example Vinayak Damodar Savarkar's *Indian War of Independence 1857*, written and published in exile in 1909, the strident title spelling out its theme.[4] The partition by the British of Bengal in 1905, seen by many as an undisguised attack on the powerbase of the INC, fuelled this new mood. Unsurprisingly, the most high-octane moments came from Indian nationalists abroad, enjoying the cleaner air of publicity in Europe and America. In 1907, for the first time, the flag of the new India was flown at a meeting of the Socialist Congress at Stuttgart in Germany, taken there by Bhikaiji Cama, co-founder of the Paris India Society.[5] London served as both a resting- and nesting-place for Indian militants. There was India House, founded as a meeting point, and home to a newspaper, the *Indian Sociologist*, edited by Shiyamji Krishna Varma. For all his vitriol, however, Krishna Varma was unclear how India would be shaped in the future, his thoughts often returning to giving more powers to the Indian princes, reconstituting them as a federation.[6] Old habits died hard.

No one exemplified the persistence of loyalism within Indian nationalism more than Mohandas Gandhi. As a young lawyer from Gujarat who had emigrated to Natal in southern Africa in 1893, Gandhi frequently invoked the 1858 proclamation in his campaign on behalf of Indians excluded from the franchise. Indians in the colony of Natal deserved the same rights as Indians in India, he claimed: they were all 'proud to be under the British Crown', and the queen's words were their 'charter of Liberty'. Gandhi also played a prominent part in the events in Natal that marked the queen's golden jubilee in 1897 and her death in 1901.[7] Gandhi would later use this personal history of loyalty to dramatic effect, highlighting the contrast between the reverence he felt for the British constitution during the queen's lifetime and his conversion to self-rule, or *swaraj*, sometime in the 1900s. In his *Autobiography* (1927), he made much of his journey of emancipation from the old politics to the new.[8] However, his faith in the British Crown endured beyond the queen's death in 1901. From his newspaper, *Indian Opinion*, he sent birthday greetings to the king-emperor in 1904 and 1905, and in 1906 he welcomed the Duke of Connaught to the colony, not least because the 'superb qualities of the late Queen Victoria' had descended to her children. A subtle shift was evident. When Edward VII died in 1910, Gandhi downplayed the king-emperor's political significance and his 'personal qualities', noting only that he would be remembered as a sovereign who followed in the footsteps of his 'revered mother'.[9] The sovereign and the system that bore his imprimatur were disentangling. Queen Victoria set the standard; it was for her successors to measure up.

In this way, the Crown continued to be written into, not out of, nationalist visions for Indian reform. Led by Annie Besant, the 'All-India Home Rule League' sought a United States of India, with its own federal parliament. The India Office would go, India would have its own army and navy, and acknowledge 'the authority only of the Crown and the Imperial Parliament, in which she enjoyed adequate representation'. This was a variation on conventional 'dominion' status, of the kind aspired to by settler colonies. The king would still appoint a governor as his representative, the governor would retain the right of veto over Indian legislation, and the Privy Council in London would remain the final court of appeal.[10] Loyalty may no longer have been so blind, but it was loyalty nonetheless. No mention was made of a republic.

Indeed, until the 1920s, the idea of an Indian republic lay far away – in California, in fact. From the exile of the west coast of the first modern republic, the Ghadhar movement led a lonely attack on the British monarchy, and colonialism in general, in India. As Ram

Chandra, leader of the Ghadhars in exile, declared, the Ghadhar party had shown that British officialdom could no longer talk blithely of the 'loyalty to the sovereign' shown by all orientals. The people of India, he asserted, 'hate tyranny and oppression exercised by monarchs, landed aristocrats and British bureaucrats as much as any other unsophisticated honest people, accustomed from time immemorial to democratic and communal life in their village republics'.[11] Here were the ingredients for an Indian republican ideology, even if a long way from home: denunciation of royalty, with no distinction drawn between monarch and government, and an inversion of orientalism, with ancient Indian ways invoked as a model for future sovereignty.

Jai Hind

The tide of opinion in India turned resolutely against the imperial monarchy after the First World War. Not only did the Great War spell the end of the European dynastic system, of which the British royal family was a component part, its aftermath also saw republics carved out of old empires, most notably the Union of Soviet Socialist Republics (1922) and the Turkish republic (1923). Britain's oldest colony, Ireland, did not get quite as far, but was granted dominion status as the Irish Free State in 1921. In India one episode, five months after the end of the First World War, pushed on Indian nationalism as nothing before: the Amritsar massacre, the shooting down by troops commanded by Colonel Reginald Dyer of hundreds of locals and pilgrims caught up in a security crackdown in the Punjab town. The killings on 13 April 1919 caused international outrage, hasty political reform in the shape of the Montagu–Chelmsford initiative, and set off the INC's non-co-operation campaign.[12] Less noticed is how the Government of India wielded royal authority and status to try and ease tension, a cack-handed manoeuvre with disastrous consequences. On 23 December 1919 a package of reform was announced in the name of the king-emperor. There would be new legislative councils and a new Chamber of Princes. The proclamation promised to send out the Prince of Wales in the following year to inaugurate the constitutional change. It also included a general amnesty releasing many of the Punjabi leaders who had been arrested in the wake of the protests that followed the killings at Amritsar.[13] With the Indian National Congress due to hold its annual meeting in Amritsar four days later, the timing of the proclamation was crucial. There was more. Acting as warm-up man for the Prince of Wales, the Duke of Connaught (the king's great uncle) inaugurated the new Legislative Council at Delhi by reading a letter from the king-emperor in which he described the new councils as instances of the Government of India's own commitment to the principles of *swaraj*. When the Prince of Wales did arrive in India he went through the motions of appeasing Indian nationalism. He laid the foundation stone of a Shivaji memorial at Poona (a school, sponsored by the Maharaja of Kolhapur), speaking of Shivaji as 'one of India's greatest soldiers and statesman', the founder of Maratha greatness.[14] All without irony. As Motilal Nehru, INC stalwart, later observed, nationalist icons that were once considered seditious were now being given royal sanction.[15]

This time the old trick of dampening Indian dissent with a message from the monarch missed the mark. The Prince of Wales's four-month tour was boycotted by the INC.[16] Mohandas Gandhi led the opposition to the royal visit. He argued that the boycott did not represent a rebuttal to the person of the Prince of Wales, but rather condemnation of the actions of the British Empire that ruled in his name. Gandhi was quite clear in this distinction. For instance he advised against defacing portraits of the king-emperor as some of the boycotters wished to do: the monarch was ignorant of the actions that debased the empire. At the same time he refused to sing the national anthem any more: he wished the king a long life but not that of the Empire. He also questioned the patriotism of some boy scouts, asking why they wore a uniform spun from foreign yarn, and why they pledged to serve 'king and country', when 'the King was an impersonal ideal existence which meant the British Empire'.[17] Gandhi had come a long way from his pre-war loyalism.

Emboldened, other Indian nationalists now directed criticism at the monarch in person. From America, Ghadhars were unfettered in their attacks on George V and his emissary son. George RI ('Rex Imperator') was labelled the 'robber of India' and his son's visit to India branded a failure, proving 'beyond any doubt that India, Ireland and other countries are not going to coddle any longer these puppet princes and kings. Such a defiant attitude as the Indian people have shown should be hailed as a signal to confine king-sheep within the British Isles'. The way forward was clear for the Ghadars, at any rate, and it was not home rule, as 'nothing short of a republic should satisfy India'.[18] Within India too, loyalism faded fast. In 1921 Hasrat Mohani, a delegate to the INC meeting in Ahmedabad, called for complete independence from foreign rule, as opposed to *swaraj* within the Empire.[19] Then in 1924 came the first mention on Indian soil of the republic. The 'manifesto' of the Hindustan Republican Association demanded a 'federal republic of the United States of India' to be achieved through 'organised and armed revolution'.[20]

The new idea spread. At the end of 1927, as the British commenced an inquiry into Indian affairs (the Statutory Commission led by Sir John Simon), some Congress leaders came out in public for the republic, a milestone moment in the history of Indian nationalism. Jawaharlal Nehru returned from Moscow, where he had been to celebrate the tenth anniversary of the Russian Revolution, to tell the inaugural meeting of the 'Republican Congress' at Madras of a new phase in the struggle against British rule. The INC, urged Nehru, needed to turn to the 'republican ideal' and, he went on, '[t]he world had adopted Republicanism. Some countries had some kind of monarchy, but almost everybody realised that Republicanism was the only thing that was necessary for the future. Monarchies, wherever they existed now, were not likely to survive very long. Republicanism had come to stay'.[21] A few months later it was the turn of Subhas Chandra Bose, general secretary of the INC. At the Maharashtra Provincial Conference in Poona in May, he described to delegates how India need not look to the west for democracy, for republics had been alive and well in ancient India. Drawing on the 1918 work of K. P. Jayaswal, Bose pointed out that originally there had been eighty-one Hindu republics.[22] Bose's discovery of old India was not new. Other INC leaders had already invoked these traditions, for example Lajpat Rai talked up the republics of the Buddhist period in his *Political*

Future of India (1919). It was Bose, however, who turned it into an axiom of Indian nationalism, returning to the idea of the antiquity of the republic in India in his *The Indian Struggle* of 1935.[23] So by the time the British finally committed to offering India dominion status in 1929, the ideal of the republic had entered the vocabulary of Indian nationalism.

But what kind of republic, and for whom? The idea of a 'United States of India' suggested a federation of equal partners. That seemed unlikely. By 1930, several of the princely states had already taken legal advice, and were persuaded that their status was guaranteed through treaty or *sannad* agreements with the Crown, not with the Government of India, so they might be excluded from any discussions about the future shape of India.[24] Moreover, dwelling on the honourable ancestry of the republic in India did not offer much hope to Indian Muslims, for it was essentially a Hindu tradition of the republic that was being exhumed by the INC. Indian Muslims now began to imagine their own nation-state, most famously in Muhammad Iqbal's presidential address to the Muslim League meeting at Allahabad in December 1930. Iqbal called for a separate Muslim state to be created in north-west India, within or outside the British Empire, but certainly free from the caliphate, from what he called 'Arabian imperialism'.[25] There were other problems too in the new republican ideal. Evoking the village community as the seed of the Indian republic, as Mohandas Gandhi's closest followers tended to do, only alienated critics of the caste system, such as B. R. Ambedkar, who saw the village as the 'Indian ghetto', preserving social hierarchy and marginalising 'untouchables' and other groups.[26] If republicanism had 'come to stay' in India, as Nehru claimed, it was clearly going to be a demanding guest.

Whatever their divisions, at least Indian nationalism could unite against the imperial monarchy. For once, however, the British had gone quiet on rolling out royalty in India. None of the king's family had gone to India since the Prince of Wales's ill-fated tour of 1921. No royal prince was on hand to cut the ribbon when the new imperial capital at New Delhi was unveiled in 1931, although the chief Indian princes – for example those of Baroda, Bikaner, Cochin, Hyderabad, Jaipur, Jodhpur, Kashmir, Patiala and Travancore – used the relocation of the seat of British power to cosy up to the viceroy by building their own annexes in Delhi.[27] Understated did not mean forgotten. In Britain, the monarchy was back in favour. From the right wing of the Conservative party – the so-called 'diehards' – the monarchy was restored to life as the figurehead of constitutional authority in India. A new battle line between monarchy and republic began to be drawn.

Cheered on by Winston Churchill, now a Conservative backbench MP, Lord Rothermere's *Daily Mail* and by the Indian Empire Society (est. 1930), the crusade to keep India as she was gathered momentum, just as the INC moved full swing into its campaign of civil disobedience. The monarchy played its part, as did the queen's proclamation of 1858, as the idea developed that the Crown in India had always been a bulwark against fanaticism and partisanship.[28] Ramsay Macdonald's Labour government tried to rein in these runaway Raj veterans, preferring to use the monarch as conciliator. George V was enlisted to open in person in the Royal Gallery of the House of Lords the first set of 'round table' discussions about the future of India in November 1930.[29] For the next two years these negotiations continued, despite dwindling Indian representation, and from them emerged the Government of India Act of 1935.[30] For the Conservative 'diehards' it went too far. In the *Saturday Review* Sir Michael O'Dwyer, lieutenant-governor of the Punjab at the time of the Amritsar massacre, claimed that the pledges of the 'Great White Queen' – the sobriquet was relatively new – were being broken by the British government.[31] In India no one was really happy about the Act either, although the INC stormed into power across the country in the 1937 provincial elections.

With the new constitution for India came a new viceroy, Lord Linlithgow. Few people believed in royal India quite as wholeheartedly as the new viceroy. Born in the year of the golden jubilee, godson of Queen Victoria, he became an aide-de-camp to the king at the end of 1915. Now Linlithgow needed to make the new constitution work. Like many a viceroy before him, he believed the name and fame of the king-emperor could be enlisted in that task. Article 2 of the 1935 Government of India Act left intact the king-emperor's powers over India. Inconveniently, the king was no more. Between the passage of the Act and Linlithgow's arrival in India in April 1936, George V had died and his successor, Edward VIII, a reluctant king at best, was wary of his Indian responsibilities, having received such a rough ride on his visit in 1921. Undaunted, Linlithgow set about organising a coronation durbar for the new king-emperor. It did not happen, and so has been passed over by historians.[32] Nonetheless the durbar that never was is revealing. Linlithgow planned that Edward VIII would arrive by air in Delhi, 'descending from the clouds upon his Indian capital', to inaugurate the new federation of India. Preparations had not got very far by the time of Edward VIII's abdication later that year, but George VI was more in favour, and the durbar was announced in the king's speech at the opening of Parliament in November, pencilled in for the cold season in either 1937 or 1938.[33]

Sixty years after Lytton's Delhi Assemblage, when Queen Victoria's new imperial title had been announced, the British were trying to conjure up the magic of monarchy once more. How times had changed. The INC passed a resolution opposing the coronation durbar. Nehru warned that the king-emperor's life would be in danger if he came to India. By February 1937, Linlithgow had abandoned the idea. It was only a temporary setback. Buoyed by the enthusiasm he saw on display in India at the time of George VI's coronation in June 1937, Linlithgow returned to his durbar project, moving it back to 1938.[34] This time provincial governors warned of the costs, and the criticism that would provoke, especially from an expanded electorate. A final line was drawn under the idea in March 1938. Failure to bring off the coronation durbar was no surprise; that a viceroy could even imagine it might work as a riposte to Indian nationalism seems remarkable, a sure sign of the dogged resilience of British belief in the monarchy-Raj.

Nehru for one thought the days of the imperial crown were done. The coronation of 1937 was the last hurrah. As he told Suresh Majumdar, secretary of the Bengal Provincial Congress Committee, '[t]he recent abdication of ex-King Edward was a blow to the monarchy in England. Because of this it became necessary to shout even more loudly at the time of the Coronation.' In India the INC boycotted the 1937 coronation.[35] Nehru became even more dismissive of the scheme for federation and the special treatment being offered to the Indian princes. As he told the All-India States' Peoples conference at Ludhiana in February 1939, the princely states were the '[o]ffspring of the British power in India, suckled by imperialism for its own purposes'. A year or so later, he was even fiercer, declaring that '[t]he Indian Princes have hitched their wagon to the chariot of imperialism. They have both had their day and will go together.'[36] Not everyone thought that forging a united India was so simple. Subhas Chandra Bose used his presidential address to the INC meeting at Jaipur in February 1938 to call for 'a federal republic in which the Provinces and States will be equal partners', warning that the British Empire should heed the lessons of the break-up of the Austro-Hungarian Empire, and not play off different states against one another.[37] Others used the same analogy to draw a different conclusion. At Lahore in March 1940, Muhammad Ali Jinnah's All-India Muslim League broke with the INC, condemning the prospect of a 'Hindu Raj', and pointing to the example of the Balkans – that is to say, the former Austro-Hungarian Empire – as a model for sovereign states sharing the same geographical region.[38] As a coherent concept, the republic of India seemed as distant as ever.

Empire to Republic

During the Second World War the monarchy remained part of the solution for the Government of India until the very last. At one end of the political spectrum, the viceroy, Lord Linlithgow, set the tone of defiance. India would only be offered dominion status if she committed fully to the war effort. For Linlithgow the Crown provided security for rule over an alien people: this was the special 'virtue of kingship' in India. In this way, George V, whose statue he unveiled in November 1939, two months into the war, had been 'everybody's king'.[39] Back in London, the secretary of state for India and Burma, Leo Amery, fought hard to retain links with the Crown in any future settlement for India, even going so far as to suggest that George VI might still undergo a coronation ceremony in Delhi once the war was over.[40] As for the king, he suggested to Winston Churchill that he undertake a royal visit to India on a morale-boosting mission to visit the troops.[41] In India's time of need, the British Conservative party still had the monarchy primed and ready to serve the Raj.

With the end of the war and change of government in Britain in 1945, Indian independence moved from dream to reality. The new Labour prime minister, Clement Attlee, whilst a member of Churchill's wartime coalition government, was appalled by Linlithgow's attitudes as viceroy. Attlee suggested that a senior political figure be sent out from Britain to end the stand-off, bringing all the parties to the negotiating table and forging a settlement, much as Lord Durham – 'radical Jack' – had done in Canada in 1838 at the start of Queen Victoria's reign, when Protestant British settlers and French Catholics were at war.[42] Sir Stafford Cripps was chosen. Known as the 'red squire', partly because of his republican views, he was very much a modern-day Lord Durham. Cripps had been sent out in 1942, and now he was despatched again, along with two other colleagues, to negotiate an all-India settlement. The Cabinet mission failed, but at least one thing was now clear. As Cripps prepared to leave, George VI was solemnly informed that going forward he would no longer be known as king-emperor.[43] The Labour party had no plans to shore up the Raj. The British Commonwealth, however, was a different matter. Keeping India inside the Empire was the Attlee government's preferred end game in India. For that they turned to the royal touch.

There was one final outing for the monarchy in India. To arrange the independence and partition of India into two new dominions, the Labour government called on a member of the royal family, Lord Mountbatten, Queen Victoria's great-grandson, who took over from Lord Wavell as viceroy in February 1947. Like Wavell he had seen military command outside the European theatre during the war, serving as supreme allied commander of SEAC between 1943 and 1946.[44] However, it was his royal credentials that recommended Mountbatten. Initially, his name had been mooted as someone who might undertake a worldwide tour of the Empire, encouraging colonies and dependencies into their new dominion status as part of the post-war British Commonwealth.[45] In India, Mountbatten's mission was more complex. He was required to set out all the alternative plans, including the partition of India, to the various parties. The goal remained to maintain dominion status.

Mountbatten oversaw the process of the partition of India into two new nations, a mainly Muslim Pakistan and a predominantly Hindu India. The haste with which Mountbatten did this, and the tragic human loss of life that followed, lie at the heart of most judgements about his short viceroyalty. There were two other matters he had to settle, however. For both it mattered very much that he was of royal blood. He was tasked with coaxing the princely states into the new settlement, and in ensuring that both India and Pakistan accepted dominion status. The first job of persuading the princes required some sleight of hand. In February 1944, the Chamber of Princes had appealed for confirmation that their independence was protected by the Crown under the terms of the queen's proclamation of 1858 as well as other agreements.[46] In June 1946 Cripps had promised that the princely states would be able to choose between accession to or independence from a partitioned India and Pakistan. Mountbatten held out hope to the Indian princes. As late as May 1947 it was assumed that the British monarch would remain king of those parts of India that attained dominion status.[47] At the same time several of the larger princely states, including Hyderabad and Bhopal, had opened up a dialogue with Jinnah about inclusion in the new Pakistan, whilst Awadh pressed Jinnah to undo its original annexation by the British from 1856.[48] Although the Chamber of Princes was dissolved in July, Mountbatten still assured doubters amongst the princely states that they would retain their independence, only having to cede control over defence, external affairs and communications. Mountbatten told the Maharaj Rana of Dolhpur on 29 July that '[i]f you accede now you will be joining a dominion with a King as Head'.[49] But Jinnah and Nehru held out, preferring to reserve dealing with the princely states until after independence. Mountbatten was left with only titbits to offer the princes: they could keep their Stars of India and other honorary titles.[50] The protection offered by the Crown was going; only the ornaments remained.

Mountbatten was also charged with keeping the two new countries within the British Commonwealth as dominions. Both Jinnah and

Nehru agreed to Pakistan and India moving to dominion status on independence for an interim period.[51] As the Raj wound down the British gave up their baubles without too much fuss. Attlee's Labour government offered to give back the imperial crown from the 1911 durbar (that never happened). Other symbols were hard to let go. The monarchy, for one. Former viceroy Lord Halifax suggested that the king and queen travel to Delhi to say 'goodbye and good luck'. Mountbatten even tried without success to have a miniature Union Jack included in the new flags of both Pakistan and India.[52] Such minutiae did not really matter. Mountbatten got what he came for. When the transfer of power was made in the middle of August 1947, sovereignty passed from the Empire not to two new republics, but to two dominions. In Karachi on 14 August, Mountbatten read out a message from the king, welcoming Pakistan to 'its place in the British Commonwealth of Nations'. The next day, from their thrones in the durbar hall in the Viceroy's House in Delhi, Lord and Lady Mountbatten presided over the handover ceremony in India.[53] Another message was read from the king, welcoming the 'fulfilment of a great democratic ideal to which the British and India people alike are dedicated'. There was no ritual lowering of the Union Jack in Delhi, although this did happen elsewhere, for example at the residency in Lucknow. Rather, the new dominion flags were run up, what Mountbatten called 'the great event of the day'. Later that evening, at a large banquet, Nehru toasted the king, and Mountbatten toasted the 'new dominion of India'.[54] Still no mention was made of a republic, either in Karachi or Delhi. Later that year, Gandhi marked the transfer of power in his own inimitable style, sending a wedding present of a table cloth to Princess Elizabeth, the heir to the throne, knitted by a Punjabi girl from yarn spun by his own hands.[55] As gifts from India to the royal family went, Gandhi's gesture was humble, a change from the tributary *nuzzars* of old, yet its meaning was clear. Until 1947, the spinning wheel, suggesting economic self-reliance, had been at the centre of the campaign for *swaraj*. Since 1921 it had featured in the INC's tricolour flag for the new nation. After independence, the *chakra* in the national flag now stood for truth and virtue, for *satya* and *dharma*, invoking Ashoka, the Indian ruler of the second century. The qualities once found in kings, emperors, queens and even empresses would now symbolise the new republic.

So the British left the Indian subcontinent, and left the interim dominion governments of India and Pakistan to debate and decide what a republic in South Asia might be. Mountbatten stayed on as governor-general of India, whilst Jinnah undertook the equivalent role in Pakistan. Statues and other wondrous signs of the Raj began to be removed from public display.[56] The constituent assemblies of the two new countries now took their time in deliberating their new constitutions. In India it became clear that the new state would be a unitary republic. A Sanskrit name was chosen for the new India, 'Bharat', meaning a universal ruler, or a *chakravati*, both words that had been used on many occasions to describe the rule of Queen Victoria. Now it had real force. The promises held out to the larger Muslim princely states by both Cripps and Mountbatten proved illusory as the Instrument of Accession was enforced across India. In Pakistan, where there were fewer princely states to manage, the process of accession was less brutal and proved more drawn out.[57] There was resistance in India, from both Muslim and Hindu princely states. The Nizam of Hyderabad, whom the British had spent decades bossing and bullying into the Empire, tried to hang on to his independence until the troops of the new Indian army moved in. Bhopal, always conspicuous in its loyalty to the queen-empress, held out too.[58] In the south, Travancore, whose raja had supplied the queen with her imperial throne way back in 1851, staved off incorporation into the new India until 1956, its prime minister, C. P. Ramaswami Aiyar, defending to the last an alternative idea of the ancient Hindu polity, one based on kingship, and refusing to accept that British paramountcy had automatically passed to the new Indian government.[59]

Something like a British monarch remained in both of the new constitutions: the figure of the president. In India, the presidential role was modelled on the British constitution, its prerogative substantial in theory – head of the armed forces, head of the executive, responsible for appointing the Chief Justice of the Supreme Court, and invested with legislative power in the event of Parliament not sitting. In practice, like the British monarch, the new president of India conceded executive authority to the prime minister, and was content to advise and warn, but never control. For guidance on how to achieve this sleight of hand, the makers of the Indian constitution turned to Walter Bagehot and his classic 1867 account of limited monarchy.[60] The royal way of doing things was admired for once. Only later when the Indian constitution came under fire did reminders of the monarchy-Raj resurface. In the 1970s Indira Gandhi was likened to an 'Empress of India', especially during the Emergency of 1975–7, when she used the 42nd amendment to curtail the functions of the Supreme Court, and to undo the independence of the Indian Parliament.[61] In Pakistan, the president was initially allotted a similar role as a simple constitutional backstop, although the 'Objectives Resolution' of March 1949 gave him more extensive emergency powers, and, by the time the new Islamic republic of Pakistan was declared in 1956, its first president, Iskander Mirza, was armed with more authority than that enjoyed by his family forebears, the Nawabs of Bengal, let alone the queen-empress of India.[62]

One area of controversy remained in India around the lingering influence of the British Crown: Indian membership of the British Commonwealth, a status that many members of the Constituent Assembly described as a new form of colonialism. During the constitutional debates, Hasrat Mohani, who had first called for national independence back in 1921, was a consistent opponent of India's hybrid 'dominion republic' status.[63] Dissent only died away after the meeting of Commonwealth heads of state in London in April 1949, when the republic of India was confirmed as a member of the Commonwealth (the offending 'British' descriptor was lopped off), an association that India had joined freely, and 'as such' recognised the king as its head. It seemed a good compromise, although Indian constitutional historians such as B. N. Rau still scrabbled around for a historical precedent, finding one in the Licchavis of Bihar, a republican state of the sixth century BC that had formed an alliance with the Gupta empire.[64] History mattered.

By the close of 1949 India had its republic. A final royal proclamation of 22 June 1948 did away with the title of king-emperor. At the end of November 1949, the new constitution was finished. It looked forward to India as a 'sovereign democratic republic' ('secular and socialist' would be added later). It looked backwards too. There was a time, Ambedkar pointed out, when India was 'studded with republics' and, he added for good measure, elected and limited monarchies too. Rajendra Prasad, shortly to become India's first president, recalled India's republics from 2,000 years before.[65] Such an invention of tradition served its purpose, underlining Nehru's claim that there was an inevitability about India's emergence from empire as a republic. In fact, there was no untrammelled path from imperial monarchy to republic, from the formation of the Indian National Congress in November 1885 to 26 January 1950, when the new nation formally commenced. Historians of modern India treat the struggle for independence in the half-century after Queen Victoria's death as a two-cornered contest, between Indian nationalism and the British government. Yet there was always a third body in the ring. That was the Crown, truly the elephant in the room of modern Indian history. Indian attachment to the idea of a patriot queen, a beneficent monarch, persisted well into the early twentieth century. Only in the 1920s did the argument emerge within Indian nationalism that the monarch, government and imperialism were one and the same thing. At that point, the idea of imperial monarchy was reappropriated by the British, in order to see off the INC, but with diminishing effects. By the end of the Raj the monarchy was as unpopular in India as the rest of the edifice of British rule. Not until 1961 did Queen Elizabeth II venture out to India and Pakistan, almost the last countries of the new Commonwealth to receive a royal visit. On that occasion all went well. Prasad and Nehru beamed with pride as the queen sat through the Republic Day celebrations of 26 January. In London, *The Times* reflected on how the visit showed up the failure of Disraeli's old romantic vision of making Queen Victoria Empress of India, how Disraeli had been wrong to push her forward as a symbol of political authority, but never one of social cohesion. Only now with the queen as head of the Commonwealth, the paper went on, was there a version of monarchy that was not alien to the Indian people.[66] As a postcolonial sentiment the observation was undoubtedly timely. Monarchy had indeed fallen from fashion in India with a resounding thud. As a historical proposition, as this book has tried to show, it was not always so. As empress, Queen Victoria had brought monarchy to life in nineteenth-century India. And in its own way, India had resuscitated royalty back in Britain.

QUEEN VICTORIA IN INDIAN VERNACULAR, 1858–1914

This listing includes all titles *published* relating to Queen Victoria and her family, of which only a small subset has survived in libraries. Unless otherwise indicated the principal source for this compilation is the annotated quarterly lists of books and periodicals published in each presidency and province as supplements to the Government of India Gazettes from 1867 onwards (IOR SV412, now available in digitised format from the British Library: https://data.bl.uk/twocenturies-quarterlylists/tcq.html).

Assamese

Moore, Reverend P. H., *Rajarajesvari Bhikitoriya* (Calcutta: Arunoday Ray, 1898)
Barua, Padma Nath, *Maharani, or Queen Victoria* (Tezpur: Assam Central Press, 1902)

Bengali

De, Muheshchundru Das, *The Illumination* (Calcutta: Mutilal Das, 1870)
Raya, Rajkrishna, *Bharat-Bhagya; or, India's Good Fortune* (Calcutta: Albert Press, 1877)
Tagore, Sourindro Mohun, *Victoria-Giti-Mala, or A Brief History of England in Bengali Verses, composed and set to music in commemoration of the assumption by Her Most Gracious Majesty, the Queen Victoria, of the Diadem 'Indiæ Imperatrix'* (Calcutta: Punchanun Mookerjee, 1877), University of Edinburgh Library, Special Collections Ma.8.27
Mookhopadhyaya, Gopal Chandra, *Victoria Rasuja, or the History of the Imperial Assemblage* (Calcutta: Srisha Chandra Bhattacharja, 1879), West Bengal State Library, http://dspace.wbpublibnet.gov.in:8080/jspui/handle/10689/3855
Biswas, Tarakanath, *Maharani Bhikitoriya Charita/Life of Queen Victoria* (Calcutta: Rajendra Lal Biswas, 1885), West Bengal State Library, http://dspace.wbpublibnet.gov.in:8080/jspui/handle/10689/10221
Tagore, Sourindro Mohun, *Bhikitoria Giti Mala, Songs in Honour of Empress Victoria* (Calcutta: Stanhope Press, 1887)
Gupta, Ambika Charan, *Maharani Victoria, or a happy reign* (Calcutta: Uchitavakta Press, 1887), West Bengal State Library, http://dspace.wbpublibnet.gov.in:8080/jspui/handle/10689/5250

APPENDIX

Sen, Chandi Charan, *Maharajni Bhiktoriya Charita Chitra Samabalita/The Memoirs of Her Majesty Queen Victoria* (Calcutta: Mani Mohan Rakshit, 1887)

Ray, Dasharathi, *Raj Putra. The Grandson of the Queen* (Calcutta: Rajendralal Ghosh, 1889)

Malik, Binod Bihari, *His Royal Highness the Prince Albert Victor Clarence Edward in India* (Calcutta: I. C. Bose & Co., 1890)

Nath, M. N., *Bharateshvari Bhiktoriya/The Empress Victoria* (Calcutta: Baptist Mission Press, 1890)

Pal, Bipin Chandra, *Rajnimata Bhiktoriya. Life of Her Majesty Empress Victoria* (Calcutta: Kartik Chandra Datta, 1891; repr. 1904), National Library Kolkata, 182.cc.904.7

Rainey, J. Rudd, *The Life of His Royal Highness the Prince Consort: Father of the Future Emperors of India. Condensed and translated into Bengali from Sir Theodore Martin's work, with the author's permission* (Calcutta: Sanskrit Press, 1892)

Rouse, G. H., *Maharanir Sakshya/The Testimony of the Queen* (Calcutta: Christian Tract Society, 1895)

Ghosh, Ambika Chandra, *Rajarajeswari Victoria* (Calcutta: Arundoday Roy, 1895), West Bengal State Library, http://dspace.wbpublibnet.gov.in:8080/jspui/handle/10689/4446

Sen, Srigovinda, *Bhikitoriya Mahotsav* (Calcutta: Sannyal & Co., 1897)

Sarkar, Purna Chandra, *Sri Srimati Maharani Bharatesvarir Hiraka Jubili Jayadhvani/The Shout of Victory on the Occasion of the Diamond Jubilee of the Maharani the Empress of India* (Chittagong: Barada Kanta Chakravati, 1897)

Banerji, Kamakhya Charan, *Bhikitoriya Charit. The Life of Queen Victoria* (Dacca: Gopi Nath Basak, 1898)

Mitra, Ananda Chandra, *Bhikitoriya Gitika, A Lyric Poem on the Life and Reign of Her Majesty Queen Victoria, Empress of India* (Calcutta: Guru Das Chatterji, 1900)

Das, Rajnarayan, *Adarsha Ramani Maharani Bhikitoriya. A Model Woman the Great Queen Victoria* (Calcutta: R. Datta, 1900)

Young, Reverend A. W., *Maha Rani O Baibel/The Queen and Her Bible* (Calcutta: Christian Tract Society, 1901)

Iyasin, Mahammad, *Matah Bhikitoriya/Mother Victoria* (Nator: the author, 1901)

Mukhopadhyaya, Pramathanatha, *Practiya-pratibha* (Calcutta: Bharat Mihir Press, 1901), National Library, Kolkata 182.cc.901.1

Chaudhuri, Mahhamad Maulavi Mokhlesar Rahaman, *Soka Bharati/The Melancholy Condolence of HGM Queen Empress Victoria* (Dinajpur: Haji Munsi Jamiruddin Chaudhuri, 1902)

Mukherji, Asutosh, *Bhutapurva Bharatesvari Bhikitoriya Bharati/Poems on the Late Empress Queen Victoria of India* (Calcutta: Gurudas Chatterji, 1903)

Bhattacharya, Kalika Prasad, *Bharate Juboraj/Prince of Wales in India* (Comilla: Ananda Press, 1905)

Anon., *Victoria Ewam Tahar Goshana Patra/ The Queen Victoria and Her Proclamation* (Benares: Jung Bahadur Singh, 1910)

Burmese

Nyun, Maung San, *Short Meanings on Victoria the Great* (Rangoon: ABM Press, 1905)

Gujarati

Prince Albert. Selections from the Prize Translation of a Gujarati Poem . . . by a Parsee Poet named Muncherjee Cawasjee (Bombay: Education Society's Press, 1870)

Chakubhai, Bulakhiram, *Yuwaraj yatra; or, the Travels of the Prince* (Ahmedabad: Ahmedabad Times Press, 1875)

Bhownaggree, Mancherjee Merwanjee, *Leaves from the Journal of Our Life in the Highlands* (Bombay: n. p., 1877), National Library of Scotland X.222.f

Wadia, Putlibai Dhanjibhai, *Her Most Gracious Majesty the Queen-Empress's More Leaves from the Journal of a Life in the Highlands from 1862 to 1882* (Bombay: the author, 1886)

Desai, Iccharam Suryaram, *Rajatejomayi maharani sri Vikṭoriyanuṃ jivanacaritra* (Bombay: Gujarati Printing Press, 1887; 2nd edn 1907), Bodleian Library, University of Oxford (IND) 14.B.74

Kabraji, K. N., *Maharaninun Yashavardhan/Narrative of the Queen-Empress Glory, Being a Brief Sketch of the Goodness and Greatness of Her Most Gracious Majesty Queen Victoria, Empress of India* (Bombay: Bairamji Fardunji & Co., 1887)

Sangle, Reverend A. M., *Our Queen Empress* (Bombay: the author, 1887)

Badshah, Bhagwanlal R., *An Elegy on the Death of Her Majesty Queen Victoria, Empress of India (being Gujarat's memorial tribute to her beloved sovereign)* (Ahmedabad: the author, 1901)

Hamirsinh, Parwatsinh, *Kaisarehinda Namdar Shri Maharniji Victoria Viraha, or In Memoriam Queen Victoria, Late Empress of India* (Ahmedabad: the author, 1901)

Vidyaram, Kavi Bhaishankerji V. (Pandit), *Victoria Virah Vilap, or In Memoriam Queen Victoria* (Ahmedabad: Aryodaya Press, 1901)

Hindi

The Queen's Travels in Scotland and Ireland, translated into Hindi by Ishwari Prasad Narayan Singh Bahadur, Maharaja of Banaras (Benares: n. p., 1875), RCIN 1053105

Harishchandra, Bhartendu, *Manomukulamala* (Benares: Medical Hall Press, 1876), University of Edinburgh Library, Special Collections Ma.7.32/2

Harishchandra, Bhartendu, *Victoria's Flag of Victory: A Poem in Hindi* (Benares: n. p., 1882), Cambridge University Library, 8833.c.52

Hara Devi, *Landan-jubili* (Lahore: Imperial Press, 1888), Bodleian Library, University of Oxford (IND) Hindi Hara 1

Anon., *Victoria Maharani ka Vrittanta/Life of the Queen-Empress of India* (Allahabad: Christian Literary Society, 1896)

Lal, Dewan Mohan, *Prabhutwa Shahanshahi. The Grandeur of the Empress* (Agra: Kewal Kishen Chand, 1896)

Sannyasi, Swami Alarama Sagar, *Bhiktoriya Raja Darpan. A Mirror of the Rule of Her Majesty the Queen-Empress* (Bankipur: Sahib Prasad Sinha, 1897)

Mehta, Lajjaram Sharma, *Srimati Maharani Bharatesvari Viktoriya ka charita, or Life of Queen Victoria, Empress of India* (Bombay: Khemraj Shrikrishnadas, 1901), Library of Congress, Washington, D. C. DS 554.M4 (Orien Hind)

Arthat, Kesarisinha Shokanjalii, *Shirmati Paramapratapi Jagatpujya Shri Bharateshvari Maharani Vikitoriya ke Dukhada Svargavas par Shokodgar, or Verses Lamenting the Death of Her Most Gracious Majesty Queen Victoria, Empress of India* (Bombay: the author, 1903)

Shukla, Cheda Lal (ed.), *Santi Siromani/The Head Jewel of Peace* (Kanpur: the author, 1908)

Kanarese

Kardguddi, Fakirappa Basappa, *Chaupadia* (Dharwad: Dnyan Vardhak Press, 1887)

Malayalam

Manavikraman, K. C. Rajah, *A Short Biographical Sketch of the Queen Empress Victoria* (Madras: Graves, Cookson & Co., 1887)

Maman, Reverend O., *A Brief Account of the Life of our Beloved Empress* (Madras: Vidya Vilsam Press, 1887)

Pillai, C. E. Govinda, *A Short Biographical Sketch of the Queen Empress Victoria* (Calicut: P. C. Achutan, 1890)

Chandran, Reverend St, *The Life of Her Majesty Queen Victoria* (Mangalore: Basel Mission, 1897)

APPENDIX

Marathi

Pitale, Ganpatarava Moroba, *Ranice pustaka, mhanaje, Maharani Viktoriya hyanca Hailanda prantantia rahivasa: va Skatalanda, Inglanda va Airlanda hya desantila saphari ani galabatanta basuna keleli paryatane hyanca vrttantal Leaves from the Journal of Our Life in the Highlands* (Bombay: Education Society's Press, 1871), Bodleian Library, University of Oxford, (IND) Mar Vic 1

Sangle, Reverend A. M., *Maharanichen Charitra, or the Life of the Queen-Empress* (Bombay: Education Society's Press, 1887)

Tilak, Pandurang Vaman, *Sangita Ranyutsava Prakash; or, the Festival of the Queen Empress in Musical Verse* (Bombay: the author, 1887)

Joshi, Purushottam Balkrishna, *Viktoria Mahotsava, or Verses in Commemoration of the Jubilee of Her Majesty Queen Victoria's Reign* (Bombay: the author, 1887)

Gunjikar, Ganesh Bhikaji, *Viktoria Maharanichen Charitra, or Life of Empress Victoria* (Bombay: Govind Moroba Karlenkar, 1888)

Phadke, Narayan Laxman, *Ranichya Rajyacha Itihas, or History of the Reign of Queen Victoria* (Poona: Balvant Ganesh Dabholkar, 1902)

'One Member of the Hindu Union Club', *Victoriya Maharanichen Charitra, or a Life of Queen Victoria* (Bombay: Nadkarni & Mandali, 1905)

Oriya

Banerji, Kalipada, *Biktoriya Rajsuya/The Imperial Assemblage* (Cuttack: Orissa Patriot Press, 1884)

Kanungo, Basudeva, *Bhikitoriya. Victoria* (Cuttack: Cuttack Printing Co., 1897)

Rao, Madhusudan, *Mahadebi Bhiktorial The Great Goddess Victoria* (Cuttack: Utkal Sahitya Press, 1901), British Library 14121.f.25(1)

Persian

Anon., *Persian Poems in Praise of the Auspicious New Year's Day of the Parsis, the Queen Empress, etc.* (Bombay: Education Society, 1881)

Bamanji, Dosabhai, *An Address of Loyalty in Persian Verse, with its English Translation to Her Most Gracious Majesty, the Queen Empress Victoria, in Celebration of the Official Jubilee in Honor of her Fiftieth Year on the British Throne* (Bombay: Bombay Education Society, 1887), British Library 14773.a.14

Bamanji Dosabhai, *Tavsife Malikae Inglistan va Kaisare Hinustan Viktoria. Or Praises of Her Imperial Majesty Victoria, the Queen of England and Empress of India* (Bombay: the author, 1887), British Library Or. 14547

Durgaprasad, Kunwar, *Gulistan-i-Hind/The Rose Garden of India* (Lucknow: Legal Press, 1889)

Punjabi

Singh, Bhai Aya, *Jubilee prakash athwa Sri Bhartesuri da sankhep samachar* (Lahore: Muifid-i-Am Press, 1889)

Nath, Lala Gopi, *Siharfi* (Ludhiana: the author, 1912)

Sanskrit

Harischandra, Bhartendu, *Offering of Flowers to the Duke of Edinburgh* (Benares, n. p., 1870), University of Edinburgh Library Special Collections Ys.10.8/3

Tagore, Sourindro Mohun, *Fifty Stanzas in Sanskrit, in Honor of HRH the Prince of Wales, Composed and Set to Music* (Calcutta: n. p., 1875), British Library 14053.cc.7.(2)

APPENDIX

Tagore, Sourindro Mohun, *Victoria-gitika, or Sanskrit Verses Celebrating the Deeds and the Virtues of Her Most Gracious Majesty Queen Victoria and her Renowned Predecessors, Composed and Set to Music* (Calcutta: I. C. Bose, 1875), British Library 14053.cc.7.(1)

Tagore, Sourindro Mohun, *Victoria Samrajyan, or Sanskrit Stanzas: On the Various Dependencies of the British Crown, Each Composed and Set to the Respective National Music, in Commemoration of the Assumption by Her Most Gracious Majesty the Queen Victoria of the Diadem, Indiae Imperatrix* (Calcutta: I. C. Bose, 1876; 2nd edn 1882), British Library 14053.cc.51

Bhattacarya, Taranatha Tarkavacaspati, *Rajaprasastih* (Calcutta: Sarasvatiyantra, 1876), Joseph Regenstein Library, University of Chicago PK3799.B487.R3 1876

Ramapati, Sri, *Shri Victoriamarahrayas/Verses in Praise of Queen Victoria* (Benares: Channu Lal, 1876)

Churamani, Pandit Ramkrishna Bhattacharyya, *Rajvarnan; or, a Description of Royalty* (Bankipur: Sadhoram Bhatta, 1878)

Nyayaratna, Benimadhaba, *Bharateswari Kabyam. Empress of India* (Calcutta: the author, 1879), SV412/8 vol. 3

Ghose, Loke-Nath, *The Victoria Jubilee Upasana or Prayers in Sanskrit Verse . . . on the Occasion of the Fiftieth Anniversary of the Reign . . . of Queen Victoria, with a Hymn Set to Hindu Music and the National Anthem in English and its Translation in Sanskrit by Professor Max Müller* (Calcutta: the author, 1887), British Library 14033.c.37

Shastri, Pandit Vaijanath, *Victoria-Prashasti; or a Eulogium on Victoria* (Poona: Bhaskar Narayan Godbole, 1892)

Sharma, Lalachandra, *Jubilee Pramodika* (Bombay: n. p., 1889), British Library 14072.ddd.2

Tagore, Sourindro Mohun, *Brief Description of the Jubilee of Her Majesty the Queen Empress in Sanskrit Poems* (Calcutta: I. C. Bose, 1892), British Library 14053.e.25(2)

Pincott, Frederic, *Rajarajesvari Maharani Viktoriya Kaisara-i-Hinda ka jivanacarita/Life of Empress Victoria* (Bankipur: Prasad Sinha, 1895), Widener Library, Harvard University IndL 2422.2

Chandra, Krishna, *Priti Kusumanjali. An Offering of a Handful of Flowers of Devotion* (Benares: Freeman & Co., 1897)

Sarma, Jaynarayan (comp.), *Vijayini Kirtimala* (Bankipur: Sahib Prasad Sinha, 1897)

Joshi, P. B., *Victoria-mahotsava; or, Verses in Commemoration of the Diamond jubilee of Her Majesty's Reign* (Bombay: Tatva-vivechaka Press, 1897), British Library 14140.a.45(1)

Tagore, Sourindro Mohun, *Srimad-Victoria-Mahatmyam, the Greatness of the Empress Victoria: A Sanskrit Poem, Set to Music, with an English Translation, and 63 Illustrations Descriptive of 60 Years of Her Majesty's Sovereignty, etc.* (London: Cassel & Co., 1897), British Library 14706.e.4

Naramsimhacharya, *Victoriyaprasastih, or Praise of Queen Victoria* (Bombay: Laxmi Venkateshwar Press, 1898), Library of Congress, Washington DC microfiche 99/61026 (P)

Sindhi

Vadhvani, Nirbdas Naraindas, *Jamma Saki Maharani Saheb Victoria Kaisar-e-Hind, or the Life of Her Majesty Queen Victoria, Empress of India* (Karachi: Sind Gazette & Commercial Press, 1900; 2nd edn 1912)

Tamil

Cupparaya Mutaliyar, Tantalam, *Mararasritiyuk Alpart perilum irajakkal perilum alankarak-kommi* (Madras: T. Cupparaya Mutaliyar, 1870), British Library Tam.A.93(e)

Jiyar, Cesattiri Aiyankar Kulattur, *Marara sri araci irantam puttirarakiya Alpart, tiyuk av Et inparo Intiyavaik kanavanta vicittiraccopanappattu* (Madras: the author, 1870), British Library pTam.B.2805

Iyengar, C. G. Psashathree, *Shopanapattu* (Madras: Vurthamanatharunginee Press, 1870)

Baboo, T., *The Queen* (Vepery: Fister Press, 1873)

Chetti, P. A. Michaelsawmi, *The Royal Messenger* (Madras: Memorial Press, 1876)

Chariar, Krishnama V., *A Jubilee Sketch of the Queen-Empress and the Empire on which the Sun Never Sets* (Madras: SPCK Press, 1887)

Anon., *The Queen-Empress of India and her Family* (Madras: CVE Society, 1888)

Rau, M. R. Krishna, *Srimat Victoria Vijayam, or the Life and Reign of Queen Victoria* (Trichinopoly: V. A. Saminada Pillai, 1889)

Chariar, Krishnama V., *A Glorious Reign of Sixty Years* (Madras: the author, 1897)

Aiyar, S. Muttu, and Aiyar, C. V. Swaminada, *Life of Her Majesty Queen Victoria, Empress of India* (Madras: the authors, 1898), Bodleian Library, University of Oxford (IND) 18.A.1

Anon., *A Brief Life of the Queen Empress* (Madras: Christian Literature Society, SPCK Press, 1901)

Duraisami, K. C., *The True Victorian Glory* (Madras: Thompson & Co., 1901), Bodleian Library, University of Oxford (IND) 18.B.27

Mudali, Munisami, *Life of Empress Victoria in Kummi Song* (Madras: the author, 1901)

Reddiar, Vidhvan Periya, *The Maharani Ammanei* (Madras: Ramalinga Swami, 1901), British Library 14172.b.7

Chettiar, P. M. Swami, *Viktoriya Makaraniyaravarkal/The Victoria Memorial* (Madras: City Press, 1901), British Library 14171.a.47

Pillai, Cankaralinkam, A., *Viktoriya makaraṇiyin carittiram* (Madras: Kumaracami Nayutu Sans, 1912), British Library pTam.B.791

Telugu

Dass, Polluri Mutyal, *Chamra Vadeyaravri Cheritramu* (Bangalore: Vicara Darpana Press, 1876)

Pantulu, Kokkonda Venkataratnamu, *The Empress of India: Nine Gems* (Madras: C. Foster & Co., 1876), British Library 14174.i.8

Baboo, T., *The Queen* (Madras: Frees Church Mission House, 1876)

Baboo, Rev. R. M., *Yuvaraju; or, the Heir Apparent* (Madras: Sattiadipam Press, 1876)

Chariar, V. Krishnama, *A Jubilee Sketch of the Queen-Empress and the Empire on which the Sun Never Sets* (Madras: SPCK Press, 1887)

Anon., *The Queen-Empress of India and her Family* (Madras: Christian Literature Society, 1893)

Adinarayanappa, C., *Vitandavada Madavedanda Kantiravamu* (Rajahmundry: the author, 1893)

Viresalingam, Kandukuri, *Life of Her Majesty Queen Victoria, Empress of India* (Rajahmundry: Vivekavardhani Press, 1897), British Library 14174.g.42(2)

Panditulu, D. Srirama, *Victoria Dwatrimsanmanjari* (Bezwada (Vijayawada): D. Vishnu Rao, 1898)

Brahmaiya, K., *Victoria Vilasamu* (Cocanada: the author, 1898)

Nissanka, Raja M., *Gita Padya Nakshatramalika* (Vizagapatam: Arsha Press, 1900)

Srinivasacharlu, P., *Kanakangi* (Madras: the author, 1900)

Sarvarayadu, S., *Life of Her Gracious Majesty Queen Victoria, the Good Late Sovereign of India* (Coconada: Sujanaranjani Press, 1901)

Bhujanga, Raja M., *Vasantakusuman, or the Life of Her Most Gracious Majesty* (Ellore: Manjuvani, 1902, 2nd edn 1908), British Library 14174.f.17(3)

Atchamamba, G., *Life of Her Majesty Queen Victoria the Great* (Coconada: Sujanaranjani Press, 1904)

Sastri, D. Suryanarayana, and Sastri, C. Sundrarama (eds), *Vasantakusumamu, Being a Poem Relating to the Life of Queen Victoria* (Madras: Royal Victoria Press, 1908)

Dorasami, Aiya, *Viktoriya Maharjni caritramu/The Life of Queen Victoria* (Madras: C. Coomarasawmy Naidu & Sons, 1912), British Library Tel.B.388

APPENDIX

Urdu

Gafur, Abdul, *Muraqqa-i-Salatin, Hissa-i-awwal-i-Asar-ul-Mutaakhkirin/The Gallery of Princes* (Delhi: Murari Lal's Press, 1875)

Nath, Bishambhar, *Tuzuk-i Jarmani* (Lucknow: Nawal Kishore Press, 1876), Rampur Raza Library, Rampur

Sahai, Ram, *Gulgasht-i-Bagh-i-Lucknow, a Description of the Visit to Lucknow of His Royal Highness the Prince of Wales* (Lucknow: Tamannai Press, 1876), Rampur Raza Library, Rampur

Karim, Abdul, *Quasidah-i-talimiyat; or, Benedictory Verses* (Patna: Sayad Fazal Karim, 1877)

Mubin, Muhammad, *Guidasta-i-Jashan Qaisarya, the Bouquet of the Imperial Assembly* (Fatehgarh: the author, 1877)

Khan, Abdur Rashid, *Guldasta-i-Rashid. The Bouquet* (Aligarh: Muhammed Muniruddin, 1878)

Mehr, Mirza Hatim Ali Beg, *I'd Qaisarya 1878. The Imperial Festival* (Agra: the author, 1878)

Das, Bulaqi, *Tawarikh-i-Jalsa-i-Shahanshahi/History of the Imperial Assemblage* (Delhi: Muir Press, 1884)

Chand, Faqir, *Tazkira-i-Malika-Victoria-i-Qaisar-i-Hind (Life of Queen Victoria Empress of India)* (Delhi: Muhibb-i-Hind Press, 1885)

Lal, Umrao Raja (trans.), *Sawanih-i-Umri-i-Hazur Malika-i-Qaisar-i-Hind/An Account of the Life of Her Majesty the Empress of India* (Delhi: Anwar-i-Muhammedi Press, 1887)

Azimabadi, Shad, *Navid-i Hind* (Patna: Subh-i Sadiq Press, 1887), Bodleian Library, University of Oxford (IND)16.c.62

Karim, Abdul, *Tuhfa-i-Jubilee, or the Jubilee Present* (Bombay: the author, 1887)

Ram, Mukand (ed.), *Akhbar-i-am* (Lahore: Matba Mitra Vilasa, 1888), Lane Medical Library, Stanford University

Das, Bulaqi, *Tarikh-i-Jubilee/History of the Jubilee of Her Imperial Majesty the Queen-Empress* (Delhi: Muir Press, 1888)

Ali, Bunyad, *Yadgar-i-jubilee Musamma, ba Talim-un-Niswan/Memorial of the Jubilee, Known as Female Instruction* (Agra: the author, 1888)

Alam, Mahbub, *Zikr-i-Mamduh/The Life of Queen Victoria, Empress of India* (Gujranwala: Punjab Press 1888; 2nd edn 1892)

Iman, Imdad, *Hadya-e-Qi Sarya. A Present to the Empress* (Arrah: the author, 1889)

Forbes, A. (comp.), *Dilchasp-i-Halat-i-Shahzadah Victor Jo Hazur Kaiser Hind ke Pote/Prince Victor, Grandson of the Empress of India* (Lucknow: the author, 1891)

Alam, Munshi Mabub, *Zikr-i-Mamduh* (Lahore: Khadim-ut-Talim Punjab Press, 1894)

Ahmad, Faizuddin, *Jubilee Malka Victoria Qaisari-i-Hind/Jubilee of Queen Victoria, Empress of India* (Kanpur: Rahmat Ullah, 1896)

Razaq, Abdul, *Ain-i-Qaisari/Regulations of the Empress* (Lucknow: Gulab Singh Press, 1897)

Das, Lala Hal Saran, *Alakh Raj/The Limitless Empire of the Queen Empress* (Lahore: Muir Press, 1897)

Abdulghani, Mirza Muhammad, *Hayati-i-Victoria al mulaqqab ba Shahanshah Nama* (Lahore: Islamia Press, 1897), University of Pennsylvania Library DA55.A87.1897

Mahapatra, Srikrishna, *Maharani. The Empress* (Cuttack: Cuttack Printing Co., 1901)

Firozeuddin, Maulvi, *Yadgar-i-Victoria ya'ni Malika Victoria ki mufassal Sawanih 'Umri aur unkeahad-i-hukumat ki mujmal tarikh* (Lahore: Sadaihind Press, 1901)

Iftikhar-ud-Din, Fakir Saiyid, *Hayat-i-Malika* (Lahore: Muifid-i-Am Press, 1901)

Ahmad, Bashiruddin, *Hayat-i-Qaisarah: yani Aliya hazrat Malikah-yi Muazzamahkuin Viktoriyah Qaisarah-i-Hind ki muktasar savnih umri* (Delhi: Matba Mujtabai, 1901), University of Pennsylvania Library, DA554.A37.1901

Zakaullah, Muhammad, *Savanih umri Hazrat Malikah-i-muazzimah Malkisifat Qaisar-i-Hind va alijanab Prins Kunsurt Alba* (Delhi: Shamsu Matabi, 1904), Centre for Research Libraries, University of Chicago, MF–11324.r282/e

292

APPENDIX

Sime, J. (trans. Lala Rej Ram), *Malka-i-Muazzuma Victoria ke Halat-i-Zindgi* (Lahore: Mufid-i-'Am Press, 1907)

Ali, Rahmat, *Wafa-i-Rahmat* (Lahore: Islamia Press, 1910)

Lal, Dori, *Sar Guzasht-i-Victoria/Life of Queen Victoria* (Saharanpur: Joti Prashad, 1912), British Library VT.3948B

NOTES

Introduction

1. Journal entry, 21 June 1872 in *Letters of Queen Victoria*, 2nd ser., ii, 218–19; Colonel Ponsonby to Earl Granville, 26 January 1873, ibid., 238–9; Duke of Argyll to Ponsonby, 1 February 1873, ibid., 242. For the visit of the Burmese envoys, see: L. E. Bagshawe (ed.), *The Kinwun Min-Gyi's London diary* (Bangkok: Orchid Press, 2006).

2. Carnarvon to Ponsonby, 24 February 1876, RA VIC/MAIN/F/16/22; Ponsonby to Queen Victoria, 17 March 1876, ibid., fols 65–6; Disraeli to Queen Victoria, 23 March 1876, RA VIC/MAIN/F/16/78; Revd Mr Farrer, 'Translation' (*c.* 23 March 1876), RA VIC/MAIN/F/16/83.

3. L. J. Trotter, *History of India under Queen Victoria, 1836–86* (London: W. H. Allen, 1886); Edwin Arnold, *Victoria. Queen and Empress. The Sixty Years* (London: Longmans, 1896), 70–7; W. W. Hunter, *The India of the Queen, and Other Essays* (London: Longmans, Green and Co., 1903), ed. Lady Hunter, ch. 1; Romesh Dutt, *The Economic History of India in the Victorian Age* (London: Kegan Paul & Co., 1906); S. Satyamurty, *Modern India (Down to the Death of the Queen Empress)* (Madras, n.p., 1909); Richard Temple, *Sixty Years of the Queen's Reign: An Epoch of Empire Making* (London: Geo. Routledge, 1897), ch. 2.

4. P. E. Roberts, *History of British India: Under the Company and the Crown* (1921); Herbert A. Stark, *India under Company and Crown: Being an Account of its Progress and Present* (1922); A. B. Keith, *A Constitutional History of India, 1600–1935* (1936); Joachim von Kürenberg, *Die Kaiserin von Indien: lebensgeschicte der Königin Victoria von England* (Hamburg: Robert Möglich: 1947).

5. Mary Ann Steegles, *Statues of the Raj* (London: British Association for Cemeteries in South Asia, 2000), 178–214; Jan Morris (with Simon Winchester), *Stones of Empire: The Buildings of the Raj* (Oxford: Oxford University Press, 2003 edn), 182–5; Maria Misra, 'From Nehruvian Neglect to Bollywood Heroes: The Memory of the Raj in Post-war India' in Dominik Geppert and Frank-Lorenz Muller (eds), *Sites of Imperial Memory: Commemorating Colonial Rule in the Nineteenth and Twentieth Centuries* (Manchester: Manchester University Press, 2016), 187–206.

6. Steegles, *Statues of the Raj*, 178, 207; Philippa Vaughan (ed.), *The Victoria Memorial Hall: Conceptions, Collections, Conservation* (Mumbai: Marg, 1997).

7. *An account of the Memorials to Queen Victoria Erected in the North-Western Provinces of India* (Agra: n.p., 1905); W. S. Meyer, W.E.A. Armstrong, R.S. Burns and E.H.S. Clarke (eds), *The Imperial Gazetteer of India*, 26 vols (Oxford: Clarendon Press, 1909–31); Somerset Playne (comp.), *Indian States. A Biographical, Historical and Administrative Survey* (1922; repr. New Delhi: Asian Educational Services, 2006).

8. See the Appendix.

9. Anindita Ghosh, *Power in Print: Popular Publishing and the Politics of Language and Culture in a Colonial Society, 1778–1905* (Delhi: Oxford University Press, 2006); Francesca Orsini, *Print and Pleasure: Popular Literature and Entertaining Fictions in Colonial North India* (Ranikhet: Permanent Black, 2009); Farina Mir, *The Social Space of Language: Vernacular Culture in British Colonial Punjab* (Berkeley: University of California Press, 2010); A. R. Venkatachalapathy, *The Province of the Book: Scholars, Scribes, and Scribblers in Colonial Tamilnadu* (Ranikhet: Permanent Black, 2012).

10. C. A. Bayly, *Empire and Information: Intelligence Gathering and Social Communication in India, c. 1780–1870* (Cambridge: Cambridge University Press, 1996), 343–4. Reports of native newspapers were made for each presidency from 1868. Quarterly lists of all publications were printed as supplements to the official government gazettes (IOR SV412).

11. Mushirul Hasan, 'Sharif Culture and Colonial Rule: A "Maulvi"-Missionary Encounter' in Mushirul Hasan and Asim Roy (eds), *Living Together Separately: Cultural India in History and Politics* (2006), 320–53; T. G. Bailey, *A History of Urdu Literature* (1928; repr. Karachi: Oxford University Press, 2008).

12. Hans Harder (ed.), *Literature and Nationalist Ideology: Writing Histories of Modern Indian Languages* (New Delhi: Social Science Press, 2010); cf. Vasudha Dalmia, *The Nationalisation of Hindu Traditions: Bharatendu Harischandra and Nineteenth-century Benares* (New Delhi: Oxford University Press, 1997); Sudhir Chandra, *The Oppressive Present: Literature and Social Consciousness in Colonial India* (Delhi: Oxford University Press, 1992).

13. The principal collection of these is in four boxes held in the India Office Records of the British Library, on loan from the Royal Collection: 'Loyal addresses to the Sovereign from the inhabitants of various places in India, Burma, and Aden, etc.', IOR Mss Eur. G55.

14. Richard S. Wortman, *Scenarios of Power: Myth and Ceremony in Russian Monarchy. Volume 2. From Alexander II to the Abdication of Nicholas II* (Princeton, NJ: Princeton University Press, 2000); Matthew Truesdell, *Spectacular Politics: Louis-Napoleon Bonaparte and the Fête Impériale, 1849–1870* (New York: Oxford University Press, 1997); Sudhir Hazareesingh, '"A Common Sentiment of National Glory": Civic Festivities and French Collective Sentiment under the Second Empire', *Journal of Modern History* 76 (2004), 280–311; Takashi Fujitani, *Splendid Monarchy: Power and Pageantry in Modern Japan* (Berkeley: University of California Press, 1996); James Shedel, 'Emperor, Church, and People: Religion and Dynastic Loyalty during the Golden Jubilee of Franz Joseph', *Catholic Historical Review* 76 (1990), 71–92.

15. Oliver Godsmark and William Gould, 'Clientelism, Community and Collaboration: Loyalism in Nineteenth-century Colonial India' in Allan Blackstock and Frank O'Gorman (eds), *Loyalism and the Formation of the British World, 1775–1880* (Woodbridge: Boydell Press, 2014), 263–86.

16. Partha Chatterjee, *The Nation and its Fragments: Colonial and Postcolonial Histories* (Princeton, NJ: Princeton University Press, 1993), 11–12; idem., *Nationalist Thought and the Colonial World: A Derivative Discourse?* (London: Zed 1986); cf. Dipesh Chakrabarty, *Provincialising Europe: Postcolonial Thought and Its Discontents* (Princeton, NJ: Princeton University Press, 2000), ch. 1.

17. Ramachandra Guha, *Gandhi before India* (London: Allen Lane, 2013), ch. 6; P. H. N. van den Dungen, 'Gandhi in 1919: Loyalist or Rebel?' in R. Kumar (ed.), *Essays on Gandhian Politics: The Rowlatt Satyagraha of 1919* (Oxford: Oxford University Press, 1971), 43–63.

18. C. A. Bayly, *Origins Of Nationality in South Asia: Patriotism and Ethical Government in the Making of Modern India* (Delhi: Oxford University Press, 1998), esp. 89–92; cf. his

'European Political Thought and the Wider World during the Nineteenth Century' in Gareth Stedman Jones and Gregory Claeys (eds), *The Cambridge History of Political Thought in the Nineteenth Century* (Cambridge: Cambridge University Press, 2011), 853; and his *Recovering Liberties: Indian Thought in the Age of Liberalism and Empire* (Cambridge: Cambridge University Press, 2012), esp. 13–14, 16–17, 26.

19. Sukanya Banerjee, *Becoming Imperial Citizens: Indians in the Late Victorian Empire* (Durham, NC: Duke University Press, 2010); Elleke Boehmer, *Indian Arrivals, 1870– 1915: Networks of British Empire* (Oxford: Oxford University Press, 2015).

20. John Mackenzie, *Propaganda and Empire: The Manipulation of Public Opinion, 1880– 1960* (Manchester: Manchester University Press, 1984); David Cannadine, 'The Context, Performance and Meaning of Ritual: The British Monarchy and the "Invention of Tradition", *c.* 1820–1977' in Eric Hobsbawm and Terence Ranger (eds), *The Invention of Tradition* (Cambridge: Cambridge University Press, 1983), 101–64; idem., *Ornamentalism: How the British Saw their Empire* (London: Allen Lane, 2001), ch. 4; William M. Kuhn, *Democratic Royalism: The Transformation of the British Monarchy, 1861–1914* (Basingstoke: Macmillan, 1996), ch. 1.

21. Monarchy as an agent of empire is at last being given due attention. See, for example, Robert Aldrich and Cindy McCreery (eds), *Crowns and Colonies: European Monarchies and Overseas Empires* (Manchester: Manchester University Press, 2016); Sarah Carter and Maria Nugent (eds), *Mistress of Everything: Queen Victoria in Indigenous Worlds* (Manchester: Manchester University Press, 2016); Milinda Banerjee, Charlotte Backerra and Cathleen Sarti (eds), *Transnational Histories of the 'Royal Nation'* (London: Palgrave, 2017). For dynastic rule, see: Johannes Paulmann, 'Searching for a "Royal International": The Mechanics of Monarchical Relationships in Nineteenth-century Europe' in Martin H. Geyer and Johannes Paulmann (eds), *The Mechanics of Internationalism* (Oxford: Oxford University Press, 2001), 145–76; Heidi Mehrkens and Frank-Lorenz Muller (eds), *Sons and Heirs: Succession and Political Culture in Nineteenth-century Europe* (Basingstoke: Palgrave Macmillan, 2015).

22. Colin Coates (ed.), *Majesty in Canada: Essays on the Role of Royalty* (Toronto: Dundurn, 2006); Philip Buckner, 'The Creation of the Dominion of Canada, 1860–1901' in Buckner (ed.), *Canada and the British Empire* (Oxford: Oxford University Press, 2008), 66–86; James H. Murphy, *Abject Loyalty: Nationalism and Monarchy in Ireland during the Reign of Queen Victoria* (Cork: Cork University Press, 2001); James Loughlin, *The British Monarchy and Ireland: 1800 to the Present* (Cambridge: Cambridge University Press, 2007).

23. For a wry and perceptive account of how the court worked politically, see: Michael Bentley, *Lord Salisbury's World: Conservative Environments in Late-Victorian Britain* (Cambridge: Cambridge University Press, 2001), 73–6, 160–4, and idem., 'Power and Authority in the Late Victorian and Edwardian Court' in Andrzej Olechnowicz (ed.), *The Monarchy and the British Nation, 1780 to the Present* (Cambridge: Cambridge University Press, 2007), 163–87.

24. Mithi Mukherjee, *India in the Shadows of Empire: A Legal and Political History, 1774–1950* (Delhi: Oxford University Press, 2010), 79–80, 89.

25. Bernard S. Cohn, 'Representing Authority in Victorian India' in Eric Hobsbawm and Terence Ranger (eds), *The Invention of Tradition* (Cambridge: Cambridge University Press, 1983), 165–210; idem., 'Cloth, Clothes and Colonialism: India in the Nineteenth Century' [1989] in Cohn, *Colonialism and its Forms of Knowledge: The British in India* (Princeton, NJ: Princeton University Press, 1996), 106–62.

26. Uday Singh Mehta, *Liberalism and Empire: A Study in Nineteenth-Century British Liberal Thought* (Chicago, IL: Chicago University Press, 1999); Jennifer Pitts, *A Turn to Empire: The Rise of Imperial Liberalism in Britain and France* (Princeton, NJ: Princeton University Press, 2005), ch. 5; Karuna Mantena, *Alibis of Empire: Henry Maine and the Ends of Liberal Imperialism* (Princeton, NJ: Princeton University Press, 2010).

27. Partha Mitter, 'Cartoons of the Raj', *History Today* 47 (1997), 16–21; Mushirul Hasan, *The Avadh Punch: Wit and Humour in Colonial North India* (New Delhi: Nyogi Books, 2007); Ritu G. Khanduri, 'Vernacular Punches: Cartoons and Politics in Colonial India', *History and Anthropology* 20 (2009), 459–86.

28. For social reform movements, see: Antoinette Burton, *Burdens of History: British Feminists, Indian Women and Imperial Culture, 1865–1915* (Chapel Hill: University of North Carolina Press, 1994). For nursing, see: Geraldine Forbes, *Women in Colonial India: Essays on Politics, Medicine and Historiography* (New Delhi: Chronicle Books, 2005).

29. Sugata Bose, 'Nation as Mother: Representations and Contestations of "India" in Bengali Literature and Culture' in Sugata Bose and Ayesha Jalal (eds), *Nationalism, Democracy and Development: State and Politics in India* (Delhi: Oxford University Press, 1996), 50–72; Sugata Bose, *The Nation as Mother and other Visions of Nationhood* (Delhi: Penguin, 2017); Sumathi Ramaswamy, *The Goddess and the Nation: Mapping Mother India* (Durham, NC: Duke University Press, 2010), 80–4.

30. 'Composite Patriotism II' (27 May 1905) in *The New Spirit: A Selection from the Writings and Speeches of Bipinchandra Pal on Social, Political and Religious Subjects* (Calcutta: Sinha, Sarvadhikari & Co., 1907), 212–13.

1 Crown and Company

1. Hobhouse to Elphinstone, 4 August 1837, IOR Mss Eur. F87, fols 13–14; entries for 14 July, 7 November in Lord Broughton, *Recollections of a Long Life*, ed. Lady Dorchester, 6 vols (London: John Murray, 1911), v, 88, 103. On Elphinstone, see: H. M. Stephens, 'Elphinstone, John, Thirteenth Lord Elphinstone and First Baron Elphinstone (1807–1860)', rev. Elizabeth Baigent, *ODNB*.

2. Leslie Mitchell, *Lord Melbourne, 1779–1848* (Oxford: Oxford University Press, 1997), 235–40; Monica Charlot, *Victoria: The Young Queen* (Oxford: Blackwell, 1991), chs 5–6.

3. On the later years of the East India Company, see especially: Cyril Phillips, *The East India Company, 1784–1834*, 2nd edn (Manchester: Manchester University Press, 1961), chs 9–10; Philip Lawson, *The East India Company: A History, 1600–1857* (Harlow: Longman, 1993), ch. 8; Anthony Webster, *The Twilight of the East India Company: The Evolution of Anglo-Asian Commerce and Politics, 1790–1860* (Woodbridge: Boydell Press, 2009), chs 5–6.

4. Eric Stokes, *The English Utilitarians and India* (Oxford: Oxford University Press, 1959); John Rosselli, *Lord William Bentinck: The Making of a Liberal Imperialist 1774–1839* (London: Chatto and Windus for Sussex University Press, 1974), 214–24; Martin Moir and Lynn Zastoupil, 'Introduction' to idem. (eds), *The Great Indian Education Debate: Documents Relating to the Orientalist–Anglicist Controversy, 1781–1843* (Richmond: Curzon, 1999), 1–70.

5. [Philip Meadows Taylor], 'The Native Princes of India', *British and Foreign Review* 8 (January 1839), 154–245; Robert Travers, 'A British Empire by Treaty in Eighteenth-century India' in Saliha Belmessous (ed.), *Empire by Treaty: Negotiating European Expansion, 1600–1900* (Oxford: Oxford University Press, 2014), 132–60.

6. For background, see: M. E. Yapp, *Strategies of British India: Britain, Iran, and Afghanistan, 1798–1850* (Oxford: Clarendon Press, 1980); James Onley, 'The Raj Reconsidered: British India's Informal Empire and Spheres of Influence in Asia and Africa', *Asian Affairs* 20 (2009), 44–62.

7. J. Sutherland, *Sketches of the Relations Subsisting between the British Government of India and the Different Native States* (1833, 2nd edn, Calcutta: G. H. Huttman, 1837); C. U. Aitchison, *A Collection of Treaties, Engagements and Sunnuds Relating to India and Neighbouring Countries*, 7 vols (Calcutta: Bengal Printing Co., 1862–5). There was a partial list presented to Parliament in 1825, and a fuller one in 1856: 'Treaties with Native

Powers in India', *Parl. Papers* (1825), Cd. 005; 'Copies of all Treaties, Conventions and Arrangements with the Native States of India, made since the 1st day of May 1834', *Parl. Papers* (1856), Cd. 341.

8. Philip J. Stern, *The Company-state: Corporate Sovereignty and the Early Modern Foundations of the British Empire in India* (Oxford: Oxford University Press, 2011); Sudipta Sen, 'Colonial Frontiers of the Georgian State: East India Company Rule in India', *Journal of Historical Sociology* 7, (1994) 368–92.

9. M. Z. A. Shakeb, *A Descriptive Catalogue of Persian Letters from Arcot and Baroda* (London: India Office Library, 1982), 5–6; J. D. Gurney, 'Fresh Light on the Character of the Nawab of Arcot' in A. Whiteman, J. S. Bromley and P. G. M. Dickson (eds), *Statesmen, Scholars and Merchants: Essays in Eighteenth-century History Presented to Dame Lucy Sutherland* (Oxford: Clarendon Press, 1973), 200–41; Natasha Eaton, 'Between Mimesis and Alterity: Art, Gift and Diplomacy in Colonial India', *Comparative Studies in Society and History* 46 (2004), 816–44.

10. Marquis Curzon of Kedleston, *British Government in India: The Story of Viceroys and Government Houses*, 2 vols (London: Cassell and Co., 1925), i, ch. 3; Jan Morris, *Stones of Empire: The Buildings of British India* (Oxford: Oxford University Press, 1983), 67–8; J. P. Losty, *Calcutta: City of Palaces: A Survey of the City in the Days of the East India Company, 1690–1858* (London: BL, 1990), 74–6.

11. Peter Gray and Olwen Purdue, 'Introduction' in idem. (eds), *The Irish Lord Lieutenancy: c. 1541–1922* (Dublin: Dublin University College Press, 2012), 3. For the wider comparisons, see: Christopher Bayly, 'Ireland, India and the Empire, 1780–1914', *Transactions of the Royal Historical Society*, 6th ser., 10 (2000), 377–98.

12. Jac Weller, *Wellington in India* (London: Longman, 1972); Kate Brittlebank, 'The White Raja of Srirangapattana: Was Arthur Wellesley Tipu Sultan's True Successor?', *South Asia* 26 (2003), 23–35; Michael Fisher, 'The Imperial Coronations of 1819: Awadh, the British and the Mughals', *Modern Asian Studies* 19 (1985), 239–77.

13. For examples of royal salute, see: *Asiatic Journal* 9 (January–June 1820), 510 (Baroda); ibid. 13 (January–June 1822), 86 (Bhopal).

14. *The Private Journal of the Marquess of Hastings, Governor General and Commander-in-Chief in India*, ed. Marchioness of Bute, 2 vols (London: Saunders and Otley 1858), i, 66–9; Abraham Eraly, *The Mughal World: Life in India's Last Golden Age* (New Delhi: Penguin, 2007), 42–52; Piyel Haldar, *Law, Orientalism and Post-colonialism: The Jurisdiction of the Lotus-eaters* (Abingdon: Routledge, 2007), ch. 6.

15. For Amherst's tour of 1827, see: *Asiatic Journal* 24 (July 1827), 92–3. For Bentinck's tour in 1831: Bentinck to Captain Wade, 9 June 1831, in *The Correspondence of Lord William Cavendish Bentinck, Governor-General of India, 1828–1835*, ed. C. H. Phillips, 2 vols (Oxford: Oxford University Press, 1977), i, 652–3.

16. James Tod, *Annals and Antiquities of Rajast'han, or, the Central and Western Rajpoot States of India*, 2 vols (London: Smith, Elder and Co., 1829–1832), ii. For Tod, see: Norbert Peabody, 'Tod's Rajast'han and the Boundaries of Imperial Rule in Nineteenth-century India', *Modern Asian Studies* 30 (1996), 185–220; Jason Freitag, *Serving Empire, Serving Nation: James Tod and the Rajputs of Rajasthan* (Boston: Brill, 2009); Florence D'Souza, *Knowledge, Mediation and Empire: James Tod's Journeys among the Rajputs* (Manchester: Manchester University Press: 2015).

17. On Akbar II, see: Salman Khurshid, 'Life in Shahjahanabad' in J. P. Losty (ed.), *Delhi: Red Fort to Raisna* (New Delhi: Roli, 2012), 207–10; John Reeve, *The Lives of the Mughal Emperors* (London: BL, 2012), 31; G. S. Mukherjee, 'Nature of Political Relationship between the Residents and Shah Akbar II', *Journal of Indian History* 60 (1982), 53–70.

18. On the *farman*, see: F. W. Buckler, 'The Political Theory of the Indian Mutiny of 1857', *Transactions of the Royal Historical Society*, 4th ser., 5 (1922), 71–100. For Akbar II, see: Mukherjee, 'Nature of Political Relationship'; Rosselli, *Bentinck*, 231. For the 1830

portrait, see: *Morning Post*, 5 July 1830, 3; and for Ram Mohan Roy's mission in 1832, see: Mary Carpenter, *The Last Days in England of the Rajah Rammohun Roy* (London: E. T. Whitfield, 1875); Lynn Zastoupil, *Rammohun Roy and the Making of Victorian Britain* (Basingstoke: Palgrave Macmillan, 2010), 20–1.

19. *The Times*, 17 March 1836, 2; *ibid.*, 22 April 1836, 6; *Short Statement Relative to the Presents Transmitted to England in 1835, by the King of Oude . . . to be Laid before their Majesties the King and Queen of England, as a Mark of Attachment and Fidelity, etc.* (London: R. Clay, 1837).

20. Foreign Dept Proceedings, 11 September 1837, P. C. 144, NAI; R. B. Boswell, *A Sermon Preached in St James' Church, Calcutta . . . on Occasion of the Ascension to the British Throne of Her Most Gracious Majesty Queen Victoria* (Calcutta: Church Mission Press, 1837), 2–3.

21. *Asiatic Journal*, n. s., 23 (August 1837), 323–5; *The Times*, 10 November 1837, 4.

22. H. Torrens to Lt. Col. N. Alves, 4 June 1838, Foreign Dept Proceedings, P. C. 41, NAI.

23. *Friend of India*, 5 October 1837, 313–14; *Calcutta Monthly Journal and General Register* (January–June, 1838), 1–3.

24. Letter of 27 October 1837, Julia Charlotte Maitland, *Letters from Madras during the Years 1836–1839*, ed. Alyson Price, orig. pub. 1846 (Otley: Woodstock Books, 2003), 54; Letter of 17 September 1837, *Letters from India by the Hon. Emily Eden*, ed. Eleanor Eden, 2 vols (London: Richard Bentley, 1872), ii, 86–7.

25. Foreign Dept Proceedings, 21 March 1838, P. C. 84, NAI.

26. In the Koran, a spring, fountain or river in paradise.

27. C. M. Wade to H. Macnaughten, 11 December 1837, Foreign Dept Proceedings, P. C. 4, NAI.

28. Edward Ingram, 'India and the North-west Frontier: The First Afghan War' in A. Hamish Ion and Elizabeth Errington (eds), *Great Powers and Little Wars: The Limits of Power* (Westport, CT: Praeger, 1993), 31–52; William Dalrymple, *The Return of the King: The Battle for Afghanistan* (London: Bloomsbury, 2013), chs 2–3.

29. Auckland to Hobhouse, 9 December 1838, BL, Add. Mss, 36, 473, fols 359–68; *The Times*, 4 February 1839, 5; *Parbury's Oriental Herald*, 4 (January–June, 1839), 258–9, 278–81.

30. C. J. Blomfield, *A Sermon Preached at the Coronation of Her Most Excellent Majesty Queen, etc.* (London: B. Fellowes, 1838), 15; 'Sermon on the Duties of a Queen' in *The Works of Sydney Smith*, 3 vols (London: Longman, 1845), iii, 293.

31. QVJl., 26 December 1837, 5 July 1838.

32. For Blomfield, see: Arthur Burns, 'Blomfield, Charles James (1786–1857)', *ODNB*. The *Life of William Wilberforce*, written by Wilberforce's sons Robert and Samuel, was published in five volumes in 1838.

33. For the background, see: Robert E. Frykenberg, 'Episcopal Establishment in India to 1914' in R. Strong (ed.), *The Oxford History of Anglicanism, vol. III: Partisan Anglicanism and its Global Expansion, 1829–c. 1914* (Oxford: Oxford University Press, 2017), 296–317.

34. *Bishop Wilson's Journal Letters . . . during the First Nine Years of his Episcopate*, ed. Daniel Wilson (London: J. Nisbet, 1863), 227–8. For Wilson, see: Andrew Porter, 'Wilson, Daniel (1778–1858)', *ODNB*.

35. For Duff, see: A. A. Millar, *Alexander Duff of India* (Edinburgh: Canongate, 1992); Philip Constable, 'Scottish Missionaries, "Protestant Hinduism" and the Scottish Sense of Empire in Nineteenth- and Early Twentieth-century India', *Scottish Historical Review* 86 (2007), 278–313.

36. Kenneth Ballhatchet, 'The East India Company and Roman Catholic Missionaries', *Journal of Ecclesiastical History*, 44 (1993), 273–88; Barry Crosbie, *Irish Imperial Networks: Migration, Social Communication and Exchange in Nineteenth-century India* (Cambridge: Cambridge University Press, 2012), 136–40.

37. Andrew N. Porter, 'Religion, Missionary Enthusiasm, and Empire' in idem. (ed.), *The Oxford History of the British Empire*, vol. 3: *The Nineteenth Century* (Oxford: Oxford University Press, 1999), 222–46; idem., *Religion Versus Empire?: British Protestant Missionaries and Overseas Expansion, 1700–1914* (Manchester: Manchester University Press, 2004); P. Van der Veer, 'The Moral State: Religion, Nation, and Empire in Victorian Britain and British India' in Van der Veer (ed.), *Religion and Nationalism in Europe and Asia* (1999), 15–43; R. E. Frykenberg, 'Christian Missions and the Raj' in Norman Etherington (ed.), *Missions and Empire* (Oxford: Oxford University Press, 2005), 107–31; Jeffrey Cox, *The British Missionary Enterprise since 1700* (London: Routledge, 2008), esp. ch. 4; Penelope Carson, *The East India Company and Religion, 1698–1858* (Woodbridge: Boydell & Brewer, 2012); Ian Copland, 'Christianity as an Arm of Empire: The Ambiguous Case of India under the Company, c. 1813–1858', *Historical Journal* 49 (2006), 1025–54.
38. R. Hartley Kennedy, 'The Suttee: The Narrative of an Eye-witness', *Bentley's Miscellany* 13 (January 1843), 256. On sati and its suppression, see: Lata Mani, *Contentious Traditions: The Debate on Sati in Colonial India* (Berkeley: University of California Press, 1998); Andrea Major, *Sovereignty and Social Reform in India: British Colonialism and the Campaign against Sati, 1830–60* (London: Routledge, 2011).
39. Kenneth Ingham, 'The English Evangelicals and the Pilgrim Tax in India, 1800–62', *Journal of Ecclesiastical History* 3 (1952), 191–200; Nancy Cassels, *Religion and the Pilgrim Tax under the Raj* (New Delhi: Manohar, 1988).
40. *Leeds Mercury*, 7 July 1838, 6; Lant Carpenter, *A Discourse on Christian 'Patriotism': Delivered to the Society of Protestant Dissenters in Hanover Square, Newcastle-upon-Tyne, on the Sunday after the Coronation of Her Majesty* (London: Longman, 1838), 26.
41. *The Times*, 28 April 1841, 6. For Blomfield's role, see: *A Letter to His Grace the Lord Archbishop of Canterbury, upon the Formation of a Fund for Endowing Additional Bishoprics in the Colonies* (London: B. Fellowes, 1840) and *A Memoir of C. J. Blomfield, Bishop of London, with Selections from his Correspondence*, ed. A. Blomfield, 2 vols (London, 1863), i, 288–9. For the background, see: Rowan Strong, *Anglicanism and the British Empire 1700–1850* (Oxford: Oxford University Press, 2007), ch. 4; idem., 'The Resurgence of Colonial Anglicanism: The Colonial Bishoprics Fund, 1840–1', *Studies in Church History* 44 (2008), 196–213; Hilary M. Carey, *God's Empire: Religion and Colonialism in the British World*, c. *1801–1908* (Cambridge: Cambridge University Press, 2011), ch. 3; Joseph Hardwick, *An Anglican British World: The Church of England and the Expansion of the Settler Empire*, c. *1790–1860* (Manchester: Manchester University Press, 2014), ch. 3.
42. *The Times*, 18 June 1841, 13. For Blomfield's encouragement, see: Blomfield to Wilson, 14 October 1844, Letter-books Diocesan, Blomfield papers, Lambeth Palace Library, vol. 41, fols 222–5; *A Memoir of C. J. Blomfield*, ii, 87–8.
43. 'Memorandum of the Bishop of Calcutta on the Subject of a Bishop's See at Agra', 25 October 1845, BL, Add. Ms. 40,874, fols 96–104; Entries for 22 January, 24 January, 11 February, 23 May, 23 July, 27 August, Wilson diaries, Ms. Eng. Misc. e. 9, Bodleian Library, University of Oxford, reprinted in *The Journal of Bishop Daniel Wilson of Calcutta, 1845–1857*, ed. Andrew Atherstone (Woodbridge: Boydell Press, 2015); Wilson to Hobhouse, 30 October 1847, IOR Mss Eur. F213/22. Joseph Bateman, *The Life of the Right Rev. Daniel Wilson, D.D., Late Lord Bishop of Calcutta . . . with Extracts from his Journals and Correspondence*, 2 vols (London: John Murray, 1860), ii, ch. 18; Bengal ecclesiastical despatches, 1852–3, 10 November 1851, IOR E/4/817, p. 1168; ibid., 1853–4, 29 March 1854, E/4/824, p. 1143.
44. For example, Sarah Tucker's *South Indian Missionary Sketches: Containing a Short Account of some of the Missionary Stations, Connected with the Church Missionary Society in Southern India, in Letters to a Young Friend*, 2 vols (London: James Nisbet, 1843), was in Queen Victoria's library, whilst the Society for the Propagation of the Gospel's *The Colonial Church Atlas, Arranged in Dioceses: With Geographical and Statistical Tables* (London: Society for the Propagation of the Gospel in Foreign Parts, 1842) was in the library of Prince Albert.

45. QVJl., 24 September 1839.
46. Ibid., 18 March 1839.
47. Bengal despatches, 29 April 1840, IOR/F/4/1932/83331.
48. 'Address from meeting of inhabitants of Bombay held at the Town Hall on 21st April 1840', Bombay despatches, IOR/F/4/1902/81001; 'Address to Queen Victoria on Occasion of Marriage', Madras despatches, IOR/E/4/956, *Bombay Times*, 26 February 1842, 134.
49. There is a copy of the Bombay government's acknowledgment of the address on the marriage, dated 28 December 1840, in Jejeebhoy letterbooks, vol. 355, University of Mumbai Library.
50. 'Letter from the Naib-i-Mukhtar of the Carnatic to Her Majesty Queen Victoria and the Court of Directors on the Occasion of the Birth of the Heir Apparent', 31 March 1842, Madras despatches, IOR/F/4/1997/88626; Alex Speirs [Gwalior] to T. H. Maddock, 9 February 1842, Foreign Dept Proceedings, 11 September 1837, F. C. 40, NAI.
51. *Bombay Times*, 12 September 1840, 589, ibid., 13 July 1842, 452.
52. Hermione Hobhouse, *Prince Albert: His Life and Work* (London: Hamish Hamilton, 1983), and Stanley Weintraub, *Albert: Uncrowned King* (London: John Murray, 1997), remain the standard accounts.
53. *The Principal Speeches and Addresses of . . . the Prince Consort. With an Introduction, Giving some Outlines of his Character*, ed. Sir Arthur Helps (London: John Murray, 1862), 81–2.
54. *The Times*, 15 April 1841, 6; John Scoble, *Slavery and the Slave Trade in British India: With Notices of the Existence of these Evils in the Islands of Ceylon, Malacca, and Penang, Drawn from Official Documents* (London: Thomas Ward, 1841); *The Export of Coolies from India to Mauritius* (London: British and Foreign Anti-Slavery Society, 1842).
55. Peel to Prince Albert, 15 February 1842, in *Letters of Queen Victoria*, 1st ser., i, 382.
56. *Principal Speeches . . . of the Prince Consort*, 134; *The Times*, 18 June 1851, 8; *Society for the Propagation of the Gospel in Foreign Parts . . . Jubilee Commemoration* (London: Society for the Propagation of the Gospel, 1851).
57. David J. Howlett, 'Ramsay, James Andrew Broun, First Marquess of Dalhousie (1812–1860)', *ODNB*; Thomas R. Metcalf, 'Canning, Charles John, Earl Canning (1812–1862)', ibid.
58. E. C. B. Lindsay, 'The Arrival of Queen Victoria in Scotland, 1842: Extracts from the Diary of Lord Dalhousie', *Transactions of the East Lothian Antiquarian & Field Naturalists' Society* 12 (1970), 32–45; idem., 'Queen Victoria in Scotland, 1842: Extracts from the Diary of Lord Dalhousie, pt. 2, ibid. 13 (1972), 61–76; Alex Tyrrell, 'The Queen's "little trip": The Royal Visit to Scotland in 1842', *Scottish Historical Review* 82 (2003), 47–73.
59. QVJl., 18 March 1842, 16 June 1842. Tagore followed the royal party to Scotland in April: *The Times*, 30 April 1842, 5.
60. *The Times*, 1 March 1842, 5; *ILN*, 1 November 1842, 440.
61. See Miles Taylor, *Wellington's World: The Duke of Wellington and the Making of the British Empire*, Fifteenth Wellington Lecture, University of Southampton, 2003, 19–20; Edward Ingram, 'The Role of the Duke of Wellington in the Great Game in Asia 1826–1842', *Indica* 25 (1988), 131–42.
62. Hew Strachan, *Wellington's Legacy: The Reform of the British Army, 1830–1854* (Manchester: Manchester University Press, 1984), 35–6.
63. David Steele, 'Law, Edward, First Earl of Ellenborough (1790–1871)', *ODNB*; A. H. Imlah, *Lord Ellenborough: A Biography of Edward Law, Earl of Ellenborough, Governor-General of India* (Cambridge, MA: Harvard University Press, 1939).
64. His first letter from India was dated 18 March 1842: Lord Colchester (ed.), *History of the Indian Administration of Lord Ellenborough, etc.* (London: Richard Bentley, 1874), 16–25. On being told that the queen corresponded with Ellenborough, Hobhouse confided his objections to this 'irregularity': '[h]e is not Viceroy, he represents the Company, not the Queen!!': entry for 24 May 1844, Broughton, *Recollections*, vi, 107.
65. Ellenborough to Queen Victoria, 18 January 1843, in *History of the Indian Administration of Lord Ellenborough*, 64–5.

2 Warrior Queen

1. The ship's log books are at: IOR/L/MAR/B/810B.
2. For an overview, see: Gerald S. Graham, *Great Britain in the Indian Ocean: A Study of Maritime Enterprise, 1810–1850* (Oxford: Clarendon Press, 1967) and idem., *The China Station: War and Diplomacy, 1830–1860* (Oxford: Oxford University Press, 1978), chs 4–8; Kaushik Roy, *The Oxford Companion to Modern Warfare in India: From the Eighteenth Century to Present Times* (New York: Oxford University Press, 2009), 262–4.
3. 'Copies of Treaties, Conventions, and Arrangements with the Native States of India Made since the 1st day of May 1834', *Parl. Papers* (1856), Cd. 341; Walter Arnstein, 'The Warrior Queen: Reflections on Queen Victoria and her World', *Albion* 30 (1998), 1–28; Paul McHugh, *The Maori Magna Carta: New Zealand Law and the Treaty of Waitangi* (Auckland: Oxford University Press, 1991), ch. 2; John M. Willis, 'Making Yemen Indian: Rewriting the Boundaries of Imperial Arabia', *International Journal of Middle-East Studies* 41 (2009), 23–38; Paul J. Rich, *Creating the Arabian Gulf: The British Raj and the Invasions of the Gulf* (Plymouth: Lexington, 2009), ch. 2; R. Derek Wood, 'The Treaty of Nanking: Form and the Foreign Office, 1842–3', *Journal of Imperial and Commonwealth History* 24 (1996), 181–96.
4. Peel to Lord Fitzgerald, 20 November [1841], BL, Add. Ms. 40,462.
5. QVJl., 29 October 1841; Ellenborough to Queen Victoria, 21 April 1842, in Lord Colchester (ed.), *History of the Indian Administration of Lord Ellenborough, etc.* (London: Richard Bentley, 1874), 28–30.
6. On the final stages of the first Afghan war, see: Edward Ingram, 'India and the North-west Frontier: The First Afghan War' in A. Hamish Ion and Elizabeth Errington (eds), *Great Powers and Little Wars: The Limits of Power* (Westport: Praeger, 1993), 31–52; Ben Hopkins, *The Making of Modern Afghanistan* (Basingstoke: Palgrave, 2008), ch. 3; Frank H. Wallis, *A History of the British Conquest of Afghanistan and Western India, 1838–1849* (Lampeter: Edwin Mellen, 2009), ch. 10; William Dalrymple, *Return of a King: The Battle for Afghanistan* (London: Bloomsbury, 2014), ch. 10.
7. QVJl., 15 April 1842. For the role of Indian forces in the first China war, see: Robert Johnson, 'The East India Company, the Indian Army and the China Wars, 1839–1860', in Peter Lorge and Kaushik Roy (eds), *Chinese and Indian Warfare, from the Classical Age to 1870* (London: Routledge, 2015), 347–67.
8. Asiya Siddiqi, 'The Business World of Jamsetjee Jejeebhoy', *Indian Economic and Social History Review* 19 (1982), 301–24; John F. Richards, 'The Opium Industry in British India', *Indian Economic and Social History Review* 39 (2002), 149–81; Amar Farooqui, 'Opium and the Trading World of Western India in the Early 19th Century' in James Mills and Patricia Barton (eds), *Drugs and Empire* (Basingstoke: Palgrave, 2007), 83–100. For the involvement of the Tagores, see: Blair B. Kling, *Partner in Empire: Dwarkanath Tagore and the Age of Enterprise in Eastern India* (Berkeley: University of California Press, 1976), ch. 3.
9. Queen Victoria to Leopold, 13 April 1841, *Letters of Queen Victoria*, 1st ser., i, 329; QVJl., 24 November 1842.
10. Steele, 'Law, Edward, First Earl of Ellenborough (1790–1871)', *ODNB*; A. H. Imlah, *Lord Ellenborough: A Biography of Edward Law, Earl of Ellenborough, Governor-General of India* (Cambridge, MA: Harvard University Press, 1939), 99–122.
11. Imlah, *Lord Ellenborough*, 108–11; Foreign Dept Proceedings (11 November 1842), S. C. 5–12, NAI.
12. Imlah, *Lord Ellenborough*, 115–19.
13. Ellenborough to Queen Victoria, 10 June 1844, in *History of the Indian Administration of Lord Ellenborough*, 131–2; Imlah, *Lord Ellenborough*, 123–47; Robert A. Huttenback, *British Relations with Sind: 1799–1843: An Anatomy of Imperialism* (Berkeley: University of California Press, 1962), ch. 5.

14. *Bombay Times*, 7 December 1842, 788; Romila Thapar, *Somantaha: The Many Voices of a History* (London: Verso, 2005), 166–76.
15. *Political Sketches by H. B.*, 10 vols (London: Thomas McLean, 1829–51), viii, 754: 'The Modern Sampson Carrying off the Gates of Somnauth' (1843); ibid., 760: 'Alarming Situation! in India from an Old Tame Elephant Running Wild!!!' (February 1843); ix, 805: 'A Lesson in Elephant Riding! Studied from Nature in the Zoological Gardens' (14 May 1844); ibid., 824: 'A Wild Elephant Trumpeting. Or A Scene from Paradise Lost!' (28 December 1844); cf. 'The "Christian" Bayadere Worshipping the Idol "Siva" ', *Punch* iv (1843), 97.
16. Anon., *India and Lord Ellenborough* (London: W. H. Dalton, 1844), 83; A Bengal civilian, *Lord Ellenborough and Lord Auckland* (London: Smith, Elder and Co., 1845); Anon. 'Lord Ellenborough's Indian Policy', *Foreign Quarterly Review* 34 (January 1845), 479–514; Anon., 'Lord Ellenborough's Government of India', *British and Foreign Review* 17 (July 1844), 646–67; *The Times*, 6 May 1844, 4.
17. HC Debs, 66 (9 February 1843), 358–64 (Inglis); ibid. (9 March 1843), 364–73 (Peel); Peel reported his misgivings about Ellenborough to the queen on several occasions: QVJl., 28 January 1843, 22 February 1843, 17 March 1843; as did Aberdeen: ibid., 8 December 1842.
18. HC Debs, 72 (8 February 1844), 342–458; Sarah Ansari, 'The Sind Blue Books of 1843 and 1844: The Political "Laundering" of Historical Evidence', *English Historical Review* 120 (2005), 35–65.
19. Stanley to Queen Victoria, 23 November 1842, *Letters of Queen Victoria*, 1st ser., i, 552–3; Fitzgerald to Queen Victoria, 1 March 1842, ibid., i, 382–3. Lady Florentia Sale's *Journal of the Disasters in Afghanistan, 1841–2* was published in 1843.
20. QVJl., 8 December 1842; ibid., 22 August 1843; Queen Victoria to Peel, 23 April 1844, in *Letters of Queen Victoria*, 1st ser., ii, 10.
21. QVJl., 15 March 1843, 30 October 1844.
22. Ibid., 14 April 1844, 2 May 1844.
23. Ripon to Ellenborough, 5 July 1843, BL, Add. Ms. 40, 865, fols 113–14.
24. Ellenborough to Queen Victoria, 27 January 1843, *History of the Indian Administration of Lord Ellenborough*, 65–6. For the history of the regiment, see: Richard Brett-Smith, *The 11th Hussars (Prince Albert's own)* (London: Leo Cooper, 1969).
25. 'Memorandum' (9 December 1842), Wellington papers, Hartley Library, University of Southampton, Wellington papers, WP2/95/41–5; Queen Victoria to Peel, 29 November 1842, *Letters of Queen Victoria*, 1st ser., ii, 10.
26. *The Waterloo Medal Roll* (Dallington: Naval & Military Press, 1992).
27. J. W. Adams, 'The Peace Medals of George III' in A. M. Stahl (ed.), *The Medal in America*, 2 vols, (New York: American Numismatic Society, 1999), ii, 1–15.
28. 'Lists of the Medals and Clasps Issued by the Indian Government (1778–1876)', TNA, MINT 16/71. For Wyon, see the family entry: Philip Attwood, 'Wyon Family (per. *c.* 1760–1962)', *ODNB*. For images of and further details about the medals referred to in this section, see: John Horsley Mayo, *Medals and Decorations of the British Army and Navy*, 2 vols (London: Constable, 1897); Andrew Whittlestone and Michael Ewing, *Royal Commemorative Medals, 1837–1977*, 7 vols (Llanfllin: Galata Print, 2008), i.
29. For the correspondence giving her approval, see: Ripon to Queen Victoria, 29 May 1843, BL, Add. Ms., 40, 864, fols 311–12; Queen Victoria to Ripon, 30 May 1843, ibid., fols 313–14.
30. *Bombay Times*, 7 October 1843, 645.
31. Prince Albert to Lord Stanley, 28 February 1844, Derby papers, Liverpool Record Office, 920 DER (14) 101/7. A proof copy of the rejected medal to which Prince Albert refers can be seen in the Fitzwilliam Museum, Cambridge: Lester Watson Collection, item no. 53.
32. Hobhouse to Queen Victoria, 20 May 1848, IOR Mss Eur., F.213/19; Hobhouse to Wyon, 4 July 1850, ibid.
33. Hobhouse to Earl Grey, 28 October 1848, IOR Mss Eur. F.213/19.

34. Bengal Military Despatches, 5 March 1851, IOR/E/4/808; Charles Winter, 'The Army of India Medal', *British Numismatics Journal* 18 (1925), 165–72.

35. 'Earl Grey's Letter. Medals', (n.d., *c.* 1849), IOR Mss Eur. F213/107.

36. Queen Victoria to Henry Hardinge, 8 April 1845, Hardinge papers, McGill University Library, C5/17, fols 30–1; Hardinge to Emily Hardinge, 23 June 1846, in *The Letters of the First Viscount Hardinge of Lahore to Lady Hardinge and Sir Walter and Lady James, 1844–1847*, ed. Bawa Satinder Singh, Camden 4th ser., 42 (London: Royal Historical Society, 1986), 177; Charles Hardinge to Walter James, 2 January 1847, in *My Indian Peregrinations: The Private Letters of Charles Stewart Hardinge, 1844–1847*, ed. Bawa Satinder Singh (Lubbock, TX: Texas Tech University Press, 2001), 130. The original sketches are now in the Royal Collections: RCIN 1070417.

37. The sequence commenced with Dalhousie to Queen Victoria, 3 July 1848, BL Add. Ms., 36, 476, fols 140–9. Hobhouse objected to the separate correspondence about Gough: Hobhouse to Queen Victoria, 15 March 1849, IOR Mss Eur. F213/13.

38. Queen Victoria to Hardinge, 6 April 1846, Hardinge papers, McGill University Library, C5/17; Queen Victoria to Hobhouse, 26 May 1849, RA VIC/MAIN/N/14/54.

39. Hardinge to Queen Victoria, 28 July 1847, BL, Add. Ms. 36, 475, fols 343–50; QVJl., 24 October 1848, 18 August. 1854. For the first Sikh war, see: J. S. Grewal, *The Sikhs of the Punjab* (rev. edn, Cambridge, 1998), 123–4; Amarpal Sidu, *The First Anglo-Sikh War* (Stroud: Amberley, 2010).

40. Dalhousie to Queen Victoria, 7 April 1849 [copy], BL, Add. Ms., 36, 475, fols 505–7. For the second Sikh war, see: Andrew J. Major, *Return to Empire: Punjab under the Sikhs and the British in the Mid-nineteenth Century* (New Delhi: Sterling, 1996); Grewal, *Sikhs of the Punjab*, 126–7.

41. Hardinge told the queen that Jung Bahadur had personally committed the murders: Hardinge to Queen Victoria, 20 April 1847, IOR Mss Eur. F213/21; Hardinge to Queen Victoria, 1 June 1849, BL, Add. Ms., 36, 475, fols 244–5; Dalhousie to Hobhouse, 7 November. 1849, ibid., Add. Ms. 36, 477, fols 103–6.

42. Lord Elphinstone, who had met Jung Bahadur in Kathmandu, and given him a ring, vouched for him: Hobhouse to Carpenter, 28 June 1850, IOR Mss Eur. F213/19; Hobhouse to Queen Victoria, 17 June 1850, ibid., F213/13; Hobhouse to Queen Victoria, 11 July 1850, ibid., F213/13. See also: *ILN*, 8 June 1850, 401–2; Orfeur Cavenagh, *Reminiscences of an Indian Official* (London: W. H. Allen, 1884), ch. 4; John Whelpton, *Jang Bahadur in Europe: The First Nepalese Mission to the West* (Kathmandu: Sahayogi Press, 1983), 188–92.

43. Ripon to Queen Victoria, 26 January 1844 [copy], BL, Add. Ms., 40, 867, fols 102–3; Prince Albert to Ripon, ibid., 30 January 1844, fols 112–13.

44. Hardinge to Hobhouse, 14 August 1847, BL, Add. Ms, 36, 473, fols 364–73; Dalhousie to Hobhouse, 15 June 1849, BL, Add. Ms. 36, 477, fols 4–13; diary entry, 15 July 1855, Dalhousie papers, National Archives of Scotland, Edinburgh, GD45/6/544. The practice of sending the shawls directly to the queen resumed in 1857: Bengal despatches, IOR/E/4/845. For some of the background, see: Chitralekha Zutshi, '"Designed for Eternity": Kashmiri Shawls, Empire, and Cultures of Production and Consumption in Mid-Victorian Britain', *Journal of British Studies* 48 (2009), 420–40; Robert A. Huttenback, *Kashmir and the British Raj 1847–1947* (Oxford: Oxford University Press, 2004), ch. 1.

45. Hobhouse to H. St. J. Tucker, 1 January 1848, Tucker to Hobhouse, 8 January 1848, IOR, F213/18. The battle axe is now in the National Museum, New Delhi: Acc. No. 58.47/3.

46. Hobhouse to Queen Victoria, 14 June 1848, IOR Mss Eur. F.213/13; Queen Victoria to Hobhouse, 15 June, ibid., F.213/12. Some of these 1846 guns are depicted in a later painting by William Tayler: *The Triumphal Reception of the Sikh Guns [at Calcutta] . . . Dedicated to the Army of the Sutledge under the Command of Gen. Sir Hugh Gough,*

Commander-in-Chief and the Rt. Honble. Sir Henry Hardinge, Governor General, Second in Command (*c.* 1858), RCIN 813908. For the arms sent the following year, see: Dalhousie to Hobhouse, 15 June 1849, BL, Add. Ms. 36, 477, fols 4–13; Dalhousie to Hobhouse, 25 June 1849, ibid., fols 14–15; Dalhousie to Hobhouse, 14 July 1849 [inc. enclosure], ibid., fols 16–18; Dalhousie to Hobhouse, 23 April 1850, ibid., fols 191–6; Duleep Singh to Dalhousie, 14 November 1850, RA VIC/N14, fol. 66. Much of the captured Sikh arsenal is now in the collection of the Royal Artillery Museum.

47. Ranjit Singh's throne is now at V&A no. 2518(IS). Diary entry, 3 November 1851, Dalhousie papers, National Archives of Scotland, Edinburgh, GD45/6/544, 467–501; Ray Desmond, *The India Museum, 1801–1879* (London: India Office Library, 1982), 41.

48. For Dalhousie's original decision to present the Koh-i-Noor to the queen, see: Dalhousie to Queen Victoria, 7 April 1849, BL, Add. Ms. 36, 476, fols 505–7; QVJl., 25 May 1849. For the journey of the diamond from Lahore to London via Bombay, see: diary entry, 17 May 1850, Dalhousie papers, GD 45/6/540, 329–40; Dalhousie to Hobhouse, 23 April 1850, BL, Add. Ms. 36, 477, fols 191–6; Queen Victoria to Hobhouse, 3 July 1850, IOR Mss Eur. F.213/12. A recent history of the jewel can be found in William Dalrymple and Anita Anand, *Koh-i-Noor: The History of the World's Most Infamous Diamond* (London: Bloomsbury, 2017).

49. Galloway to Hobhouse, 26 May 1849, BL, Add. Ms. 36, 480, fols 41–2; Hobhouse to Galloway, 28 May 1849, IOR Mss Eur. F213/16. cf. Travers Twiss, *The Law of Nations Considered as Independent Political Communities: On the Rights and Duties of Nations in Time of War* (Oxford: Oxford University Press, 1863), 123, which, without discussing the case of the Punjab, upheld Hobhouse's position on war booty. For a later 'official' account of the ownership of the Koh-i-Noor, see: 'Enquiry Regarding the Presentation of the Koh-i-Nur [sic] Diamond to Queen Victoria in 1850', IOR, L/PS/11/296.

50. Joseph Paxton's 'Crystal Palace' cost £80,000 to build. For the guarantee, see: Hobhouse to John Shepherd, 15 August 1850, IOR Mss Eur. F213/15.

51. John Shepherd to Hobhouse, 2 October 1851, BL, Add. Ms. 36, 480, fols 2 October 1851, fols 457–60, 15 October 1851, ibid., fols 467–9; QVJl., 23 October 1851.

52. RCIN 406698.

53. R. J. Moore, *Sir Charles Wood's Indian Policy, 1853–66* (Manchester: Manchester University Press, 1966); P. K. Chatterji, 'The East India Company's Reactions to the Charter Act of 1853', *Journal of Indian History* 51 (1973), 55–64; Nadine André, 'L'India Act de 1853: ruptures et continuités' in idem. (ed.), *Ruptures et continuités: mélanges offerts à François Piquet* (Lyon: Université Jean Moulin-Lyon, 2004), 363–87.

54. 'First Report from the Select Committee of the House of Lords, Appointed to Inquire into the Operation of the Act 3 & 4 Will. 4, c. 85, for the Better Government of Her Majesty's Indian Territories, etc.', *Parl. Papers* (1852–3), Cd. 627, 141, 272–4.

55. 'Report from the Select Committee on Indian Territories, etc.', *Parl. Papers* (1852–3), Cd. 533, p. 44.

56. Ibid., 211, 249, 257, 259.

57. Thant Myint-U, *The Making of Modern Burma* (Cambridge: Cambridge University Press, 2001), 104; Oliver B. Pollak, *Empires in Collision: Anglo-Burmese Relations in the Mid-nineteenth Century* (London: ABC Clio, 1979); idem., 'A Mid-Victorian Cover-up: The Case of the "Combustible Commodore" and the Second Anglo-Burmese War, 1851–1852', *Albion*, 10 (1978), 171–83.

58. 'First Report from the Select Committee of the House of Lords', 274.

59. George Campbell, *A Scheme for the Government of India* (London: John Murray, 1853), 64, 121. For Marshman's view: 'Second Report from the Select Committee on Indian Territories', qq. 4648–57. For Maddock's: HC Debs, 127 (9 June 1853), 1326.

60. 'Third Report from the Select Committee on Indian Territories', q. 5010; idem., *Remarks on the Affairs of India: With Observations upon some of the Evidence Given before the Parliamentary Committee* (London: Effingham Wilson, 1852), 89.

61. James Silk Buckingham, *Plan for the Future Government of India* (London: Partridge & Oakey, 1853). For Buckingham, see: G. F. R. Barker, 'Buckingham, James Silk (1786–1855)', rev. Felix Driver, *ODNB*.

62. Queen Victoria to Lord Aberdeen, 27 May 1853, *Letters of Queen Victoria*, 1st ser., ii, 543–4.

63. *Speech of Lieut.-Colonel Sykes, at the General Court of Proprietors of East-India Stock, on the 21st June, 1853, on the Proposed India Bill* (London: Cox and Wyman, 1853), 20.

64. Betel leaf.

65. For two slightly different versions of the same encounter, see: *The Dalhousie–Phayre Correspondence, 1852–6*, ed. D. G. E Hall (London: Oxford University Press, 1932), 377–87, and *A Narrative of the Mission to the Court of Ava in 1855*, comp. Henry Yule (Kuala Lumpur: Oxford University Press, 1968), 88; cf. J. A. Mills, 'The First Decade of British Administration in Lower Burma, 1852–1862', *Kabar Seberang* 5–6 (1979), 112–25.

3 Exhibiting India

1. RCIN 403843; QVJl., 10, 11, 13 July and 21 August 1854. For the dressing up: Lady Lena Login, *Sir John Login and Duleep Singh* (London: W. H. Allen, 1890), 347–8. For the iconography of Duleep Singh more generally: Simeran Man Singh Gell, 'The Inner and the Outer: Dalip Singh as an Eastern Stereotype in Victorian England' in Shearer West (ed.), *The Victorians and Race* (Aldershot: Scolar, 1996), 68–83; Brian Keith Axel, *The Nation's Tortured Body: Violence, Representation and the Foundation of a Sikh Diaspora* (Durham, NC: Duke University Press, 2001), 51–78.

2. Susanne Stark, 'Bunsen, Christian Karl Josias von, Baron von Bunsen in the Prussian Nobility (1791–1860)', *ODNB*. The classic study of Albert's patronage of the arts remains: Hermione Hobhouse, *Prince Albert, His Life and Work* (London: Hamish Hamilton, 1983).

3. Thomas Becker, 'Prinz Albert als Student in Bonn' in F. Bosbach and W. Filmer-Sankey (eds), *Prinz Albert und der Entwicklung der Bildung im 19. Jahrhundert* (Munich: K. G. Saur, 2000), 145–56; Franz Bosbach, 'Prinz Albert und das universitäire Studium in Bonn and Cambridge' in Christa Jansohn (ed.), *In the Footsteps of Queen Victoria* (Munster: Lit, 2003), 201–24; Franz Bosbach (ed.), *Die Studien des Prinzen Albert an der Universität Bonn (1837–1838)* (Berlin: De Gruyter, 2010), esp. chs by Amalie Fößel and Christian Recht; John R. Davis, 'Friedrich Max Müller and the Migration of German Academics to Britain in the Nineteenth Century' in Stefan Manz, Margrit Schulte Beerbühl and John R. Davis (eds), *Migration and Transfer from Germany to Britain, 1660–1914* (Munich: K. G. Saur, 2007), 93–106; Oliver Everett, 'The Royal Library at Windsor Castle as Developed by Prince Albert and B. B. Woodward', *The Library*, 7th ser., 3 (2002), 58–88.

4. Charles von Hügel, *Travels in Kashmir and the Panjab* (Karachi: Oxford University Press, 2003); QVJl., 8 August 1845, 30 January 1846, 23 March 1846, 2 March 1847.

5. Leopold von Orlich, *Travels in India: Including Sinde and the Punjab* (London: Longmans, 1845); Henry Steinbach, *The Punjaub: Being a Brief History of the Country of the Sikhs: Its Extent, History, Commerce, Productions, Government, Manufactures, Laws, Religion, etc.* (London: Smith, Elder, 1845). For Orlich, see: *The Times*, 7 June 1860, 9; and for Steinbach, see: W. H. Macleod, 'Colonel Steinbach and the Sikhs', *Panjab Past and Present* 9 (1975), 291–8.

6. *Zur Erinnerung an die Reise der Prinzen Waldemar von Preussen nach Indien in den Jahren 1844–1846*, 2 vols (Berlin: privately printed, 1853); QVJl., 2, 5, 19 July 1847.

7. Joan Leopold, 'British Applications of the Aryan Theory of Race to India, 1850–1870', *English Historical Review* 89 (1974), 578–603; Martin Maw, *Visions of India: Fulfilment Theology, the Aryan Race Theory, and the Work of British Protestant Missionaries in Victorian*

India (Frankfurt: Peter Lang, 1990), 22–5; Thomas R. Trautmann, *Aryans and British India* (Berkeley: University of California Press, 1997), 172–8; Tony Ballantyne, *Orientalism and Race: Aryanism in the British Empire* (Basingstoke: Palgrave, 2002), 41–4.

8. *The Times*, 13 January 1857, 7; G. Beckerlegge, 'Professor Friedrich Max Müller and the Missionary Cause' in John Wolffe (ed.), *Religion in Victorian Britain, vol. 5: Culture and Empire* (Manchester: Manchester University Press, 1997), 177–219. For Monier-Williams, see his *The Study of Sanskrit in Relation to Missionary Work in India: An Inaugural Lecture* (London: Williams and Norgate, 1861), esp. 39–41, and A. A. Macdonell, 'Williams, Sir Monier Monier- (1819–1899)', rev. J. B. Katz, *ODNB*.

9. QVJl., 5 January 1864. C. B. Phipps to Max Müller, 28 January 1863, Max Müller papers, Bodleian Library, Oxford, Ms. Eng. D. 2349, fol. 1.

10. Richard Sitnick, *The Coburg Conspiracy: Plots and Manoeuvres* (London: Espheus, 2008); John R. Davis, 'The Coburg Connection. Dynastic Relations and the House of Coburg in Britain' in Karina Urbach (ed.), *Royal Kinship. Anglo-German Family Networks* (Munich: K. G. Saur, 2008), 97–116.

11. Becker, 'Prinz Albert als Student in Bonn'. For Savigny, see: Margaret Barber Crosby, *The Making of a German Constitution: A Slow Revolution* (Oxford: Berg, 2008), ch. 2.

12. See Albert's 'Memorandum on German Affairs' (11 September 1847) in Theodore Martin, *The Life of the Prince Consort. Prince Albert and His Times*, 5 vols (1877; London: IB Tauris, 2012), ii, 439–46; Albert to Ernst, 14 March 1848 in Hector Bolitho (ed.), *The Prince Consort and His Brother: Two Hundred New Letters* (London: Cobden-Sanderson, 1933), 101–3; cf. Davis, 'Coburg connection', 112–13; E. J. Feutchwanger, *Albert and Victoria: The Rise and Fall of the House of Saxe-Coburg-Gotha* (London: Hambledon Continuum, 2006), 77–9.

13. 'Toast Given at the Dinner of the Trinity House' in *The Principal Speeches and Addresses of His Royal Highness the Prince Consort* (London: John Murray, 1862), 243–4.

14. *Transactions of the Royal Society of Arts* 59 (1849), p.50; Henry Labouchere to Mountstuart Elphinstone, 15 December 1849, IOR Mss Eur. F88/140/62, fols 167–70. For Albert and the 1851 exhibition, see: Hobhouse, *Prince Albert*, ch. 7; John R. Davis, 'Albert and the Great Exhibition of 1851: Creating the Ceremonial of Industry' in Caroline J. Litzenberger and Eileen Groth Lyon (eds), *The Human Tradition in Modern Britain* (Lanham, MD: Rowman and Littlefield, 2006), 95–110.

15. *The Times*, 24 May 1851, 8; ibid., 10 September 1851, 5.

16. 'First Report of the Commissioners for the Exhibition of 1851, etc.', *Parl. Papers* (1852), Cd. 1485, 72, 163–4; IOR/L/SUR/1/1, fol. 101.

17. Francis Higginson, *Koh-i-Noor, or the Great Exhibition and its Opening* (London: Pretyman and Rixon, 1851); *Hunt's Hand-book to the Official Catalogues: An Explanatory Guide to the Natural Productions and Manufactures of the Great Exhibition of the Industry of all Nations, 1851*, ed. Robert Hunt (London: Spicer, 1851), 29–32. The fullest accounts of the Indian court were in the *ILN*, 14 June 1851, 563–4; *Cassell's Illustrated Exhibitor*, 4 October 1851, 317–28; and *Dickinsons' Comprehensive Pictures of the Great Exhibition of 1851, from the Originals Painted for H.R.H. Prince Albert, by Messrs. Nash, Hague, and Roberts*, 2 vols (London: Dickinson, 1851), ii, plates 1–7.

18. *The Times*, 23 April 1851, 5; ibid., 15 May 1851, 5; cf. *Tallis's History and Description of the Crystal Palace, and the Exhibition of the World's Industry in 1851* (London: John Tallis, 1851), i, 31–8. In a large secondary literature, two accounts of the 1851 exhibition, and the place of the Indian exhibits within it, stand out: Lara Kriegel, 'Narrating the Subcontinent in 1851: India at the Crystal Palace' in Louise Purbrick (ed.), *The Great Exhibition of 1851: New Interdisciplinary Essays* (Manchester: Manchester University Press, 2001), 146–78; and Anthony Swift, '"The Arms of England that Grasp the World": Empire at the Great Exhibition', *Ex Plus Ultra* 3 (2012), 1–25.

19. *Official Catalogue of the Great Exhibition of the Works of Industry of All Nations, 1851* (London: Spicer, 1851), 860–907.

20. W. Cullen to Sir H. C. Montgomery, 7 December 1850, enc. Address from the Raja of Travancore (11 October 1850), Tamil Nadu State Archives, Political Consultations, 7 January 1851, 40.

21. Hobhouse to Queen Victoria, 14 August 1851, IOR Mss Eur. 213/13. The Raja of Travancore celebrated the receipt of the queen's letter of acknowledgment with an elaborate ceremony, depicted at the time by Frederick Christian Lewis: W. Cullen to Montgomery, Trivandrum, 19 November 1851, Tamil Nadu State Archives, Political consultations, 25 November 1851, 31; *The Durbar on the Reception by his Highness the Maharaja of Travancore of the Letter of her Majesty Queen Victoria on the 27 November 1851,* engraving by F. C. Lewis Snr after F. C. Lewis Jnr (London: Graves & Co., 1854), IOR, P384.

22. 'Minutes of the Meeting of Commissioners', 1 March 1850, 8, Archives, Royal Commission for the Exhibition of 1851.

23. QVJl., 16 July 1851.

24. East India Committee, Minutes, 13 April 1852, Archives, Royal Society of Arts, PR/GE/112/12/92; Alexander Hunter to Lyon Playfair, 9 August 1852, ibid.; Minutes, 3 November 1852, Archives, Royal Society of Arts; Bengal Public Despatch, 17 November 1852, IOR, IOR/E/4/817; Charles Grey to Henry Cole, 6 April 1853, Cole corresp., Part 2, National Art Library, Victoria & Albert Museum; *Freeman's Journal,* 25 March 1853, 3; *Official Catalogue of the Great Industrial Exhibition (in Connection with the Royal Dublin Society), 1853* (Dublin: John Falconer, 1853), 12–16, 119–122; Maggie McEnchroe Williams, 'The "Temple of Industry": Dublin's Industrial Exhibition of 1853' in Colum Hourihane (ed.), *Irish Art Historical Studies in Honour of Peter Harbison* (Dublin: Four Courts Press, 2004), 261–75.

25. *Cassell's Illustrated Exhibitor . . . of . . . the International Exhibition of 1862* (London: Cassell, Petter and Galpin, 1862), 10, 123; Desmond, *India Museum,* 103–5.

26. *The Illustrated Record and Descriptive Catalogue of the Dublin International Exhibition of 1865,* comp. Henry Parkinson and Peter Lund Simmonds (London: E. and F. N. Spon, 1866), 338–48; Nellie Ò Cléirigh, 'Dublin International Exhibition, 1865', *Dublin Historical Record* 47 (1994), 169–82.

27. 'Catalogue of the Valuable Contents of the Indian Court . . . to be Sold by Auction . . . 24th January 1887', National Art Library, Victoria & Albert Museum, 1886 Exhibition scrapbook; *Colonial and Indian Exhibition. Official Catalogue* (London: William Clowes & Sons, 1886), 10–88. Frank Cundall, *Reminiscences of the Colonial and Indian Exhibition* (London: William Clowes & Sons, 1886), 21–30. For recent analyses of the Indian 'presence' at the 1886 exhibition, see: Saloni Mathur, *India by Design: Colonial History and Cultural Display* (Berkeley: University of California Press, 2007), ch. 2; Aviva Briefel, 'On the 1886 Colonial and Indian Exhibition', http://www.branchcollective.org/?ps_articles=aviva-briefel-on-the-1886-colonial-and-indian-exhibition (accessed 4 April 2018).

28. For the queen's association with the popularity of the shawls, see Anon., *Kashmeer and its Shawls* (London: Wyman & Sons, 1875), 24, 58.

29. Felix Driver and Sonia Asmore, 'The Mobile Museum: Collecting and Circulating Indian Textiles in Victorian Britain', *Victorian Studies* 52 (2010), 353–85.

30. Joan Anim-Addo, 'Queen Victoria's Black "Daughter"' in Gretchen Holbrook Gerzina (ed.), *Black Victorians/Black Victoriana* (New Brunswick, NJ: Rutgers University Press, 2003), 11–19; Brian Mackrell, *Hariru Wikitoria!: An Illustrated History of the Maori Tour of England, 1863* (Auckland: Oxford University Press, 1985).

31. Hermann Mögling, *Coorg Memoirs: An Account of Coorg, and of the Coorg Mission* (Bangalore: Wesleyan Mission Press, 1855); *Coorg and its Rajas, by an Officer Formerly in the Service of His Highness Veer Rajunder Wadeer, Raja of Coorg* (London: Bumpus, 1857), 65–7. The Raja was required to contribute £40 per month for her upkeep: John Herries to J. W. Hogg, 26 June 1852, BL, Add. Ms. 57, 410, fols 92–3; cf. C. P. Belliappa, *Victoria Gouramma: The Lost Princess of Coorg* (New Delhi: Rupa, 2011).

32. QVJl., 6 June 1852, 7 June 1852, 26 June 1852, 30 June 1852; *Daily News*, 7 May 1852, 5; *Morning Post*, 1 July 1852, 5; *Coorg and its Rajas*, 93–4.

33. Hogg to Herries, 6 August 1852, BL, Add. Ms., 57, 410, fols 96–8, Herries to Hogg, 8 August 1852, ibid., fols 100–2; QVJl 12 September 1852; *Daily News*, 28 July 1852, 4; 1 March 1853, 5.

34. *Lady Login's Recollections: Court Life and Camp Life, 1820–1904* (London: Smith and Elder, 1916), 185–8; 'Trust of Miss E. V. G. Campbell', IOR/L/AG50/7; Robert Montgomery Martin, *Correspondence with Viscount Cranborne, H.M. Secretary of State for India, on the Ingratitude, Injustice and Breach of National Faith to the Sovereigns of Coorg* (London: W. Clowes, 1867).

35. Both Winterhalter's portrait and Marochetti's bust are now on display at Osborne House: RCIN 403841 and RCIN 41535.

36. A water carrier.

37. QVJl., 1 April 1846; Hardinge to Sarah James, 19 February 1846, in *The Letters of the First Viscount Hardinge of Lahore to Lady Hardinge and Sir Walter and Lady James, 1844–1847*, ed. Bawa Satinder Singh, Camden 4th ser., 42 (London: Royal Historical Society, 1986), 150–1; Dalhousie to Hobhouse, 22 December 1848, BL, Add. Ms., 36, 476, fols 140–9. £0.5m of jewels was sold off separately by the Government of India: *A Reprint of Two Sale Catalogues of Jewels and other Confiscated Property Belonging to his Highness the Maharaja Duleep Singh which were . . . Sold in the Years 1850 and 1851* (London: privately printed, 1885), vii. On Duleep Singh, see: Michael Alexander and Sushila Anand, *Queen Victoria's Maharaja: Duleep Singh, 1838–93* (London: Weidenfeld & Nicholson, 1980); Prithipal Singh Kapur (ed.), *Maharaja Duleep Singh: The Last Sovereign Ruler of the Punjab* (Amritsar: Dharam Parchar Committee, 1995); Nazir Ahmad Chaudry (ed.), *The Maharaja Duleep Singh and the Government: A Narrative* (Lahore: Sang-e-Meel, 1999); Peter Bance, *Duleep Singh: Sovereign, Squire and Rebel* (London: Coronet House, 2009). For a compelling new account of Queen Victoria's infatuation with Duleep Singh, see: Priya Atwal, 'Between the Courts of Lahore and Windsor: Anglo-Indian Relations and the Re-making of Royalty in the Nineteenth Century' (unpublished DPhil thesis, University of Oxford, 2017), esp. ch. 4.

38. QVJl., 6 July 1854, 26 August 1856; RCIN 403843 (Winterhalter); RCIN 41542 (Marochetti, the uncoloured version).

39. QVJl., 24 August 1854, cf. 22 August 1854, 14 November 1854.

40. *ILN*, 29 March 1856, 319; QVJl., 31 May 1856; *The Times*, 8 December 1856, 9; *Leeds Mercury*, 16 June 1860, 10.

41. The best narrative of Duleep Singh's life in England is Bance, *Sovereign, Squire and Rebel*. For details about his children, see: Anita Anand, *Sophia: Princess, Suffragette, Revolutionary* (London: Bloomsbury, 2015).

42. Kapur (ed.), *Maharaja Duleep Singh*, chs 7, 14.

43. QVJl., 21 March 1871, 5 April 1884; Martin A. Wainwright, 'Royal Relationships as a Form of Resistance: The Cases of Duleep Singh and Abdul Karim' in Rehana Ahmed and Sumita Mukerjee (eds), *South Asian Resistances in Britain, 1858–1947* (London: Continuum, 2012), 96–9.

44. Queen Victoria to the Earl of Clarendon, 23 September 1857, in *Letters of Queen Victoria*, 1st ser., iii, 315.

45. QVJl., 18 March 1868.

46. QVJl., 3 July 1886, 20 August 1886, 31 March 1891.

47. Ibid., 28 April 1854, 17 May 1854, 9 July 1855; *Extracts from Captain Colin Mackenzie's Work, Regarding the Dominions of the Late Tipoo Sultaun; and Correspondence and Memorials of Prince Ghulam Mohammad and his Family, Addressed to the Government of India and the Hon'ble Court of Directors* (Calcutta: Sandars, Cones, 1854); *The History of Hyder Shah . . . and of His Son, Tipoo Sultaun . . . Revised and Corrected by Prince Gholam Mohammed* (London: W. Thacker, 1855); *Memorial of Prince Ghulam Mohammad to the Right Honourable Secretary of State for India in Council* (London: John Edward Taylor, 1859), 33–4, 37, 39–40.

48. Catherine E. Anderson, 'Tipu's Sons and Images of Paternalism in Late Eighteenth-century Romantic British Art' in Carolyn A. Weber (ed.), *Romanticism And Parenting: Image, Instruction and Ideology* (Newcastle: Cambridge Scholars, 2007), 7–28; Sean Willcock, 'A Neutered Beast? Representations of the Sons of Tipu – the Tiger of Mysore – as Hostages in the 1790s', *Journal for Eighteenth-Century Studies* 36 (2013), 121–47.

49. Queen Victoria to Dalhousie, 24 November 1854 in *Letters of Queen Victoria*, 1st ser., ii, 54; QVJl., 21 November 1854.

4 'This Bloody Civil War'

1. *The Times*, 22 August 1856, 12, 28 August 1856, 12; *Daily News*, 22 August 1856, 4; Safi Ahmad (ed.), *British Aggression in Avadh: Being the Treatise of M. Mohammed Masih Uddin Khan Bahadur, Entitled Oude: Its Princes and its Government Vindicated* (Meerut: Meenakshi Prakashan, 1969), 3–9. There are descriptions of the delegation in Rosie Llewellyn-Jones, *Engaging Scoundrels: True Tales of Old Lucknow* (Delhi: Oxford University Press, 2000), 112–21, and Michael H. Fisher, *Counterflows to Colonialism: Indian Travellers and Settlers in Britain, 1600–1857* (Delhi: Permanent Black, 2004), 412–22.

2. *The Times*, 17 January 1857, 12; *Morning Chronicle*, 2 April 1857, 7, 6 April 1857, 5.

3. Victoria to Charles Canning, 21 August 1856, RA VIC/MAIN/N/15/17; Robert Vernon Smith to Canning, 25 August 1856, IOR Mss Eur. F231/3, fols 162–5.

4. QVJl., 4 July 1857; 'Illuminated Letter from the King of Oudh, 7 January 1857', IOR Mss Eur. C849.

5. Amongst a large literature on the Indian revolt and its background I have drawn chiefly from the following: Charles Ball, *The History of the Indian Mutiny: Giving a Detailed Account of the Sepoy Insurrection in India, etc.*, 2 vols (London: London Printing and Publishing Co., 1858–9); J. W. Kaye, *A History of the Sepoy War in India, 1857–8*, 3 vols (London, W. H. Allen, 1864–76); S. N. Sen, *1857* (Delhi: Government of India, 1957; 1995 edn); Pratul Chandra Gupta, *Nana Saheb and the Rising at Cawnpore* (Oxford: Clarendon Press, 1963); Khushhalilal Srivastava, *The Revolt of 1857 in Central India-Malwa* (Bombay: Allied Publishers, 1966); Eric Stokes, *The Peasant and the Raj: Studies in Peasant Rebellion and Agrarian Society in Colonial India* (Cambridge: Cambridge University Press, 1978); Rudrangshu Mukherjee, *Awadh in Revolt, 1857–1858: A Study of Popular Resistance* (Delhi: Oxford University Press, 1984); Joyce Lebra-Chapman, *The Rani of Jhansi: A Study of Female Heroism in India* (Honolulu: University of Hawaii Press, 1986); Michael H. Fisher, *A Clash of Cultures: Awadh, the British and the Mughals* (New Delhi: Manohar, 1987); William Dalrymple, *The Last Mughal: The Fall of a Dynasty, Delhi, 1857* (London: Bloomsbury, 2006); Rudrangshu Mukherjee and Parmood Kapoor, *Dateline 1857: Revolt Against the Raj* (New Delhi: Roli Books, 2008); Mahmood Farooqui (comp.), *Besieged: Voices from Delhi, 1857* (London: Penguin, 2010).

6. S. A. A. Risvi (ed.), *Freedom Struggle in Uttar Pradesh*, 6 vols (Delhi: Oxford University Press, 2011), ii, 150–60, iv, 604–5; Ball, *History of the Indian Mutiny*, 183–4; Kaye, *History of the Sepoy War*, 471; 'Proclamations of Nana Sahib' [2], www.csas.ed.ac.uk/mutiny/Texts-Part2.html (accessed 4 April 2018).

7. 'Correspondence on the Subject of the Despatch of Troops to India from the Colonies of the Cape of Good Hope, Ceylon, and Mauritius', *Parl. Papers* (1857–8), Cd. 2298, 28–9, 32. For the wider colonial ramifications of the rebellion, see: Jill Bender, *The 1857 Indian Uprising and the British Empire* (Cambridge: Cambridge University Press, 2016), esp. chs 3–4.

8. Canning's refusal to muster European volunteers led to a petition to Queen Victoria requesting his recall: 'Petition to Queen Victoria signed by Christian inhabitants of Calcutta' (1857), IOR/A/1/94A. For Nepal, see: Kanchanmoy Mojumdar, 'Nepal and the Indian Mutiny, 1857–8', *Bengal Past and Present* 85 (1966), 13–39. For Gwalior and Indore see: Amar Farooqui, *Sindias and the Raj: Princely Gwalior, c. 1800–1850* (Delhi:

Primus Books, 2011), 137–9; Srivastava, *Revolt of 1857 in Central India-Malwa*, chs 10–12. For the Punjab, see: Andrew Major, *Return to Empire: Punjab under the Sikhs and British in the Mid-nineteenth Century* (New Delhi: Sterling, 1996), ch. 6. For Sikh loyalty, see: J. S. Grewal and Harish Sharma, 'Political Change and Social Readjustment: The Case of Sikh Aristocracy Under Colonial Rule in the Punjab', *Proceedings of the Indian History Congress* 48 (1988), 377–82.

9. Douglas M. Peers, *Between Mars and Mammon: Colonial Armies and the Garrison State, 1810–35* (London: IB Tauris, 1995), ch. 8. For the dispersal of troops overseas, see the returns in 'Return of the Actual Military Force that was in India at the Time of the Outbreak of the Mutiny at Meerut, etc.', *Parl. Papers* (1857–8), Cd. 356, 10, 17.

10. Deep Kanta Lahiri Choudhury, *Telegraphic Imperialism: Crisis and Panic in the Indian Empire, c. 1830–1920* (Basingstoke: Palgrave Macmillan, 2011), ch. 2.

11. Merrill Tilghman Boyce, *British Policy and the Evolution of the Vernacular Press in India 1835–1878* (Delhi: Chanakya, 1988), ch. 3.

12. As Lord Broughton tartly observed to the queen's private secretary, 'We have almost ruined Dacca by pouring our Manchester Goods into India': Broughton to Col. Grey, 26 October 1851, IOR Mss Eur. F.213/13. See: Stokes, *The Peasant and the Raj*, chs 7–8; C. A. Bayly, *Indian Society and the Making of the British Empire* (Cambridge: Cambridge University Press, 1988), ch. 6.

13. Suresh Chandra Ghosh, *Dalhousie in India: A Study of his Social Policy as Governor General* (New Delhi: Munshiram Manoharlal, 1975). David J. Howlett, 'Ramsay, James Andrew Broun, First Marquess of Dalhousie (1812–1860)', *ODNB*.

14. *Memorial of the Society for the Propagation of the Gospel, on the extension of the Episcopate in India; with a statement of detailed information on the subject, an appendix of documents, and a coloured map of the present dioceses* (London: Bell and Daldy, 1857); for Mitchell and Wheeler, see: Kim A. Wagner, *The Great Fear of 1857: Rumours, Conspiracies and the Making of the Indian Uprising* (Oxford: Peter Lang, 2010), 96.

15. [Henry Reeve and John Kaye], 'India', *Edinburgh Review* 106 (October 1857), 567; cf. Alexander Duff, *The Indian Rebellion: Its Causes and Results. In a Series of Letters* (London: James Nisbet, 1858), 121 and *passim*. Others saw the outbreak as a 'long-cherished conspiracy on the part of the Mahometans' which 'inflamed' the superstitious Hindu mind: Anon., *The Indian Mutiny: Thoughts and Facts* (London: Seeley, Jackson and Halliday, 1857), 20–1; *The Trial of Bahadur Shah Zafar*, ed. Pramod K. Nayar (Hyderabad: Orient Longman, 2007), esp. 138–75.

16. Sabyasachi Bhattacharya (ed.), *Rethinking 1857* (New Delhi: Orient Longman, 2007), xvii; William Dalrymple 'Religious Rhetoric in the Delhi Uprising of 1857' in ibid., 22–43; Tariq Rahman, 'The Events of 1857 in Contemporary Writings in Urdu', *South Asia* 32 (2009), 212–29; K. M. Ashraf, 'Muslim Revivalists and the Revolt of 1857' in Biswamoy Pati (ed.), *The 1857 Rebellion* (New Delhi: Oxford University Press, 2007), 151–8; Irfan Habib, 'The Coming of 1857' in Shireen Mossvi (ed.), *Facets of the Great Revolt, 1857* (New Delhi: Tulika Books, 2008), 5–6; Marina Carter and Crispin Bates, 'Religion and Retribution in the Indian Rebellion of 1857', *Leidschrift* 24 (2009), 51–8.

17. J. A. B. Palmer, *The Mutiny Outbreak at Meerut in 1857* (Cambridge: Cambridge University Press, 1966), 133.

18. M. A. Rahim, *Lord Dalhousie's Administration of the Conquered and Annexed States* (Delhi: S. Chand, 1963).

19. Diary entries, 16 February 1851, 24 March 1851, 27 March 1851, 3 November 1851, 14 December 1851, Dalhousie papers, National Archives of Scotland, Edinburgh, GD 45/6/540.

20. [W. H. Sleeman], *Iconoclastes on the Princes and Territorial Chiefs of India* (Cheltenham, n.p., 1853), 4, 33; Dalhousie, 'Minute' (17 May 1853), Foreign Dept Proceedings, NAI, 75; cf. Dalhousie, 'Memorandum on the Future Government of India' (13 October 1852), IOR, IOR/L/PS/18/D175.

21. Bengal despatches (17 June 1856), IOR, IOR/E/4/836, p. 633.

22. Dalhousie to Queen Victoria, 19 February 1853, RA VIC/MAIN/N/15/2. For the final phase of the kingdom of Awadh, see: Fisher, *Clash of Cultures*, 227–44 and Rosie Llewellyn-Jones, *The Last King in India: Wajid Ali Shah* (London: Hurst, 2014), 109.

23. [William Knighton], *The Private Life of an Eastern King* (London: Hope, 1855).

24. Queen Victoria to Charlotte Canning, 5 July 1857, Canning papers, West Yorkshire Archives Service, WYL 250/10/42.

25. Theodore Martin, *The Life of the Prince Consort: Prince Albert and his Times*, 5 vols (London: Smith, Elder & Co., 1875–80), iv, 72–82.

26. QVJl., 16 July 1857, 18 July 1857, 20 July 1857, 25 July 1857; *The Times*, 27 July 1857, 8.

27. Queen Victoria to Lord Panmure, 29 June 1857, *Letters of Queen Victoria*, 1st ser., iii, 298–9, Queen Victoria to Palmerston, 22 August 1857, ibid., 308–12; Lord Palmerston to Queen Victoria, 15 September 1857, RA VIC/MAIN/N/15/75; Queen Victoria to Lord Palmerston, 18 September 1857, Broadlands papers, Hartley Library, University of Southampton, RC/F/845/1–2.

28. Palmerston to Queen Victoria, 15 September 1857, RA, VIC/MAIN/N/15/75; cf. QVJl., 24 September 1857. For the state day of prayer (7 October), see: Brian Stanley, 'Christian Responses to the Indian Mutiny of 1857', *Studies in Church History* 20 (1983), 277–89.

29. For example, see QVJl., 3 August 1857, 14 January 1858, 22 March 1858, 14 April 1858.

30. There is now an extensive body of work on this: Gautam Chakravarty, *The Indian Mutiny and the British Imagination* (Cambridge: Cambridge University Press, 2005); Christopher Herbert, *War of No Pity: The Indian Mutiny and Victorian Trauma* (Princeton, NJ: Princeton University Press, 2008); Salahuddin Malik, *1857: War of Independence or Clash of Civilizations? British Public Reactions* (Oxford: Oxford University Press, 2008); Eugenia M. Palmegiano, 'The Indian Mutiny in the Mid-Victorian Press', *Journal of Newspaper and Periodical History* 7 (1991), 3–11; Alison Blunt, 'Spatial Stories Under Siege: British Women Writing from Lucknow in 1857', *Gender, Place and Culture* 7 (2000), 229–46; Claudia Klaver, 'Domesticity Under Siege: British Women and Imperial Crisis at the Siege of Lucknow 1857', *Women's Writing* 8 (2001), 21–58; Catherine Hart, ' "Oh what horrors will be disclosed when we know all": British Women and the Private/Public Experience of the Siege of Lucknow', *Prose Studies* 34 (2012), 185–96; Lydia Murdoch, ' "Suppressed grief": Mourning the Death of British Children and the Memory of the 1857 Indian Rebellion', *Journal of British Studies* 51 (2012), 364–92; Andrea Kaston Tange, 'Maternity Betrayed: Circulating Images of English Motherhood in India, 1857–1858', *Nineteenth-century Contexts* 35 (2013), 187–215.

31. QVJl., 31 August 1857.

32. Adelaide Case, *Day By Day at Lucknow: A Journal of the Siege of Lucknow* (London: Richard Bentley, 1858). On Case's narrative, see: Alison Blunt, 'The Flight from Lucknow: British Women Travelling and Writing Home, 1857–8' in James Duncan and Derek Gregory (eds), *Rites of Passage: Reading Travel Writing* (London: Routledge, 1999), 92–113.

33. Virginia Surtees, *Charlotte Canning: Lady-in-waiting to Queen Victoria and Wife of the First Viceroy of India, 1817–1861* (London: John Murray, 1975); Charles Allen (ed.), *A Glimpse of the Burning Plain: Leaves from the Indian Journals of Charlotte Canning* (London: Michael Joseph, 1986).

34. Charlotte Canning to Queen Victoria, 11 December 1857, 9 January 1858, 24 January 1858, 19 May 1858, Canning papers, 250/10/4/3; QVJl., 22 March 1858.

35. Charlotte Canning to Queen Victoria, 25 November [1857], 30 August 1858, 18 December 1858, Canning papers, WYL 250/10/4/3. For Murray, see: John Fraser, 'Murray, John (1809–1898)', *ODNB*. For Beato, see: Claire Bowen, 'Memorising the Mutiny: Felice Beato's Lucknow Photographs', *Cahiers victoriens et édouardiens* 66 (2007), 195–209; Narayani Gupta, 'Pictorializing the "Mutiny" of 1857' in Maria Pelizzari (ed.), *Traces of India: Photography, Architecture and the Politics of Representation, 1850–1900* (London: Yale University Press, 2003), 216–39.

36. Barker's 'Siege of Lucknow' is now in the National Portrait Gallery (NPG 5851). On Lundgren, see: Sten Nilsson and Narayani Gupta, *The Painter's Eye: Egron Lundgren and India* (Stockholm: Nationalmuseum, 1992), 26, 29; Rosie Llewellyn-Jones, *Great Uprising*, 203–4.

37. Lady Canning drawings, Harewood House, Leeds, 1859–60 vol., fols 36–56, 59, 64–5. She also photographed the ruins of Metcalfe House, the residence of the Delhi Commissioner: 'Lord and Lady Canning Family Album', fol. 60, Gilman collection, Metropolitan Museum of Art, New York. More of her sketches of the topography of the rebellion can be found in two albums held by the Victoria & Albert Museum, starting with the depictions of Allahabad in November 1858: Dept Prints and Drawings, V&A, PD.80E.

38. Lord Palmerston to Queen Victoria, 18 October 1857, RA VIC/MAIN/N/16/9.

39. For the political background, see: Robin J. Moore, *Sir Charles Wood's Indian Policy, 1853–1866* (Manchester: Manchester University Press, 1966), ch. 2; Angus Hawkins, 'British Parliamentary Party Alignment and the Indian Issue, 1857–1858', *Journal of British Studies* 23 (1984), 79–105.

40. [John Henry Tremenheere], 'How is India to be Governed?', *Bentley's Miscellany* 43 (February, 1858), 115–16; James Silk Buckingham, *Plan for A Future Government of India* (London: Partridge and Oakley, 1858), 9; cf. Anon., *A Voice From India to the Men of Manchester* (Manchester: Joseph Pratt, 1858).

41. Lord Palmerston to Queen Victoria, 17 December 1857, RA VIC/MAIN/N/16/43; George Clerk, 'Memorandum on the Government of India' (11 November 1857), IOR, IOR/L/PS/18/D55; QVJl., 12 January 1858.

42. Vernon Smith to Queen Victoria, 31 January 1858, RA VIC/MAIN/N/17/26–7; Queen Victoria to Lord Palmerston (draft), 9 February 1858, RA VIC/MAIN/N/17/32; cf. Queen Victoria to Lord Palmerston, 24 December 1857, *Letters of Queen Victoria*, 1st ser., iii, 327–8.

43. Lord Derby to Prince Albert 25 March 1858, RA VIC/MAIN/N/17/67; Queen Victoria to Lord Ellenborough, 26 March 1858, RA VIC/MAIN/N/17/72. For the first draft of the Conservative bill, see: 'India Bill', 21–48, Derby papers, Liverpool Record Office, 920 DER (15) 27/1.

44. Michael Maclagan, *'Clemency Canning', Charles John, 1st Earl Canning, Governor-General and Viceroy of India, 1856–1862* (London: Macmillan, 1962), 196–204.

45. *Punch*, 7 November 1857, 191; Queen Victoria to Derby, 9 May 1858 (draft), RA VIC/MAIN/N/18/37; Prince Albert, 'Memorandum' (11 May 1858), RA VIC/MAIN/N/18/48; Queen Victoria to Lord Derby, 31 May 1858, RA VIC/MAIN/N/18/94.

46. Benjamin Disraeli to Queen Victoria, 24 June 1858, in *Letters of Queen Victoria*, 1st ser., iii, 372–3; HC Debs, 151 (24 June 1858), cols 350–1 (Bright). For Disraeli and India in 1857, see: Ann Pottinger Saab, 'Disraeli, India, and the Indians, 1852–58' in Wolfgang Elz and Sönke Neitzel (eds), *Internationale Beziehungen im 19. und 20. Jahrhundert: festschrift für Winfried Baumgart zum 65. Geburtstag* (Paderborn: Schöningh, 2003), 37–52.

47. QVJl., 7 July 1858; Queen Victoria to Lord Derby, 8 July 1858 (draft), RA VIC/MAIN/N/19/5; Lord Derby to Queen Victoria, 10 July 1858, RA VIC/MAIN/N/19/10; Queen Victoria to Lord Derby, 29 July 1858 (draft), RA VIC/MAIN/N/19/25; Lord Derby to Queen Victoria, 29 July 1858, RA VIC/MAIN/N/19/26; Prince Albert to Sir James Graham, 29 July 1858, RA VIC/MAIN/N/19/27; Sir James Graham to Prince Albert, 30 July 1858, RA VIC/MAIN/N/19/28.

48. HL Debs, 151 (23 July 1858), 2010–11; 'India bill', Derby papers, Liverpool Record Office, 920 DER (15), 27/1, 147–54.

49. Walter Bagehot, *The English Constitution*, ed. Miles Taylor (1867; Oxford: Oxford University Press, 2001), ch. 2.

50. 'India bill', Derby papers, Liverpool Record Office, 920 DER (15) 27/1.

51. Lord Derby to Lord Stanley, 6 August 1858, ibid., 920 DER (15) 5/1.

52. *Morning Chronicle*, 9 August 1858, 3; Benjamin Disraeli to Lord Derby, 13 August 1858, Derby papers, Liverpool Record Office, 920 DER (15) 5/1, 39a.

53. Spencer Walpole to Lord Derby, 14 August 1858, ibid., 40–1; Lord Derby to Lord Stanley, 13 August 1858, ibid., 38–9.

54. Lord Malmesbury to Lord Derby, 15 August 1858, 3rd Earl Malmesbury papers, Hampshire Record Office, 9M73/54, fols 285–6; cf. the copy in the Royal Archives which includes a long summary of the changes required by the queen: RA VIC/MAIN/N/19/38.

55. Lord Malmesbury to Lord Stanley, 15 August 1858, 3rd Earl Malmesbury papers, Hampshire Record Office, 9M73/54, fols 286–7; Lord Malmesbury to Derby, 17 August 1858, ibid., fols 287–8; Queen Victoria to Lord Derby, 15 August 1858, RA VIC/MAIN/N/19/36 (draft); Martin, *Life of the Prince Consort,* iv, 284–7.

56. Lord Derby to Lord Malmesbury, 18 August 1858, RA VIC/MAIN/N/19/41.

57. *The Times*, 10 November 1858, 9; ibid., 19 November 1858, 10.

58. Ibid., 18 October 1858, 12; cf. George Percy Badger, *Government in its Relations with Education and Christianity in India* (London: Smith, Elder & Co., 1858).

59. *The Times*, 6 December 1858, 7; [Joseph Mullens], 'The Queen's Government and the Religions of India', *Eclectic Review* 109 (February 1859), 131–5; James M'Kee, *Letter to the Right Hon. Lord Stanley . . . on the Religious Neutrality of the Government of India* (London: Nisbet, 1859), 12–13; H. B. Edwardes, *Our Indian Empire: Its Beginning and End. A lecture Delivered to the Young Men's Christian Association in Exeter Hall, 1860* (London: Seeley, Jackson and Halliday, 1886), 25–6, 32.

60. Lord Palmerston to Queen Victoria, 12 December 1857, RA VIC/MAIN/N/16/36; Queen Victoria to Lord Canning, 18 May 1859, RA VIC/MAIN/N/21/99. For Canning's enquiries in India, see the correspondence reprinted in 'Honorary Distinctions to Native Chiefs and Others', IOR, LP&S/15/1.

61. Prince Albert to Sir Charles Wood, 16 May 1860, 29 May 1860, RA VIC/MAIN/N/23/85, 94.

62. Canning to Wood, 19 July 1860 ('ancestors'), RA VIC/MAIN/N/23/115; Canning to Wood, 12 December 1860 ('Orientals'), IOR F78/LB5, fols 208–10 (copy); Wood to Prince Albert, 12 December 1860 ('Sattara'), RA VIC/MAIN/N/24/26; Prince Albert to Charles Wood, 9 January 1861 ('golden impossibility'), Halifax papers, Borthwick Institute for Archives, University of York, A4/72

63. Canning to Wood, 20 January 1861, RA VIC/MAIN/N/24/75; cf. 'Revised Table of Salutes' (20 March 1857), Foreign Dept Proceedings, NAI, F. C. 57–8.

64. For the Allahabad ceremony: *ToI*, 11 November 1861, 3. For the row over the Nizam, which nearly cost the British resident at Hyderabad his job, see: Lt. Col. Davidson to H. Durand, 1 November 1861, Foreign Dept Proceedings, NAI, 51–3, and the sequence of correspondence in IOR Mss Eur. D728/3–4.

65. On the impact of Albert's death, see: Helen Rappaport, *Magnificent Obsession: Victoria, Albert and the Death that Changed the Monarchy* (London: Hutchinson, 2011); and for the death and subsequent memorial to Charlotte Canning: Tracy Anderson, 'The Lives and Afterlives of Charlotte, Lady Canning (1817–1861): Gender, Commemoration, and Narratives of Loss' in Deborah Cherry (ed.), *The Afterlives of Monuments* (London: Routledge, 2014), 31–50.

5 Victoria Beatrix

1. [John Kaye], 'The Royal Proclamation to India', *Blackwood's Edinburgh Magazine* 85, (January 1859), 11326.

2. *Proclamation of the Queen to the Princes, Chiefs, and People of India . . . Translated into the Native Languages of British India* (Calcutta: Government of India, 1858). For details of the ceremonies: NAI, Foreign Dept (Political), 25 February 1859, 612–44; MSA, Political proceedings 1858, vol. 170, esp. fols 45–6, 61, 119, 125, 141–5.

3. Addresses (approximate number of signatures in brackets) came from Bombay (120), Poona (1,215), Royapuram (Madras) (6,000), Murshidabad (200) and Khandesh (Bombay) (920): IOR/A/1/109–113; and from Masulipatam (Machilipatnam) (822): Mss Eur. G55/32.

4. Dinshaw Wacha, *Shells from the Sands of Bombay: Being my Recollections and Reminiscences, 1860–1875* (Bombay: K. T. Anklesaria, 1920), 168–9 (Union Jack). For Madras: *Athenaeum*, 4 November 1858, 526. On the difficulties of translation: Lord Elphinstone to Canning, 28 October 1858, MSA, Political proceedings (1858), vol. 170, esp. fol. 119. For the Calcutta illumination: *ILN*, 1 January 1859, 17.

5. John Malcolm Ludlow, *Thoughts on the Policy of the Crown Towards India* (London: James Ridgway, 1859), 7, 11; Duke of Argyll, *India under Dalhousie and Canning* (London: Longmans, 1865), 106.

6. [James Fitzjames Stephen], 'Kaye's History of the Indian Mutiny', *Fraser's Magazine for Town and Country* 70 (December 1864), 757–74.

7. Thomas Metcalf, *The Aftermath of Revolt: India 1857–1870* (Princeton, NJ: Princeton University Press, 1964); Lionel Knight, *Britain in India, 1858–1947* (London: Anthem Press, 2012), 1–34.

8. NAI Mint Records, 290, Resolution 28 October 1862.

9. Mayo to the Duke of Argyll, 21 July 1871, NAI, Foreign Dept Proceedings, 15–24. For the background, see: Sanjay Garg, 'Sikka and the Crown: Genesis of the Native Coinage Act, 1876', *Indian Economic and Social History Review* 35 (1998), 359–80.

10. On the 'empire of the rupee', see: W. H. Chaloner, 'Currency Problems of the British Empire' in B. Ratcliffe (ed.), *Great Britain and Her World: Essays in Honour of W. O. Henderson* (Manchester: Manchester University Press, 1975), 179–207.

11. George Otto Trevelyan, *The Competition Wallah* (London: Macmillan, 1864), 445.

12. Charles Wood to Queen Victoria, 18 February 1860, RA VIC/MAIN/N/23/19.

13. L. L. R. Hausburg, C. Stewart-Wilson and C. S. F. Crofton, *The Postage and Telegraph Stamps of British India* (London: Stanley Gibbons, 1907); Geoffrey Rothe Clarke, *The Post Office of India and Its Story* (London: John Lane, 1921).

14. C. Stewart Wilson, *British Indian Adhesive Stamps Surcharge for Native States*, 2 vols (Calcutta: Philatelic Society of India, 1897–8), i.

15. G. F. Edmonstone to the Chief Commissioner of the Punjab, 13 December 1858, NAI Home Dept Proceedings (Public), 71.

16. Brian C. Smith, 'Sir Henry Maine and the Government of India, 1862–87', *Journal of Indian History* 41 (1963), 563–75; Gordon Johnson, 'India and Henry Maine' in Alan Diamond (ed.), *The Victorian Achievement of Sir Henry Maine: A Centennial Reappraisal* (Cambridge: Cambridge University Press, 1991), 376–88; Karuna Mantena, *Alibis of Empire: Henry Maine and the Ends of Liberal Imperialism* (Princeton, NJ: Princeton University Press, 2010). On Stephen, see: K. J. M. Smith, *James Fitzjames Stephen: Portrait of a Victorian Rationalist* (Cambridge: Cambridge University Press, 2002), ch. 6.

17. Elizabeth Kolsky, 'Codification and the Rule of Colonial Difference: Criminal Procedure in British India', *Law and History Review* 23 (2005), 631–83; idem, *Colonial Justice in British India: White Violence and the Rule of Law* (Cambridge: Cambridge University Press, 2010), chs 1–2.

18. *Reports of Monthly Meetings of the British Indian Association, 1859–61* (Calcutta: I. C. Bose), 18 (meeting of 6 April 1861).

19. For the 1861 Act, and its amendment in 1872, see: A. C. Banerjee, *English Law in India* (New Delhi: Abhinav, 1984), 193. For Maine's assertion of 24 January 1866: *Minutes by Sir H. S. Maine, 1862–9: With a Note on Indian Codification, etc.* (Calcutta: Office of the Superintendent of Government Printing, 1892), 69–70.

20. *The Indian Penal Code with notes by W. Morgan and A. G. MacPherson* (Calcutta: G. Hay & Co., 1861).

21. For the discussions in the Viceroy's Council: 'Proceedings of the Legislative Council of India', 5 June 1858, cols 241–4, 3 July 1858, col. 301, IOR V/9/4.

22. *Indian Penal Code with Notes*, 99–100.
23. John D. Mayne, *Commentaries on the Indian Penal Code, etc.* (Madras: Higginbotham, 1861).
24. V. S. Joshi, *Vasude Balvant Phadke: First Indian Rebel Against British Rule* (Bombay: D. S. Marathe, 1959), 120–1, 144–5.
25. For the case, see: Julia Stephens, 'The Phantom Wahhabi: Liberalism and the Muslim Fanatic in Mid-Victorian India', *Modern Asian Studies* 47 (2013), 22–52.
26. *The Great Wahabi Case. A Full and Complete Report of the Proceedings and Debates in the Matters of Ameer Khan and Hashmadad Khan, etc.* (Calcutta: R. Cambray & Co., 1899), 2; Fendall Currie, *The Indian Criminal Codes . . . viz., the Penal Code Act XLV. of 1860, as Amended by Later Enactments, and the Code of Criminal Procedure Act X. of 1872* (London: J. Flack, 1872), 96–8; Joseph Vere Woodman, *A Digest of Indian Law Cases, Containing High Court Reports, etc.*, 6 vols (Calcutta: Government Printing 1901), ii, 3147.
27. The peak year of the reign was 1872 when of ninety-four cases, sixty-four came from India. Figures derived from 'Return of all Appeals from Courts in India, Instituted Before the Judicial Committee of the Privy Council', *Parl. Papers* (1852–3), Cd. 358, for the years 1833–52, and from 'The Judicial Committee of the Privy Council Decisions', www.bailii. org/uk/cases/UKPC/, for the years 1853–1901. By the early twentieth century, it has been argued, the Committee functioned 'primarily as an appellate court for India': Rohit De, '"A Peripatetic World Court": Cosmopolitan Courts, Nationalist Judges and the Indian Appeal to the Privy Council', *Law and History Review* 32 (2014), 821–51. For the work in general of the Judicial Committee of the Privy Council, see: P. A. Howell, *The Judicial Committee of the Privy Council, 1833–76* (Cambridge: Cambridge University Press, 1979).
28. James Fitzjames Stephen, *Minute on the Administration of Justice in India* (Calcutta: Home Secretariat Press, 1872), 88; Arthur Hobhouse, *A Collection of Certain Notes and Minutes . . . May 15th 1872–April 17th 1877* (Calcutta: Government Press, 1906), 5 September 1872, 2; Act no. II (1863) 'To regulate the admission of appeals to Her Majesty in Council from certain judgments and orders in Provinces not subject to the General Regulations'; Act no. VI (1874), 'To consolidate and amend the law relating to appeals to the Privy Council from decrees of the Civil Courts'.
29. W. Tayler, 'Publicity the Guarantee for Justice; or, "the Silent Chamber" at Whitehall', *Journal of the East India Association* 7 (1873), 47–78.
30. E. B. Michell and R. B. Michell, *The Practice and Procedure in Appeals from India to the Privy Council* (Madras: Higginbotham, 1876), 2–4. In 1890, the Government of India advised that petitions for mercy destined for the queen should be disregarded if they were unlikely to reach London before the date set for execution: Foreign Dept Proceedings (International), NAI, 15 August 1890, 180.
31. Woodman, *A Digest of Indian Law Cases*, i, 544–5. For a recent discussion of the case, see: Rohit De, 'Constitutional Antecedents' in Sujit Choudhury, Madhav Khosla and Pratap Bhanu Mehta (eds), *The Oxford Handbook of the Indian Constitution* (Oxford: Oxford University Press, 2016), 23–6.
32. 'Disposal of Memorials Sent by Certain Persons of Bombay to Her Majesty and the Authorities in England', 30 April 1873, MSA, Pol. Proceedings, vol. 48, fols 61–146.
33. Robin Moore, 'The Abolition of Patronage in the Indian Civil Service and the Closure of Haileybury College', *Historical Journal* 7 (1964), 246–57; J. M. Compton, 'Open Competition and the Indian Civil Service', 1854–76', *English Historical Review* 83 (1968), 265–84; Clive Dewey, 'The Making of the English Ruling Caste in the Indian Civil Service in the Era of Competitive Examination', *English Historical Review* 88 (1973), 262–85.
34. 'Copy of the Memorials of Her Majesty's Covenanted Civilians in India, Praying for the Redress of Certain Grievances', *Parl. Papers* (1862), Cd. 230. For later criticism of the changes, see: J. S. Wyllie, *A Letter to the Hon'ble Sir C. E. Trevelyan, K.C.B., on the Selection and Training of Candidates for H.M.'s Indian Civil Service* (Calcutta: Home Secretariat, 1870); George Birdwood, *Competition and the Indian Civil Service. A Paper Read Before the East India Association* (London: H. & S. King, 1872).

35. Wyllie, *Letter to C. E. Trevelyan*, 9; Alfred Cotterell Tupp, *The Indian Civil Service and the Competitive System, a Discussion on the Examinations and the Training in England; and an Account of the Examinations in India, the Duties of Civilians, and the Organization of the Service, with a List of Civilians and other Appendices* (London: R. W. Brydges, 1876), 123–4.

36. QVJl., 20 October 1890.

37. 'Papers Relating to the Admission of Natives', 13–17; 'Report of the Public Service Commission, 1886–87', *Parl. Papers* (1888), Cd. 5327, p. 21; HC Debs, 13 (2 June 1893), 134 (Wedderburn).

38. HC Debs, 13 (2 June 1893), 114.

39. T. A. Heathcote, 'The Army of British India' in David Chandler and Ian Beckett (eds), *The Oxford Illustrated History of the British Army* (Oxford: Oxford University Press, 1994), 386–91.

40. 'Correspondence during the year 1858, between His Royal Highness the Commander in Chief, and the President of the Board of Control, and the Secretary of State for War, etc.', *Parl. Papers* (1860), Cd. 471; Duke of Cambridge to Prince Albert, 27 September 1858, RA VIC/MAIN/N/20/44–5; 'Memorandum' [copy], 16 October 1858, RA VIC/MAIN/N/20/70.

41. 'Report of the Commissioners Appointed to Inquire into the Organisation of the Indian Army', *Parl. Papers*, (1859, session 1), Cd. 2515, xi–xii.

42. Queen Victoria to Lord Derby, 5 February 1859, RA VIC/MAIN/N/21/26; Prince Albert to General Peel, 1 February 1859 (copy), 2 February 1859 (copy), RA VIC/MAIN/N/21/23–4; Duke of Cambridge to Lord Stanley, 30 March 1859 (copy), RA VIC/MAIN/N/21/72; Lord Derby to Queen Victoria, 6 February 1859, RA VIC/MAIN/N/21/27; 6 February 1859. General Charles Grey, Prince Albert's private secretary, provided him with very full summaries of the Commission's proceedings (12 January 1859) and its report (1 February 1860): Charles Grey papers, Durham University Library, GRE/D/I/9/111–36.

43. Queen Victoria to Charles Wood, 16 July 1859, RA VIC/MAIN/N/21/139; Sir Charles Wood to Queen Victoria, 17 July 1859, RA VIC/MAIN/N/21/140; Queen Victoria to Charles Wood, 23 September 1859, RA VIC/MAIN/N/22/51.

44. Peter Stanley, *White Mutiny: British Military Culture in India, 1825–1875* (London: Hurst, 1998), ch. 6.

45. 'Copy of Papers Connected with the late Discontent Among the local European Troops in India', *Parl. Papers* (1860), Cd. 169, qq. 21 (graffiti), 106 (dissatisfaction); 'Return of the Number of Men of the European Local Troops in India, who have Taken their Discharge since 1858, etc', *Parl. Papers* (1860), Cd. 48; HC Debs, 148 (12 February 1858), 1287 (Palmerston).

46. Neale Porter, *The Army of India Question* (London: James Ridgway, 1860), 17–21.

47. Charles Wood to Queen Victoria, 7 October 1859, RA VIC/MAIN/N/22/64. For Clyde, see: Adrian Greenwood, *Victoria's Scottish Lion: The Life of Colin Campbell, Lord Clyde* (Stroud: Spellmount, 2015), 447–53; and for Mansfield, see: T. R. Moreman, 'Mansfield, William Rose, First Baron Sandhurst (1819–1876)', *ODNB*.

48. QVJl., 26 July 1860.

49. Peter Duckers, *The British-Indian Army, 1860–1914* (Princes Risborough: Shire, 2003), 17.

50. David Omissi, *The Sepoy and the Raj: The Indian Army, 1860–1940* (Basingstoke: Palgrave Macmillan, 1994), ch. 1; Heather Streets, *Martial Races: The Military, Race and Masculinity in British Imperial Culture, 1857–1914* (Manchester: Manchester University Press, 2004), ch. 3. For a detailed case study of the Punjab, see: Tan Tai Yong, *The Garrison State: The Military, Government and Society in Colonial Punjab* (London: Sage, 2005), ch. 2; and Rajit K. Mazumder, *The Indian Army and the Making of the Punjab* (Delhi: Permanent Black, 2003), 15–18.

51. For the Sikkim and Bhutan invasions, see: I. T. Prichard, *The Administration of India from 1859 to 1868. The First Ten Years of Administration under the Crown*, 2 vols (London:

Macmillan, 1869), i, 82–4, ii, 1–43; H. Biddulph, 'The Umbeyla Campaign of 1863 and the Bhutan Expedition of 1865–6. Contemporary Letters of Colonel John Miller Adye', *Journal of the Society for Army Historical Research* 19 (1940), 34–47. For the Abyssinian campaign, see: Volker Matthies, *The Siege of Magdala: The British Empire Against the Emperor of Ethiopia* (Princeton, NJ: Princeton University Press, 2012).

52. 'Report of the Select Committee on the Army (India and colonies)', *Parl. Papers* (1867–8), Cd. 197, vi.

53. Calculated from the Indian censuses of 1871–2 and 1901.

54. Charles Wood to Prince Albert, 3 January 1861, RA VIC/MAIN/N/24/37, Charles Wood to Prince Albert, 7 January 1861, RA VIC/MAIN/N/24/40. The queen eventually purchased the crown for £500 from Major Robert Tytler, into whose custody the crown was placed after the siege of Delhi, and it is now on display at Windsor Castle (RCIN 67236). See also: *An Englishwoman in India: The Memoirs of Harriet Tytler, 1828–1858*, ed. Anthony Sattin (Oxford: Oxford University Press, 1986), 176.

55. Omar Khalidi, *The British Residency in Hyderabad: An Outpost of the Raj, 1779–1948* (London: BACSA, 2005), 33–6.

56. For an incomplete list, see: HC Debs, 118 (19 February 1903), 271–2.

57. L. Bowring, *Eastern Experiences* (London: Henry S. King, 1871), 219.

58. Canning to Lord Stanley, 20 October 1858, IOR, Photo Eur. 474; Canning to Charles Wood, 28 January 1860, IOR Mss Eur. F78/55/3, fols 57–63.

59. Elgin to Charles Wood, 5 May 1862, IOR Mss Eur. F83/2, fols 101–6.

60. For his career, see A. J. Arbuthnot, 'Aitchison, Sir Charles Umpherston (1832–1896)', rev. Ian Talbot, *ODNB*; C. U. Aitchison, *A Collection of Treaties, Engagements, and Sunnuds Relating to India and Neighbouring Countries*, 8 vols (Calcutta: Savielle, 1862–6).

61. Aitchison, *The Native States of India: An Attempt to Elucidate a Few of the Principles Which Underlie their Relations with the British Government* (Simla: Government Central Branch Press, 1875), 10, 12–13.

62. Maine, 'The Kathiawar States and Sovereignty' (22 March 1864) idem., 'The Right to Cede by Sanad Portions of British India' (11 August 1868), reprinted in Stokes (ed.) *Sir Henry Maine*, 320–25, 395–400; cf. C. U. Aitchison, *Lord Lawrence and the Reconstruction of India* (Oxford: Clarendon Press, 1894), 140–1.

63. Canning's durbar tours can be plotted from the accounts in: 'Persian Durbar Proceedings', NAI, Foreign Dept, vols 7–8. Charlotte Canning to Queen Victoria, 23 January 1861 (copy), Canning papers, West Yorkshire Archives Services, WYL 250/10/4/3. Some of Simpson's work from the tours was later reproduced in: *India, Ancient and Modern: A Series of Illustrations of the Country and People of India and Adjacent Territories Executed in Chromo-lithography from Drawings by William Simpson; with Descriptive Literature by John William Kaye* (London: Day & Son, 1867).

64. *Allen's Indian Magazine*, 13 April 1859, 276, 18 December 1859, 994; Canning to Queen Victoria, 30 May 1860, Canning papers, WYL 250/9/1/8.

65. The template *sannad* of 11 March 1862 is reprinted in Aitchison, *Collection of Treaties*, ii, 57.

66. For further details of each (date of joining the Council in parentheses), see: Maharaja of Benares (1862): *DIB*, 35; Burdwan (1864), ibid., 60–1; Maharaja of Jaipur (1868) and Maharaja of Vizianagram (1864): Bhawur Partap Singh, *The Lives of the Highnesses the Maharaja of Jeypore, the Maharaja of Vizianagram, etc.* (Vizianagram: S. V. V. Press, 1897); Nawab of Rampur (1863): *DIB*, 349. The other two princes appointed in the 1860s were Narendra Singh, Maharaja of Patiala (1862): *DIB*, 329–30; and Digvijay Singh, Raja of Balrampur (1868): *DIB*, 24–5.

67. For the well at Stoke Row, see: Laureen Williamson, *An Illustrated History of the Maharaja's Well, Stoke Row, Henley-on-Thames, Oxfordshire, the Gift of the Maharaja of Benares* (Stoke Row: Maharaja's Well Trust, 1983). For the Hyde Park fountain, see: *Morning Post*, 2 March 1868, 2.

68. Charles Grey to Charles Wood, 20 March 1862, Halifax papers, Borthwick Institute for Archives, University of York, A4/64/108.
69. For the background, see: [A native of Mysore], *The British Administration of Mysore. Part I: Fifty Years of Administration* (London: Longmans, Green & Co., 1874); Aya Ikegame, *Princely India Re-imagined: A Historical Anthropology of Mysore* (London: Routledge 2009), 22–34.
70. For the maharaja's appeal, see: 'Copies of Correspondence between the Maharaja of Mysore and the Government of India relative to His Highness's claim, etc.', *Parl. Papers* (1866) Cd. 112. For his correspondence with Queen Victoria: IOR L/PS/6/461 (1858–9), for details of the presents, including the jewellery which only got as far as Calcutta, where it was sold off, see: Wadiyar to Charles Wood, 13 March 1861, IOR L/PS/6/511, 'List of Jewellery, etc.', IOR/L/PS/6/514, and QVJl., 29 March 1862 ('pretty Indian cattle'); and addresses: Lord Elgin to Charles Wood, 30 May 1863, IOR L/PS/6/527, Pol. Dept to Charles Wood, 14 April 1864, IOR L/PS/6/532.
71. Charles Wood to Charles Canning, 31 August 1860 (copy), Mss Eur. F78/LB4, fols 98–102.
72. L. Bowring to the secretary to the Government of India, 22 April 1862, IOR L/PS/6/521; Vishwanath Narayan Mandlik, *Adoption Versus Annexation: With Remarks on the Mysore Question* (London: Smith, Elder & Co., 1866), 43–4; *Opinions of the Press on the Annexation of Mysore* (London: John Camden Hotten, 1866).
73. HC Debs, 187 (24 May 1867), 1069; Northcote to Lawrence, 16 April 1867, reprinted in 'Further Papers Relating to Mysore', *Parl. Papers* (1867), Cd. 239, 8–9.
74. John Dickinson to Holkar, 15 September 1866 (copy), John Dickinson to Holkar, 25 June 1868 (copy), Madhya Pradesh State Archives, Bhopal, Indore Foreign Dept, 41/36, file 229.
75. I. T. Prichard, *Facts Connected with the Dethronement of the Nawab of Tonk* (privately printed, 1867); *The Story of the Nawab of Tonk Written by Himself* (Simla: Simla Advertiser Press, 1868), 13; Frederick Chesson, *The Princes of India: Their Rights and Our Duties* (London: W. Tweedie, 1872), 64–5.
76. For the encouragement given by the queen's proclamation, see: I. N. Palmer to Salar Jung, 28 November 1873 (copy), Salar Jung papers, Andhra Pradesh State Archives, Hyderabad. For Palmer's role and Salar Jung's visit, see: Harriet Ronken Lynton, *My Dear Nawab Saheb* (Hyderabad: Orient Black Swan, 1991), chs 9–10; and for the background, see: Bharati Ray, *Hyderabad and British Paramountcy, 1857–1883* (Delhi: Oxford University Press, 1983), 75–7.
77. Ponsonby to Queen Victoria, 23 June 1876, RA VIC/MAIN/N/31/ 63; QVJl. 29 June 1876; Lytton to Queen Victoria, 20 August 1876, IOR Mss Eur. E218/18, 404–6. Without the wheelchair, Salar Jung's portrait was painted by Leslie Ward ('Spy') and published later in the year in *Vanity Fair.* NPG 2580.
78. Ponsonby to Salisbury, 22 July 1876, Salisbury papers, Hatfield House; Lytton to Queen Victoria, 20 August 1876, IOR Mss Eur. E218/18, 404–6; Queen Victoria to Lord Beaconsfield, 28 August 1876, RA VIC/MAIN/N/31/102 (Disraeli was ennobled earlier that month).
79. Ian Copland, 'The Baroda Crisis of 1873–77: A Study in Governmental Rivalry', *Modern Asian Studies* 2 (1968), 97–123; Edward Moulton, 'British India and the Baroda Crisis, 1874–5: A Problem in a Princely State', *Canadian Journal of History* 3 (968), 58–94; Judith Rowbotham, 'Miscarriage of Justice?: Post-Colonial Reflections on the "Trial" of the Maharaja of Baroda, 1875', *Liverpool Law Review* 28 (2007), 377–403.
80. 'Correspondence Connected with the Deposition of Mulhar Rao', *Parl. Papers* (1875), Cd. 1252, 30–1.
81. Ponsonby to Queen Victoria, 16 January 1875, RA VIC/MAIN/N/30/18; Ponsonby to Queen Victoria, 15 April 1875, RA VIC/MAIN/N/30/59; Ponsonby to Salisbury, 15 April 1875, Salisbury papers.

82. 'Correspondence Connected with the Deposition of Mulhar Rao', 31–2; Northbrook to Queen Victoria, 22 April 1875, RA VIC/MAIN/N/30/65.
83. Wood to Elgin, n.d. [c. November 1862], (copy), IOR L/PS/6/514.
84. Lawrence to Wood, 19 March 1864, Mss Eur. F78/11/1, fols 121–2, Wood to Lawrence (copy), Mss Eur. F78/LB20, fols 151–5; Northcote to Lawrence, 17 July 1868, Mss Eur. F90/2, no. 36; 'Rules as to Addresses from Native Princes and Others' (29 March 1873, 6 March 1873, 23 June 1873), IOR/L/PS/18/D72; Lawrence to Stafford Northcote, 15 August 1868, BL, Add. Ms. 50, 026, fols 37–8.
85. 'Rules as to Memorials, Petitions, Complimentary Addresses' (7 February 1878), IOR/L/PS/18/D90A; 'Rules Relating to Memorials Addressed to the Queen' (7 February 1881), IOR/L/PS/18/D73; 'Rules for the Submission and Receipt of Memorials and Other Papers to the King' (June 1906), IOR L/PS/18/D168.

6 Queen of Public Works

1. R. Montgomery Martin, *Progress and Present State of India. A Manual for General Use, Based on Official Documents, etc.* (London: S. Low, 1862), 295.
2. Dietmar Rothermund, *An Economic History of India: From Pre-Colonial Times to 1991* (London: Routledge, 1999), chs 4–5; Sabyascahi Bhattacharya, *Financial Foundations of the British Raj: Ideas and Interests in the Reconstruction of Indian Public Finance, 1852–72* rev. edn (Delhi: Orient Longman, 2005), ch. 5; Tirthankar Roy, *The Economic History of India, 1857–1947*, 3rd edn (New Delhi: Oxford University Press, 2011), ch. 3; B. R. Tomlinson, *The Economy of Modern India*, 2nd edn (Cambridge: Cambridge University Press, 2011), ch. 1.
3. William Wedderburn, *The Skeleton at the 'Jubilee' Feast: Being a Series of Suggestions Towards the Prevention of Famine in India* (1897) in *Speeches and Writings of William Wedderburn* (Madras: G. A. Natesan, 1916), 284–322; Dadabhai Naoroji, *Poverty and un-British Rule in India* (London: Swan Sonnenschein, 1901); Romesh Chunder Dutt, *The Economic History of India in the Victorian Age: From the Accession of Queen Victoria in 1837 to the Commencement of the Twentieth Century* (London: Kegan Paul, Trench Trübner & Co., 1904).
4. On railways, within a huge literature, see: Daniel Thorner, 'Great Britain and the Development of India's Railways', *Journal of Economic History* 11 (1951), 389–402; Ian Derbyshire, 'Economic Change and the Railways in North India, 1860–1914', *Modern Asian Studies* 21 (1987), 521–45; Ian J. Kerr, *Building the Railways of the Raj* (Oxford: Oxford University Press, 1995). On canals, see: Ian Stone, *Canal Irrigation in British India: Perspectives on Technological Change in a Peasant Economy* (Cambridge: Cambridge University Press, 1984).
5. Theodore Walrond (ed.), *Letters and Journals of James, the 8th Earl of Elgin* (London: John Murray, 1872), 439; W. W. Hunter, *A Life of the Earl of Mayo: Fourth Viceroy of India*, 2 vols (London: Smith, Elder & Co., 1876), ii, 207–9. For the narratives of 'progress' that accompanied technological change in India, see: A. Martin Wainwright, 'Representing the Technology of the Raj in Britain's Victorian Periodical Press' in David Finkelstein and Douglas M. Peers (eds), *Negotiating India in the Nineteenth-century Media* (Basingstoke: Macmillan, 2000), 185–209; Di Drummond, 'British Imperial Narratives of Progress through Rail Transportation and Indigenous People's Responses in India and Africa', *Zeitschrift für Weltgeschichte* 12 (2011), 107–40.
6. For 'true religion', see: Anon., 'Our Indian Railways', *Calcutta Review* 9 (1845), 21–2. For 'the truth of God's word', see: E. Davidson, *The Railways of India: With an Account of their Rise, Progress and Construction* (London: Spon, 1868), 8, 373. For the 1855 ceremony: *Report of the Opening of the East Indian Railway* (Calcutta: n.p. 1855), 2–3.
7. *Report of the Formal Commencement at Lahore of the Punjaub Railway* (Lahore: Lahore Chronicle, 1859), 17.

8. For passenger volume, see: John Hurd and Ian J. Kerr, *India's Railway History: A Research Handbook* (Leiden: Brill, 2012), 148. For the railways and the Indian famines, see: Michelle Burge McAlpin, *Subject to Famine: Food Crisis and Economic Change in Western India* (Princeton, NJ: Princeton University Press, 1983), ch. 6; Stuart Sweeney, 'Indian Railways and Famine, 1875–1914: Magic Wheels and Empty Stomachs', *Essays in Economic and Business History* 26 (2008), 147–58.

9. *Allen's Indian Mail*, 23 March 1863, 239; ibid. 26 December 1864, 1003–4; Lawrence to Queen Victoria, 21 October 1864, RA VIC/MAIN/N/27/13.

10. *ToI*, 14 June 1878, 4.

11. For the 1854 ceremony, see: Charles Cawood, *A Poetical Account of the Opening of the Ganges Canal, etc.* (Agra: J. A. Gibbons, 1854), 5. For later additions to the canal, see: A. Robertson, *Epic Engineering: Great Canals and Barrages of Victorian India* (Melrose: Beechwood, 2013), 135–8; T. Login, *Roads, Railways and Canals for India* (Roorkee: Thomason Civil Engineering College Press, 1866), ii. In March 1874, Sir William Muir, lieutenant-governor of the North-Western Provinces, opened the Agra canal 'in the name of the Queen': *ToI*, 11 March 1874, 3.

12. Freda Harcourt, *Flagships of Imperialism: The P&O Company and the Politics of Empire from its Origins to 1867* (Manchester: Manchester University Press, 2006). For the India and Australian Mail Steam Packet Company and its struggle with the East India Company, see: *Morning Post*, 31 August 1850, 1.

13. *ILN*, 17 April 1869, 392–3; W. H. Russell, *A Diary in the East during the Tour of the Prince and Princess of Wales*, 2 vols (London: Geo. Routledge & Sons, 1869), ii, 431–2. Cf. Sophie Gordon, 'Travels with a Camera: The Prince of Wales, Photography and the Mobile Court' in Frank Lorenz Muller and Heidi Mehrkens, *Sons and Heirs: Succession and Political Culture in Nineteenth-century Europe* (Basingstoke: Palgrave Macmillan, 2016), 92–108.

14. For the first ship to make the voyage see: *ILN*, 23 November 1872, 487. For Queen Victoria's reaction to the Suez Canal shares purchase, see: QVJl., 24 November 1875. For the background, see: D. A. Farnie, *East and West of Suez: The Suez Canal in History 1854–1956* (Oxford: Clarendon Press, 1969), ch. 10; Geoffrey Hicks, 'Disraeli, Derby and the Suez Canal: Some Myths Reassessed', *History* 97 (2012) 182–203; Emily Haddad, 'Digging to India: Modernity, Imperialism, and the Suez Canal', *Victorian Studies* 47 (2005), 363–96.

15. For details of the ships, see: the P&O Archive (www.poheritage.com), P&O Ref: PH-02072–00 ('Kaisar-i-Hind') and P&O Ref: AC-03173–00 ('Victoria').

16. C. C. Adley, *The Story of the Telegraph in India* (London: Spon, 1866), 4, 34–5; Deep Kanta Lahiri Choudhury, *Telegraphic Imperialism: Crisis and Panic in the Indian Empire, c. 1830–1920* (Basingstoke: Palgrave Macmillan, 2010), ch. 1.

17. *ToI*, 20 January 1872, 2; ibid., 21 February 1872, 2. For the Afghan telegrams (one to Lytton, one to Ripon), see: ibid., 7 December 1878, 3; 6 August 1880, 3.

18. Murali Ranganatahn (ed.), *Govind Narayan's Mumbai: An Urban Biography from 1863* (London: Anthem Press, 2009), esp. ch. 10; Frank Broeze, 'The External Dynamics of Port City Morphology: Bombay, 1815–1914' in Indu Banga (ed.), *Ports and Hinterlands in India* (New Delhi: Manohar, 1992), 245–72; Amar Farooqui, *Opium City: The Making of Early Victorian Bombay* (Gurgaon: Three Essays Collective, 2006). For a subtle critique of Bombay's imperial modernity, see: Rajnarayan Chandavarkar, 'Bombay's Perennial Modernities' in Chandavarkar, *History, Culture and the Indian City: Essays* (Cambridge: Cambridge University Press, 2009), esp. 12–17; and for other discourses about the city, including Marathi, see: Meera Kosambi, 'British Bombay and Marathi Mumbai' in Sujata Patel and Alice Thorner (eds), *Bombay: Mosaic of Modern Culture* (Bombay: Oxford University Press, 1995), 3–24.

19. The classic accounts are: Mariam Dossal, *Imperial Designs and Indian Realities: The Planning of Bombay City, 1845–1875* (Bombay: Oxford University Press, 1991), and Christopher W. London, 'High Victorian Bombay: Historic, Economic and Social

Influences on its Architectural Development', *South Asian Studies* 13 (1997), 99–108, and idem, *Bombay Gothic* (Mumbai: India Book House, 2002).

20. Christine E. Dobbin, *Urban Leadership in Western India: Politics and Communities in Bombay City, 1840–1885* (Oxford: Oxford University Press, 1972); Jesse S. Palsetia, *The Parsis of India: Preservation of Identity in Bombay City* (Leiden: Brill, 2001); Preeti Chopra, *A Joint Enterprise: Indian Elites and the Making of British Bombay* (Minneapolis, MN: University of Minnesota Press, 2011); Gijsbert Oonk, 'The Emergence of Indigenous Industrialists in Calcutta, Bombay and Ahmedabad, 1850–1947', *Business History Review* 88 (2014), 43–71.

21. *Proceedings in Gujarathi, of Meeting of the Native and European Inhabitants of Bombay, Held in December 1858 to Establish the Victoria Museum and Gardens* (Bombay: n.p., 1858); T. G. Mainkar (ed.), *Writings and Speeches of Dr Bhau Daji* (Bombay: University of Bombay, 1974), 366–70. The Government of India matched the 'ready liberality' of public subscriptions for the museum: George Birdwood to the secretary, Govt of Bombay, 1 March 1862, MSA, Pol. Proceedings, 77, vol. 21. For Jeejebhoy, see: Jesse S. Palsetia, *Jamsetjee Jejeebhoy of Bombay: Partnership and Public Culture in Empire* (New Delhi: Oxford University, 2015). For Shunkerseth and the museum, see: *ILN*, 3 January 1863, 12; and Mariam Dossal, 'The "Hall of Wonder" within the "Garden of Delight" in Pauline Rohatgi, Pheroza Godrej and Rahul Mehrotra (eds), *Bombay to Mumbai: Changing Perspectives* (Mumbai: Marg, 1997), 208–19.

22. Cursetjee Jamsetee Jeejebhoy to Lord Elphinstone, 21 October 1858, IOR Mss Eur. F87, fols 69–71, 3 November 1858, ibid., fols 77–8; Juganath Sunkerseth to Elphinstone, 27 February 1858, ibid., fols 127–8.

23. Khoshru Navrosji Banaji, *Memoirs of the Late Framji Cowasji Banaji* (Bombay: Bombay Gazette, 1892), 56–7. Framji Cowasji also spoke at the public meeting held to congratulate Queen Victoria on her marriage in 1840: IOR/F/4/1902/81001.

24. J. J. Cowasjee, *Life of Sir Cowasjee Jehanghier* (London: London Stereoscopic and Photographic Company, 1890); the 'Royal Albert Orphan Asylum' was inaugurated by the queen on 29 June 1867: *Daily News*, 1 July 1867, 5.

25. S. M. Edwardes, *Memoir of Sir Dinshaw Manockjee Petit, First Baronet (1823–1901)* (London: Oxford University Press, 1923), 76; *DIB*, 335.

26. On David and Albert Sassoon, see: Stanley Jackson, *The Sassoons: Portrait of a Dynasty* (London: Heinemann, 1968), 39–45; Peter Stansky, *Sassoon: The Worlds of Philip and Sybil* (London: Yale University Press, 2003), 7–9; Serena Kelly, 'Sassoon Family (per. *c.* 1830–1961)', *ODNB*.

27. R. H. Jahlboy, *The Portrait Gallery of Western India: Embellished with 51 Life-like Portraits of the Princes, Chiefs, and Nobles, from Celebrated Artists in London; Enriched with Historical, Political and Biographical Accounts from the Most Authentic Sources, in Gujarati and English* (Bombay: Education Society, 1886). The Sassoons were not included in this volume.

28. For the clock tower, see: George W. Steevens, *In India* (Edinburgh: Blackwood, 1901), 9. For the High Court: Rahul Mehrotra, Sharada Dwivedi and Y. V. Chandrachud, *The Bombay High Court: The Story of the Building* (Mumbai: Eminence Designs, 2004), 39–40.

29. *ToI*, 14 September 1887 (sculpture), 4, ibid., 1 November 1888, 4 ('best modern buildings in India'), 8 January 1891, 4 (temperance refreshment rooms), 4; Christopher W. London, 'Architect of Bombay's Hallmark Style: Stevens and the Gothic Revival' in Rohatgi et al. (eds), *Bombay to Mumbai*, 236–49; Rahul Mehotra and Sharada Dwivedi, *A City Icon: Victoria Terminus Bombay, 1887 now Chhatrapati Shivaji Terminus Mumbai, 1996* (Mumbai: Eminence Designs, 2006).

30. Asa Briggs, *Victorian Cities* (London: Odhams Press, 1963), 277–8.

31. Joubert's scheme was subsequently rejected: *ToI*, 13 March 1884, 5; Fergusson to Lord Ripon, 24 June 1884, IOR Mss Eur. E214/8, fols 207–8; Fergusson to Lord Kimberley, 11 August 1884, IOR Mss Eur. E214/4, fols 97–100, Fergusson to Kimberley, 23 September 1884, ibid., fols 125–7; Ripon to Kimberley, 6 November 1884, BL B. P. 7/3 vol. 5,

no. 58. For the abrupt abandonment of the exhibition, see: 'Proceedings of the Legislative Council of Bombay', xxiii (12 December 1884), 45–7, IOR/V/9/2802.

32. Ira Klein, 'When the Rains Failed: Famine, Relief and Mortality in British India', *Indian Economic and Social History Review* 21 (1984), 185–214; David Arnold, 'Vagrant India: Famine, Poverty and Welfare under Colonial Rule' in A. L. Beier and Paul Ocobock (eds), *Cast Out: Vagrancy and Homelessness in Global and Historical Perspective* (Athens, OH: Ohio University Press, 2008), 117–39; Peter Gray, 'Famine and Land in Ireland and India, 1845–1880: James Caird and the Political Economy of Hunger', *Historical Journal* 49 (2006), 193–215.

33. G. T. Haly, *Appeal for the Sufferers by the Present Famine in Orissa* (London: Smith, Elder & Co., 1866), 2; Arthur Cotton, *The Famine in India . . . Lecture Read at the Social Science Congress at Manchester, October 12, 1866* (London: Trübner & Co., 1866), 38.

34. James Murphy, 'Fashioning the Famine Queen' in Peter Gray (ed.), *Victoria's Ireland?: Irishness and Britishness, 1837–1901* (Dublin: Four Courts Press, 2004), 15–26; Christine Kinealy, 'Famine Queen or Faery?: Queen Victoria and Ireland' in Roger Swift and Christine Kinealy (eds), *Politics and Power in Victorian Ireland* (Dublin: Four Courts Press, 2006), 21–53; R. Arthur Arnold, *History of the Cotton Famine* (London: Saunders, Otley & Co., 1864), 196.

35. Pol. Despatches (Madras), 3 (25 February 1863), IOR.

36. Charles Grey to Queen Victoria, [21 March 1868], RA VIC/MAIN/N/27/85, Charles Grey to Stafford Northcote, 21 March 1868, RA VIC/MAIN/N/27/87; Stafford Northcote to Charles Grey, 23 March 1868, RA VIC/MAIN/N/27/88.

37. B. M. Bhatia, *Famines in India: A Study in Some Aspects of the Economic history of India with Special Reference to Food Problem 1860–1990* (Delhi: Konark, 1991), ch. 3; Edward C. Moulton, *Lord Northbrook's Indian Administration, 1872–1876* (London: Asia Publishing House, 1968), ch. 4; Richard Temple, *Men and Events of my Time in India* (London: John Murray, 1882), ch. 17.

38. For the queen's speech, see: *The Times*, 20 March 1874, 5. For details of the two funds, see: G. Colvin to Henry Ponsonby, 20 January 1874 (telegram), RA VIC/MAIN/N/29/45; Lord Northbrook to Queen Victoria, 30 January 1874, RA VIC/MAIN/N/29/49; Lord Northbrook to Queen Victoria, RA VIC/MAIN/N/29/54; *ToI*, 9 February 1874, 3; *ILN*, 21 February 1874, 167; ibid., 27 June 1874, 598–9; 'Minute by . . . Sir Richard Temple' (31 October 1874), IOR Mss Eur. F86/127, p. 80. For Hamilton's end-of-session flourish, see: HC Debs, 221 (3 August 1874), 1190.

39. 'Deputation of the British India Association to His Excellency the Viceroy and His Honour the Lieutenant Governor of Bengal' (29 December 1874), British India Association of Calcutta papers, NMML, Delhi, 2. For the Maharaja of Burdwan, see: *DIB*, 60–1, and Mary Ann Steegles, *Statues of the Raj* (London: BACSA, 200), 180. For the song of praise, see: Lord Northbrook to Queen Victoria, 1 January 1875, RA VIC/MAIN/N/30/1; Lord Northbrook to Queen Victoria, 5 February 1875, RA VIC/MAIN/N/30/21.

40. For the queen's speech, see: *The Times*, 9 February 1877, 6; Bhatia, *Famines in India*, ch. 3.

41. William Digby, *The Famine Campaign in Southern India (Madras and Bombay Presidencies and Province of Mysore) 1876–1878* (London: Longmans, Green & Co., 1878); Arthur Cotton, *The Madras Famine* (London: Simpkin, Marshall & Co., 1876); Florence Nightingale, 'The People of India', *Nineteenth Century*, 4 (August 1878), 193–221; *Graphic*, 6 October 1877, 329; Hyndman, *The Indian Famine and the Crisis* (London: Edward Stanford, 1877), 5.

42. *Punch*, 1 September 1877, 91.

43. QVJl., 3 January 1877, 2 February 1877, 25 July 1877, 17 August 1877. Lytton to Salisbury, 1 March 1878, Mss Eur, E218/20, fol. 146 (the 'famine' *Gazette*).

44. For Canadian and Australian donations, see: *ToI*, 19 March 1897, 5; Bhatia, *Famines in India*, ch. 9; McAlpin, *Subject to Famine: Food Crisis and Economic Change in Western India*, ch. 6;

Georgina Brewis, '"Fill Full the Mouths of Famine": Voluntary Action in Famine Relief in India, 1896–1901', *Modern Asian Studies* 44 (2010), 887–918; David Hall-Matthews, *Peasants, Famine and the State in Colonial Western India* (Basingstoke: Palgrave, 2005).

45. *The Times*, 11 January 1897, 6. The queen noted the Bishop of Winchester collecting donations at Windsor: QVJl., 19 January 1897.

46. 'Papers Regarding Famine and Relief Operations in India, 1896–7 (Resolutions on the Administration of Famine Relief in the North-West Provinces and Oudh)', *Parl. Papers* (1899), Cd. 8739, p. 73; 'Report of the Indian Famine Commission' (1898), Appendix, vol. I (Bengal), Minutes of Evidence, *Parl. Papers*, (1899), Cd. 9252, p. 196 (evidence of Babu Grish Chander Ghosal); ibid., vol. III (Bombay), 235 (evidence of Edulji Rumstromji).

47. For Wilson, see: Ruth Dudley Edwards, 'Wilson, James (1805–1860)', *ODNB*. For an intellectual history of these shifts in liberal political economy, see: Andrew Sartori, *Liberalism in Empire: An Alternative History* (Oakland, CA: University of California Press, 2014), esp. ch. 5.

48. Robert Knight, editor of the *Bombay Times*, claimed that 'no other country in the civilised world is so lightly taxed': *The Indian Empire and our Financial Relations Therewith, etc.*, (London: Trübner & Co., 1866), 9; cf. W. E. Forster, *How We Tax India: A Lecture on the Condition of India under British Rule, More Especially as Affected by the Mode of Raising the India Revenue: Delivered before the Leeds Philosophical & Literary Society, March 30th, 1858* (London: A. W. Bennett, 1858), 36; J. M. Maclean, *The Indian Deficit and the Income Tax* (London: F. Algar, 1871), 6–9.

49. James Wilson, *Financial Statement* (Calcutta: G. A. Savielle, 1860), 31; *The Economist*, 19 February 1859, 193–4. On the background, see: C. L. Jenkins, '1860: India's First Income Tax', *British Tax Review* 1 (2012), 87–116.

50. *Proceedings of the Native Inhabitants of Madras Held at the Hindoo Debating Society, on the 7th May 1860* (Madras: Caxton Press, 1860), 5–6.

51. Samuel Laing, 'Crisis in Indian Finance', *Nineteenth Century* 7 (June 1880), 1075. For Trevelyan's opposition to the income tax, see: *Statement by Sir Charles Trevelyan of the Circumstances Connected with his Recall from the Government of Madras* (London: Longmans, 1860), 19.

52. [James Wilson], *Cries from the East, Being Lispings from High Life and Groans from the Poor* (London: H. W. Foster, 1870), 50. Wilson's pamphlet was dedicated to Queen Victoria as 'Empress of Hindostan'. He was a different James Wilson from the late financial member of the Viceroy's Council. For other criticism of the income tax, see: 'Report of the Select Committee on East India Finance', *Parl. Papers* (1871), Cd. 363, q. 337 (evidence of Henry Stewart Reid); 'Second Report of the Select Committee on East India Finance', ibid. (1873), Cd. 194, qq. 70–1 (Charles Trevelyan); ibid., 195, 199 (Sir Charles Wingfield).

53. Abhay Charan Das, *The Indian Ryot, Land Tax, Permanent Settlement and the Famine* (Howrah: Howrah Press, 1881), ii.

54. 'A native', *Nil Darpan, or the Indigo Planting Mirror, a Drama* (Calcutta: C. H. Manuel, 1861), 2. On the drama and its influence, see: Amiya Rao and B. G. Rao (eds), *The Blue Devil: Indigo and Colonial Bengal* (Delhi: Oxford University Press 1992), chs 6–7. Ranajit Guha reads the play very differently, describing Mitra's appeal to the liberal rule of British law as an example of 'middle-class grovelling' and a 'canker that has eaten into elite nationalism at this early formative stage': Guha, 'Neel Darpan: The Image of a Peasant Revolt in a Liberal Mirror' in David Hardiman (ed.), *Peasant Resistance in India, 1858–1914* (Delhi: Oxford University Press, 1992), 76–8.

55. *Trial of the Rev. James Long for the Publication of 'Nil durpan': With Documents Connected with its Official Circulation* (London: James Ridgway, 1861), 19–21. Mitra had been a pupil at Long's school in Calcutta. For the background, see: Blair King, *The Blue Mutiny:*

The Indigo Disturbance in Bengal, 1859–62 (Philadelphia: University of Pennsylvania Press, 1966); Geoffrey A. Oddie, *Missionaries, Rebellion and Proto-nationalism: James Long of Bengal 1814–87* (Richmond: Curzon, 1999), chs 7–8.

56. 'Report of the Commission Appointed in India to Inquire into the Cause of the Riots which Took Place in the Year 1875, etc.', *Parl. Papers* (1878), Cd. 2071, p. 54. On the Deccan riots, see: Ravinder Kumar, 'The Deccan Riots of 1875', *Journal of Asian Studies* 24 (1965), 613–35; Neil Charlesworth, *Peasants and Imperial Rule: Agriculture and Agrarian Society in the Bombay Presidency, 1850–1935* (Cambridge: Cambridge University Press, 1985), ch. 4.

57. 'Second Report of the Select Committee on East India Finance', *Parl. Papers* (1873), Cd. 194, p. 58 (Trevelyan); [Henry Fawcett], 'The Financial Condition of India', *Nineteenth Century* 5 (February 1899), 193–218; idem., 'The New Departure in Indian Finance', ibid. 6 (October 1879), 639–63.

58. Calculated from data derived from East India (Finance and Revenue Accounts), *Parl. Papers* (1861), Cd. 259; (1871), Cd. 10; (1881), Cd. 221 (1890–1), Cd. 225, (1900), Cd. 225.

59. On the customs line, see: Roy Moxham, *The Great Hedge of India* (London: Constable and Robinson, 2001). Salt manufacture under the Raj awaits its historian. For a brief overview, see: W. W. Hunter, *The Indian Empire: Its People, History and Products* (London: Trübner & Co., 1886), 453–4, 622–3; Bhattacharya, *Financial Foundations of the British Raj*, 97, 356–61.

60. Lady Hobart (ed.), *The Salt Tax in Southern India: Letters* (London: Macmillan, 1878); HC Debs, 239, (2 April 1878), 457 (Lyon Playfair); John Dacosta, 'The Financial Causes of the French Revolution and their Present Bearing upon India' [1893] reprinted in Dacosta, *Essays on Indian Affairs, 1892–1895* (n.p., *c.* 1895), 1–12.

61. George Balfour, *Trade and Salt in India Free: With a Preface on the Commercial, Political, and Military Advantages in all Asia* (London: Harrison and Sons, 1875), 35–7.

62. QVJl., 16 July 1851.

63. 'Who is Responsible?', *Friend of China* 2 (April 1876), 75–6. For the background, see: J. B. Brown, 'Politics of the Poppy: The Society for the Suppression of the Opium Trade, 1874–1916', *Journal of Contemporary History* 8 (1973), 97–111; John F. Richards, 'The Opium Industry in British India', *Indian Economic and Social History Review* 39 (2002), 149–80; idem., 'Opium and the British Indian Empire: The Royal Commission of 1895', *Modern Asian Studies* 36 (2002), 375–420.

64. Arthur Evans Moule, *The Use of Opium and its Bearing on the Spread of Christianity in China, etc.* (Shanghai: 'Celestial Empire' Office, 1877), 13; Samuel S. Mander, *Our Opium Trade with China* (London: Simpkin, Marshall & Co., 1877), 24–5.

65. *The Poppy Poison in Burma* (Society for the Suppression of the Opium Trade, London: P. S. King, 1892), 8–9; James F. B. Tinling, *A Century of False Policy* (London: Society for the Suppression of the Opium Trade, 1893), 7.

66. Sunderbai H. Powar, *An Indian Woman's Impeachment of the Opium Crime of the British Government. A Plea for Justice for her Country [sic] People* (London: Dyer Brothers, 1892).

67. 'Royal Commission on Opium: Minutes of Evidence, Appendices', *Parl. Papers*, (1894), Cd. 7471, vol. iv, qq. 75–6 (evidence of Louise Dryman), 356–60 (evidence of Captain Harold Sewallis Blackburne).

68. Meaning both the sale of intoxicating alcohol or drugs and the excise levied.

69. Lucy Carroll, 'The Temperance Movement in India: Politics and Social Reform', *Modern Asian Studies* 10 (1976), 417–47; Robert Eric Colvard, 'A World Without Drink: Temperance in Modern India, 1880–1940' (unpublished PhD thesis, University of Iowa, 2013).

70. *Speech on the Liquor Traffic in India . . . at a Meeting Held by the . . . United Kingdom Alliance, May 19, 1870* in Sophia Dobson Collet (ed.), *Keshub Chunder Sen's English Visit* (London: Strahan & Co., 1871), 150.

71. On the Salvation Army in India, see: Andrew Eason, 'Religion Versus the Raj: The Salvation Army's "Invasion" of British India', *Mission Studies* 28 (2011) 71–90.

72. [Thomas Evans], *A Brief Sketch of our Indian Excise Administration, by a Loyal Briton, and a Friend to the Indian People* (Mussoorie, n.p., 1895), 3; cf. *Abkari*, 14 (July 1893), 182–4. On Evans, see: D. Hooper (ed.), *A Welshman in India: A Record of the Life of T. Evans* (London: James Clarke, 1908).

73. Lord Northbrook to Queen Victoria, 13 September 1875, RA VIC/MAIN/N/30/21.

74. For Wilberforce's trip, see: *Hampshire Advertiser*, 19 April 1890, 6. For the queen's objections to Wilberforce, see: Queen Victoria to William Gladstone, 10 February 1894, *Letters of Queen Victoria*, 3rd ser., iii, 359.

75. Mahim Chandra Chakrabati, *Dina janani* (Dacca: Luchmohan Basak, 1880), QLB (Bengal).

7 Royal Tourists

1. Canning to Wood, 22 May 1861, IOR Mss Eur. F78/55/9 fols 55.–9; Charles Wood to Prince Albert, 22 May 1861, RA VIC/MAIN/N/25/30–1; Prince Albert to Wood, 26 June 1861, RA VIC/MAIN/N/25/33.

2. Chandrika Kaul, 'Monarchical Display and the Politics of Empire: Princes of Wales and India 1870–1920s', *Twentieth Century British History* 17 (2006) 464–88; Charles Reed, *Royal Tourists, Colonial Subjects and the Making of a British World, 1860–1911* (Manchester: Manchester University Press, 2016).

3. For the world tour, including the Indian subcontinent, see: Anon., 'The Cruise of the *Galatea*', *Dublin University Magazine* 73 (1869), 72–7; John Capper, *The Duke of Edinburgh in Ceylon: A Book of Elephant and Elk Sport* (London: Provost & Co., 1871); Michaela Appel, Martin Eberle and Bernd Schäfer, *Ein Prinz entdeckt die Welt: Die Reisen und Sammlingen Herzog Alfreds von Sachsen-Coburg und Gotha (1844–1900)* (Gotha: Stiftung Schloss Friedenstein Gotha, 2008).

4. Prince Alfred to Queen Victoria, 24 January 1879, RA VIC/ADDA20/1306.

5. Gordon Pentland, 'The Indignant Nation: Australian Responses to the Attempted Assassination of the Duke of Edinburgh in 1868', *English Historical Review* 130 (2015), 57–88; Mark Stocker, 'An Imperial Icon Indigenised: The Queen Victoria Memorial at Ohinemutu' in Katie Pickles and Catherine Coleborne (eds), *New Zealand's Empire* (Manchester: Manchester University Press, 2016), 28–50.

6. 'Note by Capt. W. B. Birch', 10 February 1870, Mayo papers, Cambridge University Library, Add. Ms. 7490/80/7 (Fenian suspect). For the original itinerary in 1868: Henry Lennox to Lord Mayo, 22 October 1868, Mayo papers, National Library of Ireland, Dublin, Mss 11,223, fol. 4.

7. Mayo to Queen Victoria, 1 September 1869, RA/VIC/MAIN/N/27/129; Mayo to Argyll, 12 August 1869, IOR Mss Eur. B380/2, fols 265–72; C. U. Aitchison to T. H. Thornton, 8 December 1869, Mayo papers, Cambridge University Library, Add. Ms. 7490/81/25.

8. Prince Alfred to Mayo, 7 April 1870, RA VIC/MAIN/N/28/8; *Benares Gazette*, 27 December 1869, NNR (North-West Provinces) IOR L/R/5/47, p. 3; *Indian Daily News*, 13 December 1869, 3 (compulsory illuminations); *Bombay Gazette*, 19 February 1870, 3 (cost of lights). For the Bengal regiments, see: 'Copy of Correspondence Relative to the Military Arrangements with Reference to the Reception of H. R. H, the Duke of Edinburgh in the North-West Provinces, etc.', Judicial Proceedings B (June 1869), 271, West Bengal States Archives, Kolkata. For hunting preparations, see: Capper, *Duke of Edinburgh in Ceylon*, 2. For Indian royalty and hunting, see: Thomas Cox, 'Diplomacy on Dangerous Ground: Aristocratic Hunts in Nineteenth- and Twentieth-century Nepal', *South Asia* 33 (2010), 258–75; Julie E. Hughes, *Animal Kingdoms: Hunting, the Environment, and Power in the Indian Princely States* (Cambridge, MA: Harvard University Press, 2013), ch. 2.

9. O. T. Burne, 'Memorandum' (20 December 1869), Mayo papers, Cambridge University Library, Add. Ms. 7490/82/1

10. Sambhuchandra Mukhopadhya, *The Prince in India, by an Indian. A Description of the Duke of Edinburgh's Landing, and Stay at Calcutta, etc.* (Calcutta: Berigny & Co., 1871); N. A. Chick (comp.), *The Prince in Calcutta; Memorials of H. R. H the Duke of Edinburgh's Visit in December, 1869, etc.* (Calcutta: Barham, Hill & Co., 1870); Mayo to Queen Victoria, 27 December 1869, 3 January 1870, RA VIC/MAIN/N/27/135, 137. Nicholas Chevalier's depiction of the ball on the *Galatea* is at RCIN 920379.

11. 'Note on the Investiture of H. R. H. the Duke of Edinburgh as Knight Grand Commander of the Most Exalted Order of the Star of India', (20 November 1869), Mayo papers, Cambridge University Library, Add. Ms 7490/83/5; 'Revised Note on the Investiture of H. R. H. the Duke of Edinburgh, etc.', ibid.

12. Mukhopadhya, *Prince in India*, 102–3; Chick (ed.), *Prince in Calcutta*, 97–9. The *Gazette of India* (30 December 1869) describing the investiture is at IOR L/PS/15/3.

13. Mayo to Argyll, 4 January 1870, IOR Mss Eur. B380/4, fols 9–18.

14. Mayo to Queen Victoria, 17 January 1870, RA VIC/MAIN/N/27/140 ('native city'); Taranatha Tarkavcaspati, *Rajaprasastih* (Calcutta: Sarasvatiyantra, 1876); Harischandra, *An Offering of Flowers . . . to H.R.H. the Duke of Edinburgh* (Benares., n.p., 1870); *Pioneer*, 22 January 1870, 3.

15. Prince Alfred to Queen Victoria, 16 January 1870, RA VIC/ADDA20/1305.

16. J. W. Kaye to T. M. Biddulph, 28 March 1869, RA PPTO/PP/VIC/MAIN/1870/12912.

17. *Pioneer*, 11 February 1870, 3; *Englishman*, 14 February 1870, 3 (address).

18. *Pioneer*, 19 February 1870, 3; *Englishman*, 21 February 1870, 2; Prince Alfred to Queen Victoria, 20 February 1870, RA VIC/ADDA20/1310 (shawls); J. W. Kaye to T. M. Biddulph, 28 March 1870, RA PPTO/PP/VIC/MAIN/1870/129127.

19. Prince Alfred to Queen Victoria, 20 February 1879, RA VIC/ADDA20/1310 (flowers); Anon., *H.R.H. The Duke of Edinburgh in the Oudh and Nepal Forests. A Letter from India* (privately printed, 1870); *Pioneer*, 24 February 1870, 3. On mutiny tours, see: Manu Goswami, '"Englishness" on the Imperial Circuit: Mutiny Tours in Colonial South Asia', *Journal of Historical Sociology* 9 (1996), 54–84; David Petts, 'Landscapes of Memory: Lucknow and Kanpur in Colonial India' in Adrian Green and Roger Leech (eds), *Cities in the World, 1500–2000: Papers Given at the Conference of the Society for Post-Medieval Archaeology, April 2002* (Leeds: Maney, 2006), 195–212.

20. *Speeches Made at the Jubbulpore Banquet on the Occasion of the Opening of the Through Line of Railway Communication between Calcutta and Bombay 8 March 1870* (n.p., n.d.), Mayo papers, Cambridge University Library, Add. Ms. 7490/83/17.

21. Mayo to Argyll, 28 December 1869, ibid., Add. Ms. 7490/151, fols 377–8.

22. *Bombay Gazette*, 12 March 1870, 2; *Englishman*, 24 March, 2; Captain Clerk to O. T. Burne, 18 March 1870, Mayo papers, Cambridge University Library, Add. Ms. 7490/84/25 (Sailors' Home); Clerk to Burne 22 March 1870, ibid. Add. Ms. 7490/84/26 ('run up the score'); *An Address in Pahlavi and Zend with its English and Gujarati Translations Presented to H.R.H. . . . the Duke of Edinburgh* (Bombay: Duftur Ashkara Press, 1871). The cost of the Bombay illuminations alone were four times over budget: MSA, Pol. Proceedings (1871), vol. 30, 117.

23. *Madras Times*, 23 March 1870, 3; 'Address' (25 March 1870), Geheimes Archiv QQ XVI, Staatsarchiv Gotha, VIII/8.

24. 'Memorandum' (12 May 1870), Mayo papers, Cambridge University Library, Add. Ms. 7490/82/16 (totting up); 'Memorandum' (30 December 1870), ibid., Add. Ms 7490/82/21 (diamonds and shawls); Girdlestone to Burne, 11 March 1871, ibid., Add. Ms. 7490/82/123 (Alfred taking home all the gifts); Clerk to Burne, 1 April 1870, ibid., Add. Ms. 7490/82/11, fol. 15 (donation to schools). For Prince Alfred's Indian haul, see: *A guide to the works of art and science collected by Captain His Royal Highness the Duke of Edinburgh, K.G. during his five-years' cruise round the world in H.M.S. 'Galatea' (1867–1871) and lent for exhibition in the South Kensington Museum, February 1872* (London: John Strangeways, 1872), and *Catalogue of the collection . . . of specimens of oriental art formed by H.R.H. the Duke of Edinburgh, etc.* (London: W. Clowes & Sons, 1875). For Mayo's contribution, see:

N. A. Chick (comp.), *In Memoriam: A Complete Record . . . of . . . the Late Earl of Mayo, etc.* (Calcutta: Thomas S. Smith, 1872), xii; and *A Few Letters on the Indian Administration of the Earl of Mayo, etc.* (Simla: privately printed, 1877), 29.

25. W. H. Russell to Mayo, 22 July 1869, Mayo papers, Cambridge University Library, Add. Ms. 7490/81/7; Clerk to Burne, 22 March 1870, ibid., Add. Ms. 7490/84/26 (photographs); Prince Alfred sent on to his mother his photographic portrait taken in India: Alfred to Queen Victoria, 12 March 1870, RA VIC/ADDA20/1311. Copies (showing the Prince in a pith-helmet) are in the Staatsarchiv, Coburg.

26. *Madras Times*, 29 March 1870, 2; Frederick Tyrrell, *The Royal Viceroy* (London: Edward Stanford, 1874).

27. The fullest description of the tour remains W. H. Russell, *The Prince of Wales' Tour: A Diary in India, etc.* (London: Sampson, Low, Marston, Searle & Rivington, 1877). Two of the prince's companions later produced accounts too: Joseph Fayrer, *Notes of the Visits to India of the Royal Highnesses the Prince of Wales and Duke of Edinburgh, etc.* (London: Kerby & Endean, 1879); Lord Suffield, *My Memories, 1830–1913* (London: Herbert Jenkins, 1913). Recent analysis of the tour includes Kaul, 'Monarchical Display'; Reed, *Royal Tourists*; Milinda Banerjee, 'Ocular Sovereignty, Acclamatory Rulership, and Political Communication: Visits of Princes of Wales to Bengal' in Frank Lorenz Müller and Heidi Mehrkens (eds), *Royal Heirs and the Uses of Soft Power in Nineteenth-century Europe* (Basingstoke: Palgrave Macmillan, 2016), 81–100; Jacqueline Banerjee, 'Bertie's Progress: The Prince of Wales in India, 1875–6', http://www.victorianweb.org/history/empire/india/33.html (accessed 4 April 2018).

28. Kaul, 'Monarchical Display'; cf. Hazel Hahn, 'Indian Princes, Tigers and Dancing Girls: The Tour of the Prince of Wales through India and Ceylon, 1875–6', *Postcolonial Studies* 12 (2009), 173–92; Joseph de Sapio, 'Technology, Imperial Connections and Royal Tourism on the Prince of Wales' 1875 Visit to India' in Martin Farr and Xavier Guégan (eds), *The British Abroad since the Eighteenth Century: Volume 1. Travellers and Tourists* (Basingstoke: Palgrave Macmillan, 2013), 56–74; Ruth Brimacombe, 'The Imperial Avatar in the Imagined Landscape: The Virtual Dynamics of the Prince of Wales' Tour of India in 1875–6' in Veronica Alfano and Andrew Stauffer (eds), *Virtual Victorians: Networks, Connections, Technologies* (Basingstoke: Palgrave Macmillan, 2015), 189–214.

29. J. Drew Gray, the *Daily Telegraph's* correspondent, wrote up the journey in his *The Prince of Wales in India; or, from Pall Mall to the Punjaub* (Toronto: Belford Bros, 1877).

30. Julia Stone, *Illustrated India: Its Princes and People: Upper, Central and Farther India, up the Ganges and down the Indus: to which is added an Authentic Account of the Visit to India of His Royal Highness the Prince of Wales* (Hartford, CT: American Publishing Co., 1877); *Letters from India during H.R.H. the Prince of Wales' Visit in 1875–6, from William S. Potter to his Sister* (London: E. Lawless, 1876). Potter was a traveller, collector and erotic novelist. Mary Elizabeth Corbet, *A Pleasure Trip to India: During the Visit of HRH the Prince of Wales; Afterwards to Ceylon* (London: W. H. Allen, 1880). Corbet (née Grey-Egerton) was the wife of a Cheshire landowner and huntsman.

31. Lord Lawrence to Wood, 23 January 1865, IOR Mss Eur. F78/113/6, fols 53–4; Begum of Bhopal to Queen Victoria, 19 February 1872, NAI, Bhopal Residency Records, 134; *Calcutta Gazette*, 15 January 1872 (Queen's telegram to India), RA VIC/MAIN/N/28/70; NAI, Foreign Dept Proceedings B (October 1874), 29–30.

32. For press competition, see: Frere to Knollys, 7 October 1875, RA VIC/ADDC07/0964; Ponsonby to Queen Victoria, 13 September 1875, RA VIC/MAIN/Z/468/43. For Reuters see: William Howard Russell, 'Diary for India', News International Archives (entry for 10 February 1876).

33. *Graphic*, 20 October 1875; G. A. Sala, *India and the Prince of Wales* (London: Illustrated London News, 1875); W. and A. K. Johnston, *Map of India, to Illustrate the Travels of H.R.H. the Prince of Wales* (London: n.p., 1875).

34. Mrs Bauboo, *Iḷavaracu/The Heir-apparent: Being a Brief Account of Life His Royal Highness Albert Edward, Prince of Wales* (Madras: Satthia Theepam Press, 1875). For *The Royal Tourist*, an illustrated journal, see: *Straits Times*, 8 January 1876, 6; W. S. Thomson (comp.), *Anglo-Indian Prize Poems, by Native and English Writers in Commemoration of the Visit of His Royal Highness the Prince of Wales to India* (London: Hamilton Adams, 1876).

35. Tagore, *English Verses set to Hindu Music, in Honor of His Royal Highness the Prince of Wales* (Calcutta: n.p., 1875); *Englishman*, 7 December 1875 (portraits).

36. *The Times*, 20 March 1875, 9. For the leak, see: Knollys to Ponsonby, 20 March 1875, RA VIC/MAIN/T6/8a–8b. Mary Macmullen, the widow of a Bengal army officer, claimed the trip was undertaken 'solely at the instance of H.R.H. himself': Macmullen, *India . . . and the Prince of Wales's Visit to the Far East* (Taunton: n.p., 1876), 33.

37. Queen Victoria to Disraeli, 17 May 1875, Dep. Hughenden, Bodleian Library, 78/3, fols 267–8; cf. Queen Victoria to Lord Salisbury, 18 March 1875, 3rd Marquess Salisbury papers, Hatfield House Library, 3M/F.

38. Salisbury to Queen Victoria, 2 June 1875, RA VIC/MAIN/Z/468/13 (enclosing Fayrer's memorandum).

39. Queen Victoria to Disraeli, 9 June 1875, Dep. Hughenden, Bodleian Library, 78/3, fols 314–18.

40. 'Memorandum' (Ponsonby), *c.* May 1875, Salisbury papers, 3MF; Northbrook to Salisbury, 29 April 1875 (copy), RA VIC/MAIN/T6/10; cf. Salisbury to Ponsonby, 3 July 1875, RA VIC/MAIN/Z/468/24.

41. For the avoidance of royal honours, see: Queen Victoria to Lord Northbrook, 23 July 1875, Northbrook papers, Hants. Record Office, NP6/3/2/11, vol. II; For her disapproval of the medal, see: Ponsonby to Disraeli, 30 June 1875, Dep. Hughenden, Bodleian Library, 78/3, fols 340–1.

42. Francis Knollys to Ponsonby, 4 June 1875, RA VIC/MAIN/T6/18.

43. Northbrook to Philip Wodehouse, 3 Aigist 1875, IOR Mss Eur. D726/7; Gray, *Prince of Wales in India*, 41–2.

44. Russell, *Prince of Wales' Tour*, xviii.

45. Maharaja of Jaipur to Northbrook, 15 August 1875, Northbrook papers, Hants. Record Office, 92 M95/FS/2, fol. 69 ('future emperor').

46. John Martineau, *The Life and Correspondence of Sir Bartle Frere*, 2 vols (London: John Murray, 1895), ii, 125–6.

47. Frere to Knollys, 5 May 1875, RA, VIC/ADDC07/0969.

48. *Bombay Gazette*, 29 October 1875, 3 (carriage).

49. Disraeli to Queen Victoria, n.d. (*c.* early July 1875), RA VIC/MAIN/Z/468/33 ('royal progress'); Queen Victoria to Disraeli, 13 June 1875, Dep. Hughenden, Bodleian Library, 78/3, fols 325–6; Ponsonby to Disraeli, 4 July 1875, RA VIC/MAIN/T6/30. The queen was reported as 'still opposed' even after the House of Commons voted through the money in July: Earl of Camperdown to Northbrook 9 July 1875, Northbrook papers, Hants. Record Office, NP6/3/2/11, vol. I

50. Russell, *Prince of Wales' Tour*, xv–xvi; 'Journal of H.M.'s ship "Serapis"', 95, TNA ADM 101/271.

51. Lord Carnarvon to Disraeli, 13 September 1875, Dep. Hughenden, Bodleian Library, 79/1, fols 156–7 (Princess of Wales' residence); W. Knollys to Lord Salisbury, 15 October 1875, 23 October 1875, Salisbury papers, 3M/F (telegraphs); *The Private Life of King Edward VII (By a Member of the Royal Household)* (New York: D. Appleton & Co. 1901), 86 (carriage and ponies).

52. 'List of Chiefs from Beyond the Bombay Presidency, who are Expected to Arrive in Bombay MSA', Pol. Proceedings (1875) vol. 217, 260–2. A Telugu account was produced of the Maharaja of Mysore's trip: Polluri Mutyal Das, *Chamra Vadeyaravri Cheritramu* (Bangalore: Vicara Darpana Press, 1876) (QLB Mysore). For his tutor's report of the visit,

see: G. B. Malleson to R. A. Dalyell, 1 January 1876, Palace General Office papers, Mysore District Archives, Mys. 21, fols 71–9.

53. NAI, Foreign Dept Proceedings B (February 1877), 89–95. The controversy was set out in *H.R.H. The Prince of Wales' Visit to India. Correspondence between Sir Salar Jung . . . and C. B. Saunders . . . Relative to the Meeting Between the Prince of Wales and the Infant Nizam* (London: Yates & Alexander, 1876). For Salar Jung's arrival in Bombay, see: MSA. Pol. Proceedings (1875), vol. 214, 134.

54. Circular from secretary of the Government of India to secretary of the Government of Bombay, 3 September 1875, MSA, Pol. Proceedings, (1875), vol. 216, 129 (request for information); secretary of the Government of India to chief secretary, Government of Bombay, 12 November 1875, ibid. 21, 76–7 (solicitations); Gray, *Prince of Wales in India*, 16–17 (prisoners' decorations).

55. *Bombay Gazette*, 9 November 1875, 2–3; Gray, *Prince of Wales in India*, 56.

56. For the Baroda gift, see: *Hindoo Mythology Properly Treated: Being an Epitomised Description of the Various Heathen Deities Illustrated on the Silver Swami Tea Service Presented . . . to H. R. H. the Prince of Wales . . . by His Highness the Gaekwar of Baroda* (Madras: Gantz Bros, 1875); Ajay Sinha, 'Baroda as Provenance' in Prya Maholay-Jaradi (ed.), *Baroda: A Cosmopolitan Provenance in Transition* (Mumbai: Marg Foundation, 2015), 26–7. The ceremonial sword is now at RCIN 38023.

57. 'Laying of the Foundation Stone of the Prince's Dock, Bombay with Masonic Honours . . . 11th November 1875' (printed programme), Archives, The Library and Museum of Freemasonry, NJ63 MAN, 1. Russell, *Prince of Wales' Tour*, 162–3.

58. 'Notification' (23 December 1875), Palace General Office papers, Mysore District Archives, Mys. 21, fols 47–8; Duke of Buckingham to Disraeli, 25 November 1875, Dep. Hughenden, Bodleian Library, 121/2, fols 185–6 ('extreme disappointment').

59. *Graphic*, 25 December 1875, 628. For arrangements in Baroda, see: MSA, Pol. Proceedings (1875), vol. 221, 149–59; 'Visit of H.R.H. the Prince of Wales', Huzur Dept, Daftar 806/21–2, Baroda State Archives.

60. Russell, *Prince of Wales' Tour*, 187–210.

61. *Bombay Gazette*, 26 November 1875, 2; Fayrer, *Notes*, 46 (Monier-Williams).

62. *ILN*, 1 January 1876, 1; ibid., 8 January 1876, 48.

63. B. Bastiampillai, 'The Colonial Office and Sir William Gregory, Governor of Ceylon 1872–7: A Study in British Imperial Administration', *Ceylon Journal of Historical and Social Studies* 9 (1966) 20–43, K. M. Da Silva, *A History of Sri Lanka* (London: C. Hurst & Co., 1981), ch. 23.

64. *ILN*, 8 January 1876, 48; Russell, *Prince of Wales' Tour*, 250–2.

65. Robinson Duckworth to Ponsonby, 8 December 1875, RA VIC/MAIN/Z/468/124; *Graphic*, 8 January 1876, 25; *ILN*, 15 January 1876, 72.

66. Gregory to Lord Carnarvon, 15 December 1875, Ceylon despatches, TNA, CO54/498, fols 446–60.

67. For the drawn-out planning of the hunt, see: Bartle Frere to Carnarvon, 1 September 1875, TNA, PRO 30/6/4, fols 92–5; Russell, *Prince of Wales' Tour*, 278–86 (the kill); Cf. Jamie Lorimer and Sarah Whatmore, 'After the "King of Beasts": Samuel Baker and the Embodied Historical Geographies of Elephant Hunting in Mid-nineteenth-century Ceylon', *Journal of Historical Geography* 35 (2009), 668–89.

68. 'To His Royal Highness Albert Edward, Prince of Wales', Missions of the Society for the Propagation of the Gospel and the Missions of the Church Missionary Society; 'Translation of a Tamil Lyric, Sung at the Reception of His Royal Highness, the Prince of Wales, at Maniachi, Tinnevelly'; 'Autograph Reply of His Royal Highness, the Prince of Wales' (10 December 1875), Church Missionary Society papers, Special Collections, University of Birmingham, CMS/B/OMS/CIZ0209/14A, /15A-B, /16.

69. *Madras Times*, 23 December 1875, reprinted in *The Royal Visit to Madras, December 1st to 18th 1875* (Madras: *Madras Times*, 1875); Knollys to Disraeli, 18 December 1875, RA

VIC/MAIN/T6/64 ('hardly anyone to be seen'); *Indian Charivari*, 12 November 1875, 115.

70. Russell, *Prince of Wales' Tour*, 313–28; Russell, 'Diary for India' (entry for 13 December 1875); 'The Royal Visit to Madras', Stowe Mss, Huntington Library, San Marino, STG India Box 1 (2).

71. *Englishman*, 25 December 1875, 2–3; *Graphic*, 22 January 1876, 83–4, ibid., 29 January 1876, 104–5; *ILN*, 22 January 1876 (special supplement); Gray, *Prince of Wales in India*, 208–17; Russell, *Prince of Wales' Tour*, 351–9; NAI, Foreign Dept Proceedings (March 1877), B, 71–7 (Burmese delegation); ibid. (May 1875), B, 4–5; ibid. (June 1875), 16–17 (portable throne).

72. *Englishman*, 28 December 1875, 2; ibid. 29 December 1875, 2; 'Programme of the Undergraduates' Welcome to His Royal Highness', IOR Mss Eur. F86/163.

73. *Englishman*, 4 January 1876, 2–3; Russell, *Prince of Wales' Tour*, 370–5.

74. Russell, *Prince of Wales' Tour*, 375–6.

75. *ILN*, 22 January 1876, 92; *Graphic*, 19 February 1876, 176; C. J. Metcalfe to Richard Temple, 13 January 1876, IOR Mss Eur. F86/162 (indigo petitioners).

76. Dighton Probyn to Queen Victoria, 7 January 1876, RA VIC/MAIN/Z/469/8; Lady Couper to Queen Victoria, 13 January 1876, RA VIC/MAIN/Z/469/11; Duckworth to Queen Victoria, 14 January 1876, RA VIC/MAIN/Z/469/12.

77. Arthur Ellis to Queen Victoria, 28 January 1876, RA VIC/MAIN/Z/469/23.

78. *Graphic*, 26 February 1876 (supplement); Lord Roberts, *Forty-one Years in India: From Subaltern to Commander-in-Chief* (London: Macmillan & Co., 1901), 326–8.

79. *Indian Public Opinion*, 20 January 1876, 235–7.

80. *Graphic*, 26 February 1876, 194; ibid., 4 March 1876, 224 (Jammu).

81. 'Address from the native Christians of the Punjab' (24 January 1876), Church Missionary Society papers, CMS/B/OMS/CI1/13; Fayrer, *Notes of the Visits to India*, 93–4 (liberation of prisoners).

82. Ada Smith, 'The Prince's Visit' (24 January 1876), Church of England Zenana Missionary Society papers, Special Collections, University of Birmingham, EA4/1; Duckworth to Queen Victoria, 3 February 1876, RA VIC/MAIN/Z/469/30; Fayrer, *Notes*, 104–5.

83. *Letters from India . . . from William S. Potter*, 71–2; Gray, *Prince of Wales in India*, 328; Duckworth concurred: 'Buckingham Palace with the Tower of London dropped into the inside of it': Duckworth to Queen Victoria, 3 February 1876, RA VIC/MAIN/Z/469/30.

84. Gray, *Prince of Wales in India*, 314 (wooden whistles); *Graphic*, 18 March 1876, 272, 276. A photo survives of the scene (without the Prince) in the Jaipur City Palace archives.

85. 'Tiger-Mania', *The Prince of Wales in India, in verse* (London: n.p., 1876); *Graphic*, 11 March 1876, 242.

86. Ram Sahai, *Gulgasht-i-Bagh-i-Lucknow: A Description of the Visit to Lucknow of H.R.H. the Prince of Wales* (Lucknow: Tamannai Press, 1876), includes a depiction of the prince in an open coach; Russell, *Prince of Wales' Tour*, 512–13 (investiture).

87. MSA, Pol. Proceedings (1876), vol. 208, 144–5.

88. QVJl., 11 May 1876; *The Return of the Traveller: A Sermon Preached in Westminster Abbey by Arthur Penrhyn Stanley . . . on Sunday 14 May, 1876, being the Sunday after the Return of the Prince of Wales from India* (London: Macmillan and Co., 1876); *The Times*, 18 May 1876, 12 (Serapis); *ILN*, 1 July 1876, 19 (South Kensington display); C. P. Clarke, *Catalogue of the Collection of Indian Arms and Objects of Art Presented by the Princes and Nobles of India to H.R.H. the Prince of Wales . . . on the Occasion of his Visit to India in 1875–1876, etc.* (London: W. Griggs, 1898); William Simpson, *Shikare and Tomasha: A Souvenir of the Visit of H.R.H. the Prince of Wales to India* (London: W. M. Thompson, 1876).

89. Frere to Queen Victoria, 10 February 1876, RA VIC/MAIN/T6/77.

90. Russell, *Prince of Wales Tour*, 595.

91. *Hindoo Patriot*, 27 December 1875, 603; Cf. Madusudan Sarkar, *Bharate-Jubraj; or the Prince in India* (Barisal: Satyaprakash Press, 1875); Hemchandra Banerji, *Bharat bhiksha;*

or, India's Petition (Calcutta: Roy Press, 1878) (QLB Bengal); Narayan Krishna Dharap, *Swagatam* (Poona: Duyan Chakshu Press, 1875) (QLB Bombay).

92. George Aston, *His Royal Highness the Duke of Connaught and Strathearn: A Life and Intimate Study* (George G. Harrap & Co., 1929), chs 9, 12–14; Noble Frankland, *Witness of a Century: The Life and Times of Prince Arthur Duke of Connaught, 1850–1942* (London: Shepheard-Walwyn, 1993), chs 8–9.

93. *ToI*, 16 October 1884, 6. The Connaughts were accompanied on the trip by the artist Herbert Olivier, who later exhibited views he painted there: *Catalogue of a Collection of Drawings by Herbert A. Olivier Illustrating Life and Landscape in India and Cashmere* (London: Fine Art Society, 1885).

94. *The Times*, 13 April 1885, 9; NAI, Foreign Dept Proceedings (May 1885), 804–961.

95. NAI, Foreign Dept Proceedings (February 1889), 32–42.

96. Ibid. (January 1890), 181–5. For Prince Albert Victor, see: John Kiste, 'Albert Victor, Prince, Duke of Clarence and Avondale (1864–1892)', *ODNB*; Theo Aronson, *Prince Eddy and the Homosexual Underworld* (London: John Murray, 1994), ch. 11.

97. For the arrival at Bombay, see: Captain Charles Bateson Harvey, 'Tour with Prince Albert Victor, etc. . . . October 25th 1889 to May 2nd 1890', entry for 9 November, RA GV/PRIV/AA39A; *Civil & Military Gazette*, 11 November 1889, 2. For his stay at Poona, see: Duke of Connaught to Lord Elphinstone, 18 November 1889, RA VIC/ADDA25/87.

98. Albert Victor to Queen Victoria, 29 November 1889, RA VIC/MAIN/Z/92/75. According to *The Times*, the nizam spent £200,000 entertaining the Prince: *The Times*, 28 October 1889, 5. For the 'puffy cakes', see: Harvey, 'Tour with Prince Albert Victor' entry for 17 November.

99. 'Visit of H.R.H. Prince Albert', Chief Secretariat Records (21 of 1889), 1–7, Karnataka State Archives. For the hunting portion of trip, see: J. D. Rees, 'Prince Albert Victor in Travancore', *Macmillan's Magazine* 62 (May 1890), 71–80.

100. Harvey, 'Tour with Prince Albert Victor', entry for 17 November (throne), RA GV/PRIV/AA39A.

101. *The Times*, 16 December 1889, 5.

102. Lansdowne to the Prince of Wales, 7 January 1890, RA VIC/MAIN/N/46/54.

103. 'Message of Welcome', Cutwa municipality ('dumb millions'), RA VIC/MAIN/N/46/54; cf. Kabi Bandhu Sen, *Anshlata. The Creeper of Hope* (Calcutta: Nibaran Chandra Ghosh, 1890) (QLB Bengal). *The Times*, 9 December 1889, 5 (student disruption).

104. Diary entry for 6 February 1890, Harvey, 'Tour with Prince Albert Victor', RA GV/PRIV/AA39A.

105. Harvey, 'Tour with Prince Albert Victor', entry for 19 January (statue); Albert Victor to Queen Victoria, 19 January 1890, RA VIC/MAIN/Z/92/76.

106. *ToI*, 26 March 1890, 5; Harvey, 'Tour with Prince Albert Victor', entry for 25 March (leper asylum), RA GV/PRIV/AA39A.

8 Queen-Empress

1. 'Couronnement de l'Impèratrice des Indes' (*c.* 1881), Dorot Jewish Division, Box 171: 331, New York Public Library. Disraeli is supposed to have refused a visit from Queen Victoria on his death bed on the grounds that she would ask him to communicate with Albert: Jonathan Parry, 'Disraeli, Benjamin, Earl of Beaconsfield (1804–1881)', *ODNB*.

2. Bernard S. Cohn, 'Representing Authority in Victorian India' in Eric Hobsbawm and Terence Ranger (eds), *The Invention of Tradition* (Cambridge: Cambridge University Press, 1983), 165–210; Thomas Metcalf, *Ideologies of the Raj* (Cambridge: Cambridge University Press, 1994), 59–65; David Cannadine, *Ornamentalism: How the British Saw their Empire* (London: Allen Lane, 2001), ch. 4; Julie F. Codell, 'Photography and the Delhi Coronation

Durbars' in Codell (ed.), *Power and Resistance: The Delhi Coronation Durbars, 1877, 1903, 1911* (New Delhi: Mapin, 2012), 16–43. For a more nuanced account, see: L. A. Knight, 'The Royal Titles Act and India', *Historical Journal* 11 (1968), 488–507.

3. Queen Victoria to Crown Princess Victoria, 1 October 1873, Crown Princess Victoria to Queen Victoria, 4 October 1873 in *Letters of Queen Victoria*, 2nd ser., ii, 283–4.

4. Queen Victoria to Disraeli, 13 January 1876, Bodleian Library, Oxford, Dep. Hughenden, 79/2, fols 35–8; QVJl., 26 February 1876.

5. Disraeli to Cairns, 7 January 1876 in G. E. Buckle, *The Life of Benjamin Disraeli, Earl of Beaconsfield*, 6 vols (London: John Murray, 1910–20), v, 457; O. T. Burne, 'Memorandum', IOR/L/PS/20/MEMO31/5 (22 December 1875).

6. Disraeli to Queen Victoria, 11 January 1876, RA VIC/MAIN/N/31/3.

7. HC Debs, 227 (17 February 1876), 408–10.

8. Ibid., 410–17.

9. Disraeli to Queen Victoria, 18 February 1876, RA VIC/MAIN/F/16/1; Ponsonby to Disraeli, 19 February 1876, ibid., fol. 3; Queen Victoria to Ponsonby, 19 February 1876, ibid., fol. 4; Granville to Queen Victoria, 23 February 1876, ibid., fol. 17; Queen Victoria to Ponsonby (n.d. *c.* 24 February 1876), ibid., fol. 21; Gladstone to Granville, 18 February 1876, reprinted in Agatha Ramm (ed.), *The Political Correspondence of Mr Gladstone and Lord Granville, 1868–1876*, 2 vols Camden 3rd ser., 81–2, (London: Royal Historical Society, 1952), ii, 482–3.

10. Queen Victoria to Theodore Martin, 14 March 1876, RA VIC/MAIN/F/16/38. For hostility in the press, see for example: *The Times*, 11 March 1876, 9 ('ludicrous'), *Spectator*, 11 March 1876, 4 ('vulgarity').

11. Ponsonby to Disraeli, 15 March 1876, Disraeli papers, Dep. Hughenden 79/2, fols 130–3. Queen Victoria to Disraeli, 18 March 1876 (copy), RA VIC/MAIN/F/16/69.

12. HC Debs, 227, (9 March 1876), 1719–60; ibid., 228, (16 March 1876), 77; 'Notes' (n.d. *c.* early March 1876), Disraeli papers, Dep. Hughenden, 86/2, fols 128–9; Lord Salisbury to Disraeli, 14 March 1876, ibid., fols 147–8.

13. HC Debs, 228 (20 March 1876), 499; Disraeli to Queen Victoria, 23 March 1876, RA VIC/MAIN/F/16/78. Ponsonby to Queen Victoria, 23 March 1876, fol. 79. The geography text book referred to was John Guy, *Geography for Children, on a Perfectly Easy Plan: Adapted for the Use of Schools and Private Families.* Originally published in 1810, it was in its 89th edition by 1876; cf. *An Almanack for the Year of Our Lord 1876* (London: J. Whitaker, 1876), 64.

14. HL Debs, 228 (3 April 1876), 1047, 1049.

15. *Reynolds' News*, 2 April 1876, 5; [James Thomson], *A Commission of Enquiry into Royalty, etc.* (1876) in *The Speedy Extinction of Evil and Misery. Selected Prose of James Thomson*, ed. William David Schaefer (Berkeley: University of California Press, 1967), esp. 40–1.

16. [E. Jenkins], *The Blot on the Queen's Head; or, How Little Ben, the Head Waiter, Changed the Sign of the "Queen's Inn" to "Empress Hotel, Limited"* (London: Strahan & Co., 1876). Jenkins also criticised the bill in Parliament: 'Was this to be a new avatar to the people of India?': HC Debs, 228 (20 March 1876), 296.

17. 'Ranee Bahadoor' and 'Her Imperial Majesty the Queen of all the Britains [sic] and Sovereign Lady of India' were suggested: A Septuagenarian Tory, *Queen Alone, in every Heart and on Every Tongue* (London: Edward Stanford, 1876), 9–12; E. G. Highton, *Our Imperial Crown. A Letter Addressed to the Statesmen of the British Empire Containing an Unobjectionable Adequate Solution of the Difficulties Involved in the Proposed Extension of the Royal Titles* (London: J. Westall, 1876), 7. For attacks on and caricatures of Disraeli, see: *'God save the Queen'. Being a Last Few Words on the Royal Titles Bill, a Protest by A Loyal Subject and True Englishman* (London: C. F. Hodgson, 1876), 13–14; 'New Crowns for Old Ones', *Punch*, 15 April 1876, 147. On demonology around Disraeli at this time, see: Anthony Wohl, ' "Dizzi-Ben-Dizzi": Disraeli as Alien', *Journal of British Studies* 34 (1995), 375–411.

18. HC Debs, 228 (4 April 1876), 1181; Disraeli to Queen Victoria, 4 April 1876, RA VIC/MAIN/F/17/10; Disraeli to Queen Victoria, 26 April 1876, RA VIC/MAIN/F/17/30; Lord Derby to Disraeli, 7 April 1876, Disraeli papers, Dep. Hughenden, 79/2, fols 174–6.
19. HL Debs, 228 (7 April 1876), 1388.
20. HC Debs, 317 (25 July 1887), 1890–1; ibid., 337 (9 July 1889), 1827–8.
21. Queen Victoria suggested four names to Salisbury, Lytton not amongst them: Queen Victoria to Salisbury, 1 November 1875, 3rd Marquess Salisbury papers, Hatfield House, 3M/F; Lytton to Disraeli, 30 November 1875, Disraeli papers, Dep. Hughenden 105/1, fols 24–9.
22. For Lytton, see: David Washbrook, 'Lytton, Edward Robert Bulwer-, first earl of Lytton (1831–1891)', *ODNB*; E. Neill Raymond, *Victorian Viceroy: The Life of Robert, the First Earl of Lytton* (London: Regency Press, 1980).
23. Betty Balfour (ed.), *Personal and Literary Letters of Robert, First Earl of Lytton*, 2 vols (London: Longmans, 1906), i, 70–71, 159–70; [Lytton], 'Germany: Past, Present and Future', *Fortnightly Review* 9 (June 1871), 677–708, esp. 680–1, 706–7; idem., 'The French Constitutional Monarchy of 1830: An Enquiry into the Causes of its Failure', *Contemporary Review* 24 (June 1874), 856–74, esp. 871–4.
24. Balfour (ed.), *Personal and Literary Letters*, i, 179–81; Lytton 'Philosophy in Cunieform', *Macmillan's Magazine* 15 (April 1867), 499–509.
25. Lytton to Montagu Corry (Disraeli's private secretary), 20 April 1876, Disraeli papers, Dep. Hughenden, 105/1, fols 56–60; cf. Lytton to Queen Victoria, 4 May 1876, RA VIC/MAIN/N/31/43.
26. Lytton to Disraeli, 30 April 1876, Disraeli papers, Dep. Hughenden, 105/1, fols 68–81; Salisbury to Lytton, 30 August 1876, IOR E2183; Lytton to Queen Victoria, 4 May 1876, RA VIC/MAIN/N/31/46, partially reprinted in *Letters of Queen Victoria*, 2nd ser., ii, 460–3, but without the allusion to Austria.
27. Lytton to Disraeli, 3 October 1876, Disraeli papers, Dep. Hughenden, 105/1, fols 98–103.
28. 'Memorandum by the Viceroy' (11 May 1876, rev. 29 July and 10 August 1876), IOR Mss Eur. F86/166, fols 7–15. Cf. the original memorandum at IOR L/PS/20/MEMO33/19.
29. Lytton to Disraeli, 3 October 1876, Disraeli papers, Dep. Hughenden, 105/1, fols 98–103; T. H. Thornton to Lepel Griffin, 28 October 1876, Foreign Dept Proceedings, NAI, Pol. B., 872, fol. 4.
30. Lytton to Queen Victoria, 12 August 1876, RA VIC/MAIN/N/31/87. Lord Salisbury explained that the Order of British India was an award from the days of the East India Company, and was now 'quite full': Lord Salisbury to Ponsonby, 29 August 1876, RA VIC/MAIN/N/31/103–4. It was later revived as a campaign medal.
31. Lytton to Queen Victoria, 11 September 1876, IOR Mss Eur E218/18, fols 545–7; Salisbury to Lytton, 12 September 1876, IOR Mss Eur E218/3, fol. 481; W. H. Doyly to Temple, 3 December 1876, IOR Mss Eur F86/166. For the college of heralds and the banners, see: 'Memorandum by the Viceroy' (11 May 1876), 11, 13. For the role of Lockwood Kipling, see: T. H. Thornton to Lepel Griffin, 29 September 1876, NAI, Foreign Dept Proceedings, Pol. B. 554; Catherine Arbuthnott, 'Designs for the Imperial Assemblage' in Julius Bryant and Susan Weber (eds), *John Lockwood Kipling: Arts and Crafts in the Punjab and London* (London: Yale University Press, 2017), 151–68. For the final approval of the Indian Privy Council and suggestions for Indian members, see: Ponsonby to Queen Victoria, 7 December 1876, RA VIC/MAIN/N/32/28.
32. O. T. Burne to Richard Temple, 14 October 1876 and 16 December 1876, IOR Mss Eur F86/166; Val C. Prinsep, *Imperial India: An Artist's Journals* (London: Chapman and Hall, 1879), 35.
33. Lytton to Wodehouse, 23 July 1876, IOR Mss Eur D726/9; 'Memorandum by the Viceroy' (11 May 1876), 8; *The Times*, 16 September 1876, 7.
34. Major Davies to Col. Sir R. J. Meade, 18 September 1876, Delhi Commissioner's Records, Delhi District Archives, 192/1876 I, fol. 12.

35. 'Editors of Native Papers to be Invited to Delhi' (10 September 1876), IOR Mss Eur F86/166.
36. Lytton to Queen Victoria, 20 August 1876, IOR Mss Eur E218/18, fols 376–8.
37. Owen Tudor Burne, *Memories* (London: E. Arnold, 1907), 220. A miniature of the gold medal can be seen at RCIN 443439. For the special anna, see: Financial Dept to the Collector, 23 November 1876, NAI, Foreign Dept Proceedings, Pol. B, 878–80, of which there is an example at RCIN 445772.
38. Salisbury to Lytton, 12 September 1876, IOR E218/3, fols 366–8; T. E. Colebrooke, 'On Imperial and Other Titles', *Journal of the Royal Asiatic Society of Great Britain and Ireland* 9 (1877), 314–420; G. W. Leitner, *Kaisar-i-Hind, the Only Appropriate Translation of the Title of Empress of India, etc.* (Lahore: I. P. O. Press, 1876).
39. Lytton to Queen Victoria, 2 August 1876, RA VIC/MAIN/N/31/81 (copy of a telegram), Lytton to Queen Victoria, 12 August 1876, RA VIC/MAIN/N/31/87. For the queen's reactions to the designs, see: Queen Victoria to Salisbury, 19 August 1876, 9 October 1876, 21 October 1876, Salisbury papers, 3M/F.
40. Ponsonby to Queen Victoria, 5 November 1876, RA VIC/MAIN/N/32/15; Disraeli to Queen Victoria, 30 August 1876, RA VIC/MAIN/N/31/105.
41. Lytton to Queen Victoria, 15 November 1876, RA VIC/MAIN/N/32/20; Lytton to Queen Victoria, 11 September 1876, RA VIC/MAIN/N/32/1.
42. 'Minute by Lord Salisbury on ... Lord Lytton's proposal for a Privy Council, etc.' (2 November 1876); IOR L/PS/20/MEMO33/20 Disraeli to Salisbury, 3 September 1876 (copy), IOR Mss Eur. E218/3, fols 362–4.
43. Philip Melvill to Col. Sir R. J. Meade, 25 September 1876, Delhi Commissioner's Records, Delhi District Archives, 192/1876 III, fol. 20; Captn C. A. Bayley to Meade, 11 November 1876, ibid., fol. 66; Captain E. A. Fraser to Meade, 23 November 1876, ibid., fol. 112.
44. For the programme of entry of the Viceroy, see: *ToI*, 28 December 1876, 2. J. Talboys Wheeler, *The History of the Imperial Assemblage at Delhi held on the 1st January 1877* (1877; repr. New Delhi: Arhuja, 2007), 50–6; Lytton to Queen Victoria, 23 December 1876–10 January 1877, IOR Mss Eur E218/19, 3–19.
45. Lytton to Queen Victoria, 23 December 1876–10 January 1877, IOR Mss Eur E218/19, 13; John Robertson and L. A. Smith (comp.), *The Imperial Assemblage Directory: Being a List of the Governors, Administrators, Princes, Chiefs, Nobles and Others Present in Camp at Delhi during the Assemblage, Together with Other Information and a Map Showing the Positions of the Several Camps* (Allahabad: Pioneer Press, 1876).
46. *Calcutta Gazette*, 10 January 1877, 5–7; Talboys Wheeler, *History*, 57–9, 157; Lytton to Queen Victoria, 23 December 1876–10 January 1877, IOR Mss Eur, E218/19, 6; H. N. Miller to the under-secretary, Foreign Dept, 25 October 1876, NAI, Foreign Dept Proceedings, Pol. B, 516–18.
47. Talboys Wheeler, *History*, 70–89, is the official account. For other detailed descriptions, see: *Pioneer*, 4 January 1877, 2–3; *Bombay Gazette*, 5 January 1877, 3–4.
48. Lytton To Queen Victoria, 23 December 1876–10 January 1877, IOR Mss Eur E218/19, 18.
49. 'Reply to the Deputation of the British India Association' (30 January 1877), *Selected Speeches*, 53.
50. Government of India to the secretary of state for India, 2 February 1877, NAI, Foreign Dept Proceedings, Political A, 312.
51. Talboys Wheeler, *History*, 137–50.
52. Lytton to Hamilton, 19 January 1877, IOR Mss Eur E218/19, 44. Lytton's officials calculated the net cost of the event to be nearer 1 million rupees (about £66,000): 'Extract from the Financial Statement for 1877–8 Published in the *Gazette of India*, 15 March 1877', NAI, Foreign Dept Proceedings (December 1877), Pol. A, 495.
53. *Civil and Military Gazette*, 4 January 1877, 1; *Bangalore Spectator*, 9 January 1877, 2.

54. *Bharat Sangskarak* (Calcutta), 15 January 1877, NNR, IOR L/R/5/3; *Urdu Akbar* (Akola), 30 December 1876, NNR, IOR L/R/5/54. cf. Rajkrishna Raya, *Bharat-Bhagya; or, India's Good Fortune* (Calcutta: Albert Press, 1877), QLB (Bengal), a sarcastically titled criticism of the 'imperial rejoicings' amidst 'famines and floods'. For Tagore's work: S. Radhakrishnan (ed.), *Rabindranath Tagore, 1861–1961. A Centenary Volume* (New Delhi: Sahitya Akademi, 1961), 453.

55. *Indian Charivari*, 5 January 1877, 6–7.

56. Bernard Cohn, 'Representing Authority in Victorian India', 172; Julie Codell, 'On the Delhi Coronation Durbars, 1877, 1903, 1911', http://www.branchcollective.org/?ps_articles=julie-codell-on-the-delhi-coronation-durbars-1877–1903–1911, 6 (accessed 4 April 2018); cf. Codell, 'Photography and the Delhi Coronation Durbars', 20–2. For the memory of 1857, see: Sonakshi Goyle, 'Tracing a Cultural Memory: Commemoration of 1857 in the Delhi Durbars, 1877, 1903, and 1911', *Historical Journal* 59 (2016), 799–815.

57. *Tarjuma-e-tarikh-e-dakkan* (*c.* 1877), Mss Hist. 247, Salar Jung Museum and Library, Hyderabad.

58. Barbara Metcalf, 'Islam and Power in Colonial India: The Making and Unmaking of a Muslim Princess', *American Historical Review* 116 (2011), 1–30; Teresa Segura-Garcia, 'Baroda, the British Empire and the World, *c.* 1875–1939' (unpublished PhD thesis, University of Cambridge, 2016).

59. Mirza Hatim Ali Beg Mehr, *I'd Qaisarya/The Imperial Festival* (Agra: the author, 1878), QLB (North-West Provinces). Mehr's patron was the Nawab of Rampur. Beni Madhab Nyaratna, *Bharateswari Kabyam/Empress of India* (Calcutta: the author, 1879), QLB (Bengal).

60. The events across India receive cursory attention in Talboys Wheeler, *History*, ch. 11. A fuller account is at NAI, Foreign Dept Proceedings (December 1877), Political A, 330–496.

61. Ibid., 351a.

62. Frank Harris, *Jamsetji Nusserwanji Tata. A Chronicle of His Life* (London: Humphrey Milford, 1925), 26–9.

63. H. S. Thomas to the chief secretary to the Government of Madras, 24 November 1876, NAI, Foreign Dept Proceedings (December 1877), Political A, 330.

64. NAI, Foreign Dept Proceedings (December 1877), Political A, 337 (Benares); 344 (Cachar).

65. Ibid., 380 (Dharwad); 392 (Farrukhabad); 395 (Aligarh).

66. Ibid., 332 (Alibag); 384 (Calcutta); 415 (Secunderabad); 376 (Poona).

67. Lytton to Queen Victoria, 11 September 1876, IOR Mss Eur. E218/18, fols 454–7. The 'congratulatory poems' are listed in NAI, Foreign Dept Proceedings (December 1877), Pol. A, 439. Unless otherwise indicated the verses described here are taken from this source.

68. Sourindro Mohun Tagore, *The National Anthem: Translated into Sanskrit and Bengali Verse, and Set to Twelve Varieties of Indian Melody* (Calcutta: the author, 1882); Ponsonby to [Robert] Bickersteth, 23 February 1883, Kimberley papers, Bodleian Library, University of Oxford, Ms Eng c. 4204, fol. 32–3; Harford to A. C. Tait, 17 November 1882, Tait papers, Lambeth Palace Library, 281, fols 176–7. See: Charles Capwell, 'Sourindro Mohun Tagore and the National Anthem Project', *Ethnomusicology* 31 (1987), 407–30.

69. Kokkonda Venkatarathnamu Pantulu, *The Empress of India Nine Gems* (Madras: C. Foster & Co., 1876); cf. Mukunda Chandra Lahiri, *British-Sangita/British Song* (Calcutta: Lahihri, Chakrabati & Co., 1881), QLB (Bengal).

70. Raj Krishna Raya, *Bina/The Lute*, 1 (1879), QLB (Bengal).

71. Abdul Gafur, *Muraqqa-i-Salatin, Hissa-i-awwal-i-Asar-ul-Mutaakhkirin/The Gallery of Princes* (Delhi: Muraru Lal's Press, 1875), QLB (Punjab); Shahzada Mirza Muhammad Rais Bakht, *Mauj-i-Sultani/The Wave of Kings* (Lucknow: Nawal Kishore, 1884), QLB, (North-West Provinces).

72. Bowmanjee Cursetjee, *On British Administration in India: Consisting of Various Events and Innovations* (Bombay: Times of India, 1876).

73. 'Speech at the Convocation of the Calcutta University', 10 March 1877, in *Selected Speeches of His Excellency Robert Lord Lytton, etc.* (Calcutta: Bonnerjee & Co., 1877), 21–4, 33–4. For Lytton's private views on the BIA, 'the most pampered, pretentious, disloyal set of rascals in India', see: Lytton to Lord Cranbrook, 12 May 1879, Cranbrook papers, Suffolk Record Office, Ipswich, HA 43 T501/32.

74. Annie Besant, *England, India and Afghanistan* (London: Freethought Publishing Company, 1878), 47.

75. QVJl., 1 January 1877; Lord George Hamilton to Lytton 2 January 1877 (telegram), NAI, Political Proceedings, 865.

76. QVJl., 8 May 1878; Andrekos Varnava, *British Imperialism in Cyprus, 1878–1915: The Inconsequential Possession* (Manchester: Manchester University Press, 2009), ch. 3.

77. *The Times*, 22 April 1878, 3; Ian F. W. Beckett, 'The Indian Expeditionary Force on Malta and Cyprus, 1878', *Soldiers of the Queen* 76 (1994), 6–11.

78. 'They'd stop our Eastern pathway, very plain, / And no longer we be the Rulers of the sea, / Nor certain of our Indian domain' sang out the third verse of Fred Albert's, 'We Mean to Keep our Empire in the East' (1878); cf. 'Our "Imperial" Guard', *Punch*, 25 May 1878, 235.

79. Brian Robson, *The Road to Kabul: The Second Afghan War 1878–1881* (London: Spellmount, 1980); Alexander Morrison, 'Beyond the "Great Game": The Russian Origins of the Second Anglo-Afghan War', *Modern Asian Studies* 51 (2017), 686–735.

80. QVJl., 26 November 1878. Later, Lytton prepared a selection of photographs from the battlefield for the queen: Lytton to Queen Victoria, 30 June 1879, IOR Mss Eur. E218/21, 505–5.

81. Lytton to Queen Victoria, 7 September 1879, Mss Eur. E218/21, 712, Lytton to Queen Victoria, 13 October 1879, ibid., 895–900; Lytton to Queen Victoria, 19 December 1879, ibid., 1115–17. Rodney Atwood, *The Life of Field Marshal Lord Roberts* (London: Bloomsbury, 2015), ch. 5.

82. Gladstone, speech at Chester, *The Times*, 20 August 1879, 11; cf. HC Debs, 243 (10 December 1878), 544; Christopher Wallace, 'The Liberals and Afghanistan, 1878–80', *Historical Research*, 85 (2012), 306–28.

83. QVJl., 26 April 1880; Ponsonby to Hartington, 29 April 1880, Devonshire Collection, Chatsworth House, 340.954.

84. Queen Victoria to Hartington, 17 November 1880, Devonshire Collection, 340.1026C; cf. Ponsonby to Hartington, 3 September 1880, ibid., 340.1002; Ponsonby to Hartington, 12 March 1881, ibid., 340.1095; QVJl., 6 September 1880.

85. Hartington to Queen Victoria, 6 February 1881, Devonshire Collection, 340.1070.

86. QVJl., 17 December 1880, 31 January 1881.

87. Donald M. Reid, 'The 'Urabi Revolution and the British Conquest, 1879–1882' in M. W. Daly (ed.), *Modern Egypt, from 1517 to the End of the Twentieth Century* (Cambridge: Cambridge University Press, 1998), 217–38. For some of the domestic reaction, see: R. A. Atkins, 'The Conservatives and Egypt, 1875–80', *Journal of Imperial and Commonwealth History* 2 (1974), 190–205; Shauna Huffaker, 'Representations of Ahmed Urabi: Hegemony, Imperialism and the British Press, 1881–2', *Victorian Periodicals Review* 45 (2012), 375–405.

88. 'Composition of Force Proceeding from India to Egypt', IOR L/MIL/5/695; QVJl., 12 September 1882, 17 September 1882, 28 September 1882. The oil painting, by Richard Caton Woodville, is at RCIN 407434. For the background, see: Noble Frankland, 'Prince Arthur and the Battle of Tel-el-Kebir', *Historian* 40 (1993), 18–20.

89. QVJl., 18 November 1882; *ILN*, 25 November 1882, 538. Harry Payne's watercolour painting of the review is at RCIN 916750.

90. QVJl., 24 November 1882; Major-General Allen Johnson to the under-secretary of State for India, 15 November 1882, IOR L/MIL/7/9980.

91. Hartington to Ripon, 28 September 1881, Devonshire collection, Chatsworth House. 1881; Kimberley to Ponsonby, 7 August 1883, Kimberley papers, Bodleian Library, Oxford, Ms. Eng. 4025, fols 36–7.

92. Salisbury to the queen, 3 August 1885, RA, VIC/ADDA15/4519; Salisbury to the queen, 8 August 1885 RA VIC/ADDA15/4523; Queen Victoria to Dufferin, 31 July 1885, Dufferin papers, PRONI, D1071/H/M/1, no. 12.

93. Lord Salisbury to the queen, 9 October 1885, RA/VIC/MAIN/W/73/14; Queen Victoria to Salisbury, 12 October 1885, RA/VIC/MAIN/W/73/17; Churchill to Dufferin, 18 August 1885, IOR, Mss Eur. F130/3, no. 65; QVJl., 17 August 1885, 11 October 1885, 18 October 1885; IOR/L/MIL/16287 (25 November 1886); Queen Victoria to Dufferin, 27 August 1885, 29 October 1885, 11 December 1885, Dufferin papers, PRONI, D1071/H/M/1, nos. 16, 20, 22.

94. 'Proceedings of the Legislative Council of Bombay', xxvi (7 March 1888, 10 March 1888, 14 March 1888, 17 March 1888), IOR/V/9/2802.

95. Queen Victoria to Dufferin, 1 January 1886, 10 June 1886, Dufferin papers, PRONI, D1071/H/M/1, nos 26, 32. For the background, see: Thant Myint-U, *The Making of Modern Burma* (Cambridge: Cambridge University Press, 2001), 186–93.

9 Mother of India

1. Connaught to Kimberley, 15 June 1884, Bodleian Library, Ms Eng c 4208, ff. 137–44.

2. Geraldine Forbes, *Women in Modern India* (Cambridge: Cambridge University Press, 1996); idem., *Women in Colonial India: Essays on Politics, Medicine and Historiography* (New Delhi: Chronicle Books, 2005); Antoinette Burton, *Burdens of History: British Feminists, Indian Women and Imperial Culture, 1865–1915* (Chapel Hill: University of North Carolina Press, 1994); Philippa Levine, 'Venereal Disease, Prostitution, and the Politics of Empire: The Case of British India', *Journal of the History of Sexuality* (1994), 579–602; Barbara Ramusack, 'Cultural Missionaries, Maternal Imperialists, Feminist Allies: British Women Activists in India, 1865–1945' in Nupur Chaudhuri and Margaret Stroebel (eds), *Western Women and Imperialism: Complicity and Resistance* (Bloomington: Indiana University Press, 1992), 119–36.

3. Mrinalini Sinha, *Colonial Masculinity: The 'Manly Englishman' and the 'Effeminate Bengali' in the Late Nineteenth Century* (Manchester: Manchester University Press, 1995); Heather Streets, *Martial Races: The Military, Race and Masculinity in British Imperial Culture, 1857–1914* (Manchester: Manchester University Press, 2004), ch. 5.

4. For the queen's widowhood, see: Helen Rappaport, *Magnificent Obsession: Victoria, Albert and the Death that Changed the Monarchy* (London: Hutchinson, 2011). For widowhood in Victorian culture, see: Patricia Jalland, *Death in the Victorian Family* (Oxford: Oxford University Press, 1996), ch. 12. For widowhood in colonial India, see: Rajul Sogani, *The Hindu Widow in Indian Literature* (New Delhi: Oxford University Press, 2002); Mytheli Sreenivas, *Wives, Widows, and Concubines: The Conjugal Family Ideal in Colonial India* (Bloomington: Indiana University Press, 2008).

5. NAI Public Proceedings, Home Dept 40–41 (A) (27 January 1862), 34–5 (A) (14 March 1862), 18 (A) (20 May 1862); *Bombay Gazette*, 25 January 1862, 87; *Madras Times*, 31 January 1862, 107; *Englishman*, 11 February 1862, 2; *Allen's Indian Mail and Register*, 8 March 1862, 167; Simin Patel, 'Commemorating the Consort in Colonial Bombay' in Charles Beem and Miles Taylor (eds), *The Man Behind the Queen: Male Consorts in History* (Basingstoke: Palgrave Macmillan, 2014), 157–62.

6. [Muncherjee Cawasjee], *Prince Albert: Selections from a Prize Translation of a Gujarati Poem Written in the Year 1863 by a Parsee Poet* (Bombay: Bombay Education Society, 1870); cf. Bishambhar Nath, *Tuzuk-i Jarmani* (Lucknow: Nawal Kishore Press, 1876).

7. Queen Victoria to Sir John Lawrence, 26 July 1864, *Letters of Queen Victoria*, 2nd ser., i, 242.

8. Grey began work on the memoir early in 1864: Charles Grey to Caroline Grey, 4 May 1864, Charles Grey papers, Durham University Library, GRE/D7/2. Helps had also prepared an edition of Prince Albert's speeches for publication in 1862. For Martin's commission, see: Martin, *Queen Victoria as I Knew Her* (London: William Blackwood, 1901), ch. 1.

9. *The Early Life of the Prince Consort* was advertised in *Allen's Indian Mail*, 20 July 1867, 563. The Indian editions of the *Leaves* were: *Maharani Viktoriya hyanca Hailanda prantantala rahivasa: va Skatalanda, Iaglanda va Airlanda hya desantila saphari ani galabatanta basana kelelia paryatane hyanca vrttanta* (Bombay: Education Society's Press, 1871); *The Queen's Travels in Scotland and Ireland*, trans. Isvari Prasaad Narayan Sinha Bahadur, Maharaja of Banares (Benares: n.p. 1875); *Leaves from the Journal of Our Life in the Highlands*, trans. Mancherjee Bhownaggree (Bombay: privately printed, 1877); *The Life of His Royal Highness the Prince Consort: Father of the Future Emperors of India, Trans. J. Rudd Rainey* (Calcutta: Sanskrit Press, 1892).

10. Nassau Lees to Grey, 23 October [1867], Grey papers, Durham University Library, GRE/D/XIV/4/1.

11. The Royal Library at Windsor has three of the original presentation copies (Marathi, Gujarati and Hindi), with accompanying correspondence: Royal Library, III.60.E. The Maharaja of Benares illustrated his edition with a depiction of him presenting the book to the queen in person: RCIN 1053105.

12. *ToI*, 27 January 1877, 3.

13. Harleen Singh, *The Rani of Jhansi: Gender, History, and Fable in India* (Cambridge: Cambridge University Press, 2014), ch. 3. Cf. E. J. Humphrey, *Gems of India: or, Sketches of Distinguished Hindoo and Mahomedan Women* (New York: Nelson & Phillips, 1875); John J. Pool, *Woman's Influence in the East: As Shown in the Noble Lives of Past Queens and Princesses of India* (London: Elliot Stock, 1892).

14. T. Babu, *The Queen* (Vepery: Fister Press, 1873), this Tamil edition was followed by a Telugu one three years later (Madras: Free Church Mission, 1876); G. H. Rouse, *Maharani Sakshya/The Testimony of the Queen* (Calcutta: Christian Tract Society, 1895); A. W. Young, *Maha Rani O Baibel/The Queen and her Bible* (Calcutta: Christian Tract Society, 1901).

15. For example: V. Krishnama Chariar, *A Jubilee Sketch of the Queen-Empress and the Empire on which the Sun Never Sets* (Madras: SPCK Press, 1887), published simultaneously in Tamil and Telugu, then republished in a Tamil diamond jubilee edition as *A Glorious Reign of Sixty Years* (Madras: the author, 1897); S. Muttu Aiyar and C. V. Swaminada Aiyar, *Life of Her Majesty Queen Victoria, Empress of India* (Madras: the authors, 1898); Munisami Mudali, *Life of Empress Victoria in Kummi Song* (Madras: the author, 1901), 136.

16. Kiran Chandra Banerji, *Bharat Mata* (Calcutta: the author, 1873), QLB (Bengal); Cf. *Mahtava Jyotih, or, the Glory of the Maharaja Mahatva of Bardwan* (1876), QLB (Bengal). For this dualism, see: Indira Chowdhury-Sengupta, 'Mother India and Mother Victoria: Motherhood and Nationalism in Nineteenth-Century Bengal', *South Asia Research* 12 (1992), 20–37; idem., *The Frail Hero and Virile History: Gender and the Politics of Culture in Colonial Bengal* (Delhi: Oxford University Press, 1998).

17. Bharatendu Harischandra, *Victoria's Flag of Victory: A Poem in Hindi* (Benares: n.p., 1882). For Harischandra, see: Vasudha Dalmia, *The Nationalisation of Hindu Traditions: Bharatendu Harischandra and Nineteenth-century Banares* (Delhi: Oxford University Press, 1997); Ichharam Surayam Desai, *Life of Her Most Gracious Majesty the Queen-Empress* (Bombay: the author, 1887), cf. his earlier *Hind ane Britannia* (Bombay: Gujarati Printing Press, 1886). On Desai, see: Beatriz Martinez Saavedra, 'A History for Gujarat: The Imagining of a Region in Edalji Dosabhai'd and Ichharam Desai's Narratives' in Sharmina Marwani and Anjoom A. Mukadam (eds), *Perspectives of Female Researchers: Interdisciplinary Approaches to the Study of Gujarati Identities* (Berlin: Logos Verlag, 2016), 51–62; Bipin Chandra Pal, *Rajnimata Viktoriya/Life of H.M. Empress Victoria* (Calcutta: Kartik Chandra Datta, 1891; repr. 1904). For the attribution of the 1904 edition of this work, see: *Bipin Chandra Pal. Selected Bibliography*, ed. Bijoy Dev (New Delhi: Samskriti, 2001), 18.

18. On royal women in colonial India, see: Angma Dey Jhala, *Courtly Indian Women in Late Imperial India* (London: Pickering & Chatto, 2008); Barbara N. Ramusack, *The Indian Princes and their States* (Cambridge: Cambridge University Press, 2004), 179–82.

19. For the full list, which ran into hundreds, see: 'Returns of the Names and Designations of All Native Princes of India, or their Families, in Receipt of Pensions and Allowances, etc. 1850–64', *Parl. Papers* (1864), Cd. 82.

20. S. A. A. Risvi (ed.), *Freedom Struggle in Uttar Pradesh*, 6 vols (Delhi: Oxford University Press, 2011), ii, 528–31.

21. *Native Petition to the Imperial Parliament for the Restitution of the Raj of Tanjore, Sewajee, etc.* (Madras: Hindu Press, 1860), 9, 15; *Case of the Ranee of Tanjore* (London: Richardson, 1861). For some of the background, see: William Hickey, *The Tanjore Mahratta Principality in Southern India: The Land of the Chola: The Eden of the South* (Madras: Caleb Foster, 1873).

22. Princess of Tanjore to the Duke of Buckingham, 1 January 1881, Stowe Mss, Huntington Library, San Marino, California, STG correspondence, box 109/54.

23. Officiating chief secretary to H. S. Thomas, 8 September 1875, Political Proceedings, Tamil Nadu State Archives, 561, fols 17–18; Bartle Frere to W. Hudleston, 5 January 1876, ibid., 38, fols 17a–17b; *Proceedings Connected with the New Hospital Buildings and the Laying of The Foundation Stone of His Royal Highness the Prince of Wales Medical School at Tanjore . . . 9th November 1880* (Trichinopoly: South India Times Press, 1881).

24. HC Debs, 308 (2 September 1886), 1070–1.

25. *Memorial to Her Majesty the Queen from the (late) H. H. Suguna Bai Saheb, Rani of Sattara, etc.* (Bombay: Union Press, 1874), 7.

26. Nina Napier to Queen Victoria, 16 February 1867, RA VIC/MAIN/N/27/68–9; QVJl., 8 September 1867. For the background, see: Robin Jeffrey, *The Decline of Nair Dominance: Society and Politics in Travancore, 1847–1908*, 2nd edn (New Delhi: Manohar, 1994), ch. 3; Dick Kooiman, 'The Invention of Tradition in Travancore: a Maharaja's Quest for Political Security', *Journal of the Royal Asiatic Society* 15 (2005), 151–64; Mary Beth Heston, 'Mixed Messages in a New "Public" Travancore: Building the Capital 1860–1880', *Art History* 31 (2008), 211–47.

27. Harry Prendergast (resident of Travancore) to Henry Stokes (chief secretary to the Government of Madras), 4 June 1887, Tamil Nadu State Archives, Political Proceedings, fol. 179. The portrait is at: RCIN 404097.

28. Much has now been written about the Begums of Bhopal: Shaharyar M. Khan, *The Begums of Bhopal: A Dynasty of Women Rulers in India* (London: IB Tauris, 2000); Claudia Preckel, *Begums of Bhopal* (New Delhi: Roli Books, 2000); Siobhan Lambert-Hurley, 'Princes, Paramountcy and the Politics of Muslim Identity: The Begam of Bhopal on the Indian National Stage, 1901–1926', *South Asia* 26 (2003), 165–91 (about Kaikhusrau Jahan); idem., 'Historicising Debates over Women's Status in Islam: The Case of Nawab Sultan Jahan Begam of Bhopal' in Waltraud Ernst and Biswamoy Pati (eds), *India's Princely States: People, Princes and Colonialism* (London: Routledge, 2007), 139–56; Barbara Metcalf, 'Islam and Power in Colonial India: The Making and Unmaking of a Muslim Princess', *American Historical Review* 116 (2011), 1–30 (about Shah Jahan); Hannah Archambault, 'Becoming Mughal in the Nineteenth Century: The Case of the Bhopal Princely State', *South Asia* 36 (2013), 479–95.

29. For example, see: G. B. Malleson, *A Native State and its Rulers: A Lecture Delivered in the Dalhousie Institute, the 20th February, 1865* (Calcutta: R. C. Lepage & Co., 1865).

30. *A Princess's Pilgrimage: Nawab Sikandar Begum's A Pilgrimage to Mecca*, ed. Siobhan Lambert-Hurley (New Delhi: Women Unlimited, 2007). For the later pilgrimage of her daughter, see: Siobhan Lambert-Hurley, 'Out of India: The Journeys of the Begam of Bhopal, 1901–1930' in Tony Ballantyne and Antoinette Burton (eds), *Bodies in Contact: Rethinking Colonial Encounters in World History* (Durham: Duke University Press, 2005), 293–309.

31. Shaharyar M. Khan, 'Bhopal a Brief History' in John Falconer (ed.), *The Waterhouse Albums. Central Indian Provinces* (Ahmedabad: Mapin, 2009), esp. 138–41.

32. Shah Jahan to Lord Mayo, 17 September 1870, Mayo papers, Cambridge University Library, Add. Ms. 7490, 102/1. Henry Durand and Charles Aitchison, the Viceroy's senior officials in Calcutta, advised against any such correspondence: Aitchison to O. T. Burne, 7 November 1870, ibid., 102/4; cf. Lord Mayo to Queen Victoria, 9 November 1870 (enclosing a letter from the Begum), RA VIC/MAIN/N/28/23–4.

33. Nawab Shahjahan, *The taj-ul ikbal tarikh Bhopal, or, the History of Bhopal*, trans. H. C. Barstow, (Calcutta: Thacker, Spink and Co., 1876); Viceroy to the Begum, 15 July 1875. Foreign Dept Proceedings, NAI, 158.

34. Queen Victoria to Mary Curzon, 19 January 1900, IOR Mss Eur. F306/35, fols 12–15.

35. Dufferin to Queen Victoria, 1 September 1885, Dufferin papers, PRONI, D1071/H/M/MI/I, no. 40; Queen Victoria to Dufferin, 7 May 1886, ibid., no. 31. For Siddiq Hasan, see: Metcalf, 'Islam and Power in Colonial India'; Caroline Keen, 'The Rise and Fall of Siddiq Hasan, Male Consort of Shah Jahan of Bhopal' in Beem and Taylor (eds), *The Man Behind the Queen*, 185–204.

36. The queen agreed to the rules and insignia: Queen Victoria to Lord Salisbury, 9 October 1877, 6 January 1878, 3rd Marquess Salisbury papers, Hatfield House; cf. Sourindro Mohun Tagore, *Orders of Knighthood* (Calcutta: the author, 1884), 185–7.

37. For these three Bengali maharanis, see: Roper Lethbridge, *The Golden Book of India: A Genealogical and Biographical Dictionary of the Ruling Princes, Chiefs, Nobles, and Other Personages, Titled or Decorated, of the Indian Empire; With an Appendix for Ceylon* (London: Sampson Low, Marston & Co., 1900), 153, 171, 524. In 1876 Queen Victoria was conjoined with Sham Moini in a poem praising their 'charitable and virtuous acts': Rajinath Chatterji, *Bangangana-kavya; or, Poems on the Women of Bengal* (Barsial: Satyaprakash Press, 1876), QLB (Bengal).

38. The despatches describing the ceremonies are collected together at IOR L/P&S/15/16, a copy of which was sent on to Henry Ponsonby, the queen's private secretary.

39. For the background, see: Anil Kumar Sarkar, *British Paramountcy and the Cooch Behar State: A Study of the Anatomy of Indirect Rule in Cooch Behar* (Delhi: Abhijeet Publications, 2011); Joydeep Pal, *The Untold History of the Princely State of Cooch Behar* (Kolkata: Sopan, 2015); Lucy Moore, *Maharanis: The Life and Times of Three Generations of Indian Princesses* (London: Viking, 2004), chs 3, 5.

40. Queen Victoria to Lady Dufferin, 19 May 1887, Dufferin papers, PRONI, D1231/G/11. In retrospect, the queen thought that the Maharaja was 'too European' and that would do him harm in his own country: Queen Victoria to Lord Dufferin, 22 September 1887, Dufferin papers, PRONI, D1071/H/M/1, no. 54; cf. Suniti Devi, *The Autobiography of an Indian Princess* (London: John Murray, 1921), ch. 8.

41. Suniti Devi, *Nine Ideal Indian Women* (Calcutta; Thacker, Spink & Co., 1919); idem., *The Rajput Princesses* (New Delhi: Aryan Books International, 1992); idem., *The Life of Princess Yashodara: Wife and Disciple of the Lord Buddha* (London: Elkin Mathews and Marrot, 1929).

42. *The Times*, 22 November 1892, 6; ibid., 2 July 1900, 11. For two recent nuanced readings of the Gaekwar's 'modernity', see: Manu Belur Bhagavan, 'Demystifying the "Ideal Progressive": Resistance through Mimicked Modernity in Princely Baroda, 1900–1913', *Modern Asian Studies* 35 (2001), 385–410; Toolika Gupta, 'The Impact of British Rule on the Dressing Sensibilities of Indian Aristocrats: A Case Study of the Maharaja of Baroda's Dress' in Marie-Louise Nosch, Zhao Feng and Lotika Varadarajan (eds), *Global Textile Encounters* (Oxford: Oxbow Books, 2014), 199–204.

43. Sayagi Rao Baroda, 'My Ways and Days in Europe and India', *Nineteenth Century* 49 (February 1901), 223–4.

44. Her Highness the Maharani of Baroda and S. M. Mitra, *The Position of Women in Indian Life* (London: Longmans, Green and Co., 1911), 20–1.

45. Stafford Northcote to General Grey, 13 October 1867, RA VIC/MAIN/N/27/76; QVJl., 7 November 1867.

46. QVJl., 13 March 1868.

47. QVJl., 13 August 1870; *Keshub Chunder Sen in England*, 2 vols (Calcutta: Brahmo Tract Society, 1881–2), ii, 123–5. See also: David Kopf, *The Brahmo Sumaj and the Shaping of the Modern Indian Mind* (Princeton, NJ: Princeton University Press, 179), 261–2. For his life, see: John A. Stevens, *Keshab: Bengal's Forgotten Prophet* (London: Hurst, 2018).

48. Mary Carpenter, *On Female Education in India* (London: W. W. Head, 1868), 8. Much has been written about Mary Carpenter and India, without noting her connections to the queen: Antoinette Burton, 'Fearful Bodies into Disciplined Subjects: Pleasure, Romance, and the Family Drama of Colonial Reform in Mary Carpenter's *Six Months in India*', *Signs: Journal of Women in Culture & Society* 20 (1995), 545–74; Ruth Watts, 'Breaking the Boundaries of Victorian Imperialism or Extending a Reformed "Paternalism"? Mary Carpenter and India', *History of Education* 29 (2000) 443–56; Clare Midgley, 'Mary Carpenter and the Brahmo Samaj of India: A Transnational Perspective on Social Reform in the Age of Empire', *Women's History Review* 22 (2013), 363–85; Chieko Ichikawa, 'Jane Eyre's Daughters: The Feminist Missions of Mary Carpenter and Josephine Butler in India', *Women's History Review* 23 (2014), 220–38; Tim Allender, *Learning Femininity in Colonial India, 1820–1932* (Manchester: Manchester University Press, 2016), ch. 3.

49. Princess Alice hosted a visit by Mary Carpenter to Darmstadt in 1872: Alice to Queen Victoria, 13 October 1872 in *Alice, Grand Duchess of Hesse, Princess of Great Britain and Ireland. Letters to Her Majesty the Queen* (London: John Murray, 1885), 252–3. For Mary Carpenter's visit to India in 1876, see: *Journal of the National Indian Association*, 63 (July 1876), 195–208.

50. Duchess of Connaught to Queen Victoria, 4 February 1887, 18 March 1887, RA VIC/MAIN/Z/182/9; entry for 18 February 1887, Duchess of Connaught Diaries, RA VIC/ADD Add. Mss/A15/8445. *ToI*, 1 October 1886, 5; ibid., 3 March 1888, 3; ibid., 28 September 1888, 4. For official wives in India, see: Mary A. Procida, *Married to the Empire: Gender, Politics and Imperialism in India, 1883–1947* (Manchester: Manchester University Press, 2002), chs 6–7.

51. *ToI*, 14 December 1889, 5.

52. For Ramabai's own appeal to the queen, see: Ramabai, 'The Cry of Indian Women' (1883) in *Pandita Ramabai Through Her Own Words: Selected Works*, ed. Meera Kosambi (New Delhi: Oxford University Press, 2000), 111. For Ramabai, see: Antoinette Burton, 'Colonial Encounters in Late-Victorian England: Pandita Ramabai at Cheltenham and Wantage, 1883–1886', *Feminist Review*, 49 (1995), 29–49; Meera Kosambi, 'Multiple Contestations: Pandita Ramabai's Educational and Missionary Activities in Late Nineteenth-century India and Abroad', *Women's History Review* 7 (1998), 193–208.

53. QVJl., 13 July 1881. For the full story, see: Sean Lang, 'Colonial Compassion and Political Calculation: The Countess of Dufferin and Her Fund' in Poonam Bula (ed.), *Contesting Colonial Authority: Medicine and Indigenous Responses in Nineteenth and Twentieth Century India* (Lanham: Lexington Books, 2012), 81–96.

54. QVJl., 12 July 1883. For the 'moral influence' of the queen see: Mrs Grant Duff to Ponsonby, 10 May 1885, IOR Mss Eur. F234/54, fols 117–18. For princely support for the venture, especially from the Raja of Venkatagiri and the Maharaja of Vizianagram, see: *Report of the Victoria Hospital for Caste and Gosha Women, Madras, for 1895* (Madras: Government Press, 1895), 20–2.

55. QVJl., 22 October 1884.

56. Henry Ponsonby to Adolphus Moore, 29 September 1885 (private secretary to Randolph Churchill), Randolph Churchill papers, Churchill Archives Centre, Cambridge, 1/8/929. For the Fund, see: Lang, 'Colonial Compassion'; Maneesha Lal, 'The Politics of Gender and Medicine in Colonial India: The Countess of Dufferin's Fund, 1885–1888', *Bulletin*

of the History of Medicine 68 (1994), 29–66; Daniel Sanjiv Roberts, ' "Merely Birds of Passage": Lady Hariot Dufferin's Travel Writings and Medical Work in India, 1884–1888', *Women's History Review* 15 (2006), 443–57. For royal philanthropy in general, see: Frank Prochaska, *Royal Bounty: The Making of a Welfare Monarchy* (London: Yale University Press, 1995), 114–21.

57. 'Prospectus', *The Times*, 5 October 1885, 12; Countess of Dufferin, *A Record of Three Years' Work of the National Association for Supplying Female Medical Aid to the Women of India: August 1885 to August 1888* (Calcutta: Thacker, Spink and Co., 1888), 9, 16; idem., 'The National Association for Supplying Female Medical Aid to India', *Asiatic Quarterly Review* (April 1886), 257–74.

58. Countess of Dufferin to Queen Victoria, 7 August 1885, 14 August 1885, 6 October 1885, RA VIC/MAIN/M/59/17–18, 23; Dufferin, *A Record of Three Years' Work*, 57–8.

59. 'Minutes of the Proceedings of the Central Committee', 23 December 1886, 18 January 1888, Dufferin papers, PRONI, D1071/J/G/1A/2.

60. *British Medical Journal*, 11 July 1896, 89. cf. John Bradley (ed.), *Lady Curzon's India: Letters of a Vicereine* (London: Weidenfeld & Nicolson, 1985), 28. For the UK organisation, see: *The Times*, 15 May 1890, 5; National Association for Supplying Female Medical Aid to the Women of India, circular (n.d., *c.* 1890), Dufferin papers, PRONI, D1071 J/G/4A/3.

61. For criticism: *British Medical Journal*, 14 December 1895, 1527, 7 July 1900, 41, 17 August 1901, 423–4.

62. *ToI*, 3 February 1888, 6; Dufferin, *A Record of Three Years' Work*, 35. See also the address sent to Lady Dufferin 'On Behalf of the Benares Women' (6 April 1886), which is more of a paen to the empress: Dufferin papers, PRONI, D1071/J/D/7.

63. Countess of Dufferin to Queen Victoria, n.d. 1886, RA VIC/MAIN/M/60/4.

64. Kipling, 'For the Women' (1885) in *Early Verse by Rudyard Kipling, 1879–1889: Unpublished, Uncollected, and Rarely Collected Poems*, ed. Andrew Rutherford (Oxford: Oxford University Press, 1986), 363. For the insistence on respecting purdah: 'Minutes of the Proceedings of the Central Committee' (27 April 1888), 3, Dufferin papers, PRONI, D1071/J/G/1A/2.

65. Malabari, 'True and False Sati and Free and Enforced Widowhood' (1886), 'The Queen's Own Wards' (1887) in Dayaram Gidumal, *Life and Life-work of Behramji M. Malabari* (Bombay: Educations, 1888), 162, 220. On Malabari, see: Gráinne Goodwin, 'A Trustworthy Interpreter Between Rulers and Ruled: Behramji Malabari, Colonial and Cultural Interpreter in Nineteenth-century British India', *Social History* 38 (2013), 1–25. Queen Victoria's mother was widowed in 1814, marrying again four years later.

66. Bhownagree to Adelaide Manning, 23 August 1887, Cambridge University Library, Add. Ms. 6379/19. For the Rukhmabhai case, see: Antoinette Burton, 'From Child Bride to "Hindoo Lady": Rukhmabai and the Debate on Sexual Responsibility in Imperial Britain', *American Historical Review* 103 (1998), 1119–46; Sudhir Chandra, *Enslaved Daughters: Colonialism, Law and Women's Rights* (New Delhi: Oxford University Press, 2008), ch. 1.

67. Ponsonby to Wodehouse, 15 December 1892, 17 December 1892, 18 December 1892, Bodleian Library, Ms Eng c. 4316, fols 40–44. For the 1890 campaign, see: Malabari, *An Appeal from the Daughters of India* (London: Farmer & Sons, 1890), 20; *Story of Widow Remarriage: Being the Experiences of Madhowdas Rugnathdas, Merchant of Bombay* (Bombay: S. K. Khambataj, 1890); Jennie Fuller, *The Wrongs of Indian Womanhood* (Edinburgh: Oliphant, Anderson and Ferrier, 1900), 197.

68. For the background, see: Janaki Nair, 'Uncovering the Zenana: Visions of Indian Women in Englishwomen's Writings, 1813–1940', *Journal of Women's History* 2 (1990), 8–34; Karen E. Smith, 'Women in Cultural Captivity: British Women and the Zenana Mission', *Baptist History and Heritage* 41 (2006), 30–41; Rhonda Semple, 'Ruth, Miss Mackintosh,

and Ada and Rose Marris: Biblewomen, Zenana Workers and Missionaries in Nineteenth-century British Missions to North India', *Women's History Review* 17 (2008), 561–74.

69. *India's Women* (Church of England Zenana Missionary Society), 17 (May 1897). Cf. Mrs Malcolm Ross, *Scattered Seeds; Or, Five Years' Zenana Work in Poona* (Edinburgh: Blackwood & Sons, 1880), 31–2; Helen Lloyd, *Hindu Women: With Glimpses into their Life and Zenanas* (London: James Nisbet & Co., 1882), 43.

70. *Telugu Zenana Magazine* (March 1900) (QLB, Madras). For the background, see: Deborah Ann Logan, *The Indian Ladies' Magazine, 1901–1938: From Raj to Swaraj* (Lanham: Lehigh University Press, 2017), 14–15.

71. *Missionary Herald*, 1 April 1887, 121–4. Another organisation, the 'Helping Hands Zenana Association', welcomed an Urdu life of the queen published for the jubilee by the American mission in Lucknow: *Indian Jewels*, 4 (December 1888), 161–2. In the spring of 1897, the Church of England Zenana Missionary Society reprinted a series of leaflets and articles about the queen and her reign for distribution in India: Publications Committee Minutes, 24 March 1897, 26 May 1897, 104, 110, CEZMS papers, Church Missionary Society Archive, University of Birmingham, CEZ/G/C4.

72. *India's Women*, 21 (March 1901), 49–51.

73. Countess of Dufferin to Queen Victoria, 19 February 1885, RA VIC/MAIN/M/59/6; Duchess of Connaught to Queen Victoria, 18 March 1887, RA VIC/MAIN/Z/182/22.

74. *The Times*, 15 April 1891, 11; *The Duke of Connaught and the Bible Society* (London: British and Foreign Bible Society, 1893).

75. 'Annual Breakfast Meeting' (30 April 1890), *Our Indian Sisters* (Baptist Missionary Society Ladies' Zenana Mission), n.s., 3, July 1890, 33–9.

76. Elizabeth W. Andrew and Katherine C. Bushnell, *The Queen's Daughters in India* (London: Morgan & Scott, 1898), 57–62, 86. For Bushnell and her campaign in India, see: Kristin Kobes du Mez, *A New Gospel for Women: Katharine Bushnell and the Challenge of Christian Feminism* (New York: Oxford University Press, 2015), 67–71.

77. An Urdu book described the queen's philanthropy alongside that of Elizabeth Fry and Princess Alice: Saiyid Ahmad, *Akhlaq un Nisa/Manners of Woman* (Delhi: Akmal-ul-Matabi Press, 1891), QLB (North-West Provinces).

10 Patriot Queen

1. QVJl., 12 February, 14 February 1872.

2. W. W. Hunter, *The Indian Musulmans: Are they Bound in Conscience to Rebel against the Queen?*, 2nd edn (London: Trubner & Co., 1872), 114, 117; cf. M. Mohar Ali, 'Hunter's Indian Mussulmans: A Re-examination of its Background', *Journal of the Royal Asiatic Society* 112 (1980), 30–1.

3. QVJl., 11 May 1872, 3 August 1872; 'Major Burne's Statement of Service, with Appendices' (privately printed, 1879), 72, IOR Mss Eur. D351/1.

4. Paul Thomas Murphy, *Shooting Victoria: Madness, Mayhem, Modernisation and the Monarchy* (London: Pegasus, 2012).

5. 'Petition to the House of Commons, etc.', (n.d., *c.* June 1859), British India Association papers, NMML, Delhi; Ram Gopal Sanyal, *The Life of the Hon'ble. Rai Kristo Das Pal Bahadur, C. I. E.* (Calcutta: Ram Coomar Dey, 1886), 10, 110–12.

6. Naoroji, 'England's Duties to India', *Journal of the East India Association*, i (2 May 1867), 31–2 (Naoroji). For Naoroji and the East India Association, see: S. R. Mehotra and Dinyar Patel (eds), *Dadabhai Naoroji: Selected Private Papers* (New Delhi: Oxford University Press, 2016), xvii–xix.

7. Partha Chatterjee, *Nationalist Thought and the Colonial World: A Derivative Discourse?* (London: Zed 1986); cf. Dipesh Chakrabarty, *Provincialising Europe: Postcolonial Thought and Its Discontents* (Princeton, NJ: Princeton University Press, 2000), ch. 1.

8. Anil Seal, *The Emergence of Indian Nationalism: Competition and Collaboration in the Later Nineteenth Century* (Cambridge: Cambridge University Press, 1968), chs 5–6; Jim Masselos, *Towards Nationalism: Group Affiliations and the Politics of Public Associations in Nineteenth Century Western India* (Bombay: Popular Prakashan, 1974). For revisionist approaches to the ideology of early Indian nationalism, see: Sanjay Seth, 'Rewriting Histories of Nationalism: The Politics of Moderate Nationalism in India, 1870–1905', *American Historical Review* 104 (1999), 95–116; C. A. Bayly, *Recovering Liberties: Indian Thought in the Age of Liberalism and Empire* (Cambridge: Cambridge University Press, 2012).

9. The original petition is at: IOR Mss Eur. A/1/94. For the discussion in Parliament, see: HC Debs, 206 (13 June 1871), 2023–42.

10. Naoroji, *To the Electors of the Holborn Division of Finsbury* (London: Foulger & Co., 1886), 1.

11. *Quarterly Journal of the Poona Sarvajanik Sabha* 1 (1878), 22–46; ibid., 2 (1880), 132–3.

12. *Bengalee*, 6 January 1877, 4.

13. Syed Ahmed Khan, *The Causes of the Indian Revolt* [1873] (Karachi: Oxford University Press, 2000), 49; Syed Ahmed Khan to John Kaye, 14 December 1869, in M. I. Pani Pati (ed.), *Letters to and from Sir Syed Ahmed Khan* (Lahore: Board for Advancement of Literature, 1993), 81–4; M. Mohar Ali, 'Hunter's Indian Mussulmans'.

14. Hunter, *Indian Mussulmans*; Syed Ahmed Khan, *Dr Hunter's 'Our Indian Mussulmans – are they Bound in Conscience to Revolt against the Queen?'* (London: Henry S. King & Co., 1872), 75–6, 104.

15. *Abstract of Proceedings of the Mahomedan Literary Society of Calcutta at a Meeting Held on . . . the 23rd November, 1870 etc.* (Calcutta: Mahomedan Literary Society, 1871), 7–8, 12, 14–15.

16. Syed Ahmed Khan to Captain Evelyn Baring, 5 August 1872, Syed Ahmed Khan to Col. J. C. Ardagh, 11 May 1894, in A. A. Siddiqi (ed.), *Sir Syed's Correspondence* (Aligarh: AMU Press, 1990), 11, 186–91; Syed Ahmed Khan to Major T. Cadell, 10 February 1876, in S. Muhammed (ed.), *Sir Syed's Correspondence: Selected Documents from the Sir Syed Academy Archives* (Aligarh: AMU Press, 1995), 6–7. For some of the background, see: A. R. Khan, *The All-India Muslim Educational Conference: Its Contribution to the Cultural Development of Muslims, 1886–1947* (Karachi: Oxford University Press, 2001), chs 1–2.

17. G .F. I. Graham, *The Life and Work of Syed Ahmed Khan, C. S. I* (Edinburgh: W. Blackwood, 1885), 171–80.

18. 'List of Loyal Addresses', IOR Mss Eur. G55/44, 48

19. Sir James Fergusson, the governor of Bombay, advised against accepting an address from the Poona Sabha on the grounds that it was being sent directly to London, without going via the Government of Bombay: Fergusson to Lord Hartington, 24 March 1882, IOR Mss Eur. E214/3, fols 169–71.

20. 'Ripon our father' (in Tamil).

21. QVJl., 26 April 1880; Tony Denholm, 'Robinson, George Frederick Samuel, First Marquess of Ripon (1827–1909)', *ODNB*.

22. Ram Chandra Palit (ed.) *Speeches and Published Resolutions of Lord Ripon, etc.* (Calcutta: J. W. Thomas, 1882), 83, 86, 91.

23. Sarvepalli Gopal, *The Viceroyalty of Lord Ripon, 1880–1884* (London: Oxford University Press, 1953), chs 5–7, 14.

24. Ibid., ch. 8.

25. R. C. J. Cocks, 'Ilbert, Sir Courtenay Peregrine (1841–1924)', *ODNB*; Mary Bennett, *The Ilberts in India, 1882–1886: An Imperial Miniature* (London: BACSA, 1995). For the controversy, see: Edwin Hirschmann, *'White Mutiny': The Ilbert Bill Crisis in India and the Genesis of the Indian National Congress* (New Delhi: Heritage, 1980); Chandrika Kaul, 'England and India: The Ilbert bill, 1883. A Case Study of the Metropolitan Press', *Indian Economic and Social History Review* 30 (1993), 413–36.

26. 'Further Papers on the Proposed Alteration of the Provisions of the Indian Code of Criminal Procedure, etc.', *Parl. Papers* (1884), Cd. 3877, p. 509 ('guarded'); 'Further Papers and Correspondence on the Subject of the Proposed Alteration of the Provisions of the Indian Code of Criminal Procedure, etc.', *Parl. Papers* (1884), Cd. 3952, 465–6, 543, 546 ('specious sophism').

27. *Som Prakash*, 18 June 1883, NNR (Bengal), IOR L/5/9, p. 331. For the ladies' petition, see: 'Further Papers on the . . . Indian Code of Criminal Procedure', 461; cf. *ToI*, 6 April 1883, 3, 5 June 1883, 5.

28. *Alok*, 7 September 1883, NNR (Bengal), IOR L/5/9, p. 584; R. Krishna Singh, *Lord Ripon's Policy. Observations on the Criminal Jurisdiction Bill* (Bangalore: Caxton Press, 1883), 28.

29. James Fitzjames Stephen, *The Ilbert Bill* (London: Macmillan and Co., 1883), 29, 39.

30. *The Times*, 30 March 1883, 10; 'An Englishman', *Lord Ripon's Policy in India: An Appeal to the People of England* (London: National Union of Conservative and Constitutional Associations, 1883).

31. William Summers, *The Ilbert Bill* (Manchester: National Reform Union, 1883).

32. Surprisingly, Ilbert received support from Henry Maine: Maine to Ilbert, 26 April 1883, IOR Mss Eur. D554/15, fols 16–19.

33. 'Further Papers and Correspondence on . . . the Indian Code of Criminal Procedure', 113, 117, 145.

34. Ponsonby to Ripon, 28 April 1883, BL, Add. Ms. 43, 350, fols 137–8; Queen Victoria to Ripon, 7 June 1883, ibid., fols 139–42, Queen Victoria to Ripon, 16 August 1883, ibid., fols 143–6.

35. Queen Victoria to Ripon, 11 October 1883, ibid., 43, 530, fols 147–8; Ponsonby to [William] Maitland, 25 October 1883, Kimberley papers, Bodleian Library, Oxford, Ms. Eng. 4205, fols 61–4, Ponsonby to [Robert] Bickerstreth, 1 November 1883, ibid., fols 73–4.

36. Ripon to Kimberley, 8 December 1883, BL, B.P. 7/3, vol. 4, no. 78a; *ToI*, 12 March 1883, 6, 31 December 1883, 4.

37. *Quarterly Journal of the Poona Sarvajanik Sabha*, 4 (July 1883), 1–3; *The Public Meeting in Honour of Lord Ripon on his Retirement from the Viceroyalty, etc.* (Bombay: Bombay Gazette, 1884); *India's Farewell to Lord Ripon* (n.p., n.d., *c.* 1885), 2.

38. Wilfrid Scawen Blunt, *India under Lord Ripon* (London: T. Fisher Unwin, 1909), 325; QVJl., 5 March 1885.

39. For the early years of the INC, see: Anthony Parel, 'Hume, Dufferin and the Origins of the Indian Congress', *Journal of Indian History*, 42 (1964), 707–25; John R. McLane, *Indian Nationalism and the Early Congress* (Princeton, NJ: Princeton University Press, 1977); S. R. Mehrotra, *A History of the Indian National Congress, vol. 1: 1885–1918* (New Delhi: Vikas, 1995), ch. 1; Amitabha Mukerjee, 'Genesis of the Indian National Congress' in N. R. Ray (ed.), *A Centenary History of the Indian National Congress, vol. 1: 1885–1919* (New Delhi: Academic Foundation, 2011), 81–115.

40. Mushirul Hasan (ed.), *Proceedings of the Indian National Congress, vol. 1, 1885–1889* (New Delhi: Nyogi, 2012), 61 (Madras 1887), lv (Allahabad 1888); *The Indian National Congress: Session at Allahabad, December 1888. Impressions of Two English Visitors, etc.* (London: Indian Political Agency, 1889), 19, 21.

41. Hasan (ed.), *Proceedings of the Indian National Congress, vol. 1*, 22 (Subramania Iyer, Bombay 1885), 65 (Dadabhai Naoroji, Bombay 1885), 56, (Dadabhai Naoroji, Calcutta 1886), lvi (Madan Mohan Malaviya, Allahabad 1888), 50, 52 (Ghokale and Ali Mohamed Bhimjee, Bombay 1889); idem. (ed.), *Proceedings of the Indian National Congress, vol. 2: 1890–1894* (New Delhi: Nyogi Books, 2014), xi (Lal Mohan Ghose, Calcutta 1890), 51 (Pran Nath Sarawati, Nagpur 1891), 28 (Suredranath Banerjee, Allahabad 1892), 38 (Dadabhai Naoroji, Lahore 1893), 77–8 (Rashan Lal, Lahore 1893), 10–11 (Rungiah Naidu, Madras 1894), 83 (Surendranath Bannerjee, Madras 1894); *Report of the Twelfth*

Indian National Congress held at Calcutta, etc. (Calcutta: Star Press, 1897), 30 (Rahimatullah Sayani); *The Indian National Congress. Its Origin, History, Constitution and Objects* (Madras: National Press, 1888), 84–5.

42. Hasan (ed.), *Proceedings of the Indian National Congress, vol. 1*, 139 (Singarajee Venkata Subbraryudu Pautulu, Calcutta 1885); idem. (ed.), *Proceedings of the Indian National Congress, vol. 2*, xxviii (Ambika C. Mozamder, Madras 1894); *Report of the Twelfth Indian National Congress*, 63 (Rahimtullah Sayani); cf. 'Mother and Mother Country are more estimable than Heaven itself', in Bipin Bihari Bose, *Congress Songs and Ballads* (Lucknow: Sukh Sambad Press, 1901); *The Indian National Congress . . . Impressions of Two English Visitors*, 23 (W. S. Caine).

43. Hasan (ed.), *Proceedings of the Indian National Congress, vol. 1*, 60; Kaushik Roy, 'India' in Ian F. W. Beckett (ed.), *Citizen Soldiers and the British Empire, 1837–1902* (London: Pickering & Chatto, 2016), 112–16.

44. Hasan (ed.), *Proceedings of the Indian National Congress, vol. 1*, 50 (1886 Rajendralala Mitra).

45. Hasan (ed.), *Proceedings, vol. 1*, 1(1885), 44 (1886); Hasan (ed.), *Proceedings, vol. 2*, 2 (1892).

46. Hasan (ed.), *Proceedings, vol. 1*, 27 (1886).

47. *Northampton Mercury*, 24 November 1883, 4; *ibid.*, 29 June 1889, 3; HC Debs, 330 (9 August 1888), 148–59; ibid., 336 (31 May 1889), 1633–8. See also, Bradlaugh, 'India and the Ilbert Bill', *Our Corner* 3 (February 1884), 77–82. David S. Nash, 'Charles Bradlaugh, India and the Many Chameleon Destinations of Republicanism' in David S. Nash and Antony Taylor (eds), *Republicanism in Victorian Society* (Stroud: Sutton, 2000), 106–24.

48. *Mr Bradlaugh and the House of Commons. From a Hindoo Point of View* (London: Swan Sonnenschein, 1884), a sympathetic portrait, described Bradlaugh's position on not being allowed to take up his seat in Parliament as leaving him a 'man without caste' (p. 8).

49. Charles Bradlaugh, *The Impeachment of the House of Brunswick* (London: Freethought Publishing Co., 1874), 55–6. This pamphlet went through ten editions by 1891; HC Debs, 337 (9 July 1889), 1850–53.

50. Hasan (ed.) *Proceedings, vol. 1* (1889), lxviii–lxix; Bradlaugh, 'The Indian National Congress, What It Is and What It Demands', *New Review* 2 (March 1890), 242–53.

51. Bishan Narayan Dar, *Mr Bradlaugh's Indian Reform Bill* (Lucknow: G. P. Varma and Bros 1890); Hasan (ed.), *Proceedings, vol. 1* (1889), 17.

52. Hasan (ed.), *Proceedings, vol. 1* (1889), 86. Of the twenty addresses to Bradlaugh that have survived, seven (Awadh, Benares, Dacca, Kanpur, Madras (Triplicane Literary Society), Satara and Sirsi) lauded the queen-empress as well: Charles Bradlaugh papers, Hackney Archives, C. L. R. James Library, D/F/BRA/1/1–5, D/F/BRA/7/2–15.

53. For example, Romesh C. Dutt, 'Indian Aspirations under British Rule' in W. C. Bonerjee (ed.), *Indian Politics* (Madras: G. A. Natesan, 1898), 57.

54. *ToI*, 25 December 1888, 5. Privately, Dufferin assured Queen Victoria that the INC was not disloyal: 'the most extravagant Bengalee Baboo that ever "slung ink" . . . cherishes at heart a deep devotion to your Majesty's person', Dufferin to Queen Victoria, 31 March 1887, Dufferin papers, PRONI, D10171/H/MI/I, no. 64

55. *Audi alteram partem: Being Two Letters on Certain Aspects of the Indian National Congress Movement, with an Appendix, etc.* (Simla: Station Press, 1888); *Two Memorable Speeches of Eardley Norton, Delivered at Patchcappah's Hall, Madras, etc.* (Lucknow: G. P. Varma and Bros, 1889), 13–14; Eardley Norton, 'The Indian National Congress' in Bonerjee (ed.), *Indian Politics*, 27.

56. 'Abstract of Secret Intelligence from the Special Branch of the Thugee and Dacoity Department' (1887–8), Dufferin papers, PRONI, D1071/H/M/11/2.

57. For the UIPA's support, see: *The Seditious Character of the Indian National Congress, and the Opinions Held by Eminent Natives of India who are Opposed to the Movement* (Allahabad:

Pioneer Press, 1888), iv, xv–xxxi. For the petition: Salim al-Din Quraishi (ed.), *Correspondence of Sir Syed Ahmed Khan and his Contemporaries* (Lahore: Sang-e-Meel Publications, 1998), 139–45. For the background: Zafur-ul-Islam, 'Documents on Indo-Muslim Politics (1857–1947): The Aligarh Political Activism (1888–93)', *Journal of the Pakistan Historical Society* 12 (1964), 14–25; Francis Robinson, *Separatism Among Indian Muslims: The Politics of the United Provinces' Muslims, 1860–1923* (Cambridge: Cambridge University Press, 1974), 120–1.

58. 'Speech at Lucknow' (28 December 1887) in Syed Ahmed Khan, *The Present State of Indian Politics. Speeches and Letters* (1888; Lahore: Sang-e-Meed Publications, 1982 edn), 12; cf. Syed Khan, 'The National Congress and the Government of Madras', *Aligarh Institute Gazette*, 11 September 1888, 1023–6. For the attribution of Syed Khan's authorship of articles in the *Gazette*, see: Asghar Abbas, *Print Culture: Sir Syed's Aligarh Institute Gazette, 1866–1897* (Delhi: Primus Books, 2015), 126–37.

59. Bilgrami, 'Letter to the UIPA' in *Present State*, 52–3; cf. Raja of Bhinga, 'Democracy not Suited to India' in *Seditious Character of the INC*, 2.

60. Syed Ahmed Khan to the Maharaja of Patiala, 25 August 1888, in *Sir Syed Correspondence*, comp. Siddiqui, 116–18; Beck, 'In What Will it End?', *Aligarh Institute Gazette*, 29 May 1888, 595–603.

11 Jujubilee

1. *Bangabasi*, 12 February 1887, ibid., 26 February 1887, NNR (Bengal), IOR L/R/5/13, 202, 252. For the newspaper, see: Shyamananda Banerjee, *National Awakening and the Bangabasi* (Calcutta: Amitava-Kalyan 1968).

2. 'Lists of Addresses and Presents' (1887), TNA LC2/115. In 1897 the Lord Chamberlain's office listed only sixty-two ornamental addresses from India, out of a total from the UK and overseas of 469: 'Catalogue of Her Majesty's Diamond Jubilee Presents, 1897', TNA LC2/146. However, these comprised only a selection from those sent on by the Government of India, which itself recorded a total of 263 addresses: NAI, Home Dept Proceedings (September, 1897), 573. Even that was probably a low estimate of the total. The Bombay government listed over 140 addresses alone: MSA, Political Dept Proceedings (1897), vol. 104, *passim*.

3. Cross to Dufferin, 13 August 1886, IOR Mss Eur. E243/17; Henry Ponsonby to Charles Bradley (the Dean of Westminster Abbey), 17 October 1886, Jubilee correspondence, Muniment Room, Westminster Abbey, 394.4; Cross to Dufferin, 3 February 1887, 11 February 1887, IOR Mss Eur. F130/9, 15–18. For the 1887 jubilee, see: John Fabb, *Victoria's Golden Jubilee* (London: B. T. Seaby, 1987); Thomas Richards, 'The Image of Victoria in the Year of Jubilee', *Victorian Studies* 31 (1987), 7–32.

4. Francis Knollys to Ponsonby, 9 December 1886, RA PPTO/PP/QV/ADDX/G/16; Ponsonby to Queen Victoria, 19 February 1887, RA VIC/MAIN/F/45/81; *The Times*, 13 May 1890, 5.

5. Dufferin to Cross, 27 August 1886, IOR Mss Eur E243/22, 4; Cross to Dufferin, 22 September 1886, IOR Mss Eur. E243/17, fol. 17.

6. Charles Lawson (comp.), *Narrative of the Celebration of the Jubilee of Her Most Gracious Majesty Queen Victoria, Empress of India, in the Presidency of Madras* (London: Macmillan, 1887), 1–3; *ToI*, 30 November 1886, 5 (Bombay).

7. Dufferin to Cross, 23 November 1886, IOR Mss Eur. E243/22, fol. 6; Cross to Dufferin, 25 November 1886, 16 December 1886, IOR Mss Eur. E243/17; Dufferin to Queen Victoria (telegram), 18 December 1886, Dufferin papers, PRONI, D1071/H/MI/1, no. 59.

8. Printed circular, 8 February 1887, MSA, Pol. Proceedings, vol. 57.

9. Telegram from the Foreign Dept, Government of India to the Political Dept, Bombay, 17 January 1887, MSA, Political Proceedings, 1887, vol. 56.

10. NAI Foreign Proceedings, International A, (July 1887), 141–8 (relaxation of rules); *ILN*, 17 September 1887, 336 (Mysore); ibid., 24 September 1887, 369 (Travancore).

11. O. T. Burne, 'The Empress of India', *Asiatic Quarterly Review* 3 (January 1887), 11–31; cf. O. T. Burne, *Memories* (London: Edward Arnold, 1907), 298–301.

12. Printed circular (Imperial Institute), 24 January 1887, MSA, Political Proceedings, 1887, vol. 61; 'The Countess of Dufferin's Fund: Jubilee Year' 14 October 1886 (printed circular), Dufferin papers, PRONI, D1071 J/6/8/1.

13. *Ananda Bazar Patrika*, 14 February 1887, NNR (Bengal) IOR L/R/5/13, 203–4 (criticism of royal family involvement); *Dakar Prakash*, 2 January 1887, ibid., 78 (distribution of wealth and repeal of the Arms Act); *Sanjivani*, 15 January 1887, ibid., 101–2 (more Indians in the administration); *Mahratta*, 6 February 1887, NNR (Bombay), IOR L/R/5/112, 4 (pressure on the poor); *Indu Prakash*, 17 January 1887, ibid., 5 (reform of the Legislative Council); *Poona Vaibhar*, 16 January 1887, ibid., 5–6 (restoration of Indian rulers); *Hindi Pradip*, 27 January 1887, NNR (Punjab, North-West Provinces, etc.), IOR L/R/5/64, p. 119 (Akbar and money being forced from the poor); *Hindoo Patriot*, 17 January 1887, 27 (criticism of the Imperial Institute).

14. For the release of prisoners: *ToI*, 21 February 1887, 7; Randolph Churchill to Queen Victoria, 7 December 1886, RA VIC/MAIN/F/45/24. For the jubilee medal, see: *ILN*, 4 June 1887, 629; For criticism of native honours: *Bangabasi*, 12 February 1887, NNR (Bengal), IOR L/5/13, p.202. A Gujarati writer summed up the dilemma of the travelling princes, criticised if they went, accused of disloyalty if they stayed at home: Ambashankar Gavrishankar, *Devatai svapnun, or the Celestial Dream* (Bombay: the author, 1887), QLB (Bombay). For the list of Indian honours, see: *Englishman*, 16 February 1887, 5.

15. HC Debs, 311 (18 February 1887), 45–6; HL Debs, 311 (22 February 1887), 280–6.

16. NAI, For. Proceedings (1897), Internal B, 42.

17. MSA, Pol. Proceedings (1887), vol. 57, 22 February (Jambusar), ibid., vol. 60, 7 February 1887 (Bandora).

18. For other renditions of this theme, see: Bhai Aya Singh, *Jubilee prakash athwa Sri Bhartesuri da sankhep samachar (Jubilee Sketch of Queen Victoria)* (Lahore: Muifid-i-Am Press, 1889), QLB (Punjab); Behram Dosabhai Basla, *Poem for the Children for the Jubilee of the Queen-Empress Victoria* (Godhra: Nathabjai Lalubhai, 1887), QLB (Bombay); Pandit Lalchand, *Jubilee pramodika, or the Jubilee Rejoicings* (Bombay: Bhimsi Manak, 1887), QLB (Bombay). For criticism of government interference in the wording of addresses: *Sahachar*, 23 February 1887, NNR (Bengal), L/5/13, 250–1.

19. *Madras Standard*, 22 June 1887, 4; Hara Devi, *Landan-jubili* (Lahore: Imperial Press, 1888); *Bombay Gazette*, 21 June 1887, 5; 'A Brief Account of the Action Taken in Connection with the Celebrations of the Jubilee of Her Majesty the Queen Empress in the Various Centres in the Presidency of Bombay', 7 July 1887', MSA, Pol. Proceedings (1887), vol. 64, 12, 26, 79 (pandals, arches and palanquin processions).

20. For examples of this in Kathiawar (Bombay), see: Charles Wodehouse to William Wedderburn, 16 April 1887, MSA, Pol. Proceedings (1887), vol. 63, 190. And in Madras: Lawson, *Narrative of the Celebration of the Jubilee . . . in the Presidency of Madras*, 1–3.

21. *ToI*, 1 March 1887, 4.

22. *ToI*, 21 February 1887, 7; Cross to Dufferin, 17 February 1887, IOR Mss Eur. E243/17, fol. 382.

23. 'A Brief Account of . . . the Celebrations of the Jubilee of Her Majesty the Queen Empress . . . in the Presidency of Bombay', 3, 15.

24. Duchess of Connaught to Queen Victoria, 4 February 1887, Duke of Connaught to Queen Victoria, 17 February 1887, RA VIC/MAIN/Z/182/9, 13.

25. For a list of the addresses and gifts from India, see: *Celebration of Her Majesty's Jubilee, 1887* (London: privately printed, 1887), 136–50; *ToI*, 19 February 1887, 5 (message from the viceroy); RA VIC/MAIN/F/45/45 (Sanskrit and Telugu tributes sent onto the queen) ibid., RA VIC/MAIN/F/45/48–77 (addresses sent onto the queen). A selection of the

1887 addresses are at IOR G55, 1–10; Dufferin to Queen Victoria, 28 February 1887, Dufferin papers, PRONI, D1071/H/MI/I, no. 63.

26. 'List of Feudatory Chiefs who are Expected to be in England on the Occasion of the . . . Jubilee, etc.', IOR L/PS/18/D122. The other three Indian visitors were Kunwar Harnam Singh (the uncle of the Maharaja of Kapurthala), the Thakur of Limri and the Thakur of Gondal. For the presentation of the Cooch Behars at court, see: QVJl., 9 May 1887. For the queen's request for the escort, see: Cross to Dufferin, 11 February 1887, IOR Mss Eur. F130/9, no. 6, and for details of the escort in England, see: IOR L/MIL/7/5767.

27. Dufferin to Cross, 20 March 1887, IOR Mss Eur. F130/8a, fols 48–9; Cross to Dufferin, 22 April 1887, IOR Mss Eur. E243/17, fol. 91; Dufferin to Cross, 21 April 1887, IOR Mss Eur F130/8a, fols 68–70; Pol. Proceedings (1887), NAI, International B, 258–64 ('thoroughly European').

28. Celebration of Her Majesty's Jubilee, 11–12. The Indian guests are depicted in the far background of William Lockhart's oil painting of the occasion (RCIN 404702).

29. Celebration of Her Majesty's Jubilee, 40, 69–74; QVJl., 27 June 1887, 2 July 1887, 14 July 1887; The Times, 15 July 1887, 11.

30. For the history of the Imperial and Colonial Institute, see: William Golant, Image of Empire: The Early History of the Imperial Institute, 1887–1925 (Exeter: University of Exeter, 1984); John Mackenzie, 'The Imperial Institute', Round Table 302 (1987), 246–53; George Bremner, ' "Some Imperial Institute": Architecture, Symbolism and the Ideal of Empire in Late Victorian Britain, 1887–93', Journal of the Society of Architectural Historians 62 (2003), 50–74.

31. The Times, 5 July 1887, 10.

32. Report of the Late Organising Committee, Presented to the Permanent Governing Body (23rd July 1891), etc. (London: Waterlow and Sons, 1892), 9–10; School for Modern Oriental Studies Established in the Imperial Institute . . . Syllabus of Lectures (printed brochure), TNA PRO 30/76/13; Max Müller, School for Modern Oriental Studies Established by the Imperial Institute of the United Kingdom, the Colonies and India, in Union with University College and King's College, London (London: Judd & Co., 1890). For the commercial guides, see: David Muddiman, 'Information and Empire: The Information and Intelligence Bureaux of the Imperial Institute' in Toni Weller (ed.), Information History in the Modern World: Histories of the Modern Age (Basingstoke: Palgrave Macmillan, 2011), 108–29.

33. For membership of the Governing Body, see: The Imperial Institute of the United Kingdom, the Colonies and India, etc. (London: Imperial Institute, 1892), 9. For the fall-off in funds: ToI, 3 September 1891, 4; Indian Daily News, 20 October 1891, 3.

34. Report Presented to the First General Meeting of the Imperial Institute, etc. . . . November 26th 1892 (London: Waterlow and Sons, 1892), 12. For the donations of the Maharaja of Jaipur and Sir Cowasjee Jehangir, see: Imperial Institute, Finance Committee, Minutes, 29 July 1891, 2, 6 September 1893, 104, TNA PRO 30/76/2. For that of Bhavnagar, see: John McLeod, 'Mourning, Philanthropy, and M. M. Bhownaggree's Road to Parliament' in John Hinnells and Alan Williams (ed.), Parsis in India and the Diaspora (Abingdon: Routledge, 2007), 136–56.

35. Moonshine, 20 May 1893, 234–5; Imperial Institute. Opening Ceremony, May 10th 1893 (printed circular), TNA HO45/9871/B14351; W. E. H. Lecky, The Empire, its Value and its Growth: An Inaugural Address Delivered at the Imperial Institute, November 20, 1893 (London: Longmans, Green 1893).

36. For photographs of the Indian cavalry, see: The Sketch, 17 May 1893, 117. The Native Officer's Diary. The Diary Kept by . . . Abdul Razzak of the 1st Madras Lancers, on his Guard of Honor Duty to the Empress of India in the Imperial Institute (Madras: Higginbotham & Co., 1894).

37. Daily Telegraph, 6 May 1893, 4; Graphic, 13 May 1893, 550; ibid., 25 November 1893, 651; ILN, 20 May 1893, 591; George Birdwood, 'The Indian Metal Work Exhibition at the Imperial Institute', Magazine of Art 16 (1893), 172–7.

38. For its history see Gillian Evinson, *The Orientalist, His Institute and the Empire: The Rise and Subsequent Decline of Oxford University's Indian Institute* (2004) available at: www.bodleian.ox.ac.uk/__data/assets/pdf_file/0009/27774/indianinstitutehistory.pdf (accessed 4 April 2018); *Record of the Establishment of the Indian Institute in the University of Oxford, etc* (Oxford: Horace Hart, 1897), 6–7.

39. Herbert Sidebotham, 'Labouchere, Henry Du Pré (1831–1912)', rev. H. C. G. Matthew, *ODNB*.

40. *Truth*, 18 March 1897, 651–2.

41. *Daily News*, 29 July 1899, 6; *The Times*, 29 July 1899, 15.

42. The diamond jubilee awaits a full history, but see: Edward Ellsworth, 'Victoria's Diamond Jubilee and the British Press: The Triumph of Popular Imperialism', *Social Studies* 56 (1966), 173–80; Jan Morris, *Heaven's Command: An Imperial Progress* (London: Faber, 1973), ch. 27; Walter Arnstein, 'Queen Victoria's Diamond Jubilee', *American Scholar* 66 (1997), 591–8; Greg King, *Twilight of Splendor: The Court of Queen Victoria during her Diamond Jubilee Year* (Hoboken, NJ: John Wiley, 2007). The global reach of the celebrations beyond Britain and the Empire is conveyed in Willoughby Maycock, *The Celebration in Foreign Countries of the Sixtieth Anniversary of Her Majesty's Accession to the Throne* (London: Harrison and Sons, 1897). For the telegram arrangements, see: QVJl., 22 June 1897; Hamilton to Elgin, 11 June 1897, IOR Mss Eur. C125/2, 1–2.

43. She raised the issue as early as October of the previous year: Queen Victoria to Hamilton, [15 October 1896], IOR Mss Eur. A147, fols 3–4. For arrangements for the procession, see: Sir Fleetwood Edwards to the Bishop of Winchester, 11 February 1897, Davidson papers, Lambeth Palace, Davidson 49, fols 348–51, Arthur Bigge to the Bishop of Winchester, 29 February 1887, ibid., fols 359–60.

44. Hamilton to Elgin, 15 January 1897, IOR Mss Eur. C125/2, p. 3, Hamilton to Elgin, 26 February 1897 (copy), ibid., fol. 26; Elgin to Hamilton, 20 January 1897, Mss Eur. D509/4, fols 27–34; Steyning Edgerley to Mr Hunter, 2 February 1897, 13 March 1897, MSA, Pol. Proceedings (1897), vol. 101, 9, 41. At the beginning of June, the Viceroy sent out a *kharita* to various maharajas saying that invitations to London had not been issued because of the demands of the famine, 'one more instance of the thoughtful care and tenderness for Her people': ibid., vol. 102, 79.

45. Hamilton to Elgin, 3 June 1897 (on the Maharaja of Kapurthala), IOR Mss Eur. C125/2, 247. The other Indian rulers who came were Kunwar Dokhal Singh, Raja Ajit Singh of Khetri, Rajkumar Ennaid Singh of Shahpura. The Eton boys were the sons of the Maharaja of Cooch Behar, the Thakur of Gondal, and the prime minister of Hyderabad, Viqar-ul-Umra; QVJl., 23 June 1897; *The Times*, 24 June 1897, 6.

46. *The Times*, 23 June 1897, 14; ibid., 12 July 1897, 9; ibid., 14 July 1897, 10; QVJl. 21 June 1897. For the Thakur of Gondal's elevation: *Gazette of India*, 22 June 1897, 3.

47. For the arrangements for one of these officers, Rai Bahadur Thakur Dip Singh (of the Camel Corps), see: Proceedings of the Hazur Dept (Bikaner State), A121/5 (March 1897), Rajasthan State Archives, Bikaner. For the full list and details of their stay: 'Native Officers and Men. Deputation to England, 1897', IOR L/MIL/7/5778.

48. For the order of procession, see: *Daily News*, 22 June 1897, 2. The newsreel footage is at: http://www.britishpathe.com/video/diamond-jubilee-of-queen-victoria (accessed 9 April 2018). Charlton's painting, commissioned by the queen, is at RCIN 400211.

49. Elgin to Hamilton, 12 May 1897, D509/5, fols 135–64 (commemorative medal); Hamilton to Elgin, 25 June 1897, C125/2, 297; QVJl., 19 June 1897, 29 June 1897, 5 July 1897, 8 July 1897, 10 July 1897. For the Swoboda portraits, see: RCIN 403809, 403819, 403820, 403821; Hamilton to Sir Fleetwood Edwards, 12 June 1897, RA, VIC/MAIN/R/46/29–29a; *Daily News*, 23 July 1897, 6.

50. Elgin to Hamilton, 10 February 1897, IOR Mss Eur. D509/4, fols 51–60.

51. *ToI*, 22 June 1897, 14; *Bombay Gazette*, 22 June 1897, 5. For the Holkar's concern that proposed prisoner release was not 'consistent with public peace and safety', see Indore

Durbar to Capt. A. D. Bannerman, 15 June 1897, For. Proceedings (1897), Madhya Pradesh State Archives, 17–14, fol. 137.

52. MSA, Pol. Proceedings (1897), vol. 101, 53 (addresses to go to the government not the queen); ibid., 91 (no more than six per deputation); ibid., 107 (gifts).

53. *Hindoo Patriot*, 27 May 1897, 2; *Civil & Military Gazette*, 24 May 1897, 2 (Elgin's mocking speech); *Bombay Gazette*, 24 May 1897, 4; *Karnataka Prakasika*, 24 May 1897, NNR (Madras), IOR L/R/5/108, 125–6.

54. MSA, Pol. Proceedings (1897), vol. 104, 183–92 (Poona Sabha); NAI, Pol. Proceedings (September 1897), Public, 573 (Punjab).

55. Elgin to Hamilton, 15 June 1897, Mss Eur. D509/5, fols 323–9; Queen Victoria to Elgin, Vry 22 June 1897, telegram, no. 62, Mss Eur., F84/1, fol. 26.

56. J. P. Hewett to chief secretary, Government of Bombay, 17 April 1897, MSA, Pol. Proceedings (1897), vol. 101, p. 247.

57. Details of diamond jubilee events across India summarised here are drawn from two main sources: 'Reports on the Measures Taken for the Celebration of the Completion of the Sixtieth Year of the Reign of Her Majesty the Queen, Empress of India', NAI, Home Dept Proceedings (November 1897), 310–30, and 'Congratulatory Addresses from Public Bodies and Letters from Native Chiefs', (February 1898) NAI, Foreign Dept Proceedings (February 1898), 111–325.

58. Political Dept, Government of Bombay to the Foreign Secretary of the Government of India, 27 August 1897, MSA, Political Proceedings (1897), vol. 102, fols 297–313 (Junagadh); 'Account of the Native Jubilee Celebrations . . . in Native States under the Political Control of the Government of Madras, etc.' (Travancore), Political Proceedings (2 August 1897), 507–8, Tamil Nadu State Archives.

59. *Hindoo Patriot*, 24 June 1897, 3; 'H.M.'s Diamond Jubilee' (misc. circulars), IOR L/R/2/616/158 (for the 'Indian Princes' Health Institute'); M. R. Mehta to the Maharaja of Jaisalmer, 19 November 1898, Proceedings of the Office of the Dewan, Jaisalmer, (1898), 106/119, Rajasthan State Archives, Bikaner.

60. Karnataka State Archives, Bangalore, Chief Secretariat records (1897), 102, 112–13, 116; 'A Brief Account of the Celebration in the Mysore State of the Diamond Jubilee', IOR/R/2/Box8/63.

61. 'Memorandum Showing the More Important Points on which the Deputy Commissioners should Address the Gentlemen Assembled at the Durbars to be Held on 22 June 1897', Chief Secretariat Records, Karnataka State Archives, Bangalore, 102, fols 14–15.

62. *Mysore Gazette*, 21 May 1897, 1; Memorandum (29 May 1897), Chief Secretariat Records, Karnataka State Archives, 102, fols 153–9.

63. 'Report on the Celebrations of the Diamond Jubilee Festivities in the Minor Towns of the Bangalore District on the 21 and 22 June 1897', Chief Secretariat Records, Karnataka State Archives, 112, fol. 164; Deputy Commissioner, Shimoga District to the Secretary to the Government of Mysore, 5 July 1897, ibid., fols 204, 219.

64. MSA, Pol. Proceedings (1897), vol. 104, 651 (Bombay); 'Account of the Native Jubilee Celebration . . . in Native States under the Political Control of the Government of Madras, etc' (Pudukkottai), Tamil Nadu State Archives, Pol. Proceedings (2 August 1897), 507–8.

65. S. Muttu Aiyar and C. V. Swaminada, *Life of Her Majesty Queen Victoria, Empress of India* (Madras: the authors, 1898).

66. Durga Das De, *Yuvili yajna (The Jubilee Sacrifice)* (Calcutta: Mukerji & Co., 1897), QLB (Bengal); Rajendra Narayan Mukherji, *Hirakanjali (The Diamond Jubilee Offering)* (Calcutta: K. P. Banerji, 1897), QLB (Bengal).

67. *Madras Times*, 12 May 1897, 3 (viceregal pressure); *Maharatta*, 25 April 1897, 4 (calls for charity); *Bengalee*, 5 June 1897, 269–70 (charity and acts of grace), 26 June 1897, 304–5 (previous demonstrations of loyalty); *Dainik-o-Samachar Chandrika*, 29 June 1897, NNR (Bengal), L/R/5/23, p. 556 (sale of the queen's jubilee message).

68. *Paisa Akhbar*, 4 June 1897, *Punjab Samachar*, 19 June 1897, *Rahbari-i-Hind*, 28 June 1897, NNR (Punjab), L/R/5/181, 460–61, 515, 539–40; *The Victoria Diamond Jubilee Hindu Technical Institute, Punjab. Inaugural Address on the Commercial and Industrial Development of India, Delivered on the Evening of the 21st June* (Lahore: Tribune Press, 1897), 1.

69. *Dacca Prakash*, 20 June 1897, NNR (Bengal), L/R/5/23, 535; *Jami-ul-Ulum*, 14 June 1897, NNR (North-West Provinces and Oudh), L/R/5/74, 391.

70. Hamilton to Elgin, 25 June 1897, Mss Eur. C125/2, fol. 297.

71. *The Times*, 22 June 1897, 5; 'Report on the Measures Taken for the Celebration of the . . . Sixtieth Year of the Reign, etc.', NAI, Home Dept Proceedings (November 1897), 318 (Punjab); P. L. Malhotra, *Administration of Lord Elgin In India, 1894–99* (New Delhi: Vikas, 1979), 151–4.

72. 'Autobiography of Damodar Hari Chapekar' (Bombay Police Abstracts, 1910), reproduced at: https://cultural.maharashtra.gov.in/english/gazetteer/VOL-II/autobiography.pdf (accessed 4 April 2018). For claims about the involvement of the INC, see: Arthur Crawford, *Our Troubles in Poona and the Deccan* (London: Archibald Constable, 1897), 90–2. For the background, see: Gordon Johnson, *Provincial Politics and Indian Nationalism: Bombay and the Indian National Congress, 1880 to 1915* (Cambridge: Cambridge University Press, 1973), ch. 3; Prashant Kidambi, *The Making of an Indian Metropolis: Colonial Governance and Public Culture in Bombay, 1890–1920* (Aldershot: Ashgate, 2007), ch. 3.

73. Richard Cashman, *The Myth of the 'Lokamanya': Tilak and Mass Politics in Maharashtra* (Berkeley: University of California Press, 1975); Biswamoy Pati (ed.), *Bal Gangadhar Tilak: Popular Readings* (Delhi: Primus, 2011), esp. chs 4–5; Sukeshi Kamra, 'Law and Radical Rhetoric in British India: The 1897 trial of Bal Gangadhar Tilak', *South Asia*, 39 (2016), 546–59.

74. S. S. Setlur and K. G. Deshpande (eds), *A Full and Authentic Report of the Trial of Bal Gangadhar Tilak: At The Fourth Criminal Sessions 1897 of the Bombay High Court before Justice Strachey and a Special Jury* (Bombay: Education Society's Press 1897), 31, 73, 80, 107.

75. Arthur Godley to George Hamilton, 3 May 1897, IOR Mss Eur. D509/4, fols 413–14.

12 The Last Years of the Qaisara

1. QVJl., 21 July 1891. The progress of Bhai Ram Singh's commission can be followed in the correspondence between Henry Ponsonby, Bhai Ram Singh and Lockwood Kipling during 1890–2, in the J. L. Kipling papers, Special Collections, University of Sussex, Ms 38, 1/15. Cf. Pervaiz and Sajida Vandal, *The Raj, Lahore, and Bhai Ram Singh* (Lahore: NCA Publication, 2006), 154–68; Julius Bryant 'Kipling's Royal Commissions: Bagshot Park and Osborne' in Julius Bryant and Susan Weber (eds), *John Lockwood Kipling: Arts and Crafts in the Punjab and London* (London: Yale University Press 2017), 435–62.

2. For the Manipur crisis, see: John Parratt, *Queen Empress vs Tikendrajit Prince of Manipur: The Anglo-Manipuri Conflict of 1891* (New Delhi: Har-Anand Publications, 1992); Caroline Keen, *An Imperial Crisis in British India: The Manipur Uprising of 1891* (London: IB Tauris, 2015).

3. Ethel Grimwood, *My Three Years in Manipur and Escape from the Recent Mutiny* (London: Richard Bentley, 1891). For comparisons with 1857, see *Morning Post*, 11 May 1891, 5; M. J. Wright, *Three Years in Cachar. With a Short Account of the Manipur Massacre* (London: S. W. Partridge, 1895), 154; *Northern Echo*, 1 April 1891, 3 (an 'Indian Isandula').

4. QVJl., 10 April 1891, 19 April 1891, 3 May 1891, 4 May 1891, 7 May 1891; Cross to Lansdowne, 26 June 1891, IOR Mss Eur D558/4, fol. 27; Queen Victoria to Cross, 3 May 1891, BL, Add. Ms. 83, 315, fols 23–4; Cross, 'The Character of the Queen as Shown in her Private Letters' (n.d.), BL, Add. Ms. 51, 289, fols 59–65.

5. QVJl., 1 July 1891.

6. QVJl., 8 August 1891; Lansdowne to Cross 14 July 1891 ('catastrophic'), IOR Mss Eur. E243/30; Cross to Lansdowne, 12 August 1891, IOR Mss Eur. D558/4, fols 56–8; Manomohan Ghose, *Memorandum of Arguments on Behalf of Kula Chandra Sing, Maharaja . . . of Manipur and Tikendrajit Bir Sing, Jubraj or Senapati of Manipur, etc.* (London: W. Hutchinson & Co., 1891).

7. QVJl., 17 August 1891.

8. Queen Victoria to Cross, 5 May 1891, BL, Add. Ms, 85,315, fols 26–7.

9. Queen Victoria to Cross, 27 June 1891, BL, Add. Ms. 85,315, fols 51–2, Queen Victoria to Cross, 4 July 1891, ibid., fols 60–1.

10. Cross, HL Debs, 354 (22 June 1891), 1003; Queen Victoria to Cross, 27 June 1891, BL, Add. Ms., 85,315, fols 53–4.

11. Queen Victoria to Cross, 11 August 1891, BL, Add. Ms. 85,315, fols 66–7; Cross to Lansdowne, 15 October 1891, IOR Mss Eur. D558/4, fols 75–7.

12. IOR Mss Eur. A191 22/10/1887.

13. Sushila Anand, *Indian Sahib: Queen Victoria's Dear Abdul* (London: Duckworth, 1996); Shrabani Basu, *Victoria and Abdul: The True Story of the Queen's Closest Confidant* (Stroud: History Press, 2011); Michaela Reid, *Ask Sir James: The Life of Sir James Reid, Personal Physician to Queen Victoria* (London: Eland, 1996), ch. 8.

14. For Boehm's busts, see: https://www.sothebys.com/en/auctions/ecatalogue/lot.56.html/2011/19th-20th-century-european-sculpture-l11230 (accessed 4 April 2018); and for Swoboda's portraits, see: the Royal Collection (RCIN 403831 Abdul Karim) and (RCIN 403641 Mahomet Buksh). The queen also commissioned Heinrich von Angeli to paint Abdul Karim (RCIN 406915); 'Rules for Scotland Memorandum', 20 August 1887, James Reid Archive, Jedburgh, vol. 7; Basu, *Victoria and Abdul*, 55.

15. 'Rules for Scotland Memorandum', Reid Archive, vol. 7.

16. James Reid to Sir William Jenner, 19 July 1889, 24 August 1889, Reid Archive, vol. 9.

17. Cross to Lansdowne, 30 October 1890, IOR Mss Eur D558/3 no. 48; Lansdowne to Cross, 12 November 1890, no. 50; Lansdowne to Cross, 27 November 1890, ibid., no. 54; 29–30, no. 16: Fowler to Elgin, 17 May 1895, IOR Mss Eur F84/13, no. 16; Queen Victoria to Crown Princess Victoria, 9 December 1893, in Agatha Ramm (ed.), *Beloved and Darling Child. Last letters between Queen Victoria and her Eldest Daughter, 1886–1901* (Stroud: Alan Sutton, 1990), 163–4.

18. Reid, *Ask Sir James*, 131–2, 137–8.

19. Lambert, 'Memorandum' (March–June 1896) in 'Intelligence on Abdul Karim, *munshi* to Queen Victoria', IOR/L/PS/8/61; Basu, *Victoria and Abdul*, chs 9–10.

20. Reid, *Ask Sir James*, 137–8; Basu, *Victoria and Abdul*, ch. 11.

21. Basu, *Victoria and Abdul*, 185.

22. John Bradley (ed.), *Lady Curzon's India: Letters of a Vicereine* (London: Weidenfeld & Nicolson, 1985), 126.

23. Rafiuddin Ahmed or Ahmad (1865–1954). He later served as a minister in the government of Bombay presidency. Cf. Humayun Ansari, *The Infidel Within: Muslims in Britain Since 1800* (2004), 78–9.

24. *The Times*, 26 September 1890, 4, 13 October 1890, 3; Rafiuddin Ahmad, 'The Legal Authority of English Women Compared to Muhammadan Women', *Asiatic Quarterly Review*, 2nd ser., 1 (January 1891), 410–30.

25. Rafiuddin Ahmad, 'The Queen's Hindustani Diary', *Strand Magazine* 4 (December 1892), 551–7. Cf. his earlier 'Kaiser-i-Hind and Hindoostani', *Nineteenth Century* 29 (May 1891), 747–53.

26. *ILN*, 31 December 1892, 834; *Graphic*, 31 December 1892, 794; Rafiuddin Ahmad, 'The Royal Marriage from the Oriental Point of View', *Strand Magazine* 6 (October 1893), 447–58. RCIN 403825 (Swoboda).

27. *ToI*, 14 April 1891, 5. Ahmad claimed to have visited Balmoral in his 1891 article in *Strand Magazine*.

28. Queen Victoria to Cross, 28 May 1891, BL, Add. Ms. 83, 315, fols 38–9.

29. Cross to Lansdowne, 2 June 1892, 21 July 1892, IOR Mss Eur. D558/5, fols 39–40, 50; Lansdowne to Cross, 28 June 1892, ibid., fol. 73.

30. H. H. Fowler to Lord Elgin, 8 June 1894, 12 October 1894, IOR Mss Eur. F84/12, fols 28–30, 54–8; Elgin to Fowler, 30 October 1894, ibid., fols 109–10; *The Times*, 28 May 1894, 6; Rafiuddin Ahmad, 'A Moslem's View of the Pan-Islamic Revival', *Nineteenth Century* 42 (October 1897), 517–26.

31. *The Times*, 24 October 1894, 3; cf. Rafiuddin Ahmad, 'The Political Situation in India', *Pall Mall Gazette*, 29 January 1895, 1–2; Elgin to Hamilton, 18 September 1895, IOR Mss Eur. F84/13, fols 126–30.

32. Queen Victoria to Curzon, 30 December 1898, IOR Mss Eur. F111/135, no. 1.

33. James Reid to Lord Salisbury, 25 January 1898, Reid Archive, vol. 20.

34. Arthur Davidson to Reid, 1 May 1898 ('ruffian'), Reid Archives, vol. 20; Hamilton to Elgin, 30 April 1897, IOR Mss Eur. C125/2, fol. 169 ('Mahomedan intriguer').

35. Queen Victoria to Curzon, 13 April 1899, IOR Mss Eur. F111/135, no. 25.

36. Hamilton to Elgin, 13 October 1896, F84/14, no. 43.

37. Queen Victoria to Curzon, IOR Mss Eur. F111/135, no. 42; QVJl., 12 February 1900, 15 March 1900, 27 June 1900; Curzon to Hamilton, 14 June 1899, IOR Mss Eur. F111/158, no. 26; Curzon to Hamilton, 15 February 1900, 16 May 1900, IOR Mss Eur. F111/159, nos. 9, 28. For Curzon's support: 'Debate on the Budget, 28 March 1900' in *Speeches by Lord Curzon of Kedleston, Viceroy and Governor-General of India: 1898–1901* (Calcutta: Thacker, Spink & Co., 1901), 285.

38. *The Times*, 12 July 1900, 7.

39. QVJl., 29 October 1900; Queen Victoria to Curzon, 28 October 1900, IOR Mss Eur. F111/135, no. 71; Hamilton to Curzon, 1 November 1900, IOR Mss Eur. F111/159, no. 76.

40. Queen Victoria to Curzon, 11 January 1901, IOR Mss Eur. F111/135, no. 76; Hamilton to Curzon, 7 February 1901, IOR Mss Eur. F111/160, no. 11. The Thakur of Morbi was the only Indian prince to attend the funeral of Queen Victoria.

41. *Daily Telegraph*, 2 January 1901, 7–8; Rodney Atwood, *The Life of Field Marshal Lord Roberts* (London: Bloomsbury, 2015), 217–19.

42. *Moslem Chronicle*, 23 February 1901, 1608; 'Notifications Connected with the Demise of the Queen-Empress', Chief Secretariat records, Karnataka State Archives, Bangalore (1901), 126.

43. For the service at Calcutta Cathedral, see: *Englishman*, 2 February 1901, 4; *Service of Mourning Held on the Day of the Funeral of her Late Majesty Queen Victoria . . . in St Thomas', Cathedral, Bombay* (Bombay: n.p.), 5.

44. For criticism, see: *Mukbhir-i-Dakhan*, 30 January 1901, NNR (Madras), IOR L/R/5/110, 46–7, *Paisa Akhbar*, 2 February 1901, NNR (Punjab), IOR L/R/5/185, p. 76.

45. *Hindoo Patriot*, 5 February 1901, 5; Anon., *In Memory of Victoria, Queen & Empress, 1837–1901* (Bombay: Caxton Works, 1901), 69–71.

46. The fullest account is in A. Govindaraja Mudaliar (ed.), *India's Memorial Tribute to her Late Gracious Majesty, Queen Victoria, Empress of India* (Bombay: Thacker & Co., 1901).

47. 'Death of Her Majesty the Queen Empress' (1 February 1901) in *Speeches by Lord Curzon . . . 1898–1901*, 418. Several newspapers reproduced the text of the 1858 proclamation, e.g. *Mahratta*, 10 February 1901, 9.

48. *Al Bashir* (Etawah), 4 February 1901, NNR (North-West Provinces), IOR L/R/5/78, 90–1; *Indu Prakash*, 24 January 1901, NNR (Bombay), IOR L/R/5/156, 9–10; *In Memory of Queen & Empress* (Bombay), 66–7; *The Times*, 24 January 1901, 5; *Friend of India*, 14 February 1901, 15.

49. *Bengalee*, 23 January 1901, 1, also Mudliar (ed.), *Indian's Memorial Tribute*, 41–2; Wacha, 'Presidential Address', 17th Indian National Congress (Calcutta), reprinted in *Speeches and Writings of Sir Dinshaw Edulji Wacha* (Madras: G. A. Natesan & Co., 1920), 2–4; K. C. Duraisami, *The True Victorian Glory* (Madras: Thompson & Co., 1901), v; Lajjaram

Sharma Mehta, *Srimati Maharani Bharatesvari Viktoriya ka caritra, or Life of Queen Victoria, Empress of India* (Bombay: Khemraj Shrikrishnadas, 1901); Vidhvan Periya Reddiar, *The Maharani Ammanei* (Madras: Ramalinga Swami, 1901).

50. Primal energy.

51. Raj Johgeshur Mitter (comp.), *Bengal's Tribute to her Late Majesty the Queen-Empress. Being a Collection of Speeches Delivered at Different Memorial Meetings* (Calcutta: Standard Press, 1901), 17 (Tagore); Trailokyamohan Guha-niyogi, *Geet Bharatam: The Lays of India. The Memorial Poem-temple of Empress Victoria* (Calcutta: Sanyal & Co., 1902); *Madras Mail*, 2 February 1901, 7 (Iyer).

52. 'Queen Victoria Memorial' (6 February 1901) in *Speeches of Lord Curzon . . . 1898–1901*, 423–4, 426–7; Syed Ali Khan, *Lord Curzon's Administration: What He Promised, What He Performed* (Bombay: The Times Press, 1905), 115–16; Curzon to Hamilton, 31 January 1901, IOR Mss Eur. D510/7, fols 91–4.

53. 'Contents of the Victoria Memorial Hall' (26 February 1901) in *Speeches of Lord Curzon . . . 1898–1901*, 431–55.

54. *Maharatta*, 3 March 1903, 3.

55. Dewan of Mysore to P. H. Singh, 11 March 1901, Chief Secretariat records, Karnataka State Archives, (1901), 101; *Bombay Gazette*, 2 March 1901, 5; *ToI*, 23 March 1901, 7 (Karachi).

56. *The Victoria Technical Institute and Memorial Hall: An Account of its History and Work, etc.* (Madras: Methodist Publishing House, 1909); *ToI*, 27 February 1901, 5 (Technical Institute, Madras); ibid., 27 March 1902, 4 (Dufferin Fund); ibid., 15 February 1902, 8 (School for the Blind, Bombay).

57. Curzon to Hamilton, 14 March 1901, IOR Mss Eur. D510/7, fols 199–206; Hamilton to Curzon, 15 March 1901, IOR Mss Eur. F111/159, no. 19; Francis Knollys to Curzon, 25 April 1901, IOR Mss Eur. F111/135, no. 6.

58. H. Caldwell Lipsett, *Lord Curzon in India, 1898–1903* (London: R. A. Everett, 1903), 120. For satires of the viceregal couple, see: Harischandra A. Talcherkar, *Lord Curzon in Indian Caricature: Being a Collection of Cartoons Reproduced in Miniature, etc.* (Bombay: Babajee Sakharam & Co., 1903).

59. The principal contemporary account is Stephen Wheeler, *History of the Delhi Coronation Durbar: Held on the First of January 1903 to Celebrate the Coronation of His Majesty King Edward VII, Emperor of India* (London: John Murray, 1904). Also useful is Lovat Fraser's *At Delhi* (Bombay: Times of India, 1903). For more recent analyses, see: Stephen Bottomore, '"An Amazing Quarter Mile of Moving Gold, Gems and Genealogy": Filming India's 1902/03 Delhi Durbar', *Historical Journal of Film, Radio and Television* 15 (1995), 495–515; Julie F. Codell, 'Photography and the Delhi Coronation Durbars' in Codell (ed.), *Power and Resistance: The Delhi Coronation Durbars, 1877, 1903, 1911* (New Delhi: Mapin, 2012), esp. 37–40.

60. 'Speech on the Presentation of the Freedom of the City of London, at the Guildhall' (20 July 1904) in *Speeches on India delivered by Lord Curzon . . . whilst in England, July–August 1904* (London: John Murray, 1904), 13.

61. [C. J. O'Donnell], *The Failure of Lord Curzon: A Study In 'Imperialism': An Open Letter to the Earl of Rosebery* (London: T. Fisher Unwin, 1903), 82–5.

62. For the tour, see: Stanley Reed, *The Royal Tour in India: A Record of the Tour of T.R.H. the Prince and Princess of Wales in India and Burma, from November 1905 to March 1906* (Bombay: Bennett, Coleman & Co., 1906); G. F. Abbott, *Through India with the Prince* (London: Edward Arnold, 1906); Madho Prasad, *A Brief Account of the Tour Made by their Royal Highnesses the Prince and the Princess of Wales in India, 1905–06* (Mirzapur: Khichri Samachar Press, 1907); Theodore Morison, 'The Indian Tour of the Prince of Wales', *North American Review* 181 (December, 1905), 912–20; Sidney Low, *A Vision of India: As Seen During the Tour of the Prince and Princess of Wales* (London: Smith, Elder, 1906).

63. For the Prince's friendship with the Maharaja of Bikaner, see the correspondence beginning on 27 November 1905, Papers of the Office of the Private Secretary, Maharaja Ganga Singhi Trust, Lallgarh Palace, Bikaner. For some of the background, see: L. S. Rathore, *The Regal Patriot: Maharaja Ganga Singh of Bikaner* (New Delhi: Roli Books, 2007), 33–4; Hugh Purcell, *Maharajah of Bikaner India* (London: Haus, 2010), ch. 1.

64. The galvanising effect of the Prince of Wales's tour is described in Syed Sharifuddin Pirzada (ed.), *Foundations of Pakistan. All-India Muslim League Documents: 1906–1947*, 2 vols (New Delhi: Metropolitan Book Co., 1982), ii, 603–7.

65. A. F. Bruce to the Secretary of the Political & Foreign Dept, Bikaner, 1 September 1895, Proceedings of the Mahkama Khas (266 of 1905), Rajasthan State Archives, Bikaner.

66. *ToI*, 5 January 1906, 5.

67. 'Copies of the Proclamation of the King, Emperor of India, to the Princes and Peoples of India, of the 2nd day of November 1908, etc.', *Parl. Papers*, (1908), Cd. 324. For its gestation, see: Minto to Morley, 27 May 1908, IOR Mss Eur. D573/315, fol. 194, Morley to Minto, 7 October 1908, IOR Mss Eur. D573/3, fol. 298; Patrick Jackson, *Morley of Blackburn: A Literary and Political Biography of John Morley* (Madison, NJ: Farleigh Dickinson University Press, 2012), 406. In India the fiftieth anniversary of the queen's proclamation was marked by the publication of two new works, one in Bengali, one in Urdu: Anon., *Victoria Ewam Tahar Goshana Patra* [*Queen Victoria and her Proclamation*] (Benares: Jung Bahadur Singh, 1910), QLB (North Western Provinces); Maulvi Rahmat Ali, *Wafa-i-Rahmat* [*The Promise of Mercy*] (Lahore: Islamia Press, 1910), QLB (Punjab).

68. Telegram (31 January 1909), IOR/L/PJ/6/920 (Benares); H. G. Stokes to Arthur Godley, 1 April 1909, IOR/L/PJ/6/934 (Nagpur). In 1914 royal statues, including one of Queen Victoria, were tarred at Kolhapur: *ToI*, 28 February 1914, 8. And, three years later, the queen's statue in Clubbon Park, Bangalore, was placed under police guard: Police Dept, File 202, Karnataka State Archives, Bangalore.

69. A. Govindaraja Mudaliar (ed.), *India's Memorial Tribute to His Most Gracious Majesty King Edward VII, Emperor of India* (Madras: Selvan, 1911), 87; *The All-India King Edward Memorial* (Calcutta: n.p., 1911).

70. Ian Copland, 'Dilemmas of an Indian Prince: Sayaji Rao Gaekwar and Sedition' in Peter Robb and David Taylor (eds), *Rule, Protest and Identity: Aspects of Modern South Asia* (London: Curzon Press, 1978), 28–48; Fatesinghrao Gaekwad, *Sayajirao of Baroda: The Prince and the Man* (Mumbai: Popular Prakashan, 1989), ch. 18; Thomas G. Fraser, 'Delhi Durbar: The Coronation Investiture of 1911', *Majestas* 2 (1994), 75–91.

71. *ToI*, 5 April 1907, 7; Curzon to Morley, 14 August 1907, IOR Mss Eur. F111/458, fols 43–54.

72. Curzon to Carmichael, 15 April 1912 (draft), ibid., fols 133–8; *ToI*, 27 May 1913, 4.

73. Maharaja of Bikaner to Curzon, 13 March 1918, IOR Mss Eur. F111/458, fols 319–24; 'Proceedings of the Trustees', 11 February 1920, IOR Mss Eur. F111/460, fols 204–5; *ToI*, 1 February 1921, 5.

74. *ToI*, 29 December 1921, 7.

Epilogue

1. *Constituent Assembly Debates. Official Report*, 12 vols (Delhi: Lok Sabha Secretariat, 1946–50), i (13 December 1946), 62. For all that has been written about the ideology of Indian nationalism, the gestation of the idea of the republic has received scant coverage, e.g. D. A. Low (ed.), *Congress and the Raj: Facets of the Indian struggle 1917–1947* (London: Heinemann Educational, 1977); Jim Masselos, *Indian Nationalism: A History* (New Delhi: Sterling, 1985); R. Sisson and S. Wolpert (eds), *Congress and Indian Nationalism* (Berkeley: University of California Press, 1988); Robin Jeffrey (ed.), *India: Rebellion to Republic, Selected Writings* (New Delhi: Sterling, 1990); John Zavos, *The Emergence of Hindu*

Nationalism in Colonial India (Oxford University Press, Delhi, 2000); Bidyut Chakrabarty and Rajendra Kumar Pandey, *Modern Indian Political Thought: Text and Context* (London: Sage, 2009); Shruti Kapila (ed.), *An Intellectual History for India* (Cambridge: Cambridge University Press, 2011). A recent work that does partially address this omission is: Ananya Vajpeyi, *Righteous Republic: The Political Foundations of Modern India* (Cambridge, MA: Harvard University Press, 2012).

2. Queen Victoria questioned why both southern African colonies had broken away, and called for their restitution to the Empire: Henry Labouchere to Queen Victoria, 26 July 1856, Queen Victoria to Henry Labouchere, 8 January 1857, *Letters of Queen Victoria*, 1st ser., iii, 255–6, 285.

3. Chandra Pal, 'The Hymnology of the New Patriotism in Bengal' (October 1905) in Pal, *The New Spirit. A Selection from the Writings and Speeches of Bipinchandra Pal on Social, Political and Religious Subjects* (Calcutta: Sinha, Sarvadhikari & Co., 1907), 31, cf. 'The Shivaji Festival' (26 July 1902) in ibid., 41–2, and 'Loyal Patriotism' (25 February 1905), ibid., 218.

4. Vinayak Damodar Savarkar, *The Indian War of Independence, 1857* (Bombay: Phoenix Publications, 1947).

5. *Indian Sociologist* 3 (September 1907), 16; Sadan Jha, *Reverence, Resistance and Politics of Seeing the Indian National Flag* (Cambridge: Cambridge University Press, 2016), 79.

6. For India House, see: Nicholas Owen, *The British Left and India: Metropolitan Anti-imperialism, 1885–1947* (Oxford: Oxford University Press, 2007), 62–75; Alex Tickell, 'Scholarship Terrorists: The India House Hostel and the "Student Problem" in Edwardian London' in Rehana Ahmed and Sumita Mukherjee (eds), *South Asian Resistances in Britain, 1858–1947* (London: Continuum, 2012), 3–18. For Krishnasharma, see: Harald Fischer-Tiné, *Shyamji Krishnasharma: Sanskrit, Sociology and Anti-imperialism* (London: Routledge, 2010), 136–41.

7. 'Letter to the *Natal Advertiser*' (3 October 1893), *CWMG*, i, 63–5, 'Petition to Lord Ripon', (c. 14 July 1894), ibid., 147–57; *The Indian Franchise* (1895), ibid., 266–90; 'Letter to the *Natal Witness*' (4 April 1896), ibid., 308–11; 'Interview with the *Natal Advertiser*' (5 June 1896), ibid., 339–40; 'Address to Queen Victoria' (c. 21 June 1897), ibid., ii, 255; 'Telegram' (23 January 1901), ibid., iii, 206. For Gandhi in Natal, see: Robert A. Huttenback, *Gandhi in South Africa: British Imperialism and the Indian Question, 1860–1914* (Ithaca: Cornell University Press, 1971); Ramachandra Guha, *Gandhi before India* (London: Allen Lane, 2013), ch. 6.

8. *Autobiography* (1927), *CWMG*, xxxix, 140–1.

9. *Indian Opinion* (12 November 1904), *CWMG*, iv, 297; *Indian Opinion* (11 November 1905), (3 March 1906), ibid., v, 28, 209; *Indian Opinion* (14 May 1910), ibid., x, 251.

10. Annie Besant, *India a Nation. A Plea for India Self-Government* (London: T. C. & E. C. Jack, 1915), 153–4; idem., *India as She was and as She is* (Madras: Indian Bookshop,1923), 53; idem., *Dominion Home Rule for India* (Madras: Besant Press, 1915), ii–v. For this stage of Besant's Indian career, see: Nancy Fix Anderson, '"Mother Besant" and Indian National Politics', *Journal of Imperial and Commonwealth History* 30 (2002), 27–54.

11. Ram Chandra, 'Blind Loyalty is a Myth', *Spokesman Review*, 16 July 1916 in *Select Documents on the Ghadr Party*, comp. T. R. Sareen (New Delhi: Mounto, 1994), 146–7; Suzanne McMahon, *Echoes of Freedom: South Asian Pioneers in California, 1899–1965: An Exhibition in the Bernice Layne Brown Gallery in the Doe Library, University of California, Berkeley, July 1–September 30, 2001* (Berkeley: Centre for South Asian Studies, University of California, Berkeley, 2001), 35–8.

12. For the Amritsar massacre and its effects, see: Derek Sayer, 'British Reaction to the Amritsar Massacre, 1919–1920', *Past and Present* 131 (1991), 130–64; Kim Wagner, '"Calculated to Strike Terror": The Amritsar Massacre and the Spectacle of Colonial Violence', ibid. 233 (2016), 185–225.

13. King George V's proclamation is reprinted in A. B. Keith (ed.), *Speeches and Documents on Indian Policy, 1750–1921*, 2 vols (London: Oxford University Press, 1922), 327–32; *ToI*, 27 December 1919, 7.

14. *ToI*, 10 February 1921, 10; ibid., 21 November 1921, 9.

15. Motilal Nehru, Speech given at the unveiling of the Tilak statue at Poona, 27 July 1924: Ravinder Kumar and D. N. Panigrahi (eds), *Selected Works of Motilal Nehru*, 6 vols (New Delhi: Vikas, 1982–95), iv, 226; cf. V. G. Khobrekar (ed.), *Shivaji Memorials: The British Attitude (1885–1926), Source Material from the Maharashtra Archives* (Bombay: Maharashtra Dept Archives, 1974), ix–xx.

16. Chandrika Kaul, 'Monarchical Display and the Politics of Empire: Princes of Wales and India 1870–1920s', *Twentieth Century British History* 17 (2006), 464–88; Judith Woods, 'Edward, the Prince of Wales' tour of India, October 1921–March, 1922', *Court Historian* 5 (2000), 217–21.

17. For Gandhi and the boycott, see: *Young India* (7 July 1920), (1 August 1920), (18 August 1920), *CWMG*, xviii, 18–19, 102–3, 138–42. And for his advice regarding the king-emperor, see: *Navajivan* (11 April 1920), ibid., xvii, 311–12; *Navajivan* (29 December 1920), *Young India* (23 March 1921), ibid., xviii, 130–7, 464–7.

18. *Independent Hindustan* 1 (September 1920), 2; ibid., 1 (October 1920), 28; *United States of India* 1 (July 1923), 1.

19. 'Proceedings of the Indian National Congress, Moslem League and Other Conferences Held at Ahmedabad, etc.', 10–11, NAI, Home Pol. Proceedings (1921) F461; Francis Robinson, *Separatism among Indian Muslims: The Politics of the United Provinces' Muslims 1860–1923* (Cambridge: Cambridge University Press, 1974), 332.

20. For the manifesto, see: *The Fragrance of Freedom: Writings of Bhagat Singh*, ed. K. C. Yadav and Babar Singh (Guragaon: Hope India, 2006), 337–43. For the background, see: J. S. Grewal (ed.), *Bhagat Singh and his Legend* (Patiala: Punjab University, 2008), esp. chs by Grewal and H. K. Puri; Neeti Nair, 'Bhagat Singh as "Satyagrahi": The Limits to Non-Violence in Late Colonial India', *Modern Asian Studies* 43 (2009), 649–81.

21. 'Presidential Address at the First Session of the Republican Congress' (28 December 1927), *Selected Works of Jawaharlal Nehru*, ed. S. Gopal, 61 vols, (1964—), iii, 7–8.

22. 'Democracy in India' (3 May 1928) in *The Essential Writings of Netaji Subhas Chandra Bose*, ed. Sisir K. Bose and Sugata Bose (New Delhi: Oxford University Press, 1997), 83. On Jayaswal, see: Ratan Lal, *Kashi Prasad Jayaswal: The Making of a 'Nationalist' Historian* (Delhi: Aakar Books, 2018).

23. Lajpat Rai, *The Political Future of India* (New York: B. W. Huebsch 1919), 21; Subhas Bose, *The Indian Struggle, 1920–34* (London: Wishart, 1935), 7–11.

24. R. P. Bhargava, *The Chamber of Princes* (New Delhi: Northern Book Centre, 1991), 202; Ian Copland, *The Princes of India in the Endgame of Empire, 1917–1947* (Cambridge: Cambridge University Press, 1997), 66.

25. 'Presidential Address to the 25th Session of the All-India Muslim League Allahabad' (29 December 1930) reprinted in L. A. Sherwani (ed.), *Speeches, Writings, and Statements of Iqbal* (Lahore: Iqbal Academy, 1977), 12–13; cf. Iqbal Singh Sevea, *The Political Philosophy of Muhammad Iqbal: Islam and Nationalism in Late Colonial India* (Cambridge: Cambridge University Press, 2015), ch. 4.

26. Ambedkar, 'The Indian Ghetto' (n.d.) in *Dr. Babasaheb Ambedkar, Writings and Speeches*, 18 vols (Bombay: Govt. of Maharashtra 1979–2003), v, 19–20.

27. For the background, see: Mushirul Hasan and Dinar Patel (eds), *From Ghalib's Dilli to Lutyen's New Delhi. A Documentary Record* (Delhi: Oxford University Press, 2012); Sumanta K. Bhowmick, *Princely Palaces in New Delhi* (New Delhi: Nyogi, 2016).

28. Reginald Craddock, *The Dilemma in India* (London: Constable, 1929), 295–303. The Indian Empire Society wrote the queen's proclamation of 1858 into its constitution. For the background, see: Ian St John, 'Writing to the Defence of Empire: Winston Churchill's

Press Campaign Against Constitutional Reform in India, 1929–35' in Chandrika Kaul (ed.), *Media and the British Empire* (Basingstoke: Palgrave Macmillan, 2006), 104–24; Neil C. Fleming, 'Diehard Conservatism, Mass Democracy and Indian Constitutional Reform, *c.* 1918–35', *Parliamentary History* 32 (2013), 337–60.

29. *The Times*, 13 November 1930, 14.
30. For the Government of India Act of 1935, see: Carl Bridge, *Holding India to the Empire: The British Conservative Party and the 1935 Constitution* (New Delhi: Sterling, 1986); Andrew Muldoon, *Empire, Politics and the Creation of the 1935 India Act: Last Act of the Raj* (Farnham: Ashgate, 2006).
31. O'Dwyer, 'The Golden Age in India', *Saturday Review*, 28 February 1935, 240–1; cf. Duchess of Atholl, HC Debs, 299 (27 March 1935), 2000.
32. This account is based upon: 'Coronation Darbar', IOR/L/PO/5/19. The projected durbar for George VI is mentioned in John Glendoven, *The Viceroy at Bay. Lord Linlithgow in India* (London: Collins, 1971), 46, but not the earlier one.
33. *The Times*, 4 November 1936, 14.
34. 'Coronation of George VI: Messages of Congratulation Received through the Government of India', IOR/L/PS/13/820.
35. Nehru to Majumdar, 20 June 1937, in *Selected Works*, viii, 415–16.
36. Nehru, 'Presidential Address' (Ludhiana, February 1939) and 'The Indian States and the Crisis' (Andheri, 23 April 1940) in *The Unity of India. Collected Writings, 1937–1940* (New York: John Day, 1942), 31, 49.
37. 'The Haripura Address' in *Essential Writings*, ed. Sisir K. Bose and Sugata Bose, 198.
38. Jinnah, Speech at the annual All-India Muslim League, 23 March 1940, reprinted in W. Ahmad (ed.), *The Nation's Voice: Towards Consolidation: Speeches and Statements, March 1935–March 1940* (Karachi: Quaid-i-Azam Academy, 1992), 495.
39. *Speeches and Statements by the Marquis of Linlithgow* (New Delhi: Government of India), 64, 215–16.
40. Leo Amery to Clement Attlee, 28 February 1942, *ToP*, i, 267–8; Amery, 'Memorandum' (5 January 1945), ibid., v, 375–6; Amery, 'Notes for Discussion of an Interim Constitution' (19 March 1945), ibid., 711. See also: *The Leo Amery Diaries*, ed. John Barnes and David Nicholson, 2 vols (London: Hutchinson, 1980–88), ii, 783 (4 March 1942), 1033, (2 March 1945).
41. *Wavell: The Viceroy's Journal*, ed. Penderel Moon (London: Oxford University Press, 1973), 120 (28 March 1943).
42. 'Memorandum by the Lord Privy Seal' (2 February 1942), IOR/L/PO/6/106b. For the Attlee government and India, see: Nicholas J. Owen, 'Responsibility Without Power: The Attlee Governments and the End of British Rule in India' in Nick Tiratsoo (ed.), *The Attlee Years* (London: Pinter, 1991), 167–89.
43. Lord Pethick-Lawrence to Attlee, 4 March 1946, *ToP*, vi, 1106–7. For the Cripps and Cabinet missions to India, see: R. J. Moore, *Churchill, Cripps and India, 1939–45* (Oxford: Oxford University Press, 1979); Peter Clarke, *The Cripps Version: The Life of Stafford Cripps* (London: Allen Lane, 2002), 257–341, 393–476.
44. R. J. Moore, 'The Mountbatten Viceroyalty', *Journal of Commonwealth & Comparative Politics* 22 (1984), 204–15; Ian Copland, 'Lord Mountbatten and the Integration of the Indian States: A Reappraisal', *Journal of Imperial and Commonwealth History* 21 (1993), 385–408; Rakesh Ankit, 'Mountbatten and India, 1948–64', *International History Review* 37 (2015), 240–61.
45. R. G. Casey (Governor of Bengal) to Pethick-Lawrence, 18 January 1946, *ToP*, vi, 821.
46. Wavell to Amery, 22 February 1944, 20 April 1944, ibid., iv, 751–2, 901–3.
47. 'Cabinet C. M. (47) 50th Conclusions' (23 May 1947), ibid., x, 966.
48. *Quaid-i-Azam Mohammad Ali Jinnah Papers*, ed. Z. H. Zaidi, 18 vols (Islamabad: Oxford University Press 1993–2012), ii, 212–23, 439–53.

49. Mountbatten to the Maharaj-Rana of Dolhpur, 29 July 1947, *ToP*, xii, 391–3.
50. 'Meeting of the Partition Council' (6 August 1947), ibid., 547–9.
51. Harshan Kumarasingham, 'The "Tropical Dominions": The Appeal of Dominion Status in the Decolonization of India, Pakistan and Ceylon', *Transactions of the Royal Historical Society* 23 (2013), 223–45; A. I. Singh, 'Keeping India in the Commonwealth: British Political and Military Aims, 1947–49', *Journal of Contemporary History* 20 (1985) 469–81; Michael Brecher, 'India's Decision to Remain in the Commonwealth', *Journal of Commonwealth & Comparative Politics* 12 (1974), 62–90.
52. Attlee to Major Adeane (the king's private secretary), 12 June 1947, *ToP*, xi, 310–11; Earl of Halifax to Attlee, 12 June 1947, ibid., 435; 'Memorandum by the Secretary of State for India' (26 July 1947), ibid., xii, 361–3.
53. *The Times*, 15 August 1947, 4; Nicholas J. Owen, ' "More Than a Transfer of Power": Independence Day Ceremonies in India, 15 August 1947', *Contemporary Record* 6 (1992), 415–51; S. J. Davis, 'August the 15th, 1947: Independence Day in Calcutta', *Army and Defence Quarterly Review* 127 (1997), 271–4; Ajit Bhattacharjea, 'Tryst with Destiny', *Economic & Political Weekly*, 11 August 2007, 3278–80.
54. 'Viceroy's Personal Report no. 17' (16 August 1947), IOR/L/PO/6/123.
55. Gandhi to Mountbatten, 9 November 1947, *CWMG*, lxxxix, 507. The table-cloth (labelled as a 'lace shawl') is at RCIN 738.
56. Paul McGarr, ' "The Viceroys are Disappearing from the Roundabouts in Delhi": British Symbols of Power in Post-colonial India', *Modern Asian Studies* 49 (2015), 787–831; Maria Misra, 'From Nehruvian Neglect to Bollywood Heroes: The Memory of the Raj in Post-war India' in Dominik Geppert and Frank Müller (eds), *Sites of Imperial Memory: Commemorating Colonial Rule in the Nineteenth and Twentieth Centuries* (Manchester: Manchester University Press, 2016), 187–206.
57. Yaqoob Khan Banghash, *A Princely Affair: The Accession and Integration of the Princely States of Pakistan, 1947–1955* (Karachi: Oxford University Press, 2015).
58. Lucien D. Benichou, *From Autocracy to Integration: Political Developments in Hyderabad State (1938–1948)* (Hyderabad: Orient Longman, 2000), chs 6–7; V. P. Menon, *The Story of the Integration of the Indian States* (Calcutta: Orient Longman, 1956), 201–11.
59. 'Indian Political Theories' and 'Treaty Rights of Indian States' in P. G. Sahasranama Iyer (ed.), *Selections from the Writings and Speeches of Sachivottama Sir C. P. Ramaswami Aiyar, Dewan of Travancore*, 2 vols (Trivandrum: Government Press, 1945), ii, 1–52, 272–93. On Travancore, see: Sarath Pillai, 'Fragmenting the Nation: Divisible Sovereignty and Travancore's Quest for Federal Independence', *Law and History Review* 34 (2016), 743–82.
60. *Constituent Assembly Debates*, iv (23 July 1947) 827; x (10 December 1948) 977, 984; x (12 October 1949), 123.
61. Diego Maiorano, *Autumn of the Matriarch: Indira Gandhi's Final Term in Office* (London: Hurst & Co., 2015), 1, 28–31.
62. Humayan Mirza, *From Plassey to Pakistan: The Family History of Iskander Mirza, the First President of Pakistan* (Lanham: University Press of America, 1999).
63. *Constituent Assembly Debates*, vii (5 January 1949), 1278; viii (17 May 1949) 41–2; x (17 October 1949), 432–4.
64. B. N. Rau, *India's Constitution in the Making* (New Delhi: Orient Longmans, 1960), 348.
65. *ToI*, 23 June 1948, 1, and 'Proclamation by George VI', IOR/V/27/220/19; *Constituent Assembly Debates*, xi (25 November 1949), 978, ibid., (26 November 1949), 988.
66. *The Times*, 6 March 1961, 13. For the queen's attendance at the celebrations in January 1961 see: www.britishpathe.com/video/new-delhi-republican-day-parade (accessed 9 April 2018).

SELECT BIBLIOGRAPHY

Manuscript Sources

United Kingdom

London

British Library
Dept Printed Books
  BP7/1–5: 1st Marquess of Ripon papers, 1880–84
Dept Manuscripts
  Add. Mss 36,473–80 Broughton papers
  Add. Mss 85,315 Cross papers
  Add. Mss 7410–11 Herries papers
  Add. Mss 50,026 Iddesleigh papers
  Add. Mss 40,462 Peel papers
  Add. Mss 40,864–76 Earl of Ripon papers
  Add. Mss 43,510, 43,565–7, 53,603 1st Marquess of Ripon papers
Asian, African & Pacific Collections
  India Office Records (IOR)
    A1/94–115 Memorials
    E4 East India Company Despatches to the Court of Directors
    F4 East India Company Board Collections
    L/MIL/7 Military Collections
    L/PO/5 Private office papers
    L/P&J/6 Public & Judicial Files
    L/P&S/18–20 Political memoranda
    L/R/5/1 Native newspaper reports, 1868–1901
    R/2 Residency records
    SV/412 Quarterly List of Publications, 1867–1947
    European manuscripts (Mss Eur.)
    B380 Mayo

C144 Northbrook
D488 Edward Prinsep
D509 Hamilton
D558 Lansdowne
D594 Ilbert
D726 Wodehouse
D728 Davidson
D951 O. T. Burne
E214 James Fergusson
E243 Richard Cross
E301 H. H. Wilson
E342 James Weir Hogg
E357 George Yule
F78 Lawrence
F83 8th Earl of Elgin
F84 9th Earl of Elgin
F86 Richard Temple
F87 Elphinstone
F111 Curzon
F130 Dufferin
F213 Hobhouse
F231 Canning
F234 Grant Duff
F595 Lytton
G55 Addresses and Memorials to Royalty from India

Library and Museum of Freemasonry
Minutes, District Grand Lodge of Bengal, 1875–6

Hackney Archives, C.L.R. James Library
Charles Bradlaugh papers

Imperial College, London
Royal Commission for the Exhibition of 1851 Archive

Lambeth Palace
EW Benson papers
Bloomfield papers
Davidson papers
AC Tait papers

News International
Diaries of William Howard Russell

Royal Society of Arts
Committee minutes, 1852, 1884–6
1886 Colonial and Indian Exhibition papers

Victoria & Albert Museum
Dept Prints & Drawings
   Lady Canning topographical albums

National Art Library
    1886 Imperial and Colonial Exhibition papers
    Henry Cole papers

The National Archives, Kew
ADM 53/9778–9: 'Ship's log: HMS *Galatea*'
ADM 101/271: 'Journal of HMS *Serapis*'
CO54/98: Ceylon despatches, 1875
LC2: Lord Chamberlain Jubilee papers, 1887 and 1897
MINT 16/71: 'Indian war medals' (1896)
PRO 30/6/4: Carnarvon papers
PRO 30/12 Ellenborough papers
PRO 30/76: Imperial Institute records

Muniment Room & Library, Westminster Abbey
Dean of Westminster Abbey papers

Outside London

Public Record Office of Northern Ireland, Belfast
Dufferin papers

University of Birmingham
Church Missionary Society papers

Cambridge University Library
Add. Ms. 6379: Adelaide Manning papers
Add. Ms. 7490: Mayo papers

Churchill College, Cambridge
Randolph Churchill papers

Chatsworth
Devonshire Collection, Marquis of Hartington papers

Durham University Library
Charles Grey papers

National Archives of Scotland, Edinburgh
Dalhousie papers

University of Sussex, Falmer
J.L. Kipling papers

Hatfield House
3rd Marquess Salisbury papers

Suffolk Record Office, Ipswich
Cranbrook papers

Bodleian Library, Oxford
Dep. Hughenden, Disraeli papers

Ms. Eng. C. 4204–8, 4316–17: Kimberley papers
Ms. Eng. D. 2349, 2352: Max Müller papers
Ms. Eng. Misc. e 9: Daniel Wilson papers

West Yorkshire Archives Service, Leeds
Canning papers

Liverpool Record Office
Derby papers

Hartley Library, University of Southampton
Palmerston papers (Broadlands Mss)

Hampshire Record Office, Winchester
3rd Earl Malmesbury papers
2nd Lord Northbrook papers

Borthwick Institute York
Halifax papers

Private collections

Harewood House, Leeds
Lady Canning watercolours

Reid Archive, Jedburgh, Scotland
James Reid Scrap Books, 1887–1901
Lady Susan Reid Scrap Books, 1899–1901

Windsor Castle
Royal Archives
   GV/PRIV/AA39AAA39 Diary of Captain Charles Bateson Harvey, 1889–90
   PPTO/PP/QV/ADDX/G/16 Privy Purse Jubilee papers, 1887
   PPTO/PP/QV/MAIN/1870 Vic 12912 Duke of Edinburgh visit to India, 1869–70
   VIC/ADD Add. Mss/A15/8445 Duchess of Connaught diaries
   VIC/ADDA15 Add. Mss A15 Correspondence relating to the Duke of Connaught, 1883–90
   VIC/ADDA25 Add. Mss A25 Correspondence relating to Prince Albert Victor, 1889–90
   VIC/ADDC07 Add. Mss C07 Prince of Wales, 1875
   VIC/MAIN F/45–7 Jubilee, 1887
   VIC/MAIN/F/16–17 Royal Titles bill, 1875–6
   VIC/MAIN/M/59 Letters from the Countess of Dufferin
   VIC/MAIN/N/12–32 Indian correspondence
   VIC/MAIN/R/46–46a Diamond Jubilee 1897
   VIC/MAIN/T/6 Francis Knollys correspondence
   VIC/MAIN/Z/182 letters of the Duke and Duchess of Connaught to the Queen
   VIC/MAIN/Z/468–9 Prince of Wales in India
   VIC/MAIN/Z/92 Letters from the Grandsons, vol. 1

Europe

National Library of Ireland, Dublin, Republic of Ireland
Ms. 11,223: Mayo papers

SELECT BIBLIOGRAPHY

Staatsarchiv, Gotha, Germany
Geheimes Archiv QQ XVI: Loyal addresses to Prince Alfred

North America

Rare Books and Special Collections, McGill University, Montreal, Canada
Hardinge papers

Metropolitan Museum of New York
Lady Canning photographs

Huntington Library, San Marino, California
Stowe Mss (3rd Duke of Buckingham), Madras correspondence

India

Delhi

National Archives of India
Foreign Department proceedings, 1835–1901
Home Department proceedings
Finance Department (Mint records)
Persian Department records, Darbar proceedings, 1859–94
Residency records
    Bhopal
    Central India Agency

Alkazi Photographic Archive

Delhi District Archives
Delhi Commissioner Records

Nehru Memorial Museum & Library
Bilgrami papers
British India Association of Calcutta papers (microfilm), 1852–4

Mumbai

Maharashtra State Archives
General Department (Political) Proceedings, 1858–98

Mumbai University Library
Jejeebhoy letterbooks, 1842–56

Kolkata

West Bengal State Archives
Judicial proceedings for 1869
Political proceedings for 1876

Other Indian Archives

Bangalore
Karnataka State Archives, Chief Secretariat records, 1875–1901

SELECT BIBLIOGRAPHY

Baroda
Baroda State Archives, Huzur English Dept, Daftar files

Bhopal
Madhya Pradesh State Archives, Indore Foreign Department, 1864–82

Bikaner
Bikaner Palace papers (Maharaja Ganga Singhji Trust), Office of Private Secretary, 1905–10
Rajasthan State Archives
    Hazar Department proceedings (Bikaner), 1896–8
    Mahkama Khas proceedings (Bikaner), 1901, 1905
    Dewan Office records (Jaisalmer), 1897–1901

Chennai
Tamil Nadu State Archives
    Political Consultations, 1850–51
    Political Department proceedings, 1875–1901

Hyderabad
Andra Pradesh State Archives, Salar Jung papers
Salar Jung Museum and Library

Mysore
Mysore District Archives
    Palace General Office, 1874–95
    Palace Controller Office, 1856–1901

Rampur
Raza Rampur Library

Udaipur
Royal Palace Archives (Mewar), Photographic archive

Secondary Sources

Aldrich, Robert, and Cindy McCreery (eds), *Crowns and Colonies: European Monarchies and Overseas Empires* (Manchester: Manchester University Press, 2016)

Atwal, Priya, 'Between the Courts of Lahore and Windsor: Anglo-Indian Relations and the Re-making of Royalty in the Nineteenth Century' (unpublished DPhil thesis, University of Oxford, 2017)

Bance, Peter, *Duleep Singh: Sovereign, Squire and Rebel* (London: Coronet House, 2009)

Banerjee, Sukanya, *Becoming Imperial Citizens: Indians in the Late Victorian Empire* (Durham, NC: Duke University Press, 2010)

Bayly, C. A., *Indian Society and the Making of the British Empire* (Cambridge: Cambridge University Press, 1988)

———, *Origins of Nationality in South Asia: Patriotism and Ethical Government in the Making of Modern India* (Delhi: Oxford University Press, 1998)

———, *Recovering Liberties: Indian Thought in the Age of Liberalism and Empire* (Cambridge: Cambridge University Press, 2012)

Boehmer, Elleke, *Indian Arrivals, 1870–1915: Networks of British Empire* (Oxford: Oxford University Press, 2015)

Bose, Sugata, *The Nation as Mother and Other Visions of Nationhood* (Delhi: Penguin, 2017)

Buckler, F. W., 'The Political Theory of the Indian Mutiny of 1857', *Transactions of the Royal Historical Society*, 4th ser., 5 (1922), 71–100

Burton, Antoinette, *Burdens of History: British Feminists, Indian Women and Imperial Culture, 1865–1915* (Chapel Hill: University of North Carolina Press, 1994)

Cannadine, David, 'The Context, Performance and Meaning of Ritual: The British Monarchy and the "Invention of Tradition", *c.* 1820–1977' in Eric Hobsbawm and Terence Ranger (eds), *The Invention of Tradition* (Cambridge: Cambridge University Press, 1983)

———, *Ornamentalism: How the British Saw their Empire* (London: Allen Lane, 2001)

Carter, Sarah, and Maria Nugent (eds), *Mistress of Everything: Queen Victoria in Indigenous Worlds* (Manchester: Manchester University Press, 2016)

Chakrabarty, Dipesh, *Provincialising Europe: Postcolonial Thought and Its Discontents* (Princeton, NJ: Princeton University Press, 2000)

Chakravarty, Gautam, *The Indian Mutiny and the British Imagination* (Cambridge: Cambridge University Press, 2005)

Chatterjee, Partha, *Nationalist Thought and the Colonial World: A Derivative Discourse?* (London: Zed, 1986)

———, *The Nation and its Fragments: Colonial and Postcolonial Histories* (Princeton, NJ: Princeton University Press, 1993)

Chopra, Preeti, *A Joint Enterprise: Indian Elites and the Making of British Bombay* (Minneapolis, MN: University of Minnesota Press, 2011)

Chowdhury-Sengupta, Indira, 'Mother India and Mother Victoria: Motherhood and Nationalism in Nineteenth-Century Bengal', *South Asia Research* 12 (1992), 20–37

Codell, Julie F., 'Photography and the Delhi Coronation Durbars' in Codell (ed.), *Power and Resistance: The Delhi Coronation Durbars, 1877, 1903, 1911* (New Delhi: Mapin, 2012)

Cohn, Bernard S., 'Representing Authority in Victorian India' in Eric Hobsbawm and Terence Ranger (eds), *The Invention of Tradition* (Cambridge: Cambridge University Press, 1983), 165–210

Copland, Ian, *The Princes of India in the Endgame of Empire, 1917–1947* (Cambridge: Cambridge University Press, 1997)

Dalrymple, William, *The Last Mughal: The Fall of a Dynasty, Delhi, 1857* (London: Bloomsbury, 2006)

———, *Return of a King: The Battle for Afghanistan* (London: Bloomsbury, 2014)

Fisher, Michael, 'The Imperial Coronations of 1819: Awadh, the British and the Mughals', *Modern Asian Studies* 19 (1985), 239–77

Forbes, Geraldine, *Women in Modern India* (Cambridge: Cambridge University Press, 1996)

Godsmark, Oliver and William Gould, 'Clientelism, Community and Collaboration: Loyalism in Nineteenth-century Colonial India' in Allan Blackstock and Frank O'Gorman (eds), *Loyalism and the Formation of the British World, 1775–1880* (Woodbridge: Boydell Press, 2014), 263–86

Goyle, Sonakshi, 'Tracing a Cultural Memory: Commemoration of 1857 in the Delhi Durbars, 1877, 1903, and 1911', *Historical Journal* 59 (2016) 799–815

Guha, Ramachandra, *Gandhi Before India* (London: Allen Lane, 2013)

Jhala, Angma Dey, *Courtly Indian Women in Late Imperial India* (London: Pickering & Chatto, 2008)

Kaul, Chandrika, 'Monarchical Display and the Politics of Empire: Princes of Wales and India 1870–1920s', *Twentieth Century British History* 17 (2006)

Keen, Caroline, *An Imperial Crisis in British India: The Manipur Uprising of 1891* (London: IB Tauris, 2015)

———, 'The Rise and Fall of Siddiq Hasan, Male Consort of Shah Jahan of Bhopal' in Charles Beem and Miles Taylor (eds), *The Man Behind the Queen: Male Consorts in History* (Basingstoke: Palgrave Macmillan, 2014), 185–204

Knight, Lionel, *Britain in India, 1858–1947* (London: Anthem Press, 2012)

———, 'The Royal Titles Act and India', *Historical Journal* 11 (1968), 488–507

Kolsky, Elizabeth, *Colonial Justice in British India: White Violence and the Rule of Law* (Cambridge: Cambridge University Press, 2010)

Kuhn, William M., *Democratic Royalism: The Transformation of the British Monarchy, 1861–1914* (Basingstoke: Macmillan, 1996)

Kumarasingham, Harshan, 'The "Tropical Dominions": The Appeal of Dominion Status in the Decolonization of India, Pakistan and Ceylon', *Transactions of the Royal Historical Society* 23 (2013), 223–45

Llewellyn-Jones, Rosie, *The Last King in India: Wajid Ali Shah* (London: Hurst, 2014)

London, Christopher W., *Bombay Gothic* (Mumbai: India Book House, 2002)

McGarr, Paul, ' "The Viceroys are Disappearing from the Roundabouts in Delhi": British Symbols of Power in Post-Colonial India', *Modern Asian Studies* 49 (2015), 787–831

Mehta, Uday Singh, *Liberalism and Empire: A Study in Nineteenth-Century British Liberal Thought* (Chicago, IL: Chicago University Press, 1999)

Metcalf, Barbara, 'Islam and Power in Colonial India: The Making and Unmaking of a Muslim Princess', *American Historical Review* 116 (2011), 1–30

Metcalf, Thomas, *The Aftermath of Revolt: India 1857–1870* (Princeton, NJ: Princeton University Press, 1964)

———, *Ideologies of the Raj* (Cambridge: Cambridge University Press, 1994)

Misra, Maria, 'From Nehruvian Neglect to Bollywood Heroes: The Memory of the Raj in Post-war India' in Dominik Geppert and Frank Müller (eds), *Sites of Imperial Memory: Commemorating Colonial Rule in the Nineteenth and Twentieth Centuries* (Manchester: Manchester University Press, 2016), 187–206

Mukherjee, Mithi, *India in the Shadows of Empire: A Legal and Political History, 1774–1950* (Delhi: Oxford University Press, 2010)

Myint-U, Thant, *The Making of Modern Burma* (Cambridge: Cambridge University Press, 2001)

Patel, Simin, 'Commemorating the Consort in Colonial Bombay' in Charles Beem and Miles Taylor (eds), *The Man Behind the Queen: Male Consorts in History* (Basingstoke: Palgrave Macmillan, 2014), 157–62

Ramaswamy, Sumathi, *The Goddess and the Nation: Mapping Mother India* (Durham, NC: Duke University Press, 2010)

Ramusack, Barbara N., *The Indian Princes and their States* (Cambridge: Cambridge University Press, 2004)

Reed, Charles, *Royal Tourists, Colonial Subjects and the Making of a British World, 1860–1911* (Manchester: Manchester University Press, 2016)

Sartori, Andrew, *Liberalism in Empire: An Alternative History* (Oakland, CA: University of California Press, 2014)

Seal, Anil, *The Emergence of Indian Nationalism: Competition and Collaboration in the Later Nineteenth Century* (Cambridge: Cambridge University Press, 1968)

Seth, Sanjay, 'Rewriting Histories of Nationalism: The Politics of Moderate Nationalism in India, 1870–1905', *American Historical Review* 104 (1999), 95–116

Sinha, Mrinalini, *Colonial Masculinity: The 'Manly Englishman' and the 'Effeminate Bengali' in the Late Nineteenth Century* (Manchester: Manchester University Press, 1995)

Steegles, Mary Ann, *Statues of the Raj* (London: British Association for Cemeteries in South Asia, 2000)

Stern, Philip J., *The Company-State: Corporate Sovereignty and the Early Modern Foundations of the British Empire in India* (Oxford: Oxford University Press, 2011)

Streets, Heather, *Martial Races: The Military, Race and Masculinity in British Imperial Culture, 1857–1914* (Manchester: Manchester University Press, 2004)

Travers, Robert, 'A British Empire by Treaty in Eighteenth-century India' in Saliha Belmessous (ed.), *Empire by Treaty: Negotiating European Expansion, 1600–1900* (Oxford: Oxford University Press, 2014), 132–60

Vajpeyi, Ananya, *Righteous Republic: The Political Foundations of Modern India* (Cambridge, MA: Harvard University Press, 2012)

Wainwright, Martin A., 'Royal Relationships as a Form of Resistance: The Cases of Duleep Singh and Abdul Karim' in Rehana Ahmed and Sumita Mukerjee (eds), *South Asian Resistances in Britain, 1858–1947* (London: Continuum, 2012)

INDEX